Critical Social Studies

Editors: JOCK YOUNG and PAUL WALTON

The contemporary world projects a perplexing picture of political, social and economic upheaval. In these challenging times the conventional wisdoms of orthodox social thought whether it be sociology, economics or cultural studies become inadequate. This series focuses on this intellectual crisis, selecting authors whose work seeks to transcend the limitations of conventional discourse. Its tone is scholarly rather than polemical, in the belief that significant theoretical work is needed to clear the way for a genuine transformation of the existing social order.

Because of this, the series will relate closely to recent developments in social thought, particularly to critical theory – the emerging European tradition. In terms of specific topics, key pivotal areas of debate will be selected, for example mass culture, inflation, problems of sexuality and the family, the nature of the capitalist state, natural science and ideology. The scope of analysis will be broad: the series will attempt to break the existing arbitrary divisions between the social-studies disciplines. Its aim is to provide a platform for critical social thought (at a level quite accessible to students) to enter into the major theoretical controversies of the day.

Critical Social Studies

POLICING THE CRISIS

MUGGING, THE STATE, AND LAW AND ORDER

Stuart Hall, Chas Critcher,
Tony Jefferson, John Clarke
and Brian Roberts

© Stuart Hall, Chas Critcher, Tony Jefferson, John Clarke and Brian Roberts 1978

First edition 1978
Reprinted 1979, 1980

Published by
PALGRAVE MACMILLAN
Houndmills, Basingstoke, Hampshire RG21 6XS and
175 Fifth Avenue, New York, N. Y. 10010
Companies and representatives throughout the world

PALGRAVE MACMILLAN is the global academic imprint of the Palgrave Macmillan division of St. Martin's Press, LLC and of Palgrave Macmillan Ltd. Macmillan® is a registered trademark in the United States, United Kingdom and other countries. Palgrave is a registered trademark in the European Union and other countries.

ISBN 0–333–22060–9 hardback
ISBN 0–333–22061–7 paperback

This book is printed on paper suitable for recycling and made from fully managed and sustained forest sources.

A catalogue record for this book is available from the British Library.

Transferred to digital printing in 2002

Printed and bound in Great Britain by
Antony Rowe Ltd, Chippenham and Eastbourne

Contents

Introduction

This book started out with 'mugging', but it has ended in a different place – as the discerning reader who notes the transition from the sub-title to the main title will already have noticed. At any rate it is not about 'mugging' in the sense most readers might expect. Indeed, if we could abolish the word, that would have been our principal – perhaps our only – 'practical proposal'. It has done incalculable harm – raising the wrong things into sensational focus, hiding and mystifying the deeper causes. A moratorium should now be declared on its highly suspect use, especially by politicians, judges, the police, criminal statisticians, the mass media and our moral guardians. Unfortunately you cannot resolve a social contradiction by abolishing the label that has been attached to it. This book aims to go behind the label to the contradictory social content which is mystifyingly reflected in it: but it is *not* a book about why certain individuals, as individuals, turn to mugging; nor about what practical steps can be taken to control or reduce its incidence; nor about how awful a crime 'mugging' is. It is not a case study, a practical manual nor a cry of moral outrage. Nor does it simply reverse the terms of reference – it is *not* an 'appreciative' study of how exciting or revolutionary 'mugging' is, either. Some of those books remain to be written – though not all ought to be. But we started somewhere else, developed a different conception of the relation of 'mugging' to British society, and have consequently produced a different kind of book. We put it that way specifically to counter the view that the way books about 'social problems' are written is that investigators simply walk into the streets, their heads utterly void of any preconceptions about crime or society, look the 'empirical facts' in the face, and write about whatever 'problem' happens to sneak up behind them and hit them over the head with its presence. This is not a book like that. We doubt whether books of that order of innocence can be written about society – though there are plenty enough currently masquerading in that guise.

We *are* concerned with 'mugging' – but as a social phenomenon, rather than as a particular form of street crime. We want to know what the social causes of 'mugging' are. But we argue that this is only half – less than half – of the 'mugging' story. More important is why British society *reacts to mugging*, in the extreme way it does, at that precise historical conjuncture – the early 1970s. If it is true that muggers suddenly appear on British streets – a fact which, in that stark simplicity, we contest – it is also true that the society enters a moral panic *about* 'mugging'. And this relates to the larger 'panic' about the 'steadily rising rate of violent crime' which has been growing through the 1960s. And both these panics are about other things than crime, *per se*. The society comes to perceive crime in general, and 'mugging' in particular, as an index of the disintegration of the social order, as a sign that the 'British way of life' is coming apart at the seams. So the book is also about a society which is slipping into a certain kind of *crisis*. It tries to examine why and how the themes of *race, crime* and *youth* – condensed into the image of 'mugging' – come to serve as the articulator of the crisis, as its ideological conductor. It is also about how these themes have functioned as a mechanism for the construction of an authoritarian consensus, a conservative backlash: what we call the slow build-up towards a 'soft' law-and-order society. But it also has to ask: to what social contradictions does this trend towards the 'disciplined society' – powered by the fears mobilised around 'mugging' – really refer? How has the 'law-and-order' ideology been constructed? What social forces are constrained and contained by its construction? What forces stand to benefit from it? What role has the state played in its construction? What real fears and anxieties is it mobilising? These are some of the things we mean by 'mugging' as a social phenomenon. It is why a study of 'mugging' has led us inevitably to the general 'crisis of hegemony' in the Britain of the 1970s. This is the ground taken in this book. Those who reject the logic of our argument must contest us *on this ground*.

We came to redefine 'mugging' in this way because of how the book began, and how it developed. Until we started the study, crime was not a special field of interest to us. We became involved in a practical way when, in 1973, sentences of ten and twenty years were handed down in court to three boys of mixed ethnic background after a serious incident in Handsworth, Birmingham, in which a man on the way home from a pub was 'mugged' on a piece of waste ground, robbed and badly injured. The sentences seemed to us unnecessarily vicious; but also – in terms of the causes which produced this incident – pointless, dealing with effects, not causes. But we also wanted to do what the courts had signally failed to do: understand a problem which awoke contradictory feelings in us – outrage at the sentence, sorrow for the needless victim, sympathy for the boys caught in a fate they did not make, perplexity at the conditions producing all this. In one sense only, this starting-point proved propitious, for if you enter the 'mugging' problem with the Handsworth case, it is impossible to fall into the trap of thinking that 'mugging' is *simply* a term for what some poor boys do to some poor victims in the poor areas of our large cities. 'Handsworth' was, clearly, *also* an exemplary sentence – a sentence intended to have a social as well as a punitive impact; it was, also, the fears and anxieties which the sentence aimed at allaying. It was the *massive* press coverage, the reactions of local people, experts and commentators, the prophecies of doom which accompanied it, the mobilisation of the police against certain sectors of the population in the 'mugging' areas. *All this* was the 'Handsworth mugging'. Once you perceive 'mugging' not as a fact but as a relation – the relation between crime and the reaction to crime – the conventional wisdoms about 'mugging' fall apart in your hands. If you look at this relation in terms of the social forces and the contradictions accumulating within it (rather than simply in terms of the danger to ordinary folks), or in terms of the wider historical context in which it occurs (i.e. in terms of a historical conjuncture, not just a date on the calendar), the whole terrain of the problem changes in character. The pattern of crime, but also the nature of the social reaction, has a pre-history; conditions of existence, strikingly absent from all the publicity concentrated on the single incident. Both have a location in institutional processes and structures, apparently far away from the 'scene of the crime'. What is more, nobody is really looking at these determining conditions. Crime has been cut adrift from its social roots. Something is standing in the way of these 'conditions of existence' being treated as part of the phenomenon. And part of what is standing in the way – producing crime, so to speak, as a simple and transparent fact – is the label 'mugging' itself. It cannot be allowed to stand in all its common-sense immediacy. It has to be dismantled: dismantled in terms of its wider relations to these contradictory social forces. This is the route our investigations took. It is this path we have tried to reconstruct, to *retrace*, for the reader in the structure and argument of this book. That is why we start with 'mugging', but we end with the way the society is 'policing its crisis'. If the reader can grasp this movement, he or she will not find it difficult to see how the structure of the book follows from it.

The book has been longer in preparation than its ultimate quality deserves: partly this is because it was written while other things – working, teaching, research – had to be done; but it is also because the book has been researched, written, argued over, revised, edited and lived with as a piece of collective work. In this it owes something to where it was done – in the Centre for Cultural Studies at Birmingham, which has devoted some thought and pain to making critical social research a more collaborative intellectual practice. The book reflects something of the rewards – and the costs – of doing it as a collective enterprise. We are aware of many limitations – above all, of the necessarily unfinished nature of some of the arguments and positions we have marshalled. But its faults should not be laid at the door of collective authorship. If it is a poor effort, it would have been poorer had it been written by a single hand.

Now we have been able to draw at least a temporary line under our efforts, we find it difficult to imagine whom the book we have written will positively *please*. We have settled for the hope that, if it cannot please, it may *convince* – which is more important. The courts, the police, the Home Office will certainly find it wildly exaggerated about their negative role (to put it nicely), and inexcusably 'soft' on criminals, agitators and trouble-makers. The media will say it is biased. Academics will find it too unbalanced, too committed. Liberals, people of goodwill, active in the cause of penal reform or improving race relations, will like it at least of all – perhaps because they will approach it with more positive expectations. The lack of balance will worry them, the critique of reformism will seem churlish and sectarian, and the absence of practical solutions irresponsible. Perhaps the great majority of our readers will be worried, especially, on the last count: analysis is all very well – but where are the remedies, the practical reforms?

As to this last charge, we confess to have had our hearts hardened by what we have discovered. It is a widespread but fatal trap – precisely, a trap of 'liberal opinion' – to split analysis from action, and to assign the first to the instance of the 'long term', which never comes, and reserve only the second to 'what is practical and realistic in the short term'. In direct opposition to this most 'British' of logics, we have determined to be 'unrealistic' in the short term, in the hope that we might persuade some people to grasp the nettle of what has to be done to be 'right' in the end. So, if someone says to us: 'Yes, but given the present conditions, what are we to do now?', we can only reply 'Do something about the "present conditions".' Oscar Wilde once said that it is an outrage for reformers to spend time asking what can be done to ease the lot of the poor, or to make the poor bear their conditions with greater dignity, when the only remedy is to abolish the condition of poverty itself.

The problem is that the 'present conditions', which make the poor poor (or the criminal take to crime) are precisely the *same* conditions which make the rich rich (or allow the law-abiding to imagine that the social causes of crime will disappear if you punish individual criminals hard enough). There is something deeply 'British' about our ability to abstract individual effects from the contradictory structures which produce them. So the 'practical remedy' involves taking sides – struggling with the contradictions. This book may be disappointing to some people who know this hard truth, and who are *already* engaged in the struggle to change the structures and conditions which produce the effects analysed in this book. We greatly regret not feeling ourselves competent to take the argument further along *this* road. We hope, however, that what we have written may help to inform, deepen and strengthen their practical struggle. We hope they will read it as we have tried to write it: as an *intervention* – albeit an intervention in the battleground of ideas.

Acknowledgements

We have accumulated, already, a thousand intellectual and practical debts, only some of which we can acknowledge here. Janice Winship and Roger Grimshaw researched and wrote the original drafts for Chapters 4 and 5 respectively, and have both helpfully commented and watched with goodwill the process of further absorption and mutilation which their ideas have been subjected to in the later stages of preparation. Roger Grimshaw has kept closely in touch with the manuscript as it developed and is indeed responsible for its title. A number of other people gave us essential help in the tedious work of research at the start of the project: among them, our special thanks to Dave Cooper, Hilary Wainwright, Stephen Gee, Alan Clarke, Alasdair McGowan, Jessica Pickard, Dick Hebdige and Bob Willis. Even our slow rate of progress would have been impossible to maintain without the invaluable assistance and patience of those who typed, xeroxed and stencilled for us: Aileen Hall, Linda Owen, Judy Jefferson, Deidre Barker, Georgie Ramseyer, Anne Harris and the inestimable Joan Goode, who still − unaccountably − smiles at us when we darken her door with another request.

In our efforts to consult press cuttings, background articles and other relevant information, we were assisted by a great range of people who gave generously of their time. The files of the National Council of Civil Liberties and Ian Wolff of the B.B.C. added massively to our stockpile of mugging reports. We would like to thank the many friends and colleagues, both within and outside the Centre for Cultural Studies, who have at one time or another talked to us about the project, and offered valuable advice and criticism. We are specially grateful to Darcus Howe of *Race Today* and Ricky Cambridge of *The Black Liberator* for the time from their more important work which they gave us. We are in special debt to those who read the extremely long first draft of this manuscript: and especially to Stan Cohen, Mike Fitzgerald, Ian Taylor and Jock Young for their detailed comments and care. Although we have borrowed ideas and concepts and worked them in directions which they may not altogether approve, we have had nothing but positive encouragement and support from those people in particular, and the context in which those conversations first arose − that of the National Deviancy Conference.

To those who had their lives messed around and frustrated by the complications in ours − in so many ways, for so much longer than they bargained for − it seems somewhat redundant at this late stage to offer apologies or thanks. We confess to having been − paradoxically − much supported by the sceptical smiles with which they met our assurances that 'It's nearly finished', though that may not have been the intention! Finally, we acknowledge gratefully the material support given to this project by the Centre for Contemporary Cultural

Studies, and the constant intellectual support and encouragement of its members in the period 1973–7.

Needless to say all the errors contained in this book are somebody else's fault, and the good bits belong to the authors.

Although the final text appears in 1978, there have been a number of attempts on the way to make our on-going research more widely available. Some of those 'offshoots' of the study include:

20 years (The Paul, Jimmy and Musty Support Committee, 1973).

T. Jefferson and J. Clarke, 'Down These Mean Streets: The Meaning of Mugging', *Howard Journal*, vol. XIV, no.1, 1974; also available as *CCCS Stencilled Paper. No.17*.

J. Clarke, C. Critcher, T. Jefferson and J. Lambert, 'The Selection of Evidence and the Avoidance of Racialism: a Critique of the Parliamentary Select Committee on Race Relations and Immigration', *New Community*, vol. III, no.3, Summer 1974; also available as *CCCS Stencilled Paper No.15*.

S. Hall, *Mugging: a Case Study in the Media*, Open University television programme for course D101 *Making Sense of Society*. (Milton Keynes: The Open University Press, 1975): broadcast on B.B.C.2 on 17 April and 20 April 1975; subsequently extracted in the *Listener*, 1 May 1975.

S. Hall *et al.*, *Newsmaking and Crime*, NACRO Conference on Journalism, Broadcasting and Urban Crime, January 1975; also available as *CCCS Stencilled Paper No. 37*, and from NACRO as the pamphlet *The Media and Urban Crime*, 1976.

S. Hall *et al.*, *Mugging and Law-and-Order*, paper presented to the National Deviancy Conference at Cardiff; also available as *CCCS Stencilled Paper No. 35*.

S. Hall, *Mugging and Street Crime*, the third in a series of *Personal View* broadcasts for B.B.C. Radio (producer, Michael Green).

I

1

The Social History of a 'Moral Panic'

On 15 August 1972 an elderly widower, Mr Arthur Hills, was stabbed to death near Waterloo Station as he was returning home from a visit to the theatre. The motive was, apparently, robbery. Although the event occurred too late for the following morning's papers, the national press reported it on 17 August. They labelled it – borrowing a description proffered by a police officer – 'a mugging gone wrong'. Thus the word 'mugging', hitherto used almost exclusively in an American context, or to refer in very general terms to the general growth of crime in Britain, was affixed to a particular case, and entered the crime reporter's vocabulary. Some reporters seemed to think the 'new' word also heralded the coming of a new crime. All these notions were neatly encapsulated in the *Daily Mirror* headline of 17 August: 'As Crimes of Violence Escalate, a Word Common In The United States Enters the British Headlines: Mugging. To our Police, it's a frightening new strain of crime.'

The *Daily Mirror* offered a further development of this theme. It described the event itself, provided a definition of the word, and added supporting statistical information about 'mugging' and the escalation in crimes of violence. Since there had been no eye witnesses to the event, the description of what happened must have been imaginatively reconstructed by the reporters. Apparently, they said, Mr Hills was attacked by three young men in their early twenties. They attempted to rob him, but he fought back only to be stabbed in the ensuing struggle. So far as definitions were concerned, the paper commented that the word was American and derived from such phrases as 'attacking a *mug*: an easy victim'. American police, the *Mirror* added, 'describe it as an assault by crushing the victim's head or throat in an armlock or to rob with any degree of force, with or without weapons'. Then followed the statistics: (1) an increase in muggings in the United States by 229 per cent in ten years; and (2) the reporting of about 150 'muggings' a year, during the previous three years, on the London underground. The *Mirror* spelled out the implications of these statistics: 'slowly mugging is coming to Britain'.

Was 'mugging' a new strain of crime? The question is not as simple as it appears. In an article in *The Times* a few weeks later (20 October 1972) Louis Blom-Cooper, Q.C. expressed the view that 'There is nothing new in this world:

and mugging, apart from its omission from the Oxford English Dictionary, is not a new phenomenon. Little more than 100 years ago there occurred in the streets of London an outcrop of robbery with violence. It was called "garrotting", which was an attempt to choke or strangle the victim of a robbery.' (Mugging differs from garrotting only in its use of offensive weapons). Blom-Cooper's stress on the traditional nature of the crime seems to be the correct one; although his attempt to distinguish 'mugging' from 'garrotting' in terms of the use of offensive weapons does not square with the definition of mugging offered by the American police chief who said: 'with or without weapons'. More significant than the question of weapons is what the American definition of 'mugging' shares with the British phenomenon of 'garrotting': both refer to 'choking', 'strangling', 'an assault by crushing the victim's head or throat in an armlock'. In the effort to get a clear definition of 'mugging', the British press referred to the United States, but the similarities suggest that when Americans first defined 'mugging' they had at least one eye on Britain.

In fact the more one looks at the historical parallels, the more striking are the similarities between a number of earlier crimes and mugging. Street crimes were of course a familiar part of the general pattern of urban crime throughout the nineteenth century. Well-off travellers passing through the lonely streets of London after dark sometimes had their luggage pinched off carts by skilful 'dragsmen'. Solitary strangers might be subject to sudden attack and robbery by footpads, occasionally lured to their fate by an accomplice, a professional street-walker. Chesney reminds us of forms of robbery with violence, known variously as 'propping' or 'swinging the stick', practised by 'rampsmen'. There were outbreaks of 'garrotting' in both Manchester and London in the 1850s, and the famous outbreak of 'garrotting' in London in 1862–3 triggered off a reaction of epidemic proportions.[1] Even so, 'garrotting' itself was not new: 'Chokee Bill, the rampsman who grabbed his prey by the neck, was already a well-established underworld type.' It was the boldness and brutality of the 'garrotting' attacks in the summer of 1862, however, which triggered off a new alarm. What is striking, in terms of the parallel with 'mugging', is not just the sudden rash of garrotting cases but the nature and character of the public response. The *Cornhill Magazine* stated, in 1863, in terms which could have been transposed, without a single change, to 1972: 'Once more the streets of London are unsafe by day or night. The public dread has almost become a panic.' The outbreak in London was followed by reports of similar events in Lancashire, Yorkshire, Nottingham, Chester: 'Credulity became a social obligation' as 'the garrotters, lurking in the shadow of the wall, quickening step behind one on the lonely footpath, became something like a national bogey . . . Men of coarse appearance but blameless intentions were attacked . . . under suspicion of being garrotters.' Anti-garrotting societies flourished. Then the reaction began. More people were hanged in 1863 'than in any year since the end of the bloody code'; in July, when the epidemic had ebbed somewhat, the *Garrotting Act* was passed, providing for flogging of offenders. Several of these punishments were in fact brutally administered. Finally, the epidemic began to die away as mysteriously as it had appeared; and, though the Act and the extremity of the punishments may have had something to do with its decline,

Chesney remarks that this 'remains an open question. . . . The real significance of the garrotting scare is that the excitement and publicity it provoked made citizens readier to accept the need (and expense) of efficient, nation wide law enforcement and so speeded the general improvement of public order.'[2]

Before the 'mugging' label took its own kind of stranglehold on the public and official imagination, the police themselves seemed alert to the traditional nature of the crime concealed behind its many labels. The Metropolitan Police Commissioner, in his *Annual Report* of 1964, commenting on the 30 per cent increase in 'robberies or assaults with intent to rob', explicitly referred to the fact that 'London has always been the scene of robberies from further back than the days of highwaymen and footpads.' Were the rising numbers of robberies in 1964 the same as (or different from) 'garrotting' in the 1860s and 'mugging' in the 1970s? In Britain, there has always been a legal distinction between 'robbery' and 'larceny from the person': and the distinction turns on the fact that, in robbery, an individual is deprived of his property, in a face-to-face situation, by force or threat of force. 'Larceny from the person', in the period before the *Theft Act* of 1968, was defined as 'Pickpocketting' or 'stealing from shopping baskets', i.e. a situation involving stealth, not force or threats. Even after the *Theft Act*, when larcenies were reclassified, robbery remained as a separate category, a 'major' offence because of the use or threat of force to deprive another of his property.[3] Though, at the height of the 'mugging' scare, the police lost their sense of history, it is worth recalling that, to the end, no legal category of 'mugging' as a crime exists (though the Metropolitan Police Commissioner was able, in his 1972 *Annual Report*, to reconstruct statistics for its incidence back to 1968). The Home Secretary did, indeed, offer his own definition for clarity's sake (thereby tacitly admitting the ambiguity of the situation) when he asked police chiefs to collect statistics for the incidence of 'muggings',[4] but it never achieved proper legal status. 'Muggings' were in fact always charged as 'robberies' or 'assaults with intent to rob', or other similar and conventional charges.

It is important to remember that, though the Metropolitan Police Commissioner did not have the convenient label, 'mugging', to hand when he drafted his 1964 *Annual Report*, something out of the ordinary had indeed alerted him to this area of crime and called out his comment on its historical antecedents. What disturbed the Commissioner was the fact that in 1964 many more young people, often 'without records' – i.e. unknown to the police – were taking to robberies of this kind. Further, the Commissioner remarked, this trend was accompanied by an increasing tendency to resort to violence – a fact *not* borne out by his own statistics, which he admitted to finding puzzling. It was this coupling of young offenders and crime which had triggered his concern.

When, in 1972, Robert Carr, the Home Secretary, requested more statistical information from his police chiefs on the new wave of 'muggings', a senior county police officer of the Southampton force, in reply, once again remarked on the conventional nature of the crime to which the new title had been attached. He said he found it 'very difficult to differentiate mugging with [sic] the old traditional crime of a seaman getting "rolled" '.[5] Interestingly, in the most publicised British 'mugging' case of all – that of the three Handsworth boys in

March 1973 – the accused spoke of their intention, not to 'mug' but to 'roll' their drunk victim.[6] As the 'mugging' scare progressed, the press, which had seized on its novelty, gradually began to rediscover the historical antecedents. In response to the Handsworth case, the *Daily Mail* editorial of 20 March 1973 lifted the crime altogether outside of history and deposited it in the realms of Nature: 'a crime as old as sin itself'.

The fact is that it is extremely difficult to discover exactly what was new in 'mugging' – except the label itself. The matter is of the greatest significance for our enquiry. Let us compare the 'mugging' of Mr Hills with the following incidents. A Conservative M.P. is assaulted and kicked in the face and ribs in Hyde Park by four youths. The attackers escape with £9 and a gold watch. Has the M.P. been 'mugged'? The word 'mugged' was of course not used in this case. The date was 12 December 1968, the report from the *Daily Mirror*. Let us take a second example. In its report of the killing of Mr Hills – a 'mugging gone wrong' – the *Daily Telegraph* made a direct comparison with the street shooting and killing, four years earlier, of a Mr Shaw by two unemployed men in their early twenties. They chose Mr Shaw, the accused men had said, because they were in a 'poor position' and he was 'well dressed'.[7] The shot-gun they carried to threaten the victim accidentally went off. Although the prosecution accepted the plea that murder had not been intended, the judge gave the man who pulled the trigger 'life', his partner twelve years. Except for the choice of weapon the Shaw incident is identical with the Hills murder: amateur robbery, bungled, with unintended fatal consequences. The Shaw case, however, was not called a 'mugging'. To all intents and purposes, it was not seen at the time as a 'new strain of crime'. Perhaps it *became* a 'new strain of crime' when the *Daily Telegraph* resurrected it for comparison with the Hills case? Perhaps it was counted amongst the 'rising mugging statistics' when, in 1973, the Metropolitan Police produced for Mr Carr retrospective figures for 'mugging' going back to 1968? Was the Shaw case a 'mugging' in 1972 but not a 'mugging' in 1969? Just to make matters more complicated, the *Guardian* in 1969 quoted the two unfortunate attackers as saying that they had attempted 'to roll' Mr Shaw. . . .

What evidence we have suggests that, though the label 'mugging', as applied in a British context, was new in August 1972, the crime it purported to describe was not. Its incidence may or may not have increased (we examine the statistical evidence in a moment). Its social content may have changed, but there is nothing to support the view that it was a 'new strain of crime'. No doubt the press had some interest in stressing its 'novelty'. No doubt the use of the term with reference to American experience may have fostered the belief that something quite new to Britain had turned up from across the Atlantic. It may have been only a coincidence that the police officer who called the Hills case a 'mugging gone wrong' had just returned from a study visit to the United States. Contingency, after all, does play a role in the unfolding of history, and we must allow for it. We will try to show, however, that the facts about the 'mugging' scare, like the 'garrotting panic' of 1862 and many other 'great fears' about crime and the 'dangerous classes' before that, are both less contingent and more significant than that.

A CHRONOLOGY

During the thirteen months between August 1972 and the end of August 1973, 'mugging' received a great deal of coverage in the press in the form of crime reports, features, editorials, statements by representatives of the police, judges, the Home Secretary, politicians and various prominent public spokesmen. Before looking at this coverage in detail we want to provide a brief chronological synopsis of how public concern with this crime developed throughout those thirteen months.

The labelling of the killing of Mr Hills as 'a mugging gone wrong' in August 1972 was followed by a brief lull. This calm before the storm was broken by massive press coverage during late September, October and early November. This period provided the 'peak' of press coverage, not only for 1972, but for the whole thirteen-month period. The feature which not only precipitated this, but also sustained much of the press commentary, was the use of 'exemplary' sentences. Almost without exception, young people charged with robberies involving some degree of force (not always referred to as 'muggings') were given 'deterrent' sentences. Three years' imprisonment became the 'norm', even for teenage offenders. Traditional treatment centres for young offenders (i.e. Borstals and detention centres) were bypassed. The justifications for these severe sentences – and many judges admitted that they were unprecedented – were commonly made in the name of 'the public interest', or the need to 'keep our streets safe', or, more simply, to 'deter'. Rehabilitation was a secondary consideration to the need to preserve public safety.

In short, the judiciary declared 'war' on the muggers. Editorials quickly followed. Most of these dealt with the question of the fairness of 'exemplary' sentences. This often led on to an examination of sentencing policy in general, where the considerations affecting such policy (deterrence, retribution, public safety and rehabilitation) were variously correlated, the arguments being conducted with varying degrees of skill and subtlety. All the editorials, in the final analysis, supported the judges. Statistics also appeared to vindicate both the judiciary and the editors, since reports of the criminal statistics in the period were all headlined in terms of the rise in violent crime, especially muggings.

Feature articles also appeared during this period, written either by staff reporters or freelance writers. These attempted to provide background information on 'The making of a mugger' or 'Why they go out mugging', to quote two examples.[8] Most of these were factually well-informed and relatively informative, though the explanations they offered, with perhaps two notable exceptions,[9] neither of which appeared in the national daily press, were less than convincing. One further exception, from a different perspective, was the feature article (already quoted) by Mr Louis Blom-Cooper, Q.C., the one lone 'voice in the wilderness' raised against a harsh reaction by the judiciary.[10]

The police and the politicians took their lead from the Bench. In London the police instigated a 'clean-up-the-Royal-Parks' campaign designed to keep drug-users, prostitutes and muggers out of London's parks.[11] Local councils followed suit by setting up 'high-speed, anti-mugging patrols, equipped with vehicles, walkie-talkie radios and sometimes guard dogs' to replace conventional park-keepers.[12] Special squads were also set up by the police to 'crack-down' on mugging; patrols at London Transport underground stations were increased.[13]

As early as 22 October 1972, the *Sunday Mirror* estimated that Britain was winning its 'war' against muggers; but this did not lead to any let-up. Four days later, the new Chief Inspector of Constabulary promised an all-out drive to stamp out 'mugging' and other violent crime; he spoke of 'mugging' as his 'highest priority'.[14] Six days later, the Home Secretary was reported as having written to all Chief Constables in England and Wales for details of recent muggings. His definition of mugging – 'robberies by gangs of 2 or more youths on people walking alone in the open' – was also made public at this time. [15]This definition caused some immediate queries: terms like 'youths' and 'in the open' were, at the very least, ambiguous and the 'gang' notion seemed to rule out the possibility of an individual 'mugger'.

The Duke of Edinburgh, addressing the Royal College of General Practitioners, referred to 'mugging' as a disease of the community, for which a cure had to be found.[16] Throughout the rest of the year media coverage of 'mugging' declined considerably. However in the courts three year sentences remained fairly standard practice. There were some occasional articles on the effectiveness of various anti-mugging devices. [17] But perhaps the most significant report during this period was the publication of the results of an opinion poll in the *Daily Mail* (10 November 1972). Mugging had apparently touched a very delicate nerve in public consciousness since 90 per cent of those interviewed wanted tougher punishments and 70 per cent *greater* government urgency; and this despite the severe reaction already taking place.

In January 1973, the level of press coverage was higher than in December, but not significantly so. The Home Secretary, in a written Commons reply, said that the state of the 'war' was not 'deteriorating further' and might be 'improving in some areas':[18] cautiously optimistic. However the March headline – 'London muggings up by 129% over four years' – carried by many national papers,[19] seemed to shatter that optimism. The Special Squads, according to black community leaders, were harassing and intimidating black youngsters suspected as potential 'muggers'.[20] Then came the event which set the seal on Mr Carr's optimism: the sentencing of three Handsworth youths, one to twenty years' detention and the others to ten years, on 19 March 1973. This event revived interest in arguments about 'deterrent' sentences and feature articles reappeared; but the terms of reference had changed little, if at all. Security forces on London's underground stations were to be strengthened still further. [21] The same statistics, concerning London muggings, were resurrected and used again in April, with headlines like: 'Muggings reach four a day in London' and 'London mugging – police demand "action now" '. [22]The Old Aged Pensioners' Conference in May carried a resolution urging more drastic action be taken against hooligans. Inevitably Mr Carrr was forced to renounce his earlier optimism when he issued a special directive to police chiefs to 'hot-up' their war on teenage muggers.[23]

Five days later the Wandsworth police division was reported as having 'turned the tide' on muggers; apparently its 'plain clothes anti-mugging squads' were winning the war.[24] But four days after that on 15 May, Sir Robert Mark, then London's police chief, was reported to be 'getting every available man back on the beat to crack down on crime – particularly mugging'.[25] London had obviously not 'turned the tide' to Sir Robert's satisfaction. On 23 May, some seventeen days later, Robert Carr was again reported as 'optimistic'. He told 1200 women at the Conservative Women's Conference that Britain's police were 'winning'.[26] Despite these 'shifts' in the tides of the anti-mugging war, 'mugging' was beginning to wane as a news item. July and August produced only one 'mugging' report. This decline in media visibility was accompanied by the settling of the debate about the state of the war: it had at last been 'won'. On 29 July the Prime Minister congratulated himself on the country's progress and referred to the decline in mugging and crime in general as examples of that 'progress'.[27] On 1 October 1973 fraud replaced 'mugging' as 'Public Crime Enemy – No.1': Britain's 'Biggest criminal headache'.[28] The 'mugging' epidemic was temporarily over.

So much for the fluctuations in the mugging phenomenon. Crucially underpinning the various shifts in concern was the notion of massive increases in crimes of violence throughout the period, especially 'muggings'. Less visible, but present, if only implicitly in certain instances, were two other key themes: the notion that criminals were getting off lightly, that courts were becoming 'soft'; and the notion (really the corollary of 'soft' sentences) that the only strategy was to 'get tough'. Expressed as an equation, the argument ran: rapid increase in crimes of violence plus 'soft' sentencing policy equals need to return to traditional 'tough' (or deterrent) measures. We wish now to examine these elements in the 'rising crime rate' equation.

THE 'RISING CRIME RATE' EQUATION

This is what we might call the 'equation of concern' into which 'mugging' was inserted. It rested on an implied chain of argument: the rate of violent crime was on the increase, a trend encouraged by a 'soft-on-the-criminal' policy in the courts (as well as in the country at large, the result of 'permissive' attitudes); the only way to deal with this was to revert to traditional 'get-tough' policies which were guaranteed to have the required deterring effect on those attracted to violent crime. We want to examine each element in the argument in turn; but we start with a word of warning about statistics.

Statistics – whether crime rates or opinion polls – have an ideological function: they appear to *ground* free floating and controversial impressions in the hard, incontrovertible soil of numbers. Both the media and the public have enormous respect for 'the facts' – *hard facts*. And there is no fact so 'hard' as a number – unless it is the percentage difference between two numbers. With regard to criminal statistics, these are not – as one might suppose – sure indicators of the volume of crime committed, or very meaningful ones. This has long been recognised even by those who make most use of them, the police themselves. The reasons are not difficult to understand: (1) crime statistics refer only to *reported* crime: they cannot quantify the 'dark figure'; (2) different

areas collate their statistics differently; (3) police sensitisation to, and mobilisation to deal with, selected, 'targetted' crimes increase both the number the
police turn up, and the number the public report; (4) public anxiety about particular 'highlighted' offences also leads to 'over-reporting'; (5) crime statistics
are based on legal (not sociological) categories and are, thus, arbitrary. This
remains the case despite the deliberations of the official Perks Committee, [29] and
the efforts of the Cambridge Institute of Criminology [30] to provide more
meaningful indicators; (6) changes in the law (e.g. the 1968 *Theft Act*) make
strict comparisons over time difficult. [31]

In general it must also be remembered that everything depends on how the
crime statistics are *interpreted* (by the police), and then on how these interpretations are *reported* (in the media). However accurate or inaccurate the
statistics quoted earlier, they were used to identify the existence of a mugging
crime wave and to justify public reaction to it. W. I. Thomas once remarked:
'Those things which men believe to be true, are true in their consequences.' [32]
The statistics about mugging therefore had real enough consequences in terms
of official and public reactions. Hence we need to look at the figures 'straight'
as if they were accurate before questioning their basis in reality. But first we
ought to reiterate our purpose in making this statistical detour, i.e. we wish to
look at the statistical basis to the *first* 'mugging panic' in 1972. For this reason
we present here only statistical information up until 1972–3. For those readers
interested in the years since then we survey these briefly at the end of this particular section.

When we look at the criminal statistics and the trends that they reveal, some
interesting facts emerge. The first is that crime, *as a whole*, has been increasing
(though not uniformly) year by year *for most of this century*: since 1915 in fact
(only 1949–54 showing a net reduction, as a period, during this time). The
period which saw the greatest increase in crime generally was the period
1955–65, where the average annual increase was about 10 per cent. [33] The
seven years from 1966 to 1972 saw a decreased rate of increase, the average
increase being of the order of 5 per cent. [34] Statistically speaking, then, the
period of the greatest crime increase had passed by 1972. We were then in a
rather mixed and indeterminate period – not at the crest of a 'crime wave', as
certain public spokesmen would have had us believe. The rise, in short, was
neither particularly new in 1972, nor sudden; it was nearly as old as this century. In statistical terms, it was, temporarily anyway, past its peak. Nor, when
compared with earlier trends, was it especially alarming.

But public spokesmen usually have not meant crime generally when they
have spoken of the 'crime wave'. They have meant, specifically, the growth of
'serious' crimes, and especially the growth of 'crimes of violence'. Was this
new? Statistically speaking, no. Reginald Maudling, during his period as Home
Secretary, spoke, with concern, of 'crimes of violence' having risen by 61.9 per
cent between 1967 and 1971. [35] The figures for the years 1957–61 (i.e. a decade
earlier) reveal an even *greater* increase, one of 68 per cent. [36] (We are aware of
the problem of using statistics quoted by public figures and the press without
revealing their sources. However, this somewhat cavalier attitude is not without
intent since it is precisely such public statements – the popularisation of official

statistics – which provide the statistical 'back-up' for subsequent action. In point of fact we have checked both these statements with the official statistics, and though there are slight discrepancies due to the fact that the former appear to be taken from the *Reports of Her Majesty's Chief Inspector of Constabulary,* which only include figures for England and Wales (excepting those for the Metropolitan Police District), and the latter from the *Annual Abstract of Statistics* (1969), which combines figures for England and Wales with those for Northern Ireland and Scotland, the overall point, that the two periods are substantially similar statistically, remains valid.) So the increase, even in the specific area of 'crimes of violence', was not dramatically new.

Let us look specifically at the category, 'robbery or assault with intent to rob', the criminal statistical category nearest to 'mugging', and certainly the charge to which most 'muggers' were subject. Was the increase in *this* category as dramatic as the reaction to mugging suggested? The answer must again be no. During the ten years between 1955 and 1965 'robberies' increased by 354 per cent. [37] Between 1965 and 1972, however, they increased by only $98\frac{1}{2}$ per cent. [38] Expressed as a percentage, the average annual increase between 1955 and 1965 was 35.4 per cent but during the seven years between 1965 and 1972 it was only 14 per cent. Even if we only use statistics for 'mugging', basing ourselves on the one universally quoted, namely the rise in London muggings by 129 per cent over four years 1968–72, [39] we *still* find the average annual increase (32 per cent) is *less* than that (35 per cent) for robberies generally over the ten years 1955–65. So even the statistics most closely related to the reaction to mugging, i.e. statistics of robberies and mugging, were far from being without precedent in the post-war period. The situation with relation to crimes roughly categorisable as 'muggings' was certainly no worse in 1972 than it was between 1955–65 and, it could be argued statistically that it was, if anything, slightly better. Thus, whatever statistics are used, whether the over-all 'crimes of violence' figures, or, more specifically those referring to 'robberies' or 'muggings', it is *not* possible to demonstrate that the situation was dramatically worse in 1972 than it was in the period 1955–65. In other words, it is impossible to 'explain' the severity of the reaction to mugging by using arguments based solely on the objective, quantifiable, statistical facts. A final word of caution. We have based much of our statistical evidence on McClintock and Avison[40] since it is a large-scale, prestigious, quasi-official study, and certainly the most exhaustive survey of its kind ever undertaken in this country. Since then, McDonald has taken the authors to task on methodological grounds and especially for confining most of the analysis to the period 1955–65. [41] McDonald demonstrates, convincingly, that taking a slightly longer time span (1948–68) reduces substantially the increases that McClintock and Avison found. Anybody seriously interested in the problem of criminal statistics should undoubtedly consult McDonald's important text. However, since our purpose is not to develop more adequate ways of computing increases in crime but simply to examine the kinds of simple statistics used to justify the reaction to mugging, we feel that our use of short time spans is justified. In fact, it is precisely the *annual* statistical increase in certain crimes, dramatically presented in the media, which fuel and legitimate the concern about crime.

What about the second element in our equation: the 'softness' of the courts? How well was this grounded, statistically? There are two strands involved here: the 'acquittal versus conviction rate'; and sentencing policy. A major assumption behind some of the proposals of the Criminal Law Revision Committee, and the remarks of vociferous supporters of it, like Sir Robert Mark, was that professional criminals are being found 'not guilty' too easily. Sir Robert Mark's contention was based on the assumption that about half of the defendants who plead 'not guilty' are acquitted by juries.[42] The evidence concerning 'acquittal rates' is not nearly so easy to come by as the evidence relating to criminal statistics, but what little there is tends not to support this judgement.

McCabe and Purves, of the Oxford Penal Research Unit, found that in one-third of the acquittals they examined (fifty-three out of 173), the prosecution evidence was so thin that the judge *directed* an acquittal without leaving it to the jury;[43] and second, that most acquittals in higher courts, even where the accused had previous convictions, involved relatively *minor* offences. Elgrod and Lew re-examined the records of a firm of London solicitors for the period 1964–73 and found that the proportion of acquittals brought in by juries had remained stable and averaged out at about 31 per cent.[44] In other words, it lent support to the view of many practising lawyers of an acquittal rate of one in three of those people pleading 'not guilty', a finding which did not support Sir Robert Mark's case.

Acquittal rates appear, then, to have altered little in recent years, to affect chiefly 'minor' criminals, and to be much less than the 50 per cent claimed. But probably more pivotal to the perception of 'softness' to 'toughness' in the courtroom is sentencing policy.

Sentences for violent offences have actually been getting longer. Sparks found, using the 'year-end' figures, that those serving fixed-term sentences of seven years or more (the majority of whom were convicted for crimes of violence) had 'roughly doubled' in number between 1960 and 1967, while the numbers of those serving ten years or more had 'tripled'.[45] This finding is very different from those of the H.M.S.O. Report, *People in Prisons*.[46] One essential difference between the two documents is that the H.M.S.O. Report largely deals with *admissions* in any one year. On this basis it argues that apart from the increase in numbers serving fixed-term sentences of over fourteen years, largely consequent upon the abolition of capital punishment, there has been little change in 'intermediate' sentences. Sparks, on the other hand, using the statistics in a more complex way (and berating *People in Prisons* for its 'simple' use of the statistics), finds a very different picture: one of an increasing build-up of 'long-stay' prisoners (those serving seven-plus, ten-plus, fourteen-plus and 'life') throughout the period 1960–7, practically all of whom, by 1967, were convicted of 'violent' offences. Post-abolition, the number of 'lifers' has increased, as has the average length of such sentences.[47] Furthermore, it has been argued that 1950–7 was a period of 'lenient' sentencing which saw a twofold increase in robberies, whereas 1957–66 witnessed a reversal in sentencing policy – and a *three*fold increase in robberies. Professor Radzinowicz also notes the change, in 1960, from the lenience of the years 1950–7:

Recently the courts seem to have been taking a sterner view, and in 1960 the standards reverted to those of 1950 . . . The trend towards increased severity is also reflected in much sharper sentences for younger and for first offenders.[48]

These are hardly indexes of a growing 'soft policy' by the courts.

Whether these policies have been deterring – the third element in our equation – is another matter. McClintock and Avison,[49] reviewing the 1955–65 period in their chapter on 'The Recidivist', argue for a percentage increase of 160 per cent in the numbers coming back before the courts; with an even higher rate for the younger recidivists (aged 14 – 21). The reconviction rate for 'serious' recidivists (five or more proved indictable offences) was higher than that for other recidivists; a third of young robbers had 'high' rates of recidivism (two or more previous proved indictable offences); and 'offences of robbery and breaking showed the greatest proportion of "high" recidivism'.

As it happens, there *is* important evidence about the relation between tough sentencing and deterrence drawn specifically from 'mugging'. Baxter and Nuttall, Home Office research officers, examined the long and severe sentences passed on the three boys in the Handsworth 'mugging' case for subsequent 'deterrent' effect.[50] They experienced the same difficulty the present authors did in finding an acceptable statistical basis for 'mugging'. But, taking the 'robbery and assault with intent to rob' as their statistical base-line (and acknowledging that this figure would include 'crimes other than mugging'), the authors had to conclude: 'In none of the police areas studied did the sentence have the anticipated impact on the number of reported robberies.' In Birmingham, where the initial offence was committed, the robbery offence rate continued uninterrupted (i.e. 'relatively low throughout the two relevant years').

In short, the statistics such as we have do *not* support the 'rising crime rate' equation. An 'unprecedented' rise in robberies with violence was *not* new in 1972. Sentences for serious offences were growing *longer* rather than shorter, and *more* people were receiving them; acquittal rates seemed *not* to have changed. And these tough policies were *not* deterring. In fact, if we regard the 'toughness' in the courts throughout the 1960s as an 'experiment in deterrence', the rising rate of crime and recidivism demonstrates just how bad is the record of deterrence as an instrument of penal policy. This general picture – true for serious crime as a whole – was also true for 'mugging'.

However, in the specific case of the mugging statistics, we can go further still. We have just alluded to the difficulties that Baxter and Nuttall found in isolating a statistical base in their work on the 'mugging' figures, and we also mentioned we had similar difficulties. This point bears amplification. The much publicised 1973 headlines that London 'muggings' were 129 per cent up over the four years 1968–72 seem to have their base in *Robbery and Kindred Offences In the Metropolitan Police District, 1968–72.*[54] Their precise origin remains a deep mystery to us. Our efforts to 'crack' them have been in vain. Since there is no legal offence called 'mugging', the figures cannot be derived direct from the *Annual Reports*. Some Chief Constables expressed doubt as to what to include under 'mugging' when the Home Secretary asked for figures for 1968 (though there is evidence that, since the 1972–3 period, regional figures for crimes descriptively arranged under the 'mugging' category, together with some figures, however loose, on the ethnic identity of assailants, *have* been kept). The graph in the 1973 *Report* must therefore be a back-projection; but based on what? Since none of the existing 'robbery' figures for 1968, or the other years, square with the reconstructed 'mugging' figures, these must be a selective conflation of proportions of a number of different sub-categories within the over-all 'robbery' figures. But how much of which? (We have tried as many permutations as ingenuity allows, though without success.) And what statistical checks were there on this selective clustering under the 'mugging' label, performed in 1973 (when the 'mugging' panic was at its peak), for a year – 1968 – when the label was not in use?

We mentioned earlier that we would end with some general updating on statistics. We offer them for completeness, rather than in the hope that they will clarify much. 1973 saw practically no change in the over-all crime figures, sub-stantial percentage *reductions* in the robbery figures, substantial percentage *increases* in 'crimes of violence' generally, and a mixed set of figures for thefts from the person (a large percentage increase (12.5 per cent) in London and a largish percentage reduction in the provinces (8.4 per cent)). 1974 saw larger percentage increases in crime generally and robbery, massive percentage in-creases in theft from the person (42 per cent in the provinces, 71 per cent in London), but small percentage increases in 'crimes of violence' generally. 1975 saw smaller percentage increases in crime generally but even larger percentage increases in robbery (24 per cent in the provinces, 41.2 per cent in London). The percentage increases in theft from the person, still large, were less dramatic than in 1974, while the 'crimes of violence' category showed far larger percen-tage increases. Over all, then, the period seems 'mixed', but, for those interested in trends in statistically recorded crimes, it may be of interest that, except for sexual offences, *every* crime category recorded an increase in both the provinces and London during 1974 and 1975 – quite an unusual occurrence.

We have left the mugging statistics until last; these are, as usual, the most complicated. After the London figures produced in 1973 by the Statistical Unit for the years 1968–72, which were also reproduced in the Metropolitan Police Commissioner's *Report* for 1972, a separate 'mugging' statistic does not ap-pear again in any of the *Annual Reports* until the publication of the Metropolitan Police Commissioner's *Report* for 1975. This report carries an identical table to the 1972 *Report*, i.e. a table of robberies sub-divided into smaller categories based on the circumstances of the crime. One of these categories – robbery following an attack in the open – is clearly the mugging statistic since both the category and the figures for 1971 and 1972 tally with those in the 1972 *Report*, where it was announced that this particular category was popularly known as 'mugging'. So, despite a certain coyness on the Com-missioner's part about using the label (and this despite the fact that the original decision to sub-categorise the robbery statistics undoubtedly stemmed from, or was sanctioned by, him), we can at least be certain that the figures collected for 1975 were based on the same criteria, whatever these were, as those collected in 1972. Analysing these figures, it would appear that after the dramatic 32 per cent increase in 1972, muggings *decreased* during 1973 (by 20.7 per cent), only to *increase* by 18.7 per cent in 1974 and by 35.9 per cent in 1975. Whatever the reason for the 1973 decrease, what is certain is that the drop was only temporary. And as sentences in the courts have certainly not been getting any lighter for these offences, and police activity − in the light of much high-level concern − is unlikely to have diminished, we can only see these figures as further confirmation of the bankruptcy of policies of containment and deterrence.

However, the statistical situation regarding these figures becomes more interesting, if more confusing, during this period. In the Metropolitan Commissioner's 1972 *Report* we see the beginnings of a development which was to culminate in the production of a completely new set of crime categories in the 1974 *Report*. We have already mentioned the sub-division of the 'robbery' category which produced, as one outcome, the mugging statistics. 'Theft from the person' was similarly sub-divided, and one particular category − 'snatchings' − was included in a table showing the increases in 'selected crimes of violence, 1968–72'. We were told that 'snatchings' appear there since there was little distinction between such offences and robbery. The implication, since both were included in the table, is that the element common to both categories is that of 'violence'. But, then, in the 1973 *Report* we were told that 'snatches' were 'similar to robberies *differing only in that the victim is neither threatened nor injured by the assailant*' (our emphasis). In view of the fact that snatchings had appeared in a table of selected crimes of violence the previous year, and that it is *precisely* the element of violence which distinguishes robbery from theft, this is a very strange statement indeed. However, there is yet a further 'mystery' in the 1973 figures. We have already mentioned that this was the year which showed a dramatic drop in the numbers of robberies and muggings. 'Snatchings' followed this pattern. But 'thefts from the person' (e.g. 'pickpocketing') showed a *large increase*. How do we explain these divergent trends? Given the ambiguity surrounding all these categories and the failure to specify publicly the criteria for differentiating the categories, is it not at least plausible to mull over the possibility − without necessarily suggesting a conspiracy − that what were perceived and classified as 'muggings' in 1972 were differently perceived and classified in 1973 − as more routine examples of pickpocketing for example? Such selective perception, and the accompanying decline in the mugging statistics, would certainly retrospectively justify the control measures taken.

In the 1974 and 1975 *Reports*, the incipient unhappiness with the official legal, Home Office classifications found full expression in the production of a completely new set of 'circumstantial' categories (i.e. ones reflecting the circumstances of the crime) which appeared in addition to the Home Office classifications. Of principal interest to us was the production of a 'robbery and other violent thefts' category; though, again, the criteria for adjudging a theft 'violent' were not stated. In the light of the Commissioner's earlier sub-division of 'thefts from the person', it would appear that 'snatchings' had finally become so similar to robberies (despite being 'non-violent'!) as to warrant the production of a joint statistic. In 1975 there were 7959 such 'robberies and other violent thefts' (up 43 per cent), 4452 official robberies (up 41.2 per cent) and 1977 'muggings' (up 35.9 per cent); though the official 'theft from the person' category had no equivalent category in the Commissioner's classification. What are we to make of the new category 'robbery and other violent thefts'? Violent thefts were obviously similar to robberies; hence the joint statistic: yet official robberies were then further sub-divided without any reference to the joint statistic. This means that the mugging statistic was produced without reference to the 'violent theft' category. Yet it seems hard to believe that the introduction of these new categories – first 'snatches' and then 'violent thefts' – were entirely unrelated to the original breakdown of the robbery figures which had, as one outcome, the production of a set of figures for 'mugging'; particularly since the very reason given for the sub-division of 'thefts from the person' was to differentiate the more 'robbery-like' from the rest. Given this line of reasoning, the current publicity and concern aroused by the London mugging statistics is very difficult to understand, on purely statistical grounds, since the 1975 figures reveal that, of the 'robberies and violent thefts', only 25 per cent were actually 'muggings'. Finally, it should be emphasised that none of these statistical convolutions have ever affected the Chief Inspector of Constabulary's *Reports*, which have always stuck to the official classifications. One important result of this is that, despite the grave concern expressed in these reports about mugging (c.f. the 1973 *Report*), we have *never had any figures at all concerning the scale, and rate of increase, of provincial muggings*. If the reaction to mugging cannot then be explained by a straightforward reference to the statistics, how *can* it be explained?

When the official reaction to a person, groups of persons or series of events is *out of all proportion* to the actual threat offered, when 'experts', in the form of police chiefs, the judiciary, politicians and editors *perceive* the threat in all but identical terms, and appear to talk 'with one voice' of rates, diagnoses, prognoses and solutions, when the media representations universally stress 'sudden and dramatic' increases (in numbers involved or events) and 'novelty', above and beyond that which a sober, realistic appraisal could sustain, then we believe it is appropriate to speak of the beginnings of a *moral panic*.

A moral panic has been defined as follows by Stan Cohen in his study of the 'mods and rockers', *Folk Devils and Moral Panic*:

> Societies appear to be subject, every now and then, to periods of moral panic. A condition, episode, person or group of persons emerges to become defined as a threat to societal values and interests; its nature is presented in a stylized and stereo-typical fashion by the mass media; the moral barricades are manned by editors, bishops, politicians and other right-thinking people; socially accredited experts pronounce their diagnoses and solutions; ways of coping are evolved or (more often) resorted to; the condition then disappears, submerges or deteriorates and becomes more visible. Sometimes the object of the panic is quite novel and at other times it is something which has been in existence long enough, but suddenly appears in the limelight. Sometimes the panic is passed over and is forgotten, except in folklore and collective memory; at other times it has more serious and long-

lasting repercussions and might produce such changes as those in legal and social policy or even in the way society conceives itself. [52]

In this study we argue that there was a *moral panic* about 'mugging' in 1972–3; a panic which fits in almost every detail the process described by Cohen in the passage above. This is not to deny that, on occasions during the past few years (but also, almost certainly, for at least a century), individual men and women have been suddenly attacked, rough-handled and robbed in the street. We think, however, that it requires explanation how and why a version of this rather traditional street crime was perceived, at a certain point in the early 1970s, as a 'new strain of crime'. The number of such incidents *may* indeed have gone up – it is virtually impossible to tell from the statistical evidence which has been made publicly available. In the light of that, we think it requires to be explained why and how the weak and confused statistical evidence came to be converted into such hard and massively publicised facts and figures. It also needs to be explained how and why these 'facts' came to be identified as part and parcel – indeed, as some of the strongest evidence for – a general belief in the dramatic rise in the rate of 'violent crime'. The impression that 'violent crime', particularly 'mugging', was increasing produced a massive and intense coverage by the press, official and semi-official spokesmen, and sentences of an increasing severity in court. In short 'mugging' had consequences in the real world, quite apart from the number of people mugged on the streets; and these consequences appear to have less to do with what actually was known to be happening, than with the character, scale and intensity of this reaction. *All these other aspects are part of the 'mugging' phenomenon, too. They, too, require explanation.*

This represents a major shift of focus from conventional studies of crime. Cohen defines this in terms of a shift of attention from the *deviant act* (i.e. 'mugging'), treated in isolation to *the relation between the deviant act and the reaction of the public and the control agencies to the act*.[53] This shift of focus alters the nature of the 'object' or phenomenon which needs to be explained. In what we might call the common-sense view, sometime in the early 1970s British cities were visited by a dramatic and unexpected epidemic of 'mugging'. The police, reacting to these events, spurred on by a vigilant press, by public anxiety and professional duty, took rapid steps to isolate the 'virus' and bring the fever under control. The courts administered a strong inoculating dose of medicine. It disappeared within twelve months, as swiftly and suddenly as it had appeared. It departed as mysteriously as it had arrived. In the 'common-sense' view, *this* little sequence of events was 'mugging', at least in its primary phase. We argue, on the other hand, that there was *also* a massive blaze of publicity in the press, the use of a new 'label', widespread public comment and anxiety, a strong and vigorous official reaction. Moreover, the scale and intensity of this reaction is quite at odds with the scale of the threat to which it was a response. Thus there is strong evidence of a 'moral panic' about mugging. We insist that this 'moral panic' is also crucial to the meaning of the 'mugging' phenomenon itself. It is this whole complex – action and reaction – as well as what produced it and what its consequences were, which requires to be explained. We suggest that there is no simple 'event' here to be understood, apart from the social processes by which such events are produced, perceived, classified, explained and responded to. The more we examine this whole complex in detail, the more it seems that it is the 'moral panic' *about* 'mugging' rather than the appearance of 'mugging' itself, to which we must first give our attention.

In the following chapter, then, we bring into focus some of these so far neglected aspects of 'mugging': the way the 'moral panic' was articulated in the courts, and the reaction to it of the police – in short, the growth to visibility and subsidence, between August 1972 and the latter months of 1973, of a 'moral panic' about 'mugging' and its passage through the judicial and control apparatus.

However, before we turn to that we must make a detour back to the point from which we started: the appearance of the *label* which identified 'a new strain of crime'. It was the use of this label which provided the stimulus for the take-off of a moral panic about 'mugging'. But what was the birth and subsequent career of the 'mugging' label?

CAREER OF A LABEL

NEW YORK CITY ... the science fiction metropolis of the future ... the cancer capital, a laboratory where all the splendours and miseries of the new age are being tried out in experimental form. ... Professor Nathan Glazer, the sociologist, remarks: 'We're threatened with the destruction of the entire social fabric.'

America is where our weather comes from – the prevailing cultural winds are carrying the same challenges and threats across the Atlantic to Europe. ... The forecast does not seem very favourable ... when I last investigated New York in 1966, half a million of its citizens were living on welfare doles. Now the figure has reached a million. ... Only last week, massive cuts, the first since the second world war, were made by the state legislature in aid to the poor. ...

New York's major problem is this widespread poverty with the inevitable aftermath of growing crime, vandalism, rioting and drug-addiction. Already more than 70 per cent of the serious crimes are committed by youngsters under twenty-one. And crime means crime here – with a murder every twelve hours – many of them motiveless acts of violence with no thought of gain. ...

... the New York City Handbook |has| ... an entire section on how to deal with burglars, double-lock and protect doors and windows and the general warning: 'ON THE STREET walk where it is well-lighted and where there are people' ... one symptom |of New York's 'ills'| is the deepening bankruptcy of the city's public finances.

THE WORST RESULTS ... |are| the hatred and contempt engendered in one section of the population for another ... friends ... accept the hazards of New York rather as Londoners accepted the Blitz. (Alan Brien, 'New York Nightmare', *Sunday Times*, 6 April 1969.)

Is it a lack of courage to think big? Could not the country that thought up the Marshall plan do the same for its own good? Is it because the prejudices against race and welfare programmes are no obstacles to a grand rescue operation abroad but they assert themselves stubbornly against such a vision at home? And why is a small nation such as North Vietnam capable of resisting a super-power, despite the technical superiority of American weapons, firepower and mobility?

Such are the questions on the lips of Americans today. They are all symptoms of the doubts and anxieties that assail a large majority of the people about the trust in the America they believe in.

They are appalled by the massive confrontation at home between black and white, hawks and doves, intellectuals and non-intellectuals, between young and old, the law and the protestors. I doubt whether so many segments of American society have ever been as divided as they are today. It is more than a malaise; somehow the American spirit is temporarily unhinged.

They are afraid of walking in the streets at night and being attacked. This fear is greater than ever before. Crime in the street, unless the republican candidate for President is able to offer an alternative to President Johnson's policies in Vietnam, will be the big issue of this election campaign. (Henry Brandon, 'The Disunited States', *Sunday Times*, 10 March 1968.)

Lejeune and Alex note that 'The term *mugging* assumed its present meaning [in America] in the 1940s. Derived from criminal and police parlance, it refers to a certain manner of robbing and/or beating of a victim by petty professional operators or thieves who often work in touring packs of three or more.' [54] This is the classic meaning of the term 'mugging'. Its American location is, of course, crucial. Whatever its earlier usages. [55] it is in the United States that the term achieves its decisive contemporary definition. It was from this American context that the term was 'reimported' into British usage in the later 1960s and the 1970s.

Labels are important, especially when applied to dramatic public events. They not only place and identify those events; they assign events to a context. Thereafter the use of the label is likely to mobilise *this whole referential context*, with all its associated meanings and connotations. It is this wider, more connotative usage which was 'borrowed' when the British press picked up the term and began to apply it to the British setting. It is crucial to bear in mind, therefore, what this wider, contextual field of reference of the term was or had become in the United States. By the 1960s, 'mugging' was no longer being used in the United States simply as a descriptive and identifying term for a specific kind of urban crime. It not only dominated the whole public discussion of crime and public disorder – it had become a central *symbol* for the many tensions and problems besetting American social and political life in general. 'Mugging' achieved this status because of its ability to *connote* a whole complex of social themes in which the 'crisis of American society' was reflected. These themes included: the involvement of blacks and drug addicts in crime; the expansion of the black ghettoes, coupled with the growth of black social and political militancy; the threatened crisis and collapse of the cities; the crime panic and the appeal to 'law and order'; the sharpening political tensions and protest movements of the 1960s leading into and out from the Nixon–Agnew mobilisation of 'the silent majority' and their presidential victory in 1968. These topics and themes were not as clearly separated as these headings imply. They tended, in public discussion, to come together into a general scenario of conflict and crisis. In an important sense the image of 'mugging' came ultimately to contain and express them all.

During the 1960s, the principal venue of muggings in the United States was the black ghetto. Such areas in most of the large cities have traditionally been areas associated with high rates of crime. Following the black 'ghetto rebellions' of the mid-1960s, and against the background of an extended debate about the nature of social and family 'disorganisation' amongst ghetto blacks, the issue of black crime surfaced as a major and continuing topic of concern. Crime was taken as an index of the permanent state of tension among urban blacks: perhaps, also, as a means through which racial tension was worked out and expressed – a preoccupation no doubt supported by the fact that, of all violent offences in the United States, only robbery involves a high *inter*-racial element. [56] This equation of violent robbery with blacks was compounded by the spread of the ghettoes in most of the large cities through the 1950s and 1960s. Black crime was troubling enough when confined within the clearly demarcated zones of the ghettoes; but it became the central concern of a far more diffused and generalised threat when coupled with the spread of the ghettoes 'up-town', and the spill over of black populations into formerly white residential areas. The effects of this 'spill over' (which, in any event, compounded the many other serious problems of the large cities in the United States) was differently experienced and perceived by different sectors of the white population. Working-class whites – often of distinctive ethnic origin – perceived the 'black invasion' as a major intrusion from an even more disadvantaged group into their limited economic, social and geographical space. The tensions between these two groups have been considerably sharpened, 'white ethnics' often providing the spearhead for a white backlash against blacks and the poverty programmes (which seemed to be giving blacks an unfair advantage). This was undoubtedly one of the key sectors to which the Nixon 'silent-majority' appeal was directed, and provided active recruits into the 'law and order' campaigns. White middle-class residents were protected for longer from the black incursion; but gradually the spread of the ghettoes (and all that was associated with it) also began to make its impact here, as sectors of the cities hitherto thought 'safe' became redefined as dangerous or unsafe territory. The changing class and ethnic composition of the cities, and a shift in the whole flavour and ambience of 'urban living' for the white middle classes, precipitated not only a sense of panic but also the steady movement of whites out of the city (the so-called accelerated 'flight to the suburbs') and the adoption of a whole series of protective and defensive moves. The actual incidence of violent inter-racial crime was outstripped by the general sense of fear and anxiety on the part of the white urban dwellers; even if not actual victims, more people came to see themselves as *potential* victims, and undoubtedly a sense of 'trust' and security had been undermined. Lejeune and Alex very sensitively describe what

they call the growth of a 'defensive mentality' amongst whites; [57] and the image
of the 'mugger' erupting out of the urban dark in a violent and wholly unexpected attack or penetrating right into apartment blocks became, in many ways,
the precipitate for what were in fact much larger fears and anxieties about the
racial issue in general. By the end of the 1960s, then, the term 'mugging' had
come to stand as a referential symbol for this whole complex of attitudes and
anxieties about the general drift of American society – a cause for concern
made more urgent by the rising political conflicts relating to the Vietnam War,
and the growth of student militancy and black power.

Now this 'crisis' of American society in the 1960s was widely and vividly
covered in the British press. [58] It fitted well into a whole 'structure of attention'
in the British media. American reportage has always played an important part
in foreign news coverage in the British media, since, for both historical and
contemporary reasons, the United States is taken as a sort of paradigm case
for future trends and tendencies in the Western world, especially in Britain. In
the 1950s the United States stood, and was reported, as the symbol of affluent
success; in the 1960s it became the symbol of a modern industrial capitalist
society 'in crisis'. In both cases, the British media presentation of 'the United
States' suffered from selective exaggeration. The United States seems always to
be presented in 'larger-than-life' terms: more extravagent, more quirky, more
bizarre, more sensational than anything comparable in Britain. And when
American society began to run into serious difficulties, these too were presented in an exaggerated fashion. What is more, the British coverage of American
social problems, like race and crime, reproduced the definitions of those
problems which had been already generated in the United States. When the
British press reported on American cities, the already forged connections between black unrest, inter-racial tension, the spreading ghettoes and crime tended
to be reproduced in that form (though there is no doubt that 'selective exaggerations' solidified some of the looser connections). Thus, long before
British 'muggings' appeared in the British media, the British presentation of
'mugging' as an American crime reproduced the *whole context of 'mugging'* as
it had already been defined in the American setting. It reproduced *the idea of
American mugging* for British consumption (c.f. the extracts at the beginning of
the section). The graphic stories by Henry Fairlie – who was himself twice
'mugged' – in the *Sunday Express* in this period offer further highly specific ex-
amples of this type of coverage of American problems for British readers. [59]
Similar kinds of reports can be found at both ends of the press spectrum in
Britain in this period – for example, in Henry Brandon's pieces for the *Sunday
Times* and in Mileva Ross's 'I Live With Crime In The Fun City' in the *Sunday
Express*:

MY HOUSEKEEPER arrived one morning shaken by the experience of
witnessing the mugging and robbing of a man in front of her own house
which is just inside Washington's Negro ghetto.

It seems almost as if crime in Washington has become a sport, as if robbing for money is as easy as shopping for bread. ... In 80 percent of the
cases [of armed robberies in one day] Negroes were both assailants and vic-

tims. For the rest, whites were the victims of Negroes.

President Kennedy ... worried about Washington's reputation as culturally underdeveloped; Mr Nixon will be worrying about crime and how to live up to his election campaign promise 'to restore freedom from fear in the capital'.... Hair-raising accounts of escape from purse-snatchers or hold-up men and their easy getaways have stimulated fear, if not panic.... But many Washingtonians have become accustomed to living with crime almost in the way that Londoners learned to live with the blitz. You carry only sufficient money to keep the hold-up men satisfied.... You acquire a burglar alarm or watchdog; you don't stay out late ... you acquire your own gun.... Whites are afraid that they will be increasingly unsafe in this city where 67 percent of the population is Negro.... In the past, newspapers here have avoided racial identification of criminals.... The fact that this is now done so conspicuously ... is also an indication of how old liberal principles are being swept away by the crime wave. (Henry Brandon, 'Living round the Crime-Clock', *Sunday Times*, 26 January 1969.)

SUCH IS the amount of crime in America today that ... President Nixon ... ordered that the lights in the grounds of the White House should be kept on all night ... to stop the recent wave of attacks on Washington citizens – at least on his new doorstep.

So far ... [this] pledge of his presidential campaign – has been a notable failure.... To the harried police forces of Washington and New York, incidents [of robbery] ... are now almost as routine as parking offences.... My own experience in New York ... was a classic case of what Americans call 'a mugging'. This means that I was robbed by an unarmed attacker who jumped on me from behind.... It has happened to many of my friends.

My first-hand experience ... came early one evening.... I whirled round [upon being attacked] and looked straight ... [at] a hefty Negro youth.

Within days we seemed to be living right on top of a crime explosion.... After a few weeks the superintendent of our building ... pinned up a notice ... saying that ... a porter would be on duty ... every evening. I took all important documents ... out of my handbag. I carried the minimum of money in my purse ... One night we were awakened by a terrible noise outside ... we learned that the victim was an elderly doctor ... he was seriously hurt.... The theory was that the attackers were drug addicts.... The next morning we went out flat hunting ... we found what we were looking for ... Two doormen are on duty round the clock. And at night there is also an armed guard in the lobby. Everyone entering the building is stopped. The doorman rings me on the intercom before any visitor is allowed up.... I accept all this security as normal living now. (Mileva Ross, 'I Live With Crime In The "Fun City"': spotlighting the rising tide of violence in America', *Sunday Express*, 23 February 1969.)

We offer substantial sections of these two crime reports, one from Washington, one from New York. They range from the highly personalised and dramatised account of the *Sunday Express* reporter to the more general *Sunday Times* one. Yet, despite obvious differences in style, the same images and associations are evoked; the total 'message' is all but identical, and unequivocal, 'multifaceted', but unambiguous. The crime problem referred to here is not the problem of 'white-collar' frauds and tax evasion, nor even the problem of professional organised crime, and the legendary Mafia. What crime 'means', in these reports, is something completely different: the sudden attack, the brutal assault, the brazen threat; the 'amateur', uncouth and arrogant 'face-to-face' street and apartment encounters with young blacks/drugtakers desperate either for cash or a quick fix – in a word, the crime problem, in these reports, means *mugging*. It is *this* which is contextualised in both reports as being the 'primary' cause of the other elements mentioned: the escalation in crime; the 'resigned' acceptance of this state of affairs by both law-enforcement agencies and citizens; the fear, defensiveness and 'security-consciousness' of ordinary citizens; and, with the mention of President Nixon's electoral pledge, the notion of all this constituting a national political issue to which liberal responses have proved inadequate.

The kind of reporting exemplified in these early articles, and in a good deal of the American coverage of a similar kind in the British press in this period, acted as 'scene-setters' for the later English usage. It made 'mugging' familiar to English readers; and it did so, not by the coinage of a simple term but by transmitting 'mugging' as part of a whole context of troubling themes and images – it delivered something like *a whole image* of 'mugging' to the English reader. It presented American 'mugging' as in some ways at the centre of this complex of connected themes, drawn together with them into a single, rather terrifying scenario. Subsequent reports in the British press then employ the term 'mugging' unproblematically: the crime it indexes is already familiar to British readers, and *so are its contexts*. It is this whole composite image which was positively translated. And this helps to explain an oddity. So far as we can discover, the term 'mugging' is *not* applied to a specifically English crime until midway through 1972; but even as early as 1970, the term is *generally* and *unspecifically* applied to describe a sort of incipient breakdown in 'law and order' and general rise in violent crime and lawlessness in Britain.[60] Normally such a label would be applied in specific instances first, before gaining a wider, more generalised application. Here we find the reverse – the label is applied to Britain *first* in its *wider*, connotative sense; only then, subsequently, are concrete instances discovered. This can only be because the term was already appropriated from the United States *in its more inclusive sense* – signifying such general themes as crime in the streets, breakdown in law and order, race and poverty, a general rise in lawlessness and violence. To put it simply, if paradoxically: 'mugging' for British readers *meant* 'general social crisis and rising crime' *first*, a particular kind of robbery occurring on British streets second, and later. It is this paradox which accounts for the particular way in which the 'mugging' label is first applied to a specific British 'event' – the Hills killing near Waterloo Station. Although 'mugging' had been made thoroughly familiar to British readers – as we have seen, in the popular as well as the 'serious' press – the *specific application* of the 'mugging' label to a specific incident on a London street is problematic for the newspapers which first employ it, and seems to require some new definitional 'work' on the journalists' part. The policeman who used it first, qualifies it – 'a mugging *gone wrong*' (our emphasis). Many of the papers use quotation marks around the term – 'mugging'. Some papers (e.g. the *Daily Mirror*) offer a definition. This marks the second significant moment in the British appropriation of the 'mugging' label. The translation of 'mugging' and its context to British audiences, through the representation of American themes in the British coverage, is the first stage. But the application of the label to British events, and not in a general way but in a specific way to describe a concrete case of crime, is a shift in application and requires a new explanatory and contextualising move. This is the moment, not of the referencing of the 'mugging' idea in the American experience, but of the specific *transfer* of the label from one social setting to another: the moment of the *naturalisation* of the label on British soil.

The culmination of the English reporting of American mugging did not come until 4 March 1973 (ironically only two weeks before the Handsworth case). This was the long *Sunday Times* feature by George Feiffer on, 'New York: a Lesson for the World'. The article was in the colour supplement, and the front page of the magazine was a reproduction of a *New York Daily News* front page headed 'Thugs, Mugs, Drugs: City in Terror', which went some way towards encapsulating the article's extensive documentation of the violent decline and decay of New York. The article, which ran for eighteen pages, is too long to fully document here. It was graphically illustrated. It carried an extensive analysis, which brought together all the major themes of 'mugging' in the United States: the influx of Southern blacks, the spread of the ghettoes, the reactions of various sections of the white population, the failure of welfare programmes, the drug problem, the collapse of the education system, police corruption and ineffectiveness in dealing with growing crime, and, crucially, the major threat of violence on the streets. As the following extract demonstrates, the threat of violence on the streets was perceived as undoubtedly New York's most damaging problem. Here, more clearly than anywhere, the equation of the crime problem with the problem of 'mugging' reaches its apotheosis:

> By virtually unanimous agreement, the most damaging of New York's seemingly insoluble crises is crime. Not crime in general, not even the Mafia's illegal operations and hydra-headed leeching of former legitimate businesses. Headlines notwithstanding, most observers feel that the Mafia's great spoils are trivial in the context of New York's total lawlessness, just as gang rub-outs comprised a trifling percentage of its 1346 murders – roughly ten times the total for the whole of Britain – in the first nine months of last year. It is a new kind of crime which beleaguers the city – more accurately, an ancient, crudely simple kind: an atavism perceived as a return to the dark ages.

> 'What disturbs New Yorkers', said Roger Starr, a widely read specialist, 'is not cheating on income tax or even embezzling from firms. Millions are steadily swindled, often with official participation – but that's middle-class crime, which scares no-one. What haunts us is being mugged on your own

street or in your own elevator. The poor and desperate simply push, slash or kick the nearest victim for his purse – which is terrifying. No-one is ever fully free of that fear.'

It might be useful here to say how in general this slow translation of 'mugging' from its American setting to British ground was shaped and structured by what we might call 'the special relationship' which exists between the media in Britain and the United States. In general this coverage is sustained by the continual search for *parallels* and *prophecies*: will what is happening in the United States happen here? In the words of one famous headline, 'Will Harlem Come to Handsworth'? This is often offset by a notion of *time lag*: yes, Britain generally follows the United States but later, more slowly. There is also what we might call a 'reservation on traditions'. Britain is, it is assumed, a more stable and traditional society, and this *might* provide some buttress or defence against American experiences being reproduced here – *provided* we take immediate and urgent steps. We must learn the lessons – if necessary, in anticipation. The notion that the United States provides the 'laboratory of democracy', a preview of 'the problems of Western democracy', can be clearly seen in Henry Fairlie's *Sunday Express* article of 22 September 1968: 'In America this year one can see the politics of the future: in Britain as much as anywhere else.' There is a fuller view about how Britain might then 'learn the lessons' in Angus Maude's long article on 'The Enemy Within':

Every observer of the American scene had wondered what would become of a generation of spoiled children with too much money to spend, encouraged to behave like adults in the insecure years of immature adolescence. The spread of violence, vandalism, drugs, sexual promiscuity – in short, the growing rejection of civilized social standards – has provided the answer. Two things have contributed to this trend. First, the commercial exploitation of the prosperous teenage market, seeking to inculcate a totally material standard of values. Secondly, the propaganda of 'liberal' intellectuals who have preached the desirability and inevitability of the emancipation of the young. These are the siren voices we have been hearing, ever more brazen, in this country. As we try to grapple with our major imports from America – violence, drug-taking, student unrest, the hippy cult and pornography – our own permissive leftists have been hailing them as signs of progress. *We might as well begin to learn the lessons of America now,* [our emphasis] for our own traditional standards are under the same kind of attack. Here too, parents are becoming bemused and uncertain of their responsibilities, as authority and discipline are derided and diminished. The American radical intellectuals, who have done more than anyone to set the American people at odds with itself, have preached the rejection of patriotism, of pride in their country and its history, of all the traditions, and heritage of the past. The same gospel of anarchy is being promulgated here. We in Britain have certain advantages. We have a longer tradition of civilized living, a greater heritage of beauty and history from the past. We must treasure it and be prepared to defend it. At the same time we are going to have to fight for our future prosperity, to work harder and meet our challenges with more spirit and enterprise than are now necessary in America. This may yet be our salvation, for we have the ability to triumph if we have the will. If we fail, it will be because we have been destroyed from within – by the same kind of people who have done their best to destroy the richest and most powerful nation on earth. (Angus Maude, 'The Enemy Within', *Sunday Express*, 2 May 1971.)

Here the picture of the 'special relationship' is marginally, but significantly, redrawn. The United States is not solely a source of models and patterns ('the same kind of people', etc.), but seems to play a more active role, 'exporting' a variety of social ills to us. This indeed might stand on its own as another distinctive element of the relationship – one which comes more into play after 1968, which stresses that, because of the status of the United States as the 'richest and most powerful nation on earth', it does not simply set the pattern which Britain, like all other 'modernising societies', will follow, but may actively *impose* aspects of that pattern on our society by force of imitation and example, if not by direct cultural influence.

The underlying image of the United States, and its 'special relationship' to the British case, is central to our understanding of the way the campaign against 'mugging' developed in Britain, for it played a major part in the three stages of the transfer of the 'mugging' label from the United States to Britain. First, the idea of a 'special relationship' legitimated the *transfer* of an American term to the British situation. Second, this transfer allowed the designation of British events as *incipiently* 'American' in character. Third, the vision of the United States as 'potential future' could then be used to *legitimate* the measures being demanded and taken to control 'mugging'.

In the public debate following the extremely heavy sentences in the 'Handsworth' mugging case, the image of the United States was explicitly summoned once again in support of a policy of deterrent sentencing. A *Birmingham Evening Mail* editorial of 20 March 1973 on the sentence commented: 'Of course the innocent must be protected from assault in the streets. The more so at a time when *Britain seems to be edging too close for comfort to the American pattern of urban violence*' [our emphasis]. The American threat appeared in a more fully developed form, and made more explicitly about mugging and the safety of the streets, in a statement by Birmingham M.P., Mrs Jill Knight (quoted in the *Birmingham Evening Mail* on the same day):

> In my view it is absolutely essential to stop this rising tide of mugging in our cities. I have seen what happens in America where muggings are rife. It is absolutely horrifying to know that in all the big American cities, coast to coast, there are areas where people dare not go after dark. I am extremely anxious that such a situation should never come to Britain.

The ultimate effectiveness of the American imagery is the almost routine way in which it came to provide a basis for the justification of extreme reaction (social, judicial, political) to the crime problem. The language in this final example is almost classic, in its down-beat way, of the rhetoric of the law-and-order lobby: the cliché sensationalism of the 'rising tide of mugging' and the modest exaggeration of 'coast to coast' providing just that common touch that mobilises a silent majority and provokes it into speech. It is not at all uncharacteristic that this final use of the label – to start a crusade – should be accompanied by the mildest trace of anti-Americanism.

The 'mugging' label played a key role in the development of the moral panic about 'mugging' and the United States effectively provided both the label itself and its field of associations and references, which lent meaning and substance to the term. The mass media here was the key apparatus which formed the link and framed the passage of the term from one context to the other. This is no simple coupling. First, there is the whole American experience of 'mugging'; then there is the way an already fully elaborated and troubling theme in the United States is picked up and represented in the British press. This representation familiarises the British audience not only with the term but also with what it has come to mean, to signify, to stand for in the American context. 'Mugging' comes to Britain first as an American phenomenon, but fully thematised and contextualised. It is embedded in a number of linked frames: the race conflict; the urban crisis; rising crime; the breakdown of 'law and order'; the liberal conspiracy; the white blacklash. It is no mere fact about crime in the United States which is reported. It connotes a whole historical construction about the nature and dilemmas of American society. The British media pick up American 'mugging' within this cluster of connotative references. The term is indexical: simply by using the label, a whole social history of the contemporary United States can be immediately and graphically mapped into place. Then the label is *appropriated* and applied to the British situation. Significantly, it is applied in Britain, first, precisely in its connotative dimensions. It is used in a loose and unspecified way, to indicate rising street crime, a general breakdown of 'law and order' in certain parts of London. Only then, finally, is it applied to a particular form of crime. But this later more precise usage *also* carries with it the already powerful and threatening social themes. And gradually throughout the peak of the wave of British 'muggings' these themes, already latent in the American use of the label, re-emerge as part and parcel of the meaning of 'mugging' in Britain too. The 'mugging' label thus has a *career*: American 'mugging'/the image of American 'mugging' in the British media/British 'mugging'. This is a process, not of sudden transplantation but of *progressive naturalisation*. And this process is framed by a more general relationship – a 'special relationship', we have called it – between the United States and Britain, common to the media in many areas other than that of crime, which supports the passage of the label.

This *export-import trade in social labels* has consequences for how 'mugging' was understood in Britain, and for how the media treated it when it arrived, and for how and why the reaction to it was so rapid, intense and far-reaching. It may have helped to establish an anticipation in the minds of the British public and in official circles that 'mugging' was on its way here; and that, if and when it arrived, it would relate to other issues – such as race, poverty, urban deprivation, lawlessness, violence and the crime wave – just as it had in the United States. It may thus have helped to sensitise the British public to its troubling social features, as well as to create an expectancy that it would become an everyday occurence on British streets, and an unstoppable one at that – just as it was said to be in the United States. It may also have had an effect on the speed and direction of the official reaction, both in the 'closed' season before August 1972, when principally the police and the special Transport Anti-Mugging squads were at the forefront of containment; and subsequently, when open warfare against 'mugging' was in full spate, in the courts, the media, among the police, politicians and moral guardians. Further, it may have helped to set 'mugging' going in the public mind at a very high pitch. Given the American scene-setting, British 'mugging' had *no* career as a descriptive term referring to a version of street robbery with which, in any event, most British cities have long been familiar. The label had *no unsensational* origins in Britain. It was a complex, social theme from its inception. *It arrived in Britain already established in its most sensational and sensationalised form.* It is hardly surprising, given this pre-history, that it triggered off at once its own sensational spiral. What is more, the American representation in the British press may have helped to shape the nature of the unofficial reaction to 'mugging'; for if American 'mugging' arrived entramelled in the whole American panic about race, crime, riot and lawlessness, it was also fully entramelled in the *anti*-crime, *anti*-black, *anti*-riot, *anti*-liberal, 'law-and-order' backlash. Thus, via the American transplant, Britain adopted, not only 'mugging', but the fear and panic *about* 'mugging' and the backlash reaction into which those fears and anxieties issued. If 'mugging', by mid-1972, in Britain meant slums and cities and innocent folk and daylight robbery, it also meant liberal politicians versus decent white folks, the Nixon–Agnew coalition, the 1968 *Crime Control Act*, the politics of 'law and order' and 'silent majorities'. If the career of the label made a certain kind of social knowledge widely available in Britain, it also made a certain kind of response thoroughly predictable. No wonder police patrols jumped in anticipation, and judges delivered themselves of homilies as if they already knew what 'mugging' meant, and had only been waiting for its appearance; no wonder silent majorities spoke up demanding swift action, tough sentences and better protection. The soil of judicial and social reaction was already well tilled in preparation for its timely and long-prepared advent.

2

The Origins of Social Control

We started by looking at the emergence of a 'new strain of crime', dramatically pinpointed by the use of a new label: 'mugging'. We showed that neither the 'crime' nor its label were, in the strict sense, new. Yet the agencies of control and the media approached the phenomenon with absolute conviction of its 'novelty'. This in itself required explanation. Of course, 'novelty' is a conventional news value; but it is not necessary for the press to invent a whole new category in order to catch public attention with 'something new and different'. Moreover, the label and the conviction of novelty seemed to prevail, also, amongst the professional and expert agencies who ought to know about such things. Strictly speaking, the facts about the crimes which both police and the media were describing as 'novel' were not new; what was new was the way the label helped to break up and recategorise the general field of crime – the ideological frame which it laid across the field of social vision. What the agencies and the press were responding to was not a simple set of facts but a new *definition of the situation* – a new construction of the social reality of crime. 'Mugging' provoked an organised response, in part because it was linked with a widespread *belief* about the alarming rate of crime in general, and with a common *perception* that this rising crime was also becoming more *violent*. These social aspects had entered into its meaning. We have already travelled some distance from the world of hard facts – 'social facts as things'. We have entered the realm of the relation of facts to the ideological constructions of 'reality'. Next we examined the statistical basis to this reconstruction of events. This basis does not stand up well under scrutiny. When we first came to this conclusion, it constituted something of a controversial, even tendentious finding; but gradually the suspect nature of the 'mugging' statistics has come to be quite widely established. We concluded from this examination that the reaction to 'mugging' was out of all proportion to any level of actual threat which could be reconstructed through the unreliable statistics. And since it appeared to be a response, at least in part, not to the actual threat, it must have been a reaction by the control agencies and the media to the *perceived or symbolic* threat to society – what the 'mugging' label *represented*. But this made the social reaction to mugging now as problematic – if not more so – than 'mugging' itself. When such discrepancies appear between threat and reaction, between what is perceived and what that is a perception of, we have good evidence to suggest we are in the presence of an ideological displacement. We call this displacement a *moral panic*. This is the critical transition point in the whole argument.

Since the public has little direct experience of crime, and very few people comparatively were 'mugged', the media must bear some responsibility for relaying the dominant definition of mugging to the public at large (see Chapter 1). But this key role of the media cannot be treated in isolation. It can only be analysed together with those other collective agencies in the 'mugging' drama – the central apparatus of social control in the state: the police and the courts. It is to these apparatuses of social control that we turn first, and to the context out of which the strategies of each flowed. In Chapter 3 we shall look at how these agencies articulated with the media in order to understand how the rationales for action or dominant ideologies of the powerful complete their passage from the closed institutional world of the control culture to the forum of society as a whole.

The thirteen month period from August 1972 to the end of the following August yielded sixty different events reported as 'muggings' (if all the reports referring to one mugging – including subsequent 'follow-up' reports – count as one). If we look specifically at *how* 'muggings' were reported, the most obvious distinction seems to be between stories which are reports of 'mugging events' and stories which are reports of court cases *about* mugging events (for the exact basis of the sample, see Chapter 3).

In the 'peak' month – October 1972 – the vast bulk of the reports are of court cases. During January and February events predominate, but in March and April, when the coverage is dominated by the Handsworth case, court cases predominate once again. Over all, news reports of 'mugging' events take second place to the reports of trials and sentencing of 'mugging' in court. This becomes *massively* the case if we include the relative space and position of stories. 'Mugging' events, when reported in the following day's press, are much

TABLE 2.1

Press reports of mugging events and court cases (August 1972 to August 1973)

Month/Year	Reports of court cases	Reports of events
Aug 1972	1	1
Sep 1972	4	0
Oct 1972	15	8
Nov 1972	1	1
Dec 1972	2	2
Jan 1973	1	4
Feb 1973	1	3
Mar 1973	4	0
Apr 1973	4	1
May 1973	1	0
Jun 1973	2	3
Jul 1973	0	0
Aug 1973	0	1
Total	36	24

briefer, less prominently positioned, with shorter and smaller headlines. Court reports, especially on the day of sentencing, and most of all if they include quotes from the judge's summing up, get fuller, longer, more dramatic treatment, and are more prominently positioned. 'Sentencing', together with judges' homilies and comments, are *really* what commanded press attention during this period. The reports of court cases are not simply the 'natural' news follow-ups of events previously reported, as one might suppose. In the majority of cases, the court report is the *first* reference there is in the press to the event. The cases become prominent because of what the judges say and do, rather than because of what the offender has done or said. Strictly speaking these reports are not coverage of 'muggings' but, rather of the nature, extent and severity of the official reaction to the so-called mugging 'crime-wave'.

Most crimes that are reported in the press at the time they occur are not subsequently followed through at all, partly because the criminals are not always caught, but partly because coverage of the trial is not 'news-worthy'. These crimes and their passage through the courts are *routine*, mundane; they contravene the legal order, but in a 'normal' way; they do not threaten the normative contours or break the established expectations about crime, in general, held either by the police and the courts, the press, or the public. It is different when the crime is felt to be particularly heinous, like child rape; or particularly dramatic, like the Great Train Robbery; or when the Krays, the Richardsons and the Messinas of this world – the professionals – appear in Court. Figures like these, though no doubt also part of the world of 'normal' crime, appear, in the courts and in the media, as marked out from routine crime by a so-called pathological criminal mentality, or by the very extremity of the means they adopt. They are presented as outside what is 'normal' in our society – even 'normal' to crime.

In the press reports of these outstanding crimes and criminals, their bizarre, outrageous or threatening aspects will be centrally focused. If proven guilty, the criminals will be dealt with as harshly as the law allows. More significantly, few judges will pass sentence in such cases without a lengthy homily or admonition, which picks out what is special about the accused or crime, comments on it, usually in terms of what society will or will not tolerate, and, in closing, provides some justification for the sentence passed. Such criminals and their crimes get a treatment – in courts and the media – which consciously marks them out as different from the rest of society. It is the marking of this distinction between the 'normal' and 'abnormal', as instanced in crime, or, to put it another way, the degree to which the social order represents itself as powerfully challenged, threatened or undermined in some fundamental way by crime, which provides both the occasion for, and the nub of, the judge's remarks.[1] And it is this ritual enactment, as much as the actual sentence passed – in short, not just the crime but *the judicial response to the crime* – which leads the media to treat such court cases as 'news-worthy'. It is this element, above all, which focuses the media treatment. 'Mugging' is no exception to this rule.[2]

This ceremonial ritual act of the judge is particularly in evidence not only when the guilty are notorious and the crime grave but also when there is evidence of a 'wave' of certain kinds of crime – whether bank-snatches or shop liftings. The judge's admonitions in such cases are not restricted to the particular crime or criminals at hand; the wider social significance of the particular crime 'epidemic', society's revulsion from it and thus the social justification for exemplary sentences, are also directly invoked. These denunciations and ritual degradings of the courts are the visible response to – and thus *part of* – the perceived 'wave' of criminal events because they form an element in the 'moral panic'. For the newspapers, this official response is as news-worthy, at the height of a moral panic, as the 'real' events which are said to constitute the crime wave. Thus the shifts in the press coverage of 'mugging' from 'events' to 'court cases', and later the shift back to the 'events only', were not random: the first marks the 'peak'; the second the decline in the 'moral panic' itself.

These judicial admonitions were intended then, as much for the public (via the media) as for those accused. They are one means by which the courts contribute to the ideological construction of 'crime'. Significantly, judges' closing speeches were reported in twenty-six of the thirty-six 'court cases' reported. Thus the media concentration on 'court cases' allowed the judges to define and structure the public definition of 'mugging', and of the 'wave of muggings' in particular. These judges' speeches show a remarkable similarity: the same tone, language and images recur throughout. The effect of this uniform and weighty judicial definition in structuring the public perception of the 'moral panic' was very powerful indeed. The sense of 'moral outrage' best captures its essence. The common theme which underpinned the great majority of these observations by judges was the need to *justify* the increases in the sentences being passed. The different tacit explanations offered all appeared, therefore, as variations on the same basic theme: the response by the judiciary, *within* the court room, to public feeling, interest and pressure *outside*. To get the full flavour of what we may call the common judicial definition of the mugging crime wave in the high peak of the 'panic' (Oct–Nov 1972), we select for quotation *in full* two judges' comments as reported in the press:

> This offence is serious because it involves one person, who was alone, being set upon by three active young men, making him believe they were offering violence with a knife in order to rob him. This is the sort of offence which is so serious that the courts are taking the view that the overwhelming need is to put a stop to it. I am sorry to say that although the course I feel bound to take may not be the best for you young men individually, it is one I feel driven to take in the public interest. (Judge Hines, *Daily Telegraph*, 6 October 1972.)

> One of the worst cases I have had to deal with for a very long time. . . . Everybody in this country thinks that offences of this kind – mugging offences – are on the increase and the public have got to be protected. This is a frightful case . . . I don't see anything exceptional in the mitigating circumstances of this case. It is frightful. Had you been older the sentence would have been doubled . . . [Later, he said] I think I was lenient with him. It is because of the defendant's youth that you make the sentence less. If he had been 20 or 21 I would have doubled the prison term. Violence is on the

increase and the only way to stop it is to impose harsher sentences. It deters other people. I have talked to other judges about mugging and they are all very concerned about it. (Judge Gerrard, *Daily Mail*, 29 March 1973.)

This 'consensus of judges' – saying much the same thing in much the same way, taking leads off each other and mutually reinforcing each other – was rendered more persuasive by the lack of counter-definitions. Counter-definitions could only have come from the boys themselves, their defence counsels, or people speaking on their behalf. These were all conspicuous by their absence (the *Daily Mail* of 27 September 1972 and the *Daily Express* of 6 April 1973 carried the only two interviews 'with muggers' that we found in the national dailies during the whole period), except in the Handsworth case, where the extraordinary severity of the sentence demanded a counter-presence. If this exception is ignored (we shall be dealing with this case in full later), only five defence counsels were quoted and parents only twice – the defendants never were (except once – the cry from the dock, as the 'Oval 4' were being sentenced: 'These atrocities will be repaid when we come out'). [3] Even these quotes hardly added up to a substantial counter-definition, since the parts of the defence counsels' speeches quoted were unilaterally apologetic, bewildered and totally at a loss to make out a positive case for their clients.

THE FULL MAJESTY OF THE LAW

As our account of the press coverage of 'mugging' amply demonstrates, to pick up the trail in the press is, in large measure, the same thing as tuning in to what the judges said and thought, publicly, about 'mugging'. As we have shown, both in its reports of particular 'muggings' and in its treatment of the 'mugging' phenomenon as a whole, the press tended to orientate itself to court proceedings and the judicial process, and to treat, as a privileged point of departure, what the judges said in court about the wider meanings of the crimes they were judging and the sentences they were passing. To understand fully the context of judicial action (and its relation to the 'mugging panic'), it is necessary now to pass beyond the ideological interdependence between the media and the judiciary which we examine more fully in the next chapter, in order to look at those processes peculiar to the *internal* organisation of the judicial 'world': to look at the judicial apparatus itself, to go behind its routine practices and attempt to reconstruct the 'judicial mood' in the period leading up to 'mugging'. This task of reconstruction is not an easy one. The law stands, formally, outside of the political processes of the state, and above the ordinary citizen. Its rituals and conventions help to shield its operations from the full blaze of publicity and from the force of public criticism. The 'judicial fiction' is that all judges impartially embody and represent 'the Law' as an abstract and impartial force: individual differences of attitude and viewpoint between different judges, and the informal processes by which common judicial perspectives come to be formed, and by which the judiciary orientates itself, in a general way, within the field of force provided by public opinion and official, political or administrative opinion, are normally shielded from public scrutiny, and have rarely been studied or written about in any systematic way. The judiciary remains a closed institutional sphere within the state, relatively anonymous, represented in its institutional rather than its individual person, and protected, in the last resort, by the threat of contempt. We have therefore had to rely on reconstructing the judicial context from the rather scrappy information and public statements which are made available from time to time in the press and in quoted remarks about policy issues and public opinion passed by judges in the courts.

The factor which seems of greatest importance in shaping the 'judicial attitude' in this period is anxiety about growing 'social permissiveness'. This affected the judiciary in three ways. First, as society became generally more lax and permissive, so the boundaries between sanctioned and illegitimate activity became progressively blurred. There was undoubtedly a feeling amongst some social groups that the erosion of moral constraints, even if not directly challenging the law, would in the end precipitate a weakening in the authority of the law itself. This was specifically the case as Parliament, in the period of Roy Jenkins's Home Secretaryship, enacted a number of 'permissive' pieces of legislation in the social field; here the tide of social permissiveness could be seen as taking a distinctly official form. Second, the apprehension about 'permissiveness' was one of the factors leading to a growing preoccupation with the rise of crime, especially 'crimes of violence' committed by young offenders. The growth of crime was depicted as the inevitable outcome of this weakening of moral authority; young people were the group most at risk in this process; and violence was the index by which this vulnerability could most tangibly be measured. But, third, this coincided with a general belief that, in the face of spreading 'permissiveness' and 'rising crime', the courts had become not tougher but *softer*. In response, from the mid-1960s onwards, there is clear evidence of a stiffening of judicial attitudes towards crime, violence and sentencing policies.

We might begin to chart this swing in October 1969, a particularly rich month for predictive announcements from the judiciary. On 9 October, for example, the *Guardian* reported Mr Justice Lawton as saying: 'If violence results in bodily harm, or worse, to other people, then the police should consider very carefully whether the time has come for all such cases to be sent to trial.' Later, in response to hearing how a 21-year-old man had been put on probation and fined by magistrates for offences of violence, he added:

> With all this violence that young people are indulging in today, I am wondering whether leniency with the young is best for the public. In my view, this kind of violence to other people in our streets is not going to be cured by probation, fines or day attendance centres and the like. Word has got to go round that anyone who commits this kind of offence has got to lose his liberty.

Of particular interest here is the expressed need to 'get word round'.

On the same day, Mr Justice Roskill, a leading High Court judge, addressed the Annual Meeting of the Magistrates' Association in London. He urged magistrates not to shrink from imposing stern sentences on people convicted of crimes of violence, particularly the young. He justified this view by referring to 'public opinion' and the need for 'the courts not to lose public respect and confidence'.[4] At the end of the month Mr Justice Lawton, sentencing a 22-year-old man to eighteen months for malicious wounding, urged magistrates, once again, to send people convicted of violence to prison, rather than fining them.[5]

If we now move forward to June 1971, we can see something of the persistence of these themes: but, also, something of the reinforcement and amplification provided by the police/judiciary/media network. Speaking at York assizes, Mr Justice Willis said that the big increase in violent crime could lead to judges considering returning to 'former traditional treatment'. These comments were reported in *The Times* and the *Guardian* on 10 June 1971 – one day after the Metropolitan Police Commissioner and the Chief Constable of Yorkshire and North-East Yorkshire had had similar comments noted in the press. Lest it be thought that this convergence was coincidental, the judge himself used the actual words of the Yorkshire Chief Constable ('former traditional treatment') and one paper made the link quite explicit. *The Times* headline ran: 'Judge supports police chiefs on punishment.'

The notion of a qualitative contrast between the present and the past was also a feature of many of the judge's remarks at this time (as it was later, during the 'mugging' wave). For example, Lord Justice Lawton, rejecting the applications of two men for leave to appeal (against two-year sentences for 'causing an affray') as 'impertinent', said that until fifteen years ago such attacks (with knives and guns for 'revenge') were virtually unknown, but that now they were very common.[6] The next example is from May 1972. At the end of a general attack on 'permissive legislation' and its links with the rising crime rate, easy divorces, drug-taking and abortion for foreign girls, and on the replacement of past 'tolerance and kindness' with the present 'unkindness, intolerance, greed and no faith in anyone or anything', the High Court judge, Sir R. Hinchcliffe, speaking at a Justice Clerks' Society meeting in York, remarked on the growth of two kinds of robbery: the 'professional criminal carrying out big scale robberies', and young 'amateurs' committing small-scale robbery with violence. He warned the courts against taking 'a soft line' against the latter and urged magistrates not to fear 'unfounded, ill-informed' criticism from the media. He ended by asking for greater jurisdiction and sentencing powers for magistrates.[7] His remarks seemed to indicate the need for a shift of focus towards the 'amateurs', premised on the notion that today's 'amateurs' are tomorrow's 'professionals'. Certainly, this latter notion had become explicit by 1973 in the *Annual Report* for 1972 by the Commissioner of the Metropolitan Police. Although we cannot quantify this changing judicial mood, it seems correct to speak of a growing mood of 'anxiety' and 'concern' amongst at least conservative judges.

A number of pieces of 'permissive legislation' were enacted in the late 1960s. Most directly relevant to the shift in the judicial mood was the 'permissive legislation' affecting the exercise of the judicial function itself, especially in relation to potential young and violent offenders. Amongst the latter we would number the legislation affecting the Parole Board (1968), the *Children and*

Young Person's Act of 1969, and the *Criminal Justice Act* of 1972. This body of legislation is linked by its 'softness': the parole system because it aims to release some prisoners early; the *Children and Young Person's Act* because it aims to keep juvenile delinquents out of court; and the *Criminal Justice Act* because it aims to implement more imaginative, non-custodial alternatives to prison for some offenders. Although the impact of this legislation, in practice, has been slight,[8] and the actual drift in sentencing policy has been towards longer sentences, *especially* for the violent criminal, spokesmen for the 'control culture' have repeatedly cited it as 'evidence' (of permissiveness), the 'outcome' (of liberal 'do-gooding'), a 'justification' (for 'getting tough'), and an 'explanation' (of the 'crime wave') – in short, to support an already strong and growing impression.

The intention behind the *Children and Young Person's Act* was to treat 'very many juvenile delinquents (in common with children in trouble for other reasons) as in need of care and treatment rather than some form of punishment or disciplining'.[9] When the Conservative Government returned to power in 1970, it announced that 'it would not be implementing those parts of the Act with which it disagreed'.[10] Consequently, the changes, in so far as they affected the powers of the magistrates, were minimal: 15- and 16-year-olds could still be sent to the Crown Courts for sentencing to Borstal and detention centres and only the power to make an order sending children directly to an approved school (now a 'Community Home') had been lost. But magistrates regarded this loss of their power as crucial since they could now only place children into the care of the local authority. The decision as to whether to send a child to a Community Home was now with the Social Services Department – a 'soft' institution reluctant to make such committals, in many magistrates' eyes.

However, there were clauses available, within the Act, for overcoming the courts' 'impotence'. For example, section 23(2) of the Act gave magistrates the 'power to commit a child under seventeen to prison or to a remand centre ... for those cases where a child is "of so unruly a character that he cannot safely be committed to the care of a local authority".'[11] So if the local authority said it could not provide secure accommodation or the magistrate, in his wisdom, decided that the accommodation was not secure enough, or the child too unruly or too persistent an offender, commital to prison or remand centre could still ensue. There is good evidence that this 'option' was increasingly adopted by magistrates.[12]

The relevance for 'mugging' of this judicial way of interpreting the *Children And Young Person's Act* should now be clear. We do not know how many young persons under 17, charged with 'theft from the person' or 'robbery', were recommended for Borstal in order to 'rescue' them from 'soft' social workers and give them a taste of prison. We *do* know that many of this age, tried in the Crown Courts for such offences after Autumn 1972, had had a lengthy custodial remand and were sentenced to Borstal. If Borstal was appropriate for the 16-year-old 'mugger', something stiffer was required for the 17–21-year-olds; this could only be imprisonment; but, having settled for imprisonment, the judiciary had little alternative but to sentence to three years or more. Short, six-month sentences would normally have been suspended, despite the removal, in the *Criminal Justice Act* of 1972, of mandatory suspension. Intermediate sentences (eighteen months to two years) could not be imposed. (Blom-Cooper reminds us that the mandatory three years, embodied in the *Criminal Justice Act* of 1961, was in force, despite pressure for it to be revoked, while the whole field of the treatment of young offenders was still under review.[13]) So Borstal sentences for child 'muggers' and three-year prison sentences for older ones not only flowed from the mood of the judiciary in reaction against 'soft legislation' but were inextricably linked with the tough way legislation was being implemented in the courts – 'clearly against the philosophy and spirit of the Act', as magistrates admitted.

Another aspect of the judicial reaction against 'softness' was the desire to distinguish between the serious/hardened/unregenerate criminals and the unfortunate/mistaken/foolish/corrupted 'misfits': between 'the depraved and the deprived'. If we look at the Parole Board's terms of reference – weighing 'the interests of the prisoner' against 'those of the community' – we find this distinction at the heart of its policy.[14] Magistrates implementing the *Children And Young Person's Act* were, in practice, determined to differentiate the minor offenders from the 'unruly' and the serious recidivists in a way which fundamentally undercut the thinking behind the Act. (It should not pass unnoticed that this more traditional view of delinquency is increasingly dominating the discussion of the subject in official circles, as Morris and Giller have aptly demonstrated.[15]) While the *Criminal Justice Act* of 1972 provides non-custodial alternatives for the 'misfits', the Criminal Law Revision Committee's Report, which preceded it, has been widely regarded as an attempt to make it easier for the police and courts to secure convictions against the minority of seasoned professionals, and to make sentences, against these, tougher.[16] The legislation thus embodied, in an extreme form, the depraved/deprived distinction. This distinction between 'hard-core' and 'soft-headed' criminals is often used to underpin deterrent sentencing, directed principally against the minority of depraved offenders. But it was also a feature of the wider debate about social deviance in the period.[17] It is possible of course for the depraved/deprived paradigm to be retained, but the content of each side to alter. Once the judiciary has pinpointed 'violence' as an important threshold, *any* show of force is likely to be redefined as 'serious', and its perpetrators assigned to the 'depraved' category. The culmination of this slide may be found in the sentencing in September 1972 of young *pocket-pickers* (a skill requiring *minimal* body contact, hence by definition 'non-violent') to three years, to the accompanying rhetoric of 'violence', 'thugs', 'animals' and so on.

The judiciary occupied an extremely prominent position during the 'mugging' panic of 1972–3. But in a longer perspective the judiciary contributed in a positive way at the *beginning* of the panic, too, as well as at one of its early peaks. They seemed to share public anxiety about 'permissiveness'; they took a stringent line in implementing legislation which they interpreted as too 'soft'; they helped to generate, by some of their statements on 'violent crime', the initial concern, which, then, delivered the 'mugging' clamp-down; indeed, in the latter phase, as we shall see in the next chapter, they invoked as a justification for deterrent sentencing the public anxiety they had helped to focus, articulate and awaken in the first place.

If the 'world' of the judiciary is a closed one by custom and convention, then the 'world' of the police is closed by deliberation and intent. In the era of Sir Robert Mark, the police have become more accustomed to, and more skilled at handling, the media. But the routine tasks of crime prevention and control are certainly not regularly exposed to public scrutiny. In the 'mugging' period the police gained deliberate publicity in the media for their statements of concern about 'crime and violence'; this was part and parcel of the control strategy. More controversially, there were a few strongly partisan police statements about the general need for 'tougher action' which seem rather more like tactical indiscretions. Internal policing mobilisation – the establishment and brief of the Special Squads, or of the Anti-Mugging Squads – is, however, difficult to see, until 'after the event', or unless there is a concerted effort to bring it into the open.

The role of the police in any campaign of the sort conducted against 'mugging' is similar to that of the media, but they come in to play at an *earlier* stage in the cycle. They, too, 'structure' and 'amplify'. They 'structure' the total picture of crime in two related ways. For example, petty larcenies of under £5, though recorded and centrally collated, are no longer published in the official statistics. Since these form the great bulk of routine crime, this informal practice contributes to the sensationalising of those more serious crimes that *do* get recorded. There is also a necessary selectivity in allocating police resources to certain highlighted aspects of crime at the expense of others.

The one objective measure of police efficiency is the 'clear-up rate'. This, plus the problems of manpower and resources, makes it logical for the police to concentrate on crimes with high detection potential, at the expense of, say, petty larcenies from cars in the city centre, which are virtually unsolvable. But this logical practice is also a structuring one; it amplifies the volume of these selected crimes, since the more resources are concentrated, the greater the number recorded. The paradox is that the selectivity of police reaction to selected crimes almost certainly serves to *increase* their number (what is called a 'deviancy amplification spiral').[18] It will also tend to produce this increase in the form of a cluster, or 'crime wave'. When the 'crime wave' is then invoked to justify a 'control campaign', it has become a 'self-fulfilling prophecy'. Of course, public concern about particular crimes can also be the cause of a focused police response. But public concern is itself strongly shaped by the criminal statistics (which the police produce and interpret for the media) and the impression that there is 'wave after wave' of new kinds of crime. Of course, the contribution of criminals to 'crime waves' is only too visible, whereas the contribution the police themselves make to the construction of crime waves is virtually invisible.

Let us apply this model to 'mugging'. If there was a cluster of similar cases, appearing simultaneously in court, and labelled 'muggings' in September–October 1972, this could only be the result of police activity and arrests anything up to six or eight months earlier. The media and the courts appropriated 'mugging' as a public issue in August only because the police had been expropriating 'muggers' in January 1972. Let us look at two early 'mugging' cases. The first, involving six teenagers, was the occasion when Judge Karmel delivered his speech about 'decent citizens' being afraid to 'use the underground late at night . . . for fear of mugging' – the first media-recorded judicial invective against 'mugging'.[19] The evening paper report added that 'Mr Timothy Davis, prosecuting, said that after a series of attacks on the Northern Line British Transport Police set up a special patrol. Shortly before 11 p.m. on February 18 Det. Sgt. Derek Ridgewell got into an empty carriage at Stockwell Station – and the gang followed him'. The 'leader' then threatened him with a knife, and demanded money. The gang closed in and Ridgewell was punched in the face, it was alleged. He then signalled to fellow-officers waiting in the next carriage. A fight ensued and the teenagers were arrested. Five were found guilty of a variety of charges, ranging from 'attempting to rob' to 'assault with intent to rob' and were variously sentenced from six months' detention to three years' imprisonment. The report did not mention that this was a West Indian 'gang', or that the police themselves were the only witnesses.

The second was a case involving four West Indians aged between 20–25. This became known as the case of the 'Oval 4'. Despite the fact that the trial lasted twenty-three days at the Old Bailey, the national papers only picked up the proceedings on the final day: the day of judgement and sentence. The 'facts of the case' were, as usual, recounted through the quoted statements of the prosecution counsel. He said: 'On March 16th this year, London Transport Police were keeping observation at the Oval station when they saw the four accused hanging around and it was clear that they intended to pick the pockets of passengers.' The *Evening Standard* added: 'There were two intended victims, both elderly men. One of them was jostled on the platform and a hand was put into his pocket but nothing was taken. The other suffered a similar experience on the escalator.'[20] By a majority of ten to two the jury found all four guilty of 'attempted theft' and 'assault on the police', but they were discharged by the judge 'from giving verdicts on two counts of conspiracy to rob and conspiracy to steal'. The youngest was sentenced to Borstal, the other three to two years' imprisonment each. It was one of the accused who said: 'These atrocities will be repaid when we come out.' The paper also mentioned 'loud protests from weeping relatives and friends'.

These angry remarks of the accused become much more comprehensible if we set the case in the context of a number of additional facts (which, however, only the 'alternative press' reported). *Time Out* reminded us that:[21]

(1) these four men were members of the Fasimbas, a South London black, political organisation;

(2) on the night in question the men claimed that the plain-clothed detectives first pounced on them, swore at them, produced no identification and so initiated the fight that led to the assault charges;

(3) the defendants alleged that they were beaten up at the police station and forced to sign confessions;

(4) the police officer in charge of the arresting patrol was Detective Sergeant Ridgewell;

(5) the only prosecution witnesses were, once again, the police officers themselves;

(6) no stolen property was found on the accused;

(7) no 'victims' were approached nor produced 'in evidence' by the police;

(8) the judge himself directed the jury to consider carefully whether 'these statements are really fiction made up by Detective Sergeant Ridgewell';

(9) the judge discharged the jury from giving verdicts on the charges alleging conspiracy to rob and to steal. Thus only the charges of attempted thefts the police claim to have seen on the night in question and the assaults on the police were upheld;

(10) the charges which were not sustained related to a series of thefts of handbags and purses around markets and tube stations in Central London which the four were alleged to have confessed to.

(They were subsequently released on appeal having served eight months of their sentences.) [22]

February and March 1972: these two cases are taking place months *before* the 'mugging' panic appears. Yet, already, the police had initiated special patrols on the undergrounds. The organisational response on the ground long predates any official judicial or media expression of public anxiety. The situation was defined by the police as one requiring swift, vigorous, more-than-usual measures. This is where what came to be seen in November as a 'sharp rise in muggings' really begins.

In April of the following year, a judge stopped the trial of two black Rhodesian students – men of character and good repute, studying social work at a college in Oxford – with the remark that, 'The inconsistencies in relation to the movements of the two men on the platform are such that all six officers gave different accounts of it ... I find it terrible that here in London, people using public transport should be pounced on by police officers without a word to anyone that they are police officers.' [23] The charges and allegations in this case, resulting from an incident at a tube station, and the defence offered, were both strikingly similar to the 'Oval 4' case. The police accused them of 'attempting to steal' and 'assaulting the police'. The defendants claimed to have been set upon by five men, who produced no identification; after the ensuing fight, the two men were arrested. No 'victims' were produced. There were no other witnesses apart from the police. The group involved were the Transport Special Squad, and the operation was also led by Detective Sergeant Ridgewell.

Was there a pattern here? The 'Oval 4' judge did not believe the accuseds' story: the judge in the Oxford case did. Nevertheless, a pattern is clear. *This is the pattern of a 'focused police response'*. The Transport Police Special Squad came to be known as the 'Anti-Mugging' Squad, the prototype for others, though the precise date when this label is attached is not known for certain. No matter. This police patrol knew what kind of trouble it was looking for: who and where. There is more than a hint of anticipatory enthusiasm in the accounts of their routine emerging from all three cases. On the ground, face-to-face on the underground platforms or in the empty tube carriages – the 'mugging' panic had commenced. Demands were made for a Home Office enquiry into the activities of the 'Anti-Mugging' squad by the N.C.C.L., *Race Today*, the 'Oval 4 Defence Committee'. Later the Labour spokesman on race, John Fraser, M.P., wrote to the Home Secretary in similar vein. There was no official reply, apart from the transfer of Detective Sergeant Ridgewell to a new post, without loss of rank. According to the statistics published by the Metropolitan Police District's Statistical Unit, '1972 has seen the greatest ever growth rate in this type of crime'.[24] This suggests that it was the 'muggers' who escalated their activities in 1972. But it is clear that, throughout 1972 (and *before* the crime wave is made public in court or the media), the police, too, were extremely active in the London area against 'muggers'; the war between the police and the muggers had *already* been joined.

Once we know that the police were already alerted to, mobilised to deal with, and active against the 'mugger', in the period *before* 'mugging' had become a public issue, we must ask, whether, conceivably, this very mobilisation could have in any way *helped to produce* the 'mugging' crime wave which later appears in the courts and the media, and hence the public concern which threatened to overwhelm and displace all other crime concerns for almost a year. Did the activity of the police *amplify* 'mugging'?

One possible amplifying factor is, precisely, the decision to set up special squads in the first place. Special 'Anti-Mugging' Squads were almost certain to produce more 'muggings': an unintended but inevitable consequence of specialist mobilisation. Then there is the question of precisely what it is which these special squads were mobilised against. In the 'Oval 4' and 'Rhodesian students' cases, the Anti-Mugging Squad brought charges of 'attempted theft', i.e. pick-pocketting. Pick-pocketting is an example of 'petty larceny', not of 'robbery', i.e. involves no force or threat of force. It is a quite different situation, however, when the Anti-Mugging Squad descends on a group, accuses them of picking pockets, and then implies that they are members of a 'mugging gang'. Here a 'petty larceny' has been escalated by being relabelled a 'mugging'. Further, there are signs in these early cases of a tendency on the part of these Anti-Mugging Squads to be so eager to prosecute their task as to be prone to jump the gap between what Jock Young has called 'theoretical and empirical guilt' — in the interests of 'administrative efficiency':[25] what is sometimes called 'pre-emptive policing'.[26] In a subsequent article in the *Sunday Telegraph* on 1 October 1972 entitled 'War on Muggers', it was suggested that the police 'have tried to arrest muggers *before* they go to work, accusing them of possessing offensive weapons, loitering, trespassing and being undesirable persons' (our emphasis). Colin McGlashan echoed the same sentiment about anticipatory arrest, supporting it with some telling quotes from an unidentified 'Senior Police Officer', who referred to the Brixton Special Patrol Group as 'a bloody group of mercenaries' who were 'figure conscious all the time', concerned with the numbers of stops, arrests and crimes cleared up, and making many arrests for 'suspicion', 'loitering with intent', and so on.[27] It is of course also what countless spokesmen for the black community alleged some months later in their evidence to the Select Committee on Police/Immigrant Relations, though their evidence was not given much credence.[28] It was also the main burden of the extremely stormy meeting in March 1973 in South London on 'black people and the forces of law and order'. [29] Yet, when *Time Out* tried to get further information on the activities of the London Transport Anti-Mugging Squads, the spokesman replied that 'We have methods of dealing with this problem. But we don't disclose them – it might help the wrong people.' [30]

Another way in which police activity may serve to amplify 'mugging' is in terms of its effect on those reacted against. Jock Young calls the process whereby the behaviour of a stigmatised or deviant group comes progressively to fit the stereotype of it which the control agencies already hold as 'the translation of fantasy into reality'. [31] The actions of the police, for example, can elicit from a group under suspicion the behaviour of which they are already suspected. In the 'Oval 4' case, the police who approached the four men were in plain clothes and produced no identification; the youths were later accused of assaulting the police. But the fact that a group of politically conscious black youths resisted an unexpected arrest may tell us something about the mutual state of suspicion between blacks and the police in South London; it does not prove that the youths were 'loitering with intent' to mug. This process – where official reaction becomes a 'self-fulfilling prophecy' – may include interaction processes during the actual course of an arrest. Becker argues that much social-control activity is not so much for the enforcement of rules as for the gaining of respect. [32] Questions of 'respect' become especially important during periods of police hypersensitisation. [33] But, as John Lambert has argued, 'Police relations seem moulded on expectations of excitability and arrogance on the part of the immigrant and on immigrant expectations of police violence.' [34] The 'Oval' scene was thus already pre-set to provoke an incident through the mutual expectations by blacks and the police of one another. Deviancy amplification can depend as much on this level of *perceived* behaviour as on what people actually do.

Once the anti-mugging campaign officially opened, as we have seen, it escalated – in terms of official police mobilisation – at an extraordinarily rapid rate. There was intensified activity against 'mugging' on the ground. [35] This wave culminated in its being declared 'top priority' by the Chief Inspector of Constabulary for England and Wales. [36] There was then the request, higher up the official and political chain, by the Home Secretary to all Chief Constables for details about 'mugging', followed by the further taking of 'special measures', including the putting into the field of more special Anti-Mugging Squads. [37] The Home Secretary issued another special directive to police chiefs in May 1973. [38] Sir Robert Mark's new initiative [39] was quickly to have some effect. [40] By October, the *Daily Mirror* could report that fraud had become Britain's new 'top priority': 'Britain's biggest criminal headache.' [41] For the moment, the crime-prevention–crime-news spiral had undergone another twist.

ORIGINS OF A POLICE 'CAMPAIGN'

We have looked at the police reaction to 'mugging', and seen that, in fact, and contrary to the 'common-sense' view of how 'mugging' arose, this must be seen as occurring in *two* distinct phases. First, the period of preparation for the 'war on mugging', a period of little or no publicity, but of intense police mobilisation on the ground, targetted around particular urban trouble-spots (the underground stations and trains in London) and particular groups defined in the view of the police as 'potential muggers' – above all, groups of black youths. It is this period of closed but intensifying police reaction, when there is an institutional definition of 'mugging' already in operation, but as yet no 'public' definition which *produces*, as its effect, the *second* phase: cases in court, editorials in the papers, official Home Office enquiries about 'mugging', a publicly engaged campaign, open warfare. The whole of the first phase has been largely obscured so far in the 'history of mugging', partly because it *predates* the public panic, partly because it was a response confined to the closed institutional world of the police. The pre-history of the police reaction to 'mugging', then, has to be reconstructed for this earlier period. The origins of the panic response lie buried in this prior institutional mobilisation.

What concerns us here is *not* the individual abuses of police power by this or that policeman on this or that occasion, but effects which stem from the organisational structure and social role of the police force itself in its broad relation to 'mugging'. Cases of police corruption have grown in recent years, and so has the publicity attaching to them. Under Sir Robert Mark's guidance, the new A 10 'anti-corruption' squad, designed to weed out the 'rotten apples' in the police barrel has been extremely active – again with appropriate publicity. This is an important question, but a different one from that which engages us here. Individual members of the Anti-Mugging Squads, long before 'mugging' assumed its public shape, were intensely active in certain areas. But they were acting within an organisational framework which transcended the initiatives which individual members of the squads took within that framework. The situation in South London and elsewhere had already been defined for these specialist officers in such a way as to lead them to expect or anticipate an avalanche of 'muggings'.

Why were the police so sensitised, and how? Why was the situation already so defined? If individual members of the Anti-Mugging Squads overstepped the difficult and ambiguous line between theoretical and empirical guilt, it was – we would argue – because they were working in a situation in which such distinctions were already damagingly blurred. It cannot escape our notice *where* this institutional police mobilisation first reveals itself – the South London area and tube stations: or *who* is being picked up in the anti-mugging 'sweep' – above all, groups of black youth. So the specific targetting against 'mugging' has the closest of links with another, more inclusive, though equally powerfully charged context: the seriously deteriorated relations between the police and the black community, a feature of 'community relations' throughout the 1970s. It must seriously be asked whether the sensitisation of the police to 'mugging' was altogether unrelated to that other and troubling saga of 'police power and black people'. It is from this angle that we turn to look at a quote from Detective Sergeant Ridgewell, whose name figured so prominently in several of the anticipatory 'mugging' affairs. Ridgewell was the leader on the ground of the squad's tactics, and a former member of the Rhodesian police force. When asked at the trial of the two Rhodesian students whether he would be par-

ticularly on the look out for 'coloured young men', he replied: 'On the
Northern line I would agree with that.' [42] This squares with a great deal of the
evidence about police attitudes from other sources. This evidence suggests that
many policemen in the London area were particularly on the look out for
'coloured young men', and when they found them treated them rather differently from the way they would have been treated had they been white.

Derek Humphry[43] and John Lambert[44] have both surveyed, in different
ways, the troubled story of police–black relations in this period. Humphry's
book contains detailed case studies of the injustices suffered by blacks at the
hands of the police. Lambert's book is a more general survey of police/im-
migrant relations, and, being more sociologically orientated, is more concerned
with uncovering the structural conditions underlying police activities in relation
to immigrants. The chapter on 'The Police and Race Relations', apart from of-
fering some initial evidence of police brutality from the Campaign Against
Racial Discrimination's *Report on Racial Discrimination* (1967), is concerned,
basically, to demonstrate how the professional *role* of the policeman affects his
attitude towards immigrants. This perspective is based on a 'social' view of prejudice: 'If this "social" prejudice is an attitude of citizens at large, policemen as
citizens may be expected to share that attitude. The question raised is how such
prejudice affects the professional role of policemen.' [45] This view, which places
the individual policeman, first, within the general social framework and,
second, within his specific organisational role in order to account for prejudice,
is the kind of structural explanation of police–black relations that we intend to
adopt.

Relations between the police and the black community deteriorated so
rapidly in this period that, as we have seen, a Select Parliamentary Committee
was set up to take evidence on the matter. The evidence offered is more important than the particular implications which M.P.s drew from this evidence at
the time.[46] Clifford Lynch, on behalf of the West Indian Standing Conference,
spoke of 'The systematic brutalization of black people' and of police
'blackmail, drug planting, trumped up charges and physical assaults'. [47] Several
witnesses in the Notting Hill evidence alleged police harassment, particularly
of young West Indians.[48] The Birmingham evidence included material from
Councillor Mrs Sheila Wright, who spoke of three policemen she knew who
'went out of their way to pick on the coloured community'; and of having
received 'quite a few' complaints about police treatment of immigrants; and
from John Lambert, who said: 'A great many – even the majority – of complaints by black people about their police are justified.' [49] Black youths in
Islington 'dread harassment by the police', according to a memo submitted by
the Islington Committee for Community Relations (C.R.C.). Similar memos
were submitted by Jeff Crawford of the North London West Indian Association and the Wandsworth C.R.C.[50]

In all, only twenty-five of the forty-eight Community Relations Councils
reported good local relations, and these were mainly in medium or small towns
and in substantially Asian rather than West Indian areas. [51] The *Deedes Report*
itself was obliged to concede that 'it was made clear by all witnesses, police,
Community Relations Councils and other bodies, but chiefly by West Indians

themselves, that relations between the police and younger West Indians (by which we mean those between 16 and 25) are fragile, sometimes explosive.' [52]

The picture of relations in this period that emerges from the N.C.C.L. files is similar. Their *Annual Report for 1971* singled out 'police–immigrant' relations for special mention: 'it is clear from files that alleged harassment of immigrants far outweighs the proportion they represent in this Country'. [53] Its evidence to the Select Committee spoke of 'the worsening situation' between police and the black community. It was, they said 'Very serious indeed ... in some areas it has reached crisis proportions. There, the breakdown of communications and confidence is almost total.' [54] When an enquiry into events at Lewisham police station – which figured prominently in the evidence – was requested, the police defined the accusations as 'stereotyped'. [55] More alarmingly, the police spokesman also publicly denied knowledge of any enquiries then being investigated concerning complaints against the police, *despite* the fact that the N.C.C.L. groups said that they had referred at least fifteen cases in the previous year. [56] A major survey into race relations was carried out in May 1971 by National Opinion Polls. The poll reported:

> It is somewhat dismaying to see the extent to which coloured people are critical of the police. The West Indians in Brent were particularly critical in thinking that the police generally pick on coloured people and did not deal with them fairly in their locality. Our impression is that this criticism is too widespread to be a figment of the imagination.
>
> Eighty per cent of the white people interviewed in this survey think the police are helpful. As many as 70% of the Indians and Pakistanis also think so, but less than half of the West Indians share that view. In fact, as many as one fifth of the West Indians think that the police are positively unhelpful – a view particularly strong amongst the young working class West Indians. [57]

Finally, the special Report commissioned by the Community Relations Council on Police/Immigrant Relations in Ealing added further substantiation to this picture. [58]

This general deterioration of police–black relations produced increased hostility and mutual suspicion on both sides. On the police 'side' this meant inevitably heightened sensitivity to, and expectation of, black involvement in 'trouble', and, by extension, 'crime', especially in heavily 'immigrant' areas. These high-immigrant, multiply deprived zones of the city are, of course, in statistical fact, 'criminal' areas, [59] i.e. areas of above-average crime rates, though at the time black immigrants were *under-represented* in the crime rates of these 'criminal' areas. [60] Mutual suspicion and hostility between police and black people did not rest on this kind of 'hard' evidence. As race relations have worsened in the country generally, as black militancy and politicisation have grown, and as the number of black youths unable to find employment has multiplied (according to recent estimates at June 1974, 21 per cent of British black youths between 15 and 19 were unemployed), [61] so the police in the black communities have come, progressively, to perceive the black population as a potential threat to 'law and order', potentially hostile, potential troublemakers, potential 'disturbers of the peace', and potential criminals. It is hardly surprising that, at a certain point in time, black youths were also perceived as 'potential muggers'. In effect, this is what Detective Sergeant Ridgewell was saying.

The state of police–black relations, in the period leading up to, and after, the height of the 'mugging' epidemic, provides one strand which enables us to understand more fully the source of that *preparedness* in the police which predates the onset of the 'anti-mugging' campaign itself. Another factor is internal police reorganisation in the previous decade, which, in our view, also played a part.

Changes within the police force during the 1960s fundamentally altered the role of the policeman. There was the amalgamation of police forces into larger divisions[62] which eventually reduced the number of police forces from the 1955 figure of 125 to forty-three. More directly relevant to the 'mugging' context was the growth of squads with specialised functions and the spread of technological devices to improve the efficiency of crime control (especially the growing use of motorised transport and personal radios). These changes combined to decrease the traditional 'independence' of the policeman on the beat (incidentally an important source of the policeman's status); to accentuate the move away from 'peace-keeper' to 'crime-fighter'; and to weaken the remaining links between police and community. The 'typical' policeman was no longer the friendly, helpful 'bobby', keeping the peace and thereby *preventing* crime, knowledgeable about 'his' community and sharing some of its values, with a large degree of 'on-the-spot' independence from his immediate superiors. Today, despite the introduction of Unit Beat Policing in 1967 and Community Liaison Schemes in 1969, undertaken partly to help restore these disappearing elements in the policeman's role, the 'typical' policeman is a professional 'cop', member of a crime-fighting unit, whose cultural contact with the people he polices is minimal. He is more 'car-bound', less 'beat-bound', less likely to live on-the-spot, and, with the coming of the now ubiquitous 'walkie-talkie' and car radio, his contact with superiors, and hence dependence on them, is constant. Although both these pen-portraits are over-simplified, the *direction* of the change is undeniable.[63]

This trend towards greater professional routinisation of the individual policeman's role in crime prevention and control has been further affected by *increasing specialisation* within the force: the growing tendency to set up special squads to deal with particular areas of crime. The first of these to be established were the *Regional Crime Squads*, set up in 1964 to deal with specific 'serious' crimes. Nationally co-ordinated, and with Criminal Intelligence Bureaux as 'back-up' devices, the Metropolitan Regional Crime Squad quickly moved on from a concern with 'breaking' offences (1964) to a concern with 'organised' serious crime (1965), and then from a concern with crime to a concern with 'keeping tabs' on known professional criminals.[64] Their basic importance, however, lies in their freedom to concentrate specifically on *one* aspect of crime together with their potential for swift mobilisation against *any* type of crime or criminals: their ability to move quickly wherever and whenever needed.

A second, related development, which also provided a 'model' for later developments, was the establishment of the Special Patrol Group (S.P.G.) by Scotland Yard in London in 1965. The S.P.G. was set up (according to a senior police officer), as an 'elite force' but was later brought 'back under control' when 'the people at the top got cold feet'.[65] Today, despite Scotland Yard's insistence that the Special Patrol Group is not a 'force within a force', this apparently is the way it has developed. The Special Patrol Groups 'have their own chain of command totally separate from the senior officers in whatever area they are working in, and their own radio communications network'. Today there are six units and a total of 200 'hand-picked policemen'. The origin of the group apparently was the 1961 Home Office Working Party, set up 'to investigate the need for a "third separate policing force" in Britain'.

> The logic behind the proposals before the working party was that a gap exists between the role and practice of the Army and our security forces and the civilian police – which anyway was understrength. The gap, in practical terms, was who should deal with increasing militant industrial disputes; increasing political protest; possible racial riots; threats from abroad – 'terrorism' – and the possibility of increasing social strife as the economic and social divide between the classes in Britain widened.[66]

The Working Party took ten years to consider, and reject, the idea of a paramilitary 'third force'. Meanwhile, however, senior officers at Scotland Yard had set up their own 'third force'. Essentially the Special Patrol Group is a 'backup' squad. The 'central London commitment' (two units of the S.P.G.) provide support, for example, to 'officers on protection duties and are also available for any other serious incident. . . . In the transit vans in each of the two units on "central London commitment" duty there will always be two armed officers.' The Report also referred to their other duties. 'When not on duty as part of the "central London commitment", or involved in policing serious incidents, units of the S.P.G. are used to swamp an area that has been experiencing an increase in crime of one sort or another.' In this 'swamping' role the Special Patrol Group becomes directly relevant to our concern, since several times units of the S.P.G. 'swamped' Brixton in order to 'stamp out' mugging: and there were incidents of a similar type in Handsworth, Birmingham and elsewhere. In this way they became a sort of 'super' regional crime squad. They have been widely copied elsewhere in the country.[67]

Both these developments – the Regional Crime Squads and the S.P.G.s – have helped to loosen further the bonds between police and community. But the second development, that of the S.P.G., had additional implications. Organised outside the conventional pattern of police and community controls, and with an emphasis on preparedness, swiftness and mobility, their behaviour had something of the military style and philosophy about it. Like an army unit, they were often armed; unlike the army, they possessed the traditional power of the police arrest. The implications of these developments for the creation of Anti-Mugging Squads are not difficult to see. Based in part on the models of the Regional Crime Squads and the S.P.G.s, the new squads were organisationally committed to the specialist role, style and approach with respect to 'mugging': to expect trouble, to anticipate trouble and to take the offensive. Given this style, which was a long way from the traditional 'delicate' handling of a situation which has given the British policeman an international reputation for tolerance and good humour, some degree of harassment and intimidation was almost inevitable.

If the individual policeman is constrained by his organisation, he is also constrained by the society of which he is a part. Formally, the police enforce and apply the law and uphold public order; in this they see themselves and are seen as acting 'on society's behalf'. But in a more informal sense, they must also be sensitive to shifts in public feeling, in society's anxieties and concerns. In mediating between these two 'social' functions, Young argues, the force tends to see itself as 'representing the desires of a hypothesized "normal" decent citizen'.[68] Even where, formally, they apply the law, how, where and in what manner it is enforced – key areas of police discretion – are influenced by the prevailing 'social temperature'. In the period leading up to 'mugging' there were two contexts, directly affecting police work, where the public temperature was also rising. The police undoubtedly became sensitised in both areas. The first is that of 'law and order'; the second is the context of anti-immigrant feeling. (Both are treated in more detail in later chapters on 'Law and Order,' and are therefore only briefly sketched in here.)

Within the 'law-and-order' arena, we can identify three strands: youth, crime as a public issue, and political dissent. The 'youth' strand includes rising juvenile delinquency, the growth of the young criminal offender, vandalism and hooliganism, as well as the 'anti-social' behaviour of the succession of youth-culture movements of the period (from Teddy-Boys to Skinheads). Often spectacular in form, the restlessness, visibility and anti-authority attitudes of youth came to stand, in the public consciousness, as a metaphor for social change; but even more, for all the things wrong with social change.[69] Within the 'crime' strand, there were also a series of 'focused concerns' – the scale and professionalisation of robbery, the spread of criminal 'empires' and gang-warfare, the technological sophistication of crime, and, above all, the greater use of guns and violence and the prevalance of a 'stop-at-nothing' mentality. The police found this harder to bear in the light of their belief that it was also becoming easier for professional criminals to escape conviction.[70] The 'politics-of-dissent' strand is also a broad front, including many aspects; but, from the C.N.D. marches of the 1950s to the big demonstrations of the late 1960s, the police found themselves involved in public-order tests of strength. This was complicated by the extra-parliamentary politics of the 1960s (sit-ins, demonstrations, squatting, etc.); by the rise of the 'counter-culture' (drugs, communes, drop-outs, the pop festivals, etc.); later, by the growth of the left political sects, the student movement, and ultimately by the threat of domestic terrorism. On other fronts, rising industrial militancy, and the Northern Ireland crisis, with its threat of domestic bombings, both seemed to require a tougher, more visible police presence. (The increased involvement in 'public order' was constantly commented on in successive Chief Constables' *Annual Reports*.) In relation to all these issues, the police progressively found themselves 'in the front line' – in areas well beyond the frontiers of traditional policing, dealing with issues where the line between legality and illegality is most ill-defined and emotions run high.[71] In crowd control, one police commander commented, the police have 'got to be both quick *and* right'.[72] By making police work more exposed and vulnerable, these new policing tasks made the actual job harder, and, in requiring rest-day working, longer. These developments intersected directly with the growth of an explicit anti-police ideology on the left and a general lowering in police morale.

Between 1955 and 1965, national detection rates for all indictable crime fell from 49 to 39 per cent. This did not necessarily indicate a loss of efficiency, since the total annual volume of crime cleared up increased by 108 per cent; but it showed a striking inability of detection to *keep pace* with the increasing volume of reported crime. During the same period (1955–65) the force was consistently 'below authorised strength' (by 13 per cent in 1955, 14 per cent in 1965) and 'wastage' became a growing problem. As with detection rates, the position in London was worse.[73] The Royal Commission on the Police (1962) led to, proportionately, the biggest pay increase for the police 'this century',[74] but this failed to offset the growing arduousness of the job and the frustrating sense of losing the 'war against crime'.[75]

We have referred to the deterioration of police–black relations in this period. But, in terms of the social context of police work, we must also note its structuring context – the growth of anti-immigrant feeling in the country. Here we need only refer to a succession of key points to make the over-all tendency of the swing clear: the first *Commonwealth Immigration Act* (1962) restricting immigration, followed by the success of Peter Griffiths on an anti-immigrant ticket at Smethwick in 1964; the reversal of Labour's policy on immigration in 1965. This first phase made anti-immigrant feeling both more visible and more acceptable, officially. Then there came the burst of 'Powellism' in 1968, the mounting talk of 'repatriation', the growth of the National Front and of an anti-immigration lobby within the Conservative Party, the witch-hunting of illegal immigrants. It became progressively easier to equate blacks with 'social problems'; and as 'social problems' they were brought increasingly into contact with the police.[76]

Lambert was right when he said: 'Policemen as members of British Society may be expected to be no more or less prejudiced than their neighbours and equals'. However, the qualification he made was equally important: 'but their profession brings them in contact with coloured immigrants to a degree more marked than that of their neighbours and equals'.[77] In their roles as members of *the police force*, policemen have more opportunities to have their prejudices reinforced or negated, more scope and legitimacy to act on their feelings, than most ordinary members of the public. Lambert adds that 'because of social segregation police have little or no opportunity to meet coloured citizens except in the context of professional contact'.[78] It is in just these situations, of restricted 'professional contact', that police stereotypes about immigrants were reinforced. The police susceptibility in general to stereotypes is a function of their peculiarly isolated social position: partly self-induced, partly imposed by the ambivalence of public attitudes towards them, which range, as Jock Young has said, from 'ubiquitous suspicion to downright hostility'.[79] As Lambert observed: 'A policeman must be able to sum up a person very quickly and determine a suitable manner with which to treat him'. [80] Immigrants are only one of the easily available 'scapegoats' for the recurring economic and social ills of a system in crisis; other familiar ones in the same period were 'militants', 'subversives', 'communists', 'foreign agitators', and so on. But whereas the latter have little actual presence, though much 'mythical' media presence, immigrants are both highly visible and highly vulnerable.

The most immediate effect of these societal contexts was the growth of a particular 'mood' within the police: a mood characterised by a growing impatience, frustration and anger. This mood achieved its clearest expression in public statements about the crime 'war'. It clearly parallels the 'judicial mood' described earlier. One of the most publicised of these statements was that delivered by Sir John Waldron in his penultimate *Report of the Commissioner of the Metropolitan Police for the year 1970*. [81] In it, Sir John – then nearing retirement – said that during his service he had seen the penal sanctions become less and less punitive and at the same time had witnessed the gradual growth of violent crime in London. He complained that the small *cadre* of professional criminals had little fear of going to prison; that they built their future on hopes of parole; that they had a succession of convictions over a decade or more; and that when at liberty they had never made any endeavour to follow honest employment. His 'remedy' was to suggest long sentences in spartan, hard-working conditions. [82] The dominant police 'concerns' are here made explicit: greater leniency; the growth of violent crime; the growing 'immunity' of professional criminals; the 'softening' effect of parole; and its ineffectuality. As if to demonstrate that Sir John was not alone in his views *The Times* also carried (on the same page) an all but identical attack on the 'soft' treatment of young people by the Chief Constable of Yorkshire and North-east Yorkshire. Significantly, the latter made it explicit that he thought that his views were those of 'many police'.

The sharpest, most forthright and angriest attack on this front came two months later from two senior police officers at Scotland Yard, in a special interview with *The Times*. [83] The substance of the report was similar to Sir John's, though it went further; but the tone was altogether more strident. In it, they angrily condemned Parliament, the courts and the Home Office for their persistent leniency towards people convicted of crimes of violence. They regretted the ending of harsh prison conditions; they asserted that this 'harshness' had had a deterrent effect; they expressed alarm at the rapid increase in violent crimes. They were convinced that unless firm measures were taken, the streets of London would be as dangerous in five years' time as those of New York and Washington now; and, predictably, their suggested remedies were a return to the 'good old days' of long sentences and harsher prison conditions. Though the report appeared on the same day as that of the killing of the Police Superintendant of Blackpool, the two events were unrelated – the officers were not simply reacting angrily to the killing of a fellow officer (though this event undoubtedly strengthened their case). *The Times* editorial of the following day drew attention to the statement's political significance. [84] After citing the fact that these views were 'the corporate view of the senior ranks of the Metropolitan Police', some members of the public and the Conservative Party – a not insignificant lobby – it added an ominous 'winds of change' prediction about the statement signifying 'perhaps the direction in which the pendulum of penal treatment is about to swing'. (We should add in passing that the officers' statement was critically scrutinised by the liberal press, either directly or via eminent liberal spokesmen, and was found wanting. However, this same response was not forthcoming twelve months later when mugging 'broke' as a major media news item.[85]) In addition to this political significance, the references to the 'streets of London' and the London/New York comparisons were revealing. After all, organised professional crime – hijacking lorries, robbing banks, smuggling drugs, protection rackets, prostitution, gang 'shoot-outs' – do not, except inadvertently, take place on the streets. What *does* affect the 'safety of the streets' is 'amateur' crime: the snatched wallet or handbag, the picked pocket, the 'purse pinch', where 'everyone' is a potential victim. And here the reference to the United States is significant; it can mean only one thing – street robberies or 'muggings'. (A year later, sentencing a 'Tube knife gang', Judge Karmel made the connection quite explicit in one of the first 'deterrent' mugging sentences.[86]) The day after *The Times* interview, the *Daily Telegraph* ran a 'supporting' *editorial* on 'violent crimes'. It made explicit reference to 'senseless attacks' and 'muggings'.

> Yet anyone who reads local newspapers must have noticed the increasing number of apparently senseless attacks reported. . . . In many semi-urban areas, where there are open stretches of what used to be peaceful canal-side or common moor, local inhabitants have perforce become wary of walking on them. Muggings and pick-pocketings involving violence are becoming more frequent on London's Underground. [87]

Almost certainly, some time between this statement and the beginning of the new year, the first anti-mugging special patrol was formed.

Our narrative began with the 'first' British mugging. But it has ended with a different, and perhaps rather unexpected theme: the confrontation in our cities between 'police power and black people'. Although by no means all 'muggers' charged in this period were black, the situation and experience of black youths has, we believe, a *paradigmatic relation* to the whole 'mugging' phenomenon. We hope to enforce this link by evidence, illustration and argument as the book proceeds. However, let us recall at this point how we arrived at the connection in the first place. Our focus initially was on the period when 'mugging' became publicly visible, in the courts and the mass media, as a social problem, through to its relative 'decline': roughly, August 1972 to October 1973. The intersection between the courts, the media and 'mugging' in this period are not hard to discover. We then turned to the internal organisation of the judicial world and to some of the developments taking place there. Then we turned to the police. But, in contrast with the courts and the media, the role of the police seemed to us peculiarly, though not perhaps surprisingly, 'invisible'. In some senses this 'invisibility' was only to be expected. The police *do* figure in certain ways in the media and in public debate. But the *internal* organisation of the police, by contrast, is not, normally, much publicised; and their plans, contingency schemes, mobilisation on the ground, and so on are very reticently handled indeed – as, given their role in crime detection, apprehension and prevention, is only to be expected.

This partial 'invisibility' of the police role seemed to us especially significant, because what evidence there was seemed clearly to point to the fact that a major mobilisation of police resources, attention and energies had taken place some months *before* 'mugging' came to be signified, by the courts and the media, as a pressing social problem. Indeed, the courts could not have been overflowing with 'mugging' cases in September 1972 unless the police had been active on this very front some months before. This forced us to look at the role of the police in the 'mugging' panic in a somewhat different way. If the police were so sensitised to the real or perceived threat from 'muggings' *before* 'mugging' had been appropriated to the public domain, then that prior activity must have been predicated on an *institutional* definition of certain kinds or patterns of crime as 'adding up to', or 'being interpretable as', the beginnings of a 'mugging' wave – a 'new strain of crime'. In looking at the police, then, we are pushed back, behind the headlines and before the judges' homilies, to an earlier, 'pre-mugging', period; to activities which belong to the restricted rather than to the public aspects, of the state; or to relations between the police and the society which predate, and postdate, the immediate exchanges between the police and the mugger. On the margins of the 'mugging' epidemic, then, there arises *its pre-history*: the longer and more complex story of the striking deterioration in police–black relations, especially between the police in certain areas of the big cities and sections of black youth. It is only in this context that the *innovatory* role of the police, in the generation of a moral panic, can be properly assessed and understood.

The examination of the role of the media, the judiciary and the police undertaken in these chapters points to the *social* rather than the strictly legal or statistical nature of the kind of crime under discussion here, which produces different sorts of response from within the state. Once this point has been grasped, it is difficult to continue to consider the agencies of public signification and control, like the police, the courts and the media, as if they were passive reactors to immediate, simple and clear-cut crime situations. These agencies must be understood as actively and continuously part of the whole process to which, also, they are 'reacting'. They are active in defining situations, in selecting targets, in initiating 'campaigns', in structuring these campaigns, in selectively signifying their actions to the public at large, in legitimating their actions through the accounts of situations which they produce. They do not simply respond to 'moral panics'. They form part of the circle out of which 'moral panics' develop. It is part of the paradox that they also, advertently and inadvertently, *amplify* the deviancy they seem so absolutely committed to controlling. This tends to suggest that, though they are crucial actors in the drama of the 'moral panic', they, too, are acting out a script which they do not write.

3

The Social Production of News

The media do not simply and transparently report events which are 'naturally' newsworthy *in themselves*. 'News' is the end-product of a complex process which begins with a systematic sorting and selecting of events and topics according to a socially constructed set of categories. As MacDougall puts it:

> At any given moment billions of simultaneous events occur throughout the world. . . . All of these occurences are potentially news. They do not become so until some purveyor of news gives an account of them. The news, in other words, is the account of the event, not something intrinsic in the event itself. [1]

One aspect of the structure of selection can be seen in the routine organisation of newspapers with respect to regular types or areas of news. Since newspapers are committed to the regular production of news, these organisational factors will, in turn, affect what is selected. For example, newspapers become predirected to certain types of event and topic in terms of the organisation of their own work-force (e.g. specialist correspondents and departments, the fostering of institutional contacts, etc.) and the structure of the papers themselves (e.g. home news, foreign, political, sport, etc.) [2]

Given that the organisation and staffing of a paper regularly direct it to certain categories of items, there is still the problem of selecting, from the many contending items within any one category, those that are felt will be of interest to the reader. This is where the *professional ideology* of what constitutes 'good news' – the newsman's sense of *news values* – begins to structure the process. At the most general level this involves an orientation to items which are 'out of the ordinary', which in some way breach our 'normal' expectations about social life, the sudden earthquake or the moon-landing, for example. We might call this the *primary* or *cardinal news value*. Yet, clearly 'extraordinariness' does not exhaust the list, as a glance at any newspaper will reveal: events which concern elite persons or nations; events which are dramatic; events which can be personalised so as to point up the essentially human characteristics of humour, sadness, sentimentality, etc.; events which have negative consequences, and events which are part of, or can be made to appear part of, an existing newsworthy theme, are all possible news stories. [3] Disasters, dramas, the everyday antics – funny and tragic – of ordinary folk, the lives of the rich and the powerful, and such perennial themes as football (in winter) and cricket (in summer), all find a regular place within the pages of a newspaper. Two things follow from this: the first is that journalists will tend to *play up* the extraordinary, dramatic, tragic, etc. elements in a story in order to enhance its newsworthiness; the second is that events which score high on a number of these news values will have greater news potential than ones that do not. And events which score high on *all* dimensions, such as the Kennedy assassinations (i.e. which are *unexpected* and *dramatic*, with *negative* consequences, as well as *human tragedies* involving *elite persons* who were heads of an extremely *powerful nation*, which possesses the status of a *recurrent theme* in the British press), will become *so* newsworthy that programmes will be interrupted – as in the radio or television news-flash – so that these items can be communicated immediately.

When we come later to consider the case of mugging, we will want to say something about how these news values tend to operate together, as a structure. For our present purposes, however, it is sufficient to say that news values provide the criteria in the routine practices of journalism which enable journalists, editors and newsmen to decide routinely and regularly which stories are 'newsworthy' and which are not, which stories are major 'lead' stories and which are relatively insignificant, which stories to run and which to drop.[4] Although they are nowhere written down, formally transmitted or codified, news values seem to be widely shared as between the different news media (though we shall have more to say later on the way these are differently *inflected* by particular newspapers), and form a core element in the professional socialisation, practice and ideology of newsmen.

These two aspects of the social production of news – the bureaucratic organisation of the media which produces the news in specific types or categories and the structure of news values which orders the selection and ranking of particular stories within these categories – are only part of the process. The third aspect – the moment of the *construction* of the news story itself – is equally important, if less obvious. This involves the presentation of the item to its *assumed* audience, in terms which, as far as the presenters of the item can judge, will make it comprehensible to that audience. If the world is not to be represented as a jumble of random and chaotic events, then they must be identified (i.e. named, defined, related to other events known to the audience), and assigned to a social context (i.e. placed within a frame of meanings familiar to the audience). This process – identification and contextualisation – is one of the most important through which events are 'made to mean' by the media. An event only 'makes sense' if it can be located within a range of known social and cultural identifications. If newsmen did not have available – in however routine a way – such cultural 'maps' of the social world, they could not 'make sense' for their audiences of the unusual, unexpected and unpredicted events which form the basic content of what is 'newsworthy'. Things are newsworthy because they represent the changefulness, the unpredictability and the conflictful nature of the world. But such events cannot be allowed to remain in the limbo of the 'random' – they must be brought within the horizon of the 'meaningful'. This bringing of events within the realm of meanings means, in essence, referring unusual and unexpected events to the 'maps of meaning' which already form the basis of our cultural knowledge, into which the social world is *already* 'mapped'. The social identification, classification and contextualisation of news events in terms of these background frames of reference is the fundamental process by which the media make the world they report on intelligible to readers and viewers. This process of 'making an event intelligible' is a social process – constituted by a number of specific journalistic practices, which embody (often only implicitly) crucial assumptions about what society is and how it works.

One such background assumption is the *consensual* nature of society: the process of *signification* – giving social meanings to events – *both assumes and helps to construct society as a 'consensus'*. We exist as members of one society *because* – it is assumed – we share a common stock of cultural knowledge with our fellow men: we have access to the same 'maps of meanings'. Not only are we all able to manipulate these 'maps of meaning' to understand events, but we have fundamental interests, values and concerns in common, which these maps embody or reflect. We all want to, or do, maintain basically the same perspective *on* events. In this view, what unites us, as a society and a culture – its consensual side – far outweighs what divides and distinguishes us as groups or classes from other groups. Now, at one level, the existence of a cultural consensus is an obvious truth; it is the basis of all social communication. [5] If we were not members of the same language community we literally could not communicate with one another. On a broader level, if we did not inhabit, to some degree, the same classifications of social reality, we could not 'make sense of the world together'. In recent years, however, this basic cultural fact about society has been raised to an extreme ideological level. Because we occupy the same society and belong to roughly the same 'culture', it is assumed that there is, basically, only *one* perspective on events: that provided by what is sometimes called *the* culture, or (by some social scientists) *the* 'central value system'. This view denies any major structural discrepancies between different groups, or between the very different maps of meaning in a society. This 'consensual' viewpoint has important political consequences, when used as the taken-for-granted basis of communication. It carries the assumption that we also all have roughly the same *interests* in the society, and that we all roughly have an equal share of power in the society. This is the essence of the idea of the political consensus. 'Consensual' views of society represent society as if there are no major cultural or economic breaks, no major conflicts of interests between classes and groups. Whatever disagreements exist, it is said, there are legitimate and institutionalised means for expressing and reconciling them. The 'free market' in opinions and in the media is supposed to guarantee the reconciliation of cultural discontinuities between one group and another. The political institutions – parliament, the two-party system, political representation, etc. – are supposed to guarantee equal access for all groups to the decision-making process. The growth of a 'consumer' economy is supposed to have created the economic conditions for everyone to have a stake in the making and distribution of wealth. The rule of law protects us all equally. This consensus view of society is particularly strong in modern, democratic, organised capitalist societies; and the media are among the institutions whose practices are most widely and consistently predicated upon the assumption of a 'national consensus'. So that, when events are 'mapped' by the media into frameworks of meaning and interpretation, it is assumed that we all equally possess and know how to use these frameworks, that they are drawn from fundamentally the same structures of understanding for all social groups and audiences. Of course, in the formation of opinion, as in politics and economic life, it is conceded that there will be differences of outlook, disagreement, argument and opposition; but these are understood as taking place within a broader basic framework of agreement – 'the consensus' – to which everyone subscribes, and within which every dispute, disagreement or conflict of interest can be reconciled by discussion, without recourse to confrontation or violence. The strength of this appeal to consensus was vividly encapsulated in Edward Heath's prime ministerial broadcast, following the settlement of the miners' strike in 1972 (suggesting that open appeals to consensus are particularly prevalent when conflict is most visible):

> In the kind of country we live in there cannot be any 'we' or 'they'. There is only 'us'; all of us. If the Government is 'defeated', then the country is defeated, because the Government is just a group of people elected to do what the majority of 'us' want to see done. That is what our way of life is all about. It really does not matter whether it is a picketline, a demonstration or the House of Commons. We are all used to peaceful argument. But when violence or the threat of violence is used, it challenges what most of us consider to be the right way of doing things. I do not believe you elect any government to allow that to happen and I can promise you that it will not be tolerated wherever it occurs.[6]

Events, as news, then, are regularly interpreted within frameworks which derive, in part, from this notion of *the consensus* as a basic feature of everyday life. They are elaborated through a variety of 'explanations', images and discourses which articulate what the audience is assumed to think and know about the society. The importance of this process, in *reinforcing* consensual notions, has been recently stressed by Murdock:

> This habitual presentation of news within frameworks which are already familiar has two important consequences. Firstly, it recharges and extends the definitions and images in question and keeps them circulating as part of the common stock of taken-for-granted knowledge.... Secondly, it 'conveys an impression of eternal recurrence, of society as a social order which is made up of movement, but not innovation'.[7] Here again, by stressing the continuity and stability of the social structure, and by asserting the existence of a commonly shared set of assumptions, the definitions of the situation coincide with and reinforce essential consensual notions.[8]

What, then, is the underlying significance of the framing and interpretive function of news presentation? We suggest that it lies in the fact that the media are often presenting information about events which occur outside the direct experience of the majority of the society. The media thus represent the primary, and often the only, source of information about many important events and topics. Further, because news is recurrently concerned with events which are 'new' or 'unexpected', the media are involved in the task of making comprehensible what we would term 'problematic reality'. Problematic events breach our commonly held expectations and are therefore threatening to a society based around the expectation of consensus, order and routine. Thus the media's mapping of problematic events within the conventional understandings of the society is crucial in two ways. The media define for the majority of the population *what* significant events are taking place, but, also, they offer powerful interpretations of *how* to understand these events. Implicit in those interpretations are orientations towards the events and the people or groups involved in them.

PRIMARY AND SECONDARY DEFINERS

In this section we want to begin to account for the 'fit' between dominant ideas and professional media ideologies and practices. This cannot be simply attributed – as it sometimes is in simple conspiracy theories – to the fact that the media are in large part capitalist-owned (though that structure of ownership is widespread), since this would be to ignore the day-to-day 'relative autonomy' of the journalist and news producers from direct economic control. Instead we want to draw attention to the more routine *structures* of news production to see how the media come in fact, in the 'last instance', to *reproduce the definitions of the powerful*, without being, in a simple sense, in their pay. Here we must insist on a crucial distinction between *primary* and *secondary definers* of social events.

The media do not themselves autonomously create news items; rather they are 'cued in' to specific new topics by regular and reliable institutional sources. As Paul Rock notes:

> In the main journalists position themselves so that they have access to institutions which generate a useful volume of reportable activity at regular intervals. Some of these institutions do, of course, make themselves visible by means of dramatization, or through press releases and press agents. Others are known to regularly produce consequential events. The courts, sports grounds and parliament mechanically manufacture news which is ... assimilated by the press. [9]

One reason for this has to do with the internal pressures of news production – as Murdock notes:

> The incessant pressures of time and the consequent problems of resource allocation and work scheduling in news organisations can be reduced or alleviated by covering 'pre-scheduled events'; that is, events that have been announced in advance by their convenors. However, one of the consequences of adopting this solution to scheduling problems is to increase the newsmen's dependance on news sources willing and able to preschedule their activities. [10]

The second has to do with the fact that media reporting is underwritten by notions of 'impartiality', 'balance' and 'objectivity'. This is formally enforced in television (a near-monopoly situation, where the state is directly involved in a regulatory sense) but there are also similar professional ideological 'rules' in journalism.[11] One product of these rules is the carefully structured distinction between 'fact' and 'opinion', about which we have more to say in a later chapter. For our present purposes, the important point is that these professional rules give rise to the practice of ensuring that media statements are, wherever possible, grounded in 'objective' and 'authoritative' statements from 'accredited' sources. This means constantly turning to accredited representatives of major social institutions – M.P.s for political topics, employers and trade-union leaders for industrial matters, and so on. Such institutional representatives are 'accredited' because of their institutional power and position, but also because of their 'representative' status: either they represent 'the people' (M.P.s, Ministers, etc.) or organised interest groups (which is how the T.U.C. and the C.B.I. are now regarded). One final 'accredited source' is 'the expert': his calling – the 'disinterested' pursuit of knowledge – not his position or his representativeness, confers on his statements 'objectivity' and 'authority'. Ironically, the very rules which aim to preserve the impartiality of the media, and which grew out of desires for greater professional neutrality, also serve powerfully to orientate the media in the 'definitions of social reality' which their 'accredited sources' – the institutional spokesmen – provide.

These two aspects of news production – the practical pressures of constantly working against the clock and the professional demands of impartiality and objectivity – combine to produce a systematically structured *over-accessing* to the media of those in powerful and privileged institutional positions. The media thus tend, faithfully and impartially, to reproduce symbolically the existing structure of power in society's institutional order. This is what Becker has called the 'hierarchy of credibility' – the likelihood that those in powerful or high-status positions in society who offer opinions about controversial topics will have their definitions accepted, because such spokesmen are understood to have access to more accurate or more specialised information on particular topics than the majority of the population.[12] The result of this structured preference given in the media to the opinions of the powerful is that these 'spokesmen' become what we call the *primary definers* of topics.

What is the significance of this? It could rightly be argued that through the requirement of 'balance' – one of the professional rules we have not yet dealt with – alternative definitions do get a hearing: each 'side' *is* allowed to present its case. In point of fact, as we shall see in detail in the next chapter, the setting up of a topic in terms of a debate within which there are oppositions and conflicts is also one way of *dramatising* an event so as to enhance its newsworthiness. The important point about the structured relationship between the media and the primary institutional definers is that it permits the institutional definers to establish the initial definition or *primary interpretation* of the topic in question. This interpretation then 'commands the field' in all subsequent treatment and sets the terms of reference within which all further coverage or debate takes place. Arguments *against* a primary interpretation are forced to insert themselves into *its* definition of 'what is at issue' – they must begin from this framework of interpretation as their starting-point. This initial interpretative framework – what Lang and Lang have called an 'inferential structure'[13] – is extremely difficult to alter fundamentally, once established. For example, once race relations in Britain have been defined as a 'problem of numbers' (i.e. how many blacks there are in the country), then even liberal spokesmen, in proving that the figures for black immigrants have been exaggerated, are nevertheless obliged to subscribe, implicitly, to the view that the debate is 'essentially' *about numbers*. Similarly, Halloran and his co-workers have clearly demonstrated how the 'inferential structure' of violence – once it became established in the lead-up period – dominated the coverage of the second Anti-Vietnam Rally and the events of Grosvenor Square, despite all the first-hand evidence directly contradicting this interpretation. [14] Effectively, then, the primary definition *sets the limit* for all subsequent discussion by *framing what the problem is*. This initial framework then provides the criteria by which all subsequent contributions are labelled as 'relevant' to the debate, or 'irrelevant' – beside the point. Contributions which stray from this framework are exposed to the charge that they are 'not addressing the problem'. [15]

The media, then, do not simply 'create' the news; nor do they simply transmit the ideology of the 'ruling class' in a conspiratorial fashion. Indeed, we have suggested that, in a critical sense, the media are frequently not the 'primary definers' of news events at all; but their structured relationship to power has the effect of making them play a crucial but secondary role in *reproducing* the definitions of those who have privileged access, as of right, to the media as 'accredited sources'. From this point of view, in the moment of news production, the media stand in a position of structured subordination to the primary definers.

It is this structured relationship – between the media and its 'powerful' sources – which begins to open up the neglected question of the *ideological role* of the media. It is this which begins to give substance and specificity to Marx's basic proposition that 'the ruling ideas of any age are the ideas of its ruling class'. Marx's contention is that this dominance of 'ruling ideas' operates primarily because, in addition to its ownership and control of the means of material production, this class also owns and controls the means of 'mental production'. In producing their definition of social reality, and the place of 'ordinary people' within it, they construct a particular image of society which represents particular class interests as the interests of all members of society. Because of their control over material and mental resources, and their domination of the major institutions of society, this class's definitions of the social world provide the basic rationale for those institutions which protect and reproduce their 'way of life'. This control of mental resources ensures that theirs are the most powerful and 'universal' of the available definitions of the social world. Their universality ensures that they are shared to some degree by the subordinate classes of the society. Those who govern, govern also through ideas; thus they govern with the consent of the subordinate classes, and not principally through their overt coercion. Parkin makes a similar point: 'the social and political definitions of those in dominant positions tend to become objectified in the major institutional orders, so providing the moral framework for the entire social system.' [16]

In the major social, political and legal institutions of society, coercion and constraint are never wholly absent. This is as true for the media as elsewhere.

For example, reporters and reporting *are* subject to economic and legal constraints, as well as to more overt forms of censorship (e.g. over the coverage of events in Northern Ireland). But the transmission of 'dominant ideas' depends *more* on non-coercive mechanisms for their reproduction. Hierarchical structures of command and review, informal socialisation into institutional roles, the sedimenting of dominant ideas into the 'professional ideology' – all help to ensure, within the media, their continued reproduction in the dominant form. What we have been pointing to in this section is *precisely how one particular professional practice ensures that the media, effectively but 'objectively', play a key role in reproducing the dominant field of the ruling ideologies.*

MEDIA IN ACTION: REPRODUCTION AND TRANSFORMATION

So far we have considered the processes through which the 'reproduction of the dominant ideologies' is secured in the media. As should be clear, this reproduction, in our view, is the product of a set of *structural imperatives*, not of an open conspiracy with those in powerful positions. However, the whole cycle of 'ideological reproduction' is not completed until we have shown the process of *transformation* which the media themselves must perform on the 'raw materials' (facts *and* interpretations) which the powerful provide, in order to process these 'potential' stories into their finished commodity news form. If the former section stressed a relatively passive orientation to powerful 'authoritative' definitions, in this section we are concerned to examine those aspects of news creation in which the media play a more autonomous and active role.

The first point at which the media actively come into their own is with respect to *selectivity*. Not every statement by a relevant primary definer in respect of a particular topic is likely to be reproduced in the media; nor is every part of each statement. By exercising selectivity the media begin to impose their own criteria on the structured 'raw materials' – and thus actively appropriate and transform them. We emphasised earlier how the criteria of selection – a mixture of professional, technical and commercial constraints – served to orientate the media in general to the 'definitions of the powerful'. Here, on the other hand, we wish to stress that such criteria – common to all newspapers – are, nevertheless, *differently* appropriated, evaluated and made operational by each newspaper. To put it simply, each paper's professional sense of the newsworthy, its organisation and technical framework (in terms of numbers of journalists working in particular news areas, amount of column space routinely given over to certain kinds of news items, and so on), and sense of audience or regular readers, is different. Such differences, taken together, are what produce the very different 'social personalities' of papers. The *News of the World*'s dominant orientation towards the 'scandalous' and the sexual, and the *Daily Mirror*'s concern with the 'human-interest' aspect of stories, are but two obvious examples of such internal differences in 'social personalities'. It is here – as each paper's own 'social personality' comes into play – that the transformatory work proper begins. [17]

An even more significant aspect of 'media work' is the activity of transforming an event into a finished news item. This has to do with the way an item is *coded* by the media into a particular language form. Just as each paper, as we have just argued, has a particular organisational framework, sense of news and readership, so each will also develop a regular and characteristic *mode of address*. This means that the same topic, sources and inferential structures will appear differently even in papers with a similar outlook, since the different rhetorics of address will have an important effect in inflecting the original item. Of special importance in determining the particular mode of address adopted will be the particular part of the readership spectrum the paper sees itself as customarily addressing: its target audience. The language employed will thus be the *newspaper's own version of the language of the public to whom it is principally addressed: its* version of the rhetoric, imagery and underlying common stock of knowledge which it assumes its audience shares and which thus forms the basis of the reciprocity of producer/reader. For this reason we want to call this form of address − different for each news outlet − the *public idiom* of the media.

Although we have stressed here the *different* languages of different papers, this emphasis should not be taken too far. It is not the vast pluralistic range of voices which the media are sometimes held to represent, but a range *within certain distinct ideological limits*. While each paper may see itself as addressing a different section of the newspaper-reading public (or different types of newspapers will be in competition for different sectors of the public), the 'consensus of values' which is so deeply embedded in all the forms of public language is *more limited* than the variety of the forms of public 'language in use' would suggest. Their publics, however distinct, are assumed to fall within that very broad spectrum of 'reasonable men', and readers are addressed broadly in those terms.

The coding of items and topics into variations of the public language provides a significant element of variation in the process of transforming the news into its finished form; but, as with 'objectivity' and 'impartiality' before, this variation is not necessarily structurally at odds with the process we have called 'ideological reproduction' − for translating a news item into a variant of the public language serves, also, to *translate into a public idiom the statements and viewpoints of the primary definers*. This translation of official viewpoints into a public idiom not only makes the former more 'available' to the uninitiated; it invests them with popular force and resonance, naturalising them within the horizon of understandings of the various publics. The following example will serve as an illustration. The *Daily Mirror* of 14 June 1973 reported the presentation by the Chief Inspector of the Constabulary of his *Annual Report*, in which he claimed that 'the increase in violent crimes in England and Wales had aroused justifiable public concern'. What the *Mirror* does in this case is to *translate* the Chief Inspector's concern with rising violent crime amongst the young into a more dramatic, more connotative and more popular form − a news headline which runs, simply, 'AGGRO BRITAIN: "Mindless Violence" of the Bully Boys Worries Top Policeman'. This headline invests the sober *Report* with dramatic news value. It transposes the *Report*'s staid officialese into more newsworthy rhetoric. But it also inserts the statement *into* the stock of popular imagery, established over long usage, including that usage created by the paper's own previous coverage of the activities of 'aggro' football hooligans and skinhead 'gangs'. This transformation into a public idiom thus gives the item an *external public reference* and validity in images and connotations already sedimented in the stock of knowledge which the paper and its public share. The importance of this external public reference point is that it serves to *objectify* a public issue. That is, the publicising of an issue in the media can give it more 'objective' status as a *real* (valid) issue of public concern than would have been the case had it remained as merely a report made by experts and specialists. Concentrated media attention confers the status of high public concern on issues which are highlighted; these generally become understood by everyone as the 'pressing issues of the day'. This is part of the media's *agenda-setting* function. Setting agendas also has a reality-confirming effect.

The significance of using a public idiom with which to 'set the agenda' is that it inserts the language of everyday communication *back into the consensus*. While it is true that 'everyday' language is already saturated with dominant inferences and interpretations, the continual process of translating formal official definitions into the terms of ordinary conversation reinforces, at the same time as it disguises, the links between the two discourses. That is, the media 'take' the language of the public and, on each occasion, return it to them *inflected with dominant and consensual connotations*.

This more 'creative' media role is not obviously fully autonomous. Such translations depend on the story's potential-for-translation (its newsworthiness) and on its anchorage in familiar and long-standing topics of concern – hooliganism, crowd violence, 'aggro' gang behaviour. This process is neither totally free and unconstrained, nor is it a simple, direct reproduction. It is a transformation; and such transformations require active 'work' on the part of the media. Their over-all effect is nevertheless to help close the circle by which the definitions of the powerful become part of the taken-for-granted reality of the public by translating the unfamiliar into the familiar world. All this is entailed in the over-simple formula that journalists, after all, know best how to 'get things across to the public'.

THE MEDIA AND PUBLIC OPINION

So far we have been addressing the question of the production of *news reports*. In the next chapter we shall be looking more closely at differences between types of news, feature articles and editorials. At this stage we want simply to draw attention to the relationship between a newspaper's 'public idiom' and its editorial voice. We have so far discussed the transformations involved in transposing a statement made by a primary definer into an everyday language: into the code, or mode of address customarily used by that paper – its 'public idiom'. But the press is also free to editorialise and express an opinion about topics of major concern; it is not limited to 'reproducing', through its own 'code', the statements of the powerful. Now, one common kind of editorialising is for the press to speak *its* own mind, to say what *it* thinks, but *expressed in its public idiom*. In other words the paper's *own* statements and thoughts on an event – the product of editorial judgement – are represented in the paper's public language in the same way as the statements of primary definers: the process is very similar. Whether arguing for or against a line of action, the language employed is that customarily used by the particular paper. However, there is a second type of editorial which adds a further transforming twist; i.e. the editorial which actively claims to *speak for the public* – the editorial which goes beyond expressing *its own views in a public idiom* and actually *claims to be expressing the public's views*. We call this more active process, *taking the public voice* (as opposed to simply *using a public idiom*). Some such editorial voices are so distinctive (e.g. *The Times*) that it might be more accurate to talk of these as the paper's *own* 'voice'. However, it is unlikely that such a voice is ever completely independent in its rhetoric of the editor's sense of the 'public idiom' of his assumed audience. The essence of the difference, which we shall exemplify when we consider briefly some mugging editorials in the final part of this chapter, is that between the editorial which says 'We believe . . .' and that which says. 'The public believes . . .' This 'taking the public voice', this form of articulating what the vast majority of the public are supposed to think, this enlisting of public legitimacy for views which the newspaper *itself* is expressing, represents the media in its most active, *campaigning* role – the point where the media most actively and openly shape and structure public opinion. This kind of editorial usually takes the form either of support for some countervailing action which has been taken, or, even more frequently, of a demand that strong action *should* be taken – because the majority demand it.

In either form of editorialising, the media provide a crucial mediating link between the apparatus of social control and the public. The press can legitimate and reinforce the actions of the controllers by bringing their own independent arguments to bear on the public in support of the actions proposed ('using a public idiom'); or it can bring pressure to bear on the controllers by summoning up 'public opinion' in support of its own views that 'stronger measures are needed' ('taking the public voice'). But, in either case, the editorial seems to provide an objective and external point of reference which can be used either to justify official action or to mobilise public opinion. It should not be overlooked that this playing back of (assumed) public opinion to the powerful, which is the reverse of the earlier process described of translating dominant definitions into an (assumed) public idiom, takes the public as an important point of reference on both occasions (legitimation), while actually bypassing it. By means of a further twist, these representations of public opinion are then often enlisted *by the controllers* as 'impartial evidence' of what the public, in fact, believes and wants. The spirals of amplification are, in this last instance, particularly intricate and tight. (We shall look at some examples from 'mugging' later.)

What we are concerned with here is the general role of the media in the process of actively shaping public opinion. In societies where the bulk of the population has neither direct access to nor power over the central decisions which affect their lives, where official policy and opinion is concentrated and popular opinion is dispersed, the media play a critical mediating and connecting role in the formation of public opinion, and in orchestrating that opinion together with the actions and views of the powerful. The media do not only possess a near-monopoly over 'social knowledge', as the primary source of information about what is happening; they also command the passage between those who are 'in the know' and the structured ignorance of the general public. In performing this connective and mediating role, the media are enhanced, not weakened, by the very fact that they are, formally and structurally, *independent* both of the sources to which they refer and of the 'public' on whose behalf they speak. This picture may now tend to suggest a situation of 'perfect closure', where the free passage of the dominant ideologies is permanently secured. But this tightly conspiratorial image is not an accurate one, and we should beware of its apparent simplicity and elegance. The central factor which prevents such a 'perfect closure', however, is *not* a matter of technical or formal controls, or the randomness of chance, or the good sense and conscience of the professionals.

If the tendency towards ideological closure – the prevailing tendency – is maintained by the way the different apparatuses are structurally linked so as to promote the dominant definitions of events, then the counter-tendency must also depend on the existence of organised and articulate sources which generate *counter*-definitions of the situation. (As Goldmann remarked,[18] social groups and collectivities are always the infrastructure of ideologies – and counter-ideologies.) This depends to some degree on whether the collectivity which generates counter-ideologies and explanations is a powerful countervailing force in society; whether it represents an organised majority or substantial minority; and whether or not it has a degree of legitimacy within the system or can win such a position through struggle.[19] Primary definers, acting in or through the media, would find it difficult to establish a complete closure around a definition of a controversial issue in, say, industrial relations without having to deal with an alternative definition generated by spokesmen for the trade unions, since the unions are now a recognised part of the system of institutionalised bargaining in the industrial field, possess an articulate view of their situation and interests, and have *won* 'legitimacy' in the terrain where economic conflict and consensus are debated and negotiated. Many emergent counter-definers, however, have no access to the defining process at all. Even regularly accessed definers, like official trade-union spokesmen, must respond *in terms* pre-established by the primary definers and the privileged definitions, and have a better chance of securing a hearing and influencing the process precisely if they cast their case within the limits of that consensus. The General Secretary of the T.U.C. has an easier passage if he makes a 'reasonable' trade-union case against a reasonable employers' one, if he is arguing and debating and negotiating within the rules, rather than if he is defending unofficial strike action, and so on. If they do not play within the rules of the game, counter-spokesmen run the risk of being defined out of the debate (because they have broken the rules of reasonable opposition) – labelled as 'extremist' or 'irrational' or as acting illegally or unconstitutionally. Groups which have not secured even this limited measure of access are regularly and systematically stigmatised, in their absence, as 'extreme', their actions systematically de-authenticated by being labelled as 'irrational'. The closure of the topic around its initial definition is far easier to achieve against groups which are fragmented, relatively inarticulate, or refuse to order their 'aims' in terms of reasonable demands and a practical programme of reforms, or which adopt extreme oppositional means of struggle to secure their ends, win a hearing or defend their interests. Any of these characteristics make it easier for the privileged definers to label them freely, and to refuse to take their counter-definitions into account.

The media thus help to reproduce and sustain the definitions of the situation which favour the powerful, not only by actively recruiting the powerful in the initial stages where topics are structured, [20] but by favouring certain ways of setting up topics, and maintaining certain strategic areas of silence. Many of these structured forms of communication are so common, so natural, so taken for granted, so deeply embedded in the very communication forms which are employed, that they are hardly visible at all, as ideological constructs, unless we deliberately set out to ask, 'What, other than what has been said about this topic, *could* be said?' 'What questions are omitted?' 'Why do the questions — which always presuppose answers of a particular kind — so often recur in this form? Why do certain other questions never appear?' In the arena of industrial conflict, for example, Westergaard has recently observed:

> The exclusion of wider issues is itself a result of the general 'balance of power' between unions and employers — far more crucial for the analysis of the situation than the upshot of particular disputes within the terms of that restriction. . . . The locus of power has to be sought primarily in the limits which define areas of conflict and restrict the range of alternatives effectively put into dispute. Often indeed, they may be so tightly drawn that there are no alternatives ventilated. There is then no 'decision making' because policies appear as self-evident. They simply flow from assumptions that render all potential alternatives invisible. . . . It follows that the locus of power cannot be seen except from a standpoint outside the parameters of everyday conflict; for those parameters are barely visible from within. [21]

In this section we have tried to indicate the way in which the *routine structures and practices* of the media in relation to news-making serve to 'frame' events within dominant interpretative paradigms, and thus to hold opinions together within what Urry calls 'the same sort of range'. [22]

Since the media are institutionally distinct from the other agencies of the state, they do not automatically take their lead from the state. Indeed, oppositions can and frequently do arise *between* these institutions within the complex of power in society. The media are also impelled by institutional motives and rationales which are different from those of other sectors of the state; for example, the competitive drive to be 'first with the news' may not be immediately in the interest or to the advantage of the state. The media often want to find out things which the primary definers would rather keep quiet. The recurrent conflicts between politicians — especially Labour Party politicians — and the media indicate that the aims of the media and those of the primary definers do not always coincide. [23] Despite these reservations, however, it seems undeniable that the *prevailing tendency* in the media is towards the reproduction, *amidst all their contradictions*, of the definitions of the powerful, of the dominant ideology. We have tried to suggest why this *tendency* is inscribed in the very structures and processes of news-making itself, and cannot be ascribed to the wickedness of journalists or their employers.

CRIME AS NEWS

Now we wish to specify how the general elements and processes of news production operate in the production of crime news as one particular variant of news production. We began by noting that news is shaped by being set in relation to a specific conception of society as a 'consensus'. Against this background newsworthy events are those which seem to interrupt the unchanging consensual calm. Crime marks one of the major boundaries of that consensus. We have already suggested that the consensus is based around legitimate and institutionalised means of action. Crime involves the negative side of that consensus, since the law defines what the society judges to be *illegitimate* types of action. Ultimately, the law, created by Parliament, executed in the courts, embodying the will of the population, provides society with the basic definition of what actions are acceptable and unacceptable; it is the 'frontier' marking 'our way of life' and its connected values. Action to stigmatise and punish those who break the law, taken by the agents formally appointed as the guardians of public morality and order, stands as a *dramatised symbolic reassertion* of the values of the society and of its limits of tolerance. If we conceive of news as mapping problematic reality, then crime is almost by definition 'news', as Erikson has suggested:

> It may be important to note in this connection that confrontations between deviant offenders and the agents of control have always attracted a good deal of public attention. . . . A considerable portion of what we call 'news' is devoted to reports about deviant behaviour and its consequences, and it is no simple matter to explain why these items should be considered newsworthy or why they should command the extraordinary attention they do. Perhaps they appeal to a number of psychological perversities among the mass audience, as commentators have suggested, but at the same time they constitute one of our main sources of information about the normative outlines of our society. In a figurative sense, at least, morality and immorality meet at the public scaffold, and it is during this meeting the line between them is drawn.[24]

Crime, then, is 'news' because its treatment evokes threats to, but also reaffirms, the consensual morality of the society: a modern morality play takes place before us in which the 'devil' is both symbolically and physically cast out from the society by its guardians – the police and the judiciary. Lest this statement be thought over-dramatised, it should be compared with the following *Daily Mail* comment (headed 'The men we take for granted') on the killing of three policemen in 1966:

> The Shepherd's Bush crime reminds Britain of what it really thinks about its police. In Britain the policeman is still the walking sign which says that

society has reached and takes for granted a certain stable normality of public order and decency. Bernard Shaw once said that for him the picture of unchanging Britain was symbolized by a policeman standing with the rain glistening on his cape. He is still the man you ask the time, or the way to the Town Hall or whether the last bus has gone. He is still the man, who, when society asks him, goes along into the unlit alley to investigate the noise. That is why the death of a policeman by violence is felt so deeply by us all. The deaths of the three men at Shepherd's Bush, senselessly and deliberately gunned down on the job of maintaining that order and decency, come as a frightful shock that seems to rock the very earth. A dazed incredulity is followed by the realization that order is not to be taken for granted. The jungle is still there. There are still wild beasts in it to be controlled. [25]

Crime news is not of course uniformly of this dramatic nature. Much of it is routine and brief, because the bulk of crime itself is seen as routine. Crime is understood as a permanent and recurrent phenomenon, and hence much of it is surveyed by the media in an equally routinised manner. Shuttleworth, in his study of the reporting of violence in the *Daily Mirror*, has noted the very different kinds of presentation used, depending on the nature of the violence being treated. [26] He commented especially on the relatively small space, and the impersonal and abbreviated manner in which many 'mundane' forms of crime are reported. (The brevity of these reports are further constrained by the *sub judice* rule which prevents the press commenting on a case which is before the courts, and the recent strengthening of the rules against the press presuming guilt before it has been proven.) Many news items about crime therefore do little more than note that another 'serious' crime has been committed. Nevertheless, the media remain highly sensitised to crime as a potential source of news. Much of this 'mundane' reporting of crime still fits our over-all argument – it marks out the transgression of normative boundaries, followed by investigation, arrest, and social retribution in terms of the sentencing of the offender. (The routine work of the police and the courts provide such a permanent category of news that many 'cub reporters' are assigned, as their first task, to the 'crime beat'. If they survive this routine job – most senior editors learn to assume – then they are ready for bigger and more testing news assignments.) The reporting, at greater length, of certain dramatic instances of crime, then, arises from and stands out against the background of this routinised treatment of crime. The alteration in the visibility of certain crime-news items works in conjunction with other organisational and ideological processes within the news media – for example, the relative 'competitiveness' of other news items for space and attention, the item's novelty, or its topicality, and so on. Crime, here, is not significantly different from other kinds of regular news items. What selects particular crime stories for special attention, and determines the relative degree of attention given to them, is the same structure of 'news values' which is applied to other news areas.

One special point about crime as news: this is the special status of *violence* as a news value. Any crime can be lifted into news visibility if violence becomes associated with it, since violence is perhaps the supreme example of the news value 'negative consequences'. Violence represents a basic violation of the person; the greatest personal crime is 'murder', bettered only by the murder of a law-enforcement agent, a policeman. Violence is also the ultimate crime against property, and against the state. It thus represents a fundamental rupture in the social order. The use of violence marks the distinction between those who are fundamentally *of* society and those who are *outside* it. It is coterminous with the boundary of 'society' itself. In the speech quoted earlier, Mr Heath drew the crucial distinction between 'peaceful argument', 'what most of us believe to be the right way of doing things', and 'violence', which 'challenges' that way. The basis of the law is to safeguard that 'right way of doing things'; to protect the individual, property and the state against those who would 'do violence' to them. This is also the basis of law enforcement and of social control. The state, and the state only, has the monopoly of *legitimate* violence, and this 'violence' is used to safeguard society against 'illegitimate' uses. Violence thus constitutes a critical threshold in society; all acts, especially criminal ones, which transgress that boundary, are, by definition, worthy of news attention. It is often complained that in general 'the news' is too full of violence: an item can escalate to the top of the news agenda simply because it contains a 'big bang'. Those who so complain do not understand what 'the news' is about. It is impossible to define 'news values' in ways which would not rank 'violence' at or near the summit of news attention.

We saw previously how the production of news is dependent on the role played by primary definers. In the area of crime news, the media appear to be more heavily dependent on the institutions of crime control for their news stories than in practically any other area. The police, Home Office spokesmen and the courts form a near-monopoly as sources of crime news in the media. Many professional groups have contact with crime, but it is only the police who claim a *professional* expertise in the 'war against crime', based on daily, *personal* experience. This exclusive and particular 'double expertise' seems to give police spokesmen especially authoritative credence. In addition, both the formal and informal social relations of news-making from which the journalist derives his 'crime' material are dependent on a notion of 'trust', e.g. between the police and the crime correspondent; i.e. on reliable and objective reporting by the journalist of the privileged information to which he is allowed access. A 'betrayal' of that trust will lead to the drying up of the flow of information. [27] The Home Office, which is invested with the ultimate political and administrative responsibility for crime control, is accredited because of its responsibility to Parliament and hence, ultimately, to the 'will of the people'. The special status of the courts we have noted earlier. Judges have the responsibility for disposing of the transgressors of society's legal code; this inevitably gives them authority. But the constant media attention to their weighty pronunciations underlines the importance of their *symbolic* role: their status as representatives and 'ventriloquists' for the good and the upright against the forces of evil and darkness. What is most striking about crime news is that it very rarely involves a first-hand account of the crime itself, unlike the 'eye-witness' report from the battlefront of the war correspondent. Crime stories are almost wholly produced from the definitions and perspectives of the institutional primary definers.

This near-monopoly situation provides the basis for the *three* typical formats for crime news which together cover most variants of crime stories. First, the report based on police statements about investigations of a particular case – which involve a police reconstruction of the event and details of the action they are taking. Second, the 'state of the war against crime report' – normally based on Chief Constables' or Home Office statistics about current crime, together with an interpretation by the spokesmen of what the bare figures mean – what is the most serious challenge, where there has been most police success, etc. Third, the staple diet of crime reporting – the story based on a court case: some, where the case is held to be especially newsworthy, following the day-to-day events of the trial; others where just the day of sentencing, and especially the judge's remarks, are deemed newsworthy; and still others which consist merely of brief summary reports.

However, the reason why the primary definers of crime figure so prominently in media crime reporting is not exclusively a function of their especially authoritative status. It has also to do with the fact that crime is *less open* than most public issues to competing and alternative definitions. A C.B.I. statement is usually 'balanced' by a T.U.C. statement, but a police statement on crime is rarely 'balanced' by one from a professional criminal, though the latter probably possesses more expertise on crime. But, as an opposition, criminals are neither 'legitimate' nor organised. By virtue of being criminals, they have forfeited the right to take part in the negotiation of the consensus about crime; and in the nature of most criminal activity itself, they are a relatively unorganised, individualised and fragmented stratum. It is only in very recent times that prisoners have become sufficiently organised and articulate on their own behalf to win access to the debate, say, about penal reform, even when this is about prison conditions or methods of prison discipline. By and large, the criminal, by his actions, is assumed to have forfeited, along with other citizenship rights, his 'right of reply' until he has repaid his debt to society. Such organised opposition as does exist – in the form usually of specific reforming groups and experts – often shares the same basic definition of the 'problem' as the primary definers, and is concerned merely to propound alternative means to the same objective: the returning of the criminal to the fold.

What this amounts to, where there seems to be a very wide consensus, and counter-definitions are almost absent, is that dominant definitions command the field of signification relatively unchallenged. What debate there is tends to take place almost exclusively *within the terms of reference* of the controllers. And this tends to repress any play between dominant and alternative definitions; by 'rendering all potential alternatives invisible', it pushes the treatment of the crime in question sharply on to the terrain of the *pragmatic* – given that there *is* a problem about crime, what can we do about it? In the absence of an alternative definition, powerfully and articulately proposed, the scope for any reinterpretation of crime by the public as an issue of public concern is extremely limited. Consequently, one of the areas where the media are most likely to be successful in mobilising public opinion within the dominant framework of ideas is on issues about crime and its threat to society. This makes the avenue of crime a peculiarly one-dimensional and transparent one so far as the mass media and public opinion is concerned: one where issues are simple, uncontroversial and clear cut. For this reason, too, crime and deviance provide two of the main sources for images of pollution and stigma in the public rhetoric. [28] It is not merely coincidental that the language used to justify action against any potential group of trouble-makers deploys, as one of its critical boundary markers, the imagery of criminality and illegality, applying it either directly, or indirectly, by association; [29] for example, the signification of student protestors as 'student hooligans', or 'hoodlums', or academic 'thugs' (discussed more fully in Chapter 8).

MUGGING AND THE MEDIA

So far we have been discussing the general characteristics of news production; then more tightly focusing on the forms these take in relation to the production of crime-as-news. In this section we shall connect these analyses of news production with the press treatment of 'mugging' news stories specifically. In examining, chronologically, the changing nature of this press treatment, we shall be able to see not only the application of specific news values, but, more importantly, how these operate as a *structure* in relation to a particular topic – in this case a particular kind of crime – to maintain its newsworthiness.

It might help to start with Table 3.1, which illustrates the general pattern of press reporting of mugging events during our sample period – August 1972 to August 1973; but first we need to say something about its empirical basis. Our sample was based on a daily reading of both the *Guardian* and the *Daily Mirror* for the thirteen-month sample period. We also had access to substantial files of cuttings referring to mugging events in this same period, which had been collected as a result of an extensive, but not exhaustive, reading of other national dailies, the national Sunday papers and the London evening papers. Because of the slightly different news emphases in both the Sunday papers and the London ones, we have not included stories from these sources in Table 3.1 or the accompanying text, though we have used material from these papers, in illustration, elsewhere in the book. Our search, based only on the national dailies, yielded thirty-three different events reported as muggings in the *Daily Mirror*, eighteen in the *Guardian*, and sixty over all. In arriving at these figures, we decided to count all the different reports referring to one particular mugging (i.e. 'follow ups' of the same event through to the later stages such as court case, appeal, etc.) as one; and we also decided that the first month in which the event was mentioned should become the month in which it was recorded in the table. Further, we also decided that the 'whole sample' column should include only the total number of different events. Thus in arriving at our figures for each month, the same event reported in, say, four different papers was counted as only one event. In the separate columns for the *Guardian* and the *Daily Mirror*, on the other hand, if the same event appeared in both papers it was recorded in both columns. Foreign mugging reports were excluded from the table. (Those interested in press coverage of mugging generally, as opposed to the coverage of mugging events – reports of crimes or court cases – should consult Table 3.2 at the end of this chapter.)

It should be clear from Table 3.1 that the peak of the press coverage of mugging events occurred in October 1972. Thereafter there is a decline in press interest. The maintenance of interest beyond the new year, through March and April, probably owes a lot to the effect of the Handsworth case. After that, only a spate of stories in the *Daily Mirror* in June provide mugging with any appreciable media visibility. Although, as we now know, August 1973 was by no means the end of 'the mugging story', it seems fair to conclude that by August 1973 mugging had concluded 'one cycle' of its newsworthiness. While the figures involved are admittedly small, and not very revealing on their own, when we turn to the *changing* nature of the coverage, a more distinct pattern does emerge – and one which bears out the notion of a 'cycle' of newsworthiness'.

'Mugging' breaks as a news story because of its extraordinariness, its novelty. This fits with our notion of the extraordinary as the cardinal news value: most stories seem to require some novel element in order to lift them into news visibility in the first instance; mugging was no exception. The Waterloo Bridge killing, defined by the police as a 'mugging gone wrong', was located and signified to its audience by the *Daily Mirror* as a 'frightening new strain of crime'. Someone stabbed or even killed in the course of a robbery is by no means novel. What *lifts* this particular murder out of the category of the 'run of the mill' is the attribution of a *'new'* label; this *signals* its novelty. Importantly, in line with our earlier argument, this event is *mediated* by the police investigating it; *they* provide the mugging label, and hence the legitimation for its use by the press. The journalist then builds on this skeletal definition. He frames and contextualises the details of the story in line with the operating logic of news values; he emphasises its novelty (a 'frightening new strain of crime') and the American connection.

TABLE 3.1

Mugging events reported in the press (August 1972 to August 1973)

Month/Year	Daily Mirror	Guardian	Whole sample
Aug 1972	1	2	2
Sep 1972	4	1	4
Oct 1972	12	9	23
Nov 1972	2	0	4
Dec 1972	0	1	2
Jan 1973	3	2	5
Feb 1973	1	0	4
Mar 1973	2	2	4
Apr 1973	2	0	5
May 1973	0	1	1
Jun 1973	5	0	5
Jul 1973	0	0	0
Aug 1973	1	0	1
Total	33	18	60

Galtung and Ruge have hypothesised that 'once something has hit the headlines and been defined as "news", then it will continue to be defined as news for some time',[30] and our example certainly validated this. Perhaps more importantly though, for a time, the simple attribution of the mugging label was sufficient to bring many discrete and commonplace crime events into the orbit of the newsworthy. The clearest examples of this process were provided by some of the most publicised early 'mugging' court cases; as we saw in Chapter 2, these were, in fact, trials for pickpocketting (or even 'attempted pickpocketting'). Other examples were the small spate of stories in September/October of attacks committed by girls. Mugging, it would seem, provided something of a focusing element for a latent concern about the growth of female violence – a concern which has since become manifest and independent from the concern about mugging. This process – what Hall has called the 'generative and associative' effect of new labels[31] – was also much in evidence during the period when the 'mod'/'rocker' labels had some novelty.[32]

However, the news value of 'novelty' is eventually expended; through repetition the extraordinary eventually becomes ordinary. Indeed, in relation to any one particular news story, 'novelty' clearly has the most limited life span of all the news values. At this point in the 'cycle' of a news story, other, more enduring news values are needed in order to supplement declining newsworthiness, and so sustain its 'news-life'. Two in particular seemed to play such an augmenting role in relation to mugging: those of the 'bizarre' and 'violence'. In respect of both of these news values, we find a growth in the number of mugging reports, throughout our sample period, which seemed to gain news visibility primarily because of the presence of such supplementary news values. Although the numbers involved are small, they do seem to us to be sufficiently marked to warrant our making inferences about them. On the other hand, the news-value 'elite or famous person' does not appear to play, in our sample anyway, such an augmenting role. In all we found only five stories which seemed to gain news visibility primarily because of the famous name of the victim: two appeared in 1972,[33] and three in 1973.[34]

By the 'bizarre' report we mean one with highly unusual, odd, eccentric, quaint, strange or grotesque characteristics. In our sample such reports could be sub-divided into two – those with a humorous twist and those with more menacing and grotesque overtones – but the term 'bizarre' seems adequate to cover the element of newsworthiness common to both types. During 1972 we found only one such report: the *Guardian* story of 10 November 1972 of a youth marching a man, who had no money, into a bank at knife-point in order to cash a cheque. But between March and July 1973 we found five – some humorous, some grotesque. As an example of each we have chosen two *Daily Mirror* stories.[35] The first, headlined 'Muggers pick on the wrong man', 5 June 1973, was a humorous story full of unusual twists and reversals. The report spoke of an unsuccessful mugging by three 'would-be' muggers. Their intended victim 'waded in with fists flying', left them 'lying dazed and battered', and then called at the nearest police station to inform them of the incident. The police then went to look for the men, not, apparently, to charge them but to see if any of them were 'seriously hurt'. Later in the same month, 27 June 1973, came a report with strange and menacing overtones: the story of the hurling over a cliff, in the small hours, of a hairdresser ... 'for 30p'.

The bizarre base for this last story is obviously the strange and extreme form that the assault took. But implicit in the story line is a second news angle, which casts an interesting light on the broader social understanding of crime. This second angle is carried in the juxtaposition, in both the headline and the story itself, between the assault and the reward gained by the muggers – 'for 30p'. The juxtaposition can only work (creating a dissonance between the two elements) given an implied 'rational calculus' about crime, and especially about the relation between violence and the results gained from its use. The implication of the *Mirror*'s juxtaposition is that '30p' is not a *rational* motive for the degree of violence involved in the assault. This implied calculus is often at work in the public signification of mugging – an implied *disparity* between the violence used in mugging attacks and the 'loot' taken. The contrast implicitly identifies a subordinate theme which came to be associated with the social concern about mugging – what was identified by police spokesmen as its 'gratuitous violence'.

Since we found it very difficult to differentiate precisely the purely 'gratuitous' from more 'instrumentally' violent mugging reports – for example, a 'gratuitously violent' headline might belie a more ambiguous, 'instrumental' report[36] – we have no precise, quantitative evidence of an increase in 'violent' reports of a specifically gratuitous kind. However, we do have evidence of a relative increase in the number of 'violent' mugging stories in general which bears out our notion about violence having an important role to play as a *supplementary* news value in the case of mugging.

Taking the coverage as a whole, of the sixty different mugging cases found, thirty-eight were reports of 'violent' muggings (i.e. involving actual physical assault), whereas only twenty-two were 'non-violent' (i.e. instances where there was only the threat of violence or no reported violence): a ratio of slightly under two-to-one. (Our estimates were based on the reported descriptions of the crimes, not on the formal charges brought against the defendants.) Yet if we contrast the reports found during 1972 (twenty violent and fifteen non-violent) with those found during 1973 (eighteen violent and seven non-violent), we find a change in the ratio from just over one-to-one to nearly three-to-one; and if we take only the last five months of the sample period (April – August 1973) we get a ratio of five-to-one (ten violent reports and two non-violent ones).

Of course, these ratios, and the pattern of intensification around the violence theme that they reveal, would not be particularly significant if they corresponded with the official statistics used to justify the reaction to mugging. Obviously, as our earlier section on statistics should have demonstrated, the problems of using official crime statistics as a base – and especially mugging statistics – are many. However, we offer the following evidence as our basis for saying that of the cases collectively perceived by the police to be 'part of the mugging problem' in the 1972–3 period, about 50 per cent were 'non-violent', and the ratio of one-to-one that this revealed remained fairly constant:

So far this year about 450 cases have been reported to the squad [set up to deal with South London 'muggings']. Of these 160 have been substantiated as violent robberies and a further 200 confirmed as thefts from the person, either by snatching or pocketpicking. (*Sunday Times*, 1 October 1972.)

Nor is there such a thing as a typical mugger. But there is a pattern. Go to Brixton Police Station, for example, and it's all there on the wall charts and in the statistics. In the past year, 211 robberies with violence or threats – 40 more than the previous year. Snatching without violence – 300 cases. (*London Evening News*, 22 March 1973.)

The ratio between the statistics for 'robberies' and 'snatchings' is similar in both sets of statistics, though one set refers to 1972 and the other to early 1973. In fact there are slightly *more* 'non-violent' than 'violent' cases. Since neither article gives any further, separate, figures for 'muggings', it seems fair to assume that both 'robbery' and 'snatching without violence' were being treated, for all practical purposes, as muggings. As a further vindication of this view, we would refer readers to the *Report of the Commissioner of the Metropolitan Police for the Year 1972* which explicitly states that there is little difference between 'snatchings' and 'robbery': 'Although they are not strictly crimes of violence, "snatchings" are included in the table [crimes of violence (selected)] because there is no great distinction between these offences and those of robbery and because a similar increase is evident over the last two years.' [37] The Commissioner is talking – though he claims not to like the term – of 'muggings'. Although the tendency of the media to over report violent crime in general has frequently been noted, [38] what we have been drawing attention to here is the way 'violence' is increasingly used, as a structuring element, in relation to the life cycle of one particular news theme.

In Roshier's look at the selection of crime news in the press, he found four sets of factors to be particularly important: '(1) the seriousness of the offence ... (2) "Whimsical" circumstances, i.e. humorous, ironic, unusual ... (3) Sentimental or dramatic circumstances ... (4) The involvement of a famous or high status person in any capacity (although particularly as offender or victim).' [39] These are very similar factors to the news values we found to be important as supplementary sources of newsworthiness, i.e. the 'famous personality', the 'bizarre' and violence. However, our emphasis has been on how these news values operate as a structure or set: how they operate in relation to the primary value of novelty, principally as different ways of reviving a 'flagging' news story. This emphasis, we believe, justifies our talking of a 'cycle of newsworthiness', and supports our conclusion that by August 1973 this particular cycle was at, or very near, its end.

RECIPROCAL RELATIONS

Finally, we want to look at the *relations of reciprocity* between the primary definers and the media, as exemplified in the mugging case. On 26 September 1972 the *Daily Mirror* carried a story with the headline 'A Judge Cracks Down On Muggers In City Of Fear.' The story perfectly illustrates the role and status for the media of privileged definitions: the use of the term 'muggers' in the headline is justified by the judge's statement in the main report: 'Mugging is becoming more and more prevalent certainly in London. We are told that in America people are afraid to walk the streets late at night because of mugging.' We must also take note here of the judge's use of American 'mugging' as a reference point against which his sentencing is contextualised; but primarily this example illustrates the 'anchorage' of news-stories in the authoritative pronouncements of privileged definers *outside* the media.

In October 1972, we find an example of how the media utilises a 'base' in such definitions for its *own* definitional work on such an issue. The *Daily Mirror* on 6 October 1972 accompanied a report of Judge Hines's sentencing three teenage youths to three years' imprisonment for 'mugging' with an editorial which picked up his statement that 'The course I feel I am bound to take may not be the best for you young men individually, but it is one I must take in the public interest.' The editorial *adds its own campaigning 'voice'* – its 'public idiom' – to that of the judge: 'Judge Hines is right. There are times when deterrent sentences which normally would seem harsh and unfair, MUST be imposed ... if mugging is not to get out of hand as it has in America, punishment must be sharp and certain.' Here we can see the press in a more active role – justifying (but simultaneously using as its justification) judicial statements about 'mugging' as a public issue. The circle has become tighter, the topic more closed, the relations between media and primary definers more mutually reinforcing. (Indeed for the *Mirror there is no debate left*: 'Judge Hines is right.')

A week later (13 October 1972), the *Sun*, in an editorial entitled 'Taming the Muggers', moved another step towards closure by aligning 'the people' with the dominant definition of the judiciary. In this example, the *Sun* does not bring its 'public idiom' to bear – rather, it *takes the public voice*; it becomes the people's 'ventriloquist':

WHAT ARE the British people most concerned about today? Wages? Prices? Immigration? Pornography? People are talking about all these things. But the *Sun* believes there is another issue which has everyone deeply worried and angry: VIOLENCE IN OUR STREETS ... Nothing could be more utterly against our way of life, based on a common sense regard for law and order.... If punitive jail sentences help to stop the violence – and nothing else has done – then they will not only prove to be the only way. They will, regrettably, be the RIGHT way. *And the judges will have the backing of the public.*

If we disregard for a moment differences between individual papers and treat all the newspapers as contributing to a sequence in which critical definitional work on the controversial topic of 'mugging' is carried out, then we can see, in abbreviated form, how the relations between primary definers and the media serve, at one and the same time, to define 'mugging' as a *public issue,* as a matter of *public concern*, and to effect an ideological closure of the topic. Once in play the primary definition commands the field; there is now in existence *an issue of public concern*, whose dimensions have been clearly delineated, which now serves as a continuing point of reference for subsequent news reporting, action and campaigns. For example, it now becomes possible for the police, who are somewhat circumspect about appearing to involve themselves in controversial matters which are not yet settled, to *demand wider powers* to act on an issue of crime control which has now been unambiguously installed as an urgent public matter. Thus:

> *Police may seek more powers on 'mugging'.*
> Police superintendents, alarmed by the increase in violent crime, particularly among young people, may ask the Home Office for stronger powers to combat 'mugging'. (*The Times*, 5 October 1972.)

A few months later it is the judiciary which *recruits the public concern about 'mugging'* (or *takes the public voice*) as a defence for *their* deterrent sentencing policies:

> *Mugger jailed for 3 years. 'And I was lenient', says the judge.* The judge added, 'everybody in this country thinks that offences of this kind – mugging offences – are on the increase and the public have got to be protected. This is a frightful case' (*Daily Mail*, 29 March 1973.)

In this last example 'public opinion' has been *imported back into* the judicial discourse as a way of underpinning and making legitimate a judicial statement about crime. Whereas before the media grounded *its* stories in evidence provided by the courts, now the courts use the public ('everybody thinks') to ground *their* statements. This is an exceedingly limited circle of mutual reciprocities and re-enforcements. But even this twist of the amplification spiral should not blind us to the starting-point of the process: the point where it began and from which it is continually renewed – the role of the primary and privileged definers, who, in classifying out the world of crime for media and public, establish the principal categories across which the news media and newsmen run their secondary themes and variations.

A week previously another judge had added the final twist to the 'spiral', and effectively 'closed the circle'. Sentencing two youths whose counsel had made reference to the heavy sentences handed down in the Handsworth case the previous day, the judge commented that 'The press had now made it known that sentences for street attacks involving robbery "would no longer be light".'[40] Here we see the *reciprocity between the different parts of the control culture* in an extremely clear and explicit form. We have here *exactly the reverse side* of the process we noted earlier in which the media legitimated its coverage in evidence provided by the courts. Now the media themselves have become the 'legitimator' of the control process. We are now at the very heart of the inter-relationships between the control culture and the 'signification culture'. The mutual articulation of these two 'relatively independent' agencies is by this stage so overdetermined that it cannot work in any way other than to create *an effective ideological and control closure* around the issue. In this moment, the media – albeit unwittingly, and through their own 'autonomous' routes – have become effectively an apparatus of the control process itself – an 'ideological state-apparatus'.[41]

TABLE 3.2
The press coverage of 'mugging' (August 1972 to August 1973)

Month/Year	Guardian (1)	Daily Mirror (2)	(1) and (2) combined	Other dailies	Monthly totals
Aug 1972	5	1	6	3	9
Sep 1972	2	5	7	5	12
Oct 1972	7	18	25	19	44
Nov 1972	5	5	10	13	23
Dec 1972	0	2	2	4	6
Jan 1973	4	5	9	4	13
Feb 1973	0	1	1	7	8
Mar 1973	7	9	16	37	53*
Apr 1973	4	4	8	13	21
May 1973	2	0	2	4	6
Jun 1973	0	5	5	0	5
Jul 1973	0	0	0	0	0
Aug 1973	1	1	2	0	2
Total	37	56	93	109	202

* Includes thirty-four stories on the Handsworth case.

NOTES: (1) As in Table 3.1, the *Guardian* and the *Daily Mirror* were read exhaustively, while the figures for 'other dailies' were reconstructed from press cuttings supplied by N.C.C.L. and the B.B.C.

(2) All items mentioning 'mugging' were counted. Most referred to particular crimes but a substantial number were of a more general kind: reports of Home Office/police activity; features; editorials, etc. Consistently, across papers and months, this latter kind of report provided about a quarter or more of all items.

II

4

Balancing Accounts: Cashing in on Handsworth

On the evening of 5 November 1972, Mr Robert Keenan was walking home from a pub in the Villa Road area of Handsworth, Birmingham, when he met three boys, Paul Storey, James Duignan and Mustafa Fuat. They stopped him and asked for a cigarette. Then they knocked him to the ground and dragged him to a nearby piece of wasteground, where they robbed him of 30p, some keys and five cigarettes. After this they left him, but returned about two hours later, found he was still there, and attacked him again; on this occasion James and Mustafa kicked him, while Paul attacked him with a brick. Again they left the scene, but came back to attack him once more.

Some time later, Mustafa Fuat and James Duignan phoned for an ambulance and told the police that they had found an injured man. In the following two days they were interviewed on several occasions, and on 8 November, following what James, Mustafa and two girl witnesses told the police, all three boys were arrested and charged. It seems from the statement of one of the girls that at least one other person saw either one of the attacks on the unconscious body of Mr Keenan. There were about two hours between the first and second attacks.

On 19 March 1973, the three boys appeared in the court in Birmingham before Mr Justice Croom-Johnson and were charged as follows: Paul Storey with attempted murder and robbery; James Duignan and Mustafa Fuat with wounding with intent to cause grievous bodily harm and robbery. The three boys pleaded guilty to all charges. The prosecution presented the facts as outlined above. The defence counsel did not substantially challenge them, but pleaded mitigating circumstances: in Paul's case that he came from a broken home, with some history of violence in the family which might lead to the 'conclusion that this sort of background can affect the human mind so as to lead to otherwise completely unexplainable behaviour'. In James's and Mustafa's defence, it was argued that Paul had been the instigator of, and main participant in, the offence.

The judge said that it was a 'serious and horrible case'. To Paul Storey he said, 'Storey, you were clearly the ringleader. You clearly took the most active part in the attack on Mr Keenan. You went back for the purpose of assaulting him. You kicked him, you hit him over the head with a brick, and on a third occasion, you went back and kicked him three or four times in the face as he lay insensible on the ground. You are nothing more or less than a wild animal.' He then went on to pass sentence on Paul, saying: 'It is quite impossible for me to do other than to order you to be detained in such a place and in such conditions as the Secretary of State may direct. I fix the period at twenty years.' The detention order was made under the *Children and Young Person's Act* of 1933, section 53 (2). Under the same Act, James and Mustafa were given sentences of ten years' detention each.

On 21 March, the three boys were recalled before the judge; he had omitted, he said, to pass separate sentences on the robbery charges. He said he had reread the medical reports on Mr Keenan, about the extent of his injuries and how they had been caused (though he had not, it seemed, reread the welfare and psychiatric reports on the boys). He went on: 'Robbery involves the use of violence and the sentences must reflect the degree of violence . . . the effects can only be described as sickening. The public must be protected from you.' He then passed sentences of twenty years' detention for Paul, and ten years each for James and Mustafa, to run concurrently with those given previously.

The previous minor misdemeanours of the accused, such as they were, were not referred to by the judge. Paul Storey had been fined £10 for a 'disorderly act' the previous May (he took a car and drove it around Handsworth until it ran out of petrol), and at school he had been at the receiving end of a minor stabbing. James Duignan had spent some time in an approved school for minor, non-violent offences. Mustafa Fuat had no record.

On 14 May Lord Justice James considered an application for leave to appeal for a reduction in the length of the sentences, made on behalf of all three boys. He refused the appeal on the grounds that the boys would be eligible for parole, and that it was unlikely that they would serve anything like their full sentences.

On 28 June, in the Court of Appeal, Lord Chief Justice Widgery (in a judgement analysed more fully later) upheld Lord Justice James's decision and refused leave to appeal.

This is the bare outline of the Handsworth case which marked the culmination of the mugging panic in its first phase: one reason for our concentration on it here. Additionally, though, the 'Handsworth case' prompted intensive press coverage. We have treated this as a case study in which the analysis of the media made in the previous chapter can be exemplified. Although the extent of coverage was unprecedented, this does not undermine our representation of it as typical of previous coverage. The same set of core news values shapes the construction of the initial front-page leads; the assumptions and formulations of the editorials closely resemble earlier positions taken by papers. [1] The feature articles, too, mobilising possible explanations of 'mugging', had similar precursors;[2] while the debate between 'experts' and 'lay' opinion served to sharpen rather than alter the shape of arguments about crime and punishment which had for some time occupied space in letter columns.

The Handsworth case, then, crystallises the operation of the media, so that in one moment we can observe the shape of a whole news process. It also allows us to see how the different forms of the process (news, editorials, features) handled the elements in the case, and how these forms of news production related to each other. Finally, we are concerned with the dependence of the forms on meanings, references and interests rooted outside the specific sphere of media operation. As we have seen, news values define as newsworthy that which is abnormal, thus mobilising a sense of what constitutes normality. In the Handsworth case a whole range of such assumptions – about the routine operation of the legal system, the basis of sentencing policy, the extent to which young people can be held responsible for their actions, their immediate motives, more long-term consideration of social causes – were operative. All these provided a structured framework within which the media worked out its variations.

This framework of beliefs and ideas about how the social order normally works constitutes a sort of folk ideology about crime and punishment in society. The handling of the Handsworth story in the press was an 'ideological' process, not only because certain social interests were realised in its treatment, but because it had meaning only by leave of ideological constructs which generated it as a meaningful and 'newsworthy' set of items. In the analysis which follows, we are less concerned with the immediate content of the news coverage, and more concerned with the way the Handsworth story was constructed by these folk ideologies, and, reciprocally, with the way these ideologies articulated and tested themselves through the construction of the story as a news item. We are concerned, not with the news content of the press, so much as with the 'ideologies of crime and punishment': with an ideological not a content analysis. It must be added, however, that ideologies are not simply sets of ideas and beliefs about the world hanging loose in people's heads. They are made active and realised in concrete practices and apparatuses – for example, the practices and apparatuses of news construction. These ideologies are present only when they are realised, objectivated, materialised in concrete instances, actions or forms, through concrete practices.

PRIMARY NEWS

JAILED FOR 20 YEARS – SHOCK SENTENCE ON A MUGGER AGED 16 (*Daily Mirror*, 20 March 1973)

20 YEARS FOR MUGGERS – Boy 16 weeps after sentence (*Daily Express*, 20 March 1973)

20 YEARS FOR THE MUGGERS AGED 16 (*Sun*, 20 March 1973)

20 YEARS FOR BOY, 16, WHO WENT MUGGING FOR FUN (*Daily Mail*, 20 March 1973)

16 YEAR OLD BOY GETS 20 YEARS FOR MUGGING (*Guardian*, 20 March 1973)

20 YEARS FOR 16 YEAR OLD MUGGER – five cigarettes and 30p from victim (*Daily Telegraph*, 20 March 1973)

MUGGER AGED 16 GIVEN 20 YEARS DETENTION AND COM-
PANIONS 10 YEARS (*The Times*, 20 March 1973)

16-YEAR-OLD BOY GETS 20 YEARS IN 'MUGGING' CASE
(*Morning Star*, 20 March 1973)

Headlines are frequently an accurate, if simple, guide to the themes implicit in a story which the newspapers consider to represent its most 'newsworthy' angle. The 'news value' of a story is frequently augmented by counterposing, in the headline, two apparently contrasting or oppositional themes or aspects. It is relatively rare for *all* the national papers to select *the same* angle or angles around which to pivot a story. It is therefore striking, in this instance, that every newspaper chooses to signify the Handsworth story by means of the same contrasting or juxtaposed themes: the *youth* of the offenders versus the *length* of the sentences. Some papers expanded the story's news value by the addition of the newsworthy label 'mugging' or 'mugger'. The juxtaposition of the eldest offender's age, as contrasted with the unusual length of the sentence, testifies to the reliance by the press on the court-room as the principal source for its front-page story. The story, in other words, was first signified through the news exploitation of its judicial or penal aspect. Within this unanimity, there are important differences of emphasis: notably, between those who put *the age* of Paul Storey first (*Guardian, The Times, Morning Star*) and those who put *the sentence* first (*Daily Express, Daily Mail, Daily Mirror, Sun, Daily Telegraph*). The *Guardian, Daily Mail*, and *Morning Star* did not direc- tly label the offenders as 'muggers'; the *Morning Star* uses inverted commas around mugging; the *Telegraph*'s emphasis is 30p; and the *Mail* stresses the motive of 'fun'. Some of these are indicative of *real* differences of emphasis which become apparent in the subsequent coverage (e.g. the *Star* challenging the mugging definition), as we hope to demonstrate.

The formal function of a headline is to draw the readers' attention; to do this it must dramatise the event or issue, and hence the oft-satirised tendency to use reinforcing words like 'shock', 'sensation', 'scandal', 'drama'. But what it must also do is to indicate why this item is important and problematic. Here, the use of the mugging label and the juxtaposition of the 16-year-old/20 years themes are enough for us to recognise and situate this event as part of the 'mugging' pattern – a climax to the earlier exemplary sentences of late 1972, which at the same time poses a series of complex choices about the treatment of young of- fenders. The Handsworth case does not appear as a story; it appears as a set of questions, touching on a problematic area – questions about penal policy. We should add that the term 'mugging' was not used in court, so far as we know, so that its appearance in the headlines here demonstrates again the 'creative' role of the media, which we saw in Chapter 3, and the way in which the cons- tant search for augmenting news values – in this case the use of the 'mugging' label – ensures that the 'debate' which follows will be heavily 'inferentially structured' from the outset.

To pursue this group of 'open questions' behind the sentence, the newspapers sought the reactions of the immediate actors – the offenders' relatives and friends, and then those of social advocates – those seen as having the right or duty to express an opinion or pronounce judgement on the sentence. Most papers, then, quickly moved beyond the report of the court hearing, which was presented with considerable similarity: opening with the judge's comments, a presentation of the prosecution case, and extracts from the pleas in mitigation. Here there were only two significant variations, both of which proved important indicators of subsequent coverage. The *Daily Mail* and the *Sun* omitted the pleas offered in mitigation and thereby prefigured their heavy emphasis on the suffering of the victim; and the *Morning Star* prepared its own opposition to the sentences by omitting the judge's comments.

As we can see, in the Handsworth case the exploration of the 'issues behind the event' was not added to a common objective summary of the court proceedings; it was rather, built into the very way the story was first presented as a news item – and not only in the headlines and the text. Most of the newspapers – *The Times, Telegraph* and the *Morning Star* being the exceptions – carried photographs of some kind. Four of the remaining five had insets of Paul Storey, two of the judge, two of Mustafa Fuat, and one of Paul Storey's mother. No paper had more than two at this stage. Perhaps because of the limited stock of family photographs, some of them were of the offenders as very young children and others were indistinct and blurred. Their over all effect, especially if juxtaposed with the bewigged judge, is to reflect in highly personalised terms the themes – youth/innocence versus adulthood/the law – already signified in the headlines. This *individualising* of the abstract issues was further accomplished by the reproduction of the boys' mothers' comments. The *Express, Mail* and *Sun* quote all three; the *Telegraph, Guardian* and *Star* none; *The Times* just Paul Storey's mother, as does the *Mirror*. There is perhaps here – in the extent to which opposition to the sentences was represented as located immediately in the boys' families rather than through detached consideration of the issue – a real distinction between a populist and a more abstract approach. *The Times* here, exceptionally, unbends itself a little.

These, then, were the actors given credence because of their personal and intimate involvement in the event. But the event was also presented as having wider implications, as marking a new development in the on-going judicial process of sentencing around which a public debate had already been established. The terrain of this debate was occupied by interest groups and pressure groups, elected representatives and academic experts on crime and penal policy. Locked in combat here were the penal reformers – concerned with the implications of the sentences for these and other offenders – and the law-enforcers, willing to greet with enthusiasm a sentence they believed to be both deterrent and justly retributive. Only the *Sun* and the *Morning Star* did not use these forces in opposition as a more generalised representation of the implicit opposition between the judge and the boys' mothers: an indication of their unequivocal handling of the issue. The *Mail, Telegraph, Mirror* and *Guardian* used quotes from such institutions as PROP (the prisoners' rights organisation), the National Council for Civil Liberties and the Howard League for Penal Reform, which all condemned the sentence, in contrast to those who supported it, the Police Federation and various Tory M.P.s. The *Express* and

The Times preferred to describe the controversial nature of the sentences in their own words, as 'without precedent'.

There is, then, a pattern common to most of the newspapers: a 16-year-old/20-year mugging headline, a photograph or two, an account of court proceedings, some statements from the affected, more general comments from institutionalised spokesmen. Before considering two papers in detail, we wish to note two additions to some of the stories which warrant comment. The first is the use by *The Times* and the *Guardian* of a series of politico-juridical statements about the need for heavy sentences against 'muggers'. Both quote speeches of the previous eighteen months made by Lord Colville, Minister of State for the Home Office, the Home Secretary, Robert Carr, and Lord Hailsham, the Lord Chancellor. The effect of these quotations is to suggest that these sentences were, if not directly approved by the government, at least in line with their general thinking on the subject. It moves the sentence from a judicial to a political level, and in so doing acknowledges – in a way which breaches the conventional representation of the judiciary as an independent arm of the state – the relationship between them. It is an ambiguous insertion, not only because it raises the question of whether the government might or should have intervened in sentencing policy, but also because it begins to situate this sentence as part of the larger mugging campaign and that, in turn, as part of the highly politicised law-and-order issue.

In the event, the *Guardian* did not pursue the line of enquiry, and *The Times* settled the ambiguity by using the second addition we mentioned. It followed these political statements by recalling the 129 per cent rise in muggings claimed by Scotland Yard, thus implicitly justifying the sentences as being no more than a legitimate reaction to an unprecedented crime wave. A similar 'statistical' tactic was used by the *Telegraph*. These additions affected a particular closure of the topic: whatever the long-term issues might be, the hard evidence supported the necessity for drastic action; and legitimated a 'political' interest in the 'judicial' handling of the case. These, then, were two distinctive and significant variations on otherwise common themes. We now wish to demonstrate how two newspapers, different in readership, lay-out, style and overt political allegiances, can adopt very different routes through the issues behind the Handsworth event, and yet never breach the agreed boundaries of news exploration. These papers are the *Daily Telegraph* and the *Daily Mirror*.

The *Telegraph* shared with the rest of the press a common sense as to what was primarily newsworthy about the Handsworth case – 20 years/16-year-old. This common ground was, however, significantly inflected by the 'Five cigarettes and 30p' strapline, which underscores the senselessness and irrationality of the crime (significantly, the 'lack of motivation' was the main reason subsequently cited by the Court of Appeal when confirming the sentences). Technically, the story was written in a classic 'objective' style. In keeping with this, a formal balance was maintained within the story, which reports the criticism of the sentence by penal reformers. But this balance is framed by the 'legalistic' nature of the over-all report. This is strongly instanced by the *Telegraph*'s use of a statement by Mr Colin Woods, Assistant Commissioner (Crime), Scotland Yard, that 45 per cent more people were hurt in robberies in

London than in previous years. His declaration that 'We are not going to let the thugs win', and shock at the callousness of the muggers, tended to swing the *Telegraph* report firmly into the judicial camp, through the strategic use of a primary definer. So does the subsequent capsule biography of the judge and his earlier remarks about the insecure backgrounds of young offenders. The formal balance and objective style of the report was thus outweighed by the paper's alignment with the 'judicial' perspective. Its 'balance' was legalistic and institutional, rather than 'humane' and personalised. The first day's report contained no quotes from parents, no reference to parental background or to neighbourhood (though some of these are treated in the feature story on 21 March 1973). The *Telegraph* case was, therefore, an unusually consistent one in its adoption of a judicial frame of reference as a 'resolution'.

The *Mirror* presented a contrast to this: as we might expect, the event is here personalised, dramatised, and the differing views quoted were cast in publicly available moral 'common-sense' terms, as befitted the *Mirror*'s popular-demotic style. The story contained many of the same elements as the *Telegraph*: but its presentational arrangement was very different. The age/sentence juxtaposition was stretched in the headline to a contrast between main and supporting headlines, the first taking the most dramatic angle (20 years) the second the youth's age. This may, however, be simply a matter of the *Mirror* not having available space for long headlines in the tabloid format, rather than a difference of stress. The 'mugging' reference was general ('mugging' not 'a mugging') and unequivocal (no inverted commas). The forces 'pro' and 'con' the sentence were stated with equal balance. Both were seen, however, as appealing to public morality as final arbiter: the reformers' appeal against an outdated severity in the courts; the Police Federation spokesman citing 'society's' exhausted patience. There was thus no swift judicial conclusion available here. And, as if to signify that the case 'opened out into' a public debate not yet resolved, the *Mirror*, in its supplementary page two story, *literally* displayed the two sides of the argument in perfect balance. Beneath a four-column headline, 'The Case of the Teenage Muggers', lay two stories, two columns long each, in straight juxtaposition:

20 YEARS IS A LONG TIME FOR A YOUNG BOY (Storey's mother)	GANGS SEEM TO REGARD MUGGING AS A SPORT (Police Federation)

This was a particularly strict exercise in 'news balance'. No crime statistics or data belong here. The opposition hinged on two controversial *images* of the criminal – 'young boy'/gangs. Which, it asked, is the correct way to perceive these criminals? To fill out this juxtaposition, the left-hand column consisted almost entirely of personal comments by Storey's mother – 'a good boy', 'bad company', 'very shocked', 'the environment': statements which personalised the accused, grounding the abstract stereotype of the criminal in the figure of a real person and a real environment. The right-hand column adds, to the Police Federation, the ubiquitous Assistant Commissioner Woods, with his observation on the violent and pointless nature of these crimes, and his comment on 'The mugger [as] ... a reflection of the present violent society.'

As between the *Telegraph* and the *Mirror*, there were significant similarities and differences to be noted. The *Telegraph* story already arrived at a provisional closure, via the use of the judicial perspective. The *Mirror* left the issues more polarised, more open and unresolved. Both papers, however, picked up the same newsworthy themes; both provided a certain balance of views; both quoted; both weaved their inflections around basically the same elements of the story.

In constructing this item as a news story, then, all the papers went for the most troubling and problematic aspect. The story was thematised around these troubling concerns, and the formal exploitation of this thematic shaped the handling in different papers. The story gained in news value as a result of being sharply polarised between its two key aspects – age of offenders/length of sentence. Orchestrated as a quasi-argument between these two 'sides', the news treatment then took the form of contrasting them and elaborating on them. Most papers did this through quotation of sources represented as falling on one or other side of the 'debate'. Almost all treatments work in the direction of balancing off the two viewpoints. The very formal way balance was represented (often literally in the typography and lay-out) signified that the matter was controversial, open to more than one interpretation, with some strong arguments on either side, on the basis of which the reader could make up his or her mind. Strict balance was not always present: one or other side was sometimes ignored (*Sun, Morning Star*). In others, the story was so structured as to leave one side in command of the field (*Telegraph, The Times*). Nevertheless, the principal form of the primary-news treatment of Handsworth was to cast what first appeared as a 'report' on a factual event into the form of a *question or issue*. Except in one or two cases, the 'closure' effected at that stage was, at best, partial. Of course, formal balance is not the whole story. Arguments, formally balanced, can nevertheless be inflected so as to favour one side or the other. This may arise from the particular 'personality' of the paper, or from how such subjects are 'normally' angled (see the previous chapter). Or a closure can be effected by the statement of an editorial judgement on it – usually by taking it over into the opinion part of the paper: its editorial columns. Alternatively, the answer which the formal juxtaposition seems to require can be relocated by recasting the question – going behind it to another level of exploration. This movement consists of replacing the original terms of 'the question' by a search for more background explanations and causes, suggesting that the immediate causes implicit in the primary-news treatment have not exhausted its possibilities. Both developments of a primary-news story mark a shift from foreground news to some other level. This shift is both formal and ideological. The formal shifts – from news to editorials, or from news to features – both depend on elaborating some of the themes already present in first-order news presentation. But they inflect these themes in opposite directions: the first (editorials) towards a judgement, the second (features) towards 'deeper explanations' or 'background'. The separation is therefore not a technical matter of good journalistic practice, but arises from two different ways of effecting an ideological closure (simple and complex). If primary-news stories are presented in 'the form of a question', editorials and features provide two, different kinds of 'answers'.

THE EDITORIALS

Primary-news stories provide the foundation for most editorials; indeed the decision to produce an editorial at all is some indication of the significance accorded such stories by a newspaper. Editorials, also, are related to feature articles in that both are ways of developing further elements of primary news: they are two different kinds of 'answers', and often, as we shall see, contradictory ways of handling the same event. Thus one focus of attention here will be the relationship between editorials and other news forms. The other focus relates to the fact that it was in some editorial columns particularly that the panic about mugging was fostered and the campaign against muggers vociferously waged. We are, therefore, interested in the range of explanatory arguments deployed about crime and sentencing, and the implicit theories of human nature and society underpinning these. It is here, then, that we get a first glimpse of the kinds of explanations and ideologies that constitute the core of Chapter 6. Since much of our evidence in that chapter comes from letters – the 'personal viewpoints' of correspondents – it is not surprising that it is in the editorial columns – the 'personal viewpoints' of newspapers – that we begin to encounter, perhaps more clearly than anywhere else in the news coverage of the event, these explanatory paradigms. Finally, since these editorials also produced a *judgement* on the event, we are also interested in these; i.e. in the forms of 'resolution' adopted. As it happened, there was a striking unanimity in the judgements arrived at. With few exceptions, editorials on Handsworth supported the sentences. Our concern here, then, is the fact of this unanimity – the closure around the traditional viewpoint – and the consequent absence or failure of the 'liberal' nerve.

Only three of the eight daily national newspapers failed to carry an editorial: the *Daily Mirror*, the *Sun* and the *Guardian*. We suspect that but for an industrial dispute the *Daily Mirror* would have carried an editorial and that it would have argued – given its particular mix of populism and progressivism – for *both* strong action to stamp out mugging *and* progressive reforms to alleviate social deprivation. (Although it falls outside our sample, this is precisely the line followed by the *Sunday Mirror* editorial.) The reason the *Sun* failed to carry one is related to the way it strictly delimited the story's themes from the outset, collapsed the distinctions between different kinds of news coverage, and thus made an editorial superfluous. The editorial judgement was already built into the news treatment. (This 'one-dimensional' treatment was exceptional and explains why we have chosen to look at the case of the *Sun* separately later.)

The case of the *Guardian* is undoubtedly the most interesting, and revealing. Its primary-news story was relatively open and its use of quotations from both social-work agencies and politicians opened up various possibilities of editorial development. Furthermore, the *Guardian* habitually gives favourable and sympathetic coverage to penal-reform groups and, of all the papers, most consistently gives a liberal voice to a series of neglected social issues. Yet, in this instance, it was speechless. The reason, we suggest, is related to the fact that the *Guardian* had hoisted itself on the same headline pivots as everybody else: an indication of its failure to resist the lure of the mugging panic and its terms

Unable, given this starting-point, to challenge the validity of the mugging campaign, and unable. given that there is a 'problem of crime' and that the sentences were, in theory, flexible, to offer a realistic alternative, it had nothing to
say and fell into silence. This failure of the liberal nerve, this ambiguity, is
sometimes a characteristic of the *Guardian* when issues present themselves as
a choice between hard alternatives, but is also symptomatic of the deep contradictions inherent in the liberal position itself. It is, perhaps, in relation to
crime more than in any other single area that the liberal voice is most constrained; that conventional definitions are hardest to resist; that alternative
definitions are hardest to come by. In Chapter 6 we shall attempt to say why
we think this is the case. Nevertheless, this general lack of a liberal editorial
voice, at the high point of the mugging panic, ought to be strongly emphasised.

Of the five papers which carried an editorial, only the *Morning Star* opposed
the sentences. Its uncompromising radicalism is in stark contrast with the
Guardian's liberal evasiveness. Reversing the conventional terms, it called the
sentences 'savage' and the boys 'victims'. It drew out the sentences' political
implications – to appease those who 'campaign for the punitive society' – as
well as denouncing the sentences on the more normal pragmatic grounds of the
unproven effectiveness of deterrent sentences and the 'criminalising' effect of
prison. As for what should be done, it suggested that 'the sentences should be
slashed and the boys given remedial treatment'. Despite the failure to challenge
the use of the mugging label – a possibility in view of the use of inverted
commas around the term in the headline – the argument is certainly the most
consistent in the press, and is carried through all stages of its coverage.

The remaining four papers supported the sentences: most circumspect and
'balanced' was *The Times*; most aloof and legalistic was the *Telegraph*; while
the *Mail* and the *Express* were most whole-heartedly in support of the judge
and in condemnation of the 'savagery' of the crime. *The Times*, perhaps
because of its relatively restricted primary coverage and lack of secondary or
feature coverage, had a lengthy and detailed editorial, headed '20 years for attempted murder'. Here it takes up, unlike any other paper, both sides of the
headline juxtaposition (20 years/16-year-old) and weighs up the two sides. It
criticises a twenty-year sentence on a boy of 16 from a disturbed home
background, but notes that the crime was a 'savage one'. It concludes: 'It is
always hard to be sure how much an exemplary sentence really does act as a
deterrent but it would be very strange if it had no deterrent effect at all. The
public are justifiably alarmed at the increase in violent crime and look to the
law for what protection it can provide.'

In sum, this was a very tortuous exercise in balance, and undoubtedly the
one best exemplifying the dilemma facing 'liberals' when a choice is necessary
between hard alternatives; although *The Times* does finally choose, it is an uneasy, conscience-wracked choice. The note on which *The Times* ends – the appeal to the autonomous abstraction of 'the law' – is one which informs the
whole of the *Telegraph*'s editorial 'scales of justice'. By making this particular
case merely an example of the difficulties faced by properly constituted
authority – the judiciary – in finding appropriate sentences in a period of growing violent crime, the *Telegraph* could admit the severity of the sentences,

justify them in the context of rising crime, and ignore the peculiarities of the case. This was a general 'view from the top'. Untroubled by particular details, which must inform primary-news treatment, it had shifted the argument, and hence the issue, to a manageable level.

If the *Telegraph* was an example of one way of resolving the 'dilemma' of *The Times*' balancing act, the *Express* and the *Mail* offered a very different route. For them it was precisely the detailed characteristics of this crime as typical of the 'mugging trend' which pointed to the necessity for the sentences. Thus the *Daily Mail*, under the headline 'Terrible deterrent', employed a short, stabbing style, reflecting, typographically, the viciousness of the attack and the notion of mugging as 'in vogue'. It also picked up the primary-news headline emphasis 'for fun':

> They went in with boots and bricks. . . . *Their victim* an Irish labourer may suffer permanent behaviour changes. . . . *Their haul* – five cigarettes etc. . . . *Their ages* 15 to 16. . . . Yesterday the savagery of the crime was matched by justice at its most harsh. . . . Only as a deterrent can society contemplate such terrible punishment. Mugging, the trendy term for a crime as old as sin itself, is in vogue with young thugs. The law should make it known by every propaganda means at its disposal, that deterrent sentences are in vogue too.

The *Express* followed substantially the same lines: the meagreness of the haul compared with the viciousness of the attack; the historical continuity of mugging (in strong contrast with its 'novel' representation in news): 'Today's footpads are no different from their predecessors.' There was slightly more emphasis on the offenders' personalities – 'callous', 'casual', 'without motive', 'for fun', 'blood lust' – and the court's duty was seen, unlike the *Mail*'s stress on deterrence and an 'eye for an eye', as being to 'reflect the people's will'.

Underlying both editorials, not elaborately but certainly implicitly, we can see the essence of the conservative vision of crime. Environmental factors as determinants of behaviour – the essence of the liberal view of crime, as we shall see – have no place here; instead, crime is seen as trans-historical, eternal, always essentially the same. ('A crime as old as sin itself. . . . Today's footpads are no different from their predecessors.') Its source, in other words, lies within – in human nature, which is faced perennially with the same stark *choice* – between 'good' and 'evil'. This essentialist view of human nature, with its accent on the freedom to choose and on the forces of good and evil, has obvious roots in various religious ideologies: the *Mail*'s reference to 'sin' indicates this. Yet there are also strong secular theories of instincts – which have uneasily and somewhat contradictorily found their way into this traditionalist viewpoint. Thus the notion of 'blood lust' as an explanation of mugging in the *Express* suggests somebody not only totally, but pathologically 'free' – somebody at the mercy of uncontrollable instincts or, in Freudian terms, somebody at the mercy of a completely untutored *id*. Paradoxically, then, this 'freedom to choose' is often really predicated on an unstated theory of *psychological determinism*.

Both these papers are characterised by a sharp disjunction between the rhetoric of the editorials and that of their feature stories, where the latter, being committed primarily to *exploration* not judgement, tried to get inside some of the ambiguities before, if at all, attempting any kind of 'resolution'. In our sample this meant, in every case, rehearsing, however fitfully, variants of determinist explanations of crime. Only in editorials, it seems, can complexities and ambiguities be ironed out in favour of open advocacy; and in all the papers, despite the differences, such advocacy was there: the appeal to the law as ultimate protector of all 'our' interests. Whether it is represented as a way of balancing the interests of the individual and society (*The Times*), a difficult institutional process of essentially judicial decision (*Telegraph*), or as the last bastion of civilised and decent people against the (recurrent) forces of evil (*Mail* and *Express*), it is in the law we must trust. The contradictions of everyday social experience were suppressed by shifting the debate to the more abstract level of the law.

There were, however, two dissenting voices from this avoidance of issues on the ground and the open advocacy of the sentences to which it leads. Both occurred in papers which for different reasons did not carry editorials, and both were in the form of regular, idiosyncratic, provocative 'personal viewpoints'. These were those of Jon Akass in the *Sun* and Keith Waterhouse in the *Daily Mirror*. Because they occupied a special position outside the formal news structure, they were expected and able to dissent from its formulation of issues, though, in the case of the *Sun* particularly, they clearly demonstrated the contradictory tensions between different aspects of news coverage. Thus Akass, in the paper which most clearly identified with the victim and ignored all protesting voices, was able, under the headline 'Putting the legal boot in won't solve the problem of muggers', to describe the sentences as 'a punishment almost as barbarous as the crime itself', talk of the need to 'transform society in such a way that kids like Paul Storey no longer exist' and even quote China as an example of such a transformation. His final appeal however – rather undercutting the transformation argument – was an appeal to the experts to deliver some answers: 'otherwise what are all those sociologists for'. Although there must be some doubts about Akass's sincerity in view of his intermittently flippant tone, this was an inherently radical approach. Equally radical, and more consistent, was Keith Waterhouse's column in the *Mirror* – 'Order in Court'. His argument was pivoted on the misrepresentation of the image of 'law and order' – 'Public order is not simply a state of suspended animation where nothing is going on and nobody gets mugged.' Waterhouse argued that the sentence had no relevance to our right 'to get on with our business free from hindrance', and that it made no attempt to deal with the social conditions which breed violence. Finally, he forestalled a major line of counter-argument by saying it was in the interest of any victim – especially the next one – that the larger questions of social policy be tackled.

The existence of these pieces should not be underestimated. In challenging the definitions of mugging and law and order and in insisting on the need for radical social change, they sought to transform the very terms of the debate, and thus it must be said, the news values of the papers for which they write. Yet it would be equally unwise to overestimate them. Neither would get away with such dissent as editorial leader-writers. They were able to do it only because they had been incorporated within the newspaper as a form of institutionalised dissent, which could, in the hands of other licensed dissenters, equally go to the other 'extreme' (cf. John Gordon in the *Sunday Express*). The presence of Akass and Waterhouse demonstrates that a view about law and crime in a popular newspaper can be both radical and accessible; but their over-all effect, when compared with the massive coverage dominated by conventional news values, is scarcely more than token. The sheer weight of the institutional news values undoubtedly dominates over the idiosyncratic opinion, however radical and well-argued.

From these editorials we can also glean the outline of a common response (with the exceptions of the *Morning Star* and the two dissenting *personal viewpoints*):

(1) this crime was an especially bad one of its kind; and
(2) it was symptomatic of an increase in violent crime which must be dealt with in sentencing policy; or
(3) this crime was part of an eternal struggle between good and evil;
(4) of paramount consideration was the protection of the public; and
(5) in such a situation it was the law's responsibility to act firmly.

It needs strongly emphasising that these arguments could only be supported on three conditions: one was the unqualified acceptance of certain propositions, i.e. that violent crime was spiralling; that there *was* a strain of crime identifiable as mugging; and that the protection of the public was more important than reform of the criminal. The second was that the issue was taken out of any particular social context so that society became an abstraction. This involved excluding the opinions and perceptions of all those groups and individuals without whom most of the primary and feature articles could not have been written. And the third was that the law was perceived in a particular way: autonomous, functioning in the interests of all, responsive to public opinion. It should be clear from this that editorial parameters were *not* those of news coverage: society-wide interests – the 'public' – replaced a series of particular interests as the focus. But since the 'society' involved was an abstraction, composed of no particular groups or interests, the relationship between particular groups, and between particular groups and particular social institutions, could not be explored. Thus we got editorials on 'law and society' and features on 'police and criminals'. Concrete social experience was dissolved by the editorial discourse into an abstraction – 'society' – so that the morally totalising viewpoint aimed for in editorials was both generalised and mystifying.

THE SUN

The primary-news and feature articles in the *Sun* merit separate consideration because they took virtually no account of the formal and ideological variations apparent in the other papers. A characteristic headline on 20 March, '20 Years For The Mugger Aged 16', introduced a story by Richard Saxty which in some of its most salient features was altogether untypical of national press coverage. There was, for example, a brevity, firmness and certitude in the paper's own early statement of the significance of the sentence – 'a surprise crackdown on mugging violence' – and the social categorisation of the main offender as 'former skinhead Paul Storey'. Similarly, the details of the crime were described in language which other papers tended to reserve for editorial rhetoric – the boys 'put the boot in' and 'learned yesterday the new price the courts put on violence for kicks'.

In the context of such a tight and exclusive encoding of the story, the reaction of the 'shocked' mothers was represented as the human face of the drama rather than as any source of opposition. The *Sun*, alone of the papers, felt no obligation to quote any penal reforming groups or any institutionalised Birmingham opinion. Conversely, it did not quote the sentences' supporters nor situate the crime as part of a pattern other than 'violence-for-kicks'.

The major news angle for the *Sun* was that of *the victim*. At the end of the primary-news story was a short piece with its own heading – 'What it means to be the victim of muggers', which prefigured the massive front-page lead on 21 March, the only feature article to be a front-page lead. Most of the story's space was in fact covered by the headline and accompanying head and shoulders photograph of Mr Keenan. The main caption read 'I'm Only Half a Man', with a smaller supplementary line –' "My Life Is In Ruins" says Tragic Victim of Boy Muggers'. The main body of the story was familiar: Keenan's (approving) opinions about the sentence and his (stupid) attackers, his hospitalisation, loss of job and psychological instability resulting from the crime. Peculiar to the *Sun*, however, was the subordination of all other aspects of the story to the focus on *the victim*, which in the distress it described and pity it sought to evoke has to be read as tacit approval for the sentence. Debate and conflict are both ignored through empathy with the victim as citizen: the story of how such a criminal act may reduce a normal, hard-working, law-abiding man to a fearful, impecunious and unemployable wreck. Precisely because it does not raise its position to that of an abstract proposition, precisely because the extent of the victim's suffering is regarded as sufficient in itself to justify such a retributive sentence, the *Sun* could avoid the need to take account of any contrary opinion. Any ambiguities such dissenting opinion might have highlighted had been forestalled in advance through this exclusive perspective.

The reasons for the superfluousness of an editorial should by now be apparent. These were further enhanced by the refusal – comparable only to the dismissal of the problem in the *Telegraph* – to examine the area of Handsworth in any depth. Even less was the relationship of biography and background acknowledged as a focus of concern. Thus what was in most other papers a central problematic requiring some kind of resolution was 'solved' in the *Sun* by the way in which it was formulated – a series of labels which proscribed further analysis.

> Handsworth, the sprawling Birmingham slum where the three muggers grew up is a violent playground. . . . Paul Storey, son of a mixed marriage, tried drugs, then theft – and finally violence in a bid to find excitement in his squalid environment. Paul's mother, 40-year-old Mrs. Ethel Saunders, said 'What chance have young people got in a lousy area like this?'

Violence, race, drugs, theft, youth – a series of random labels. In such a context the strategy suggested by Tory M.P. Charles Simeons that muggers should be herded into a compound and ridiculed, quoted by the *Sun*, does not seem to be at all out of place.

Formally, the *Sun* did cover the main elements common to other feature articles – victim, mugger, area – but its particular treatment of each rendered exploration and analysis superfluous. The *Sun*'s particularly linear news treatment (sentence–crime–victim) made it unique in both its ideological interpretation and the journalistic forms it adopted. The *Sun* had implicitly abolished the traditional distinctions between 'news fact', 'feature exploration' and editorial opinion in favour of an exclusive shaping of the event through its own arbitrary and transparent definition.

The implications of this ideological straitjacket for the construction of news cannot be too heavily emphasised. It involves the abandonment – in this case and other arenas of social life – of any nominal commitment to different kinds of analysis and explanation by precluding the possibility of argument and debate. Marcuse, whose work in general we find only fitfully useful, has, on the question of 'one-dimensional' language, offered a useful summary of its main features – he could well have been talking about the *Sun*:

> As a habit of thought outside the scientific and technical language, such reasoning shapes the expression of a specific social and political behaviourism. In this behavioural universe, words and concepts tend to coincide, or rather the concept tends to be absorbed by the word. The former has no content other than that designated by the word in the publicized and standardized usage, and the word is expected to have no other response than the publicized and standardized behaviour (reaction). The word becomes cliché, and as cliché, governs the speech or the writing; the communication plus precludes genuine development of meaning. . . . The noun governs the sentence in an authoritarian and totalitarian fashion, and the sentence becomes a declaration to be accepted – it repels demonstration, qualification, negation of its codified and declared meaning. . . . This language which constantly imposes images militates against the development and expression of concepts. In its immediacy and directness, it impedes conceptual thinking; thus, it impedes thinking. [3]

FEATURES IN THE NATIONAL PRESS

Even the most cursory examination of the continued press coverage of the Handsworth case on 21 March reveals a significant shift in emphasis. Whereas both the primary-news stories and editorials pivoted around the controversy over the sentence, thematised in terms of 'mugging'/youth/deterrent sentencing, the specific problem of the sentence was widened on the next day to explore, as the *Guardian* sub-headed one of its pieces, 'the background problem'. This movement from foreground (event, issue, dilemma, problem) to background (cause, motivation, explanation) took the form of a development from primary news to feature articles. A secondary set of *feature news values* came into play: conceptually distinct from primary-news values, yet dependent on cues provided in the initial news thematisation. Most importantly, this stage in the news process drew on a wider ideological field. The problem was extended from that of the rightness of the immediate strategy adopted to control a given outbreak of crime, to considerations about how such a 'wave' comes about in the first place.

The movement from 'hard' or primary news to features operated at several different levels, which we have represented in tabular form (see Table 4.1). At the level of the professional sub-culture of journalists – their working sense of what features are about – it involved a recognition that 'there is more to this story than meets the eye', that the discreet news event had a 'background'. In the Handsworth case the 'background' took the form of a series of questions: What kinds of youths perpetrated this crime? What sort of social background did they come from? What other problems went along with this kind of crime?

For the examination of these kinds of questions there are established journalistic conventions. Journalists sent out into the field are primed to look for 'elements' in the background: people, places, experiences, which lay down the parameters of the background problem. These are individually explored using grass-roots opinion, local experts (councillors, M.P.s, social workers) and even, on occasion, 'academic' reports or enquiries; then, crucially, weighed against each other, producing in some features typographical formats which explicitly balance one set of elements against another.

These two levels – what we have called 'journalistic common sense' and 'feature dynamics' – are *inherently* ideological, for what they seek to do is to contextualise the event, place it in the social world. In their selection of background elements they identify further issues or social problems which may be either merely noted or pursued in some detail. These themes are thus brought into an implicit or explicit relationship with the original 'problem' of crime. These kinds of people commit that kind of crime in a certain kind of area: a pattern identified and combatted by those charged with responsibility for control, who may include political figures, social workers, or the police. In the selection of elements, the credibility accorded to particular accounts of the situation, and the weighing or balancing of considerations against each other, the feature articles must negotiate with available analyses, explanations or images of the 'background problem'. It is at the 'moment' of features in the journalistic discourse that the connection between media processes and more widely distributed lay ideologies of crime becomes most visible; and it is to the mobilisation of these 'lay ideologies' that we wish to draw most attention.

The movement to this wider set of problematics did not, however, involve a wholesale abandonment of the original issue of the sentence. In some papers, most notably the *Star* ('Anger flares at savage sentence on muggers') and the *Guardian*, there were further protests from liberal pressure groups. Equally explicit was the *Daily Mail*'s incorporation into its feature of an interview, on the effectiveness of deterrent sentencing, with prominent criminologist Terence Morris. More inferentially, the *Express* portrait of the liberal reputation of Judge Croom-Johnson implied that the sentence demonstrated the exhausted patience of even the most tolerant members of the judiciary. Most powerfully of all, the 'foreground' was inserted into the 'background' through interviews with *the victim*, which were carried by all the national newspapers. At the level of 'journalistic common sense', the universality of this focus on the victim had much to do with his availability for interview, and the special privilege to be given to the views of the person on whose behalf the sentence was passed. An interview and photograph could be incorporated at the level of feature dynamics into a dramatic confrontation of mugger *versus* victim. But these alone are not sufficient to explain what is after all an unusual focus: victims of crimes are not normally asked to comment on the sentences of those who have committed crimes against them. Although both the *Star* and the *Guardian* (' "I am sorry about sentences" says victim of mugging attack') represented Keenan as expressing some empathy with the three boys, he was more often used as an implicit justification of the sentence, either through his own opinion ('Sympathy? They didn't feel any for me' – *Daily Express*), or through, as we have seen in the *Sun*, a re-emphasis of the extent of his injuries ('I can hardly climb the stairs now' – *Daily Mail*). We are not seeking here to play down the extent of the real and permanent injury done to Robert Keenan or to deny his right to an opinion on the sentence. We are rather attempting to demonstrate how his suffering and opinions were ideologically appropriated in these feature articles to become an implicit justification of the sentence. The features, then, not only weighed elements within the background problem but also weighed them as a whole against the foreground. Thus the implicit determinism we shall identify as characteristic of many of the pieces on Paul Storey and Handsworth – suggesting that here the criminal was almost not responsible for his actions – was partly undercut by this refocus on the victim, drawing us back to the actions – from the focus on their possible causes – and thus, implicitly, to a concern with the defence of innocent victims.

Most clearly in the *Mail* and the *Express* the victim was counterpointed by *the criminal*, who was labelled in these two papers respectively as 'gang boss' and 'mugger'. In those simple labels we can see the attempt to 'place' Storey – *to typify him*. In one, he is the gang boss, with connotations both of the professional criminal world and its Mafia-type leaders and of the established images of deviant youth groupings: the leaders and the led, the hard core and the periphery, the depraved and the deprived. Less crude perhaps, but no less powerful than the *Sun*'s more lurid characterisation of him. In the other, more simply, he is the 'mugger' – an image, by now fully developed, of undisciplined, violent youth. However, the search for typifications or 'criminal careers' in the biographies of Storey was blocked by the denial by friends, relatives and social workers that he exhibited recognisably 'pathological' tendencies. In the *Mail* the supplementary headline to 'Gang Boss' read 'Violent? He wasn't a bad lad – he really wasn't' – a comment from a local cafe owner. In the absence of specific signs of personality disorder, there was a more general sketch of his 'career': separated parents; a brief period of casual work; involvement in petty crime; on the streets much of the time. The stress on school, family and employment is apparent in the shorter portraits of the other two boys, though in the case of Mustafa Fuat, with a relatively stable family and no criminal record, only the imminent demolition of his home is any evidence of what these

TABLE 4.1

The dimensions of feature news values: a model

Stage	Journalistic common sense	Feature dynamics	Ideological framework
(1) 'Hard' news story	Dramatic/sensational/novel elements (i.e. length of sentence and type of crime)	'Hard' news dynamics stress *immediate* 'facts' and their implications (i.e. for general penal policy)	The sense of what is 'newsworthy' derives from, and reinforces, an ideologically-charged conception of society
(2) Move to feature	Assessment of events as having a background not covered by hard news story (i.e. crime and criminal have a social background)	Commissioning reporter(s) to dig around for 'reactions' and interpretations by accredited sources (i.e. contacting those immediately involved and/or lobbyists and experts)	Explanation/contextualisation: placing the events and the actors on a 'map' of society
(3) Kind of feature	Selecting those background elements *cum* explanations considered *relevant* (i.e. not politico-judicial links nor drugs and violence, but Handsworth, its inhabitants and experts)	Picking up cues provided by sources as to typicality of events or as symptomatic of underlying issues (e.g. Ethel Saunders and 'lousy area'; Handsworth M.P. and 'war against crime')	Identification of social issues: channelling public concern (i.e. Handsworth as a 'problem area')
(4) Elements of feature	Seeking out the actors and locations carrying the relevant experiences and quasi-explanations (i.e. the victim; the mug-	Placing the actors and locations in relationship to each other; 'setting it up' typographically, use of photographs and re-	Subsumption of *themes* under *images* (i.e. housing, employment, race, police under 'violence', 'the ghetto', 'youth', 'the

ger; the police; the street or area)	porters' 'feel pieces' (e.g. *Daily Express* two-page spread)	Making the event and its implications 'manageable' i.e. not destructive of, or demanding changes in, basic structure of society)
(5) Reintegration of feature into paper's dominant discourse	Possible solutions to defined problems (e.g. praise of voluntary work/police; calls for crash youth programme/research)	Surface coherence: pulling elements together into one focal point (e.g. *Guardian*'s use of community worker's comment on sentence being as insensitive as the crime itself)

indices sought to measure: social disorganisation. Implicit in them is the search for points where these boys had 'gone off the rails'. Equally implicit is the counterpoint of these: the patterns which keep the rest of us 'on the right road'; the right influences and achievements at home, school and work. To fail in all or any of these, runs the implicit explanation of deviance operating here, is to be 'at risk'.

The *Express* portrait was almost identical, though with a more deterministic headline – 'The boy who was sentenced before he was born', supplemented by an image of youth at risk – 'too much time on his hands'. His family background, school record and inability to find a job were again reviewed with emphasis on the all-too-brief time when, with a regular job, money in his pocket and a girl friend, he looked capable of leading a 'normal life'. In both the *Mail* and the *Express* there was no explicit attempt to explain the boys' involvement in a violent crime in terms, for example, of genetic defects, 'bad company', or other consistent and explicit causal explanations. Rather what we have is a portrait of failure at all the points of social integration which 'normally' apply. The inference is that we are all potentially at risk, but most of us, through a good environment and a positive attitude, are able to pursue the appropriate goals of regular work, established family life and legitimate enjoyment.

Yet in both articles there is a further and more ambiguous way in which these youths were differentiated from the rest of society: through the index of race. Both papers introduced early on Storey's 'West Indian' father: in both, his racial resentment was reported. The *Mail* pursued the race theme with some determination, reproducing an allegedly local definition of the street where James Duignan lived as 'Mini United Nations' and pursuing the Cypriot connections of the Fuat family in a sentence which, in its search for local colour, underlined the otherness of an alien cultural background – 'The walls are hung with Oriental mats.'

These specifically racial connotations, with their implications for the portraits of Handsworth in the same features, and for the future trajectory of the 'mugging' panic, were absent from the *Daily Telegraph*'s biographical portrait. There was also less emphasis on the family than in the *Express* and *Mail*, though school attendance and unemployment were reviewed in much the same terms. Overall there was a much stronger typification: 'The recent life of Paul Storey is typical of many cases in the files of social workers in the Handsworth district.' Unless it be taken that all such 'cases' are potentially violent criminals, there is little in this 'placing' of Storey to account for the criminal act: the typification is strong yet unspecified. Rather the *Telegraph* follows through with approval Ethel Saunder's comments on the social environment – 'Mrs Saunders is not alone in blaming the problems of Handsworth for the difficulties faced by young people there.' An Assistant Chief Constable and a local councillor emphasised the poor quality of the environment.

For the *Telegraph* the particular course of Storey's biography was subsumed under the general problem of a poor environment. And it is the problem of *the environment*, specifically the area of Handsworth, which was the third universal element of the features. It was apparently triggered off by the comments of Paul's mother about the 'lousy area'. But this is not sufficient explanation of the presence of this theme, since she said other things, about Paul being on drugs, for example, which were not pursued in the features. The rationale of 'journalistic common sense' is insufficient to account for the stress on Handsworth. The focus on Handsworth is more fully explained by its connection with a long-standing, ideological structure: that of the 'criminal patch' or slum, and the ghetto/crime connection elaborated in so many stories about American muggings. It has assumed the status of a 'social fact', that some areas produce more crime and criminals than others. This background theme was picked up very early on, frequently in the primary-news story – and not only through the intervention of the liberal lobby, with their environmentalist explanations of 'mugging'. In the *Express*, for example, where no such pressure groups appeared, we had a highly charged description of the venue of the crime. The victim 'met the boys in a tumble-down immigrant area of Handsworth where they live'. The reverberations of such an image in a paper so long committed to 'immigration control' need no emphasis from us.

It was thus hardly surprising to find the immigrant theme introduced early on in the *Express*'s portrait of Handsworth headed 'It is not a safe place to walk alone/The ghetto/Handsworth/Poor housing and no jobs.' Crime, race and poverty are the essential characteristics – with the first two predominating over the last – as the *Express* joined in the old game of trying to sort out what's wrong with the neglected area; whereas the *Telegraph* found local experts who agreed with Ethel Saunders's condemnation of the area, those used in the *Express* considered it 'unfair'. The Chairman of the City's Community Relations Committee was at pains to stress that the crime could have happened anywhere, and that one crime should not condemn a whole neighbourhood. He unwittingly colluded in a redefinition of the problem in primarily racial terms: not all Handsworth youth was the problem, but black youth, unemployed, angry, aggressive, with an 'anti-social' sub-culture. There was a circle of associations here in which crime and race defined the ghetto and were defined by it; yet nowhere was there any indication of the ghetto's origins. Though Councillor Sheila Wright was allowed to reintroduce the problem of housing, it was a coloured community worker, recounting the resentment of black youth, who was allowed the last 'expert' word. In the face of this active reshaping of the problem from slum area to black youth in the ghetto, the concluding optimism of the *Express* piece was perfunctory – a throwaway humanism, marginal to the argument:

> There are too many places like Paul Storey's grotty little street around Handsworth – ironically once the 'in place' to live in Britain's second city. But happily there are an awful lot of people trying to make Handsworth a better place to live in.

The placing of Handsworth on the social map was not conducted at the level of the structures which made it what it was. The nature of the housing market, for example, and the deprived position of immigrants within it, received no explicit attention; rather, what was at work was a *description of associations* – race, crime, housing, unemployment – out of which, in some unspecified way, there

emerged the problem of 'anti-social, black youth'. The heavy racial emphasis in
the biography of Paul Storey made more sense set in such a context: he
became an index of the problem behind crime – that of race. Although there
was a kind of determinism at work, the surface manifestations of social
pathology were located, by implication, in the presence of *outsiders* in this '90
per cent immigrant area', which was at the root of the problem.

The *Daily Mail* followed similar leads to the Express, although it played its
own variations. Its first description of Handsworth in its primary-news report
picked up the familiar themes of race and crime:

> All the sentenced youths are either coloured or immigrants and live in one of
> Birmingham's major problem areas. Police and social workers have been
> battling for five years to solve community problems in Handsworth, where
> juvenile crime steadily worsens and there are continuous complaints about
> the relationship between the police and the predominantly coloured public.

As in the *Express* it was Handsworth which provided an overarching theme,
again caught in an organic metaphor – 'where violence breeds', and there was a
loose and ambiguous suggestion of communal responsibility for such areas –
'Handsworth ... "a blot on any country that claims to be civilized" ... and the
home of Paul Storey.'

To do the *Mail* credit it did introduce some detail on the exact nature of the
area's housing problem. It described Handsworth as 'a problem area – scruffy
and neglected and two miles from the city centre.... A sprawl of Victorian-
built houses occupy most of the area. Property values are low. Private
landlords are common. They find no shortage of tenants especially among the
immigrants.' For depth, however, the *Mail* turned to a fairly straight rendering
of the opinions of three 'experts': a (radical) Labour councillor, the Assistant
Chief Constable (Crime) and the local M.P. (Tory). The first was quoted at
some length, emphasising how 'deplorable housing conditions, high unemployment and pressure on local schools' brought about high rates of delinquency
and children in care. The feature reproduced her adverse comments on the
Council's 'herding together' of poorer families into such areas. The reporters
added the statistic that 25 per cent of Handsworth's inhabitants were under 15,
and said that the Education Department did not deny that their resources were
stretched. However, the openness of the *Mail* feature broke down with the next
expert – the local M.P., who presented himself as standing at the forefront of
the 'war against crime' in Handsworth. It is this which turned out to be the
'blot on any country which claims to be civilized', producing the 'atmosphere
... where some people are afraid to walk alone'. The phrasing, the crime
statistics used, were exactly the same as in the *Express*; and so was the reversal
in logic which was employed – an argument beginning with environmental factors ended with the fear of crime; and, like the *Express*, the race theme
followed on almost immediately and was baldly introduced: 'It is estimated
that 70% of Handsworth's population are coloured and the area poses Birmingham with its biggest ghetto problem.' The final image was one of the
historical decay of the area: 'Handsworth once housed wealthy industrialists
living in well-swept tree-lined streets. The streets are now littered and the

children play on demolition sites.' It is striking that both the *Express* and the *Mail* should have ended with such similar evocations of urban decay. It is an image of the city in decline: powerfully descriptive yet without explanatory dimensions. There was no attempt to offer an account of how the decay came about, but instead a tightening of the circle of associations: housing, race, crime.

The *Guardian* might reasonably have been expected to have a more complex approach. It is after all the paper to which the poverty lobby and 'caring professions' look for support. It too picked up the area theme early but in a more specific and pointed way than the *Express* or *Mail*:

> The Villa Road area is one where the police do not enjoy a good relationship with the largely immigrant community and where teenage unemployment is high ... last month 31 voluntary workers in the area signed a letter to Birmingham's Chief Constable alleging that there was police harassment of the West Indian population and claiming that police methods were unhelpful in dealing with Handsworth's growing problem of violence.

Teenage unemployment and crime were common themes; the radical insertion was that of immigrant/police tension. The analysis remained, however, at the level of symptoms: early on in the feature, headlined 'Depressed and depressing', a whole list of such symptoms was given: 'Handsworth is both depressed and depressing and the Soho ward where most of the trouble happens has a reputation for violence, poor housing, unemployment and racial resentment.' This comprehensive list of indices of 'depression' remained descriptive: no causal connections were provided. Perhaps surprisingly the *Guardian* did not pull on established social-work orientated analysis of 'multiple deprivation'. Rather there was an emphasis – unique in the national press – on telling how Handsworth must have been experienced by those who live there: 'From the point of view of the locals it is a district where the police harass, the City Council does not care and there are "more rats than human beings" as a coffee bar owner puts it.' Subsequently, the environment problem was appropriated in a manner very similar to that in the *Express* and the *Mail*. The question posed was of how crime was somehow an outcome of a situation where 'The terrace houses are in disrepair and the garden fences broken down'. It is into this problematic that Paul Storey's biography was inserted – 'The street where Paul Storey lived for nine years is littered with broken bricks and milk bottles.' This loosely framed thematisation of the environment was carried, together with the more specific 'social problem' of which Paul Storey was part; and with a dose of 'unstable family background' for good measure: 'There is chronic unemployment in the area for black youngsters, and Paul's father, whom he never knew, is West Indian.'

The *Guardian* was rehearsing a wider range of potential explanations than any other paper: multiple symptoms of social pathology; the specific social problem of unemployed black youth; an unstable family background – yet none of these were followed through consistently. Instead we revert back to the 'environment' problem, with the introduction of Mr Corbyn Barrow and council leader Stan Yapp, who stressed that Handsworth's problems were not unique and that properly funded urban renewal would (in some unexplained way) eradicate the problems. Even the police recognised the role of 'poor social conditions' and resented being blamed for 'factors outside their control'. The conclusion, in the form of a remark by a local community worker, pushes us back to the original issue of the sentence: 'It's not that we don't want mugging stopped, but this sentence is as insensitive a weapon as the brick Paul Storey used.' The *Guardian* was in certain specific ways distinguishable from other papers, in its approach to Handsworth, by a liberal perspective. There was no attempt to label the area in terms of race, or to suppress the real problem of police–immigrant relationships, and there was a genuine attempt to empathise with local inhabitants. Yet in the end the *Guardian* allowed itself to be trapped by the simplistic environment/behaviour model which did not provide connections between the two elements. Handsworth remained not only unsolved but was impossible of solution given the terms in which the *Guardian* had approached it. Unable to break with those terms – a measure of its inability to rupture dominant ideological formulations – the *Guardian* was left in distress and depression.

We can see, then, that in the feature pieces on the boys' biographies and the area of Handsworth, there were several loosely formulated quasi-explanations and highly structured images of crime causation. The move from news to features had, across all the papers, involved exploration of the 'background problem' and there had been a remarkable similarity in their selection of the main focal points of attention – 'victim', 'mugger', 'area'. We have been concerned here to show how limited the perspective of all the papers was. Yet it would be misleading to assume that there was no room at all for editorial intervention or that it was impossible to orchestrate the range of explanations and images in different ways – especially at the moment of weighing elements against each other.

There was, indeed, the option taken up by *The Times* of not doing a feature at all. That this newspaper does not include feature articles at all in its journalistic repertoire may be sufficient explanation – though this is more than a formal question and indicates, if nothing else, a supreme confidence in the ability of its news coverage to thematise and contextualise dramatic or problematic issues.

If *The Times* eschewed any kind of exploration, that pursued by the *Morning Star* remains unique. It pivoted around opposition to the sentences expressed by various pressure groups, with the specific addition of an adverse comparison, made by a Birmingham Campaign against Racial Discrimination (CARD) representative, of these sentences with the more lenient treatment accorded to two white youths who had permanently disfigured a Pakistani man. There were no biographies of the youths; only one phrase – expressing 'sorrow' – from the victim; and Handsworth was briefly characterised as 'one of Birmingham's biggest problem areas', though the protest letter about police tactics mentioned in the *Guardian* was treated more fully. It seems likely that lack of resources restricted the *Star*'s ability to explore the issue: it had to rely on the secondary material available through its own circuit of contacts. How far the *Star* might have broken with the formal and ideological constraints of feature news apparent in the other papers must thus remain a matter of conjecture.

Outside of *The Times* and the *Morning Star*, a common pattern of feature treatment emerged. Essential background elements – universally those of victim, mugger and area – were selected, individually explored, and set against each other. It is the specific journalistic feature form which provides the mechanism of balance; the final weighing is not arrived at by a process of argument or analysis but is built into the feature form as it is initially constructed. Thus one strategy used by more than one newspaper was to juxtapose (either within the same feature article or in the same paper in a 'feature spread') a number of ways of interpreting the connection between crime and environment, biography and background. This way of balancing off a number of different readings is a sort of *feature by montage* effect and was most obvious in the case of the *Daily Express* and the *Daily Mail*. In the *Express* the 'balance' was set out on the double-page – on the left Handsworth and the mugger, on the right the suffering victim, the liberal judge unusually incensed, and a highly flattering portrait of the local police (pre-empting more critical versions of police policy towards immigrant groups such as those appearing in the *Star* and the *Guardian*). Although the whole feature had a severely deterministic headline – 'Caught for Life in a Violent Trap' – we have seen how the Handsworth/ mugger side of the equation had been so undermined by particular images of the race–crime connection that the overall effect was to cut away the grounds of the argument it otherwise contained. Balance here was represented typographically but the *ideological weight* was tilted to one side.

The *Mail* similarly counterpointed victim and mugging underneath the portrait of Handsworth headed 'Where Violence Breeds'. The heavy emphasis on race and crime in that article again undermined the formal commitment to 'balance', while the interview with expert criminologist Terence Morris relocated the 'real' problem as that of policy and treatment rather than crime causation – suggesting, moreover, that it remained insoluble.

In the case of the *Telegraph* the 'montage' effect was less immediately visible, yet still the same process of weighing victim against mugger, environment against law and order, was at work. The *Telegraph* had its own particular resolution which denied the dimensions of the problem, mainly through its use of a police spokesman: 'The police were not complacent about mugging but did not think it was an overall problem.' Hence the *Telegraph* was only formally at the level of feature exploration, since it systematically rejected the formulations on which such exploration was based elsewhere: Handsworth was not a breeding ground for crime; Storey was only a species of well-known delinquent; the victim's suffering and the exceptionally brutal nature of the attack were sufficient explanations of the issue. The feature followed closely the lines of explanation laid down in the primary-news story and editorial.

The *feature by montage* conveyed an impression of comprehensiveness (covering all points of view) as well as of balance: 'hard-line' councillors or policemen againt 'soft-centred' community workers; local residents against figures of authority; or (as in the *Birmingham Evening Mail*'s version) mothers of the accused against anxious mothers in the street. Formally, the issue was left unresolved: evidence was not ignored, but these elements were simply left contradicting each other. It would have been possible for this variety and contradictoriness to be tolerated by the paper (reserving its own judgement for the editorial); in practice, the montage was so selected and shaped that a 'resolution' on one side or other of the ideological paradigm did appear to emerge of its own accord.

An alternative feature strategy was to try to distil the essence or the problematic core of the problem by finding all the general themes condensed into a local instance. This was the *feature by microcosm* effect. Here the general issue of crime/poverty/violence was perceived and portrayed through the particular story – for example, of Handsworth. This was most evident in the local papers (as we shall see). In the nationals, it was principally at work in the *Guardian*. That paper physically – and thus ideologically – separated out the elements of its feature exploration. The interview with the victim and extended protests from pressure groups provided the material of the front-page, follow-up story, but consideration of Paul Storey's biography and the social environment of Handsworth were reserved for the 'background problem' on the features page. This separation – while something of a break with otherwise dominant feature news values – also represented a kind of equivocation. For by going 'behind' the immediate issue of liberal penologists *versus* law-and-order adherents, the *Guardian* also displaced the problem so that there appeared no relationship between the sentences and policies towards deprivation. The *Guardian*, unable to confront the 'moral panic' to which it had itself contributed through conventional news coverage, sought the safer ground of social policy. Hence the *Guardian* provided less of an effort to balance competing interests around the case than to balance competing interests within the area: not victim *versus* mugger but local residents *versus* those in authority. The sharpness of these conflicts of interest were noted, yet there was no attempt to choose between them any more than the paper could produce an editorial coming down on one side or the other of the controversy over the sentence. This 'equivocation' is a central element in the repertoire of modern liberalism, which has been effectively dissected by Roland Barthes in his designation of it as 'Neither-Norism':

> By this I mean this mythological figure which consists in stating two opposites and balancing the one by the other so as to reject them both (I want neither this nor that). It is on the whole a bourgeois figure, for it relates to a modern form of liberalism. We find again here the figure of the scales: reality is first reduced to analogues; then it is weighed; finally, equality having been ascertained, it is got rid of. Here also there is magical behaviour: both parties are dismissed because it is embarrassing to choose between them; one flees from an intolerable reality, reducing it to two opposites which balance each other only inasmuch as they are purely formal, relieved of all their specific weight ... a final equilibrium immobilizes values, life, destiny, etc.: one no longer needs to choose, but only to endorse. [4]

THE BIRMINGHAM PAPERS

We have separated out the Birmingham provincial papers for analysis on the grounds that their particular local interests affected their news treatment of the case. In terms of concrete journalistic practices they were 'nearer the ground' than the national papers, and had more immediate access both to those immediately involved and to local experts or opinion leaders. They also produced more stories and coverage. Ideologically, there was an emphasis on the *local* origins of victim and criminals, and some consideration of the implications for the city of Birmingham as a whole. This had particular implications for the range of explanations and images mobilised in the feature treatment; and while we shall note some characteristics of the primary-news treatment evident in the three papers – the *Birmingham Post, Evening Mail* and *Sunday Mercury* (all owned by one combine) – it is on the local feature-news treatment that we wish to concentrate. The *Birmingham Post* – a daily newspaper of conservative views and format – carried six pieces on the Handsworth case, as follows:

Mother blames 'lousy area' for son's crime
Judge sentences boy aged 16 to 20 years (20 March 1973)

Boys may appeal against sentences
The Grove, Birmingham 19 [feature] (21 March 1973)

30p assault boys will appeal on sentences
Detained [editorial] (22 March 1973)

Like the *Daily Mail*, the *Post* did not lead with the Handsworth story, and its front-page story outlined the family's reactions to the sentence while the back page had the court report. More strikingly, the *Post* restricted its use of the 'mugging' label to a police statistic in the back-page story, and – in inverted commas – in the editorial. It *never* appeared in a headline. While the characterisation of the offenders as '30p assault boys' carried its own connotations of motiveless crime, the avoidance of the label was a significant variation from most news treatment. This persistent absence of the 'mugging' label was so consistent that we would suspect it was the result of a specific editorial decision, the rationale for which remains closed to us. For the rest, however, the *Post* may be distinguished from the nationals only by its much earlier introduction of feature concerns. Interviews with Ethel Saunders and Robert Keenan appeared alongside the court report to form the focus of the news treatment of 20 March, at the expense, it would appear, of 'institutionalised' debate, which was represented only by two local figures: Rex Ambler and Harold Gurden, M.P. for Selly Oak. The initial front-page story was 'rounded-off' by an extract from the Colville speech and the '129%' mugging statistic. The two stories of 21 and 22 March concerned themselves mainly with the details of appeal procedure, one or two further reactions (notably from the Birmingham-based secretary of the British Association of Social Workers), and, on 22 March especially, the intricate workings of the parole system as applied to detention sentences. This last insertion was linked to the editorial of the same day. Headed 'Detained', it sought to eradicate a 'misunderstanding' over the 'mugging case' caused by the nature of a detention sentence. The *Post* therefore sought to explain the processes of review and parole which enabled release of Storey when 'the authorities into whose care his violence has led him are satisfied that his obvious psychotic problems have been rectified'. The fixing of a twenty-year period was therefore more symbolic than real: a *show* of retribution. That this may have been necessary and effective was suggested by reference to the allegedly successful campaign of deterrent sentencing adopted by the Recorder of Birmingham which 'stamped out' telephone-box vandalism. The *Post* thus tried to have it two ways – on the one hand, twenty years did not mean what it says, and on the other hand, it was a necessary deterrent.

This legalistic argument hinged on the consignment of Storey to the all-embracing category of 'psychotic' (though the argument was inconsistent since psychotics are presumably by definition incapable of the rational calculation necessary on the criminal's part if deterrence is to be successful). But this solution to the biography/environment problem was not one adopted by the news and feature treatment. The front page of the two stories on 22 March, for example, heavily emphasised the criminals as members of *city* families. Parents were interviewed and brief family histories given: dates of arrival in the city, composition of the family. The boys' biographies outlined those indices of failure we noted in the national press: poor education, lack of employment, bad environment. At one and the same time the boys were 'normalised' into recognisable city families, though their general circumstances were portrayed as 'abnormal'. This tension was never resolved and it is not surprising to find that in its most explicit feature piece the *Post* should concentrate wholly on the environment background and omit biographical considerations altogether.

The *Post*'s Handsworth feature attempted to encapsulate the environment problem, not in the area as a whole but in one street. Hence its heading 'The Grove, Birmingham 19' underneath a photograph which, in its presentation of debris, neglect in the background, and the fenced-off scene of the crime in the foreground, provided a powerful image of a social vacuum. It was a new slum image: not overcrowded, claustrophobic, old industrial back-to-backs, but decadent, run-to-seed ex-suburbia. It is on these superficial aspects of the environment that the text concentrated. Some representative local inhabitants – Mrs Worrall, mother of eleven children ('whose family is by no means the biggest of the Grove families'), afraid to go out at night; Mrs Hill ('when I came here 19 years ago, this was a respectable neighbourhood'), living through the experience of decay – were called upon to give eye-witness accounts. But it is at the level of *appearance* that the environment problem was represented:

> Surely no street in Birmingham is less aptly named. Even on a sunny spring day its ambience is dispiriting; at night it is full of noisome menace . . . the street is the natural – indeed, the only playground of the many children, a large proportion of them coloured, who live in the Grove.

There is something deceptive here about the way certain key connections, which produce a sort of 'explanation' of the Handsworth event, are ambiguously fused together in a visual image. Here we are back with the 'dirt = deviance' version of the environmentalist theme, and it is to this aspect of the sentence on Storey that the sociologists should direct their attention – 'then perhaps what happened to him could lead to an improvement in the kind of background which fostered his crime'. What the *Post* did not, could not, recognise was the arbitrary formulation of its own question – its ignoring of the structural and cultural determinations which occupy that space between environment and crime.

The *Evening Mail* is more populist in format than the *Post* and was at the time marginally less conservative; though subsequently, under changed editorship, it has become more stridently right wing and has earned itself a bad reputation amongst liberal circles for its massive over-reporting of black immigrants as problems – especially of 'mugging' in its more recent phase. Its coverage of the Handsworth event reached saturation point:

> 20 years Detention For City Boy 16 (19 March 1973)
> Mothers Fight for Boy Muggers
> Outsiders [editorial]
> Twenty year sentence: what the MPs think
> Society 'At Limit of Leniency'
> Call for enquiry into truancy
> Behind The Violence (20 March 1973)
> Mugging judge says it again: 20 years
> Mugging: Friends rally to appear for youths
> The night Handsworth was minding its own business
> Meanwhile back in the Juvenile Court
> One Paul Storey is too many [personal viewpoint] (21 March 1973)
> City Mugging Victim to Claim (22 March 1973)
> 'Nightmare Week' by Mrs Storey (23 March 1973)

The *Mail* picked up the 'mugging' label earlier than the *Post*, though not in the story appearing the same day as the sentence. In that headline 'city boy' is an indication of the *Mail*'s identification of a *local* theme which structures its news treatment from the beginning. Initial thematisation and background exploration were not at all sharply separated. The *Mail* moved very early into feature-news coverage. The lead story of 20 March – 'Mothers fight for boy muggers' – took the form of a 'feature by montage'. But of the three main elements in the nationals (victim, muggers, area) the *Mail* used only the victim.

Instead of the muggers, we had their mothers; instead of the area, we had the 'terror'; and under the heading 'the reaction' the on-going controversy was presented. The 'balance' was heavily weighted in favour of the sentence, as the main sub-headings indicate:

> 'My son has done wrong – but 20 years is too much'
> 'They nearly finished me'
> 'We're not so afraid now' – mothers
> 'Severity needed to combat crime' – police

The issue was here thematised in local forms: the debate took place not across the society but within the city. The mothers' protests were here opposed by other local mothers, who saw themselves as potential victims; so the opposed interests existed, not between the people of Handsworth and those outside, but within the population itself. The local grounding was pursued in the various inside-page stories – some of the most active participants in the petition were

Storey's friends; the debate about the sentences was conducted between local M.P.s, councillors and local social workers.

If the case was a problem *for* the city, it was also a problem *of* the city. Not unexpectedly, the exploration of this theme led to an examination of Handsworth, but that was situated in a particular context: not poverty in the city, nor even the ghetto in the city, but *youth in the city*. The case was inserted, without too much friction, into the *Mail*'s on-going 'file' on violent youth. On 20 March the *Mail* expanded a pre-planned series on a local experiment in youth work (the *Double Zero* club) into a full-page feature called 'Behind The Violence'. To the vicar's account of his youth-club experiment were added two pieces – one by a local magistrate on the problems of dealing with violent young offenders, the other some comments on the effects of long-term imprisonment by an eminent psychiatrist. It is thus not surprising to find 'violent youth' providing the theme and heading for the *Mail* editorial of the same day: 'Outsiders'. Here the area of Handsworth – and thus the whole complex crime/environment, biography/background problematic – was subsumed under the youth theme. The need for deterrent sentencing having been acknowledged by the long-established reference to the 'American pattern of urban violence', there was an explicit appeal for remedies to be applied to 'root causes', specifically to 'the explosive situation in socially deprived areas' like Handsworth. Hence the conclusion was double-edged: 'Tough sentences for savage crimes may be a necessary short-term expedient. But the community must look deeper if long-term solutions are to be found.'

On the following day this heavy thematisation of the case was continued, and it is into this perspective that the portrait of Handsworth was inserted. 'The night Handsworth was minding its own business' appeared alongside letters on the sentence, and above a piece whose title reveals its topic ('Meanwhile back in the Juvenile Court'), and all under the general heading 'Spotlight on violence and its causes as the 20-year sentence debate continues'. While the *Mail* had not denied the relevance of the 'environment', this was particularised so as to fit with the violent-youth theme. The focus was very much on the children of Handsworth:

> In the Grove, Villa Road, home of the sixteen year old, there is paper scattered on broken paving stones, grey soil sprouting wizened grey plants, crumbling fences, and gaps in the brickwork where the mortar has lost heart. Many children too. Healthy beautiful children with dirty knees, yes, but with young expressions and soft, ungrained complexions. Ebullient, as they offer to show 'where he lived with his mum'. In a flat in the Grove's only detached house. Are these youngsters at risk because all around them gardens wilt, paper drifts and paint flakes from Victorian artisan's dwellings? Is a way of life decided behind a front door or on the streets? How many Handsworth kids make good but not news by gaining university places, then degrees?

The same technique of speculative, subjective exploration – the most extreme form of 'feature by microcosm' – was applied to the homes of the other two offenders. The article ended with an admission that no progress had been made in the study of 'detritus and dereliction' – 'We find ourselves back at the beginning: what goes on behind those front doors?' There had been no examination of the structural constraints operating on Handsworth, not even the cursory kind we found in the nationals; no attempt either to fit the boys' backgrounds – covered through the mothers in the earlier 'feature-by-montage' piece – into their social environment. The background issue here took the form – implicit and by no means fully formed – of a cultural problematic: how a 'way of life' was formed, and whether it was 'the family' or 'the streets' which were the determining influence.

A measure of the integrated approach of the *Mail* is that this cultural theme provided the pivot for Brian Priestley's personal viewpoint of 21 March – 'One Paul Storey is too many.' While Priestley was accorded the same licence as Waterhouse in the *Mirror* and Akass in the *Sun*, he did not contradict, but took to its logical conclusion, the definition of the background problem which had been built into the news treatment. The problems faced by Paul Storey, Priestley argued, were similar to those faced by youths in other inner-city areas – Hockley, Balsall Heath, Aston. They had 'typical' histories: trouble at home, poor school achievement, distrustful of adults, searching for excitement, perhaps as an extra burden they were coloured. On this (by now familiar) talk of the fracturing of social ties, Priestley's portrait depended. He was clear about the responsibility for this situation: the Community Relations Committee, youth organisations, the City Council, all were variously failing in their duty. The results were disastrous:

> At the moment too many youngsters are deprived of decent homes, playing space, youth facilities, fresh air, opportunities for lawful adventure, chances of escaping from the areas in which they live, the sort of adult leaders who they feel understand their problem; and the prospect of a happy future. It must be time that these young folk were seen as the crash priority of our youth programme.
> Even one Paul Storey is too many.

The resort to crime here was thus portrayed as an option in the field of leisure. Although there was some minimal acknowledgement of structural factors – housing, for example, curiously on a par with 'fresh air' – the 'missing link' to retie these young people to society was primarily that of leisure provision. Only nominally was youth situated in particular areas of the city. Employment, education and income, the lack of which helped to define those areas, were not of real relevance. What Priestley did was to fill the gap between physical environment and social behaviour, so troubling to the Handsworth feature writer, with the mediation of leisure. Larger questions about social inequality were thus circumvented, and, equally importantly, a real pragmatism – a crash youth programme – could be advocated. Analysis and solution had been localised, not only in geographical but in political terms also. The solution was within the city's grasp, if only the council had recognised the need.

A whole complex of redefinitions had been at work in the *Mail*'s handling of the issue: from 'muggers' to 'violent city youth', from 'problem area' to 'way of life', from 'law and order' to 'leisure', from 'juvenile courts' to 'youth courses'.

The complexities of explaining one crime, a pattern of crime, a criminal area; the possibly crucial roles of family, school, work-place; the over-all factors of housing, poverty, race: all these – and more – had been subsumed under the image of 'culturally-deprived youth prone to violence because of the vacuum in their leisure time'. This reformulation of the 'background problem' may have more validity than some we have examined, but it remains, in its omission of structural factors, patently inadequate as an analysis. Its power is that of an image – that of 'bored' youth who became 'at risk' through doing nothing.

The Birmingham-based *Sunday Mercury* is a difficult paper to characterise. In appearance and perspective, it is more like a local weekly than the *Post* and the *Mail*: deliberately, proudly, old-fashioned in views and news treatment, it eschews sex and sensationalism in favour of the moral and the mundane. Its feature treatment of the Handsworth case appeared at first glance idiosyncratic in the extreme. It did not focus at all on the victim, the criminal or the area, but presented two case studies of how it was possible not merely to survive but to succeed from the beginnings of a slum background. The feature took up the whole editorial page. Two interviews with prominent Birmingham men, one a self-made businessman, the other an ex-Cabinet Minister, covered the middle and right-hand parts of the page; the editorial column was on the left and the weekly Christian column appeared, as always, at the bottom left of the page. The *Mercury* had chosen the theme of mugging for its Sunday sermon. Both interviewees were pictured: the businessman in a small facial inset, the politician, in a larger picture, standing in the street in Lozells where he went to school.

It can scarcely be said that the *Mercury* spelt out its argument. The drift of the argument, from the controversy over a twenty-year prison sentence to the present decay of family life in society as a whole, was not *articulated* in any clear or systematic fashion. The editorial, for example, discussed youthful crime in terms of changing family life, but made no specific reference to 'mugging'. The interviews contained *implicit images* of society and explanations of 'deviance', but made hardly any direct reference to the Storey case. The overall effect was actually quite subtle. By avoiding any attempt to explain specific crimes, it was much easier to pull on unfocused common-sense concerns and assumptions, to weave them into an implicit image of society and (apparently) to offer a *generalised* explanation of recent events in terms of the breakdown of family life.

The selection of 'experts' in relation to this theme was quite crucial. For the *Mercury*, no doubt, the fact of previous exhaustive newspaper treatment of the subject led to the search for a more original approach. But here, as elsewhere, this technical explanation of the *Mercury*'s feature treatment is of limited and distorting value. It would in any event have been quite out of line with the *Mercury*'s provincial common-sense 'world-view' to have consulted those sociologists, criminologists, community workers and voluntary agencies which even the most conservative of the daily national newspapers used in some form as reference points. Thus it is entirely appropriate that the 'expertise' sought by the *Mercury* was not that of intellectual analysis or professional concern but one of lived experience. The biographies chosen were not simple accounts of rampant individualism, celebrations of exceptional men. What the *Mercury* required was not morality tales of competitive success but images of an integrated society, and, within that, of the stable social life and culture of the slum – thus the emphasis on the family, especially on the mother figure. Each man talked about his own mother, enabling the editorial to pinpoint *the mother* as the key integrative mechanism which had now broken down. Hence the headings. The interview with the businessman was headed 'My widowed mother ruled five of us'; that with the politician, 'Miss Hayman, the Lozells shepherd' – a reference to the politician's primary-school teacher, who, according to his description, acted as a supplementary and communally available mother-figure. It is Mr Howell who raised the description of his experience to the level of explanation: ' "Environment", asserts Mr Howell, "is very very important. If it is bad or poor or overcrowded then this may not matter if the other things are there – the social anchors – the family life and fellowship that we had." ' This became the theme of the accompanying editorial, which inserted the new problem of violent, juvenile crime into an ultra-traditionalist framework. What was required was not new thinking but the reassertion of old values. The analysis of urban deprivation had become a panegyric for traditional motherhood and the old culture. The point was simply made:

Mother it seems is no longer the formidable force she used to be. The economic and social pressures of modern life have diminished her dominant role in the family. Instead of running the home full-time as mentors, cooks, confessors, comforters, cleaners and arbitrators, about half a million in the Midlands are now breadwinners; part career-women and only part-time mothers. Just how high a price society is paying for mother's wage packet nobody yet knows. Some sociologists, magistrates and others think it may be a frightening one. Who can tell how much idleness, fecklessness, vandalism and educational subnormality is due to the simple fact that many schoolchildren do not know what it is to go home to mother, to tea on the table and a sympathetic ear for the chatter of the day? . . . Rootless, underdeveloped and insecure children become inadequate, deprived teenagers whose social and emotional needs are fulfilled in gangs of other inadequates. The streets replace the anchorage of home. Violence becomes a form of self-expression and vandalism as way of filling the vacuum left by mum. Evidence is mounting that traditional family life, often derided as too restrictive, too cloying, too limiting to freedom and too old hat in an age when youth is emancipated, is still a priceless asset. To be a mere mother running a home and family is to play as vital a role in our society as there is. It is worth more than pin-money, more than keeping up with the Joneses and much more than can be expressed in material terms. If the problems of rootless urban youth are to be tackled with any determination, perhaps we should start with a Government-sponsored campaign to put mother back where she belongs – in the home.

This was a powerful appeal. It did not draw on the self-perpetuating images of the media which may have ultimately provoked cynicism in the audience. It drew much more directly on the ideology of *traditional common sense*, known to all 'normal' people as the right and proper way of life, exemplified in the lives of these two men, enshrined in the Christian platitudes of the *Mercury*'s resident common sense preacher.

There is a strong case for considering the *Mercury*'s treatment of the Handsworth event as more ideologically coherent than that of any other paper. There were no gaps in the *Mercury* of the kind we found in the *Daily Mail* and *Daily Express* between relatively wide-ranging features and narrow-minded editorials. The *Mercury* did not feel it necessary even to go through the motions of handling a debate about Paul Storey's character and education, the correctness of the sentence, or the problems of Handsworth as an area. In one sense, its advantages were temporal. It did not have to follow closely on previous news treatments or take account of the definitions and reactions of experts. As a weekly (i.e. Sunday only) provincial paper, it was the paper least tied by the established emphases of news treatment, least constrained by how the topic had already been defined. It was free to establish its own stresses and themes, and to draw the story (now several days old as a news story) into its own ideological orbit. This gave it the opportunity for a more consistent and coherent thematic treatment. It was cast in a form – the biography as a moral tale for our times – quite independently constructed (independent, that is, of the details and contingencies of the particular news values surrounding the Handsworth event), quite distinctively conceived.

This, then, was a distinctive type of feature – one more characteristic of the popular Sunday paper than of the daily: the feature as moral tale, or 'sermon'. Its 'feature' aspect sprang almost entirely from the freedom the paper had to 'stand back' from the event itself, and handle the 'deeper questions', 'larger themes' which it raised. It did not consider closely questions of social problems in a 'sociological' way; nor did it go for graphic first-hand reporting; nor, even, did it construct an explanation out of the medley of expert opinions and voices. It *bent* the subject *back* towards one of its great, persistent, overarching moral themes: the sanctity of family life, its cohesion, its supportive framework, its contribution to the maintenance of traditional ways of life. With a certain, technical, journalistic flair, the *Mercury* then chose to 'feature' this great conservative social theme in an interestingly 'personalised' way, through the exemplary lives of local worthy men. But there can be no mistaking the continuity of ideological themes which this novelty of treatment and story somewhat conceals. A hundred different stories, cast in a hundred different ways, lead *Mercury* readers, every week, down the narrow path back to the great, conserving, central verities of life. In its capacity to combine novelty of treatment and angle, or personalisation with an instinctual traditionalism, in its ready feel for the grooves of consensual, common-sense wisdoms and unchanging patterns, the *Mercury* shares a great deal with that other section of the conservative press, the national Sunday 'populars'. It inhabits much the same moral-social landscape, in which the heady, restless world of change, movement, disturbance – the modern spirit – is contrasted, unfavourably, with the 'old truths', the old patterns, the old concerns, the old and tried ways of doing things. It is a *deep affirmation* of the social order, underscored by a rooted popular traditionalism. The contrasts across which its particular weekly features are cast are simple, abstract and broad: rootlessness, insecurity, emotional deprivation, vandalism, educational subnormality and 'other inadequacies' are all woven together as the anomic price of change – against that, the steady, solid, rootedness of 'home to mother . . . tea on the table and a sympathetic ear for the chatter of the day'.

The image here evoked, then, related not to the problem, but the solution. It was positive rather than negative, yet contained within it an explicit model of historical decay, not of the city, but of mother-centred family life. The *Sunday Mercury*'s response to the problem of a new age was to insist that the clock be turned back.

CONCLUSION: EXPLANATIONS AND IMAGES IN THE MEDIA

The great majority of the features on the Handsworth case selected victim, mugger and area as their principal feature themes. The press found irresistibly problematic the connections between a horrific crime, the dramatic response in the court, and the new slum conditions which provided the venue of the crime and the background of the criminal. It was this link which required exploration and hence provided the pivot for the move into feature treatment. Above all, the move to exploration encountered the problem of the relationship between physical environment and social conduct. The condensed explanations of this relationship presented in the headlines were various: the organic stress of the *Daily Mail* ('Where violence breeds') or the severe yet imprecise determinism of the *Daily Express* ('Caught for Life in a Violent Trap'). The boys' biographies were sometimes worked into the background (as in the *Guardian*), but were more often separated out (*Daily Mail, Daily Express, Birmingham Post*). The links between biography and background were represented in different ways – here by the common reproduction of the race theme, there by the identification of other Handsworth children as potential criminals.

While some of these techniques effected spurious kinds of connection between environment and crime, there is evident a search for a more satisfactory solution. One strategy, especially evident in the 'features by microcosm', was the attempt to make a direct connection between 'decay' and 'criminal conduct'. Two processes are necessary here. One is to reduce the definition of the environment from one embracing the hidden mechanisms of housing, poverty and race to one involving simply the surface appearance of dirt and dereliction. The second is to suppress the possible mediations between environment and crime. The social ties of family, school and job, are displaced into the biographical pieces, and their function as structural/cultural institutions within the area can thus be ignored. It becomes possible, then, to short-circuit the environment/crime relationship. Rather than trace the complex links between the deteriorated physical environment, patterns of cultural organisation and individual acts of crime, the inference is that a derelict and neglected house or street infects the inhabitants with a kind of moral pollution. The litter in the streets becomes the sign of incipient criminality.

While this strategy was found most openly in the provincial conservatism of the *Birmingham Post* and *Evening Mail*, cosmopolitan liberalism, as represented in the *Guardian*, fared no better in its attempt to crack the crime/

TABLE 4.2
Press coverage of the Handsworth case

	Front-page lead (20 March 1973)	Inside stories (20 March 1973)	Editorials (20 March 1973)	Features (21 March 1973)	Second sentence (22 March 1973)
Daily Express	Boy 16 weeps after sentence 20 YEARS FOR MUGGER		Let us protect the innocent	Caught For Life In a Violent Trap – The Ghetto – The mugger – The victim – The judge – The police	Battle over jailed boy. Vital issues raised says lawyer
Daily Mail	Storm over boy muggers	20 years for boy 16 who went mugging for fun – Where sons went wrong, by mothers	A terrible deterrent	Where violence breeds – Handsworth – The gang boss – The victim – An expert's view	Boy muggers: same again Judge forgot robbery charges
The Sun	20 YEARS FOR THE MUGGER AGED 16 Two friends given 10 years – Boys with a debt to pay	What it means to be a victim of the muggers	None ('Putting the legal boot in won't solve the problem of the muggers' – J. Akass, 21 March 1973)	'I'M ONLY HALF A MAN My life is in ruins' says tragic victim of boy muggers	Another 20 years for 'Mug' boy
Daily Mirror	JAILED FOR 20 YEARS Shock sentence on mugger aged 16	THE CASE OF THE TEENAGE MUGGER Storey's mother vs Police Federation	Industrial dispute ('Order in Court' – K. Waterhouse, 22 March 1973)		Young mugger gets another 20 years

Newspaper			Savage (21 March 1973)		
Morning Star	16 year old boy gets 20 years in mugging case			Anger flares at savage sentence on muggers	
Guardian	16 years old boy gets 20 years for 'mugging'			'I am sorry about sentences,' says victim of mugging attack Depressed & Depressing	Another 20 years for boy in mugging case
Daily Telegraph	20 YEARS FOR 16-YEAR-OLD MUGGER Five cigarettes and 30p from victim		Scales of Justice	30p muggers so stupid says victim	
The Times	Judge sentences three Birmingham boys for 'serious and horrible' offences against man going home MUGGER AGED 16 GIVEN 20 YEARS DETENTION AND COMPANIONS 10 YEARS	Mother says boy is 'very shocked'	20 years for attempted murder		

environment problem. The list of pathological symptoms on which that paper's portrait of Handsworth was based remained essentially descriptive. Out of the list of crime, prostitution, poor housing, poverty and inter-racial strife, which were causes and which effects? If the environment determines crime, what determines the environment? These are difficult questions: but that is not the main reason for evading them. There is hardly any way of tackling those problems without calling into question some fundamental structural characteristics of society: the unequal distribution of housing; the low levels of pay in particular industries; the nature of welfare benefits; the lack of educational resources; racial discrimination. It was the directly political nature of these determinants which necessitated the appropriation of environmental determinism in such crude and unresolvable terms. It was into this vacuum that there emerged the most powerful mechanisms for resolving these problems ideologically – *public images*.

A 'public image' is a cluster of impressions, themes and quasi-explanations, gathered or fused together. These are sometimes the outcome of the features process itself; where hard, difficult, social, cultural or economic analysis breaks down or is cut short, the resolution is achieved by orchestrating the whole feature so as to produce a kind of composite description-*cum*-explanation – in the form of a 'public image'. But the process is somewhat circular, for these 'public images' are frequently already in existence, derived from other features on other occasions dealing with other social problems. And in this case the presence of such 'public images' in public and journalistic discourse feeds into and informs the feature treatment of a particular story. Since such 'public images', at one and the same time, are graphically compelling, but also stop short of serious, searching analysis, they tend to appear *in place of analysis* – or analysis seems to collapse into the image. Thus at the point where further analysis threatens to go beyond the boundaries of a dominant ideological field, the 'image' is evoked to foreclose the problem. The over-arching 'public image' which dominated the national papers feature treatment of the Handsworth case was that of the *ghetto* or *new slum*. It was this image which was inserted at the moment when the crime/environment relationship was most pressing, ideologically. The 'transparent' association between crime, race, poverty and housing was condensed into the image of the 'ghetto' but not in any causal formulation. Any further demand for explanation was forestalled by this essentially circular definition – these *were* the characteristics which made up the ghetto. The initial 'problem' – the crime – was thus inserted into a more general 'social problem' where the apparent richness of description and evocation stood in place of analytic connections. The connections which were made – with the death of cities, the problem of immigration, the crisis of law and order – were fundamentally *descriptive* connections. Through the 'public image of the ghetto' we were pushed back up the scale where generalised analogy replaced concrete analysis and where the image of the United States as precursor of all our nightmares came back into play. It was a powerful and compelling form of *rhetorical closure*.

The ghetto/new slum image was dominant in the national press feature treatment: more explicitly in the *Daily Mail* and the *Daily Express*; less so in the

Guardian and *Daily Telegraph*. It was also implicit in the approach of the *Birmingham Post*, but the other two local papers, the *Evening Mail* and the *Sunday Mercury*, provided their own unique imagistic resolutions. Less public than provincial perhaps, certainly feeling, in the national context, dated. But the images of *youth* and *the family* mobilised by those papers fulfilled the same ideological role as the ghetto in the nationals, and in their particular settings they had a similar evocative power.

Both involved specific redefinitions of the environment. In the *Mail*'s evocation of youth we were taken out of Handsworth into a whole ring of such areas in the city. What drew them together was not housing, race or poverty but the presence in them of a particular group: young people without adequate recreational facilities. Thus redefined, the problem became open to forms of pragmatic resolution. Since it was a problem of the young rather than a whole population; since it was one of recreation not of work; since it was one internal to the city and not present in the society as a whole; since, in short, the problem had been *localised*, it was amenable to *local solutions*. Hence Priestley's stirring call to the city council for a 'crash youth programme'. This image – of deprived, restless youth looking for excitement – drew on a whole post-war definition of the 'youth problem': from the Teddy-Boys to the muggers the same images have been evoked.

Social dislocation of a rather different kind informed the *Sunday Mercury*'s feature. Here the mediation absent in the national press between physical environment and social conduct was provided by a cultural formation: that of the family. Poor housing and poverty need not have led to crime if a proper home with 'mother in her rightful place' was provided. The novelty of the environmental situation was denied: there had always been areas like this. What was missing was the cultural source of respect and discipline which – alone it would appear – could guarantee our adherence to the rules of proper social behaviour. That the image of family life evoked is historically dubious, and the examples given hardly typical, should not blind us to the pull such an evocation is likely to have on those who inhabit the world of the *Sunday Mercury*: the appeal to everyday decency, accepted morality, established ways of living. Crime is the price we must pay for having forsaken these values. If the 'ghetto' is an image of urban decay then this appeal to the family is an image of moral decline. Different in so many ways, both images share a sense of social loss. It is on the relationship between images, explanations, ideologies, and precisely such a sense of loss, that Chapter 6 is focused.

5

Orchestrating Public Opinion

'Letters to the editor' have not been much studied as a journalistic form, [1] nor their function much examined. In the Letters' column, readers' opinions appear in the press in their least mediated public form. The selection *is* ultimately in the hands of the editor, but the spectrum of letters submitted is not (apart, that is, from occasional 'plants'). This does not mean that a Letters' column offers a representative slice of public opinion; nor that it is free of the shaping processes of news construction (defined earlier). Letter columns in different papers have different flavours – compare the prestige spot in *The Times* with the *Daily Mirror*'s 'Old Codger's; and these flavours, though reflecting something about the paper's regular readers, must also to some degree be the result of a positive editorial selection by the newspaper itself, in keeping with its own 'social image' of itself. There is a good deal of mutual reinforcement here: because papers are known to carry a certain kind of letter from a certain type of correspondent, such people write more frequently; or others, hoping to get space, construct their letters in terms they know will be acceptable. This is a structured dialogue. That structure is not simply a matter of style, length or mode of address. Committed nationalisers write differently to the *Daily Express*, which would be hostile, than to the *Guardian* which might be tolerant. The difference in the kinds of letters printed will also have something to do with the paper's position in the hierarchy of cultural power. 'Conversation' in *The Times* or *Daily Telegraph* is conducted 'between equals'. The paper of this type can 'take for granted a known set of subjects and interests, based for the most part on a roughly common level of education': they can 'assume a kind of community – in this society, inevitably either a social class or an educational group'. [2] The position of *The Times* depends on its power to influence the elite from within; its readership, though small, is select, powerful, knowledgeable and influential. It and its correspondents speak within the same conversational universe. In the letters it prints, therefore, it is making public one current of opinion within the decision-making class to another section of the same class. When the popular press, by contrast, addresses its readers as 'you', they mean 'everyone who is not us: we who are writing the paper for "you" out there'. Readers here are not of the same 'community': they are essentially consumers, 'a market or a potential market'. [3] The basis of the power of the popular press is that, though their readers lie outside the nexus of decision-making, the populars can 'represent their opinions and feelings' to those who *are* at the centre. They articulate on their readers' behalf; they speak *to power*. Their letters, therefore, must principally be of the 'ordinary-folks' variety; they must show their capacity to pull readers, normally invisible, into the public conversation. These are two different kinds of 'cultural power'; and the difference is reflected in the letters they print and the kinds of people who write them.

The papers' choice of letters over time will also reflect the operation of a certain kind of 'balance' (balance within the spectrum of letters they receive, of course). If a newspaper editorial takes a strong line, it may feel obliged to print some letters which are critical. If an issue is controversial, it will print some letters on either side of the debate. This 'balance' is notional. It is *not* a statistical balance between all the letters received, and certainly not a true index of the balance of opinion in the country or amongst the readership. But the fact that 'balance' is a criterion remains important. It indicates one of the main functions which letter columns serve: to stimulate controversy, provoke public response, lead to lively debate. Letters are also there, in part, to sustain the claim that the mind of the press is not closed, and that its pages are open to views it does not necessarily approve. Letters are therefore also part of the democratic image of the press – they support its claims to be a 'fourth estate'.

Letters will also be chosen for the status of the letter writer. Very special people will tend to have their letters printed: so will very un-special people – 'grass-roots' voices'. Papers will differ according to which end of that spectrum they are orientated towards. Most letter columns are, in part, a 'sounding board' for the opinions of the 'man in the street', but most will aim for some balance between these sorts of letters, and letters from 'influentials' – the 'balance' is struck by editors for editorial effect, rather than for strict numerical equality.

Letter columns, then, *do* permit certain viewpoints on controversial issues to surface in the public domain; in this sense they do help to widen the representation of views expressed on topics, and perhaps to indicate viewpoints which do not normally get publicly expressed. But they are in no sense an accurate representation of 'public opinion', and that is because they are not an unstructured exchange but a *highly structured* one. Their principal function is to help the press organise and orchestrate the debate about public questions. They are therefore a central link in the shaping of public opinion – a shaping process the more powerful because it appears to be in the reader's keeping and done with his or her consent and participation. We stress the organised form, the *formal* nature, of the medium in which this takes place. People do not write letters to the press like they write to friends. A 'letter to the editor' marks an entry into the public arena: letters are public communications, coloured by 'public motives'. Their intention is not simply to tell the editor what they think, but to shape policy, influence opinion, swing the course of events, defend interests, advance causes. They occupy a mid-way position between the 'official statement' and the private communication; they are public communications. Whoever writes a letter to the editor means to cash, publicly, a position, a status or an experience.

There were letters to the editor on the Handsworth case in both the national and local press. Those in the national press in a fortnight sample period were distributed as follows:

Morning Star	1	(2 April 1973)
Guardian	8	(22, 26, 28, 31 March 1973)
The Times	3	(24, 30 March 1973; 2 April 1973)
Daily Telegraph	7	(22, 23, 28 March 1973)
Daily Mirror	3	(24 March 1973)
Daily Mail	4	(23 March 1973)
Total	26	

(There were some letters that dealt with 'matters arising' from the case; they did not comment on the case itself. Such uncommitted letters were excluded from the analysis and the totals given above.[4])

Most of the letters were about the sentence passed rather than about the 'mugging' itself. In this respect – as often – letters, like features, 'take off from' the points of newsworthiness first identified in the *news* treatment. *News* defines 'what the issues are', for letters as for other parts of the paper. News is the primary structure.

First, the letters which *criticised* the long sentences passed on the three Handsworth boys – these fall within what we shall term a 'liberal' perspective on crime. These may be divided into two groups: those which argued principally about the sentence itself – framed, that is, within a 'penological' perspective (i.e. concerned with the debate about which methods most effectively accomplish the reduction of crime): and those which, beginning there, adopted a wider frame of reference. The 'penological' perspective took the definition of crime for granted, and argued about strategies of containment and control. The letters were about either reform and rehabilitation (of the guilty) or deterrence (of others). Few thought a judge might be tempted by retribution: only one referred to it as a possible excuse for what was really 'savage overkill'. Four correspondents, at least, did not stray at all outside this tight frame. The arguments deployed (critical of the sentence) were 'liberal' ones: shorter prison sentences give greater hope of rehabilitation, they argued; longer sentences do not really deter. Sometimes statistical studies from other countries were quoted. Sometimes 'rehabilitation' carried a psycho-therapeutic overtone: the criminal is 'sick' – sentences must be 'curative'. These 'liberal' letters seemed aware that they were arguing a rather unpopular case, in a climate set by those with opposing positions. So they often situated themselves *within* the dominant position first – declaring their credentials, so to speak – before launching a counter-argument. A strong traditionalist argument was that 'liberals' forget the victim. So one writer argued that, in the long term, it is the 'tough' not the 'soft-on-crime' lobby which shows no compassion for the victim. Traditionalists often call criminals 'uncivilised'. The liberal correspondents tried to turn the tables: two called the *sentences* uncivilised; one referred to 'blood lust', another called them 'savage'. Another asked whether Judge Jeffreys had 'also been resurrected'.

Some of the 'liberal' letters moved beyond the *immediate* question of the efficacy of sentencing measures. Three picked up the topic of 'inner-city areas' and their problems. The most hard-hitting of these identified 'bad areas' with race discrimination, suggesting that the sentence is the end-product of this trend. This letter referred to the 'Oval 4'; Pakistani youths killed in an affray with the Special Patrol Group (S.P.G.); S.P.G. activities in black areas; Enoch Powell; fire bombing in Brixton; a racist film by the Monday Club. This letter had to work hard to take the topic that far, within the discourse of the letters' column. The crime was not to be excused, it argued – but the sentence was unfair and dealt with 'symptoms' rather than 'the causes' of crime. No other letter got this far. But another said the sentences would antagonise youth in inner-city areas, the majority of whom were poor and black; they would 'divide and destroy our society'. Birmingham was not an area where robbery with violence was increasing – a telling argument, subsequently supported by the official statistics, but *not* picked up by other correspondents or editorials. This letter also referred to a 'civilized, tolerant and just society'. The notion of 'civilization' seemed to be a critical criterion in the discussion of crime and punishment; both the liberal and traditionalist positions attempting to recruit it for their own advantage. Traditionalists regarded the crimes, liberals regarded harsh sentences, as failing to meet the test of 'civilized' conduct.

The requirements felt by critics of the sentence to 'pay their dues' and insert their opinions *within* a more accepted mode of conceiving crime and punishment are strikingly illustrated by another letter, headed 'Deprived Communities can help themselves', which also takes up the inner urban theme:

> I would not deny offenders' responsibility for their acts, except for the mentally ill; but all of us are also subject to outside pressures and some have been almost totally deprived of the beneficient influences and opportunities which have made us what we are. Self-made men, from the Prime Minister downwards, may say, 'I overcame my surroundings – why can't everyone else?' But others have not his ability and in Birmingham slums the opportunities for employment let alone advancement are strictly limited.

The response of the criminal to his situation, the letter continued, was 'natural'; a healthy young dog locked up in a dingy room, with enough to eat but nothing to do, would become unruly. The writer called for urban aid projects to 'help deprived communities to help themselves'. This letter seemed to be trying to *translate* sophisticated theories of crime into simple, comprehensible terms understandable by a reader with a traditionalist outlook. It tried to win consent to a liberal argument by capturing positions within the traditionalist perspective. It was not only a complex, condensed piece of reasoning, but it was reasoning which encompassed a wide selection of the 'lay ideologies' of crime, which structure all public debates on this issue.

There were fourteen letters which supported the sentence. The strongest theme here was the need to *protect the public from crime*. The need to 'protect' was sometimes coupled with the need to impose discipline: 'If parents won't control these thugs, the State must.' Reform of the criminal – a liberal point – occurred far less often, though one letter mentioned 'guidance' and 'help', and another doing 'something constructive with the boy'. The deterrent value of long sentences was mentioned only four times; 'just deserts' only twice; four writers urged us to think of the victim. The contextualisation of crime, which occurred less frequently in these letters than in the 'liberal' ones, also moved in a different direction. One letter, which did go outside the limited frame, invoked the government's 'election pledge on law and order'; another referred to the crisis in the nation's morals, the decline of the family, the abolition of capital punishment, the prevalance of abortions and the recent case of a Hell's Angels' 'gang bang', where the group had been cleared of rape. Whereas 'liberal' letters contextualised by referring to 'social environment', 'traditionalists' contextualised by generalising the theme of moral pollution and the decline of discipline and order. *Society* was at the heart of the 'liberal' case against the sentence; the question of *morality* was at the centre of the traditionalist case.

Another feature of some traditionalist letters was a toying with brutalist solutions to crime. One writer said that if an animal had made the attacks on a person which Paul Storey made on Mr Keenan, 'it would have been shot or destroyed instantly'. But, having arrived at this brink of retribution, the writer relented: Storey being 'something more than an animal' (though, clearly, not 'something' *fully human*) will have to be dealt with differently. But a second letter did step across the threshold. This was the letter that suggested that offenders should be put in cages to withstand the gaze of the outraged public: 'human nature ... after 2000 years remains unchanged basically'.

Traditionalist letters were often buttressed by appeals to *ordinary personal experience*. One writer, mother of two teenage boys, used this similarity to the mother of the offenders not to sympathise but to strengthen the demand for tough sentences: 'If I were to have to face that sort of thing from my own children, I would, of course be broken hearted but I would own that they deserved every single day.' A second suggested that 'If do-gooders were to have a loved one murdered or badly hurt in a mugging, they would not be so quick to stand up for these thugs.' Here the appeal to 'personal experience' was aimed at undercutting soft-hearted, do-gooding liberalism: first-hand experience of crime, they suggested, would provide the cold touch of realism which was missing from the abstract, distanced 'intellectualising' of the liberal position. These references to 'personal experience', to 'ordinary people' and to 'common-sense realism' constituted a widely diffused argument in *all* the letters on the sentence, and on both sides of the argument, though, in general, they overwhelmingly were recruited in support of retributive attitudes to crime.

This contrast between 'concrete experience' (supporting realism – i.e. traditionalist social attitudes) and 'abstract reformism' (based on attitudes which are too 'soft on crime') was a *consistent deep-structure* in letters on this kind of topic to the press: its roots in popular ideology are discussed more fully below.

The 'traditionalist' case was carried as much in the writer's tone and style as in the content of what he or she was arguing. Mr Charles Simeons, M.P., the correspondent with the suggestion about 'cages', perhaps best – because most extensively (he had two letters) – typified this tone of bluff, breezy, confident common-sense: the 'plain man' thinking aloud, and speaking his mind. 'Unchanging human nature' was confidently asserted in a dependent clause. Moral statements were made with blanketing assertion: 'Bullies have always been cowards who fear personal inconvenience.' On his proposal to put muggers in cages, he added: 'Far from being sadistic, I visualise no customers or one at most.' This plain-speaking, frankly brutalist style was typical of letters which, because their arguments seemed to rest on the *felt legitimacy* of popular, long-standing 'folk wisdoms' (often forgotten, of course), carried, in their whole tone and approach, the implication: 'everyone knows'. The same breezy colloquialism was to be found in another letter, which complained of 'wails from the bleeding hearts'; adding 'If bashing the motorist is effective, so is bashing the hooligan.' On the whole, the 'liberal' tone simply could not afford to be so confident, assuming instant support for incontrovertible truths. 'Liberal' letters had to *argue* their way by a much longer, less assertive, more 'rational' route to their less popular conclusions. So far as crime, retribution, toughness and authority were concerned, traditionalists proceeded with the certain conviction that Truth was already in their pockets. It is important to add that, though this 'populist traditionalism' was most evident in the popular press – the *Mail* and the *Mirror* in our case – there were at least three letters in the *Telegraph* which could be placed close to this category. It was by no means the prerogative of the popular press, nor was it simply a function of the requirement of brevity. It was a social 'voice', not attributable to technical constraints.

The distribution of arguments within these letters to the daily national press can now be summarised as follows:

Guardian	Liberal 6 Traditionalist 2 (of which 4 are penologically orientated)
The Times	Liberal 1 (penological)
Daily Telegraph	Traditionalist 5 Liberal 2
Daily Mirror	Traditionalist 3
Daily Mail	Traditionalist 4
Morning Star	Radical 1 [6]

The distribution of the arguments employed thus fits squarely with what we might think of as the newspapers' respective 'position' in the spectrum of attitudes on social and moral questions. The *Guardian* contained not only the most 'liberal' letters, but also those which contextualised crime in social-problem terms: the *Telegraph* was the most 'traditionalist'. The position of the *Mail* was the expected one – in the traditionalist camp. The position of the *Mirror* was the most classic – left-liberal in politics, but often solidly conservative on social, moral and penal questions: the ventriloquist of working-class corporatism.

LOCAL CHANNELS

In the *Birmingham Post* and *Evening Mail* there were, in a seven-day period, twenty-eight letters in all, twelve categorised as *liberal*, sixteen *traditionalist*. [7] The differences between those in both papers were slight enough to enable us to consider them together. (Again, we exclude peripheral, uncommitted letters from the totals. [8])

The Handsworth case clearly had a different resonance and greater salience for Birmingham than for other parts of the country; the more so since a city area – Handsworth – itself figured as a protagonist in the debate. The spread of opinions was thus more sharply polarised as between 'liberal' opinion and professional 'healers', and those drawing on traditionalist common-sense argu-ments. Here, the split referred to earlier appears more starkly. It was felt that liberals took an abstract and theoretical attitude, treating daily experience as an instance, merely, of a more general case; traditionalists were orientated solidly to common-sense experience, rooted in the discrete specific everyday life in the 'real' world – fighting fire with fire.

A strong theme amongst the *critics* of the sentence, as in the national press, was the penological one: harsh sentences did not reform offenders. Some added that they did not deter potential criminals either. Four of these letters were focused on the *specific* question of sentencing – including one which based op-position to deterrent sentencing on personal expert experience: it is by a prison psychologist. Even where the focus is on sentencing, we can see how there is a movement towards theories of *explanation* of crime in the 'liberal' letters. For example, the prison psychologist's letter contained a theory of crime embedded in his argument. Criminals may be 'immature, irresponsible types of people who do not plan their lives' but act 'in a spontaneous way'. Another writer, deploying an 'environmentalist' rather than a 'psychological impulse' model of crime, referred to the 'ways in which society itself has contributed to producing violent and deviant minorities'. The remedy proposed (the liberal alternative to deterrence/retribution) was an extension of the 'caring' social services: 'more effective preventive services both social and educational'.

The author referred to above – a representative of the Association of Social Workers – also attempted a startling reversal of the traditionalist concern with the victim, with the argument that: 'In a very real sense, Paul Storey himself emerges as a "victim".' There were consistent references in this group of 'liberal' letters to *social* influences: 'the fault of his surroundings'; 'bored or . . . had a bad upbringing'. There was also a quite startling attempt to use the 'personal-reference' argument against, rather than for, the sentence – the following is from an ex-prisoner: 'I have done a fair bit of bird. I know that the longer the sentence, the worse the person gets . . . if you get mixed with rubbish you can turn out like "rubbish".' This was not, however, the sort of 'personal experience' likely to carry much weight with the 'tough-sentencing' lobby. In one or two letters the 'environmentalist' case was very fully deployed: 'There seems little doubt that there are groups in our society who can be described as relatively under-privileged, whether one uses social, emotional, economic or educational measures.' These 'have their origins somewhere in history'. Social scientists 'would be able to give us some fairly sound guesses as to how these factors affect individual behaviour'. Slums, poverty and unemployment remain, while Concorde is produced with the result that 'small wonder that some have little difficulty in applying a Marxist model to the situation and explaining it in terms of opposing class interests'. This was, perhaps, the fullest and most elaborated statement of the sociological perspective on crime to be encountered in the letters; and the fact that it is cast in rather general terms, and stops short within a 'social environment' explanation, does not diminish its emergent radicalism. It was, incidentally, written by a probation officer. Three dimen-sions of welfare state care were represented in this batch of 'liberal' anti-sentence letters: prison psychologist, social worker and probation officer. But there were no letters of this kind from the 'hard' side of social control: no policemen, no prison warders, no borstal governors.

The majority of letters in the local press were in fact from the 'traditionalist' camp; and not surprisingly the most powerful theme there was the challenge and reply to the position of liberal environmentalists: frequently supported by references to 'personal experience' and common-sense realism. 'Why do do-gooders always blame the environment? I and thousands of others were brought up in slums, but I cannot recall any case of mugging during my youth.' 'I was one of eight children brought up between the wars in poverty in a small two bedroom terrace house. We were kept clean, honest and God-fearing. . . . It made us all good citizens and proud to accept only what we worked for.' 'I am proud of my old girls who have made good despite sordid childhood homes, and whom I still meet' (this last from a teacher). Respec-tability, the struggle to do good and lift oneself by one's moral bootstraps despite everything, could hardly be more eloquently – because so *experientially* – expressed.

In these letters, the model of crime based on environmental factors was solidly opposed by the appeal to *moral discipline*. Morality *overcomes* environmental disadvantage. For youth said to be roaming the streets, with 'nothing else better to do', one correspondent recommended, 'Guides, Scouts, Boys' Brigade, youth clubs and various other things attached to school and churches.' A former Teddy-Boy, born and raised in Handsworth, had found 'a lack of things to do during the evenings' but 'we certainly didn't go around beating people up'. Most of the arguments against the environmentalists stem-med from this reassertion of the individual's capacity to triumph over adver-sity. Some uncommitted writers countered the negative image of the environ-ment given by the critics, not by an appeal to self-discipline but by an appeal to a positive image: in many roads 'several communities live perfectly happily together' and, 'if Handsworth is such an awful place, why is the competition for houses so intense?'

Many of the letters in the traditionalist camp called on personal or personal-expert experience to support their rejection of the environmentalist proposition. Two of these were connected with the 'hard' wing of social control: a prison officer's wife and the 'grandson of a magistrates' chairman and the son of a practising solicitor'. More commonly, those appealing to personal situation and everyday experience were signed – 'A working class mother of three teenagers', 'the father of a son who was attacked near Camp Hill a few years back'. These 'generic' correspondents, especially if they hinted at a personal experience of crime, tended to take up strongly the *discipline theme* considered above: not self-discipline, but the need for social and moral discipline, given the breakdown of law and order. The correspondent who alleged that 'Older people are afraid to walk the streets and our children are unable to go out alone to play in the streets or park' blamed the softness of the courts and thought the police were doing 'a wonderful job'. Others took a similar line: 'Already people in this area say they would rather risk crossing the busy main road than use the underpasses.' Others in this group referred directly to the institutions responsi-ble for the growth of indiscipline: 'With the lessening of a firm and stable family life for children the proportion of hostile young people in our society will increase'; 'The lack of home and school discipline is appalling.' Another asserted, 'Only stiff deterrents will make life tolerable.' Yet another, which identified the rise in crime with the end of National Service and the 'abolition of capital punishment', called for 'a national disciplinary service, based on a civilian type army, where the strict teaching of discipline should be a major priority'. The number of such letters, together with the similarities in tone, content and attitude would certainly support our view that *here* was the heart of the traditionalist case on crime. We would include in this characterisation of the traditionalist heartland, *both* those letters which opposed 'do-gooding' by an appeal to self-discipline, *and* those which, pivotting on the fears of ordinary folk, traced crime to moral causes and the collapse of an orderly way of life. The traditionalist case was pre-eminently a *moralist* argument.

All the letters, for or against the sentence, came from Birmingham or the Birmingham area, except one from a social workers' representative. A Birmingham expatriate wrote from Florida to warn his home city of an American-style mugging threat. There was a batch of letters from 'schoolboys', all roughly Paul Storey's age, intended, no doubt, to represent the views of normal, decent, respectable teenagers; they came out four to three critical of the sentence. Again, as we indicated in the previous section, those critical of the judge wrote letters on average over twice as long as the traditionalists – having to argue harder to establish a reasoned case. But the general effect was one of scrupulous balance: the greater number of traditionalist letters being 'balanced' by the fact that critics' letters were often printed first. One letter, fully within the traditionalist perspective, added a theme which may have underlain others taking a similar position, but which was rarely openly expressed. It simply said: 'surely the English in their homeland are entitled to protection against such thugs as this boy'. 'In their homeland' is a specially nice touch, in view of the fact that, for good or ill, England was Paul Storey's 'homeland' too.

PRIVATE–PUBLIC CHANNELS: THE ABUSIVES

The next group of letters takes us to the boundary between 'private' and 'public' discourse, and permits us a brief, selective glimpse into the 'underworld' of public opinion. These were the abusive letters sent at the time of the Handsworth affair. They were, of course, 'private' in the sense that they were personally addressed, *not* transmitted in a public medium. Thus they may be thought to fall outside the network of public communications. On the other hand, they expressed 'public' rather than private sentiments; they were from people who are not known to the recipient – indeed, most of them were deliberately anonymous. They were not intended to form the basis of an exchange or a relationship – for example, they clearly did not anticipate a reply. There is good evidence for saying that they were 'private' only because they contained attitudes too violent or language too abusive for public taste. It is *this* fact essentially – their extremism – which switched them into the private channel. 'The work of cranks', 'the lunatic fringe' are two common dismissive responses to such letters. Our aim is to demonstrate two things: first, the abusive letters contained some attitudes which were *not* expressed in 'letters to the editor'; second, and more important, many attitudes in the 'abusives' were *transformations* of attitudes widely held but expressed in more restrained ways in the public correspondence.

Indeed, the transformation referred to was often only formal. Abusive letters are written 'person to person' rather than 'citizen to fellow-citizen'. A different tone is to be expected in the move from public to private discourse – and this indeed is what we find. The more difficult question is the extent to which private and public letters, though different in form, language and tone, nevertheless represent different points along *the same* spectrum of public opinion as was found in 'letters to the editor': expressions in which the same 'lay ideologies' were operative. A significant number of the 'abusives' did go far beyond the limits that the 'citizen in the public forum' accepted for himself. And this might lead us to think that the two channels were quite distinct. Abusive letters would then indicate the existence of systems of meaning quite separate from those available to the society of 'reasonable' readers and writers whom the media address. The public media, however, do not in any sense reflect the full scale of social discourse. The social communication through which public opinion is formed consists of everything, from conversations between neighbours, discussion at street-corners or in the pub, rumour, gossip, speculation, 'inside dope', debate between members of the family at home, expressions of opinions and views in private meetings, and so on, all the way up to the more formal levels, with which the mass media intersect. The organising of 'public opinion' takes place at *all* these levels of social interchange. The idea that the mass media, because of their massive coverage, their linking of different publics, their unilateral power in the communications situation, therefore wholly absorb and obliterate all other, more informal and face-to-face levels of social discourse, is not tenable. We must therefore examine these 'private' letters as excluded or *displaced* portions of the social 'talk process', in which *ordinary* people figure.

The question then arises: from what source do these more 'extreme' attitudes to crime arise? They are not simply irrational. As we hope to show, a certain rationality or 'logic' is clearly also present in these letters. Most abusive letters assume that there is a wider public there which – had it read the letters – would no doubt agree with what is being said, even if it would not 'go so far'. Abusive-letter writers assume the invisible presence of this 'public', not only in the empirical sense ('many people do agree with me') but also in a more normative sense ('people *should* agree with me; after all, its obvious that since P and Q then X and Y follow'). In other words, despite their private form, they remain – paradoxically – embedded in and draw upon a social and 'public' discourse about crime. The 'lunatic fringe' and the 'crank' are, in this sense, not to be dismissed as eccentric as some may be tempted to do. In any case, the line which sometimes separates private and public obsessiveness is not as clear cut as is suggested, and can be hard to draw when one is working from the evidence of the written text alone. When events or issues touch a public nerve on the raw, powerfully obsessive feelings and ideas can be 'domesticated' enough to find expression in the public domain; and, even when not prepared to go fully 'public', they may form the real basis of actions and influence what people feel and think.

Thirty letters of an abusive kind were received by Paul Storey's mother and two of a sympathetic kind. The proportions can be explained by reference to widespread values in society, of which the comments in the press give us some indication. While there was disagreement over the sentences given to the boys, there was universal condemnation of their crime. The features of the crime reported in the press corresponded to a model of crime widely detested and feared. The boys were pictured as archetypal violent criminals: merciless, cold-blooded in pursuit of gain, yet prepared to heap seemingly gratuitous violence on a lone and eventually defenceless innocent man. This picture provided the premise for many of the letters.

Ten of the thirty fell in the category of 'the reasonable citizen writing privately' to the boy's mother (who had been featured in the press coverage of the crime). We examine these first. We have called them 'retributivist' – they all clearly demand that the law must exact retribution from the criminal for his actions. This category of writer certainly overlaps with *one* category of press letters:

> How dare you say your son isn't bad? He has stolen cars and is a layabout. What about the man whose whole life has been ruined by his wickedness? He deserves to be locked away from decent people, and you are probably partly to blame. Go back to Jamaica.

This kind of letter was characteristic in its speech-forms. The 'bad' identity of Paul Storey was *fixed* in a simple, graphic, stereotypical way. 'Layabout' was probably derived from press reports that he had been unemployed: the unemployed = layabout = scrounger = bad equation is a common one in conservative social ideology. The cry, 'what about the victim?', now extremely active, directs attention back to the gravity of the offence. The moralising chain of words pulls together the theme of 'moral degeneracy well punished': bad-wickedness-deserves-blame. The only moderation is in the idea that the mother is only 'partly' to blame. The final sentence picks up the 'homeland' idea quoted at the end of the previous section; but here the nation is firmly identified with the 'moral community', from which both Storey and his mother are ritually expelled. (This is of course *wholly* symbolic: Storey was not born in Jamaica, and his mother is white.) The conception of moral indignation and retributive justice informing this letter is crystal clear from its whole moral structure. It sounds extreme because of its clarity, condensation, its abruptness and lack of qualifications. But, in content, it stands firmly *within an accepted public ideology of crime and punishment*.

This type of letter-writer is likely to believe that extra measures (in addition to the sentence) should in justice be taken against the offender. Corporal punishment or an extended sentence was often recommended. But all such recommendations stopped short of thoroughly extreme or repulsive violence. They did not advocate the death penalty nor did they go far beyond what the judiciary itself might be thought capable of recommending, or indeed in some cases had recommended in the comparatively recent past. The writers thus remained within the circle of what we might call 'acceptable extremism'.

One writer, a widow, evidently from Birmingham, incorporated such an appeal for discipline and vengeance in an account of her own experience at the hands of a mugger, 'a Boy 16 years old':

> He kicked me to the ground into the ground, [sic] and would have killed me if he had not got my bag. I wonder if it was *your son* who did this to me, and you have the damn cheek to say 20 years [is] too much. What would you do if your son was the one who was left to die, I bet you would soon cry for vengeance. You don't know what it is like to be beaten up and robbed in the city while your children are waiting for you to come home. This city is getting that you cannot go out after dark. You are afraid to visit your friends in case you will never get back home. If I had my way the cat of nine tails should be brought back and whip everyone of them and then lock them up. You should get 20 years with him and your worry is over.... You ask the C.I.D. in Steele House Lane [sic] the state I was in, a *Woman*.

Here a whole, clearly terrifying personal experience of violent assault was mobilised behind the indictment of the mother of the offender (there was also a passing reference to a daughter who had had a serious accident), and found its correlative in the judgement that 'he should get 100 years and lashed across the backside also'. Again, all the elements of the picture of a crisis of 'crime in the streets' were present here. The same was true of another example: 'We are afraid to go out in the evening in London. We have our clubs to go to and are afraid to go out.... If we didn't have our police, what would it be like? The swines, they are better off inside.' Both letters, as well as expressions of genuine anxiety (the second is signed 'Pensioner from Bethnal Green'), pulled on a very vivid public definition of mugging: streets infested with violent hoodlums, the police a bulwark against the breakdown of law-abiding society. Again, though somewhat extreme in their language, they shared, with many 'letters to the editor' and press editorials, a picture of society as crime-ridden, followed by an appeal to 'bring back the birch'. Correlatively, eighteen letters of the total sample displayed a strong concern for the *victim's* suffering, a feeling legitimised by the same tight moral structure.

Other letters, on the margins of respectability, invoked *capital* punishment as a suitable method of dealing with the offender in this case. One of these gave an extremely clear insight into the mechanics of a retributive definition of crime:

> *The victim who counts the cost*
> Mr. Keenan thanks to your son is now unable to follow his occupation – and you ask for mercy. What mercy did your son show Mr. Keenan – NONE. Therefore your son must pay the penalty.

We can see here how the ideas of 'cost' and 'payment' were used to organise the definition of crime and punishment, which was interpreted through a notion of 'equal exchange': no mercy to victim, *therefore* no mercy to the offender; violence to one, violence to the other. The writer added – in a tone reminiscent of the judiciary during the 'mugging' panic: 'Society will not stand for muggings.' This particular letter was set out in a self-conscious and symmetrical way, with capital letters, headings and deliberate spacing of the lines; two colours of type were used. A newspaper photograph of Paul Storey had been affixed to the paper. This obsessive care in 'making an appropriate impact' was a feature of the more extreme kind of letter. It concluded:

HE SHOULD HAVE BEEN ... HANGED!

Some letters seem to belong more appropriately to a category of subterranean rather than near-public viewpoints. These were *exclusively* concerned with the racial aspect of the case. A writer from Liverpool began: 'So you are shattered, pity about you.' The two boys, Storey and Fuat, were described as 'niggers'. The writer went on: 'by her name the woman who has 12 kids is an alien too, an R.C., she should be in Southern Ireland and you and the nigs and pakis back in the Jungle.' This kind of open racism allowed the writer to construct an interpretation which excluded all other issues. The stereotyped associations here became indiscriminate: almost any 'alien' attribute – 'niggers', 'R.C.', 'Southern Ireland', 'Pakis' – will serve. These labels were then linked to a political analysis which was also by no means unfamiliar: 'The 3 of them have no rights in this country, just living off the Welfare State. Oh for Enoch Powell to clear the lot of you, back to your own land. You know where you are well off.' In this part of the letter, the violent racial–alien epithets have been transmuted into a more 'acceptable' form, since the assertion of the rights of the 'native born' could be presented as a national not a racist concern, once the out-group had been defined as alien, with their 'own land'. It is not suprising that, in this scenario, the alien should be associated with the archetypal deviant – the lazy layabout being kept by the Welfare State. The idea that 'nigs' and the 'Pakis' live off the Welfare State is one of the commonest ideas now in the lexicon of racism. Another of these racist letters bore a signature with a vague address, the only one of its kind. None of the three advocated, within our terms, an exceptionally brutal punishment. We should note that twelve writers in all brought in the question of race, though it was a theme discerned less commonly in the 'reasonable' letters.

These letters, with their racist structure, bring us to the edge of the more extreme group of abusive letters, which we call 'super-retributivist' or 'revengist', either because of the level of abuse they contained or because of the exceptionally brutal punishments they recommended. They shared with the 'racist' letters the tendency to abuse the mother; and this involved the mobilisation of subterranean racial–sexual themes – accusations of sexual promiscuity, over-large families, miscegenation, and so on.

There were two fully 'extreme' letters which set all these themes in, again, a purely racialist context. Eight letters of this general 'revengist' type advocated forms of execution to get rid of the offender, including two who wished to see Paul Storey lynched. There were two recommendations that he be castrated and one that his mother be sterilised for her 'crime' in giving birth to him. Other methods of punishment included: daily corporal punishment and 'smashing in' Paul Storey's face. Another correspondent, presumably recalling the treatment of Mr Keenan, suggested that every week the offender by struck in the face with a brick. One writer suggested that Paul Storey's body be finally thrown in the Thames. By contrast 'retributivists' mentioned life sentences or a judicial equivalent more often.

The 'revengists' presented their subjects in abusively stereotypical terms: 'thug', 'vermin', 'animal', 'scum', 'bastard', etc. These labels invite us to envisage the offenders as 'beyond the pale', i.e. *so* wicked that 'normal' punishments are rendered irrelevant and even dangerous. The violence of the language used to describe criminal and crime served to *legitimate* the correspondents' crossing of the boundary from tough but legal retribution to sadistic vengeance.

In these letters particular wicked acts appeared as but a token of their perpetrators' basically *evil nature*. Like vermin, they were *naturally*, not humanly, dangerous. Thus they must be dealt with by absolute measures. For some writers the only human touch they retained was that they could be held responsible for what they did. For instance, two of the writers hoped that Paul Storey might 'rot in hell'. This notion helped to bring him back into the realm of humanity, but only in a limited and inauthentic sense. A more grim morality informed the hope of six writers that Paul Storey would die during his prison sentence. It was hoped that Nature will come to the aid of 'justice'. One writer's opinion that the offender's mother be sterilised for giving birth to him becomes intelligible in the context of an ideology that considers him in some literal way an abnormal 'monster' – 'vermin'. Another writer felt that the boy's mother should be destroyed for 'spawning' him.

Here we must notice how crime has been transformed into a theory of evil human nature – made tangible in the images of the abnormal and monstrous. Condensed in, and adding powerful weight to, these images are themes of race and degraded sexuality – and their outcomes are to be found in the demands for brutalised and sadistic punishments. This unpleasant triad – race, sexuality and sadism – have, as the work of the Frankfurt School and others have shown us,[9] formed the deep-structure of the 'authoritarian personality'. More importantly, this deep-structure also underpins the more displaced (and therefore publicly acceptable) themes and images of *other* letters we have seen. The transmutation from this triadic basis to its 'more acceptable' expression in the call for discipline, the tendency to scapegoat, the drive for remoralisation and the rigidity of stereotyping is as alarming as the unmodified expressions in the letters we have just considered. We can see some of these elements of abnormality, sexuality and the rigid commitment to stern measures in this next extract:

So you are going to appeal against the sentence you shameless . . .; his conduct is a tribute to the bringing up you gave him. I hope he never comes out alive: it's men like Mr Justice Croom Johnstone [sic] we need in this country, God bless him. We can do without your half cast bastard with his evil eyes and murderer's forehead. I am a good judge of character, he was born to kill. If I was in prison I would consider it a great insult to live cheek by jowl with the likes of him. I hope they will bring back the hanging [sic]. In

America a mob would surround the jail and lynch him. Don't worry about your bastard, but the victim, poor man.

This letter contains what we might think of as every theme in the lexicon of revenge, as well as representing a 'structure of thought' very close indeed to the 'authoritarian' one, identified by Reich, Adorno and others. It also recapitulates themes sounded in a more fragmented form in other letters of the same kind. The style is fundamentally a demotic one, just emerging from speech. It projects acute hostility against Paul Storey's mother. It attributes his conduct to her faulty rearing of him. It unashamedly – and deferentially – identifies with the authority figure of the judge, and in a specially 'traditionalist' manner ('God bless him'). In the next sentence it links race ('half caste'), sexuality ('bastard'), with the criminal ('murderer') – and it defines them all in abnormal, monstrous and non-human terms. In so doing it also places itself squarely within the tradition of Lombrosean biological positivism – that is, it takes these monstrosities as forms of 'un-natural' (not human) perversion, fixed in the biological–criminal type once and for all; and it claims to be able to detect and read this type in terms of its genetic and physical characteristics ('evil eyes . . . and murderer's forehead'). Finally, it calls, first, for the extreme legal sanction – hanging – then *passes beyond* this to fantasy mob violence, the lynching. Both are predicated on a reference to 'the victim, poor man', with its typically sentimental cadence.

A number of themes in the 'revengist' letters connect with ones expressed in a more moderate form in both the public and the 'retributive' abusive letters. For example, several letters rejected the environmentalist or 'sociological' explanation of the crime: 'Your son got what he deserved. . . . You cannot blame the area, it must be the way he was brought up.' Or: 'Your classic response of blaming his area for his degeneracy is a lot of crap. Your son should die and his soul rot in hell.' Motives were not frequently discussed, though one 'retributive' letter which brought in the motive of 'fun' also gave a clearly voluntaristic account of the crime: 'they knew what they were doing'. A 'revengist' letter echoed the same theme: 'he knew what he was doing'. But fundamentally, motives remained irrelevant because to the writers it was transparent that 'evil is evil'. There was a striking absence of any argued defence of the sentence, in anything like the clear and explicit terms we found in the 'letters to the editor'. The deterrent value of severe punishment, which appeared again and again in the public correspondence, hardly surface in the private letters – there were only three brief references.

Finally, we must note the recurrence in these letters of certain fundamental 'root-concepts' or images. They are fundamental because they stand for basic, bed-rock sentiments and certainties about the world in which their authors live. They are not solely restricted to the private letters – but appear more forcibly here in the context of the more immediate, less publicly structured, form of address. We shall consider these more fully later, but we point briefly here to the centrality in all of them, of the *family*. This theme constantly recurs in terms of its centrality in the bringing up of the child – the 'normal' family produces 'normal' children; therefore it *must* have taken an abnormal family to produce the 'monster'. This connects with the other themes – *race* and *sexuality* – which we noted earlier: a half-caste boy, whose mother is living with a man who is not the boy's father provide the raw material for those who 'understand' how 'monsters' are 'spawned'.

A personal letter is a written form of communication which is predicated either on intimacy or recognition. Either it attempts to recreate an immediate stream of 'speech' from writer to reader; or it anticipates a response. Its force springs from its personal tone, its informality of tone and address. It is always signed, often with friendship or affection. It opens or continues a relationship, through the exchange of the written word. Personal *abusive* letters are shocking precisely because they open this avenue of direct address and reciprocity – but only to abuse and exploit it; they insinuate, along channels exposed to receive a greeting, instead, a venomous abuse. Most of them are anonymous. They invoke a form of reciprocity, which their anonymity then refuses. The source of the abuse remains unseen, unidentified, mysterious, unlocatable. They therefore carry with them an overtone of menace. It is their 'refusal of sociality', as much as their extremity of language and feeling, which constitutes the measure of their 'abuse'.

PUBLIC OPINION AND IDEOLOGY

Looking at a local crime in its local setting, and reading both the local and the private correspondence, gives us some insight into the maze of communicative channels which support the formation of *public opinion*. Many of these lie, in the first instance, outside the formal channels of the public media altogether. Yet these 'informal' channels of public opinion should not be neglected. In a locality as dense, socially, and as complex, ethnically and politically, as Handsworth, such 'informal' channels are thick on the ground. The interplay of knowledge, rumours, folk-lore and opinions constitutes a critical, and primary, level at which opinion begins to shape up about an event as dramatic as the 'mugging' of a local resident, long before the media appropriate it. In the days immediately following the Handsworth 'mugging', the locality was full of rumour, 'informal news' and views. Only a small proportion of this found its way into the local press, in the form either of 'letters to the editor', or of local witnesses and local experts called on by the media to express a view. Already such opinions are framed by interpretation, shaped by common-sense views and received wisdom about crime. Opinion, however, cannot remain long at this informal or disorganised level. The very actions of the control culture, and of the media, in mapping the event into society-wide perspectives and contexts serve to raise the threshold of public opinion. Local communication channels are swiftly and selectively integrated into more public channels.

The crystallising of 'public opinion' is thus raised to a more formal and public level by the networks of the mass media. It is true that, in societies like ours, individuals often live highly segmented lives, embedded in local traditions and networks. But it is also true that, precisely in such societies, the networks which *connect* are pivotal. Events and issues only become *public* in the full sense when the means exist whereby the relatively 'separate worlds' of professional and lay opinion, of controller and controlled, are brought into relation with one another, and appear, for a time at least, to occupy the same space. It is communication and communication networks that *create* that complex creature we call 'public opinion'. In monitoring the passage of the Handsworth case through the media, we are at the same time watching the process by which public opinion is formed; and specifically, the process by which crime ascends into the public arena and assumes the form of a 'public issue'.

'Public opinion' about crime does not simply form up at random. It exhibits a shape and structure. It follows a sequence. It is a social process, not a mystery. Even at the lowest threshold of visibility – in talk, in rumour, in the exchange of quick views and common-sense judgements – crime talk is not socially innocent; already it is informed and penetrated by the lay opinions and ideologies *about* crime as a public topic. The more such an issue passes into the public domain, via the media, the more it is structured by the dominant ideologies about crime. It is these which form the infrastructure of any public debate. The more a crime issues on to the public stage, the more highly structured it becomes, the more constrained by the available frameworks of understanding and interpretation, the more socially validated feelings, emotions and attitudes are mobilised around it. Thus the more public – the more of a public issue – a topic becomes, the more we can detect the presence of larger networks of meaning and feeling about it; the more we can discern the presence of a highly structured, though by no means complete, or coherent, or internally consistent, set of *ideologies about crime*. It is these which concern us in the following chapter.

In Chapter 3 ('The Social Production of News') we looked at one of the major sources of knowledge and interpretation about crime in our society: that critical intersection between the courts and the media. Without falling into a conspiratorial reading of this link, we suggested how and why the intimate connection between the sources of crime news (the courts and the control culture) and the means of public dissemination (the media) served powerfully to structure and mould public knowledge about crime, and at the same time to inflect that understanding with 'dominant interpretations'. This is a powerful, indeed a determining source in the analysis of how public opinion is formed; and in what follows we should not forget how powerfully the so-called 'conversation' by means of which public opinion is supposed to arise is structured by its institutional sources – how much, that is, 'public opinion' is something 'structured in dominance'. In Chapter 4 ('Balancing Accounts') we looked, via the particular instance of the Handsworth case, at what then happens when a particularly dramatic piece of crime news is appropriated and processed by the mass media (in this instance, by the press). Here we observed several stages in a process which serves to further construct and elaborate a crime topic. In particular we examined, not only the differences in ideological inflection between one paper and another, but the different structures of interpretation accreting around the topic at the different points in the process: its primary-news construction; its passage into the domain of exploration and explanation – the domain of 'second-order' news or feature treatment; its passage into the domain of judgement – the arena of the editorial statement. In this chapter, we followed that process through further, in the particular case of Handsworth, to the letters. But 'letters' provide a sort of tip-over point in our examination. For here – in both 'letters to the editor' and in the private abusives – we encounter, at last, public opinion beginning to come back the opposite way, *up* the channels of private and local 'news' *into* the domain of public opinion. Without forgetting for a moment how subject this apparently 'spontaneous' swell of public opinion about the Handsworth crime from below was to the shaping power of those institutional forces discussed earlier, it is of crucial importance to note *the character and forms of the 'response from the lay public' which crime news awakens.* For it is the awakening of lay public attitudes, and their crystallising in forms which underpin and support the viewpoints already in circulation, which help to close the consensual circle, providing the lynch-pin of legitimation.

Now, exactly what is involved in this apparently spontaneous *rendezvous* of dominant interpretations passing down and 'public opinion' passing up? The nature of this 'circle' is something we examine in the following chapter. But it is not quite the spontaneous, miraculous process it at first appears to be. For a moment, let us consider only the *forms* in which this seemingly spontaneous public opinion is arising. At first, expressions of 'lay attitudes' to crime *appear* altogether different in form from those which are being transmitted and constructed higher up in the chain of communication. As against splash headlines, full-page features, lengthy quotes, expert examinations, we have here, brief, personal 'letters to the editor'; as opposed to weighty whispers and conversation in high places, we have the furtively scribbled, shame-facedly delivered, abusive missive. But, if we look again, below the variety of surface forms, to the more generative level, we discover the presence of ideological structures, which might hitherto have escaped our attention. At each stage – in the courts, in the news, in the editorial judgements, in the letters, in the abusives – despite their many and significant differences, a familiar lexicon appears to be at work, informing the discourse. The same, very limited *repertoire* of premises, frameworks, and interpretations appear to be drawn upon whenever the topic of crime and punishment has to be deployed. The differences must not be expunged. The police speak one way about street crime – the language of crime control and containment; the courts cast it a different way – in the language and idiom of judicial reasoning and motive. The opinions expressed by different experts are strongly inflected by their respective professional worlds and outlooks; even there, the 'social-work' perspective of the professions of social care differs from the 'pathological' perspective of the criminologist, that of the local community worker from the local councillor. When we pass into the media, differences are, again, significant: the *Daily Telegraph* and the *Guardian* do not pass by the same route when seeking to explain crime; features exist, one might almost say, to take up angles which news did not exhaust. Again, when we look at letters, differences, both between lay and professional letter-writers, or between public and private letters, are apparent. In any account which attempts to 'map' the public ideologies of crime, these differentiations must be taken into account. We insist that, so far as we can tell, there is no such thing as a single, coherent, unified, consistent English 'public ideology of crime' (in the singular) which we have been able to discover. On the other hand, we also insist that the very different forms and explanations about crime, whose differences seem overwhelming at the phenomenal levels of their appearance, *seem to be generated by a far more limited set of ideological paradigms.* By 'paradigms' here, we mean the themes, premises, assumptions, the 'questions presuming answers', the matrix of ideas, through which the variety of public 'opinions' about crime take coherent form. It is to this structured field of ideological premises that we now turn. What are the deep-structure paradigms about crime in our society? What are *the English ideologies of crime?*

6
Explanations and Ideologies of Crime

In looking at the 'English ideologies of crime' we want to consider more fully certain points touched on earlier and give them more sustained attention than was possible while dealing with the specific elements of the public reaction to the Handsworth case. The first of these is the 'cluster' of recurrent themes and images in the letters about the Handsworth case – a cluster organised, we suggested, around questions of the family, discipline and morality in relation to crime. Second, since these occurred within what we termed the 'traditionalist' view of crime (in opposition to the 'liberal' perspective), we wish to look at some of the roots of this 'traditionalist' world-view. Most importantly, since the division between the 'traditional' and 'liberal' views both *organised and formed the limits of* the public discussion of crime at each of the levels of discourse which we considered (in the various aspects of the press, and in the public and private letters), we wish to give some attention to the 'explanations and ideologies' underpinning these perspectives. Specifically, we intend to attempt to answer a number of questions. What are the conditions under which these themes and images of the traditionalist position are reproduced across the various circuits of public opinion? How, in a complex, divided and structured society, does the traditionalist perspective come to exert such a powerful appeal on *both sides* of the lines of structuration? Why, in a society which since the late 1960s has been increasingly polarised economically and politically along class lines, should the same social and moral perspective on crime address, and be carried with such apparent unanimity, by different classes? Why should traditionalism be the dominant form of an apparent *cross-class consensus* on crime? Finally, how does the traditionalist perspective come to hold the dominance over the liberal position which we have seen it did in the debate about the Handsworth sentences?

The first part of this chapter, then, is an attempt to identify what the organising elements of this *traditionalist consensus* are, and how they come to be mobilised around the question of crime. In the final part of the chapter, we shall return to the relation between the traditionalist and the liberal perspectives on crime, and consider the apparent failure of the liberal position to 'generalise' itself across society.

IMAGES OF SOCIETY

We begin by attempting to unpack some of the core images which seem to us to form central elements in the 'traditionalist' ideology of crime. Gouldner once argued that all social theories contain 'domain assumptions' about society embedded in them. We would argue that all social ideologies contain powerful images of society at their heart. These images may be diffuse, quite untheorised in any elaborate sense; but they serve to condense and order the view of society in which the ideologies are active, and they constitute both its unquestioned substratum of truth — what carries conviction — and the source of its collective emotional force and appeal. Together, these images produce and sustain an uncodified but immensely powerful, conservative *sense of Englishness*, of an English 'way of life', of an 'English' viewpoint which — it also, by its very density of reference, asserts — *everyone* shares to some extent. We do not make any claim to offer here an exhaustive inventory of this traditional English ideology, only to have identified some of the major images around which this traditionalist definition of 'Englishness' is constructed and organised. Our aim here is to open a discussion which we regard as of considerable importance, and to touch on two related but distinct aspects. First, can we begin to identify the social content which is being carried in these images, around which a traditionalist view of crime is organised? Second, can we begin to make sense of its power to generalise itself across social and class divisions — its claims to 'universality'? The traditionalist ideology is not the only active ideology in society by any means; but it is a *dominant* ideological field. And this dominance, and its claims to general representativeness, are connected. It is dominant because it appears to be able to *catch up* quite contradictory life and class experiences within its master framework. Ideologies are easier to understand when they seem, within their own logic, to reflect or adequately correspond to the experiences, positions and interests of those who hold them. But though ideologies do include this practical relation, they cannot be wholly explained in this way; indeed, when we speak of the practical social role of ideologies, we are speaking of the power of ideologies to translate into convincing ideological terms the outlooks of classes and groups who are not, even in a collective sense, its 'authors'. So we are also concerned here with what it is in the social and material condition of subordinate classes which allows the dominant traditionalist ideologies to gain some real purchase, and to carry conviction, to win support. How is this traditionalist ideological 'unity' constructed out of disparate and contradictory class formations? How does *this* version of 'the English way of life' provide the basis of ideological consensus?

We turn, first, to the notion of *respectability* — at once, so different for different social classes, and yet so 'universal' a social value. It is an extremely complex social idea. It touches the fundamental notion of self-respect: men who do not respect themselves cannot expect respect from others. But respectability also touches the more 'protestant' values of our culture; it is connected with thrift, self-discipline, living the decent life, and thus with observance of what is commonly held to be upright, decent conduct. It is strongly connected with ideas of self-help and self-reliance, and of 'conformity' to established social standards — standards set and embodied by 'significant others'.

The 'others' are always those who rank and stand above us in the social hierarchy: people we 'look up to', and in turn respect. The idea of respectability means that we have taken care not to fall into the abyss, not to lose out in the competitive struggle for existence. In the middle classes, the idea of 'respectability' carries with it the powerful overtones of competitive success; its token is the ability to 'keep up appearances', to secure a standard of life which enables you to afford those things which befit – and embody – your social station in life. But in the working classes, it is connected with three, different ideas: with work, with poverty, and with crime in the broad sense. It is *work*, above all, which is the guarantee of respectability; for work is the means – the only means – to the respectable life. The idea of the 'respectable working classes' is irretrievably associated with regular, and often skilled, employment. It is labour which has disciplined the working class *into* respectability. Loss of respectability is therefore associated with loss of occupation and with poverty. *Poverty* is the trap which marks the slide away from respectability back into the 'lower depths'. The distinction between the 'respectable' and the 'rough' working class, though in no sense an accurate sociological or historical one, remains an extremely important *moral* distinction. If poverty is one route downwards out of the respectable life, *crime* or moral misconduct is another, broader and more certain route. Respectability is the collective internalisation, by the lower orders, of an image of the 'ideal life' held out for them by those who stand higher in the scheme of things; it disciplines society from end to end, rank by rank. Respectability is therefore one of the key values which dovetails and inserts one social class into the social image of another class. It is part of what Gramsci called the 'cement' of society.

Work is not only the guarantee of working-class respectability, it is also a powerful image in its own right. We know how much our social and indeed personal identities are caught up with our work, and how men (*especially* men, given the sexual division of labour) who are without work, feel not only materially abandoned but spiritually de-centred.[1] We know in fact that this is the product of an extremely long and arduous process of historical acculturation: all that is involved in the erection, alongside the birth of capitalism, of the Protestant Ethic, and all that was involved in the insertion of the labouring industrial masses into the rigorous disciplines of factory labour.[2] Work has gradually come to be regarded more as 'instrumental' than as 'sacred', as manual labour under capitalism is disciplined by the wage contract; leisure, or rather all that is associated with non-work and with the private sphere, has come to rank even higher than once it did in the hierarchy of social goods, as family and home have been progressively distanced from work. Yet, for men above all, the workaday world of work, and the formal and informal values associated with it, seem in many ways coterminous with the definition of 'reality' itself. And this, though endowed with extremely powerful ideological content reflects a material fact: without work, the material basis of our lives would vanish overnight. What matters here, with respect to crime, however, is not so much the centrality of work, and our feelings about it, as what we might call the *calculus of work*. The calculus of work implies the belief that, though work may have few intrinsic rewards and is unlikely to lead to wealth, prosperity and riches for the vast majority, it provides one of the stable negotiated bases of our economic existence: a 'fair day's wage for a fair day's work'. It also entails the belief that the valued things − leisure, pleasure, security, free activity, play − are a *reward* for the diligent application to long-term productive goals through work.[3] The former come after, and as the result of, or recompense for, the latter.

Of course, some professional crime could, technically, be seen as 'work' of a kind, and there are certainly testimonies by professional criminals which would support such an interpretation. But few people would see it that way. The sharpest distinction is made between the professional or organised life of crime, and the petty pilfering and 'borrowing' from one's place of work, which is regarded as a customary way of setting a fundamentally exploitative economic relation to right, and is thus not understood as 'crime' in the ordinary sense at all. Crime, in the proper sense, when involving robbery or rackets for gain, is set off *against* work in the public mind, precisely because it is an attempt to acquire by speed, stealth, fraudulent or shorthand methods what the great majority of law-abiding citizens can only come by through arduous toil, routine, expenditure of time, and the postponement of pleasure. It is through this contrast that some of the most powerful moral feelings come to be transferred against deviants who thrive and prosper, but do not work. One of the most familiar ways in which the moral calculus of work is recruited into attitudes to social problems is in the way people talk about 'scroungers', 'layabouts', those who 'don't do a stroke' or 'live off the Welfare'. The characterisations are often applied indiscriminately, and without much evidence, to various 'out-groups': the poor, the unemployed, the irresponsible and feckless − but also youth, students and black people. These are seen as getting something without 'putting anything into it'. The image implies instant moral condemnation. At the same time it is important to remember that again, a real, objective, material reality is distortedly expressed in these negative images of the 'scrounger' and the layabout. For the vast majority of working people, there is absolutely no other route to a minimal degree of security and material comfort apart from the life-long commitment to 'hard graft'. It must be remembered that this feeling that 'everyone should earn what he gets by working for it' also informs working-class feelings about the very wealthy, or those who live on unearned incomes, or accumulate large pieces of property, or about the unequal distribution of wealth. There is evidence that what is sometimes called a 'pragmatic acceptance' of the present unequal distribution of wealth is matched by an equally strong feeling that there is something intrinsically wrong and exploitative about it. So sentiments stemming from the prevailing 'work calculus' have their progressive aspect too,[4] though they are often used to underpin root conservative attitudes to all who transgress it.

Another social image with special importance for public ideologies of crime has to do with the need for social *discipline* − and with England as a disciplined society. Once again, there are different versions of this very general social idea across the different class cultures; the idea is interpreted and applied differently within different cultural systems of meaning, while retaining sufficient common elements to appear to carry a more universal validity. The idea of a 'disciplined society' is enshrined in popular mythology – the whole nation 'at prayer' having been long ago supplanted by the whole nation in an orderly queue. It is especially strong at those high points of popular history, like 'the War', where a country of free individuals 'pulled itself together' to defeat the enemy. The 'discipline' of English society is not the rigorously organised tyranny of the bureaucratic or regimented state, but that 'self-discipline', flexible yet tenacious, which holds the nation together from the inside when it is under stress. In the English ideology, 'discipline' is always linked and qualified by an opposing tendency which tempers its authoritarian harshness: in the upper classes, the idea of discipline and anarchism (as caricatured, for example, in the roles played by John Cleese in the television comedy series, *Monty Python's Flying Circus*). Lower down the social scale, discipline is often qualified by the image of a sort of petty-bourgeois 'anarchy' (as, for example, in post-war Ealing comedies or *Dad's Army*). However, the capacity of popular mythology to counter or qualify the respect for 'social discipline' in these ways does not mean that it is not a strong sentiment – only that it is held, like so many other traditional social values, in a peculiarly British way, and with a very special English sense of irony.

Nevertheless, the appeal to 'discipline' draws on very different roots in the different class cultures. In the middle-class context, it means or includes self-reliance, self-making, self-control, the self-sacrifice for long-term goals and the competitive struggle which alone yields rewards for the individual and his family. More generally, it means the disciplined giving of deference to *authority*, the expectation of obedience from those over whom authority is exercised, the *responsible* discharge of that authority, and so on. Discipline means something different amongst many working-class people, where it has more to do with the practice of thrift – making do – in the face of adversity, the self-sacrifices necessary to maintain the collective nature of social life and organised efforts against the odds. Transgression of the idea of discipline therefore means different things in these different class contexts.

The traditional idea of social discipline is closely linked, on the one hand, with notions about *hierarchy* and *authority*. Society is hierarchical, in the dominant view, by nature. Competitive success may promote individuals up through this hierarchy, but does not destroy the notion of a hierarchical order itself. But the hierarchy, in turn, depends upon the giving and taking of authority. And the exercise of authority, both on the part of those who exercise it, and of those who give obedience to it, requires discipline. This trinity – the hierarchical nature of society, the importance of authority and the acclimatisation of the people to both through self-discipline – forms a central complex of attitudes. In this version of the dominant social image, indiscipline is seen as a threat both to the hierarchical conception of the social order and to the exercise of 'due authority' and deference; it is thus the beginnings, the seed-bed, of social anarchy. (The failure to adhere to traditionally sanctioned working-class codes of conduct and solidarity, on the other hand, threatens, not the social order itself, but rather the *local* order – of class, neighbourhood, family, group – generated from below by 'sub-cultural' definitions of right conduct.) Hence, in traditional usage, 'youth' may be condemned as much for its lack of respect as for its technical delinquency; for whereas the latter is an infringement of the rules, the former unpicks the cement provided by authority and deference which binds rebellious youth to the social order. We must stress, here, that contrary to the much-popularised idea that large tracts of the working classes are deferential to authority in all its concrete social detail, the ascription to a hierarchical social order entailed in the dominant idea of social discipline is quite *abstract*, contrary to real experience and therefore riven with contradictory feelings among working-class people. One study of traditionalism and conservatism in English political cultures reaches the not-unexpected conclusion that:

> On the one hand there is consensus across all classes and party groups on dominant values, elites and institutions at the symbolic level . . . on the other hand . . . disaffection and dissensus is particularly marked in the subordinate classes who . . . have confused and ambivalent attitudes towards the dominant social, economic and political order. [5]

(The discipline of working-class organisation, struggle and defence has, of course, quite different roots. It is pitched *against* this traditionalist definition of 'social discipline'.)

The other side of 'social discipline' is perhaps more relevant to traditionalist public sentiments about crime. This is the fact that in English culture the preferred forms of discipline are all *internalised*: they are forms of *self*-discipline, *self*-control. They depend on all those institutions and processes which establish the internal self-regulating mechanisms of control: guilt, conscience, obedience and super-ego. The exercise of self-discipline within this perspective has as much to do with *emotional* control (and thus with sexual repression, the taboo on pleasure, the regulation of the feelings) as it does with *social* control (the taking over of the 'morale' of society, the preparation for work and the productive life, the postponement of gratifications in the service of thrift and accumulation). It follows that the three social image clusters we have so far discussed – *respectability, work* and *discipline* – are inextricably connected with the fourth image: that of *the family*.

In the traditionalist lexicon, the sphere of the *family* is of course where moral-social compulsions and inner controls are generated, as well as the sphere where the primary socialisation of the young is first tellingly and intimately carried through. The first aspect has to do with the repression and regulation of sexuality – the seat of pleasure – in the family nexus; and thus with authority. The second has to do with the power which the family has, through its intimate exchanges of love and anger, punishment and reward, and the structure of patriarchy, to prepare children for a competitive existence, work and the sexual division of labour. The *family*, too, is a complex social image; different forms, functions and habits may be found in the different social classes. Thus the structures of sexual identity and repression within the working-class family, though in some respects reproducing the dominant structures of sex roles in the organisation of the family, are also profoundly shaped by the material experiences of the class – the construction of practices and a definition of 'masculinity' and masculine work and values in the world of production which are transposed into the sexual organisation of the family. Similarly, the apparently cross-class conception of the family as 'refuge' carries a particular weight and intensity when the world from which the family forms a 'refuge' is the daily experience of class exploitation in production and work. But the 'sense of family' is a strong value because it is an absolutely pivotal social institution. Few would deny its central role in the construction of social identities, and in transmitting, at an extremely deep level, the basic ideological grid of society. Family ideology is undoubtedly also changing; and we have learned to think of the family, also, in more positive, less punitive terms. But, when we come 'right down to it', the dominant *image* of the family – perhaps across classes – still has more to do with the duty of instilling a basic understanding of fundamental 'do's and don'ts' than it does of providing a mutually sustaining and releasing framework. Love is what we hope and pray will emerge from the family, but disciplining, punishing, rewarding and controlling is what we seem actually to do in it a great deal of the time. Reich, [6] with some justification, called it a 'factory for creating submissive people'. And, as we have increasingly come to see, the fundamental images of authority, power and discipline, along with the primary origins of what Giles Playfair calls 'the punitive obsession', [7] are experienced and internalised *first* within its tiny kingdom. The alignment of the sexual and the social – a fundamental task of the family – is just the homology of structures which creates inside us those *repertoires* of self-discipline and self-control for which, later, the wider world is to be so thankful. It is little wonder, then, that fears and panics about the breakdown of social discipline – of which crime is one of the most powerful indices – centre on the indiscipline of 'youth', 'the young', and on those institutions whose task it is to help them internalise social discipline – the school, but above all, the family.

The next image is rather different, but equally significant in relation to crime. It is the image of the *city*. The city is above all the concrete embodiment of the achievements of industrial civilisation, both in terms of its embodiment of wealth and as the concentration of the sources of wealth, but also in its history – the conquest of the threats of the city in the nineteenth century: the threats of disease, insanitariness, crime, and political unrest. [8] The 'state of the city' is, in a sense, the 'tide-mark' of civilisation; it embodies our level of civilisation and the degree to which we are successful in maintaining that level of achievement. However, this image does not connect with working-class experience at this general level – it is not the idea or ideal of the city which the working-class grasps and comprehends. The working-class experience of the city is more segmented – it is carried in specific and concrete *local* ties and connections. At its broadest, it is an identification with a particular city and its own distinctive characteristics ('Sheffield born, Sheffield bred, strong in the arm and weak in the head'). It is embedded in particular forms of industrial development, particular local achievements, both of work and leisure. Even more, however, this connection with the city is carried in the patterns and organisations of specific localities within the city – the social and economic patterns of the particular working-class neighbourhood, with its specific traditions, membership and definite limits. It is where people live, talk, play, shop and sometimes work – it is their 'bit' of the city, to which people are concretely and directly attached. Working-class experience is crucially *parochial* in this sense. The effective relation of crime and the city is thus not *felt* by the working class at the level of a wave of shoplifting, bank raids and a rash of suburban burglaries. It occurs only with the invasion of the sense of their 'space' and its seemingly eternal patterns by 'public' forms of crime. In the period we are concerned with, however, the registration of crime on these areas is profoundly effective because crime *coincides* with *other* experiences of the dislocation, decline and undermining of those local patterns of material and social organisation – the destabilisation of its own complex internal system of social ordering. We shall return to this question subsequently when dealing with 'social anxiety'.

Nevertheless, these concrete local ties provide the material from which the working class can be connected with the city. The productive and political achievements of that class have often been mobilised within the city in the form of 'civic pride' – for example, in the quality of 'craftmanship' in particular industries (ship-building, cloth-making, steel production, and so on), in the development of 'municipal socialism' and the construction of publicly provided facilities and services (whose lasting monument in the northern towns are the architectural wonders of town halls). Similarly, those local loyalties have also been mobilised in local cross-class alliances through leisure provision – most obviously in the organisation of football clubs by the local bourgeoisie for working-class crowds. In this sense there have been provisional and contingent alliances across the classes about the city as a focusing source of local identity.

Overarching these social images and holding them together is the only image of the totality which sometimes seems to have achieved anything like universal currency: that of *England*. There are as many 'ideas of England' as there are classes and regional cultures, but it is appropriate here to speak of two dominant facets. The first is internal: it relates to all those things which, it is felt, the English 'do well', those intrinsic national qualities which have before, and will again, 'see us through'. Orwell has touched on many of them: they are *core* national strengths and virtues – and by 'core' we mean that they are felt to be what *most* people are *really* like *underneath*. The obvious signs that the English can be quite otherwise, the recognition of faults, limitations and weaknesses does not touch this core: 'underneath it all' the English are fundamentally decent; 'basically', they are a tolerant and moderate people; 'ultimately', most people will 'see sense', face realities, plump for the practical, common-sense line – each value is predicated on this reference to what is *ultimately* true of the culture, behind all surface appearances to the contrary. It is an image of the culture and the nation which is true only 'in the last resort'. The English can be stupid, pig-headed, blimpish, refuse to face reality, stubbornly individualistic, but 'in the last resort' people compromise, or 'rally round', or organise themselves if they have to. These qualities are reluctant to show themselves at first: it is only 'finally' that they emerge. That is why they are most apparent during a crisis, at the height of war, facing defeat, or at some other, similar 'finest hour'. In normal times, Orwell observed, 'the ruling class will rob, mismanage, sabotage, lead us into the muck'. Yet 'the nation is bound together by an invisible chain', and 'in any calculation about it one has got to take into account its emotional unity, the tendency of nearly all its inhabitants to feel alike and act together in moments of supreme crisis'.[8] It is an extremely powerful cluster of patriotic sentiments, and it feeds into, and off, a sense of, and a real devotion to, all the diverse aspects of locality, neighbourhood and region which precisely give to this rather nebulous 'national' image its rich and diverse actual content and purchase.

The second aspect of 'England', however, is external. It is forged in relation to the superiority of the English over all other nations on the face of the globe. This is basically an imperial image – its myths and ideological power are rooted in the policies and populist justifications of the high noon of British imperialism; into it has fed centuries of colonisation, conquest and global domination. It is present in the Englishman's divine right to conquer 'barbaric' peoples, a right which is then redefined, not as an aggressive economic imperialism, but as a 'civilising burden'. The Empire, backed by military, naval and economic supremacy, helped to form the belief that the English possessed special qualities as a people which protected them from military defeat, and kept the country independent and secure. The experience of Empire has its own long and complex effects on the English working class. Primary among these is the creation of a material and ideological superiority of that class over 'native' labour forces through the establishment of imperial dominance – making the English working class what Marx and Engels termed 'a bourgeois proletariat'. This superiority is complexly interwoven with the experience of competition between the metropolitan working class and the 'cheap labour' of the peripheral economies (for example, in the cotton and textile industries). This experience of competition was of course intensified by the partial *internalisation* of the periphery's 'cheap labour' during the post-war expansion of English capitalism and its dependence on immigrant labour. The assumption of superiority over all other peoples is often a quiet, unspoken one, but it is largely unquestioning; and though it is especially strong with respect to former 'natives' – colonised or enslaved peoples, especially if they are black – it includes 'wops', 'froggies', 'paddies', 'eye-ties' and 'yanks', as well, who, of course, are good at a lot of things, but can be shown to lack just that combination of qualities which make the English what they are. Inside the 'idea of England', then, lies a commitment to what Britain has shown herself to be capable of, historically, as well as a more common-or-garden commitment just to the 'English way of doing things'. Feelings about the flag, the Royal Family and the Empire belong here, though – as we have noted before – this is neither an unswerving commitment to these institutions themselves in their present form, nor to the abstract principles which the institutions embody – for example, the 'rule of law'; it is more a vague image of the rightness, 'fair play' and reasonableness of the British way – for example, of the British 'system of justice' (including the near-total faith in the honesty and uncorruptibility of the only unarmed police left in the developed civilised world).

The final image we must deal with here is that of *the law*. We have left it till the last because the law is the most profoundly ambiguous of these connecting images, and because (contradictorily) it is the law which is summoned in defence of these images 'in the last instance'. The law appears as the only institutionally powerful defence of the other aspects of Englishness. They are pre-eminently self-regulatory; they are dependent on the mutually self-respecting practices of 'reasonable men'. But when men become 'unreasonable', when the stability of that free ordering is unhinged, the law is the only barrier between 'freedom' (in its particular English form) and 'anarchy'; it is the only recourse for 'reasonable men'. The relation of the working class to the law is an extremely complex one, involving particular forms of connection *and* disconnection. It is captured in the paradox of the coexistence of two images of the police – the appeal of the image of the 'bobby on the beat' and the strong sense that 'all coppers are bastards'. To understand this contradictory relation, we must look at how the law articulates with a sense of a working-class 'code of behaviour'. This fundamental code of respectable and acceptable behaviour by and for the members of a 'community' has a content which does not exactly parallel that of the law. It makes different types of distinction – for example, the formal definition of theft is given a different shape in this code: distinctions are made about the nature of theft according to its victim. Theft from work and 'fiddles' have an acceptability which they would not be accorded by the law – they are seen as an integral part of redressing the economic balance. On the other hand, 'internal' theft within the constitutive circle of friends, relatives and neighbours forms a fundamental breach of the code; it fractures the concrete relations of mutual support. Similarly, some forms of violence have been deemed either normal (after Saturday-night drinking) or 'private' (domestic violence) and are not seen as the proper business of the law; while others – 'un-provoked' or 'unnecessary' violence (especially where perpetrated by 'out-siders') are seen as infractions of the social space of the community. Similarly, some members of the locale are proper victims (because of their concrete rela-tions – husband/wife, or because of their ability to respond – young men), whereas violence to others (e.g. old ladies) appears 'senseless' because it falls outside the organising matrix of the code.

The law, then, has a specific and very complex relation to this code. It has a role to play and can be summoned against infractions of the code; but inter-ference in practices vindicated by the code is the action of 'interfering busy-bodies'. Thus the law appears as both a necessary support to the code (where this cannot be maintained by internal control) and as unnecessary and external irrationality.[10] Nevertheless, when this code and its material conditions are un-dermined – and can no longer be maintained internally – the law has a regulative appeal. Its connection with the code becomes more significant than its disconnection. The law, then, can be used as a *mobiliser* when it becomes the only institutional and powerful force which can maintain the conditions of that 'way of life'; it appears to secure those other more personalised social habits and images – thus it can be summoned to protect those conditions.

It is on the level of the law, and its negative, crime, that the conservative ideology can most powerfully tap the ambiguities of the experience of the sub-ordinate class. The proclamation of the openness of the law to all, irrespective of their station, is a promise to defend the interests of all the members of the society against the criminal, no matter how large or small the matter may be. Life and property – to whomsoever they belong – will be protected. This equality of protection connects with the experience of the working class, for it is they who bear the brunt of most property crimes. *Certain kinds of crime* are a real, objective problem for working people trying to lead a normal and respectable life. If street crime rises, it will be primarily in *their* streets. They have a real stake in defending what little property and security they have managed to store up against the threat of poverty and unemployment. Crime threatens the limited range of cultural goods which make life worth living at all with a measure of self-respect. The demand that crime must be controlled – that people be free to walk about unmolested, that since the property of the wealthy and powerful is constantly and sophisticatedly protected there is no reason in the 'just society' why the property of the poor should be exposed to theft and vandalism – is not from this point of view an irrational one. This 'traditionalist' attitude to crime has its real, objective basis in the material situation and cultural position of the subordinate classes:

> Members of the working class also have a considerable stake in the notion (and the achievement) of social justice; they want a fair return for their labour, and are antagonistic to those who obtain easy money parasitically upon the work of others. Bourgeois ideology plays upon this genuine fear, arguing that all will be rewarded according to their utility and merit, and that those who cheat at these rules will be punished. In this way, ideology aspires to acceptance as a universal interest, although in reality it conceals the rampant particular interests of the ruling classes as displayed in both their legal and illegal aspects. [11]

Of course, if crime really could be controlled, and all could be free to go about their business, the 'freedom' which this impartial law would provide for working people would be the freedom to go on being poor, and exploited. The law does not have to be 'bent' in order to facilitate the reproduction of class relations (though it may be bent on occasions). It achieves this through its normal, routine operation as an 'impartial' structure of the state. But this long-term view of the role of the state as a 'class state' is hard to reconcile with the short-term view that the poor should not have what little they possess snatched from them. The ideology of the law exploits and functions within this very gap – producing, on the one hand, a misrecognition in the working class of its contradictions of interest, and, on the other hand, serving to split and divide sections of the class against each other.

Images of society need not be less powerful because they are imprecise, ambiguous or elusive. We claim no comprehensiveness for the sketch towards a traditionalist 'English ideology' which we offered above; but we would argue the need for such a 'map' when considering how the popular imagination 'thinks' the problem of crime. Of course, we have approached it from what might seem an unusual angle: we have tried to depict some of the image clusters which stand as collective representations of order against which images of crime and the criminal are counterposed.

Each of the themes we have touched on within this traditionalist version of the 'English ideology' *organises* crime within it. Each one connects with and identifies crime – and inserts it into a discourse about normality, rightness and their inverse. Crime both touches the material conditions in which life is lived, and is appropriated in the ideological representations of that life. Given the depth and breadth of these connections, crime appears to be inserted within the very centre of this conception of 'Englishness' – it has a crucial dividing and defining role to play in that ideology. This complex centrality of crime gives 'crime as a public issue' a powerful mobilising force – support can be rallied to a campaign against it, not by presenting it as an abstract issue, but as a tangible force which threatens the complexly balanced stabilities which represent the 'English way of life'. Crime is summoned – through this ideology – as the 'evil' which is the reverse of the 'normality' of 'Englishness', and an 'evil' which if left unchecked can rot away the stable order of normality. The reaction to crime, then, is deep-rooted, both materially and ideologically. This combination is an extremely powerful one, and, for the dominant classes, an extremely fruitful one. Crime allows all 'good men and true' to stand up and be counted – at least metaphorically – in the defence of normality, stability and 'our way of life'. It allows the construction of a false unity out of the very different social conditions under which this 'way of life' is lived, and under which crime is experienced.

ROOTS OF THE TRADITIONALIST WORLD VIEW: COMMON SENSE

We turn now to a theme only lightly touched on so far. This is the strength of the appeal to 'common sense' and personal experience we noticed in the letters. It is a theme which performs a double role, and consequently we consider it separately here. To avoid confusion, we should indicate just what we consider the 'doubleness' of this experiential common sense to consist of. First, it is a specific part of the traditional 'English ideology', as we shall describe below; but it is also the *form* in which that ideology is carried. That 'way of life' is experienced and expressed as being 'natural': 'that's the way things are'; 'it's just common sense'.

There are powerful historical reasons why this appeal to the practical and the concrete plays such a role in the 'English ideology'. Almost all the commentators on the development of English ruling-class ideology are agreed that it is centrally organised around 'empiricisms'. [12] The empirical cast of mind is one of the defining 'peculiarities of the English'. The complex social and political inheritance of a developed agrarian capitalism before the emergence of industrial capitalism, and the political alliances between industrial capital and landowning political representatives produced a ruling-class ideology which is peculiarly 'empirical'. Anderson defined this 'fusion' as follows:

> The hegemony of the dominant bloc in England is not articulated in any systematic major ideology, but is rather diffused in a miasma of commonplace prejudices and taboos. The two great chemical elements of this blanketing English fog are 'traditionalism' and 'empiricism': in it visibility – of any social or historical reality – is always zero. Traditionalism was the natural ideological idiom of the landed class as soon as its pure monopoly of political power was challenged. . . . Empiricism . . . faithfully transcribes the fragmented, incomplete character of the English bourgeoisie's historical ex-

perience. . . . Traditionalism and empiricism henceforward fuse as a single
legitimating system: traditionalism sanctions the present by deriving it from
the past, empiricism shackles the future by rivetting it to the present.

Marx locates the empiricism of English thought in a connected but slightly
different way from Anderson's somewhat dismissive observation on the lack of
development of the English bourgeoisie. Instead, he sees it as occurring as a
function of their *practical* achievements. Marx castigates Bentham – the per-
fecter of utilitarian philosophy – for 'genius in the way of bourgeois stupidity'.
However, he goes on to add that 'in his avid and simple way ... [Bentham]
assumes the modern petty bourgeois, above all the modern English petty
bourgeois, to be the normal man'. Marx's point here is that utilitarianism, even
its dismal Benthamite form, was, in England, already normalised, naturalised
and universalised as a habit of thought – not because it was a profound
theoretical system, but because it reflected its massive existence in daily practice; it reflected as 'natural' the daily experience of life under an accomplished
capitalist system of relations. Marx points to how certain seminal ideas and
ways of thinking have become so sedimented in social *practice* as to define the
whole texture and ethos of English ideas – they have become 'taken for granted' because they are so massively present in our experience. Marx captures
this peculiar combination of English material development and intellectual
backwardness in a comparison with its opposite – Germany's theoretical
sophistication and economic backwardness: 'If an Englishman transforms men
into hats, the German transforms hats into ideas.' [13] English 'common sense',
then, in one sense reflects the real, practical establishment of a 'natural' order
of society – bourgeois society. We can trace the effectiveness of this reference
to the concrete, the 'natural' order of things, by going back to some of the elements we found when we first encountered the public expression of lay opinion
about 'mugging' – in the 'letters to the editor' columns in the national and
provincial press, and in the abusive letters. One of the most forceful arguments
deployed in letters was the privileged appeal which ordinary folk made to
everyday *personal experience*, the reference to *concrete instances*. Although
these rhetorical appeals were to be found in both what we called the 'liberal'
and the 'traditionalist' letter-writer, it was far more widespread and carried far
greater conviction when mobilised under the banner of a traditionalist world
view. Now the reference to personal experience and concrete instances may
seem at first sight to require no further explanation. After all, those who really
have experience of a social problem at first hand have something original to say
– something of an insider's viewpoint – about social issues. In the public discourse otherwise dominated by the expert and the sociologist, 'personal experience' is often the only claim to be heard which the 'man or woman in the
street' can make. The tendency to generalise must be made sensitive – the
English believe – to these, inevitably more *particularised* points of view, since
otherwise it would blur important aspects of the question in its sweeping
glance. Editors of letter columns especially value this kind of personal
testimony, grounded in known experience and referring to concrete evidence.
In fact, few of the letters we looked at are really *concrete* in this sense. They do

not go into the actual detail of the experience which they are drawing on – say, of being robbed or 'mugged'. They refer to personal experience – but principally to give extra weight to their opinions. So the experiential reference is often indirect – 'He might change his views if he or a close relative suffered one of these attacks.' Or it is obliquely invoked, through personal characterisation: *Signed* 'Working class mother of three teenagers'.

Experience, here, means something specific – primary experience, unmediated by theory, reflection, speculation, argument, etc. It is thought superior to other kinds of argumentation because it is rooted in reality: experience is 'real' – speculation and theory are 'airy-fairy'. Often the reference to experience is used in exactly this way – 'cut the talking and listen to someone who *really knows*'. Ann Dummett, talking about this English impatience with theory, and reverence for 'sense experience', has observed that the English remember Sir Isaac Newton not for the discovery of calculus but 'for having an apple fall on his head while snoozing in the warmth of late summer in an orchard'.[14] This ironic example serves to remind us that the primacy of experience and of common-sense thought is a glue which solidifies English culture from its most exalted to its most everyday and mundane level. English philosophy, epistemology and psychology are all, also, powerfully *empiricist* in their typical modes. The privilege of common sense is therefore not something reserved to those who stand outside of intellectual culture, and who may, for that reason, be tempted to pit brute experience against intellectual reasoning. Empiricism is a cultural force *both* inside and outside of English intellectual culture; hence the legitimacy of the reference to empirical experience which attaches to it.

The appeal to common sense also draws some of its power from English anti-intellectualism. Although this is in no way an exclusive English value, there is some evidence to suggest that it is particularly strong in English culture. It is a value which exalts 'common sense' over the intellectuals, the 'theorisers'. Theorisers regard life as a 'talking shop' – they never do anything. They are people who 'really don't know' what goes on in real life, who are bemused by their own abstractions, who argue in ways which are irrelevant to the life of the great mass, and, what is more, propose, from these theoretical heights, explanations and policies which do not take majority experience into account. We also found this suspicion of 'intellectuals' in many of our letters to the press, and it is a stable element in the moralising rhetoric of the popular press. It has, of course, its own rational core. It represents the response of a subordinated social class to the established hierarchical class system and the social distribution of 'valid' knowledge that accompanied that hierarchy (especially as marked out educationally by certificates, examination passes, diplomas, degrees, and so on). Its 'anti-intellectualism' is a *class* response to that unequal distribution of knowledge: a response from a class which emphasises practical knowledge, first-hand experience of *doing things*, because it is the response of a *working* class. This working-class 'anti-intellectualism' is a classic instance of Poulantzas's proposition that subordinated classes 'often ... live even their revolt against the domination of the system *within the frame of reference of the dominant legitimacy*'. (our emphasis).[15] It is a defining characteristic of that form of consciousness which Lenin once called 'trade union consciousness', and which other writers have defined as 'labourist'. [15]

But 'common sense' has other more positive roots in English society and culture. In the *Uses of Literacy* Richard Hoggart discussed at length the sources of what he called the 'us/them' structure in working-class life and culture:

> 'They' are 'the people at the top', 'the higher ups', the people who give you your dole, call you up, tell you to go to war, fine you, made you split the family in the thirties to avoid a reduction in the Means Test allowance, 'get yer in the end', 'aren't really to be trusted', 'talk posh', 'are twisters really', 'never tell you owt', 'clap yer in clink', 'will do y' down if they can', 'summons yer', 'are all in a click together', 'treat y' like muck'. [17]

'Us', by contrast, means the group, those who belong, who stand together, who have to 'muck in' and take the good times with the bad, the neighbourhood, the community. In the final instance, it is the sense of a common position and common experience which makes 'Us' *a class* – though it is class in the *corporate* sense, a defensive community which is caught by this contrast, not the class which takes power or transforms the whole of society in its image: what Marx called 'class-in-itself'.

This kind of *corporate class consciousness* has both positive and negative features. From it stems both the debunking, 'putting a finger to the nose' attitude towards authority *and* the deferential attitude. From it arises both the strong solidarities of working-class culture, and the toleration it sometimes shows towards its own containment: both its massive collective strengths and its willingness to 'live and let live', to 'take things as they come'. Hoggart has also closely linked this 'us/them' structure with what he calls 'The "Real" World of People – the world of "the personal and the concrete".'

> Holding fast to a world so sharply divided into 'Us' and 'Them' is, from one aspect, part of a more important general characteristic of the outlook of most working class people. To come to terms with the world of 'Them' involves in the end, all kinds of political and social questions, and leads eventually beyond politics and social philosophy to metaphysics. The question of how we face 'Them' (whoever 'They' are) is, at last, the question of how we stand in relation to anything not visibly and intimately a part of our local universe. The working class splitting of the world into 'Us' and 'Them' is on this side a symptom of their difficulty in meeting abstract or general questions. . . . They have had little or no training in the handling of ideas or in analysis. Those who show a talent for such activities have increasingly . . . been taken out of their class. More important than either of these reasons is the fact that most people, of whatever social class, are simply not, at any time, going to be interested in general ideas; and in the working classes this majority . . . will stick to the tradition of their group; and that is a personal and local tradition. [18]

The 'common sense' which is formed in this historical space has its own, peculiar, dense structure. Hoggart notes the manner in which it is *grounded* in the concrete relations, environments, networks and spaces of the working-class family and neighbourhood (and, though he pays it less attention than it deserves, of work). This culture does yield 'views and opinions' on general matters and on the world, 'but these views usually prove to be a bundle of largely unexamined and orally-transmitted tags, enshrining generalizations, prejudices and half-truths, and elevated by epigrammatic phrasing into the status of maxims'.[19]

However, 'common sense' is not peculiarly English *per se*, though the English variant is no doubt particularly distinct and powerful. Other writers have concerned themselves with it as a *recurrent* way in which subordinate social classes are connected with the dominant ideology of a society. In another context, Gramsci remarked that common sense is always 'a chaotic aggregate of disparate conceptions ... fragmentary ... in conformity with the social and cultural position of those masses whose philosophy it is.' [20] It has strong links, Gramsci noted, with what Hoggart also calls 'primary religion' – again we should note the strongly ethical note in some of the letters discussed. It connects with fate and with a certain root patriotism (again, very different from middle-class jingoism). In a fundamental way (again quite distinct from any abstract notion of our national heritage), common sense represents a 'traditional popular conception of the world',[21] a conception formed in the closest relation to practical, everyday life.

Although the structure of common sense is therefore often directly in touch with the practical struggle of everyday life of the popular masses, it is also shot through with elements and beliefs derived from earlier or other more developed ideologies which have *sedimented* into it. As Nowell-Smith observes:

> The key to common sense is that the ideas it embodies are not so much incorrect as uncorrected and taken for granted ... Common sense consists of all those ideas which can be tagged onto existing knowledge without challenging it. It offers no criterion for determining how things are in capitalist society, but only a criterion of how things fit with the ways of looking at the world that the present phrase of class society has inherited from the preceding one.[22]

The world bounded by 'common sense' is the world of the subordinate classes; it is central to that subordinate culture which Gramsci, and others following him, call 'corporate'.[23] For the subordinate classes, ruling ideas tend to be equated with the whole structure of ideas *as such*. This does not mean that working-class people 'think' the world with the same ideas as the ruling classes. The dominance of one class over another does not mean that the latter disappears into the former. Subordinate class cultures maintain their autonomy, by struggle and by establishing their own defensive culture. But ruling ideas tend to form the outer limit and horizon of thought in a society. This is never simply a matter of *mental* subordination alone. Ruling ideas are embodied in the dominant institutional order: subordinate classes are bounded by these dominant relations. Hence, in *action* as well as in thought, they are constantly disciplined by them.

Parkin has argued that what he calls 'subordinate value systems' reflect the ways of life and material conditions of existence of subordinate classes;[24] but since these are experienced and thought within the framework of the dominant classes, they represent, not coherent alternatives to, but *negotiations* of, the latter. Negotiations, he argues, produce a culture which is *both different and subordinate*: a 'corporate', as contrasted with a 'hegemonic', culture. A corporate culture often arises, then, as a series of negotiations, qualifications, limited situational variants *within* or the result of partial struggles *against* the more 'hegemonic' sweep of the dominant culture. What the subordinate culture 'owes' to the hegemonic order is not a positive and grateful identification, but rather a reluctant confirmation of its hegemony – what has come to be called 'pragmatic acceptance'.[25] 'Pragmatic acceptance' often is the outcome of the class struggle in ideas – a struggle which here has taken the form of a 'negotiated truce'. The difference between 'corporate' and 'hegemonic' cultures often emerges most clearly in the contrast between *general ideas* (which the hegemonic culture defines) and more contextualised or *situated* judgements (which will continue to reflect their oppositional material and social base in the life of the subordinate classes). Thus it seems perfectly 'logical' for some workers to agree that 'the nation is paying itself too much' (general) but be only too willing to go on strike for higher wages (situated); or for parents to demand that children should be better disciplined, but complain when their own children are beaten. The accommodated settlements of a subordinate culture are necessarily contradictory. 'People often maintain unreconciled contradictions in their viewpoint, contradictions expressed in different contexts. ... It is in this linkage between opinion about national policy and immediate experience that many of the most obvious contradictions arise.'[26] The important point is not only that common-sense thought is contradictory, but that it is fragmentary and inconsistent precisely *because* what is 'common' about it is that it is not subject to tests of internal coherence and logical consistency. What is important is the disjunctures in scale, position and power which these inconsistencies reflect. 'Logical inconsistencies' are often the product of just the degree of difference in contextualisation which enables distinct class cultures and subcultures to coexist 'structured in dominance'. So the right to 'make exceptions and qualifications' to the structure of dominant ideas really helps to keep dominant ideas intact. Dominant ideas are more *inclusive* in range: they encompass a wider slice of reality; they explain and reference things which take place on a larger plane, outside of 'immediate experience'. The ideas which arise from 'immediate experience', which are situationally or contextually bound, then appear as mere exceptions, brackets, qualifications, *within this larger structure of thought*. In this way the dominant and subordinate position of the different classes is refracted through the relation between dominant and subordinate structures of ideas.

The important point is that the contextualised judgements, the 'exceptions' to the general rule, do not often spawn counter-ideologies capable of challenging the over-all hegemony of 'ruling ideas', thus leading on to alternative strategies of struggle which take the transformation of society as a whole as their object. The content of material social experience which informs subordinate value systems is, in fact, very different from that which is expressed in 'ruling ideas'. But this structured difference is concealed and harmonised under the tutelage of the dominant framework. It is through this unequal complementarity that the hegemony of dominant ideas *over* subordinate ones is sustained. This complementarity is the basis for *cross-class alliances*, where subordinate attitudes are mobilised and made active in support of interests and attitudes which reflect a quite different, antagonistic class reality.

Ann Dummett gives a trivial example which effectively makes the point. For the middle classes, she argues, 'tea' in the afternoon 'means . . . a leisured and unnecessary refreshment between lunch and dinner. You take it around four o'clock; the bread and butter will be cut thin, and you will not, except at a children's tea party, eat it in the dining room or kitchen.' But tea 'to the majority of the population is the meal of the evening, eaten about five-thirty when father gets back from work and has had time to wash and change his clothes'. Here, 'something accepted both here and abroad as . . . characteristically English means, in fact, quite different things to different groups of people in England'.[27] Nevertheless, it is the first (minority) not the second (majority) meaning of 'tea' which is thought 'characteristically English'; the first not the second which has a privileged place in English popular mythology. A practice restricted to the English upper-middle classes has come to represent something universal for the English as a whole: a class custom has become 'hegemonic'. The ruling classes have learned 'to give its ideas the form of universality, and represent them as the only rational, universally valid ones'.[28] We can now see how, because of their pervasiveness and hegemonic quality, this structure of 'ruling ideas' comes to be equated simply with 'how things are', and thus with common sense itself − the one structure of ideas which everybody shares. This universalising of 'common sense' masks the important differences between class experiences; but it also establishes a *false coincidence* of ideas between different classes. *This coincidence then becomes the basis for the myth of a single, English kind of thought.*

SOCIAL ANXIETY

The question is not why or how unscrupulous men work . . . but why audiences respond.[29]

We have been traversing the terrain of traditional ideas and their historical roots. But now we must look at the way in which specific historical forces operated on this traditional ground-base to produce, in the 1960s and 1970s, a strong upsurge of conservative moral indignation about crime. Engels noted that 'in all ideological domains tradition forms a great conservative force. But the transformations which this material undergoes springs from class relations.'[30]

We have discussed some of the central images providing society with a degree of ideological unity around the traditional pole. Crucially, those images cohere in a vista of *stability* − of solid, bedrock and unchanging habits and virtues, presenting a sense of permanence even in 'bad times', a kind of base-line that, no matter what, remains 'forever England'. Here we are concerned to show how a set of specific social changes combined to undercut some of the crucial supports to this set of images of social order among sections of the population who have no alternative ideological structure which could perform a similar cohering function. This undermining produces an effect in these class fractions which we have called 'social anxiety' – a product of both the dissolution of the material supports of that ideology, and the weakening of the broad social commitment to that ideology itself. We would suggest that one consequence of this 'state of flux' into which sections of the population are thrown in times of dislocation is the emergence of a predisposition to the use of 'scapegoats', into which *all* the disturbing experiences are condensed and then symbolically rejected or 'cast out'.[31] These scapegoats have attributed to them the role of *causing* the various elements of disorganisation and dislocation which have produced 'social anxiety' in the first place. However, these scapegoats do not just 'happen', they are produced from specific conditions, by specific agencies, *as scapegoats*. First, however, we must pay attention to the erosion of 'traditionalism' as a particular cross-class alliance, and to the production of social anxiety. There seem to us to have been two distinct but related reasons for this.

In the post-war period we can identify two 'breaks' in the traditional ideologies, each of which produced a sense of the loss of familiar landmarks and thus provided the basis for growing 'social anxiety'. The first had to do with 'affluence'. The basis of 'affluence' was the post-war boom in production. But it was experienced as a particular kind of consumption – personal and domestic spending – and as a particular transformation of traditional values and standards. The association of 'affluence' with an attitude of 'unbridled materialism', hedonism and pleasure was seen as quickly leading on to 'permissiveness' – a state of the loosening of moral discipline, restraint and control. The 'new values' were distinctly at odds with the more traditional Protestant Ethic. And the groups or class fractions which most directly experienced the tension between the Protestant Ethic and the New Hedonism were those – the non-commercial middle classes, above all, the lower-middle classes – who had invested everything in the Protestant virtues of thrift, respectability and moral discipline.[32]

The second development tending to awaken and heighten 'social anxiety' arises in roughly the same period, but directly affected a rather different stratum. The scale of social change in the period was wildly exaggerated. But the adaptation of society to post-war conditions did indeed set in motion social changes which gradually eroded some of the traditional patterns of life, and thus the supports, of traditional working-class culture. Change *of a kind* was to be seen everywhere; and nowhere was it more concentrated in its effects than in the erosion of the 'traditional' working-class neighbourhood and community itself, and its 'hard core' – the respectable working class. (By 'traditional' here, we mean, as Hobsbawm and Steadman-Jones have argued, that pattern of working-class life which established itself in the final decades of the nineteenth century – some aspects of which Steadman-Jones has dealt with under the title 'the re-making of the English working class'.[33] In a sense, the English working class was to a certain degree 'remade' once again, in the post-war years. Urban redevelopment, changes in the local economies, in the structure of skills and occupations, increased geographical and educational mobility, relative prosperity supported by the post-war recovery boom, and a spectacularised 'religion of affluence', though in one sense distinct processes, had a combined and decomposing effect, in the long-term sense, on the respectable working-class community.[34] The close interconnections between family and neighbourhood were loosened, its ties placed under pressure. Communal spaces and informal social controls, which had come to be customary in the classic traditional neighbourhoods, were weakened and exposed. The cultural and political response to these forces was considerably confused – a confusion which, there is little need to say, is most inadequately expressed in the familiar quasi-explanations of the period: 'embourgeoisement' and 'apathy'; but also in modifications within the traditional working-class ideologies of 'labourism'. In part, as we have argued elsewhere,[35] there was a strong tendency – the product of considerable ideological manipulation of reality – to reduce this complex and uneven process of change to the famous 'generation gap'. The distance – marked by the war – between the generations of the pre- and post-war eras exaggerated the 'sense of change'.

Middle-aged and older people clearly experienced these contradictory developments primarily as a 'sense of loss': the loss of a sense of family, of a sense of respect, the erosion of traditional loyalties to street, family, work, locality. In ways which are hard to locate precisely, that 'sense of loss' also had something to do with the experience of the war and the decline and loss of Empire – both of which had contributed, in their different ways, to the ideological 'unity' of the nation. Many familiar patterns of recreation and life were being reconstructed by the commercialisation of leisure and the temporary onset of a conspicuous and privatised consumption: the transformation and decline of the English pub is, in this respect, as significant a sign as the more publicised exaggerations of teenage leisure and life. The 'springs of action' were unbent – but they did not immediately take another shape; instead there was a sort of hiatus, a degree of permanent unsettledness. Local integration was weakened – but not in favour of any alternative solidarities, outside the scope of the family circle, itself narrower, more nucleated. Poverty as a way of life was widely said and thought to be disappearing – though poverty itself refused to disappear; indeed, not long after it was, magically, rediscovered.

One could begin to pinpoint this seed-bed of social anxiety at several points. One event which seems to bring all sorts of strands together, and to expose the reservoir of unfocused post-war social discontent in a particularly sharp and visible form, is the Notting Hill race riots of 1958. Although overtly about 'race', it is clear that these events also served as a focus of social anxiety, touching many sources by no means all of which were, in any specific sense, racial.[36] Put another way, Notting Hill was complicated because there was a need to condemn both the violence of white youth, and yet point to the bad habits of immigrants which had caused the tension. There was, to use Stan Cohen's terminology, uncertainty as to whether the 'folk-devils' were white working-class youth/Teddy Boys or black immigrants. In time the racial issue was to be made clearer, but for the moment it was blurred.

No such general ambiguities surrounded the 'mods' and 'rockers'. Cohen notes many sources of disquiet which came to be focused on groups of teenagers in conflict at seaside resorts:

> The Mods and Rockers symbolized something far more important than what they actually did. They touched the delicate and ambivalent nerves through which post-war social change in Britain was experienced. No one wanted depressions or austerity, but messages about 'never having it so good' were ambivalent in that some people were having it too good and too quickly.... Resentment and jealousy were easily directed at the young, if only because of their increased spending power and sexual freedom. When this was combined with a too-open flouting of the work and leisure ethics, with violence and vandalism, and the (as yet) uncertain threats associated with drug-taking, something more than the image of a peaceful Bank Holiday at the sea was being shattered. One might suggest that ambiguity and strain was greatest at the beginning of the sixties. The lines had not yet been clearly drawn and indeed, the reaction was part of this drawing of the line. [37]

A genuine sense of cultural dislocation, then, came to focus not on structural causes but on symbolic expressions of social disorganisation, e.g. the string of working-class youth sub-cultures. That these were themselves often 'magical solutions' to the same cultural or structural problems – attempts to resolve, without transcending, inherent contradictions of the class – was not the least of the ironies. [38]

What were in fact related but distinct developments were collapsed into three composite and overlapping images of unsettledness: youth, affluence and permissiveness. It was possible to perceive these challenges to the normal patterns in terms of a limited number of oppositions: undisciplined youth *versus* maturity; conspicuous consumption *versus* modest prosperity; permissiveness *versus* responsibility, decency and respectability. The residual resistance to these new ways thus first began to find articulation as a movement of moral reform and regeneration – whether rooted in the desire for a return to the concrete certainties of the traditional working-class respectability, or in the form of a campaign for the restoration of middle-class puritanism.

As these contradictory thrusts continued to afflict and challenge the dominant morality, and the axes of traditional working-class life continued to tilt at an alarming angle, so the general sense of dislocation increased. For those moral crusaders used to formulating their discontent in organised ways, there were the possibilities of joining movements – to clean up television, cleanse the streets of prostitutes, or eliminate pornography. But for those whose traditional forms of local articulation had never assumed these more public, campaigning postures, there was left only what one writer described as a nagging bitterness:

> Most old people I met expressed resentment of the forces in society which have robbed them of the crushing certainty that all their neighbours shared the same poverty and the same philosophy, and were as uniformly helpless and resourceless as themselves.... But now they feel they were deceived.... The values and habits that grew out of their poverty have been abolished with the poverty itself. While they were still striving for social justice and economic improvement, they took no account of any accom-

panying change that would take place in their value-structure: they simply transposed themselves in imagination into the house of the rich, and it was assumed that they would take with them their neighbourliness and lack of ceremony, their pride in their work, their dialect and common sense. . . . Instead of imposing their own will upon changing conditions they allowed themselves to be manipulated by them, not preserving anything of their past, but surrendering it like the victims of a great natural disaster, who flee before the elements and abandon all that they have painstakingly accumulated. Perhaps, if they had understood what was happening, they would have preserved something of the old culture, but instead they raise their voices in wild threatening querulousness against the young, or the immigrants or any other fragment of a phenomenon that is only partially and fitfully available to them. [39]

Seabrook is at pains to emphasise that this hostility to outsiders is not simple prejudice; it is grounded in the social reality and material experience of those who have such fears:

The immigrants act as a perverse legitimation of inexpressible fear and anguish. What is taking place is only secondarily an expression of prejudice. It is first and foremost a therapeutic psychodrama, in which the emotional release of its protagonists takes precedence over what is actually being said. . . . It is an expression of their pain and powerlessness confronted by the decay and dereliction, not only of the familiar environment, but of their own lives, too – an expression for which our society provides no outlet. Certainly it is something more complex and deep-rooted than what the metropolitan liberal evasively and easily dismisses as prejudice. [40]

This 'expression of pain and powerlessness' is a root cause as well as an early symptom of social anxiety.

In the vocabulary of social anxiety blacks and Asians were ready-made symbols for, and symptoms of, a succession of dislocations: in housing, neighbourhood, family, sex, recreation, law and order. To communities beset by a 'sense of loss', their race and colour may well have mattered less than their simply *otherness* – their alienness. We say this in part because in this period social anxiety does not seem always to need to go outside its social and ethnic boundaries to discover the demons on which to feed. In some parts of the country, the language of race and the language used about travellers are interchangeable. [41] And, even closer to home, so far as the respectable poor are concerned, are always the *very* poor – the rough, the marginals, the lumpen-poor, the downwardly mobile, the disorganised outcaste and misfits. The lumpen-poor, being too close for the respectable working class to take much comfort from their suffering, have always been available as a negative reference point. Here, again, powered by pain and powerlessness, negative reference points become the source of an escalating sense of panic and social anxiety:

Those who emerge from the collapsed and dwindling matrix of traditional working class life often believe that their projection upwards is a great personal achievement. They tend to acquire the social attitudes of the groups they aspire to ... in a rather extravagant and extreme form. In their anxiety to identify themselves with the successful they often show great lack of charity and compassion with the poor and the weak. Those who are successful often seem pregnant with a sense of blame and indignation, which they lodge vociferously with a wide range of social deviants – the workshy, the young, the immigrants, the immoral.... People who are successful believe that success is a reflection of some moral superiority. They rate enterprise and initiative as the most worthwhile of all human characteristics, and what they rather vaguely call fecklessness or spinelessness as the most contemptible. But because their own success stems from virtue, its opposite must be true, that failure stems from vice. People at the bottom of the scale are felt to be a vaguely menacing influence, not in any obvious revolutionary way, but they do undermine the beliefs which legitimate those who are in positions of superiority. This is why the references to criminals, shirkers, drunks, are so venomous. The suspicion lingers that perhaps the ascription of total responsibility to the failures is no more justified than the arrogation of it by the successful.... It is not solicitude about social justice and order which prompts people to invoke the gallows and the birch and all the other agencies of punishment and repression. It is the knowledge that any attenuating concessions made to the failure and the wrong-doer would imply a consequent diminution of their own responsibility for their achievements. And this is a surrender they are not prepared to contemplate. [42]

The Folk Devil – on to whom all our most intense feelings about things going wrong, and all our fears about what might undermine our fragile securities are projected – is, as Jeremy Seabrook suggested above, a sort of alter ego for Virtue. In one sense, the Folk Devil comes up at us unexpectedly, out of the darkness, out of nowhere. In another sense, he is all too familiar; we know him already, before he appears. He is the reverse image, the alternative to all we know: *the negation.* He is the fear of failure that is secreted at the heart of success, the danger that lurks inside security, the profligate figure by whom Virtue is constantly tempted, the tiny, seductive voice inside inviting us to feed on sweets and honey cakes when we know we must restrict ourselves to iron rations. When things threaten to disintegrate, the Folk Devil not only becomes the bearer of all our social anxieties, but we turn against him the full wrath of our indignation.

The 'mugger' was such a Folk Devil; his form and shape accurately reflected the content of the fears and anxieties of those who first imagined, and then actually discovered him: young, black, bred in, or arising from the 'breakdown of social order' in the city; threatening the traditional peace of the streets, the security of movement of the ordinary respectable citizen; motivated by naked gain, a reward he would come by, if possible, without a day's honest toil; his crime, the outcome of a thousand occasions when adults and parents had failed to correct, civilise and tutor his wilder impulses; impelled by an even more frightening need for 'gratuitous violence', an inevitable result of the weakening of moral fibre in family and society, and the general collapse of respect for discipline and authority. In short, the very token of 'permissiveness', embodying in his every action and person, feelings and values that were the opposite of those decencies and restraints which make England what she is. He was a sort of personification of all the positive social images – only *in reverse*: black on white. It would be hard to construct a more appropriate Folk Devil.

The moment of his appearance is one of those moments in English culture when the suppressed, distorted or unexpressed responses to thirty years of unsettling social change, which failed to find political expression, nevertheless surfaced and took tangible shape and form in a particularly compelling symbolic way. The tangibility of the 'mugger' – like Teddy Boy, rocker and skinhead before him – his palpable shape, was a prompt catalyst: it precipitated anxieties, worries, concerns, discontents, which had previously found no constant or clarifying articulation, promoted no sustained or organised social movement. When the impulse to articulate, to grasp and organise 'needs' in a positive collective practice of struggle is thwarted, it does not just disappear. It turns back on itself, and provides the seed-bed of 'social movements' which are collectively powerful even as they are deeply irrational: irrational, to the point at least where any due measure is lost between actual threat perceived, the symbolic danger imagined, and the scale of punishment and control which is 'required'. These streams of social anxiety and eddies of moral indignation swirled and bubbled, in the 1960s and 1970s, at some level right beneath the surface ebb and flow of electoral politics and parliamentary gamesmanship. Seabrook remarked:

> Most people I met who said they were socialists offered a ritual and mechanistic account of their convictions, which could not compete with the drama of the Right, which talks of the guts of the nation having been sapped by the Welfare State, and of a coddled and feather-bedded generation of shirkers and scroungers and loafers – words with an emotive power which the lexicon of the left has lost. The ascendancy of the Right is no less real for its relative failures to be collected in voting patterns: these have become institutionalised. Most people are not aware that there is any connection between their social beliefs and their voting habits. [43]

And that is precisely the gap, the opening into the mouth of Hell, from which the mugger was summoned.

However, this combining of the defence of the traditional world view with its appropriate scapegoats does not take place by magic. The necessary connections have to be made, publicly forged and articulated – the 'sense of bitterness' described by Seabrook has to be worked on to come to identify its scapegoats. Ideological work is necessary to maintain the articulation of the subordinate class experience with the dominant ideology – 'universal' ideas do not become so or remain so without these connections constantly being made and remade. The devils do, indeed, have to be *summoned*.

In the period with which we are concerned this leads us to a second source of the traditionalist view – to an altogether different and more powerful voice than that of the working class. It is a voice which takes both the dominant ideology and subordinate anxieties and moulds them together in a distinctive tone: that of moral indignation and public outrage. We have in mind here the 'appeal to common sense', to the 'experience of the majority' (often, nowadays, called the 'silent majority', just to enforce the point that it is not sufficiently heeded in the counsels of the experts and decision-makers), voiced by certain middle-class and, especially, lower-middle-class or 'petty-bourgeois' social groups. Their presence has increasingly been felt in public debates about moral and social problems; they have led the campaign against 'permissiveness', and are especially active in writing letters to the local press and airing views on 'phone-in' programmes. (We may think of this voice, collectively, as the *ideal audience* for the radio programme, *Any Questions*, or as the ideal correspondents of *Any Answers*.) Common sense – good stout common sense – is a powerful bastion for those groups which have made many sacrifices in exchange for a subaltern position 'in the sun', and who have seen this progressively eroded on three fronts: by what they think of as the 'rising materialism' of the working classes (too affluent for their own good); by the shiftless, work-shy layabouts who 'have never done an honest day's work in their lives' – the lumpen-bourgeoisie as well as the lumpen-proletariat; and by the high-spending style of consumption and progressive culture of the wealthier, more cosmopolitan, progressive upper-middle classes. These petty-bourgeois groups have been somewhat left behind in the pace of advancing social change; they have remained relatively static in jobs, position, attachments, places of residence, attitudes. They are still firmly in touch with the fixed points of reference in the moral universe: family, school, church, town, community life. These people have never had the upper-class rewards of wealth or the working-class rewards of solidarity to compensate them for the sacrifices they have made to compete and succeed. All the rewards they have ever had are 'moral' ones. They have maintained the traditional standards of moral and social conduct; they have identified – over-identified – with 'right thinking' in every sphere of life; and they have come to regard themselves as the backbone of the nation, the guardians of its traditional wisdoms. Whereas working people have had to make a life for themselves in the negotiated spaces of a dominant culture, this second petty-bourgeois group projects itself as the embodiment and last defence of public morality – as a social ideal. Although often similar to other middling groups in the society, the old middle classes and the old petty bourgeoisie -- the 'locals' – find themselves opposed to the 'cosmopolitans', who have moved most and fastest in terms of jobs and attitudes in the last two decades, who feel themselves 'in touch' with less localised networks of influence, who therefore take 'larger', more progressive views on social questions – the *real* inheritors of that degree of post-war 'affluence' which Britain has enjoyed. As the tide of permissiveness and moral 'filth' has accumulated, and the middle and upper classes have lowered the barriers of moral vigilance and started to 'swing' a little with the permissive trends, this lower-middle-class voice has become more strident, more entrenched, more outraged, more wracked with social and moral envy, *and* more vigorous and organised in giving public expression to its moral beliefs. This is the spear-head of the moral backlash, the watchdogs of public morality, the articulators of moral indignation, the moral entrepreneurs, the crusaders. One of its principal characteristics is its tendency to speak, not on its own behalf or in its own interest, but to identify its sectional morality *with the whole nation* – to give voice on behalf of everybody. If subordinate class interests have come, increasingly, to be projected as a universal cry of moral shame, it is above all this petty-bourgeois voice which has endowed it with its universal appeal. The point, once again, is not that the two sources of traditionalism – working class and petty bourgeois – are the same, but that, through the active mediation of the moral entrepreneurs, the two sources have been welded together into a single common cause. This is the mechanism which is activated wherever the moral guardians assert that what *they* believe is also what the 'silent majority' believes.

The split within the middle class between its 'local' and 'cosmopolitan' fractions has produced two opposed 'climates of thought' about central social issues since the war. The split is to be found in the debate about 'permissiveness' and moral pollution, sexual behaviour, marriage, the family, pornography and censorship, drug-taking, dress, mores and manners, etc. The same polarisation is evident also in the area of social welfare, crime, penal policy, the police and public order. In promoting some more liberal attitudes to crime and punishment, as well as in showing itself more tolerant towards deviant moral and sexual behaviour, 'progressive' opinion – as the traditionalists see it – has directly contributed to the speed at which moral values have been degraded, to the erosion of society's standards of public conduct. The 'progressives' have prepared the ground for the moral and political crisis which we are all now experiencing. It is easy to see why the lumpen should want to pollute respectable morality. But how have good, stalwart middle-class people been so bemused and misled? One explanation is that they have been misled by a conspiracy of intellectuals – the liberal establishment, united in a conspiracy against the old and tried ways of life, feeding on its vulnerable heart. This was the *traison des clercs* which drove the Nixon administration into justifying to themselves the excesses of Watergate. But another, even more convenient explanation is that the 'progressives' have simply lost their way – because they have been consistently out of touch with what the great, silent majority think and feel (they feel, of course, conservatively). Thus liberals have been betrayed into talking and acting *against common sense*. In this scheme of things, the silent majority, common sense and conservative moral attitudes are one and the same, or mutually interchangeable. So the reference to 'common sense' as a final moral appeal also contracts quite complex affiliations with this larger debate. In this convergence, common sense is irrevocably harnessed to a traditionalist perspective on society, morality and the preservation of social order. The appeal to common sense thus forms the basis for the construction of traditionalist coalitions and alliances devoted to stoking up and giving public expression to moral indignation and rage.

What has been vital to this 'revivalist' movement in traditionalist ideology is its ability to use that thematic structure of 'Englishness' which we discussed earlier, to connect with and draw out the otherwise unarticulated anxieties and sense of unease of those sections of the working class who have felt 'the earth move under their feet'. And it is the potency of those themes and images (work, discipline, the family, and so on), rather than any detailed specification of their content, which has made those connections possible.

By comparison, the 'liberalism' which has been the ethos of the cosmopolitan middle class has failed to touch those deep roots of experience. Identifying itself with 'progressive' developments of whatever nature, it has to all intents and purposes presented itself as the prime-mover and guardian of 'permissiveness', with all its attendant affronts to the traditional values and standards. Similarly, its liberal position on crime and social problems has been too distant, too academic to make connections with everyday experience. It has argued its case in statistics, abstract analysis and in the 'quality' Sunday newspapers – and failed to offer anything comparable to the direct impact or pragmatic immediacy of the traditionalist world view.

It is of critical importance not to confuse these two sources of traditionalism in English culture in the debate about crime, not to treat their appearance inside common public forms as a 'natural' process. It is important to distinguish the 'rational core' of working-class traditionalism from that of its petty-bourgeois form. Two different class realities are expressed inside this apparently single stream of thought. We must remember the roots which both have in the real, concrete social and material experience of their subordination.

EXPLANATIONS AND IDEOLOGIES

What we have tried to do so far in this chapter is to reconstruct the deep-structure or social matrix of the 'traditionalist' views on crime which proved so instrumental in the public reaction to 'mugging' and which provides the support for conservative popular campaigns on crime in general. Moral panics come into play when this deep-structure of anxiety and traditionalism connects with the public definition of crime by the media, and is *mobilised*. Now we can at last go back to the questions we posed at the beginning concerning 'explanations and ideologies'. How is crime commonly explained? What 'vocabularies of motive', what social ideas already arranged in credible chains of explanation are drawn on, across the class and power spectrum, to provide an account of why 'mugging' suddenly occurred out of the blue? What general lay ideologies about crime inform these explanations?

First, we have to make clear what we mean by an 'explanation'. We are not here discussing fully coherent and adequately theorised explanations of crime, such as we might find in the different schools and tendencies which make up criminological theory. We shall see, at the end, that the more fragmentary, more incoherent and contradictory kinds of explanations which have explanatory power at the level of judicial reasoning, news and feature presentations in the media, public expert and 'lay' opinion, and so on, do indeed relate to the more elaborate 'criminological theories' which have gained currency at different times in Britain, and other developed capitalist societies. But we have started, in fact, at the opposite end. When the journalist, or the judge, or the members of the ordinary public have to respond to, or explain, troubling events, like 'mugging', they tend to draw, often in a piecemeal and unreflexive manner, on the social images, the 'ideas of society', the sources of moral anxiety, the scattered meanings which frame their everyday experience in order to construct, out of them, social accounts which carry credibility. These accounts are not constructed afresh out of each individual's head. They draw on the publicly objectivated 'vocabularies of motives' already available in the public language – the available field of practical ideologies. To find an explanation for a troubling event, especially an event which threatens to undermine the very fabric of society, is of course the beginnings of a sort of 'control'. If we can only understand the *causes* of these events, then we are half-way to bringing them under our control. To give shocking and random events 'meaning' is to draw them once again into the framework of the rational order of 'things understood' – things we can work on, do something about, handle, manage.

The explanations we construct are not in the normal sense 'logical'. They are not internally consistent and coherent. They do not obey a strict logical protocol. In part this is because (as we shall see in a moment) we do not construct such 'explanations' out of nothing. We work with the elements of explanation which are already available, which lie to hand, which seem to have some relevance to the problem at hand. These bits and pieces are really the fragments of other, often earlier, more coherent and consistent theoretical elaborations which have lost their internal consistency over time, fragmented, become sedimented in ordinary 'common sense'. Gramsci calls them *traces*: 'the historical process . . . has left an infinity of traces gathered together without the advantage of an inventory'. [44] So when we use these fragments of other ideological systems to construct explanations, we are operating rather like Levi-Strauss's primitive myth-maker, the *bricoleur*, who assembles the oddments and fragments of his culture, combined in ever new ways, to construct meanings and to reduce the world to orderly shape and meaningful categories: the bricks and mortar for a 'house of theory'. [45] It is perfectly clear, for example, that, though Britain is by now a thoroughly secularised society, in one sense, there is hardly a developed argument or an important social or moral attitude we are likely to encounter about, say, marriage or sexuality, which does not, in either a positive or negative way, draw on or refer to religious – indeed often specifically Christian – modes of thought. Christianity continues to provide 'traces' which enable secular men to 'think' their secular world. Thus, as Marx once observed, 'The tradition of all the dead generations weighs like a nightmare on the brain of the living.' [46]

When the ordinary lay public constructs explanations, it imagines that it is doing so free from ideological and societal constraint, far away from theorising and scientific discourse; but in fact, all explanations are constructed, not by being produced out of the internal fabric of the mind, but by being cast within the existing fields of explanation, the socially maintained 'vocabularies of motive', objectivated over time. It is from these larger 'systems of thought' that, in fact, their credibility as well as their coherence derives.

We can simply indicate here the three main levels at which explanations of crime arise: in the judiciary, in the media, and amongst the 'ordinary lay public'. Judges do often elaborate on the social and moral 'meaning' of the crimes they are judging or the criminals they are sentencing. But, on the whole, they do not provide very elaborated 'explanations'. Retribution, condemnation, deterrence are the primary tasks of the judge, not providing convincing explanations of crime. This does not mean that the act of explaining is not involved in judicial homilies – only that they are extremely condensed, and tend to be drawn from a very limited stock. A long disquisition on the psychological or societal causes for a crime would be considered unusual, and is normally bracketed out of consideration by the alternative 'logic' which the judiciary operates: the 'logic' of judicial reasoning and legal precedent, of plausibility, not motivation. Crime for gain, judges perfectly well understand. It is a piece of wickedness, of course, but does not require much further speculation. Crime by insanity requires much greater argument and skill for defence lawyers to establish, and judges are notoriously reluctant to accept such pleas. When in the Handsworth case the motivations of the 'muggers' could not be made easily to fit either of these ready-to-wear explanatory models, Lord Chief Justice Widgery experienced some considerable logical unease:

> His lordship also obtained some assistance from the observations of Lord Justice James, the single judge who refused the applications (for appeal) in the first instance. He had pointed out that in Storey's case the court was quite ignorant of what his motivation was and that the only date when it could be said with any confidence that he should have fully matured and rid himself of whatever personality defect that caused the activity was when he would reach his early thirties and 'this particular tendency has burnt out'. [47]

Paul Storey would have had an easier passage from the Lord Chief Justice had his actions been more palpably and conveniently explicable within one or another of the already established explanations of crime. (We note, at the same time, that a 'theory' of crime resulting from a psychological defect and the notion of criminals at the mercy of uncontrollable impulses (which then in maturity 'burn themselves out') are both *implicit* in the judge's remarks; a whole psychologistic theory of crime is, in fact, embedded and condensed within the Lord Chief Justice's remarks.)

Perhaps the most elaborated attempts to develop explanations of crime occur in the press, especially in feature articles. That, we suggested, was because it is the essential function of feature articles to probe into the backgrounds and causes of events, and to explore explanatory models. As we saw earlier, there seem to be a variety of explanatory models of crime in play in the press, though in fact the range – looked at in terms of their 'logics' rather than in terms of the specific arguments they deploy – is much more limited. Even 'environmental' explanations, which figure strongly where the Handsworth 'mugging' was concerned, really operate within a very tight set of constraints.

The range of explanatory paradigms, then, is very limited, and these limited basic structures of thinking about crime form the framework within which the variety of specific explanations have to be constructed. These basic paradigms operate by providing answers to a *common* set of shared questions or problems – it is these which pose the 'criminal question' for these paradigms. We have seen earlier how the debate around the Handsworth sentences was more or less polarised around the 'liberal' and 'traditionalist' positions – in the various forms of press treatment, in judicial comments, and in both the public and private letters. The reason why these two positions (and their complex concrete variants) are able to take the role of positions *within a 'debate'* is that they are fundamentally organised by, and address themselves to, the same set of questions.

Central to this set of questions is the 'nature' attributed to the criminal – his motivation or state of mind, which polarises the liberal and traditional positions around the degree of choice involved in action, or – in more legalistic terms – the degree of responsibility the criminal has. This connects with deeper assumptions about the conception of 'human nature' which is attributed to the criminal, and thus with conceptions of the *relation* between the criminal and society. Only from these *fundamental* positions about the nature of crime, the individual and society (i.e. the underpinnings of 'causal' explanations of crime) is the final question answerable – what the society's response to crime should be: the objectives of penal policy and punishment.

We do not find elaborate and extensive responses to these questions within the various 'bits' of lay explanations which we saw earlier, but nevertheless very similar positions are *implicit* in the attribution of motive, 'nature', causation, and so on to the criminal in everyday speech. But they are not derived from criminological theorising or judicial reasoning – they are precisely the attempt at lay explanation which must 'make sense' of crime – connect it with their experience – in common-sense terms: that is, with whatever 'bits' of cultural knowledge are at hand and seen to connect.

In this final section, we shall try to develop a typology of these explanations which will show how the answers to the different questions cohere, but, also, how what appear to be the two *polar* positions in the lexicon of crime – the liberal and traditionalist – are themselves interconnected: how they form a 'unity in difference' of the available ideologies of crime. In very simplified terms, we can identify two basic 'lay ideologies' of crime, two basic explanatory frameworks.

The *conservative* explanation of crime lays fundamental stress on the primitiveness of crime, and the state of mind leading up to it. It is predicated on the eternal struggle between Good and Evil. Human nature is fundamentally nasty, brutish and vile. But the seed of Good is planted in us all. It requires, of course, eternal vigilance on the part both of society and of conscience. All of us are involved in this perpetual spiritual warfare against the 'evil that is in us'. Most of us manage to subdue the Devil. For the explicitly religious version, the submission to the authority of God and the moral law; for the secularised version, the submission to social authority and hierarchy, are the armour-plates of conscience which help us to surmount Evil and do Good. The criminal, however, has chosen not to fight the good fight. He has embraced Evil. This puts him outside the human community, makes him something 'less than human', something pre-human, uncivilised. That is his choice; but the wages of choosing Evil are heavy. The criminal represents a threat to us all, both to our physical safety, our moral duty and our social code. We must be protected against him. And a clear warning must be delivered to all others who for the sake of gain, impulse or base motive are tempted to follow him in this path to unrighteousness. There is a sort of calculus – both divine and utilitarian – by which the greater the crime, the more severe the punishment.

The *liberal* theory of crime is different. Here, the criminal is seen as backward, or bored, or confused, or ignorant, or poor, or under-socialised: 'Forgive them, for they know not what they do.' If the conservative view of crime is pure Old Testament, the liberal view is the New Testament in the form of a social gospel. The individual agent is a weak vessel, with the power of forces larger than himself. Only the mechanisms of socialisation and good fortune keep the majority of us on the straight and narrow. When these 'socialising' mechanisms break down, all of us are vulnerable to the revival of anti-social instincts and impulses. Crime is at root a 'social problem'. It arises, not from some fundamental premises of the whole moral universe, and not from some major structural fault of the social or moral system, but from particular failures, particular lapses in a structure which remains, in large measure, sound. Social problems require solutions. If the social or psychological processes can be remedied and improved, the possibility of such behaviour reoccurring can be minimised. Meanwhile, of course (here the liberal version makes its vital concession to the greater fundamental coherence of the conservative paradigm), public safety must be preserved, the guilty punished (for few are totally without responsibility) as well as rehabilitated, the innocent protected.

These are caricatures, no more. They are not intended as exhaustive sketches of the content of public consciousness about crime; and, even as sketches, they are patently adequate. We offer them simply to indicate one of the most fundamental principles of structuration in the body of common attitudes widely diffused in our society on the theme of crime and punishment. They provide a line of articulation which distinguishes between the idea that crime is an evil thing, part of the dark forces of nature and human nature, beyond our rational control, against which men and society in their deep revulsion must be protected – a fundamental breach in 'the order of the moral universe' – and the idea that crime derives from the weakness and fallibility of human arrangements, whether of our society or our personalities, part of the structure of human frailty, which, in punishing, we must also rescue, buttress, protect and gradually strengthen by reform. It is hard to give these root-images any more precise legal, ideological or indeed historical content. Yet, between them, they command and construct the skeletal syntax, the elementary forms, of the collective mental discourse of a great many English people about crime and its control.

A great host of diverse ideas are gathered under the shadows of these two structures of thought and feeling – and the 'order' they exhibit is by no means a coherent one in terms of the way these ideas fit together. For example, the 'traditional' or conservative structure exhibits many of the features of a system of religious thought, though it is only ambiguously related to religious themes and ideas, and by now draws explicitly on religious beliefs very obliquely, if at all. The 'order of the moral universe', to which this view of crime is attached, often assumes a hierarchical shape; it carries a deep commitment to the idea of social hierarchy and order. But when we ask what lies at the summit of that 'order' and guarantees it in its defence against evil and disorder, we are hard put to decide whether it is some notion of God, or 'good', whether these are the ideological correlatives of Custom, Tradition or of Society itself as an abstract entity. Similarly, when we speak of the 'frailty of human arrangements' – a central idea in the liberal structure – we must be aware that there are an enormous variety of ways in which this 'frailty' reveals itself: the sick and the mad are 'weak' – but so are the 'poor'. And the idea that these groups of the frail and vulnerable have found themselves 'at risk' in the struggle for human existence may entail three contrary notions: first, that the weakness is inside us, it is a vulnerability of the mind, of the spirit, of character; second, that it is the result of social arrangements which must be amended; third that it results from social forces outside us, which shape us 'what e're we will'. There are psychologistic, reformist and deterministic *variants* in the liberal ideology about crime.

These two broad structures of common-sense ideas are best thought of as 'workings up' of our pre-theoretical knowledge about crime. They embody the 'sum total of what everybody knows about' crime; an 'assemblage of maxims, morals, proverbial nuggets of wisdom, values and beliefs, myths and so forth, the theoretical integration of which requires considerable intellectual fortitude in itself'.[48] These are the categories which most of us who have no professional knowledge of, or responsibility for, crime and its control, employ in order to 'think' the reality of crime which confronts us every day. These are the *practical ideologies* which supply 'the institutionally appropriate rules of conduct' for the majority.[49] This is the level at which ideologies become real, enter experience, shape behaviour, alter conduct, structure our perception of the world – the level of ideas as a 'material force'.[50] 'What is taken for granted as knowledge in society comes to be coextensive with the knowable, or at any rate provides the framework within which anything not yet known will come to be known in the future.'[51] 'That atmosphere of unsystematised and unfixed inner and outer speech which endows our every instance of behaviour and action and our every "conscious" state with meaning.'[52]

Behind and informing these practical ideologies, though in no simple one-to-one correspondence, lie the more articulated, 'worked-up', elaborated and theorised ideologies of crime which have shaped the operation of the juridical apparatuses of the state and the work of its intellectual exponents over time. Once again we can do no more than crudely sketch in some of the main positions which have emerged at this more theoretical level. The purpose of attempting this complicated – and largely unwritten – 'social history' of the theories of crime and punishment in summary form at all is twofold. First, because when we try to give the content of our two fundamental common-sense structures any greater richness of detail, then we are obliged to acknowledge that this detail, and the logics which inform them, have been imperfectly and haphazardly *borrowed* from the larger 'universes' of social discourses about crime: the theories of crime have left their 'trace', though not their 'inventory', as Gramsci remarked, on the structure of common-sense ideas about crime. But the second reason is that these theories did not elaborate themselves out of thin air; they are not only mental constructions. They arose because of the particular needs, the historical position, of the great social classes and class alliances which have had the control and containment (and thus the definition) of crime at their command – at different points through the development of the British (and related) social formation. Or, rather – since this way of putting it suggests, erroneously, that each emergent class carries its conception of law and crime 'like a number plate on its back' [53]— they are the great constructions of crime and the law which have emerged through the struggle between the dominant and subordinate classes at particular moments and stages in the development of capitalist social formations and their civil, juridical, political and ideological structures: 'Each mode of production produces its specific legal relations, political forms, etc.' [54] Laws, Marx stated, help to 'perpetuate a particular mode of production', though the influence they exert 'on the preservation of existing conditions of distribution and the effect they thereby exert on production has to be examined separately'. The ways of conceiving crime, society and the law, elaborated in these different theoretical perspectives, and materialised in the practices and apparatuses of the legal and criminal justice systems, remain active in structuring common sense and 'weigh on the brain of living'. Thus, unconsciously, often incoherently, in thinking the question of crime within the framework of common-sense ideas, the great majority of us have no other mental equipment or apparatus, no other social categories of thought, apart from those which have been constructed for us in other moments of time, in other spaces in the social formation. Each of the phases in the development of our social formation has thus transmitted a number of seminal ideas about crime *to* our generation; and these 'sleeping forms' are made active again whenever common-sense thinking about crime uncoils itself. The ideas and social images of crime which have thus been embodied in legal and political practices historically provide the present horizons of thought inside our consciousness; we continue to 'think' crime *in them* – they continue to think crime *through us*. In conclusion we want to identify one or two of these seminal ideas which still seem to carry force in our common-sense ideas of crime and the law.

Early ideas of law were closely bound up with the notion of their divine origin and guarantee. Although law regulated the intercourse of men, including their secular life, it had come from God or the gods; and in so far as its dispensation and interpretation was exercised by priestly caste or by ruler and king, these preserved the divine, god-given element in the law – as well as the anti-god, rebellious element against the given order – entailed in the notion of 'crime'. Ancient law had another source – custom. The customs and folk-ways of the group or community constituted something as 'sacred' as the word of the gods; and indeed, since custom powerfully regulated such a large proportion of man's secular relations – especially the crucial relations of kinship and property – the 'breach of custom' (i.e. the going against the customary ways of the people) entailed the most powerful of sanctions. Although far away from us now in time, there can be little doubt that some of these ideas – carried forward and embedded, in modified form, in more modern systems of law and ideas of crime – provide the base-line for many of the ill-defined but powerful sentiments which go to make up what we have called the 'traditionalist' attitude: the belief that crime is a breach, both against the divine moral law and against the community; the association of crime with Evil; the link between 'the law' and the traditional customary 'ways' of the people; the concept of punishment as a sanction against deviation; above all, the association of the law and right conduct with hierarchy, authority and with the weight and precedent – the 'sacredness' – of the past. It would be hard to comprehend some of our more primitive feelings about the law and crime without understanding their roots in ancient ideas and forms of the law.

Maine conceived the shift from ancient to modern ideas of the law in terms of two, connected movements: the shift 'from Status to Contract'; and the shift, 'Starting, as from one terminus of history, from a condition of society in which all the relations of persons are summed up in the relations of the Family ... towards a phase of social order in which all these relations arise from the free agreement of Individuals.' [55] The latter conception of law, which Maine called 'contract societies', was the product of The Enlightenment; or, to put it another way, it was part of that immense revolution in structures and outlooks which signalled the emergence of bourgeois society. Classical conceptions of the law and the 'classical' definition of crime stem from this early 'liberal' form of bourgeois society. To this the great exponents of 'possessive individualism' and the great 'social contract' theorists (Hobbes, Locke, Montesquieu, Rousseau), as well as the great codifiers of the criminal law (Beccaria) made their contribution. The 'free individual' was enshrined at the heart and centre of this idea of the law – as well as of its opposite, crime; the 'possessive individual' was driven not by 'sin' but by interest and egoism; law, the state and 'society' were the self-imposed constraints which free and sovereign individuals took upon themselves – in the form of a 'contract' in society. This conception was given a classic form by Beccaria:

> Laws are the conditions under which men, naturally independent, united themselves in society. Weary of living in a continual state of war ... they sacrificed one part of it, to enjoy the rest in peace and security. But ... it was also necessary to defend it from the usurpation of each individual who would always endeavour not only to take away from the mass his own portion, but to encroach on that of others. Some motives, therefore, that strike the senses, were necessary to prevent the despotism of each individual from plunging society into its former chaos. Such motives are the punishments established against the transgressors of the law. [56]

Although the classical conceptions of law and crime were often cast in 'natural' terms – natural rights, natural law – the particular interests and historical destiny of the emergent bourgeoisie, linked with the protection of property, the rationality of the market and the 'rational' basis of state power, of Leviathan, were all clearly 'universalised' within it. Without the traces of these ideologies and the practices which realised them, we literally could not now think certain modern legal concepts. The doctrine of 'individual responsibility', which is a corner stone of judicial practice, begins here; so does the concept of the inviolability of 'contracts freely entered into', and of the 'contract of free individuals with one another in society', the sacred foundation and guarantee of all other contracts; so does the equation of the 'person' in law with private property; so does the root-belief that the law defends and protects that which, in turn, protects and defends *us* – and thus that crime is a sign that egoism has escaped the disciplining bonds of social life, and 'gone on the rampage'. Since the 'free individual' was sovereign, men could choose conduct conducive to, or destructive of, 'society' — hence the doctrine of responsibility for crime. But because men were also 'rational', they had given up something to secure everything. Man's rationality was identified with the social consensus of free individuals — equal before the law; it was also 'in practice always pitted against the passions of an unthinking self-interest'.[57] This highly specific image of rationality was made the basis for a theory of 'universal man': as in its counterpart, political economy, bourgeois man became the paradigm for 'natural' man, for man as such.

The conceptions of freedom, of contract, of responsibility and of 'the rational' generated in the liberal or classical revolution constitute the core of some of our most profound 'modern' ideas about law and crime. But the actual processes of the legal system, in their day-to-day manifestations, though based on these presuppositions, have been extensively modified by a subsequent change in the structure of legal ideas: the impact of positivism and the beginnings of the 'deterministic positions', which have so profoundly shaped modern notions of crime, and which were enshrined at the heart of the criminal system in what has been called the 'neo-classical revision'. The neo-classical revision was the product, not of competitive market bourgeois society, but of industrial capitalism as an increasingly organised corporate social system. Into the classical conceptions of free contract there gradually penetrated the sense of all those powerful forces which modified and constrained the free play of free wills. Bentham, whose rationality so often drove him beyond the limits which the rationality of market individualism assumed in his own time, had, as early as 1778, called for a systematic study of crime and periodical statistical returns on criminals; they would, he said, constitute 'a kind of political barometer'.[58] And as industrial capitalism remade the world in its image, it became progressively clear that not the contracted individual but the contracted classes, and the social conditions they lived and worked in, were the shaping historical agencies. In this new framework, the 'working classes' and the 'dangerous and criminal classes' assumed a new and menacing identity: what Chevalier has called the metamorphosis of 'the criminal theme into the social theme' had commenced.[59] The impact of Marx and Durkheim on legal ideas was a consequence of this attempt to think crime in terms of its social origins. In the neo-classical tradition, though the doctrine of 'individual responsibility' remained undiminished at its centre, men's actions gradually came to seem more and more shaped by forces which were not under his control, in societies which in their size and complexity dwarfed man's reason and will. The great English investigations into the social conditions of the industrial and criminal classes, from Mayhew to Booth, and the great amassing of 'moral statistics', using crime as a 'barometer' of social disorganisation — to which the French investigators, Durkheim's forerunners, made such a contribution — began to reshape popular as well as legal conceptions of crime. The era of biological, psychological positivism and of sociological determinism — alongside the era of developed industrial capitalism — had commenced; beside the law there arose the 'science of crime' — criminology, the study of the conditions and etiology of the criminal impulse, with its root in earlier 'moral statistics'.

We must note that the movements which shape this second transformation of legal thought and practice – like the first transformation – do not occur *within* the legal apparatus, but modify it through their impact on it from outside. As Pearson has noted,[60] some elements of this new strain of thought about crime are visible in the work of many of the nineteenth-century 'moral investigators' of city life; but its codification and systematisation took place within criminology and in its relations to (and borrowings from) other 'human sciences' – sociology, psychology and psychiatry. We cannot here leave our main theme to follow the shifts and developments in the theorising of the aetiology of crime,[61] but merely focus on the emergence of psychologistic and environmentalist determinism as two of the crucial tendencies along which legal practice aligned itself.

There is no direct and simple transference of these ideas into legal practice from criminology, though as Cohen has argued,[62] the deeply *pragmatic* nature of English criminology has promoted persistent and close connections with policy-making, especially in the humanitarian reform of correctional institutions. However, the actual modification of the law to take account of this 'positivist revolution' depended on the expansion and organised intervention of professional and semi-professional agencies. The two crucial apparatuses with respect to the criminal law are the 'psychiatric professions' and the development of social-work agencies within the state. These institutions have been the 'practical bearers' of these ideologies in the modification of the law. They have been the agencies which have not only modified the *ideas* of criminal responsibility in the law, but provided practical alternatives for the disposition of the criminal – therapeutic and treatment-based alternatives to 'correctional' penal policy. If classical law was formulated within the *laissez-faire* state of early capitalism, these reformulations have taken shape within the organisation of an interventionist Welfare State.

We cannot trace the complex development of these two main strands in the modification of the criminal law in this context any further.[63] We can only note its broad parameters. First, both are organised by an *individualist* determinism – the boundaries of their theoretical horizons are largely limited to the psychological interaction of the individual and the family, though social work is theoretically more ambiguous than clinical psychiatry in this sense. Indeed, the (historically derived) individual-centred case-work orientation of social work was one of the predisposing factors leading to its being professionally submerged under what has been called the 'psychiatric deluge' – with psychiatry as social work's main 'theoretical organiser'. Both, then, occupy the same 'theoretical space' (individualism) though with rather different origins and outcomes.

Second, both have historically modified the criminal law – but as 'exemptions' from its central principles, rather than transforming those principles. They operate on the basis of demonstrating that *individual cases* do not meet the criteria of 'individual responsibility' because of *exempting factors* – the individuals have in some sense a 'diminished responsibility'. In the psychiatric instance, this is demonstrated 'clinically': the individual is in need of 'treatment'.

The principles of exemption in social work are looser – they include predisposing inadequacies of various sorts; and the possibility is held out to the court that the individual will respond to rehabilitative personal contact – supervision. The only exception to this essentially *marginal* status of the liberal revisions to classical positions on crime within the legal apparatus has been restricted to the sphere of operation of the juvenile court, where children have been accepted as incapable of 'criminal responsibility' *as a social category.* [64] This is the one element of the legal apparatus within which social-work principles have actually come to dominate classical legal principles. (Current demands for the reorganisation of the court and the removal or modification of the 1969 *Children and Young Person's Act* are aimed in part at removing the 'welfarist' dominance in this sector.)

Third, we must note the reflection of this marginal position of liberalism within the law in the failure of the 'liberal imagination' fundamentally to touch and reorganise popular conceptions of crime and law. The psychiatric frame connects only in the broadest sense – in adding some materials and illustrations for the more fundamental common-sense designation of the incomprehensible as 'he must be made' – while the social-work development has, more often, been seen as 'soft' – *excusing* the criminal for his actions. Fuel has been added to this conception in the recent highly publicised 'misjudgements' and 'errors' of social workers in relation to cases of 'child-battering' and the 'sexuality' of their young charges. These instances have provided powerful ammunition to the traditionalist assault on the 'soft liberalism' of the welfare agencies.

The connections of this liberal 'reforming' ideology to the working class are extremely complex. At the most fundamental level, it has been the organised struggle of the working class which has played a crucial role in forcing the expansion of the state in a welfare-orientated direction. However, the social-policy orientation of the Labour Party (Fabian reformism) has been massively shaped by the new petty bourgeoisie. [65] The social-democratic demands for equality, welfare and the 'caring society' have taken a form which is strongly structured by the conceptions of these 'disinterested' liberal professions and semi-professions.

Thus, at one level, there are powerful material connections between this reformist ideology and the social-democratic reformism of much of English working-class politics – it touches crucial demands for material improvement, security in the face of the vagaries of capitalism, and the greater equality of provision of material and cultural resources, etc. But there are crucial ambiguities in the way the class experiences its own apparent achievement. Suspicions of 'state snoopers', distrust of the activities of middle-class 'do-gooders', 'bleeding heart' liberals who are over-interested in 'good causes', a Welfare State which spends their money on immigrants and 'scroungers', and which has at the same time failed to fulfil its promises to the diligent and hard working – all these recapitulate both the division of 'mental' and 'manual' labour which we noted earlier, and the internal segmenting of the working class itself: the 'respectables and the rough' and the 'racial' fractioning. This contradictory working-class attitude to 'welfare reformism' in the legal-criminal area reflects a fundamentally contradictory reality – one which differs from the promises held out by the Welfare State as the means of achieving the ideal of the 'just society'.

In addition, the liberal-reforming ideology – though it connects most concretely with these material questions – is least sure-footed on the terrain of *crime*. We saw earlier how each of the central themes of the traditionalist world view touched and drew into its ambit the question of crime. The liberal ideology manages no such concrete address to the working-class experience of crime – it remains distanced and abstracted. Even within the Labour Party, the otherwise solid alliance with the liberal ideology has always been profoundly ambiguous on the topic of crime – involving both 'liberalising' legislation, e.g. on the juvenile court, but also profoundly repressive measures, e.g. the implementation of the Mountbatten report on secure accommodation for long-term prisoners.[66] The relative weakness of the liberal position on crime, in all the different terrains we have examined (within the legal apparatus, in relation to popular consciousness, and at the level of organised politics), constitutes a crucial feature of that position – its fundamentally *defensive* nature. In relation to crime, liberal reformism remains essentially on the defensive – reasonably strong in good times, and capable for a time of setting the pace of reform, but capable also of being rapidly eroded when times are not so good, and placed under pressure by the more conventional structure of beliefs about crime. One of the most notable features of the 'mugging' episode, for example, is the fact that, under the pressure of a mounting public scare about muggings, this liberal-humanitarian-reformist perspective more or less temporarily disappears from, for example, editorials in the newspapers, and appears in subordinated and defensive positions elsewhere. In terms of the common-sense imagination, liberal views on crime represent a fragile and compensatory structure of ideas. Under conditions of stress they do not possess enough of a social base or real ideological purchase to determine the nature of public reactions to crime, once the traditional categories of thought have been mobilised by way of social anxiety and moral entrepreneurship.

In this chapter we have tried to pull together, in an inevitably speculative way, a number of themes and problems. By trying to trace the reaction to crime from its source in the media (where it is subject to complex structuring) right through to its varied expression in 'public opinion', we have been trying to undermine two, apparently opposed, but actually *complementary*, false propositions which impair much of radical thought on the question of crime. The first is that the traditionalism of the public temper on crime is the product of a conspiracy on the part of the ruling classes and their allies in the media. The second is that there really is a single thing called 'English culture' or 'English thought', and that it is overwhelmingly conservative in its essence. Neither, we argue, adequately accounts for the contradictory character of 'English ideologies'. It is of the utmost importance, then, to try to penetrate beneath these convenient 'unities' to their underlying antagonisms. This led us to explore some of the processes by which ideas have been *hegemonised* by the ruling classes in capitalist society. Such a critique will not, of itself, rupture the structures of hegemony, but it forms one of the first requirements, a necessary condition, of that break. Beyond that rupture lie alternatives which are as yet only partially and fitfully glimpsed – which are present only when the dominated classes align themselves with their historical movement, and develop strategies of action and modes of thought which have broken the internal structures which maintain their subordination. In that alternative space *also* lies the termination of the existing processes of 'criminalisation': an alternative view of crime and the law as the product of antagonistic social forces, and of their incidence and operation as one of the principal means by which class domination is secured. The law remains one of the central coercive institutions of the capitalist state; and it is *coupled* in the most fundamental way with the structure of crime, with the way crime is perceived, and in the way crime forces those who are subordinate in society to shelter beneath a hegemonic order:

> But when men become separated or feel themselves separated from traditional institutions, there arises, along with the spectre of the lost individual, the spectre of lost authority. Fears and anxieties run over the intellectual landscape, like masterless dogs. Inevitably in such circumstances men's minds turn to the problem of authority. [67]

It is with the posing of this problem – the 'problem of authority' – that our analysis can no longer remain at the level of analysing ideologies of crime. We have tried in this chapter to pose and answer questions about how complex ideologies of crime provide the basis, in certain moments, for cross-class alliances in support of 'authority'. But authority itself is not discoverable here – the conditions and forms of its exercise, the conditions under which *support* for authority needs to be mobilised actively, cannot be formed in ideologies of crime. The 'problem of authority' directs us to a different level of analysis, a different terrain of social organisation: as Gramsci put it:

> A 'crisis of authority' is spoken of: this is precisely the crisis of hegemony, or general crisis of the State. [68]

III

7

Crime, Law and the State

At the simplest level, what the term 'mugging' refers to is a crime; hence the reaction to 'mugging' can be understood as a normal exercise of judicial power. This is the common-sense view of the 'mugging' phenomenon, and we must acknowledge, once again, the force which it commands. As an explanation, however – as we have tried to show – the conventional crime/crime-control perspective is wholly inadequate. The immediate, common-sense reference which 'mugging' carries is once again in wide usage: a pattern of street crimes against innocent victims perpetrated, sometimes with unexpected violence, for gain. But the moment we ask: where did the term come from, and how did it enter into its common-sense usage, and what meanings and associations does it mobilise, its immediacy and transparency cloud over. There is more here than meets the eye. The police became, somewhere between 1971 and 1972, alerted to its growing menace; and the popular sensitivity to it remains high, especially in certain urban areas (see Chapter 10). But as soon as we ask what groups are most involved, against whom are the police mobilising in this period, we find ourselves, again, in deeper water than we expected. Hypothetically, relations between black youth and the police in the ghetto areas *could* have reached their present low ebb *because* blacks have become progressively engaged in 'muggings'. It is a deduction which lacks plausibility. The long deterioration in relations between the police and blacks began in the late 1960s not the early 1970s; it pre-dated the 'mugging' panic. The evidence to the House of Commons Select Committee on Police/Immigrant Relations refers to a range of issues contributing to the serious and mutual erosion of trust between the two groups;[1] 'mugging' is not prominent among them. The many cases reported in Derek Humphry's book *Police Power and Black People* pre-date the 'mugging' panic.[2] If a simple sequence of any kind can be deduced here, then it is deteriorating relations between police and blacks, followed by a rise in 'mugging'. This is not yet a causal sequence; the chain of circumstances lacks all its proper mediations. But the hypothetical sequence posed above is actually a more plausible one than the common-sense one, now – we believe – widely accepted. The 'mugging' panic emerges, not from nowhere, but out of a field of extreme tension, hostility and suspicion sustained by the relations between the police and the black communities. Crime, alone, does not explain its genesis.

Once it did appear, the scare about 'mugging' in the 1972–3 period clearly touched a nerve of public anxiety. Again, this looks, on the face of it, as if street crime rose, the public grew alarmed, and that alarm triggered off an official and judicial response; that is the common view. It carries greater credibility if 'mugging' is the first panic of its kind to appear, and if the genesis of public anxiety was based clearly in the 'hard evidence' of the rising rate of street crime. That is not the case. We have indicated, and will examine in greater detail shortly, the *succession* of 'moral panics' focused on the deviance and anti-social behaviour of youth which spiral through the whole post-war period. In this cycle 'mugging' is a relative latecomer. Indeed, it arises in the middle of a general moral panic about the 'rising rate of crime'; far from triggering into existence what does not previously exist, it clearly *focuses* what is already widespread and free-floating. The *fit*, here, between a predisposition to discover 'crime' as the cause behind every general social ill, and the specific production of the 'mugger' Folk-Devil, is, indeed, almost too neat and convenient to be true. But then we must ask, why *is* society *already* predisposed to panic about crime? How does this predisposition relate to the way society reacts when a tangible cause for concern is discovered and produced – in the 'hard' and compelling figures of the 'mugging' headlines? These questions lead us outside and beyond the common-sense framework. They raise questions which cannot be resolved within a conventional crime/crime-control perspective. They subvert, the naive, common-sense wisdom about 'mugging'. Clear as the case seems, it is inadequate. In each instance we seem to approximate closer to the truth if we reverse or invert the common-sense account. Accordingly, we were forced in our examination to look at the 'mugging' phenomenon again, not only on a much broader historical canvas, but, as it were, in reverse: through the eye of its paradoxes. If a label precedes a crime, and the judicial arm of the state is increasingly locked in a struggle with a section of the community which then produces its criminals, and the society shows a clear predisposition to panic about this aspect of 'rising crime' before it discovers a particular instance of the crime to panic about, then it is necessary to turn, first, not to the crime but to what seems most problematic: *the reaction to crime*. Thus we pose the problem now in its most paradoxical form: could it be possible – historically plausible – that a societal reaction to crime could precede the appearance of a pattern of crimes?

This question does not – let us emphasise – entail a simple inversion. The requirement to begin an explanation of 'mugging' somewhere other than with the question of who first committed what, when, does *not* entail an argument that no such crime ever existed. It is *not* our view that the police or some other agency of the state has simply conjured 'mugging' and street crime up out of thin air. Undoubtedly, between 1971 and 1973, and indeed since, people on the streets or in open spaces have been robbed, pickpocketted or otherwise relieved of their property, often accompanied with rough physical treatment; a number of victims have been assaulted in the course of robbery, and some have been badly and seriously injured. 'Mugging' was not produced, 'full blown' from the head of the control culture; it is not simply a ruling-class conspiracy. Moreover, it has – when accompanied by violence – sometimes resulted in serious physical and emotional consequences for its victims, many of whom are old or unable to cope with the shock of the encounter, and few of whom have very much of the world's wealth at their command. This is not a pretty social development to contemplate, and it is not part of our argument that it should be 'excused'. Indeed, we are *not* in the business of individual, moral judgement at all. But, to counter any misunderstanding, let it be clear that, just as we do not believe that 'mugging' was invented by the state, so we do not believe that street crime is a romantic deviant adventure. There is a political position which suggests that *anything* which disrupts the social order or even tenor of bourgeois life is a *good thing*. It is a tenable position, but it is not ours. Apart from anything else, no existing social order that we know of has ever been changed by the exploits of individuals ripping off other individuals of their own, much-subordinated, class. Our argument is simply not conducted within this individual frame of reference, or within the given, common-sense calculus of individual blame or praise. To blame the actions of individuals within a given historical structure, *without taking that structure itself into account*, is an easy and familiar way of exercising the moral conscience without bearing any of its costs. It is the last refuge of liberalism.

We insist, however, that it is still far from proven that: (i) there were *more* such crimes in the 1972–3 period than at any previous time; or (ii) that any rate of increase corresponds precisely to the official figures produced in the criminal statistics. Let us, without forcing the argument too far at this moment, merely suggest an alternative *scenario*, which must be taken in conjunction with the earlier critique we levelled at the nature, presentation and 'use' of the criminal statistics (see Chapter 1). A crime like 'mugging' – which, as we suggested, bears *many* similarities to traditional and long-standing forms of street crime (and is, indeed, presently being applied to what are clearly pickpocketing offences) [3] – *could* easily become the focus of official and public attention, not because its numbers rise but because a quite distinct new social group appears to be involved. For example, suppose the vast majority of street crimes in working-class urban districts suddenly began to be perpetrated by white, upper-middle-class public school boys; or suppose the majority of street crimes were suddenly to be accompanied by a sign bearing the slogan, 'For a liberated Ulster and a United Irish Republic'. The examples are hypothetical and far-fetched. But they help to reinforce the point that a simple *rise in numbers of crimes committed* is by no means the only reason why public attention might suddenly focus on a 'dramatic new strain of crime'. This could also happen because of a significant change in the social composition of the offenders, or if the crime became invested with an overt political purpose and meaning. Here, again, the common-sense view does not stand up for long to sceptical inspection.

We have refused, therefore, to orientate ourselves in the accepted and conventional accounts of the 'mugging' panic. No doubt someone will shortly write the book telling us exactly how many 'muggings' were perpetrated, who were the victims and whom the aggressors. Our account attempts, not to shore up a shaky set of starting propositions, but to interrogate the matter from its most problematic side. Why does society react to 'mugging' as it does, when it does? To what, exactly, is this a reaction? This starting-point derives from an initial hypothesis to which all the evidence points, once the grip of common sense over it has been broken: this is that *there appears to be a vigorous reaction to 'mugging' as a socio-criminal phenomenon before there are any actual 'mugg-*

ings' to react to. Let us fill out what this altered starting-point entails, the shift in terrain which the new vantage-point brings about. Why is Britain in a moral tail-spin about 'crime' in the early 1970s? Why is the 'control culture' so sensitised and mobilised against a potential 'mugging' threat, and why does this prior sensitisation occur against such a distinctive social and ethnic group in the community? Why does the very idea of 'mugging' trigger off such profound social fears and anxieties in the general public and the press? In short, what is the repressed social and historical content of 'mugging' and the response to it? What does this tell us about the nature of social control, the ideologies of crime, the role of the state and its apparatuses, the historical and political conjuncture in which this cycle appears? These questions point to aspects and levels of the society far removed from the 'normal' terrain of 'normal' crime and its 'normal' prevention. Perhaps the most immediately troubling feature is the clear discrepancy between the scale of the 'threat' – even on the basis of the official estimates – and the scale of the measures taken to prevent and contain it. That discrepancy alone points us towards new dimensions of explanation.

This shift is sometimes characterised as a move in the argument from a traditional criminological to a transactional view of crime: 'mugging' considered now as the consequence, largely, of the labelling of deviance, and the outcome of transactional encounters between 'muggers' and law-enforcement agencies. No doubt such transactional processes were indeed at work on the ground; and they may have had some of the amplifying consequences to which transactional explanations of deviance have so acutely pointed. Anti-Mugging Squads, formed specifically to look out for and prevent criminal exploits on the London underground, may well, through specialisation and concentration of resources as well as through anticipatory policing, have produced more instances – and thus a 'higher' crime rate – than if the statistics had reflected simply the routine instances of reported 'theft', 'robbery' or 'pickpocketting' by victims. If the Transport Police believed that pickpocketting and snatching were increasing on the London underground, and stood around in plain clothes waiting to pick the snatchers up, they no doubt did find some – and the number may have included youths who looked suspicious, threatening or hostile to the police on general grounds, and whose ambiguous actions were therefore resolved into the convenient category of 'snatching'. In short, the initiation of a period of intense policing can of itself amplify the rapid volume of crime. Another effect of increasing the intensity of crime control and surveillance is often to clear the area of potential offenders – people whose looks, bearing, demeanour could be construed as law-breaking. In this sense – quite apart from the deterrent effect of the fear of apprehension and sentencing – crime prevention and control do sometimes *work*. But another, alternative, effect of increased police control, if the political 'definitions of the situation' are sufficiently pointed that way, is that youths who see themselves as locked in a sort of running battle with the forces of 'law and order' – and not necessarily because they are already confirmed criminals – may *take to* snatching because snatching becomes, so to speak, the defined site of a continuing struggle with 'the law' and the social system it protects. There are signs, in the period after 1973, that 'mugging' does, indeed, *acquire* a quasi-political meaning of this sort, in the context of continuing conflict between young blacks and the police. Another way of putting it is that the hidden social content of this crime may have been brought, progressively, to the fore as a result of 'transactions' between the police and the criminals, and this content may then be positively appropriated by some criminals. There are signs of this evolution taking place, both in the way first-hand accounts by young, black 'muggers' *change* between 1972–3 and 1975, and in the way 'mugging' is discussed by social workers and community activists in the areas where it has become a topic of burning concern. In these different ways, something important is to be gained by examining the transactions between 'muggers' and the police, as the definitions of the situation by each of the other alter. (The Spaghetti House 'affair' in 1975, in which three black men kidnapped and held hostage a number of people at an Italian restaurant in London, identifying themselves at one point as political activists rather than as simple criminals, though it was not an incident which involved a 'mugging', is one of the clearest and most publicised instances of the shifting definitions and emergent 'social' content of black crime during this period.)

On the whole, though, we have chosen to replace a conventional crime interpretation of 'mugging', not by a 'transactional' analysis of crime, but by a more historical and structural view. There are, we argue, clear historical and structural forces at work in this period, shaping, so to speak, from the outside, the immediate transactions on the ground between 'muggers', potential muggers, their victims and their apprehenders. In many comparable studies, these larger and wider forces are merely noted and cited; their direct and indirect bearing on the phenomenon analysed is, however, left vague and abstract – part of 'the background'. In our case, we believe that these so-called 'background issues' are, indeed, exactly the critical forces which *produce* 'mugging' in the specific form in which it appears, and push it along the path it took from 1972–3 through to the present. It is to this shaping context, therefore, that we turn: attempting to make precise, without simplification or reduction, the other contradictory connections between specific events of a criminal-and-control kind, and the historical conjuncture in which they appear. Of course, the transactional view contains important and critical insights, and we have profited from them. They remind us that there is no such thing as crime, here, and crime prevention, there; only a *relation* between the two – crime-and-control. They remind us that deviance is a social and historical, not a 'natural', phenomenon; that for acts to be 'deviant' they must be recognised, labelled and responded to as 'crimes'; there must be a society whose norms, rules and laws are transgressed, control institutions whose task it is to enforce the norms and punish the infractor. But the transactional perspective tends to view this process of labelling and reaction largely at the level of the micro transactions out of which the relations between the law and the law-breaker are constructed. Without wishing to deny that 'social order' is, indeed, constructed and sustained, time and again, in these myriad interactions, we feel the need of a vantage-point which is able to consider the longer-term, larger role which the legal institutions play, through the control of crime, in the maintenance of the stability and cohesion of the whole social formation from which, under certain

conditions, acts defined as infractions of the law develop. We are also anxious
not to tell the story as if the initial acts of law-breaking and crime have no
rationale or authenticity. For this would be to return, by a strangely circuitous
route, to the strictly functionalist view that, after all, society is an integrated,
fully consensual 'whole' and that infractions, discrepancies and antagonisms
within it are the result of the actions of those who know not what they do, or –
to reverse the case – that their actions are the imaginary constructs of the controllers, so that deviancy becomes simply a nightmare of the state. Again, to
put the matter in the form of a paradox: it is important to reject the common-
sense view that, when all is said and done, muggers mugged, the police picked
them up, and the courts put them away, and that is that. But it is also important to insist that some muggers *did* mug, that 'mugging' *was* a real social and
historical event arising out of its own kind of struggle, that it has its own
rationale and historical 'logic' which we need to unravel.

All this points to a need for a more differentiated, historically located
analysis. We must begin to draw distinctions, however provisionally, between
crimes which are 'deviant' with respect to their means, but consonant with the
over-all structure and 'norms' of the society, and crimes which seem to express
– however fitfully and incompletely – an element of social protest or opposition
to the existing order. We need to distinguish, again provisionally, between those
occasions where the scale of criminal activity and the scale of measures taken
to contain crime stand in some rough balance to one another – where crime
control is best understood as a part of the 'normalised repression' of the state,
and its defence of property, the individual and public order; and those occasions when there is a radical discrepancy between the nature of the 'threat' and
the scale of 'containment', or when the incidence of certain kinds of crime does
appear, suddenly, to increase or assume a *new* pattern, or where the pace of
legal repression and control rapidly increases. For these latter moments have
tended, both in the past and in the present, to coincide with moments of a wider
historical significance than is contained by the play of normalised repression
over the structure of normal crime. Such moments of 'more than usual alarm'
followed by the exercise of 'more than normal control' have signalled, time and
again in the past, periods of profound social upheaval, of economic crisis and
historical rupture.

'NORMAL' CRIME AND SOCIAL CRIME

The complex relationships between crime, political movements and economic
transformation have not yet had the attention they seem to deserve from social
historians, though the recent work of Hobsbawm, Rudé, Thompson and others
has given it a fresh and welcome impetus. The connections are not, of course,
simple; no simple evolutionary traces can be drawn across historical time, as if
the links were simple and linear. The connection between popular protest and
the maintenance of public order is relatively easy to see in the eighteenth and
nineteenth centuries, whether one is looking at food riots, rural protest,
machine-breaking and the actions of the city 'mobs', or at political assemblies
declared illegal, the reform movements, the great Chartist agitation, the birth of

trade unions or working-class political struggle. But here, the social and political content is relatively clear and undisputable in retrospect, even if difficult to sort out at the time. When the reform movements of the 1860s were forbidden the right of free speech in Hyde Park on the grounds that the 'Royal Parks are intended for the recreation and enjoyment of the people', few can have been in doubt that the enforcement was political rather than simply 'public order' in character. In a support meeting after the Trafalgar Square fracas in February 1886 – Black Monday – John Burns is reputed to have addressed his audience as 'Friends and fellow-workers and detectives'. Paradoxically, in this period it is the actions of the socialists, radicals and the urban casual poor which defended the thoroughly 'bourgeois' liberty of free assembly. Yet Engels did not think much of the political philosophy of the crowd – 'poor devils of the East End' a 'sufficient admixture of roughs' who, having completed their work, returned to the East End singing 'Rule Britannia'! [4] Burns was 'done' for 'sedition of some sort' (he was acquitted); many of those who vented their anger on the property surrounding Trafalgar Square were charged with criminal damage – one thing leading on to another. . . . Throughout the period, the clearly political containment of popular protest was effected under the ambiguous cover of 'public order' and its sanctions. [5] The connection is more difficult to establish where popular protest assumes a mainly 'criminal' rather than political form. [6] It is even more difficult where what is defined as 'crime' has a clear social or economic content, which however remains implicit, [7] or where professional crime is tightly interwoven with social unrest or appears as its literal or figurative forerunner. [8]

Historians have also begun to identify a distinction between 'ordinary' and 'social crime'. Hobsbawm speaks of 'types of criminal activity which could be classified as "social" in the sense that they expressed a conscious, almost political challenge to the prevailing social and political order and its values', and asks whether 'such social criminality could be clearly distinguished from other forms of delinquency (all of which can of course be defined as "social" in a wider sociological sense)'. [9] The differences are important, but extremely difficult to sustain in any definitive way. Thompson has remarked of eighteenth-century crime that, 'though there is a real difference in emphasis at each pole' between 'normal' crime and 'social' crime, the evidence does not sustain 'a tidy notion of a distinction between two kinds of crime'. [10] Normal and social crime are not fixed statuses or 'natural' categories to which classes of people can be permanently ascribed. The assignation to one or another category, and indeed the very use of the 'criminal' tag, is often part of a broader strategy of repression and control, only some aspects of which belong to the exercise of crime-prevention and control in any normal sense. To take the eighteenth-century definition of 'crime' for granted is to take the eighteenth-century definition of property-right and class for granted. If we are examining processes rather than categories, the routes which individuals take into and out of crime are enormously variable. Even more, that which, at a certain historical period, leads certain classes of people to take up what is currently defined as 'crime' as part of a collective strategy in the face of the conditions in which they find themselves is a matter requiring the most delicate historical judgement and reconstruction. Most important of all, the study of 'criminal sub-cultures' as distinct entities commits the easy but serious historical error of separating out sociological categories from a wider and more inclusive history of the fractions and strata composing a class as a whole, in the more fundamental sense of the term. In such a perspective, it is precisely the whole *repertoire* of struggle – strategies, positions and solutions – which must inform the analysis, and which throws a revealing light back on to those sections of the class taking or driven along the specific path of 'criminalisation'. The concept of a criminal subculture can be a fruitful or a sterile starting-point for an investigation, depending on whether 'crime' is treated as a given, self-evident ahistorical and unproblematic category, or whether it serves as the provisional category through which to construct the more complex accounts and 'real relations' of an adequate class history. This is, indeed, true, not only for the study of criminal sub-cultures, but for the study of class cultures and 'sub-cultures' *tout court*. They must be related to the wider class problematic of which they are a historically differentiated part.[11]

The point is easy to illustrate from the social history of nineteenth-century London. The criminal 'fraternities' of East London were clearly parts of the wider class ecologies, class cultures and class formations of the London of the period. To reserve them for a special category would be simply to lose any grip on a central aspect of the history of the urban working class and the urban poor of the period. In the historical sense, 'crime' was a well-articulated part of the working-class cultural *repertoire* of the period: how some members of the labouring and casual poor 'lived' the contradictory experience and exploitative relationships which characterise class relations as a whole – to which other class members found a variety of alternative personal and collective 'solutions'. Of course, distinct criminal networks existed, with their distinct activities, territories, underworlds, professional specialities and 'trades'. At their margins, and sometimes right within them, some men, women and children engaged in what can only be described as authentic, often quite self-consciously pursued, 'criminal careers'. Nevertheless, it would be an odd account which did not recognise that the activities of the labouring poor – especially the great body of destitute families and casual male, female and child labour which composed a sizeable chunk of the city's population – in securing the basic elements of physical and material survival often embraced 'skills' which the authorities and investigators would certainly, and did indeed, describe as 'criminal' or illegal. The contribution of the children of the East End poor to the meagre family income included a number of activities – tasks, errands, message jobbing, street performing, begging, buying of stale bread, collecting scraps and rotten fruit, and so on. For the children of those families which had arrived at the terminal point on the poverty line, it must have been a very thin, often imperceptible, margin indeed between getting what they had to, legally, and scrounging where and however they could; and the margin, for all practical purposes, was not between 'legality' and 'illegality' so much as between survival and sheer destitution.[12] Describing the normal ways in which the rural poor had often to survive in the previous century, Thompson has observed that 'if this is a "criminal sub-culture" then the whole of plebian England falls within the category'[13]. Similarly, if all the things which the East End poor had to do to survive were 'criminal', then indeed that convergence between the 'labouring' and the 'dangerous' classes which so transfixed the middle classes in the early part of the century, or between the 'respectables' and the contaminating influence of the 'casual residuum' which returned to haunt the official mind in the 1880s and 1890s, had a real material basis. [14] It would be a poverty-stricken account, indeed, which hived off 'crime' from that dialectic of work–poverty–unemployment–crime which is the defining matrix of working-class London through much of the century. Even when the intersections were not immediate, the fear that they might come to pass powerfully transfixed the minds of the governing classes throughout (cf. Stedman-Jones's account of the *grande peur* accompanying the demonstrations of the London unemployed following 'Black Monday' [15]). Some people undoubtedly graduated out of the twilight zone between crime and poverty, survival and destitution, into full-time criminal careers; and the people of the East End no doubt themselves registered, in the complex of feelings and attitudes which enabled them to 'make sense' of their situation and conduct, the difference: 'regular' professional thieves, who set out for their 'work' each night as others set out for theirs in the early morning, are said sometimes to have referred to themselves as 'honest' thieves, to mark their distinction from the 'casual' crime of the casual poor. But this whole story of crime, work and poverty – a major theme of the life of the London labouring classes throughout the nineteenth century – could hardly be reconstructed at all unless, alongside the internal differentiations of the various strata of the class, the complex unity of the position of the class as a whole is continually articulated along a differentiated continuum of responses and solutions – what we have called elsewhere the 'working-class repertoire'. [16]

This first argument about the relation between crime and its social context connects closely with a second: the obvious but frequently neglected point that 'crime' is differently *defined* (in both official and lay ideologies) at different periods; and this reflects, not only changing attitudes amongst different sectors of the populations to crime, as well as real historical changes in the social organisation of criminal activity, [17] but also the shifting *application* of the category itself, by the governing classes, to different groups and activities, in the course of – and sometimes for the purpose of preparing the ground for – the exercise of legal restraint and political control. As well as the changing structures of crime, and popular attitudes to crime, we must also take account of the role which *criminalisation* – the attachment of the criminal label, to the activities of groups which the authorities deem it necessary to control – plays in legitimising the exercise of judicial control. As we argued earlier, there is something appealingly simple about the 'criminal label': it resolves ambiguities in public feeling. The appeals to the right of free assembly in the London demonstrations of 1886 and 1887 must have touched an ambiguous nerve amongst the middle classes; but about the sight of 'the West End . . . for a couple of hours in the hands of the mob', *The Times* was in no doubt. Crime issues are clear-cut; political conflicts are double-edged. But a governing class which can assure the people that a political demonstration will end in a mob riot against life and property has a good deal going for it – including popular support for 'tough measures'. Hence the 'criminalisation' of political and economic conflicts is a central aspect of the exercise of social control. It is often accompanied by heavy ideological 'work', required to shift labels about until they stick, extending and widening their reference, or trying to win over one labelled section against another. (A short history of ideological repression could be reconstructed around the transformations effected between the following couplets: deserving/undeserving, labouring/dangerous, 'true working'/residual, respectable/rough, moderate/extremist.)

In his study of the introduction, over a century earlier, of the infamous *Black Act*, Thompson has written:

> What is at issue is not whether there were any such gangs (there were) but the universality with which the authorities applied the term to any association of people which fell outside the law ... For the category 'criminal' can be a dehumanising one ... and the categories then prepare us exactly for the conclusions.... The behaviour of the 'Blacks' was a 'real danger to peaceable men' and therefore 'the provisions of the Black Act had justification at this time'. 'Something needed to be done'. [18]

The use of labelling and criminalisation as part and parcel of the process of legitimating social control is clearly not confined to the past. In the political domain it has time and again taken the form of a fear of, or discovery of, conspiracies, either from within or without, e.g. the typical 'Red Scare'. But there are many other recent examples where legal controls have been sustained precisely by an inspired convergence of criminal and ideological labels. [19] Of course, not all the convergences are convergences of labels. Some mark real, historical developments. There are many unambiguous historical examples of 'political groups self-consciously adopting traditionally criminal strategies and styles', [20] from the Bonnot Gang and other conspiratorial fraternities on the fringes of the anarcho-syndicalist movement earlier in the century, to the Angry Brigade, Baader-Meinhof and other more contemporary forms of the 'political gang'. And if these are taken as representing instances of the convergence from political into criminal activities, there are, equally, many significant recent examples which move the other way – from the criminal to the political: the autobiography of *Malcolm X*, [21] and the politicisation of black criminals in the recent American prison movements, [22] are only two of the most obvious instances.

To put the matter more simply, in a class society, based on the needs of capital and the protection of private property, the poor and propertyless are *always* in some sense on 'the wrong side of the law', whether actually they transgress it or not: 'the criminal sanction is the last defence of private property'. [23] All crime control (whether against crimes undertaken for conscious 'social' motives or not) is an aspect of that larger and wider exercise of 'social authority'; and in class societies that will inevitably mean the social authority exerted by the powerful and the propertied over the powerless and the propertyless. We can see this clearly, again, in the eighteenth century, where the law was far more openly and explicitly an instrument of class domination and authority. Thompson's argument in *Whigs and Hunters* seems to be that the disguised and blackfaced poachers of deer and game in the royal parks and chases, and the Whig 'hunters' who took them on (supported by one of the most sweeping and draconian measures ever devised within the English criminal code – the *Black Act*, backed by the Walpole junta in power, and surrounded by whispers of Jacobite conspiracies and strange gatherings in the night), were engaged in the long, deep and protracted struggle, in progress throughout the century, between customary rights and traditions, and the encroaching bourgeois notions of property and law. [24] The crimes of the forest were only one episode in the longer story of the 'remaking' of English life and society in its bourgeois form – a process which often depended rather more on the selective use of terror and force than on more 'civilising influences'. [25]

> From another aspect, it appears as if it is not just a matter of 'crime' enlarging but equally of a property-conscious oligarchy redefining, through its legislative power, activities, use-rights in common or woods, perquisites in industry, as thefts or offences. For as offences appear to multiply so also do statutes. ... And the ideology of the ruling oligarchy, which places a supreme value upon property, finds its visible and material embodiment above all in the ideology and practice of the law. [26]

The fact that the law did not always act in simple and perfect consonance with this larger purpose, and that judicial terror was frequently tempered with mercy, does not undermine the argument that, in their longer historical trajectory, the changing concepts and practices of the law and the changing concepts and structures of bourgeois property were moving, during the eighteenth century, in 'rough harmony'; and that the law became one of the privileged instruments, not simply in enforcing the conformity of the populace to the new structures, but in securing for property its ideological sway – its proper authority: 'The courts dealt in terror, pain and death, but also in moral ideals, control of arbitrary power, mercy for the weak. In doing so they made it possible to disguise much of the class interest of the law. The second strength of an ideology is its generality.' [27] Hence, when the emergency concerning the 'Blacks' arose:

> What made the 'emergency' was the repeated public humiliation of the authorities; the simultaneous attacks upon royal and private property; the sense of a confederated movement which was enlarging its social demands, especially under 'King John'; the symptoms of something close to class warfare, with the loyalist gentry in the disturbed areas objects of attack and pitifully isolated in their attempts to enforce order. [28]

The connections are made, on a wider canvas, in Douglas Hay's essay on 'Property, Authority and the Criminal Law', already quoted from, which argues that in the eighteenth century, 'terror alone could never have accomplished these ends. It was the raw material of authority, but class interest and the structure of the law itself shaped it into a much more effective instrument of power.' [29] 'Throughout the period,' Hay concludes, 'the importance of the law as an instrument of authority and a breeder of values remained paramount.' [30] 'A ruling class organizes its power in the state. The sanction of the state is force, but it is force that is legitimized, however imperfectly, and therefore the state deals also in ideologies.' [31] In this period, then, the law played a crucial role, not simply in the maintenance of a certain kind of public order in the service of a certain type of ruling oligarchy — the political representatives of an agrarian capitalism — but also as one of the principal public 'educators' to a certain idea of property: hanging some, as it were, for the larger purpose of tutoring the rest. And part of that tutorship to authority rested, precisely, in the law's majesty, its arbitrariness, its panoply and ritual — ceremonies which embodied the very notion of 'authority' itself, and which, as Thompson notes, [32] 'were at the heart of the popular culture also' — were indeed publicly situated *at* its heart, through the court rituals, visitations of the magistrates, the public executions, the ballads and broadsheets, with their exemplary moral force. (When we say that in English popular ideology there is a powerful respect, if not for 'the law' then for 'The Law', it is well to remember how it got there, who put it there and for what purpose.) If, in the eighteenth century, property became the measure of all things, the law was one of the most effective of measuring rods. Hay reminds us, too, of the nature of this concept of 'property' around which the law embroidered its complicated skein of respect and forced obligation: a concept defined, as well as anywhere, by Blackstone, one of the foremost jurists of his time: 'there is nothing which so generally strikes the imagination, and engages the affections of mankind, as the right of property; or that sole and despotic dominion which one man claims and exercises over the external things of the world, in total exclusion of any other individual in the universe'. [33] This was no simple matter of the legal consolidation of class rule. Linebaugh, writing of the same period, has noted:

> It is by looking at crime from the point of view of capital in the Eighteenth Century that we can best appreciate its importance in 'the perennial struggle between capital and labour'. . . . Eighteenth Century crime was an integral aspect of the organisation and creation of a 'free' mobile labour force, of the formation of a home market, and of the transformation of the wage: that is, crime was both the result and a part of the main tasks of 18th Century capitalist development. [34]

Yet, as Thompson has argued: 'At petty and quarter sessions the JP's sentenced for poaching, for assaults, for wood-theft . . . and for the theft of chickens. At assizes the judges sentenced coiners, rioters, sheep-stealers, and servant girls who had run off with their mistress's silk and silver spoons. Research has not yet confirmed that they were sentencing different kinds of people from different sub-cultures.' [35]

The class character of the law, the class administration of justice, the articulation of both with the objective requirements of capital, the distribution of property and what Gramsci called the 'education' of the subordinate and propertyless classes through the law are complex matters. Their developments cannot be traced in a linear evolution, predicated on the assumption of some necessary 'functional fit' or natural correspondence between the different levels of a social formation. The eighteenth-century complex, in which the law played so open a role, is profoundly modified in the succeeding centuries. This does not mean the law steadily improved; indeed during the Jacobin scare and in the upsurge following the end of the Napoleonic War, it became, if anything, more coercive and draconian. Further, its development cannot be told simply in terms of crime and the law, since precisely one of the things which changes is the *position* of the law, the juridical apparatuses and the state in the constitution of the modes of hegemony characteristic of *laissez-faire* and then later of monopoly industrial capitalism, as compared with its role in a social formation in which agrarian capital dominates. No simple 'law of evolutionary succession' is to be observed here.[36] The law does become – gradually and of course *unevenly* – less arbitrary, more 'impartial', more rational in its conduct, more 'autonomous'. The sanguinary penal code is modernised: the identification between the rural gentry and the magistracy becomes progressively less direct; the regular and professional police force replaces the army, the yeomanry and amateur law enforcement. It remains true that, at every critical political turning point in the nineteenth century – the struggle against the unreformed parliament, the formation of the unions, the disturbances of the 1820s, the Chartist agitation, the great popular reform demonstrations of the 1860s, the unemployment agitations of the 1880s, the unrest accompanying the new unionism at the end of the century, the high tide of militancy just before and after the First World War – the 'law-enforcement agencies', and then the law itself, was on hand, in a crucial role: the last fortress and fortification of the existing state of things, whatever they happened to be at the time. But not only was the law forced, above all by the growing working-class presence, to perform this task more circumspectly and 'impartially', legitimating itself, not in the prerogatives of a propertied class but in the universal appeal to 'public order' and the general interest; it was constantly, forced back to a more impartial position. It is open to question whether the law continued to play quite the direct *educative* role which it did a century before.[37] The position can only properly be assessed when set within the framework of the transformation of the modes of capital, as the regime of industrial capital gradually wins out over landed capital, transforming everything in its wake, including that to which the role and position of the law must most directly be referred: the nature and position of the capitalist state itself, as the organising centre of a new set of ruling-class alliances. In this long transformation, we must not neglect the contradictory effect of the progressive 'autonomisation' of the judicial apparatus through the more rigorous application of the 'rule of law' and the 'separation of powers'. For if this continued to obscure the class nature of the law and its exercise, it at the same time secured a *real* and significant measure of justice for the poor and the powerless, and distanced everyday legal practice from the immediate influence of the executive. The working-class movement must count the extension of the rule of law, the freedom of speech and assembly, the right to strike and to organise in the work-place, as its own victories – not simply as 'bourgeois concessions' magnanimously granted. Such advances were of course won only as a consequence of more or less continuous struggle at key points and moments – it is this ruptured history which is now retrospectively smoothed out into the consoling myth of the civilising advance of the law and its contribution to the 'conquest of violence'. In the long term, in the routine premising of the civil law on the inviolability of contract, and of the criminal law in the defence of private property, and in its repressive, 'public-order' work on behalf of social stability and order in the face of social movements and political dissent, the law continued to do the state some service. The articulations between the law, a bourgeois social formation and the advance of industrial capital become more complex, different in character as compared with the eighteenth century. Yet it would be impossible to sustain the argument that all coupling ceases, or that the connection is wholly dissolved. As John Griffith has recently argued: 'The political neutrality of the judiciary is a myth, one of those fictions our rulers delight in, because it confuses and obscures. . . . Our political system thrives on obfuscations. . . . The judiciary does not of course call its prejudices political or moral, or social. It calls them the public interest.' [38] We shall come in a moment to consider some of these contradictory developments – they belong not to the internal history of the law so much as to the 'regional' history of the capitalist state and to the changing modes of hegemony. But, historically, as in the present, the case ought to have been sufficiently strongly established by now that crime and crime prevention are not discrete and autonomous areas; and thus that it cannot be only 'social' crime which requires historical explanation.

FROM 'CONTROL CULTURE' TO THE STATE

At one level, of course, 'The Law' – the legal system, the police, the courts and the prison system – is manifestly part and parcel of the judicial organisation of the modern capitalist state. But this is so largely in a descriptive or purely institutional sense. Most criminological theories – including much of 'radical criminology' – have no concept or theory of the state. In conventional theories, the exercise of state power through the operation of the law is acknowledged only formally, and its mode of operation is treated as unproblematic. This is quite unsatisfactory, even if we remain within the perspective of the legal system. And once we widen the perspective to include the relations between the juridical and other levels and apparatuses of the state, we are clearly in need of a more developed framework than is provided by the well-worn and oft-repeated common-sense wisdoms of liberal democratic theory, cast as they are within that most English of ideologies – British constitutionalism. Lord Denning himself has acknowledged that:

> In theory the judiciary is a neutral force between Government and the governed. The judge interprets and applies the laws without favour to either. . . . British judges have never practiced such detachment. . . . In the criminal law the judges regard themselves as at least as much concerned as the executive with the prosecution of law and order. [39]

In the earlier stages of this study, we examined concretely the relationship between the different apparatuses of control in relation to 'mugging': the police, the judiciary, the media. Lemert has used the term 'societal control culture' to refer to the concerted actions of such agencies in relation to particular crimes. The 'societal control culture' is, in Lemert's terms, 'the laws, procedures, programs and organizations which, in the name of a collectivity, help, rehabilitate, punish or otherwise manipulate deviants'.[40] This definition has provided a useful starting-point in the generation of more radical theories of crime and deviance. It highlighted the relationship between different control agencies as of critical importance in the designation and control of crime. The term 'culture' in this context also serves to remind us that, at one important level, these agencies were linked, not only by their control function, but by their shared 'definitions of the world', their common ideological perspectives. Above all, as compared with more strictly 'transactional' theories, where deviance and crime appeared to depend on the ebb and flow between different 'definitions of the situation', more or less equally ranked on the scale of power, Lemert's emphasis serves to remind us that, if labelling is an important aspect of the identification and control of deviance, then the question of who has the power to label whom – what Becker came subsequently to call the 'hierarchy of credibility'[41] – is of even greater importance. Thus the notion of a 'societal control culture', institutionally based, ideologically supported, with some stability and continuity over time, and reflecting the massively skewed distribution of power between law-makers and law-breakers, was of considerable theoretical significance in neutralising the incipient tendency of 'transactional' theories to operate in a historical and material void, denuded of the concept of power (and thus of the complementary concepts of opposition, struggle, conflict, resistance and antagonism).

The 'control-culture' approach, however, appears too imprecise for our purposes. It identifies centres of power and their importance for the social-control process; but it does not locate them *historically*, and thus it cannot designate the significant moments of shift and change. It does not differentiate adequately *between* different types of state or political regime. It does not specify the kind of social formation which requires and establishes a particular kind of legal order. It does not examine the repressive functions of the state apparatuses in relation to their consensual functions. Thus many different types of society – 'plural' societies, where some are more plural than others, or 'mass societies', where power is alleged to be distributed between the elites, or a 'democratic society' with countervailing powers – are all made compatible with the concept of a 'social-control culture'. It is not a historically specific concept. In short, it is not premised on a theory of the state: even less on a theory of the state of a particular phase of capitalist development – e.g. class democracies in the era of 'late capitalism'. For these reasons, we have abandoned it for all but general descriptive purposes.

Instead, we return 'The Law' to the classic terrain of the theory of the state. General questions of law and crime, of social control and consent, of legality and illegality, of conformity, legitimation and opposition, belong, and must ultimately be posed unambiguously in relation to, the question of the capitalist state and the class struggle. We have suggested that the law, in both its civil and criminal roles, and in both its routine and 'exceptional' modes, is centrally connected, in bourgeois social formations, with the problem of fundamental modes of hegemony. In our case, the form of state in question is its post *laissez-faire* or Welfare State form: installed in and through a specific type of political regime – the fully developed parliamentary democracy; at a specific historical conjuncture – what we shall come to identify more fully as a 'crisis in hegemony'. In this part of the study, we attempt to situate 'mugging' systematically at this *level* of analysis: in relation to the state, the politico-juridical apparatuses, the political instance, the modes of consent, legitimation, coercion and domination – the elements which contribute to the maintenance or disintegration of a specific mode of hegemony.

In filling out this connection between the state and crime, we have tried to work with and to contribute to the development of a specifically Marxist theory of the state, and of the relationship between law, crime and the state. Unfortunately, there is no fully elaborated theory of this kind to be found in Marx and Engels. The elements of such a theory are of course present but they require – in the light of contemporary developments – to be worked out, not drawn upon and used at will. As is often the case in those areas where Marxism is not yet fully developed, the simple formulae are often too simple, too reductive for our purposes. The idea, for example, that, broadly speaking, legal norms and rules in a bourgeois society will reflect and support bourgeois economic relations, or that, in class societies, the law will be an instrument of class domination, may provide the first, basic step in such a theory, but it remains too general, too abstract, too reductive, too sketchy and epochal in form to be of much service. It is a useful but not an adequate point of departure. It is necessary, therefore, at the risk of a necessary detour into some general theoretical questions, to state more fully and explicitly the concept of law, crime and the state on which we draw in the subsequent analysis.

In locating the origins of his materialist theory in a critique of idealist forms of thought, Marx remarked that his enquiry had led him to the conclusion 'that neither legal relations nor political forms could be comprehended whether by themselves or on the basis of so-called general development of the human mind, but ... originate in the material conditions of life',[42] whose totality Hegel and the French and English theorists called 'civil society'; the anatomy of civil society, 'however, has to be sought in political economy'. The crucial level of determination on this complex of social relations – civil society and the state (what Gramsci called 'the two great floors of the superstructure') – was the mode of the production and reproduction of material life. This general proposition had to be made historically specific: 'each mode of production produces its own specific legal relations, political forms, etc.'[43] Law, then, like other superstructural forms, served to 'perpetuate a particular mode of production'. Yet, Marx insisted, 'the influence exercised by laws on the preservation of existing conditions of distribution, and the effect they thereby exert on production has to be examined *separately*.[44] 'But the really difficult point,' he repeats in the Introduction to the *Grundrisse*, 'is how relations of production develop *unevenly* as legal relations. Thus e.g. the relation of Roman private law ... to modern production' (our emphasis).[45] It seems clear here that Marx is arguing both for a long-term or 'epochal' determination of the level of a mode of production over legal relations, and *at the same time*, for no simple, transparent or immediate correspondence, for their 'relative autonomy', as the phrase goes. Engels seems to be echoing Marx's mature concept of 'unevenness', in at least one of its dimensions, when, in discussing the relationship between economic development and the law, he notes that in

England a bourgeois content is given to 'old feudal laws'; while a 'classic law code of bourgeois society' like the *Code Civil* could serve, in France, as a successful, but in Prussia as an ill-adapted, legal form for capitalist development. In another context, it is Engels who notes that 'once the state has become an independent power vis-a-vis society, it produces forthwith a further ideology. It is indeed among professional politicians, theorists of public law and jurists of private law that the connection with the economic facts gets lost for fair. Since in each particular case the economic facts must assume the form of juristic motives in order to receive legal sanction. . . .' [46] Here the crucial problem of a Marxist analysis is posed: how to understand the nature of the 'uneven correspondence' between legal relations and other levels of a social formation; how to comprehend that the state can serve 'the supremacy of this or that class in the last resort . . . the development of the productive forces and relations of exchange', while at the same time assuming the appearance of an independent power, 'apparently standing above society' moderating its contradictory antagonisms. [47]

In the *German Ideology* Marx and Engels stress that those who rule, 'besides having to constitute their power in the form of the State, have to give their will . . . a universal expression as the will of the State, as law'. [48] The state is therefore not independent of the class struggle; but it is, or *comes to be*, the structure which enables a ruling-class alliance to 'give its ideas the form of universality, and represent them as the only rational, universally valid ones'. [49] Lenin also insisted that the state is 'the product and manifestation of the irreconcilability of class antagonisms'; 'it creates "order",' he continued, 'which legalizes and perpetuates this oppression by moderating the collisions between classes'. Here, the same apparent paradox is repeated: the state is the product of class antagonisms, and perpetuates a class order – by appearing to moderate the class struggle. [50] Thus the moderating and conciliating role of the state, 'above the classes', is itself one of the forms in which the essential class nature of the state *appears* at a certain moment in the historical development of the productive life of capitalist societies. Its 'determination in the last instance' – to put it paradoxically – is exercised, at a certain moment, most effectively, indeed *only*, in and through its 'relative autonomy'. (Althusser insists, quite correctly, that we must grasp these 'two ends of the chain' at once.) In the necessary attempt to undermine any simple and immediate 'correspondence' between the mode of production, the form of the state and the character of the law, and in stressing the necessarily 'uneven' character of the relations between the different levels of a social formation, the necessity to 'think' the precise nature of its uneven correspondences can, however, sometimes be altogether lost. It is important to observe that even Poulantzas, who most forcefully elaborates the non-correspondence between the different levels of a social formation (the 'relative autonomy' of the economic, the political, the ideological), has, of necessity, to return to the classical premise that the dominance of 'private capitalism involves a non-interventionist state and monopoly capitalism involves an interventionist state'. [51] Poulantzas's elaboration of 'relative autonomy' has too frequently been quoted at the expense of any recognition of the premising of his analysis on what he himself calls these 'tendential combinations'.

But how does the class struggle reappear through the state, as the conciliation of the class struggle? The argument turns on Marx's usage of the term,
'appearance' and its cognates. [52] Marx always uses 'appearances' in the *strong*
sense. The notion of 'appearance' as used in Marx is not the same as the
common-sense meaning of the term 'false appearances', if by that we understand something which is simply an optical illusion, a fantasy in men's imagination. The term 'appearance' in Marx implies a theory of *darstellung* or
representation – a theory that a social formation is a complex unity, composed
of different levels and practices, where there is no necessary identity or
correspondence between the effects a relation produces at its different levels.
Thus 'appearances' in this sense, are false, not because they do not exist, but
because they invite us to mistake surface effects for real relations. As Gramsci
puts it: 'The terms "apparent" and "appearance" mean precisely this and
nothing else. . . . They are the assertion of the perishable nature of all
ideological systems, side by side with the assertion that all systems have an
historical validity and are necessary.' [53] Thus the unequal exchange of capital
with labour power in the sphere of capitalist production *appears as* – is
transformed into – the 'equal exchange' of commodities at their 'value' in the
sphere of exchange. Thus the unequal extraction of surplus value in production
appears as 'a fair day's wage for a fair day's work' at the level of the wage contract. So, also, the 'reproductive' work which the capitalist state performs on
behalf of capital, assumes the appearance of the class neutrality of the state –
standing above the class struggle and moderating it – at the politico-juridical
level: 'In order that these antagonisms . . . might not consume themselves and
society in sterile struggle, a power *apparently* standing above society becomes
necessary for the purpose of moderating the conflict and keeping it within the
bounds of "order".' [54]

We can see this theory of 'representation' at work in *Capital*, in for example,
the discussion of the 'wage-form'. Both in everyday life, in bourgeois common
sense and in political economy, the wage is 'experienced' and theorised as the
form of 'equal exchange' between the capitalist and the labourer, regulated only
by the 'hidden hand' of the labour market. Marx argues that this form of 'equal
exchange' is in fact founded 'in the depths', on relations of production, by
which surplus labour is extracted by the capitalist in the form of surplus value
– relations which are neither free nor equal. These relations are, however, apparently 'lived' as market relations of equality. The wage relation, in the sphere
of exchange, is a relation 'standing in' for another relation which, at the same
time, it obscures. It is clear of course that this does not mean that the wage
relation is a figment of the imagination, an imaginary construct. The wage relation is a tangible and necessary relation for capital. Wages do exist. Indeed,
they are absolutely necessary to capitalist 'relations of production' since they
are the form in which capital advances part of itself – 'variable' capital – in order that labour power can reproduce itself through subsistence in the family,
the sphere of 'reproduction'. Wages are also the means by which the wage-
earners are attracted from one labour market to another, and thus distributed
to the various branches of production. Thus wages are a part of productive
capital, the necessary part which capital advances for the reproduction of
labour power. However, they assume under capitalist conditions a 'form' which

appears to belong to the sphere of circulation alone, and thus as the labourer's 'just reward' for a 'fair day's work'. The appearance which capital assumes in this sphere (i.e. money) conceals or obscures from the labourer the fact that what he is paid is only a part of what he already produces – and that this payment favours the capitalist because it enables the labourer to reproduce that labour power which he will need for the cycle of production to continue:

> Within the limits of what is strictly necessary, the individual consumption of the working class is therefore the reconversion of the means of subsistence given by capital in exchange for labour power, into fresh labour-power at the disposal of capital for exploitation. It is the production and reproduction of that means of production so indispensable to the capitalist: the labourer himself. . . . The maintenance and reproduction of the working class is, and must ever be, a necessary condition to the reproduction of capital. [55]

Earlier, Marx notes that 'The conversion of a sum of money into means of production and labour-power . . . takes place in the market, within the sphere of circulation.' However, he adds: 'the simple fundamental form of the process of accumulation is obscured by the incident of the circulation which brings it about, and by the splitting up of surplus value'. [56] The transaction of capital, he argues, 'is veiled by the commodity-form of the product and the money-form of the commodity'. In this connection, he says, 'The bourgeois economist' has a 'narrow mind' which is 'unable to separate the form of appearance from the thing that appears'. The 'forms' which 'capital assumes while in the sphere of circulation', as well as 'the concrete conditions of its reproduction', are 'hidden under these forms'. [57]

Capital must therefore constantly *pass through* the web of circulation and the forms which effect its transformation at that level, in order to complete its circuit, 'flowing on with incessant renewal'. So the sphere of circulation is *necessary* to the circuit of capital, even though at the same time it is precisely its exchange *forms* which 'hide the play of its inner mechanism'. Clearly, the forms of exchange cannot *adequately* express or grasp the relations of production between capitalist and labourer as a whole, for they appear in exchange as one 'moment' only of the realisation of value. It is about this sphere of exchange, however, that Marx observes: 'this sphere . . . within whose boundaries the sale and purchase of labour power goes on, is in fact a very Eden of the innate rights of man. There alone rule Freedom, Equality, Property and Bentham.' [58] In short, it is from this one-sided appearance which capital assumes in circulation that there arise all the concepts and discourses which organise the domains of the superstructures – political, legal and ideological.

We must try to think the problem of the capitalist state on the analogy of the things Marx has been saying about the wage form in *Capital*. The State, apparently independent of any particular class interest, composed of the politico-juridical apparatuses, embodying the 'general interest', 'universal' rights and obligations, is precisely the form (and after a certain stage in the development of the capitalist mode of production, the *only* form) in which particular class interests can be *secured as a 'general interest'*.

In the *Eighteenth Brumaire* and his other historical writings, Marx analysed in concrete detail this 'relative independence' of the sphere of politics and the juridical system from the mode of production. The crisis of December 1851 in France, and the failure of any one class or class alliance to seize power in the state, leading to the 'Bonapartist' stalemate, reflected, Marx argued, the *backwardness* of the French mode of production at the time; the latter's 'under-development' set the limits within which the 'Bonapartist' political resolution was effected. But it did not determine the specific class content of each moment of the political crisis, which, Marx showed, assumed a succession of different forms of regime – social republic, democratic republic, parliamentary republic – each representing an attempted equilibrium between different class forces, before falling back 'on the despotism of a single individual'. [59] These different forms of regime – in which the relations of class forces and the struggles between them appeared – were generated at the level of *politics*: each stage in the resolution producing, in turn, a different form of the state. Each, in its own way – Marx added – 'methodically' developed the French state as an independent power. The less each attempted class alliance proved able to rule on its own, the more it required a strong state to rule on its behalf; yet none could finally command this state and rule from its base. The class which finally came nearest to securing its interests through the rule of Napoleon and his 'ideas' was, in the event, a section of a backward and declining class – the conservative sections of the smallholding peasantry. This class could not rule on its own or command the state in its own name. Hence it attempted to 'rule through' Napoleon. In fact Napoleon for a time succeeded in ruling through it. This class fraction did, Marx observes, 'prosper in a hot house fashion' under Napoleon; but in the long term it undoubtedly retarded rather than advanced the development of the productive forces and capitalist relations in France. The *Eighteenth Brumaire*, the most dazzling analysis of the political instance in Marx's mature historical work, thus offers an exceptionally lucid insight into the complexities of the 'uneven correspondence' between the forms of the state and other levels of the social formation. The political crisis which finally assumed its Bonapartist 'resolution' was precipitated by the contradictory development of the French mode of production. The complex of classes and class fractions 'in play' in the crisis corresponded to the underdeveloped stage of that development: the fact that industrial capital was not yet in dominance in the French economy, and several different modes of production were still in an uneven combination. The level of development of the French mode of production thus set certain critical *limits* to the forms of the political resolution which were possible at that moment in French history. The peculiar nature of 'Bonapartism' Marx clearly understood as a stalemate resolution which was also a postponement: 'France therefore seems to have escaped the despotism of a class only to fall back beneath the despotism of an individual.' [60] This 'resolution' does not advance – it retards the further development of the productive forces. The essay is therefore a brilliant exposition of the way the political domain is both 'connected with' and at the same time 'relatively independent' of the economic movements of society. It is an object lesson in the attempt to 'think' the relative-autonomy/determination-in-the-last-instance of the politico-juridical level of a social formation.

THE LEGAL AND POLITICAL ORDER OF THE STATE

It is the legal and political aspects of the capitalist state which principally concern us here. Although the modern capitalist state is constituted principally at the political level, it has many other functions – including directly economic ones – which cannot be examined here. The observations which follow should not therefore be taken as standing, even in bare outline, as a *general* account of the modes of operation of the modern state. It is to the role of the state in the establishment of hegemony – as this is achieved in the political, juridical and ideological domains, and within civil society and its association – that our attention here must necessarily be limited.

Gramsci, whose work has considerably enlarged our conception of the state and its functions, speaks of the capitalist state as 'the instrument for conforming civil society to the economic structure'. That is to say, the state plays a critical role in *shaping* social and political life in such a way as to favour the continued expansion of production and the reproduction of capitalist social relations. This may be considered a 'general function of the state in so far as, since the development of relatively complex social formations, some developed form of territorial and juridical authority has been necessary to organize and consolidate the basic productive relations'.[61] But the manner and scale on which the state performs this role *under capitalism* is historically specific and distinct from any other type of social formation hitherto known. Capitalism is the first mode of production to be based on the historic appearance and dominance of 'free labour'; that is, labour which is not bound by traditional, juridical or political ties of force, obligation, caste or custom; which is denuded of its own means of production (as labour under domestic production was not); and which enters into a productive relation with capital in its 'free' form, organised only by the contract and the labour market, the buying and selling of labour power. Similarly, the exchange of money for commodities in a society of generalised commodity exchange, where again only the market relation rules, and each individual appears as 'mutually indifferent' to the other's interest, represents a quite specific historical phase of social development. The first aspect belongs to the expanding sphere of private capitalist production, the second to the extending terrain of what was called 'civil society'. Although the economic level is, in this form of society, massively determining, the social relations which characterise such societies of private capital and the market cannot be sustained, recreated and reproduced within the sphere of production alone. The conditions for capitalist production and the reproduction of its social relations must be articulated through *all* the levels of the social formation – economic, political, ideological. Thus, for example, a society based on private capital and 'free labour' in the *economic* sphere requires the *juridical* relations of private property and the contract. Hence it requires a legal code in which these relations are institutionalised; a legal ideology in which these economic motives can assume the form of 'juridical motives'; a juridical apparatus which can give the economic relation a legal expression and sanction. So far as capitalist production is concerned, what matters is the exchange of capital against labour power and the extraction of the surplus. But this labour power has to be physically reproduced. New generations of workers must take the place of old or dead ones; the worker must return refreshed sufficiently each day to labour productively again. The site of this side of the physical and cultural reproduction of labour power – on which economic production depends – is not within production, but (through the instrument of the 'living wage') actually performed within the sphere of consumption of the family and thus in part through the sexual division of labour. Labour power has also to be reproduced at the level of knowledge and skills, which the advancing technical division of labour in capitalist production requires. Increasingly, this 'task' is performed, not within production, but through the distinct sphere of the education system – over which, progressively, as a separate apparatus, the capitalist state increasingly takes command. Labour must also be tutored to 'the rules of morality, civic and professional conscience, which actually means rules of respect for the socio-technical division of labour and ultimately the rules of the order established by class domination'.[62] This 'task' of ideological conformity is, increasingly, the work of the cultural apparatuses – over which, again, the state comes to exert an increasing organisational sway. Hence, even in a social formation over-determined by the laws of motion of capitalist production, the conditions for that production – or what has come to be called *social reproduction* – are often sustained in the apparently 'unproductive' spheres of civil society and the state; and in so far as the classes, fundamentally constituted in the productive relation, also contend over this process of 'social reproduction', the class struggle is present in all the domains of civil society and the state. It is in this sense that Marx called the state 'the official resumé of society'[63], the 'table of contents of man's practical conflicts'. It 'expresses *sub specie rei publicae* (from the political standpoint) all the social conflicts, needs and interests'.[64] Gramsci paraphrased this by calling the state essentially 'organisational and connective'.

For Gramsci, the type of 'order' which the state imposed and expressed was of a very specific kind: an order *of cohesion*. Of course, cohesion can be achieved in more than one form. One side of cohesion clearly depends on force and coercion. In a system based on capitalist reproduction, labour has, if necessary, to be *disciplined* to labour; in bourgeois society, the propertyless have to be disciplined to the respect for private property; in a society of 'free individuals', men and women have to be disciplined to respect and obey the overarching framework of the nation-state itself. Coercion is one necessary face or aspect of 'the order of the state'. The law and the legal institutions are the clearest institutional expression of this 'reserve army' of enforced social discipline. But society clearly works better when men learn to discipline themselves; or where discipline appears to be the result of the spontaneous consent of each to a common and necessary social and political order: or where, at least, the reserve exercise of coercion is put into effect with everyone's consent.

In this respect, Gramsci argued, the state had another, and crucial aspect or role besides the legal or coercive one: the role of leadership, of direction, of education and tutelage – the sphere, not of 'domination' by force, but of the 'production of consent'. 'In reality, the State must be conceived of as an "educator", in as much as it tends precisely to create a new type or level of civilization. . . . It operates according to a plan, urges, incites, solicits, and "punishes".' The legal system – the site, apparently, of coercion – also had a positive and educative role to play in this respect:

> for once the conditions are created in which a certain way of life is 'possible', then 'criminal action or omission' must have a punitive sanction, with moral implications. . . . The Law is the repressive and negative aspect of the entire positive, civilizing activity undertaken by the State . . . praiseworthy and meritorious activity is rewarded, just as criminal actions are punished (and punished in original ways, bringing in 'public opinion' as a form of sanction).[65]

In Gramsci, this management of consent was not conceived simply as a trick or a ruse. For capitalist production to expand, it was necessary for the whole terrain of social, moral and cultural activity to be brought, where possible, within its sway, developed and reshaped to its needs. That is what Gramsci meant by the state 'creating a new type or level of civilization'. The law, he added, 'will be its instrument for this purpose'.[66]

Gramsci clearly recognised that the capitalist state involved the exercise of *both* types of power – coercion (domination) and consent (direction). Even the coercive side of the state worked best when perceived as legitimately coercing – i.e. with the consent of the majority. The state enforces its authority through both types of domination; indeed, the two types are present within each apparatus of the state.[67] Nevertheless, Gramsci argued, the capitalist state functioned best when it operated 'normally' through leadership and consent, with coercion held, so to speak, as the 'armour of consent', for then the state was free to undertake its more educative, 'ethical' and cultural roles, drawing the whole edifice of social life progressively into conformity with the productive sphere. The liberal-democratic state, he argued – with its elaborate structure of representation, its organisation of social interests through Parliament and the formation of parties, its representation of economic interests in trade unions and employers' federations, its space for the articulation of public opinion, its organisational sway over the multitude of private associations in civil life – achieved its *ideal* form, its fullest crystallisation, when rooted in popular consent. These were the essential preconditions for the exercise of what Gramsci called 'hegemony'. Hegemony was no automatic condition; its very *absence* from Italian political life was what focused Gramsci's attention on it. But it was the condition to which liberal-bourgeois society 'aspired'. And its achievement – this universalisation of class interests – *had progressively to pass through the mediation of the state.* Gramsci spoke of 'the decisive passage from the structure to the sphere of the complex superstructures'. Only when a dominant class fraction could *extend* its authority in production through to the spheres of civil society and the state could it be said to exercise 'hegemony'. Through the state, a particular combination of class fractions – an 'historical bloc' – was able to 'propagate itself throughout society – bringing about not only a unison of economic and political aims, but also intellectual and moral unity, posing all the questions around which the struggle rages, not on a corporate but on a "universal" plane, and thus creating the hegemony of a fundamental social group over a series of subordinate groups.' [68]

Gramsci conceived the fundamental level of determination over a social formation to be constituted 'in the last instance' at the level of productive relations; hence he speaks of the fundamental classes of capitalist production as 'the fundamental social groups'. But he recognised that there is no such simple and homogenous formation as *a*, or *the*, ruling class; and he recognised that under different historical conditions the objective interests of such a 'fundamental class' in production could only be realised through the political and ideological leadership of *a particular fraction* of that class, or an alliance of class fractions. The state was thus, for him, of crucial importance in the very *formation* of such ruling alliances, including the welding of the interests of *subaltern* groups under the authority of a particular alliance, thus forming the basis of a 'bloc' which could extend and expand its social authority over the whole *ensemble*. The state was also the terrain in which *subordinate* social classes could be 'won' to support the authority of the ruling alliance. If hegemony was to be secured without destroying the cohesion of the social formation, and without the continual exercise of naked force, then certain 'costs' might have to be extracted from the dominant class to secure consent to its social and political base. Only the state could, when necessary, impose these political costs on narrower ruling-class interests. Undoubtedly, Gramsci believed that the liberal form of the capitalist state was well adapted to this complex exercise in hegemony. In and through political representation, parties, the play of public opinion, there was room for the formal representation of the needs and interests of subordinate social groups within the complex of the state; by these means their loyalty and consent could be 'cemented' to the hegemonic fraction. Similarly, the 'rule of law' established that equality of all citizens, giving the law an autonomous position, while enabling it to perform certain critical tasks, within the legally established framework of hegemonic class power. The same was true at the economic level:

> Undoubtedly the fact of hegemony presupposes that account be taken of the interests and tendencies of the groups over which hegemony is exercised, and that a certain compromise equilibrium should be formed . . . the leading groups should make sacrifices of a corporate-economic kind. But there is also no doubt that such sacrifices and such a compromise cannot touch the essential; for though hegemony is ethical-political, it must also be economic, must necessarily be based on the decisive function exercised by the leading group in the decisive nucleus of economic activity. [69]

More and more, the formation of such 'unequal equilibria' has been the peculiar 'task' of the state.

The state is therefore the key instrument which enlarged the narrow *rule* of a particular class into a 'universal' class leadership and authority over the whole social formation. Its 'task' is to secure this broadening and generalising of class power, while ensuring also the stability and cohesion of the social *ensemble*. The *relative independence* of the state (the 'relative autonomy' of the political from the economic) is, in capitalist societies, the *necessary condition* for this 'task' of cohesion and unity. For this reason, the view of the capitalist state as 'the executive committee of the ruling class' is not a particularly helpful one. It pinpoints the essential class nature of the state but it obscures what is specific to the state under capitalism – the basis of its independence. The temptation is to 'read' the political level of the state as always and *directly expressive*, either of the 'needs' of the productive forces or of the narrow class interests of one ruling class fraction. This obscures the fact that a fundamental class can exercise power through the mediation, at the political level, of a ruling or 'governing' class fraction different from itself. It renders unintelligible the fact that the English industrial bourgeoisie 'ruled' for a substantial part of the nineteenth century, *through* a Parliament dominated by the landed aristocracy; or that the English working class was, for a long period, represented politically through the radical wing of the Liberal Party.

Only a proper understanding of the basis of the form of 'independence' which the state assumes under capitalism enables us to reconcile Perry Anderson's observation that the English industrial capitalist class never becomes the 'governing' class,[70] with Marx and Engel's insistence that England in the nineteenth century was the most bourgeois nation on earth.[71] This otherwise perplexing fact has something to do with Marx's insistence that the bourgeoisie was the only 'ruling class' incapable of ruling on its own. This point is often clearly put in Marx and Engels's writings on Britain and France.[72] Engels thought it almost 'a law of historical development that the bourgeoisie can in no European country get hold of political power . . . in the same exclusive way in which the feudal aristocracy kept hold of it during the Middle Ages'.[73] And the reason for this lay in the tendency of the various capitals increasingly to enter into competition with one another, and for these internal conflicts to represent themselves through internal struggles between different fractions of the bourgeoisie. Hence *Capital itself* – social capital – comes to require a strong, interventionist state, capable of functioning as the 'ideal total capitalist', 'serving the interests of the protection, consolidation and expansion of the capitalist mode of production as a whole, over and against the conflicting interests of . . . the "many capitals" '.[74] The state, Engels said, is a 'capitalist machine . . . the ideal personification of the total national capital'.[75]

In Gramsci's sense, then, the state is not so much an entity, or even a particular complex of institutions, so much as it is a particular site or level of the social formation: with its specific forms and 'tasks', irreplaceable by any other structure, even if, in the last analysis, it is superstructural. The state is the *organiser*. In its economic function it helps to organise on behalf of capital – more and more so as capitalism moves from its *laissez-faire* to its state-monopoly form. It secures the conditions for the reproduction of capital and maintains the society as a site for profitable investment. But it also organises through its juridical function – the 'set of rules which organizes capitalist exchanges and provides the real framework of cohesion in which commercial encounters can take place'.[76] It organises ideologically, through the cultural sphere and the education system – once again, progressively expanded and complexified as the productive needs it serves develop; through the means and media of communication and the orchestration of public opinion. Increasingly, it organises the civil and social life of society – especially of the family and the poor, through the 'mediated' structures of the Welfare State. Above all, it organises *through politics*, the system of political parties and political representation: through 'the maintenance of order in political class conflict'.[77] This organisation of hegemonic domination at the level of politics and the law is, indeed, what, above all, is specific to the functions of the capitalist state. Through the political and juridical sides of its activity, the state secures a certain kind of political order, enforces a certain type of legal order, maintains a certain kind of social order, in the service of capital.

One effect of erecting a complex of state apparatuses in this way is to render the economic aspect of class relations invisible. The classes are represented, politically, as if composed only of 'individual citizens'. The relation of citizens to the state is defined in the law (legal subjects) and through the political institutions (political subjects). The state represents itself as the repository of all these individual wills – it is the 'general will', while standing above and apart from the sordid struggle between particular interests. It reconstitutes class subjects as *its own* subjects: itself as 'the nation'. The political-juridical domain establishes the central points of reference for other public ideologies. The ideological concepts of *this* sphere predominate over others: the language of liberties, 'equality, rights, duties, the rule of law, the legal state, the nation, individuals/persons, the general will, in short all the catchwords under which bourgeois class exploitation entered and ruled in history' becomes paramount.[78] Poulantzas even argues that under capitalism other ideological spheres – philosophy, religion, moral discourse – borrow their key notions from the political-juridical domain.

The 'autonomy' of the liberal capitalist state thus gives a *universal* form to the domination by a succession of ruling-class alliances. That 'universalisation' of the state to the 'general interest' is underpinned by its base in popular representation and popular consent. The capitalist state is the first, historically, to root itself in a universal suffrage. Gradually, through a prolonged political struggle, the emergent working classes won a position in 'political society', and were by the early twentieth century incorporated formally into it. This gradual, uneven, often bitterly resisted drawing of all the political classes within the formal framework of the state, at one and the same time, widened its representative base (and thus its legitimacy), and forced it to appear increasingly 'autonomous' of any one particular class interest. A fundamental recomposition of the form of the capitalist state followed. Hereafter, the state could only provide the 'theatre' for the organisation of hegemony, by working *through consent*. Its work as an 'organiser of consent' thus becomes more critical – as well as more delicate, more problematic. Only by winning consent can the state exact both obligation and obedience.

The law, also, is progressively 'autonomised' as part of this general recomposition; but it remains an integral part of the equation of consent and compliance. The law is the site of the more coercive aspect of the capitalist state: but this exercise in coercion remains legitimate because the law, too, has its base ultimately in popular representation and the 'will of the people through Parliament' which legislates. The strict and impartial observation of the 'rule of law' and the classical doctrine (long ago enunciated by Montesquieu) of the 'separation of powers' are the formal expressions of this pact of civil association in the state, and thus also the soil in which the impartiality of the law is rooted. Hunt has remarked that, because the 'separation of powers' tends to conceal the class character of the judicial apparatus, its critics have been wrongly tempted to exaggerate the *coincidence*, at all times, between the state, the needs of capital, the ruling class and the law. We have suggested the reasons why this simple inversion is not acceptable; it does not explain enough, or adequately. For example, it cannot explain how and why the law can and does sometimes intervene against the overt interests of a particular ruling-class fraction. In the face of this, the expressive view is driven back to a conspiracy theory. Similarly, it cannot explain what the material basis is for the belief – to which working people often subscribe (and which cannot be dismissed as 'false consciousness') – that the law affords *them* some protection of life, limb and property *too*. In fact, the arbitrary, openly class nature of the law, remarked on earlier in relation to the eighteenth century, reflected the *limited* basis of the consent and participation which sustained the coalitions of the emergent agrarian capitalist state – 'Old Corruption'; and demonstrated its imperfectly developed 'bourgeois' character. The wider the political foundations of the state, the stronger the presence of the great 'unenfranchised' classes in it, the more – slowly and unevenly, to be sure – the law, in its routine operations, is driven towards a formal separation from the direct play of the class interests of the governing fraction of the ruling class. This 'recomposition' of the juridical instance within the capitalist state occurs through the most complex dialectic. The law is propelled, by the development of the political class struggle, to appear more independent: this provides a degree of judicial 'space' which the working classes sometimes appropriate for their own defence and protection; but it also gives the law a measure of freedom, as it were, to 'police' – and thus to regulate – capital itself. This task of superintendence and reconstruction 'from above' is a function which, at certain moments, the dominant class fractions require but which they cannot carry through in their own name, and which they don't always like. The 'autonomisation' of the law does not therefore mean that it ceases to perform certain critical judicial tasks on behalf of the development of the capitalist mode of production. In some ways, it now possesses greater freedom and legitimacy to do so. It does, however, mean that these tasks have to be performed in different ways, through profoundly modified legal structures and legal ideologies. It suggests, in short, how this 'perfecting' of the juridical apparatuses of the liberal capitalist state was a process driven forwards by the attempt to find a solution, at a higher level, to contradictions which could not otherwise be overcome: a solution which – like the 'rule of law' itself – remains contradictory.

The consequence of this dialectical movement for the position of the juridical apparatus in the state must be borne in mind throughout what follows – above all, for its contradictory result. A 'Law' which is 'above' party and class can and must, from time to time, impose its legal authority on sections of capital itself. It must enforce its universal legal norms and sanctions against 'illegal' capitalist transactions. Thus 'decisions by the court do not always please the holders of state power.' [79] It must extend its sway to all 'legal subjects' – giving everyone a substantive interest in the preservation of legal order. The substantial gains which working people have made from the enforcement of the 'rule of law' and other legally sanctioned rights must not be overlooked in a hasty but one-sided unmasking (cf. Thompson's eloquent, but itself somewhat one-sided, defence).[80] On the other side, we should not neglect what it performs – not necessarily in a concealed, but often in a perfectly open and 'legitimate' way – in the long-term service of capital. The inscription within its legal forms of the key relations of capital – private property, the contract – is no well-kept secret. If the law demarcates illegal forms of appropriation, it makes the legal forms public and visible – the norm – and sanctions them positively. It protects life and limb. But it also preserves public order; and, under this rubric, it frequently secures, in moments of open class confrontation, just that stability and cohesion without which the steady reproduction of capital and the unfolding of capitalist relations would be a far more hazardous and unpredictable affair. It preserves society against its enemies, within and without. It raises existing social relations – for example those stemming from the social and sexual division of labour – to the level of universal norms. By operating strictly within judicial logic, juridical norms of evidence and proof, it constantly brackets out those aspects of class relations which destroy its equilibrium and impartiality *in practice*. It equalises, in the formal eye of the law, things which cannot be equal. In the famous words of Anatole France: 'in its majestic impartiality it forbids the rich and poor alike to sleep under the bridges of Paris'. It addresses 'class subjects' as individual persons; in Althusser's phrase it constantly 'interpellates the subject' – the legal subject.[81] It even treats corporate structures as 'persons'. 'It is important to stress,' Hunt reminds us, 'that the legal rules do not create the social relations that make up capitalist society. But by stating them as principles and by enforcing them, the Law operates not only to reinforce these relations but to legitimise them in their existing form.' [82] The law thus comes to represent all that is most impartial, independent, above the play of party interest, within the state. It is the most formal representation of universal consent. Its 'rule' comes to stand for the social order – for 'society' itself. Hence a challenge to it is a token of social disintegration. In such conjunctures 'law' and 'order' become identical and indivisible.

MODES OF HEGEMONY, CRISIS IN HEGEMONY

So far we have been speaking of certain general features of the capitalist state. In earlier stages of capitalist development the state performs its work on behalf of the capitalist system, not necessarily by assuring jobs within its bureaucracies or within its political apparatuses for the sons of a rising bourgeoisie, but by other means: first, by destroying those structures, relations, customs, traditions which, deriving from the past, from past modes of life, stand in the way, fetter and constrain capital's 'free development'; second, it performs the work of actively tutoring, forming, shaping, cultivating, soliciting and educating the emergent classes to the new social relations – which enable capitalist accumulation and production to begin 'freely' to unroll. This is a crude but *essential* starting-point for approaching the more difficult issue of the different *types* of state, throughout the historical development of capitalism, which perform this 'work'; and the different *tasks* which arise from different moments in the development of capital; and thus of the different *modes of hegemony* which it is possible for ruling-class alliances to establish and organise through the mediation of the state.

Historically, a great variety of political regimes have been compatible with the capitalist mode of production. This does not undercut Gramsci's argument that certain mechanisms are crucial for the capitalist state *in any* of its 'normal' forms. The qualification, 'normal', is important. Although the precise nature of the relationship between fascism and capitalism in a degenerate phase is still a matter of considerable controversy, it must now be acknowledged that capitalism is also compatible with – and may required to be 'rescued' by – certain quite *exceptional* forms of the state (e.g. the fascist state), in which many of its normal modes are suspended. Gramsci had cause to understand the significance of these 'exceptional' moments, since it was precisely one such state, the state of Mussolini's fascist Italy, which imprisoned him. However, while bearing this 'exceptional' possibility in mind, it is necessary to retain the concept of the 'normal' modes of the liberal and post-liberal state. And this has, centrally, to do with the fact that, however this is actually organised, the capitalist state tends towards founding and establishing its dominance over civil life and society through *the combination* of modes of consent and modes of coercion – but with *consent* as its key, legitimating support. How this 'rule through consent' may actually underpin several very different kinds of state, or how a particular form of the state may shift from one principal modality to another, in moments of crisis, may be illustrated by looking, schematically, at three key moments in its historical development in Britain.

It is becoming increasingly clear that the idea of a 'pure' version of the non-interventionist *laissez-faire* state in Britain in the mid-nineteenth century is a fiction. In the hey-day of the 'liberal' state – roughly, the period between the defeat of Chartism at the end of the 1840s and the onset of the Great Depression – though the state tended to a position of 'non-intervention' in economic affairs and in the market, it remained a significant educative and regulatory force throughout. As Polanyi argues, for the economic liberals of the mid-century, *laissez-faire* was an end to be realised – if necessary through state intervention – not a description of an existing state of things. [83] Radical utilitarians, following Bentham, certainly believed in intervention, precisely to secure the conditions in which untramelled individualism could flourish. This is of course the period of the progressive stabilisation of industrial capital as the dominant mode of production at home over all other modes, including, gradually, that of landed capital; and of the enormous productive expansion of capital across the face of the globe – the creation for the first time of that 'global net' which Marx predicted and which Hobsbawm, in the *Age of Capital* has recently so vividly recreated. [84] The introduction of what Marx calls 'machino-facture' on a large scale transforms the existing basis of production, and in the same moment, transforms existing modes of labour and recomposes the labour force internally. In this period, the role of the state is at once 'minimal' and critical. It is through the state and Parliament that many of the traditional economic arrangements stilf fettering the growth of industrial capital are dismantled; the crucial passage of the repeal of the Corn Laws is a key example here – one of many. It positively 'cultivates' the new working classes to the regime of steady, regular, regulated, unbroken wage labour – the assault by economic liberalism in its most aggressive phase on the 'paternalism' of the old Poor Laws, and the drawing of even the poor and destitute directly into the net of 'productive work' is another key instance. Marx observes how the criminal law and the penal system are related to this disciplining of even the most recalcitrant sectors of the potential labour force to the habits of wage labour. [85] At the same time, the state begins to concern itself with – first through fact-finding, then through administrative intervention, regulation and inspection – the *conditions* of labour (the factory legislation of the period), and the *consequences* of industrial upheaval (the urban reform of health, sanitation and the city). Many of these tasks are 'recuperative': without them capitalism could become neither so self-regulating nor so 'automatic'. Some of them – for example, factory legislation on child and female labour, and then the critical restriction on working hours – the state accomplishes *against* the immediate short-term interests of industrial capital. Here, the state has to accommodate the growing strength, power and organised presence of the working class, and, *apparently* at capital's expense, initiates those legislative measures which provide a stabilising 'equilibrium' for the dominance of capital to continue without massive working-class revolt. We can see in this instance both the 'work' which the state does *for* capital, *against* capital, and its contradictory consequences. For the controls on the length of the working day contravened the crucial means by which capital expanded its surplus: through the lengthening of the working day. Once a barrier had been established to this method, capital is driven to another mode of 'self-expansion' – increasing the productivity of labour through the extension of 'dead' labour (machines) in relation to 'living' labour: that shift from the extraction of 'absolute' to the extraction of 'relative' surplus value which inaugurates a whole new cycle of capitalist development. So the 'relative autonomy' of the state has some contradictory consequences for the very mode of production which it superintends.

In this period it is *politics* which provides the key mechanism of *consent*: and it is through the political system that the dominant economic class exercises its hegemony. We have shown already how important it is that this is executed, not in its own name or person, but through the occupancy, in government and politics, of fractions of landed capital. This displacement of power, from what Marx called the 'economically ruling class' to the 'politically governing caste', is critical for an understanding of the shifting alliances of mid-century politics. It is also critical for an understanding of how the working classes came, throughout this period, to be formally represented, politically, as what Marx and Engels called a 'tail' or appendage to the Whig–Radical alliance – a fact which was to have the greatest consequences for the 'political re-education' of the new industrial masses. The period is framed, at either end, by the two great struggles over the reform of parliamentary institutions. The industrial bourgeoisie first enfranchises itself and its 'tenants'; and then, through the century, is progressively forced to extend the franchise to the working classes. This process, too, is contradictory. On the one hand, the reforms bring the working classes into formal political representation, thereby modifying the undiluted exercise of political power in the interests of capital (thus each stage of enfranchisement is vigorously resisted); yet, on the other hand, the enfranchisement of the masses (which, we must remember, is not completed until the beginning of the next century) creates that base of popular consent which makes the structures of economic and political power legitimate. It finally founds the regime of capital on the stable basis of 'universal consent'. This could not have happened without the *enormous expansion* of the whole sphere of operation of the state – for only in and through a 'universal' state, capable of representing itself as standing above the contending struggles between the classes and 'conciliating them', could the state provide the bridge between the extension of formal political power at the base, and the exercise of limited class domination at its apex. In this contradictory development, then, the state itself is recomposed, enlarged – but also utterly altered in its internal composition and in its spheres of operation. This process is already visible in the period, but as yet no bigger than a cloud on the horizon. The reforms of education, which gradually widen the role of the state in the distribution of skills and knowledge, complementary to the growing complexity of the industrial labour process, which is also taking place in this period, is one aspect of its expansion. But many of those 'tasks' which, later, are to become the privileged arena of state power, are, crucially, still left to the private initiatives of 'civil society' and its associations. The moralising of the poor, the tradition of paternal welfare, the religion of domesticity, the nurturing of the ethos of 'respectability' and self-help – those critical ideological tasks of the mid-century – are the prerogative, not of the state itself, but of the religious and private charities and institutions. Equally important is the delicate balance, already beginning to be established, between central state and local government initiatives. Without this complex of related but 'autonomous' institutions and decentered relations, the classical liberal state of the *laissez-faire* period would have been neither as 'free' nor as 'residual' as, in fact, it appeared.

We cannot examine here in any depth the complex history of the intervening period between the 'non-interventionist' state of the mid-Victorian period, and the 'interventionist' state installed in our day; but it constitutes, of course, a critical period of *transition*. What we have already identified as the shift from absolute to relative surplus value, and the changes required for capitalism to base itself in a new mode of generating its surplus and guaranteeing accumulation, provides the internal stimulus to an extensive and sweeping modification of English society through and through; externally, the declining rate of profit for capital following its first, tumultuous phase of expansion, and the rise of competing national capitals, provide a complementary stimulus. The first leads to that profound shift in capitalism's productive processes at home, which creates the base for a modern capitalism: the raising of the productivity of labour, the application of science and technology as a 'material force' directly to production, the modifications in the labour process itself and in the regime of labour and its real subsumption, the massive recomposition of the structures of capital through centralisation, concentration and vertical integration. The second leads into that period of intensified rivalry between national capitals, the fevered export of capital and the securing of markets and raw materials overseas which produced, first, the 'high noon' of Imperialism, and then the First World War and the Depression. Both, together, constitute an *epochal shift* in the nature of capitalism – and hence in the character, position and mode of operation of the state: what Lenin named the transition from *laissez-faire* to 'monopoly' capitalism. In that transition, the modes of operation of the state change on both its fronts. In the direct confrontations with organised labour, in the revolutionary ferment before and after the First World War, the capitalist state serves a more openly coercive function – attempting to break labour directly, to dilute its skills, recompose it from 'above', to destroy its organised defences – perhaps than it had performed at any point earlier, at least since the end of the Chartist threat. In this confrontation with labour the law is by no means absent or strictly neutral. This lasts through the period of 'retrenchment' and reaches a point of culmination in the imposed defeat of the General Strike, from which the labour movement took twenty years to recover. Yet, at the very same moment, through a different sphere of the state, the exercise of containing, rather than breaking, the working class is also in motion. The early beginnings of a 'welfare state' and the raising of the 'social wage' are, like the sinuous movements of Lloyd George, its great architect, pointed at the very same end – though operating through a different *mode* – to which the coercive regime was directed: establishing the *terms* on which the working classes were to be at one and the same moment *enfranchised* (in the enlarged sense, socially as well as politically) *and contained*. Once again, the expansion of the state is a key factor in this process – an attempt to establish a hegemony over the working class, by a combination of force and consent, which immediately *fails*, though the basis of its long-term success is laid. This whole period is one transfixed from end to end by the question of 'labour'. It is a transitional phase when the capitalist state is just able to *dominate* the class struggle, although it cannot lead.

We have only to turn to the change in scale, position and character of the post-war 'welfare' capitalist state to recognise the difference. The capitalist state has been thoroughly recomposed in the intervening period, and by the very processes which have also been responsible for transforming Britain into an 'unsuccessful' monopoly capitalist social formation from that of a 'successful' *laissez-faire* capitalist one. This can be easily registered, even if, for the moment, we confine ourselves to a descriptive account of the enlarged spheres of state intervention. *First*, in the post-1945 period, the state has itself become a major, direct factor in the economic relations of the society. It took over into 'public ownership' ailing and under-capitalised but vital supportive industries, public utilities, and became a major employer of labour in the productive as well as in the 'unproductive' and service or welfare sectors. *Second*, through the use of neo-Keynesian techniques, it directly undertook what capital, left to itself, could no longer undertake: a superintending of the major movements of the economy, intervening directly to regulate the level of demand, to influence investment, to protect employment levels, and later to manage the movement of wages and prices and to oversee the differential imposition of the 'costs' of recession; that is, the state considerably expanded its over-all function of managing crises and superintending the 'general conditions' of capitalist production and accumulation, and of defending the rate of profit. *Third*, in order to contain working-class pressures for greater security of life and employment, and to consolidate itself on the basis of popular consent, it assumed responsibility, through taxation and the 'social wage', for great stretches of welfare – redistributing parts of the social surplus and considerably expanding its administrative bureaucracies at the same time. *Fourth*, it gave the impetus to a considerable expansion of technical and other kinds of education (including the linked spheres of scientific research and development), in keeping with the technological needs of the economy, the growing division of labour and the requirements for more interchangeable skills in the labour process. *Fifth*, the state became more prominent in the ideological sphere: attempting the integration of the worker into capitalist production and consumption, and of the organised working class into the management of the economy as a 'social partner'; the management of political and social consent; the dissemination of the ideals of 'growth', technical rationalisation and a pragmatic politics which 'get things done'; the propagation of the image of a society of participation and of growing 'equal opportunities for all' – these and other ways of ideologically reinforcing the legitimacy of the new 'mixed' capitalist economy became, to a greater extent than before, the direct, rather than the indirect, responsibility of the state. Its involvement in the field of political communication, in the cultural sphere and the media, is one of the many features of this extensive ideological intervention. Another form which this ideological intervention of the state assumed was the attempt to depoliticise politics itself, and thus to dismantle where it could, and to incorporate where it could not dismantle, working-class politics, labour institutions and organisations. *Sixth*, it greatly promoted the integration and centralisation of capital in the key economic sectors, both through indirect influence, in the administrative mechanisms of joint committees and planning boards, as well as through active measures to promote rationalisation. *Seventh*, it sponsored a major shift in the exercise of state power from the political and parliamentary to the administrative and bureaucratic spheres of government. *Eighth*, through its participation in the complex of international institutions and bodies, it attempted to harmonise the global effects of international capitalist competition as a whole, shoring up the failing currencies of some, establishing free-market zones of specialised production and trade amongst others, in an attempt to keep the system as a whole on an even economic keel – though these efforts at the level of the capitalist nation-states have been persistently undermined by renewed competition between them, even more by the growth of the great multinational forms of capital, so to speak, within or beside the state – the states within the state.

As the limits to the system have increasingly become apparent – a sharpening in competition for declining world markets, shifts in the terms of trade against the metropolitan capitalist countries from the primary-producing developing world, a tendency of the rates of profit in the developed countries to fall, deepening cycles of boom and recession, periodic currency crises and a growing level of inflation – so the *visibility* of the state has increased. It has altogether ceased to be – if ever it was – a 'night-watchman'. It has become increasingly an interventionist force, managing capital where capital could no longer successfully manage itself, and thereby *drawing the economic class struggle increasingly on to its own terrain*. With this increase in its social and economic role, has gone a more overt and direct effort by the state to manage the *political* class struggle. It is through the state that the 'bargains', increasingly, are struck which are intended to give the working classes a 'stake' in the system: it is here that the organised labour movement has progressively been incorporated into the management of the economy as one of its major corporate supports; here, that the balance between periodic concessions and periodic restraints have been regulated in such a way as to favour the long-term growth and stability of capital. To ensure these conditions for capital in the productive and economic life of societies, the state itself has also increasingly been concerned with the 'social equations' which make it possible – with the spheres of social and cultural *re*production, as well as with economic production itself. In Britain, where the attempt to bring off this transition successfully has had to be mounted in extremely unfavourable economic conditions, and in the face of a strong, though often corporate, working class with rising material expectations, tough traditions of bargaining, resistance and struggle, each crisis of the system has, progressively, taken the overt form of a crisis in the management of the state, a *crisis of hegemony*. Increasingly, the state has appeared to absorb all the pressures and tensions of the economic and political class struggle into itself, and then been torn apart, by its conspicuous lack of success. And because the state has assumed a far greater, more autonomous and direct role of superintending the political and economic needs of a capitalism in crisis, so progressively the forms of the class struggle have been reorganised, appearing more and more as a direct conflict between the classes *and* the state. Progressively, the various crises take the form of a general crisis of the state *as a whole*, and rapidly reverberate upwards from their initial starting-points to the higher levels of the legal and political order itself.

In this new form of an 'interventionist' capitalist state the securing of popular consent is more than ever its *only* basis of legitimacy. The governments and political regimes which arise within this new type of state result from, and are supposed to be responsive to, the formal process of consultation established through political representation. It is this process which is supposed to make the state sensitive to, and therefore representative of, the 'sovereign will of the people'. True, that 'will' is expressed through the electoral system only at periodic intervals. The complexities of government and administration are increasingly divorced from that kind of disorganised pressure which ordinary electorates can bring to bear on the constituted bureaucracies. But this centralisation of power through the state is said to be countermanded by the play of public opinion and the independence of a free press. But, without directly absorbing the agencies of opinion formation, it is clear that governments, directly through the decisions they make and the policies they put into effect, through their monopoly of the sources of public knowledge and expertise, and indirectly through the mass media, political communications and other cultural systems, have the most powerful effect in shaping the 'popular consent' which they then consult. The source of administrative power has moved progressively from Parliament to the executive and the great, powerful battalions organised around and increasingly within the orbit of the state itself. In the light of these changes, simpler versions of democratic liberal theory have had to be emended to take account of the simple discrepancies of power which manifestly appear as between the great corporate institutions of the modern economy and state, and the ordinary elector. Nowadays 'consent' is therefore said to depend on the fact that the large but competing corporate entities will cancel out or 'countervail' each other's influence. There is a third and wider meaning now given to consent, which may be called 'sociological'. And it is this which is now said to provide the necessary back stop to the exercise of arbitrary power by the state. The suggestion is not that power has been effectively dispersed in modern democratic mass societies but that the vast majority of people are united within a common system of values, goals and beliefs − the so-called 'central value system'; and it is this *consensus on values,* rather than formal representation, which provides the cohesion which such complex modern states require. The dominant and powerful interests are therefore 'democratic', not because they are directly governed in any sense by the 'will of the people', but because they, too, must ultimately refer themselves and be in some way bound by this 'consensus'.

Now consensus as the unseen regulator or 'hidden hand' of the modern corporate capitalist state is of critical importance − though not exactly in the way in which it appears in the pluralist theorists of political democracy. It has played a critical role in the post-war history of the British state. It was the consensus which provided the political underpinning for that period of social unity and cohesion in the 1950s. And, as such 'common causes' as did provide the basis of this government from centre ground have been progressively eroded, so the cry for consensus, the search for consensus, the wheeling in of consensus as the ultimate test of every political problem and argument, has become more pronounced. Consensus is therefore important for the modes of operation of the modern state. We would define it as the form in which the *consent* of society is won. But won *for what?* Won *by whom?* Although there may be no simple 'ruling class' in a homogeneous sense, the so-called 'democratisation of power' in modern capitalist societies has nowhere effectively replaced either the fundamental fractions of capital and its representatives, at the economic level, nor the dominant succession of ruling-class alliances which organise it at the political level. These coalitions of class fractions, organised as a bloc together with certain subaltern class interests, form the continuing basis of capitalist political class power. And it is precisely such groups which are able to use the enlarged sphere of the state to organise their power.

When a ruling-class alliance has achieved an indisputed authority and sway over all these levels of its organisation − when it masters the political struggle, protects and extends the needs of capital, leads authoritatively in the civil and ideological spheres, and commands the restraining forces of the coercive apparatuses of the state in its defence − when it achieves all this on the basis of consent, i.e. with the support of 'the consensus', we can speak of the establishment of a period of hegemony or hegemonic domination. Thus what the con-sensus really means is that a particular ruling-class alliance has managed to secure through the state such a total social authority, such decisive cultural and ideological leadership, over the subordinate classes that it shapes the whole direction of social life in its image, and is able to raise the level of civilisation to that which the renewed impetus of capital requires; it encloses the material, mental and social universe of the subordinated classes, for a time, within its horizon. It naturalises itself, so that everything appears 'naturally' to favour its continuing domination. But, because this domination has been secured by con-sent – on the basis of a wide consensus, as the saying goes – that domination not only seems to be universal (what everybody wants) and legitimate (not won by coercive force), but its basis in exploitation actually *disappears from view*. Consensus is not the opposite – it is the complementary face of domination. It is what makes the rule of the few disappear into the consent of the many. It ac-tually consists or is founded on the conjunctural mastery of class struggle. But this mastery is displaced, through the mediating form of 'the consensus', and reappears as the *disappearance* or pacification of all conflict; or, what in con-sensus theory once held pride of place under the title, 'the end of ideology'. No wonder, when Harold Macmillan won his third successive electoral victory for the Conservatives in 1959, on the basis of an extremely wide convergence in the society, such that all the economic and sociological trends appeared 'naturally and spontaneously' to be favouring his continued mastery of the political scene, and through him, the domination of that fraction of capital which had gained grounds under his political tutelage – no wonder he announ-ced (no doubt hoping it would become a self-fulfilling prophecy) that 'The class struggle is over'. Perhaps he added, *sotto voce*, 'and we have won it'.

Gramsci speaks in 'The State and Civil Society' of that point 'in their historical lives' where 'social classes become detached from their traditional parties' which are 'no longer recognized by their class (or fraction of a class) as its expression'. Such situations of conflict, though having no doubt their mo-ment of origin deep within the economic structure of the mode of production it-self, tend, at the political level, to 'reverberate out from the terrain of the parties . . . throughout the State organism'. The content of such moments, Gramsci argued, is:

> the crisis of the ruling class' hegemony, which occurs either because the ruling class has failed in some major political undertaking for which it has requested, or forcibly extracted, the consent of the broad masses. . . . Or because huge masses . . . have passed suddenly from a state of political passivity to a certain activity, and put forward demands which, taken together, albeit not organically formulated, add up to a revolution. A 'crisis of authority' is spoken of: this is precisely the crisis of hegemony, or general crisis of the State.[86]

We would argue that a crisis of hegemony or 'general crisis of the state', precisely as Gramsci defined it, has indeed been developing in Britain since the spontaneous and successful 'hegemony' of the immediate post-war period: that, classically, it first assumed the form of a 'crisis of authority'; that, exactly as described, it first reverberated outwards from the terrain of the parties of 'represented and representatives'.

A crisis of hegemony marks a moment of profound rupture in the political and economic life of a society, an accumulation of contradictions. If in moments of 'hegemony' everything works spontaneously so as to sustain and enforce a particular form of class domination while rendering the basis of that social authority invisible through the mechanisms of the production of consent, then moments when the equilibrium of consent is disturbed, or where the contending class forces are so nearly balanced that neither can achieve that sway from which a resolution to the crisis can be promulgated, are moments *when the whole basis of political leadership and cultural authority becomes exposed and contested.* When the temporary balance of the relations of class forces is upset and new forces emerge, old forces run through their *repertoires* of domination. Such moments signal, not necessarily a revolutionary conjuncture nor the collapse of the state, but rather the coming of 'iron times'. It does not follow either that the 'normal' mechanisms of the state are abrogated. But class domination will be exercised, in such moments, through a modification in the *modes of hegemony*; and one of the principal ways in which this is registered is in terms of a tilt in the operation of the state away from consent towards the pole of coercion. It is important to note that this does not entail a suspension of the 'normal' exercise of state power – it is not a move to what is sometimes called a fully exceptional form of the state. It is better understood as – to put it paradoxically – an 'exceptional moment' in the 'normal' form of the late capitalist state. What makes it 'exceptional' is the increased reliance on coercive mechanisms and apparatuses already available within the normal *repertoire* of state power, and the powerful orchestration, in support of this tilt of the balance towards the coercive pole, of an *authoritarian* consensus. In such moments the 'relative autonomy' of the state is no longer enough to secure the measures necessary for social cohesion or for the larger economic tasks which a failing and weakened capital requires. The forms of state intervention thus become more overt and more direct. Consequently such moments are also marked by a process of 'unmasking'. The masks of liberal consent and popular consensus slip to reveal the reserves of coercion and force on which the cohesion of the state and its legal authority finally depends; but there is also a stripping away of the masks of neturality and independence which normally are suspended over the various branches and apparatuses of the State – the Law, for example. This tends further to polarise the 'crisis of hegemony', since the state is progressively drawn, now in its own name, down into the arena of struggle and *direction*, and exhibits more plainly than it does in its routine manifestations what it is and what it must do to provide the 'cement' which holds a ruptured social formation together.

In the two chapters which follow, we try to locate the mugging phenomenon squarely within this historically developing 'crisis of hegemony' in the British state. The reaction to 'mugging', we shall argue, is and continues to be one of the forms in which this critical 'crisis of hegemony' makes itself manifest.

8

The Law-and-Order Society: the Exhaustion of 'Consent'

In this and the following chapters, our aim is to establish precisely in what sense, in what historical context, the reaction to 'mugging' can be said to constitute an aspect of a general 'crisis of hegemony' of the British state. Because 'mugging' provides our privileged point of departure, our account is pitched at the level where hegemony is won or lost: that is, in the civil, political, juridical and ideological complexes of the social formation – in 'the superstructures'. This inevitably results in an account of the British crisis from the top downwards. Thus our analysis gives greater attention to changing relations of force in the political class struggle, to shifting ideological configurations, the changing balance within and between the state apparatuses, etc. than it does to fundamental economic movements. This is a necessary, but one-sided accentuation. No adequate conjunctural analysis of the post-war crisis yet exists on which we could hang our more immediate concerns. An analysis of the British social formation at the level of the changing composition and structure of capital, the recomposition of classes, the technical division of labour and the labour process has only recently been initiated. Our account reflects these absences by the very limits within which it moves. It does not follow that hegemony is unrelated to fundamental contradictions in the structure of capitalist relations. Quite the reverse. Hegemony, in Gramsci's sense, involves the 'passage' of a crisis from its material base in productive life through to 'the complex spheres of the superstructures'. Nevertheless what hegemony ultimately secures is the long-term social conditions for the continuing reproduction of capital. The superstructures provide that 'theatre' where the relations of class forces, given their fundamental form in the antagonistic relations of capitalist production, appear and work themselves through to a resolution.

In the analysis which follows, the principal movement to which we relate the 'mugging' panic is the shift from a 'consensual' to a more 'coercive' management of the class struggle by the capitalist state. The analysis traces the formation of a certain hegemonic equilibrium in the immediate post-war period; its erosion and break-up; then the attempt to secure 'consent' by a more coercive, non-hegemonic use of 'legitimate force'. This process is subject to a rough periodisation: the construction of consensus, as the condition for the post-war stabilisation of capitalism in the circumstances of the Cold War; the establishment of a period of extensive hegemony in the 1950s; the disintegration of this 'miracle' of spontaneous consent; the sterner, more troubled and unsteady attempt to put an essentially 'Labourist' variant of consent together, drawing on the social-democratic *repertoire*; its exhaustion, coupled with the rise of social and political conflict, the deepening of the economic crisis and the resumption of more manifest forms of class struggle; the attempt to rely on a more 'exceptional' form of class domination in the 1970s through the state. 'Mugging' and the reaction to it is structurally, as well as chronologically, linked with this last movement in the rupture of ruling-class hegemony.

The problem of the periodisation of a conjuncture is posed, but not resolved theoretically within the form of analytic reconstruction chosen. In the arrangement of themes, we hope the reader will be able to discern what are, in fact, the overlapping of different periodisations, of structurally different forces developing at different tempos and rhythms of, in fact, different 'histories'. The depth of the crisis, in this sense, is to be seen – only fitfully established here – in the accumulation of contradictions and breaks, rather than in their net sequential or chronological identity. The political, juridical and ideological forms in which the crisis is appropriated provide the dominant moments but not the determinate level of the analysis. They provide us with our key focus – on the state and the organisation of class power through the state. In recent years, this central question in Marxist theory has attracted increased attention, following its too long neglect. We subscribe to its centrality. But – against what might seem to be the logic of our own analysis – we must beware of making 'the state' a convenient catch-all. Poulantzas, for example, whose writings have greatly stimulated and informed our work, sometimes appears to go to the other extreme and virtually absorb everything which is not part of the 'economic anatomy' of capitalism into the terrain of the state. This blurs and obscures key distinctions which need to be retained. Many of the moments to which our narrative refers are of course precisely points in the shifting modality of class power as represented in and mobilised through the state. We hope our analysis penetrates at least far enough to suggest the underlying movements behind these surface forms to whose 'absence' they point.

THE CHANGING SHAPE OF 'PANICS'

In the truncated account of the 'crisis of hegemony' which follows we shall be concerned with different moments in the 'relations of forces', but also with their ideological signification. The two strands have been combined in the analysis. This ideological dimension of a crisis is crucial, as we have argued earlier. In formally democratic class societies, the exercise of power and the securing of domination ultimately depends, as we have argued, on the equation of popular consent. This is consent, not simply to the interests and purposes but also to the interpretations and representations of social reality generated by those who control the mental, as well as the material, means of social reproduction. A conspiratorial interpretation is not intended here. As Althusser has argued:

> the ruling class does not maintain with the ruling ideology, which is its own ideology, an external and lucid relation of pure utility and cunning. When, during the eighteenth century, the 'rising class', the bourgeoisie, developed a

humanist ideology of equality, freedom and reason, it gave its own demands the form of universality, since it hoped thereby to enrol at its side, by their education to this very end, the very men it would liberate only for their exploitation. [1]

Thus, 'the bourgeoisie *lives* in the ideology of freedom, the relation between it and its condition of existence: that is, *its* real relation (the law of a liberal capitalist economy) but invested in an imaginary relation (all men are free, including the free labourer) '. Popular consent, the basis of this form of the state, is all the more pivotal in those liberal democracies where the working classes have won formal political representation. The class struggle, in such societies, does, therefore, *define* what the state can and cannot do to secure the national interest. The capitalist state cannot remain securely founded on the legitimacy of popular representation, *and* take severe and unusual measures to contain a threat to its foundation which the vast majority of the population does not believe exists. It must therefore continually shape and structure that 'consent' to which, in turn, it refers itself.

The mass media are not the only, but they *are* among the most powerful, forces in the shaping of public consciousness about topical and controversial issues. The signification of events in the media thus provides one key terrain where 'consent' is won or lost. Again, as we have argued earlier, the media are formally and institutionally independent of direct state interference or intervention in Britain. The signification of events, in ways which reproduce the interpretations of them favoured by those in power, therefore takes place – as in other branches of the state and its general spheres of operation – through the formal 'separation of powers'; in the communications field, it is mediated by the protocols of balance, objectivity and impartiality. This means both that the state cannot directly command, even if it wished, precisely how public consciousness will be attuned on any particular matter, and that other points of view do, of necessity, gain access and have some right to be heard. Although this is a process which is heavily structured and constrained (cf. our earlier analysis in Chapter 3), its result is to make the 'reproduction of the dominant ideologies' a problematic and contradictory process, and thus to recreate the arena of signification as a field of ideological struggle. In analysing the way the post-war crisis came to be signified, then, we shall not expect to find a set of monolithic interpretations, systematically generated by the ruling classes for the explicit purpose of fooling the public. The ideological instance cannot be conceived in this way. There is, in any event, evidence enough to suggest that in this period the ruling classes themselves substantially believed the definition of an emergent social crisis which they were propagating. Nevertheless, as we have already shown, there are mechanisms at work which tend to ensure the favourable and extensive reproduction of the interpretations of the crisis subscribed to by the ruling-class alliance, even when the media then place their own constructions and inflexions over these in the course of public signification. There is of course no simple consensus, even here, as to the nature, causes and extent of the crisis. But the over-all tendency is for the way the crisis has been ideologically constructed by the dominant ideologies to win consent in the media, and thus to constitute the substantive basis in 'reality' to which public opinion continually refers. In this way, by 'consenting' to the view of the crisis which has won credibility in the echelons of power, popular consciousness is also won to support to the measures of control and containment which this version of social reality entails.

Statements by key spokesmen – what we have called 'primary definers' – and their representation through the media therefore form a central part of our reconstruction. But in order to understand how these played a part in the shifts in the nature of hegemony within the state and the political apparatus over the relevant period, a number of intermediary concepts need to be introduced. The problem concerns the relation to our analysis – which is pitched at the level of the state apparatuses and the maintenance of forms of hegemonic domination – of the phenomenon described earlier as the *moral panic*. The concepts of 'state' and 'hegemony' appear, at first sight, to belong to different conceptual territory from that of the 'moral panic'. And part of our intention is certainly to situate the 'moral panic' as one of the forms of appearance of a more deepseated historical crisis, and thereby to give it greater historical and theoretical specificity. This relocation of the concept on a different and deeper level of analysis does not, however, lead us to abandon it altogether as useless. Rather, it helps us to identify the 'moral panic' as one of the principal surface manifestations of the crisis, and in part to explain how and why the crisis came to be *experienced* in that form of consciousness, and what the displacement of a conjunctural crisis into the popular form of a 'moral panic' accomplishes, in terms of the way the crisis is managed and contained. We have therefore retained the notion of the 'moral panic' as a necessary part of our analysis: attempting to redefine it as one of the key ideological forms in which a historical crisis is 'experienced and fought out'.[2] One of the effects of retaining the notion of 'moral panic' is the penetration it provides into the otherwise extremely obscure means by which the working classes are drawn in to processes which are occurring in large measure 'behind their backs', and led to experience and respond to contradictory developments in ways which make the operation of state power legitimate, credible and consensual. To put it crudely, the 'moral panic' appears to us to be one of the principal forms of ideological consciousness by means of which a 'silent majority' is won over to the support of increasingly coercive measures on the part of the state, and lends its legitimacy to a 'more than usual' exercise of control.

There is a tendency, in the early years of our period, for there to develop a succession of 'moral panics' around certain key topics of controversial public concern. In this early period, the panics tend to be centred on social and moral rather than political issues (youth, permissiveness, crime). Their typical form is that of a dramatic event which focuses and triggers a local response and public disquiet. Often as a result of local organising and moral entrepreneurship, the wider powers of the control culture are both alerted (the media play a crucial role here) and mobilised (the police, the courts). The issue is then seen as 'symptomatic' of wider, more troubling but less concrete themes. It escalates up the hierarchy of responsibility and control, perhaps provoking an official enquiry or statement, which temporarily appeases the moral campaigners and dissipates the sense of panic. In what we think of as the middle period, in the later 1960s, these panics follow faster on the heels of one another than earlier; and an increasingly amplified general 'threat to society' is imputed to them (drugs, hippies, the underground, pornography, long-haired students, layabouts, vandalism, football hooliganism). In many instances the sequence is so speeded up that it bypasses the moment of *local* impact; there was no upsurge of grass-roots pressure required to bring the drugs squad crunching in on cannabis smokers. Both the media and the 'control culture' seem more alerted to their occurrence – the media quickly pick up the symptomatic event and the police and courts react quickly without considerable moral pressure from below. This speeded-up sequence tends to suggest a heightened sensitivity to troubling social themes.

There is indeed in the later stages a 'mapping together' of moral panics into a *general panic* about social order; and such a spiral has tended, not only in Britain, to culminate in what we call a 'law-and-order' campaign, of the kind which the Heath Shadow Cabinet constructed on the eve of the 1970 election, and which powered Nixon and Agnew into the White House in 1968. This coalescence into a concerted campaign marks a significant shift in the panic process, for the tendency to panic is now lodged at the heart of the state's political complex itself; and from that vantage-point, all dissensual breaks in the society can be more effectively designated as a 'general threat to law and order itself', and thus as subverting the general interest (which the state represents and protects). Panics now tend to operate from top to bottom. Post-1970, the law-and-order campaigners seem to have effectively sensitised the social-control apparatuses and the media to the possibility of a general threat to the stability of the state. Minor forms of dissent seem to provide the basis of 'scapegoat' events for a jumpy and alerted control culture; and this progressively pushes the state apparatuses into a more or less permanent 'control' posture. Schematically, the changing sequence in moral panics can be represented as follows:

(1) *Discrete moral panics* (early 1960s, e.g. 'mods' and 'rockers')
Dramatic event ⟶ public disquiet, moral entrepreneurs (sensitisation) ⟶ control culture action
(2) *'Crusading' – mapping together discrete moral panics to produce a 'speeded-up' sequence* (late 1960s, e.g. pornography and drugs)
Sensitisation (moral entrepreneurship) ⟶ dramatic event ⟶ control culture action
(3) *Post-'law-and-order' campaign: an altered sequence* (post-1970 e.g. mugging)
Sensitisation ⟶ control culture organisation and action (invisible) ⟶ dramatic event ⟶ control culture intensified action (visible)

But what are the signifying mechanisms – in the media and the sources on which they depend – which sustain these shifts in the sequence? What 'signification spirals' sustain the generation of the moral panic?

Signification spirals

The *signification spiral* is a way of signifying events which also intrinsically escalates their threat. The notion of a signification spiral is similar to that of an 'amplification spiral' as developed by certain sociologists of deviance.[3] An 'amplification spiral' suggests that reaction has the effect, under certain conditions, not of lessening but of increasing deviance. The signification spiral is a *self-amplifying sequence within the area of signification*: the activity or event with which the signification deals is *escalated* – made to seem more threatening – within the course of the signification itself.

A signification spiral seems always to contain at least some of the following elements:

(1) the identification of a specific issue of concern;
(2) the identification of a subversive minority;
(3) 'convergence', or the linking, by labelling, of this specific issue to other problems;
(4) the notion of 'thresholds' which, once crossed, can lead to an escalating threat;
(5) the prophesy of more troubling times to come if no action is taken (often, in our case, by way of references to the United States, the paradigm example); and
(6) the call for 'firm steps'.

There are two key notions – 'convergence' and 'thresholds' – which are the escalating mechanisms of the spiral.

Convergence: In our usage 'convergence' occurs when two or more activities are linked in the process of signification so as to implicitly or explicitly draw parallels between them. Thus the image of 'student hooliganism' links 'student' protest to the separate problem of 'hooliganism' – whose stereotypical characteristics are already part of socially available knowledge. This indicates the manner in which *new* problems can apparently be meaningfully described and explained by setting them in the context of an old problem with which the public is already familiar. In using the imagery of hooliganism, this signification equates two distinct activities on the basis of their *imputed* common denominator – both involve 'mindless violence' or 'vandalism'. Another, connected, form of convergence is listing a whole series of social problems and speaking of them as 'part of a deeper, underlying problem' – the 'tip of an iceberg', especially when such a link is also forged on the basis of implied common denominators. In both cases the net effect is *amplification*, not in the real events being described, but in their 'threat-potential' for society. Do such convergences *only* occur in the eye of the signifying beholder? Are they entirely fictional? In fact, of course, significant convergences do and have indeed taken place in some areas of what might be described by the dominant culture as 'political deviance'. Horowitz and Liebowitz have pointed out that the distinction between political marginality and social deviance is 'increasingly obsolete' in the United States of the late 1960s.[4] Similarly, Hall has argued that in respect of certain areas of British protest politics in the late 1960s and 1970s: 'the crisp distinction between socially and politically deviant behaviour is increasingly difficult to sustain'.[5]

Convergences, for example, take place when political groups adopt deviant life-styles or when deviants become politicised. They occur when people, thought of in passive and individual terms, take collective action (for example, claimants), or when supporters of single-issue campaigns enter into a wider agitation or make common cause. There can be real convergences (between workers and students in May 1968) as well as ideological or imaginary ones. However, signification spirals do not depend on a necessary correspondence with real historical developments. They may represent such real connections accurately, or they may mystify by exaggerating the nature or degree of the convergence, or they may produce altogether spurious identities. For example, in the 1970s some homosexuals involved in the Gay Liberation movements *did* belong to the radical or marxist left. A signification which, however, assumed that all homosexual reformers were 'marxist revolutionaries' would be one which inflected a real convergence in an ideological direction – an exaggeration whose credibility would nevertheless no doubt depend on its kernel of truth. Such an inflection would also be a misrepresentation – misrepresenting both the many reformers who were without overt political commitment, and the critique which even those who were marxists regularly made of traditional 'left' attitudes towards sexual issues. Such an inflection would be 'ideological' exactly because it signified a complex phenomenon in terms of its problematic part only. It would also entail 'escalation', since it exaggerates out of all proportion the one element most troubling and threatening to the established political order. The earlier example of 'student hooliganism' works in much the same way, this time connecting and identifying two almost wholly discrepant phenomena. But this example also shifts the political terms of the issue – that posed by the emergent student movement – by resignifying it in terms of a more familiar and traditional, non-political (hooliganism) problem; that is, by translating a *political* issue into a *criminal* one (the link with violence and vandalism) – thereby making easier a legal or control, rather than a political, response from the authorities. This transposition of frameworks not only depoliticises an issue by *criminalising* it, but also singles out from a complex of different strands the most worrying element – the violent one. The resignification process thus also simplifies complex issues – for example, by 'making plain' through elision what would otherwise have to be substantiated by hard argument (e.g. that all student protest is mindlessly violent). Thus the movement's 'essential hooliganism' comes to pass for substantiated truth. Such significations also carry, embedded within them, concealed premises and understandings (for example, those referring to the exceedingly complex relation between politics and violence). Finally, by signifying a political issue through its most extreme and violent form, signification helps to produce a 'control' response – and makes that response legitimate. The public might be reluctant to see the strong arm of the law arbitrarily exercised against legitimate political protesters. But who will stand between the law and a 'bunch of hooligans'? Imaginary convergences therefore serve an ideological function – and that ideological function has real consequences, especially in terms of provoking and legitimating a coercive reaction by both the public and the state.

Thresholds: In the public signification of troubling events, there seem to be certain thresholds which mark out symbolically the limits of societal tolerance. The higher an event can be placed in the hierarchy of thresholds, the greater is its threat to the social order, and the tougher and more automatic is the coercive response. *Permissiveness*, for example, is a low threshold. Events which break this threshold contravene traditional moral norms (e.g. taboos on premarital sex). They therefore mobilise moral sanctions and social disapproval – but not necessarily legal control. But the struggles which take place, and the moral crusades which are mounted to defend the shifting boundary of 'permissiveness', can be resolved if some aspect of a 'permissive' act *also* infringes the law, if it breaks the *legal threshold*. The law clarifies the blurred area of moral disapproval, and marks out the legally impermissible from the morally disapproved of. New legislation, of either a progressive or restrictive character, is thus a sensitive barometer of the rise and fall of traditional moral sentiment, e.g. the shifts around the question of abortion. The transgression of the legal threshold raises the potential threat of any action; impermissible acts contravene the moral consensus, but illegal acts are a challenge to the legal order and the social legitimacy which it enshrines. However, acts which pose a challenge to the fundamental basis of the social order itself, or its essential structures, almost always involve, or at least are signified as leading inexorably across, the *violence threshold*. This is the highest of the limits of societal tolerance, since violent acts can be seen as constituting a threat to the future existence of the whole state itself (which holds the monopoly of legitimate violence). Certain acts are of course violence by any definition: armed terrorism, assassination, insurrection. Much more problematic are the whole range of political acts which do not necessarily espouse or lead to violence, but which are thought of as 'violent' because of the fundamental nature of the challenge they make to the state. Such acts are almost always signified in terms of their *potential for social violence* (violent here being almost a synonymn for 'extremism'). Robert Moss has recently argued that 'The conquest of violence is the signal achievement of modern democratic societies.' [7] By 'conquest of violence' here he must mean not its disappearance but its confinement to the state, which exerts a monopoly of *legitimate* 'violence'. Therefore every threat which can be signified as 'violent' must be an index of widespread social anarchy and disorder – perhaps the visible tip of a planned conspiracy. Any form of protest thus signified immediately becomes a law-and-order issue:

> When the state is not seen to be fulfilling this basic function, in the face of a serious and sustained upsurge of violence – either criminal or political – we can be sure of one thing: that sooner or later, ordinary citizens will take the law into their own hands or will be disposed to support a new form of government better equipped to deal with the threat. [8]

We may represent some of the thresholds employed in signification spirals diagrammatically, as in Figure 8.1. The use of convergences and thresholds together in the ideological signification of societal conflict has the intrinsic function of *escalation*. One kind of threat or challenge to society seems larger, more menacing, if it can be mapped together with other, apparently similar, phenomena – especially if, by connecting one relatively harmless activity with a more threatening one, the scale of the danger implicit is made to appear more widespread and diffused. Similarly, the threat to society can be escalated if a challenge occurring at the 'permissive' boundary can be resignified, or presented as leading inevitably to a challenge at a 'higher' threshold. By treating an event or group of actors not only in terms of its/their intrinsic characteristics, aims and programmes, but by projecting the 'anti-social potential' across the thresholds to what it *may* cause (or, less deterministically, lead to), it is possible to treat the initial event or group as 'the thin edge of a larger wedge'. The 'permissiveness' of the counter-culture appears far more menacing when 'long hair' and 'free sex' are seen as the inevitable forerunners of drug-taking, or where every pot-smoker is signified as a potential heroin addict, or where every cannabis buyer is an incipient dealer (i.e. involved in illegal acts). In turn, the threat to illegality is immeasurably escalated, if drug-taking inevitably makes every user 'prone to violence' (either because drugs lower his reason, or provoke him to rob to sustain the habit). Similarly, peaceful demonstrations become more threatening if always described as potential scenarios for violent confrontations. The important point is that, as issues and groups are projected across the thresholds, it becomes easier to mount legitimate campaigns of control against them. When this process becomes a regular and routine part of the way in which conflict is signified in society, it does indeed create its own momentum for measures of 'more than usual control'.

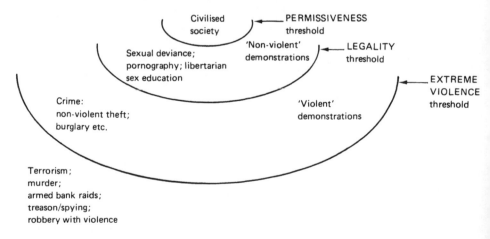

FIGURE 8.1

In what follows, we treat the emergence of an 'exceptional form' of the state, and the ideological signification of the crisis which shadows this development, as two aspects of the same problematic. For the sake of conciseness, we have drawn the majority of our references from two newspapers, the *Sunday Express* and the *Sunday Times* – papers sufficiently different (one 'popular', one 'serious'; one conservative, one liberal) to catch the range and sequence of signification through the period, and to pinpoint internal discrepancies of emphasis; though we have consulted the press much more widely in the general reconstruction of the period and frequently quote other sources.

POST-WAR HEGEMONY: CONSTRUCTING CONSENSUS

Undoubtedly the fact of hegemony presupposes that account be taken of the interests and tendencies of the groups over which hegemony is to be exercised, and that a certain compromise equilibrium be formed – in other words, that the leading group should make sacrifices of an economic-corporate kind. But there is also no doubt that such sacrifices and such a compromise cannot touch the essential; for though hegemony is ethical-political, it must also be economic, must necessarily be based on the decisive function exercised by the leading group in the decisive nucleus of economic activity. (Gramsci)[9]

Socialism is no class movement. . . . It is not the rule of the working class; it is the organization of the community. (Ramsey Macdonald) [10]

The class war is over. (Harold Macmillan) [11]

The reconstruction of a ruling-class hegemony in Britain in the aftermath of war must be located, however briefly, in the international stabilisation of the capitalist world. Three factors are of critical importance here. In economic terms, the stabilisation of capitalism on a world scale, against the background created by world wide depression in the 1930s followed by total war, was accomplished by modifications in the internal structure of capital, and by its further global expansion, leading to a period of unparalleled productive growth – perhaps the most sustained period of growth ever experienced in the history of the system. In political terms, the period also witnessed the extensive stabilisation, in Europe especially, of parliamentary democracy based on the augmented role of the state in economic affairs – a development which had also been thrown in doubt by the growth of fascism as an extraordinary political response to the extraordinary circumstances of economic depression. In ideological terms, we find the marshalling of the Western democracies in the face of the challenge from the Communist world, and the generation of refurbished doctrines of 'free enterprise' as a counter to Soviet power in the conditions of Cold War. Britain, in her own special way and within the limits of her own historical position, entered into this stabilisation by a 'peculiar route', to which the two governing parties – Labour in the period up to 1951, and then the Conservatives, in a period of unrivalled hegemonic domination – made significant, though distinct contributions.

The 1945–51 Labour government – often conceived as marking the high water-mark of social democracy, and laying the base for a peaceful, parliamentary transition to socialism – represented, in fact, the end of something, rather than the beginning; everything that had matured during the extraordinary conditions of a popular war, was then, even in its heyday, beginning to pass away. Labour constructed the Welfare State, took some declining industries into public ownership, and managed the transition from a war economy to peacetime production by the exercise of a fierce austerity. It tried to graft certain humane ideas of social reform on to a system of production it did not reconstruct. It is possible, R. H. Tawney once remarked, to peel an onion layer by layer, but it is not possible to skin a tiger stripe by stripe. Employment was kept full. But the real redistribution of income between classes had taken place during, not after the war;[12] the working classes bore the brunt of a severe Crippsian wage freeze in 1948 and a massive devaluation in 1949, triggered by the Korean War inflation. These set the outer parameters of the Labourist experiment. Labour also committed Britain firmly to the American side in the Cold War, which erected a sort of 'Berlin Wall' around political life. Anything drifting left of centre seemed in imminent danger of falling off the edge of the world into the clutches of the Kremlin. *Encounter* and the Congress for Cultural Freedom patrolled this perimeter of the 'free world'. All the political solutions were contained within its limits. Throughout Western Europe, the Cold War had the effect of driving every major political tendency into middle ground, where political life was stabilised around the key institutions of parliamentary democracy and the 'mixed economy'. Although in electoral terms in Britain the Left was in power, ideologically and politically the 'Left' was already in retreat. The sacrifice of 'free prescriptions' to the rearmament programme marked the end of the road. In 1951, the loss of nerve floated Labour – and with it the whole social-democratic interlude – out on the tide.

Yet the foundations of the post-war consensus were laid in this critical interlude. They were, in sum: the construction of the Welfare State; the adaptation of capitalism, and of the labour movement, to the 'mixed-economy' solution; and the commitment to the 'free-enterprise' side of the Cold War. These established the limits of a new sort of social contract, the principal effect of which was to confine the labour movement within the framework of capitalist stabilisation. On the basis of security of employment and of welfare – banishing the twin spectres of the Depression – the labour movement was committed to finding a solution to the class struggle within the framework of a mixed economy in which private capital set the pace, and of the parliamentary structures of the capitalist state. Contrary to some assessments, this trajectory of accommodation had been a feature of Labourism from its inception;[13] but its open acknowledgement set in train a profound modification of post-war social democracy.

Labour planted the seed; but the Tories reaped the harvest. To the construction of consensus they made their own contribution. They accepted the Welfare State as a 'necessary social cost' – a modifying principle – of the new capitalism: capitalism 'with a human face'. The same applied to the principle of full employment. By these concessions, under the leadership of a reformed party under Lord Woolton and the 'new men', Conservatism paid its dues and moved into centre territory. Although it returned to power in 1951 with the promise to burn the controls and restore free enterprise, its success marked the triumph of a new, rather than the refurbishing of an old, 'Conservatism'. [14] The new Conservatives acknowledged that the state should assume responsibility for the general management of employment and demand. The nationalisation of a small public sector proved no embarrassment to these 'new men', except when, in the case of steel and sugar, it threatened productive industry itself; this they successfully turned back in its tracks. In these ways they put themselves 'on the side of the future', while at the same time securing the conditions for a return to an economy harnessed to the imperatives of free-enterprise capitalism. The concessions on welfare and full employment secured just the measure of popular legitimacy the revival of capitalism required. From this centrist ground – prophetically labelled 'Butskellism' – the expansion of a popular consumers' capitalism was launched.

Analysts have sometimes been tempted to read Labour's contribution to the laying of this foundation to capitalism's unparalleled expansion as a sort of plot. It was nothing of the kind. Welfare was indeed an inroad into unbridled capitalism conducted at the open expense of the working class; full employment meant something to a class long used to the dole and the unemployment queue. What mattered was that these innovations were made within the logic of capitalist development, not against it. And this permitted such inroads as they represented to be *redefined in practice* by the party of capital into its key and legitimating supports. Capitalism has frequently developed by way of such unintended consequences, driven forward by the contradictions, often put on the agenda by enlarged working-class strength, which it must surmount. In absorbing these contradictory structures British capitalism was forced to recompose itself, further along that long path from *laissez-faire* to monopoly initiated in the latter years of the nineteenth century; and in doing so, also to recompose the capitalist state itself and the political structures of the working class. The Taylorist and 'Fordist' revolution, opened up in the early years of the century and extended (on the back of the depression) in the inter-war period, leading to the introduction on a very wide scale of new productive methods which greatly extended the productivity and intensification of labour, came to its fulfilment in the post-war era. The gradual adoption of the Keynesian instruments of economic regulation not only made possible the abandonment of doctrinaire *laissez-faire* in the interests of capital itself, but provided the lever with which a whole new institutional framework for the modern development of capitalism could be refashioned. Both made possible the high-wage, mass-production, domestic-consumer-orientated modern economy, under the governance of an expanded and interventionist 'state regulator'. And these in turn provided the basis for post-war economic expansion. The harnessing of Keynesian instruments made it possible, for a time, to counteract the capitalist tendency to uncontrolled boom and recession. The abandonment of an economy of cheap labour and the market control of unemployment made possible a vast expansion of the mass market for domestic-consumer commodities. The base for this productive boom was the post-war 'managerialist' corporate enterprises, rooted in the exploitation of cheap energy and new technologies. [15] This kind of capitalist development required a major refashioning of the capitalist state. The expansion of an 'interventionist state' was thus set in motion by, and related to,

far more fundamental economic functions for capital than its normal association with the formation of the Welfare State suggests. This was no longer the
state of 'competitive capitals'; it superintended a form of capital requiring
massive co-ordination and an institutional framework of harmonisation – if
necessary, at the expense of individual capitalists. The sphere of this
progressive harmonisation was often the enhanced state – the state of what
Marx called *social capital* as 'a concrete force'. [16] The co-ordination of the
market itself, of consumption, of a strategy across capitals – and of the incorporation and containment of a working class whose political strength had to be
accommodated but whose wages, no longer so easily controllable through unemployment and wage cuts, had to be disciplined in another way – these
become key strategic processes lodged in the capitalist state itself.

At the level of consumption and exchange, the rise in money wages and the
surge in consumer goods served, in the 1950s, to mask those crucial changes in
the labour process, and the division of labour consequent on them, through
which the system tried to become, once again, cost-effectively productive on a
new scale. It also tied the working class, through the mass market, hire
purchase and the well-timed budget, to the Conservative Party's success at the
polls. The fortunes of the system and the fortunes of the Conservative Party
now became indissolubly linked. In the course of this renewed productive surge
every vestige of Labour's innovations was reshaped and redefined into the support for a new 'people's capitalism' and a vigorous Tory populism. Witness
Anthony Eden: 'Our objective is a nation-wide property-owning
democracy.... Whereas the socialist purpose is the distribution of ownership
in the hands of the State, ours is the distribution of ownership over the widest
practicable number of individuals.' [17]

This was the first leg in the post-war construction of consensus. The second
was its political realisation – the 'politics of affluence' – over which Harold
Macmillan presided with such consummate adroitness. In 1955 the Tories went
to the country under the slogan, 'Invest in Success'. Macmillan's 'Never had it
so Good' slogan was first unveiled at a speech in Bradford in 1957. It was
sustained, with increasing assurance and much public-relations vigour, in the
run-up to the key 1959 election, directly capturing the sheer, heady experience
of an apparently unending upward curve in the nation's fortunes by its vulgar
opportunism. 'You've had it good. Have it better. Vote Conservative.' They
did. By now the Tories had identified themselves with every favourable social
trend. 'In short,' conceded Mr Gaitskell, 'the changing character of labour, full
employment, new housing, the new way of life based on the telly, the fridge, the
car and the glossy magazines – all have had their effect on our political
strength.' 'The Tories identified themselves with the new working class better
than we did', remarked another Labour Minister (Patrick Gordon-Walker). Mr
Macmillan's resumé was pithier, and more to the point. It had, he observed,
'gone off rather well'. Besides, it demonstrated that 'the class war is obsolete'.
Labour was plunged into the dark night of the soul: no short-term electoral
swing but the whole sociology of post-war capitalism seemed set against them.

The third phase was constituted by the manufacture of the ideology – the
religion – of the 'affluent society'. Its success lay principally in the way

economic forces beyond anyone's control appeared to be sustaining it. It also had some basis in the immediate changes in social life which the revival of capitalism in its new form brought in its train. The boom, the onset of more rapid social mobility and the temporary blurring of class distinctions had the immediate effect of diminishing the sharpness of class struggle. So did changes in housing, in the patterns of working-class life in the new estates, and the enlarging of opportunities for some through the expansion of state education. Working-class living standards appeared permanently underpinned from below by welfare, and stimulated above by rising money wages. Once the great trade unions, under the leadership of those whom Addison has called, with justice, 'moderate social patriots',[18] lined themselves up behind the mixed-economy solution, certain structural changes were temporarily closed off; there seemed more to be won by pushing within the system than by overturning it. Capital now appeared to sustain, rather than eat into, working-class living standards. The new corporate enterprises, with their self-financed expansion programmes, their new technologies and their rising, public-spirited mangerial elites, were hard to equate with the system's earlier hard-faced entrepreneurs. At a deeper level, new technologies and modifications in the labour process had produced new structures in the technical division of labour, generating new occupational strata and cultures within the working class. The rise of the state and tertiary sectors expanded the size of the intermediary classes, which, though they too had nothing to sell but their labour, had their work differently organised from that typical of the pre-war skilled labourer. These social changes unhinged many traditional patterns of class relations in the immediate sphere of social life, reorganising some attitudes and aspirations, dismantling some of the stable forms of working-class consciousness and solidarity, and setting aside some of the familiar landmarks of traditional pre-war society. Distinctions between the old, declining industrial regions of the 'north' and the new, bustling 'scientific' industries of the 'south' accentuated the impression of the new unevenly replacing the old. The media caught and transfixed, in graphic visual terms, the surface flux of social change, and provided the immediate reflection of an unplanned social upheaval. But the key factor was the effect of these shifts, working together, partially to confine the working class and the labour movement within the limits of the system: the containment of working-class politics within the logic of capitalist development. This partial incorporation was not at all incompatible with a vigorous, instrumental wage militancy – milking the system for what it was worth: a form of the continuation of class struggle 'by other means' which was obscured, for a time, by the more personalised and privatised ways of 'making it' within the system. The drift towards a centrist consensus in politics, with its consequent fragmentation in the classic forms of class struggle, had the long-term consequence of shifting the locale of struggle away from the institutionalised front and towards a more localised, more syndicalist type of shop-floor politics. In the centre, what united people – whether in terms of real achievements or unrealised aspirations – appeared stronger than what divided them. On this basis a general consensus appeared spontaneously to produce and then to reproduce itself to infinity: a permanent Conservative hegemony.

Gradually, an ideological reading of the post-war condition was installed. In the heady economic climate of the times, unplanned social change came to be designated, ideologically, as the tokens of the new, 'classless' consumer, post-capitalist society. The unevenness of social change, experienced in serialised and fragmented ways, was resolved in an ideological form: the myth of affluence. As the pace of change gathered speed, so change itself became a national preoccupation. Here the idea of the United States – now the leading capitalist nation – provided the comforting point of reference; even Mr Crosland's vision of 'the future of socialism' resembled nothing so much as a cross between Harlow New Town and a mid-West suburban enclave. Consensus was constructed, ideologically, on top of this perplexing sweep of social transformation. The people had to be convinced that capitalism had changed its nature, that the boom would last forever. Since the millenium had patently not arrived for the majority, ideology was required to close the gap between the real unequal distribution of wealth and power and the 'imaginary relation' of their future equalisation. This inflexion of the contradictory reality into the illusion of permanent progress-to-come was grafted on to something real; but it also transformed that rational core. Like all social myths, 'affluence' contained its sub-stratum of truth – the transformations in the structures of capitalism and the recomposition of the capitalist state and its politics. But it consistently inflected this antagonistic reality in a consensual direction. It extrapolated the present into a future by its favourable side only, a 'trend' without contradiction or historical break. Myth, Barthes reminds us, is dehistoricised, depoliticised speech.[19] It suppresses the historical nature and antagonistic content of what it signifies, the temporary conditions of its existence, the possibilities of its historical transcendence. It converts discontinuity into continuity, History into Nature. The operation of the myth of affluence – the 'religion of affluence' – on the contradictory reality of post-war capitalist reconstruction was accomplished by just such a profound ideological displacement. Within its terms monopoly capitalism was represented as 'the post-capitalist era'. The incorporation of capitalist property became 'the managerial Revolution'. The Welfare State was transcribed as 'the abolition of poverty'. The rise in money incomes became the 'redistribution of wealth'. Political convergence on middle ground dictated by the fundamental rhythms of capitalist production and circulation was inverted into the 'end of ideology'. The lowering of political goals was hymned as the birth of 'political realism' – the art of the possible. The ideological closure aimed for was complete. Above all, the transformations it entailed appeared to come, spontaneously, from nowhere, a natural tendency of all good men and true to come together consensually to support the same goals and celebrate the same values: getting and spending; getting ahead; private space in a do-it-yourself world – a new form of democratised possessive individualism. But though Harold Macmillan artfully impersonated this 'consensus-without-tears' – look, no hands! – the whole enterprise required the most skilful political and economic management. The main economic trends which underpinned the affluent illusion had to be sustained. So had those social trends favouring the continuing hegemony of the few still wielding power over the powerless majority: above all, the stabilisation of the institutional commitment of the masses to the system, binding the people to the *status quo* by consensual hoops of steel. The first was the task of the economic, and now the state, managers of the conditions for the continued realisation of capital. The second was achieved through the deep adaptation of Labour into an alternative party of capitalism. The third was, principally, the object of the ideology of affluence. Over this last Macmillan and his entourage presided – nothing short of the stage-managed *production of popular consent*.

The closure was of course never completed or secured. In part, its economic base was structurally unsound. Britain participated in the world-wide capitalist boom, but more slowly and hesitantly than her major rivals. The long imperialist inheritance, coupled with the ancient nature of her industrial infrastructure and the slow rate of technological innovation, set her at a striking disadvantage. In economic terms, she was a third-rate post-imperial, not a first-rate new capitalist power. Inflation began to rise, though, because of the relative strength of labour, wage settlements were struck for a time, at increasingly high levels. Ultimately, of course, inflation ate into real wages: 'inflation is the economic enemy of *consensus*'.[20] Cost inflation also began to eat into profit margins. Coupled with the low rate and level of investment, Britain's competitive position declined, resulting in a diminishing share of the world market for manufactured goods. The heavy reliance on 'invisible exports' produced a dramatic gap in her rate of growth as compared with her competitors. The ascendancy of the financial fraction of the ruling class produced the regular export of capital overseas in the search for short-term profits, and the defence to the death of sterling as a world currency. The failure of technical investment slowed down the recomposition of capital and produced a declining rate of profit. The Conservative economic managers exhibited a certain short-term wizardry in tying budgets to electoral chances. But every 'go' had its 'stop', each 'stop' accompanied by more damagingly inflationary packages inducing a pervasive structural stagnation. The state was increasingly drawn to intervene to maintain the national economy as a site for profitable investment.

Consensus, moreover, was constructed across highly paradoxical phenomena. The high point of 'affluence' in 1956 coincided with such highly un-consensual events as: the Suez adventure (with its stirring impact on the Labour movement); the Hungarian Revolution (with its dramatic effects on the Communist Party); the birth of the New Left; the *Uses of Literacy, Look Back in Anger* and Elvis Presley. The emergence of a section of the radical intelligentsia from the conformist cramp of the Cold War, the birth of extra-parliamentary politics in the anti-nuclear movement, the emergence of a flourishing, commercially sponsored youth culture – all were discrepant phenomena of an 'affluent society' floated out on the consensual tide. Here and elsewhere, it seemed clear that consensus, affluence and consumerism had produced, not the pacification of worry and anxiety – their dissolution in the flux of money, goods and fashion – but their reverse: a profound, disquieting sense of moral unease. Mr Macmillan's dazzling high-wire act was conducted on top of the highly un-Edwardian world of supermarkets and motorways, jukeboxes and jets, jeans and guitars, scooters and televisions, demonstrations in the streets and the systematic abuse of the middle classes from the stage of the Royal Court. Although consumption represented a real and effective economic motive, the British remained uneasy with the gospel of unbridled materialism. One of the sterner members of the Cabinet had warned the Tory Party Conference that economic success should 'help to satisfy man's desire to serve a cause outside himself'. But it was not at all obvious that a 'people's capitalism' was delivering, alongside the cornucopia of goodies, a sense of moral purpose. When *The Economist* enjoined 'modern Conservatives' to look up 'at the TV aerials sprouting above working class homes' and 'down on the housewives in tight slacks on the summer road to Brighton' and find in them 'a great poetry', it had to admit that there was still the 'old-fashioned Conservative who looks out at the comforts made achievable by rising incomes and the hire purchase revolution and who feels vaguely that the workers ... are getting above their station'.[21] In the late 1950s and early 1960s, the two topics most calculated to catch the imagination of grass-roots Tories at the Party Conference were crime and immigration – themes of disturbance, not of consensus and success. Significant social groups in society felt abandoned by the scramble of some for the affluent, 'progressive' middle ground, and threatened by rising materialism below; amidst the 'never had it so good society', they yearned for a firmer moral purpose. They provided the backbone for the entrepreneurs of moral indignation.

This mechanism is crucial for our story. On the surface, everything appeared to be 'going well'. Displaced from its centre in public moral discourse, and unable to find a foothold in the pragmatic, incremental politics of consensus, a generalised moral anxiety about 'the state of things' tended to find expression in themes which appeared at first marginal to society's main movements. This is the source of the post-war 'moral panic'. It first precipitated with respect to 'youth', which came to provide, for a time, a metaphor for social change and an index of social anxiety.[22] Every troubling feature of post-war social change was refracted in its highly visible prism. In youth, social change was not simply projected, but magnified. Inheritors of the Welfare State, harbingers of the post-war world, 'youth' was, at once, the vanguard of the Golden Age, and the vanguard party of the new materialism, the new hedonism. All of social change was inscribed, in microcosm, in its innocent face. The public response was, predictably, ambivalent. That ambivalence is registered in the 'moral panic' about the Teddy Boys in the mid-1950s,[23] where the public gave vent to its collective horror at the spectacle of youth of the white under-class, with its rising social ambitions and its expressive violence, dressed up in off-the-peg, lumpenised versions of an Edwardian style, jiving to what Paul Johnson once described as 'jungle music', floating out of its proper habitat 'up town', spilling over into the respectable enclaves, dance halls and cinemas, and occasionally running amok to the beat of *Rock Around The Clock*.[24] The link with violence provided the *frisson* on which moral panics feeds. A few years later, the remnants of the Teds found their way into the streets of Notting Hill in the first full-scale race riots ever seen in Britain. *The Times* editorial ('Hooliganism is Hooliganism') made the straight transposition from hooliganism and 'teenage violence' into lawlessness and anarchy. The growth of racism was neglected; but the existence of blacks as a 'problem' was tacitly acknowledged.[25]

The affluent consensus was thus founded on an unstable base. Its career

was, in any event, destined to be short lived. It began to disintegrate shortly after Macmillan's triumph at the polls in 1959. In the middle of 1960 a massive
balance-of-payments crisis developed – a crisis which unmasked the depth of
Britain's real economic decline. It was followed by Selwyn Lloyd's gigantic
'stop' Budget of 1961; a Cabinet purge; the Cuba crisis; the collapse of
Britain's bid to enter the E.E.C.; and a rise in the unemployment rate to 4 per
cent. On a broader front, critics had begun to unearth the dark side of
affluence, inscribed in a series of reports and studies – Galbraith, Titmuss,
Albemarle, Buchanan, Pilkington, Milner-Holland, Crowther, Robbins, Plow-
den – which added up to the 'rediscovery of poverty'. On the cultural front, the
legitimacy of the Establishment was submerged in a wave of cynicism and disbelief, especially in the 'satire' movements. In March 1960, George Wigg, basing himself on a story in *Private Eye*, raised the 'little matter' of a scandal 'involving a member of the front bench'. The Profumo Affair brought on stage the
whole 'affluent' cast of performers: a West Indian, three call girls, a property
speculator, an osteopath with country-house connections, a Secretary of State
and a Soviet naval attaché. When the Profumo Affair reached its sordid conclusion, the 'Macmillenium' had also closed. Typically, what had begun in
politics and economics had found its consummation in a splurge of moral
indignation.

CONSENSUS: THE SOCIAL-DEMOCRATIC VARIANT

> The peculiar character of Social Democracy is epitomised in the fact that
> democratic-republican institutions are demanded as a means, not of doing
> away with two extremes, capital and wage labour, but of weakening their
> antagonism and transforming it into a harmony. (Marx) [26]

The period between 1961 and 1964 is transitional: not between Prime
Ministers but between two variants of the consensus management of the state.
The self-regulating, spontaneous cohesion of British social and political life, underpinned by the consumer boom, was destroyed during this transition. In its
place, Labour attempted – drawing on an alternative *repertoire* – to construct
a 'social-democratic' variant, based on an appeal, not to individualism, but to
the 'national interest', and to a prosperity which would have to be struggled for,
defended at home and abroad, and for which belts – especially those of the
working classes – would have to be tightened. This dominates the period, up to
the Heath victory in 1970. There were, in fact, many overlaps between the two
phases. Indicative planning was introduced, not by Wilson but by Selwyn
Lloyd. Growth, out of which alone 'more' could be provided, and modernisation, without which labour could not be productive, had already become
national goals, before Mr Wilson rephrased them into the new social
democratic litany. But these overlaps – by which, silently, the new structures of
capitalism and the modern corporate state were matured – conceal the quality
of the 'leap' which Labour initiated on its return to power.

What Macmillan had never essayed, and only Labour was in a position to
initiate, was the full slide into *corporatism*. Labour had no alternative strategy
for managing the economic crisis. By committing itself to capitalist structures,

it had guaranteed the existing distribution of inequality. Since the present equilibrium could not be further disturbed without destroying the goose which laid the golden eggs, only an over-all leap in production – growth – could provide what the working class demanded (more) while preserving the existing mechanisms of surplus realisation and profitability. The secret was to expand productivity: to make labour more productive – which, in conditions of low investment, meant raising the rate of the exploitation of labour. The potential sharpening of conflicts of interest between the classes could only be dampened down by subsuming everyone into the 'higher' ideological unity of the national interest. Panitch has called the theory of a 'redistribution' which did not touch the existing inequalities of class power the 'doctrine of socialism in one class'. [27] The subsumption of class interests within the national interest he has defined as Labour's 'nation-class synthesis'. He adds: 'the new social contract in this context is a contract not only between unequals but one in which the guarantor of the contract – the state . . . is not and cannot be disinterested and neutral between the classes.' [28]

The only way in which such goals could be politically realised was by drawing all sides into an active partnership with the state: to make labour and capital equal 'interests', under the impartial chairmanship of the 'neutral' state; to commit each side to national economic targets; to persuade each to regulate the share which it took out of the common pool; and thus to establish a tripartite corporate bargain at the centre of the nation's economic life, based on the harmonisation of interests between capital, labour and the people – the latter appearing in the heavy disguise of the state. This was to provide the basis for a common corporate strategy for capital as a whole – social capital. Each party had its constituency; each its duties – principally of discipline. Capital defended business, and would be rewarded with profits. Labour defended the working man, and would be rewarded with a higher standard of living. The state represented 'the rest' – the nation – and stabilised the contract, enforcing it on the community. This idea of a permanent alliance – 'for the national good' – between labour, capital and the state is the pivotal idea, the practical basis, of the social-democratic experiment in consensus-building: the corporate consensus of the 'big batallions'. Mr Callaghan's 'social contract' is only another variant of the same strategy – adapted for seige conditions. It depended, above all, on disciplining the nation to consent – and on the institutionalisation of the class struggle. Capital would constrain its free-enterprise mavericks, committing them to national targets. The unions would discipline their shop-floor militants. Both antagonistic elements could be 'won for the centre'. The state would be responsible for establishing the network of institutional frameworks within which 'the bargains' could be struck. In this form, the state, while appearing to subsume into itself the best interests of everyone, in fact firmly assumed command over the long-term conditions of capital – if necessary at the expense of short-run market considerations of individual capitalists.

This pacification and harmonisation of the class struggle was accomplished in part through the generation of its own distinctive ideology. It was announced and indexed by the Wilsonian rhetoric of 'modernisation', of 'all sides pulling together', with its clarion call to 'productive workers by hand and brain', and its ringing denunciation of 'backwoodsmen' on all sides – unregenerate free-enterprisers here, militant shopstewards and leftists there. Modernisation had the key ideological effect of translating Britain's economic decline into its *technical* aspects alone. Growth subsumed the historical into the technological. Within this form of political 'Newspeak', technico-pragmatic rationality was installed as the only form of politics left. This ideological convergence was underpinned by one of the most heroic attempts in the post-war period – a decisive shift – to put together a new social *bloc*: an alliance between the modernising industrial managers and the new technical working class. The 'New Britain' was to be 'forged in the white heat of the technological revolution'. Immediately, in the run up to the election and its aftermath, this ramshackle social configuration seemed poised for success. The new Labourist gospel was just efficacious enough, just vague enough, to forge a temporary alliance between managers, technicians and the few fragmented constituencies for social change created by the 'rediscovery of poverty'. It had no other logic or historical base. In fact, no side in the alliance could redeem its stake without disturbing the bargain – thereby interfering with its fundamental basis: the generation and redistribution of the surplus in capital's favour. As soon as economic pressures sharpened, the concoction began to fall apart. Once tested, it revealed its true internal logic: the attempt to conserve British capitalism and manage the crisis by the construction of a disciplined form of consent, principally under the management of the corporate state.

Once again this effort to construct a disciplined consensus appeared strikingly at odds with social movements and the spirit of the times. 1964 was also the year of the Beatles' rise to cultural pre-eminence; of massive record sales and the 'beat' boom; of 'mod' styles, the flourishing artisan capitalism of the Kings Road boutiques, and the whole phenomenon of 'swinging London'. For those committed to an older, Prostestant ethic, or responding to the call of Wilson's 'New Methodism', with its simple contrasts of Ancient and Modern, the narcissism of the 'mods', the flaunted sexuality of the Rolling Stones, the transformations of masculinity in fashion, and the generalised hedonism, registered as a deep shock. Once again, the accumulating social anxieties were displaced from centre to periphery, and assumed the form of righteous moral indignation. The staged 'mods–rockers' confrontations on the holiday beaches attracted massive public attention, wild press over-reporting and a campaign of intense social reaction from the moral entrepreneurs, the police and the courts.[29] The drama was thematised in terms of the continuing moral struggle between the guardians of society and the affluence, boredom, indiscipline, hedonism, vandalism and 'mindless violence' of 'youth'. It provided a sort of recapitulation, in a minor key, of the themes Mr Wilson was orchestrating elsewhere.

Labour inherited the biggest deficit on the balance of payments in British peace-time history. The response was a cringing return to the most ancient tune in the book – the religion of sterling. 'The first essential', the Prime Minister remarked, 'is a strong economy. This alone will enable us to maintain the value of the pound.' But when the chips were down, that company of loyal souls in the City sold sterling for all they were worth. Labour rallied to its defence; and the international financiers, who alone could ransom the government, named their price. Wage freeze, cuts in public expenditure, the sabotage of the 'social package', which alone had attached Labour's radical wing to the corporate strategy. The government borrowed furiously, and persuaded the T.U.C. to accept a statutory wages policy. The 1966 election was handsomely won. Then the incomes policy became the centre plank of Labour's New Testament. The sharp edge of Labour policy was turned against the unions − the anarchy of wage bargaining, and restrictive practices. There was a further call for discipline. Then, in the middle of this revivalist campaign, came the seamen's strike.

The seamen's strike threw the whole strategy into the balance. What was at issue, the Prime Minister said, was nothing less than 'our national prices and incomes policy'. Only a defeat of the strikers would convince foreign investors of 'our determination to make the policy effective'. Mr Wilson then brought into play the major paradigm of social control, which, with the help of the media, was to dominate the ideological signification of industrial conflict from that point forwards to the present. He raised the level of threat to national proportions: the strike, he said, was against the national interest, because it was 'against the state, against the community' − a fateful convergence. It was thus, figuratively, and could therefore be signified, literally, as a *conspiracy*: 'this tightly knit group of politically motivated men . . . who are now determined to exercise back-stage pressures, forcing great hardship on the members of the unions and their families, and endangering the security of the industry and the economic welfare of the nation'. Time and again, in the succeeding decade, the class struggle was to be reconstructed, ideologically, in these terms: the conspiracy against the nation, holding the innocent to ransom; the stark contrast between the subversive clique and the innocent worker and his family − the seducers and the seduced. How else, in a consensual world, in which the state had become, for all practical purposes, the nation, could conflict be explained? The long march of those twin ideological demons − extremists and moderates − to which the mass media have lent their assiduous support had its point of departure in the post-war period just here.

Immediately, the 'red scare' was a success: the seamen settled. But the credibility of Labour as a reforming party of the working class evaporated with this 'victory'. Mr Wilson's 'historical bloc' fell apart. Worse, the run on sterling began again. Two deflationary packages followed. Labour now stood as the last, not very convincing, governor of the economic crisis, the bastion of the most backward sectors of British capital. The magic of the social democratic consensus began silently to depart. Mr Wilson − looking more Churchillian with every passing hour − now presided over what can only be described as *managed dissensus*.

DESCENT TO DISSENSUS

the crisis of the ruling class' hegemony . . . occurs either because the ruling class has failed in some major political undertaking for which it has requested or forcibly extracted the consent of the broad masses . . . or because

... huge masses ... have passed suddenly from a state of political passivity to a certain activity and put forward demands which taken together, albeit not organically formulated, add up to a revolution. A 'crisis of authority' is spoken of: this is precisely the crisis of hegemony, or general crisis of the State. (Gramsci) [30]

1966 provides a sort of early turning-point in the passage Gramsci describes from the 'moment of consent' through to the 'moment of force'. It is observable, as much in the spheres of moral authority and civil society as it is in the domain of politics and the state. The more fluid and open atmosphere of the 1950s and early 1960s had found their official apotheosis, if anywhere, in the liberalising reforms identified with Roy Jenkins's period in the Home Office, in the sphere of censorship, divorce, abortion, licensing, Sunday Observance, etc. But by the mid-1960s the calculated innocence of 'swinging London' had been redescribed as 'pornographic Britain' by the populist guardians of public morality. The moral backlash had commenced. The Police Federation, antagonised by a lost pay claim, the threatened abolition of capital punishment and the killing of three policemen by Harry Roberts, warned that the police were 'losing the war against crime'. The capital-punishment debate became, indeed, one of the pivotal points of popular reaction. More widely, the Moors murders were interpreted as the inevitable result of the pornographic society. The argument, persuasively put by Pamela Hansford-Johnson in *On Iniquity*, [31] was recapitulated by the press and public spokesmen. The ex-head of Scotland Yard, Sir Richard Jackson, in an authoritative series in the Sunday press, expressed his disgust at 'the rapid growth of public slop and sentiment about criminals and of propaganda against the police, the courts and all forms of established order, and for the weird, mongrel, yapping pack ... of misguided, soft-hearted liberals'. [32] In the same paper, Percy Howard charged the 'leaders of the Permissive Revolution' with moral responsibility for the Moors murders ('Are Brady and Hindley the Only Guilty Ones?'). [33] The media not only, in general, began to draw these telling connections together around the threshold of 'permissiveness', but they adopted the paradigmatic explanation of which Sir Richard had availed himself: the soft, misguided 'liberals' leading an innocent public into decadence, the 'hard core' mopping up in their wake, as moral life sank into a den of iniquity. The conspiratorial form of this paradigm matched, in the moral sphere, the explanatory figure which the Prime Minister himself was manipulating in the political domain. The hunt for 'subversive minorities' and 'liberal dupes' had begun.

The turning of the tide against liberalism, at the 'permissiveness' frontier, was taking place, simultaneously, on other fronts. Whereas in the 1950s the American example was the harbinger of all good things to come, in the 1960s, it was the American 'crisis' − student movements, the anti-Vietnam campaigns, the civil-rights rebellions and growing black resistance, the blossoming of the hippie and 'flower-power' generation − which set the pace. Between 1966 and 1967, these themes began to have their resonance 'on native ground' in Britain too. 1967 is the year of the great English 'panic' about drug use, [34] identified with the whole hippie scene: the new Regional Drug Squads were formed in

July of this year. Like other panics, this one too was sponsored by a dramatic incident – the trial of Mick Jagger for possession in June. No figure was more designed to fit the stereotype and trigger moral alarm: overtly if androgynously sexual, flamboyant, hedonistic – and guilty. Here, in the drug scene – as we suggested earlier – the moral entrepreneurs discovered the criminal edge of permissiveness. Shortly after, Marianne Faithfull was apprehended after an overdose, and another Rolling Stone, a first offender, was sentenced to nine months for smoking Indian hemp. The press described this as an 'exemplary martyrdom'. As part of his liberalising programme, Mr Jenkins had pushed through his *Race Relations Act* in 1965. But the Smethwick election of 1964 marked the emergence of overt racism into the official electoral politics of Britain for the first time in the post-war period. And, as Paul Foot's study clearly documents, the racist rot had penetrated deeply into the base of the Labour movement itself.[35] Mr Jenkins's liberalism was, here also, rapidly outstripped by events. At the impending promise of the arrival of the first wave of Kenyan Asian passport-holders, the anti-immigrant lobby took to the field for the first time. Mr Powell's observation that, though 'the comparison with the U.S. is not exact . . . it is startling'; Sir Cyril Osborne's friendly warning that 'the English people have started to commit race suicide'; Mr Sandy's fear that 'the breeding of millions of half-caste children would . . . produce a generation of misfits'; Mr Cordle's amiable estimate that 'In thirty years we would be a coffee-coloured nation'. All are from deep in the heart of Conservative official territory.[36] When the trouble arose at the London School of Economics over the appointment of Dr Adams as Director, the press instantly attributed the trouble to 'a handful of student agitators'.[37] When the British protests against American involvement in Vietnam began, Mr Hogg, remarking on the 'well-oiled machinery of indignation', observed that 'It has been activated when the Communists have pursued the matter. It has been silent and ineffective whenever they have not.'[38] The drift across the thresholds had also commenced.

1968/(1848): CATACLYSM – THE NATION DIVIDES

A spectre is haunting Europe – the spectre of Communism (Marx and Engels, *Communist Manifesto*) [39]
A spectre is haunting Europe – the spectre of student revolt (Danny and Gabriel Cohn-Bendit, *Obsolete Communism*) [40]

1968 is the year of a remarkable cataclysm: a parting of the waters. Like its predecessor (1848), it was an incomplete and unfinished 'revolution'. Its seismic impact reverberated outwards from its principal terrain in social and political life; its eddies are not yet fully spent. It consisted above all of the attempt to instigate 'revolution from above' – to transmit the spark of rebellion from the 'little motor' of student revolt to the great, inert engine of the labouring masses, envisaged as Marcuse's 'cheerful robots' in their 'one-dimensional' sleep. It was an assault on the culture and superstructure of late capitalism mounted by the system's own vanguard – a 'lumpen-bourgeoisie': a class fraction without a tangible productive base. In so far as this fraction embodied certain contradictions and antagonisms of the system they were those which stemmed from the 'higher nervous system', the overdeveloped 'social brain' of late capitalism. It was a revolt in, but also *of*, the superstructures. It propelled, by an act of collective will, the breaks and ruptures stemming from the rapid expansion in the ideology, culture and civil structures of the new capitalism, forwards in the form of a 'crisis of authority'.

Once again the United States led. The hippie 'golden summer' had scattered the seeds of disaffiliation far and wide, alongside acid rock, flower power, beads, kaftans and bells, the L.S.D. 'high' and the Haight Ashbury 'down'. Slowly the great exodus of America's 'brightest and best' from the cultural pathways of Middle America and the liberal-corporate state began, and parallel with that the organised students' movements, with their libertarian origin, and – now on a separatist trajectory – black rebellion in the cities. Norman Mailer had long ago foreseen just such a conjuncture: 'In such places as Greenwich Village, a *menage-a-trois* was completed – the bohemian and juvenile delinquent came face to face with the Negro and the hipster was a fact in American life.'[41] It was not the United States alone which found itself 'quite briefly in a revolutionary condition'.[42] From Berlin to Naples, Paris to Tokyo, the university – the ideological 'factory' – became the centrepiece of an astonishing reversal and confrontation. An entirely novel *repertoire* of confrontation tactics, theatrical and dramaturgical in inspiration, was generated. Temporarily, the politics of the street replaced the politics of the convention and the ballot box. Street and community became the sites for a series of politico-cultural happenings. In France and West Germany the movement was more 'orthodox' – the solid presence of the Communist mass party in the one, and the critical stream of Marxist theories in the other, marking one dimension of the difference. Both began with the ideological dismantling of corporate-liberalism from the left: the 'critique of pure tolerance'. Following the massive uprising of the Sorbonne students, a wave of strikes and worker demonstrations spread across France. But though the 'May events' came closest, outside of Italy, to sparking a working-class movement into life, they remained essentially a 'festival of the oppressed' – the figuratively oppressed, that is: the revolutionary dream of participation, worker control and creativity holding a more central role than Leninist conceptions of the vanguard party and state power. This very hesitancy before the citadel of the state was to be its undoing. The legitimacy of the Gaullist state, compounded by the 'legitimacy' of the French Communist Party, conspired, in a bizarre coalition, to turn the flank of revolution into reforms. When, in response to the growing signs of worker-student collaboration, the General incorporated 'participation' into his Referendum proposals, 200,000 massed in protest in the forecourt of the Gare de Lyon. Then Pompidou released the C.R.S.: 'Crush them', he advised, 'without weakness.' The young – workers and students – bore the brunt. A million respectable Frenchmen marched for Gaullism. Negotiations and elections were resumed. The Gaullist state had survived Armageddon. The counter-revolution had begun. Not long after, Mailer's 'Armies of the Night' retreated before the advancing grey dawn of the Nixon–Agnew triumph at the polls – revenge of

the 'silent majority'. The slogan under which this counter-revolution advanced
was 'law-and-order'.

As in 1848, Britain moved into this cataclysm more cautiously and sedately.
No workers marched, no factories were occupied, few heads were broken by
police batons. What in Paris divided the capital, in Britain tended only to
polarise the Common Room. Nevertheless, in her own 'peculiar' way, Britain
experienced her '1968'. The social and political polarisation which characterises the next decade began from this point. As elsewhere, Britain was
profoundly shocked by the 'great refusal' of those very sons and daughters
whom the system had chosen. They had undermined morality and civil society;
now they challenged the foundations of the state. The resolution of the state to
resist, and the panic and fear of the 'silent majority' at having their routinised
way of life threatened and shattered, made a fateful *rendezvous*. Out of this
convergence the drift into reaction and authoritarianism was born. In Britain
the greatest casualty was the disintegration of liberalism. Outflanked on its student left, intellectual liberalism threw in the sponge without a fight, and many
of its outstanding stalwarts, eloquent about academic freedom in general only
up to the point where some actual, particular freedom was threatened,
emigrated speedily to the extreme right, and made themselves over into the
range-riders of discipline. This reaction proved to be all the sharper since the
threat arose, not from some guerrilla group trained in Outer Mongolia, but
from the children of affluence itself, those destined to inherit the neo-capitalist
earth: the apprentice-managers of the world.

If the near cataclysm of 1968 shook the citadels of the state, civil society
proved remarkably impermeable. Nightly, the images of helmetted and shielded
riot-control police advancing on lines of students with headbands and combat
jackets, looking down the muzzles of machine-guns or scattering before the
C.S. gas, flooded on to the television screens, and provided a spectacle for
sober citizens at home before the box. The scenes themselves frequently contained, on one side, demonstrators and police locked in combat, and on the
other private citizens threading their way home through the debris, going about
their private business, not more than a canister's throw away. Much has indeed
been written about the apathy and privatisation which marked civil life under
corporate capitalism in this period – the massive disjuncture between the
'private world' of the citizen and the apparatuses and processes of the state.
The buttressing of the 'little world' of private wants and needs, of family and
home, appeared as a defence against the encroachments of the abstract
bureaucracies of politics, the economy and administration; but the two were,
nevertheless, intimately co-ordinated, the fullness of the one compensating for
the 'emptiness' of the other. 'Apathy' and the consolidation of the corporate
capitalist state were bedfellows. Yet each appeared unrelated – the state's
augmented role at the centre was experienced only as a set of private, serialised
grouses at the margins. The split was recapitulated in the rhetorics of public
ideology: workers by day went home only to be addressed by politicians and
advertisers, by night, as altogether different beings – consumers. Politics itself
became progressively 'privatised'. In its indistinct way, the student revolt was
mounted as a challenge to *this* hegemony of the state over the privatised
sphere. Much of the violence and confrontation, like the participatory slogans,

were directed against the invisible walls which rendered citizens the unwitting colluders with their own powerlessness. So was the communitarian stress, and the summons to reappropriate power at the base. Finally, this trajectory failed to intersect with or penetrate the veil of the privatised kingdom; this was the measure of its objective lack of centrality. But the novelty of its content and forms, and its targetting in on the 'revolution of everyday life', was not irrelevant, as the orthodox revolutionaries assumed (the French Communist Party called the 1968 militants 'pampered adventurists'). Situationism was directly germane – a simple 'negation' – to the new forms of state power, and left its profound trace in the revolutionary culture, though there were precious few 'situationists'.

The inner trajectory of the student movement's attack was, however, a godsend to the state itself and to the media, for it gave just enough substance to the massive, overwhelming efforts of the media and their licensed spokesmen to resolve the whole complex scenario into the simplifying terms of 'violence'. Confronting the first big Grosvenor Square anti-Vietnam demonstration in April, the *Observer* was cool enough to remark that 'these student demonstrations are not serious political movements pursuing real aims: they are more like a highbrow version of football hooliganism'. But when, after 'May', the press faced the even more massive October demonstration, the *Sunday Express* could observe, without fear of successful contradiction, that 'This is not primarily an Anti-Vietnam war demonstration. It is a cold and deliberate exercise in violence by evil men using the young and gullible to their own ends. It is a calculated effort by skilled left-wing agitators to bring our police into disrepute and terrorise the community.' This reduction of all forms of dissent or protest to the search for agitational cliques bent on violence, coupled with the arithmetic of consensus, in which 'majorities' were continually reckoned up against 'minorities', marks the whole ideological signification of student protest in Britain. It was gradually to become a dominant signification paradigm [43] for the whole gamut of social conflicts and political troubles. It also marks a shift in the signification spiral (discussed earlier) up through the thresholds towards their outer perimeter. By the time the second anti-Vietnam demonstration arrived, in October, the conviction that this would be a 'violent confrontation of the forces of law and order ... and the forces of anarchy' proved so overwhelming an 'inferential structure' in the collective minds of the politicians, the police and the media that (as the Leicester study, *Demonstrations and Communication* has shown) [44] it determined the whole shape of the subsequent coverage and dominated the news values, even though the great proportion of the march passed off peacefully: 'Today the heart of London will be in a state of seige ... And for what? Because the demonstrators feel strongly about what is happening in Vietnam? Rubbish.' [45] When the violence the press itself had predicted failed to arise, the police were congratulated for preventing it: 'Police Win Battle of Grosvenor Square'; 'The Day The Police Were Wonderful'. [46] The face caught on several front pages cheering on the troops was that of the new Home Secretary, who, in keeping with the time, had replaced the 'liberal' Mr Jenkins: someone destined for higher things – 'Honest Jim' Callaghan.

The appearance of a renewed panic about race, in the very moment of this intense polarisation of the political scene and just when the shift from a managed to a more coercive variant of consensus is occurring, cannot be wholly fortuitous. In 1967, Mr Powell had remarked, apropos the race issue, that 'we must act and act soon. We dare not look across the Atlantic and say, as we sit with folded hands, "It Can't Happen Here".' [47] Now, in 1968, as the floodgates of social dissent opened, race – not for the last time – becomes a salient theme: one capable of carrying intense but subterranean public emotions forward on a wave of reaction.

By comparison with the great abstract themes of the student movement – 'participatory democracy', 'community power' – the race theme was concrete and immediate. Its reference to 'everyday life', as lived by the 'silent majorities' of private citizens in the visibly declining parts of the post-imperial city, was *direct*. It touched the disappointed aspirations and frustrated hopes of those in the 'respectable' and lower-middle classes who had invested their last savings in Mr Macmillan's 'property-owning democracy', only to have the equally respectable (but black) family moving in next door send property values plummetting. No first immigrant generation had sacrificed more for the 'quiet life' than the early black immigrants to Britain in the 1950s. Yet, objectively, they were destined to signify the dark side of the 'affluent dream' – to embody the repressed content of the affluent nightmare. Their imputed taste for big American cars – the direct expression of the over development of under development in their native land – caricatured the affluent life. Their Saturday-night parties were a constant reminder of the sacrifices demanded by the regime of work and the taboo on pleasure enshrined in the Protestant ethic. Their presence in the job queue recalled a century of unemployment and summary dismissal – evidence that a few years of 'full employment' cannot liquidate a whole class experience of economic insecurity. The black immigrant moved into the declining areas of the city, where Britain's 'forgotten Englishmen' lived on the very tightest of margins; he entered this 'tight little island' of white lower-middle and working-class respectability – and, by his every trace, his looks, clothes, pigmentation, culture, mores and aspirations, announced his 'otherness'. His visible presence was a reminder of the unremitting squalor out of which that imperial noon had risen. The symbolism of the race–immigrant theme was resonant in its subliminal force, its capacity to set in motion the demons which haunt the collective subconscious of a 'superior' race; it triggered off images of sex, rape, primitivism, violence and excrement. Out there, in the great suburban world of money and power, where few black men or women walked, a suitably high-minded view of 'racial integration' in the lower depths could be taken; what *these* white men and women feared above all was that they would suddenly lose their position and power – that they would suddenly become, in all senses of the word, *the poor*. What the white poor feared, however, was that, after all this time, they might become *black*. (Every social stratum, Fanon suggests, uses the stratum beneath it as material for dreams, fantasies or nightmares.) When polarisation and revolt began to transmit shock-waves through the body politic of the state, those in power felt the *status quo* on which they stood *shift*; they felt the earth move. But what their most articulate spokesmen chose to *say* to their constituents was not that the 'earth' of consensus politics had *moved*, but that the blacks were *moving in*. Mr Powell struck a rich vein when he offered journalists his story of the little white old lady of Wolverhampton (the one nobody ever found), who had 'excreta pushed through her letter box' and endured the racialist abuse of 'charming, wide-eyed, grinning piccaninnies'; or the sad tale of the 'quite ordinary working man', who suddenly confessed, 'If I had the money to go I wouldn't stay in this country . . . in 15 or 20 years the black man will have the whip hand over the white man.' Such stories and phrases intersected directly with the anxieties among ordinary men and women which come flooding to the surface when life suddenly loses its bearings, and things threaten to go careering off the rails. An outcast group, a tendency to closure in the control culture, widespread public anxiety: Mr Powell himself provided the 'dramatic event'. No wonder, unlike Mr Heath, he poured such scorn on the three-day wonder of the 'I'm Backing Britain' movement, which surfaced and faded. Politicians worth their salt must know what issues will connect, which themes will mobilise a popular groundswell, launch a crusade, bring out the troops. Mr Powell had evidence of what he himself had earlier called 'combustible material'. [48]

In fact, most blacks who knew the score at local level had long since given up the promise of 'integration', even as Mr Jenkins was making his most eloquent defence of it. First-generation immigrants silently abandoned 'integration' as a practical aspiration, and turned to other things – like making a living and a tolerable life for themselves, among their own people in their own areas. But the second generation emerging from the difficult experience of an English education into a declining labour market were in a quite different mood. The better equipped, educated, skilled, languaged and acculturated they were, the sharper their perceptions of the realities of discrimination and institutionalised racism, the more militant their consciousness. West-Coast acid rock may have been blowing the mind of white youth; but down there in the ghetto the most popular record was 'Shout it Loud, I'm Black And Proud'. Black Power had arrived. The summers of 1967 and 1968 were crucial in terms of the penetration of the most advanced and conscious sectors of black youth by the ideas and concepts of the American black revolution. For several months the media and race-relations officials refused to believe that anything so 'violent' and un-British as Black Power could take root amongst 'our West Indian friends'. Typically, they dubbed anyone who tried to describe or influence young blacks in the cities as 'racialist' and 'extremist'. A well-organised, vigorous anti-immigrant lobby now rapidly developed within the Conservative Party. In his speech at Walsall on 9 February 1968 Mr Powell called for a virtual end to the entry voucher system and a virtual embargo against the Kenyan Asians. The lobby immediately won ground. The Labour government, responding to the most immediate, pragmatic and self-interested calculations, spirited a Bill through Parliament introducing an entry voucher system for Kenyan Asians. This only whetted the appetite of the anti-immigrant lobby. In April, as President Johnson announced a bombing 'pause' in Vietnam and his own decision to retire – both significant victories for the anti-war left – a white assassin murdered Martin Luther King. A prolonged nightmare of looting and arson followed in the United States – what *Time* described as a 'black rampage that subjected the U.S. to the most widespread spasm of racial disorder in its violent history'. It had a sharp impact amongst black militants in Britain. On 20 April on the eve of the Race Relations Bill, Mr Powell delivered his 'rivers of blood' speech in Birmingham. 'Those whom the gods wish to destroy they first make mad. We must be mad, literally mad, as a nation to be permitting the annual inflow of some 50,000 dependants. ... It is like watching a nation busily engaged in heaping up its own funeral pyre.' Discrimination, Mr Powell continued, was being experienced, not by blacks, but by whites – 'those among whom they have come'. This invocation – direct to the experience of unsettlement in a settled life, to *the fear of change* – is the great emergent theme of Mr Powell's speech. It is whites who have 'found their wives unable to obtain hospital beds in childbirth, their children unable to obtain school places, their homes and neighbourhoods, changed beyond recognition, their plans and prospects for the future defeated'. The River Tyber, he ended, was 'foaming with much blood. ... That tragic and intractable phenomenon which we watch with horror on the other side of the Atlantic is coming upon us here by our own volition. ... Indeed it has all but come.' [49]

Long term, 'Powellism' was symptomatic of deeper shifts in the body politic. Mr Powell once wrote that Conservatism was 'a settled view of the nature of human society in general and our own society in particular'. But gradually, through the 1960s, and then explosively in 1968, English society had become distinctly *un*settled. The unrelieved pragmatism of Mr Wilson and Mr Heath in this period was a living testimony to the bankruptcy of consensus politics in a period of renewed social conflict. The gap was filled from the right. Mr Powell employed race – as subsequently he was to use Ireland, the Common Market, defence of the free market, and the House of Lords – as a *vehicle* through which to articulate a definition of 'Englishness', a recipe for holding England together.[50] On race Mr Powell was often accused of skewing 'the facts', of illogicality. This is to miss the point and meaning of his political intervention. The themes which are closest to his heart – a Burkean sense of tradition, the 'genius' of a people, constitutional fetishism, a romantic nationalism – do not obey the pragmatic imperatives of a Wilsonian or Heathian 'logic'. They are ordered by more subliminal nationalist sentiments and passions. It was one of Mr Powell's gifts to be able to find a populist rhetoric which, in the era of rampant pragmatism, bypassed the pragmatic motive, and spoke straight – in its own metaphorical way – to fears, anxieties, frustrations, to the national collective unconscious, to its hopes and fears. It was a torpedo delivered straight to the boiler-room of consensus politics itself.

The country now began to lurch smartly to the right, punctuated by continuing trouble on the university campuses, moving in close tandem with events elsewhere. In the United States, for example, the movements from the left opened the rifts within the Democratic Party – McCarthy on the radical wing, Wallace on the right, students, blacks, Yippies and Mayor Daley's troops in the park: 'already, weeks in advance [of the Democratic Convention] there is a smell of bloodshed'. [51]But it was the Nixon–Agnew ticket which gathered up these threads into a law-and-order platform which mobilised the silent majorities: an example not lost on the Conservative Shadow Cabinet. The polls revealed substantial majorities, in Britain, on the right for all the major social issues. The consensus, it was said, had been undermined by 'extremism' on both sides.

The period is so punctuated by shocks and alarms that it seems gratuitous to conclude with a reference to two issues, not yet mentioned, which emerge strongly towards the end of 1968, and which not only compound the crisis then, but come more and more to dominate the scene. In September, the strike at the Ford plant at Halewood made 1968 the worst year for industrial stoppages in the motor industry, and initiated a period of prolonged and bitter struggle in the multinational giant. In October and November, the newly formed Northern Ireland Civil Rights movement organised a series of 'moral-force' demonstrations against the Protestant ascendancy and Orange discrimination in the province, and were opposed by the Reverend Paisley and the Royal Ulster Constabulary. It is not the first time in English history that the coming of 'iron times' has been heralded by trouble in Ulster.

1969: THE 'CULTURAL REVOLUTION' AND THE TURN INTO AUTHORITARIANISM

If the Underground really intends to go underground and become an active resistance movement, it must try to discover its real roots in the specific conditions of the English social structure. It must expose the process of pacification which holds the whole thing together.... But any attempt to explode this con ... is itself put down as 'violence' and then crushed with all the real violence of due legal and/or therapeutic process.... The only force at present capable of hitting back are the kids who are trying to fight their way out of their parents' culture, whether this is working or middle class.... If it is to stop playing this sort of game, the underground must begin by dissolving the ideological split between its political and cultural 'sectors'. [52]

The rupture which 1968 marks with the immediate past is sustained in 1969. Polarisation moves more rapidly, and into new areas. Many of the same themes which provided the fulcrum of official and popular reaction in the preceding two or three years are resumed again in 1969, but now in what, from the point of view of the state, must have looked like an advanced stage of social disintegration. This advanced condition of the crisis is marked ideologically – as we have come to expect – by extensive *convergences* between its different themes. The themes of protest, conflict, permissiveness and crime begin to run together into one great, undifferentiated 'threat'; nothing more nor less than the foundations of the Social Order itself are at issue. Perhaps, after all, the students will not precipitate a takeover in the factories by the working class in the classic revolutionary scenario. But there are more ways than one of bringing a society toppling down like a house of cards. Its moral fibre can be eaten away by the cancer of permissiveness, or so Mrs Whitehouse persistently asserts. It can be penetrated by organised crime, as the *Sunday Express* believes. It can be subverted by 'ideological criminals' (i.e. student militants), as the American Attorney-General, John Mitchell (subsequently to be swept out in the 'non-ideological' Watergate tide) asserted. It can be 'held up to ransom' by industrial militancy, as the crusaders for industrial-relations legislation are persuading the nation. It can be 'soft-pedalled' to death, as Mr Quintin Hogg keeps warning his Sunday readers. Above all, it can be outraged and brutalised by violence and anarchy. These two themes are really the upper *thresholds* of the crisis; they stake the crisis out, not in this or that area, issue, problem or question, but as a progressively deteriorating *general* condition. Violence is the outer limit. It marks the point where civilised social organisation descends into brute force. It is the end of *law*. Anarchy is its result – the disintegration of social order. Mr Powell put it succinctly in September: 'Violence and mob law are organized and expanding for their own sake. Those who organize and spread them are not seeking to persuade authority to act differently, to be more merciful or more generous. Their object is to repudiate authority and destroy it.' [53]

Let us turn once again to the black–race issue. If the first response in the black community to the onslaught, led by Mr Powell and the 'radical right' lobbies within the Conservative Party, was shock, fear and dismay, the second response was a degree of politicisation and organisation *in depth* hitherto unknown in the post-war history of black migration. This is the period of the formation of militant black groups and groupings – the British Black Panther Party, the Black People's Alliance, etc. – the organisation of anti-police harassment demonstrations, and the recruitment of, especially but not exclusively, second-generation blacks into the orbit of 'Black Power', and a more militant black cultural consciousness. Desmond Dekker's Ras Tafarian record, *Israelite*, with its kaballa-like millenarianism, was at the top of the black record charts at the time, and 'Reggae' began to penetrate into white society via the media and through its paradoxical adoption amongst young, white 'skinheads'. Dilip Hiro's estimate at this time that not only had the ranks of the militant black organisations enormously expanded but that there were a dozen or more sympathisers for every committed black activist, has not been seriously challenged. [54] On the other side, the white thrust was also 'hardening'. The formal cover-stories and anecdotes were abandoned, and Mr Powell led the advance into the hard bargaining about 'numbers' and its equally tough corollary: repatriation. The initiative, here as elsewhere, passed, more or less for good, from the well-meaning liberal centre to more extreme points on the compass; and the extremes exerted a retroactive effect on the centre. Paul Foot has reminded us that only two months separated Mr Heath's condemnation of Mr Powell's speech as 'character assassination of one racial group', and Mr Heath's espousal of the idea that immigrant admissions should be 'for a specific job in a specific place – for a specific time', with renewed annual permits and no 'absolute right to bring their relatives, however close': the nefarious 'patrial/non-patrial' distinction which was to be enshrined in the Tory Commonwealth Immigration Bill of 1971. [55]

A sensitive British chord is undoubtedly touched, in 1969, by the vivid coverage in the media of the United States and the connections there between black power and black crime. A random check in two newspapers throws up Henry Brandon's '24 hours of armed robbery and street crime in Washington'; [56] Mileva Ross's classic 'I Live with Crime in the Fun City'; [57] Allen Brien's 'New York Nightmare'; [58] and the Henry Fairlie *Sunday Express* reports. These pieces not only fixed British minds on the complex chain connecting race, politics and crime, but they drew explicit lessons *for* Britain, and they chewed over possible scenarios of reaction – the law-and-order platform, the appeal of the Wallace bid, Nixon's proposal to transfer juvenile violent offenders to adult courts, etc.

Crime itself also delivers one of its climacterics at home in 1969, with the sensational trial and jailing of the infamous Kray twins, those archetypal East End villains whose combination of professionalism and psychopathology kept them week after week in the headlines. More significant is the nagging, persistent worrying-away at the whole question of crime, authority and society which rises and falls like a fever chart through the year. In February, Mr Heath, anticipating the review deadlined for 1970, called for a serious study of the effects of the abolition of capital punishment. Before the month's end, he and Quintin Hogg were locked in a debate with Mr Callaghan about Labour's alleged failure to handle the 'drive against crime'. Capital punishment, the murder rate, the rising arc of crimes of violence, the trend towards softer sentences – these now-archetypal concerns of the crime-news domain continued to dominate public debate. The *Sunday Times* was far-seeing enough to predict that the crime/capital-punishment debate of 1969 provided a sort of rehearsal for 'a sharp debate on law and order' to come – in 1970. [59] In October Mr Hogg was at the crime hustings again, accusing Labour of the more sweeping charge of helping to undermine *all* morality and authority. [60] By the end of the year – one Piccadilly squat and a Springboks tour later – Mr Hogg's rhetoric had escalated into its now-familiar stark and simple oppositions: the law versus the threat of anarchy. His tendency to enlarge and expand the nature of any threat to 'order' by sliding quite different things together beneath a single rubric is already in evidence here: 'When Unions, when University teachers and others, when students, when demonstrators of various kinds, when Labour and Liberal M.P.'s announce their deliberate detestation of all forms of authority save their own opinions, how can you expect the police and the courts to enforce the law.'[61] Here, as appears to be the case whenever separate issues, categories and problems begin to be blurred in a general and specious ideological convergence, one can assume that the pressures towards sterner control measures, more widely and indiscriminately applied, are also escalating. We can also assume that the explicit themes mentioned are beginning, ideologically, to provide a sort of 'cover' for other concerns. Naturally, recourse to the law as a last defence – in both the practical and abstract sense – comes more prominently to the fore as these forms of amplification extend. We can see this at work, in a moment, when we turn to the other active fronts of permissiveness and protest. Meanwhile the role of the legal and violence thresholds, drawing increasingly sharp lines of distinction between the permissible and the impermissible, cutting into and through the rising tide of social conflict, reducing it to polar oppositions, becomes more insistent. Sir Alec Douglas Home, writing early in the year in the *Sunday Express* about Ulster, gave a good example of it: 'Civil violence in modern conditions simply opens the way to the looter, whose stock in trade is social chaos. . . . In a democracy like that of the United Kingdom and Northern Ireland, it is a government's plain duty to sustain the constitution and the law.' It is noticeable, in the same month, on a quite different topic, and from a traditionally far more liberal source. An editorial in the *Sunday Times* argued that once the 'encrusted totem' of trade-union immunity from legal sanction was destroyed, then governmental action on strikes could take place in a more 'rational atmosphere': 'only legal reform can strengthen the validity of collective agreements. . . . [and] protect thousands of men from being put out of work by the wildcat striker . . . and strengthen the hand of official union leadership.' [62] In a subsequent editorial the *Sunday Times*, while recognising that introducing the law into trade-union affairs was not *the* answer, nevertheless greeted the proposals to that effect beginning to be sounded by the prospective Tory front bench with the thought that the law was the necessary first step to combat the recent strike figures which 'depict a type of anarchy'.[63] The language of crime, violence, chaos, anarchy – and The Law, apostrophised in that way, is beginning to slide like a Dickensian fog into unexpected places.

The Wootton Report on drugs had been published at the end of 1968. It proposed a firmer distinction in sentencing between possession of and selling marihuana, and a recategorisation of cannabis to a group different from that for heroin and other dangerous drugs. Its proposals were modest, its lineage impeccable, its precedents (the American Report was, if anything, bolder) auspicious. The popular press, however, labelled it as a 'Conspiracy of the Drugged' (*Daily Mirror*), a 'Junkie's Charter' (*Evening News*). There was also a 'conspiracy' on the other side – in Parliament – when the Report came to be debated. Mr Callaghan attributed its follies to the polluting effect on the Committee of a 'soft-drugs lobby', and defended his decision to reject its main findings with the remark that he was pleased to have contributed to 'a halt in the advancing tide of so-called permissiveness'. [64] His Shadow, Mr Hogg, could only tread willingly in his master's footsteps. The ebb and flow of this debate left its mark on the rest of the year. The opponents of permissiveness also won through in the rejection of the Arts Council's report recommending the repeal of the Obscenity Law (as if in accord with Mrs Whitehouse's warning that any politician promoting this 'Pornographer's Paradise' would be committing 'political suicide') [65] and in the new Drugs Bill introduced by Mr Callaghan, contrary in spirit and practice to the Wootton Report. [66]

The apogee of 'official' permissiveness was reached when Roy Jenkins attempted to redefine the word 'permissiveness' as 'civilisation' – 'the achievement of social reform without disruption . . . avoiding excessive social tensions'.[67] Thereafter permissiveness was assured of a universally adverse and hostile press. When, at the end of August, the whole counter-culture assembled in the Isle of Wight for the first British pop-festival, the media constructed an image of the event which contained a run-down of just about every permissive demon that had ever haunted the imagination of the morally indignant: '100,000 fans threatened to riot'; 'security guards with dogs raced'; 'near pandemonium'; 'filled with hippies and weirdies'; 'the whole scene was one of chaos'; 'hippies swimming in the nude'; '73 people arrested for drugs'; a 'youth found critically injured at the foot of the cliffs'; 'drugtaking'; 'scantily-clad youths'; and – not long after – 'a bizarre happening where boys and girls dance wildly in the nude'; 'a good excuse for a mass orgy'; and so on. This 'Woodstock nightmare' was counterposed by the media to 'local residents' and 'sedate island folk' [68] – the 'silent majorities' of 1970, here no more than a hair's breadth, a naked body, away. Still, had not the moral entrepreneurs consistently warned that a lenient sentence here, a corrupt intellectual there, another 'soft' Report, and the inevitable consequences would be nudity, drugs, orgies in the street, a 'diet of depravity'? Had not Mrs Whitehouse eloquently reminded us of the striking parallels with 'the decadence of the Weimar Republic which had paved the way for Hitler's Germany'? [69]

The wave of student unrest did not fade away in 1969. In January, the London School of Economics was once again closed following the 'affair of the gates' – an incident which ended in discipline and dismissals of staff. It also provoked one of the finest examples of what we have elsewhere called 'the numbers game' – the attempt to separate moderates from extremists, to cast the former as innocent, well-meaning dupes and the latter as 'a tiny clique of politically motivated men'. Mr Short, the Labour Secretary for Education, for example, explained, in a convincing statistical display to the House of Commons, that the 'LSE has about 3,000 students. The disruptions which have taken place involve about probably 300 of these. . . . The real perpetrators are a tiny handful of people – fewer than one-half of 1 per cent . . . are the thugs of the academic world.' [70] He added, for good, memorable measure, the reflection that they were 'Brand X revolutionaries'. Acts of 'hooliganism, vandalism and terrorism at Keele',[71] the Cambridge 'Garden House affair', the mass read-in of the Vice-Chancellor's files at Warwick,[72] and the slow-motion near-breakdown of Essex, were all still to come.

Politically, in Britain, as elsewhere, the 1968–9 period represents a watershed: the whole fulcrum of society turns, and the country enters, not a temporary and passing rupture, but a prolonged and continuous state of semi-siege. Its meaning and causes, then, and its consequences since, have been neither fully reckoned with, nor liquidated. The political polarisation which it precipitated fractured society into two camps: authority and its 'enemies'. This spectacle mesmerised the right, the centre and the apolitical, precisely because it refused to assume the recognised forms of classical class conflict and the politics associated with it. But it also marked the left; and its legacies remain, active and unexorcised, in the spectrum of radical and revolutionary politics to this day. At the time it involved, in effect, two separate but related developments: the transmission of the spark of student politics to a wider constituency and field of contestation – the 'politics of the street'; and the partial politicisation of the counter-culture. Although the first somewhat resembled some wild anarcho-libertarian scenario, and the second sometimes assumed the form of 'the revolt of the bourgeoisie', in truth there was no recipe for either in the classical revolutionary cook-books. One example of the first is related to racial issues – the Rhodesia House demonstrations in January 1969, and the tactically brilliant Stop The Seventies Tour (S.T.S.T.) rehearsal during the Springboks' rugby tour from October onwards. The latter exhibited all the concentrated force of a single-issue campaign, limited in scope, but wide enough to involve young liberal people. It provoked – such was the atmosphere of the moment – a vigorous and on some occasions a vicious response (at Swansea the police appeared to make room for anti-demonstrator vigilantes to rough-house the protesters; the Home Secretary had subsequently to intervene to limit the scope of the rugby 'stewards'). [73] S.T.S.T. was a strange enough coalition of forces, to be sure. The South African paper, *Die Beeld*, classically described it as a 'bunch of left-wing, workshy, refugee long-hairs', neatly catching all the clichés. But very considerable numbers of young people, sensitised by the events of 1968, were recruited into the politics of the demonstration by the clarity of its anti-apartheid appeal.

The politicisation of the counter-culture was more complicated and uneven. The underground press, deriving much of its style from the American 'outlaw press', its counter life-style fired on the hippie trail and the 'summer of love', advanced a radical critique of straight society, but maintained an ambivalent stance, at first, to the politics of protest. Nevertheless, a profoundly anti-authoritarian, libertarian 'politics' of a kind, transfusing public issues with the language and feeling of the personal, was sustained by the counter-culture, and disseminated in the network of 'alternative' institutions – the Arts Labs, Free University, Gandalf's Garden network, with its street theatres and community activists – transforming what Peter Sedgwick called 'these common refusals and affirmations' into something more like Abbie Hoffman's 'Invisible Nation'. Somewhere in this period the American counter-culture encountered the spectre of 'repressive tolerance' in its all too-real form of the State Troopers, and lost its political virginity. Some turned back into commune life, whole-earth foods and the countryside: others went on to build 'the Movement'. In September, when the Chicago Conspiracy Trial opened, the full spectrum of the enemies of the state were on view. On one of those long evenings in jail, Abbie Hoffman explained to the Black Panther leader, Bobby Seale, that 'Yippie is the political aspect of the Hippie movement and the hippie is the part of the group that hasn't necessarily become political yet.' [74] By October, however, Seale was appearing bound and gagged before Judge Hoffman.

The British route was, as usual, more sedate. The drugs and life-style bust and police harassment of the alternative press were the principal forms in which the counter-culture first engaged with the law. In March, Jim Morrison was arrested for obscenity. In May, Jagger and Marianne Faithfull were pulled in again for possession. In July, Brian Jones of the Rolling Stones drowned – an exemplary death commemorated in Hyde Park by a quarter of a million young people. In October, the police raided *Oz*. One convenient instance of the escalating conflict between straight society and the disaffiliates – and one which reveals how the partial politicisation of the counter-culture was accomplished – was the 144 Piccadilly Squat by the London Street Commune in September. It was consciously planned as an 'improvisation' designed to bring together several different tributaries of the counter-culture: quasi-anarchists, political 'hard men', hippie drop-outs, working-class layabouts, hard-core bohemians and the Hell's Angels. To the organisers' regret, the 'skinheads' finally lined up outside with the police and the newsmen: their entry to the squat would have completed its 'logic'. Borrowing an old form of working-class politics – squatting – they adapted this to 'post-capitalist' conditions (occupying a fashionable town residence) for the *new* homeless – London's drop-out youth community. This was a spectacle calculated to scandalise traditional moralists like Mrs Whitehouse, traditional politicians like Lord Hailsham, traditional academics like John Sparrow – but also, traditional Marxist groups like the International Socialists, and 'traditional' squatters like Jim Radford. The police broke up the commune with energy – allowing the 'skinheads' a bit of 'aggro' first.

The backlash had indeed begun. The silent majority were rallied by the more active of the moral entrepreneurs in campaigns to 'clean up' Britain (beginning, symbolically, with the B.B.C.). Closer to the ground, the police were now goaded and prodded into action, especially over drugs, the alternative press, obscenity. The counter-culture gradually acclimatised itself to the continuous presence of 'the Law'. The dream that 'straight society' might simply abandon the struggle, throw the towel in, and turn on, proved to be a mirage: one which had survived so long only because the counter-culture did not itself fully understand the nature of the society it aimed to subvert, or its vulnerability. The London Street Commune Manifesto, aimed at ending this innocence, stated that they claimed 'the miserable capitalist streets' because 'they are the only possible space from which the reorganisation of the Underground could take place'.[75] In 1969 the police began to close down this informal street occupation. This brought the counter-culture up against 'the Fuzz'; and, more than any other single force, the 'Fuzz' *almost* succeeded in converting the Underground into an active political resistance movement. The counter-culture had named straight society, conventional attitudes and life-styles, possessive individualist hang-ups, as 'the enemy'. They failed to recognise these things as the armature of bourgeois society until its agencies of defence – the police – converted one kind of 'repression' into another.

There followed considerable recruitment of a section of the counter-culture into the ranks of the revolutionary left groups and sects: International Socialists, the newly formed International Marxist Group, the anarchists, Solidarity, the various Maoist fractions. As had already taken place in, for example, the Italian 'hot autumn' of 1969, a small but active and influential left had arisen on the outer flank of the Communist Party. Wider political influences – from the anti-Vietnam War solidarity committees, from Guevarist and other Third World developments – played into this pre-revolutionary milieu. From *within*, the variegations appeared infinite – from life-style politics, rock music and psychedelia, to Trotskyism, libertarianism, and community politics of no known affiliation: a seemingly bewildering and diverse scenario of intense activism, lacking cohesion, theoretical clarity or tactical perspective. From *without*, however, it presented the spectacle of a hydra-headed conspiracy against *a whole way of life*, its organisational looseness, spontaneous, free-wheeling character precisely constituting its threat to a stable and orderly civil life – the return of King Mob. A sector of that largely invisible creature, the English intelligentsia, had become loosed from its proper moorings, detached itself from its traditional mode of cultural insertion, and hovered, in a pre-revolutionary ferment, suspended in its own milieu. The populist guardians awaited something further: its precipitation as an overtly political force.

This was not always to occur where either its sponsors or its opponents expected. *Oz* and *IT* were solidly 'for' the sexual revolution – but this was undoubtedly a revolution envisaged from the dominant male position, a fantasy of
the never-ending 'lay'. In the spring of 1968 a woman called Lil Bilocca had
spearheaded a militant campaign among the wives of Hull fishermen to improve trawler safety, and Rose Boland led a group of sewing machinists at the
Ford Dagenham factory in a strike for the women's right to work on machines
and at skilled trades hitherto reserved for men. But as a *movement* Women's
Liberation undoubtedly had its origins and was precipitated within the same
'oppositional milieu' we have been describing. The radical version of feminism
it began to develop was snatched from the male-chauvinist hearts of its own
'revolutionary' men: post-war feminism began as a 'revolution within the
revolution'. However, its impact was profound. Internally, within the ranks, it
made concrete the connection between the 'personal' and the 'political' which
the counter-culture had advanced often in abstract terms only; it pinpointed the
specific mechanisms which articulated abstract 'ideological oppression' with
the specific forms of a capitalist culture founded on the principle of patriarchy.
Externally, through its critique, it touched issues as close to the nerve cells of
civil society under capitalism as anything in the more outrageous catalogue of
alternative 'happenings': sexuality, the family, male domination. It emerged at
the very moment when capitalist culture entered one of its most dangerous moments: a period of *repressive degeneration*.

The year 1969 represented the last moment when the 'cultural revolution', as
distinct from other strands of political struggle, might have crystallised as an
autonomous political force. The precipitation did not occur. Had it *coincided*
with the forms of struggle to come, in the 1970s, its subsumption into a wider
trajectory might have had revolutionary consequences. It did not. The history
of radical politics in this period is the history of missed conjunctures. But why
had it crystallised *at all*? What did its threatened precipitation *mean*, in terms
of capitalism's capacity to hold together as a viable way of life?

The counter-culture was 'superstructural' in two senses. In social composition, the majority of its bearers probably came from middle-class backgrounds,
from parents not engaged in skilled or unskilled productive labour in the
traditional sense; though some of its most active recruits were from strata
which had only recently experienced social mobility – products of the
'educational revolution', first-generation grammar-school or new comprehensive children, art school or college as well as university boys and girls.
Whatever their class origins, they were potential recruits to the *new organic intelligentsia* – those trained to fill intermediary or subaltern positions, but with
critical tasks to perform in terms of social reproduction, those whom the com-
plexifying social and technical division of labour in capitalism needed both to
recruit (actually) and win over (ideologically) if it was to survive.

But the counter-culture was also, in its thrust, directed *at* the superstructures
of modern capitalism. In character, it was intrinsically 'anti-bourgeois': aimed
at the overthrow of Protestant Man, the ushering in of a new reign of Reason,
presiding over an Aquarian Age of Pleasure. It demanded, above all, a revolution *in* consciousness – because it was, in essence, a revolution *of*

consciousness. It threatened a reversal in the superstructures, in ideology, where bourgeois civil life was cemented and reproduced; and though, in focal concerns and in its critique and mode of struggle it tended, consistently, towards a radical idealism, this is bound to be the prevailing tendency when social contradictions accumulate at the level of the superstructures, when ideological struggle for the moment 'takes command'. It was a revolution led by a key fraction of the dominant class, against the hegemonic culture to which, by any logic, that fraction ought to have made allegiance. It thus indexed a severe rupture *within* the hegemonic ideology — a rupture which, as Juliet Mitchell has argued, is likely to be led, in the first instance, 'from within the ideologically dominant class'.[76] The superstructures, as Gramsci has argued, have the function of ensuring the reproduction of a certain type of civilisation, of producing a certain kind of 'man' and citizen', a certain 'ethic' in correspondence with the long-term needs of the economic structure, though with no degree of functional fit — indeed, with what Althusser has called a 'sometimes teeth-gritting harmony'. Especially through its organisation in the state, its task is to establish the always problematic and contradictory conformity of social, political and civil society to the needs and requirements of the mode of production itself.[77] This is the sphere we have called *social reproduction*: the 'reproduction of the social conditions of production'. The 'cementing' of society, in this more extended sense, requires its own modes and mechanisms. Any profound restructuring of the inner organisation and composition of capitalist relations — such as characterises the long transition from *laissez-faire* to monopoly, or the more intense section of this arc where British capitalism found itself in the post-war period — requires and precipitates a consequent 'recomposition' of the whole social and ideological integument of the social formation.

Why these ruptures occurred, at just this moment, in the superstructural level of capitalist social formations has never been properly charted — despite the movement's overwhelming tendency to self-analysis. '1968' has never been thoroughly comprehended; it has been largely bypassed. Certainly, the ideology of thrift, respectability and security, through which the middle classes had morally and ideologically associated themselves with the system and acclimatised themselves to its needs, was constantly eroded in this period by the appeals to consumption and self-gratification which underpinned the post-war affluent boom. At a deeper level, the bourgeois character and the bourgeois family, with its patterns of emotional restraints and introjected repressions, its 'Protestant ethic' of work, rational dedication to and fulfilment through one's vocation, its emphasis on self-discipline and internalised authority and its taboo on pleasure, which formed the dense, ideological integument in civil society for the developing capitalist mode of production, became *disarticulated* as capitalism moved into a more advanced monopoly form. A certain type of rationality, related in a complex way with certain forms of sexuality and certain styles of authority and discipline, had been as necessary, in the earlier phases of capitalism, to its capacity to reproduce itself as the relations of capitalist production themselves. Indeed, these *were* also 'social relations' of capital — outside the productive sphere, but vital to its continuation. These tangled strands began to unwind in the post-war period. In the spheres of work (productive and unproductive), and above all in the expanding spheres of the state in its welfare-capitalist form, capitalism came progressively to assume a bureaucratic and impersonal form, routinising and regulating more and more of the private and the personal world as the capitalist state assumed responsibility for, and direction over, domains which the *laissez-faire* state had left to civil society. This apotheosis of 'possessive individualism' and 'bureaucratic man', under the leadership of an increasingly interventionist and corporate state, made everyday life appear, at one and the same time, regimented and empty. At the more structural level, the complex nature of advanced capitalist societies posed problems of the most radical kind in terms of ensuring the consent and affiliation of all its members to its logic. This 'crisis of legitimation' we have encountered before; but, in this context, it meant an enormous extension in the ideological apparatuses – what Enzensberger has called the 'consciousness-making industries'. Moreover, these industries had a real material base in the productive technologies and infrastructures of the new capitalism, as Enzensberger and others have shown. Not only were they tied to the new frontier of the 'third industrial revolution' – that based on electronics and cheap energy-sources – they were also co-ordinated with the changing social organisation of the labour process, management and the circulation system of capital itself. In the recomposition of capital, the media and the education apparatuses (now far more directly superintended by the state) were key 'productive' supports – and were, consequently, massively expanded. The organisation of science and technique, its practical application to production, with the consequent recomposition of skills, of labour and the labour process were unthinkable without 'a decisive development in the forces of mental production', in 'the mental universe' – in the means and techniques of mental and ideological reproduction, and in the size and character of the 'new intelligentsia'. Sections of that 'new intelligentsia' were, on the one hand, favoured, with respect to skilled and semi-skilled productive workers, but they were also more closely and 'organically' co-ordinated with the technical processes of capitalist reproduction than ever before. These 'brightest and best', formed in the expanding horizons of knowledge opened up in the tertiary sectors of education, often faced the prospects of what has come to be recognised as the phenomenon of intellectual proletarianisation: a new qualitative kind of deskilling. In general, 'The greater the development of Capital, the higher the rate of reproduction that is necessary to maintain it.' [78] And, ' "Advanced capitalism" . . . is impossible . . . without a parallel expansion of the social "brain" and nerves of communication.' [79]

The counter-culture was the translation of this uneven development at the ideological and superstructural levels. It first appeared in, and then took as its target, the very institutions which had formed it. It attacked and criticised the very goals and values to which these institutions had tried to attach them. Especially, it focused on the institutions which manufacture 'attachment', which try to internalise consent, which produce and reproduce the dominant ideology:

Women, Hippies, youth groups, students and school children all question the institutions that have formed them, and try to erect their obverse: a collective commune to replace the bourgeois family; 'free communications' and counter-media; anti-universities – all attack major ideological institutions of society. The assaults are specified, localized and relevant. They bring the contradictions out into the open. [80]

The list could be infinitely expanded. The counter-culture did not arise from the experience of repression, but rather from the 'repressive tolerance' of the liberal-capitalist state. It *redefined* this liberalism, this tolerance, this pluralism, this consensus, *as repressive*. It renamed 'consensus' as 'coercive'; it called 'freedom' 'domination'; it redefined its own relative affluence as a kind of alienated, spiritual poverty. Summoned to the intellectual vocation, students chose to see themselves as 'new kinds of workers'. They renamed the 'institutions of higher learning' – the liberal 'community of scholars' – a bureaucratic technical machine – the 'multi-versity'. They called society's bluff, they broke open its cover-up. One of the unintended consequences was that in challenging the 'institutions for the propagation of consensus' they unleashed its obverse side – 'the powers of coercive state violence that are always there as a background support'. [81] This point of origin *within* the crisis of the dominant culture may help to explain why the 'counter-culture' could not stand on its own as a political formation. Its thrust could be better defined as a 'systematic inversion', a symbolic up-turning, from within, of the whole bourgeois ethic. Some of its sharpest engagements were engendered, not by taking 'another' path, but by pushing the contradictory tendencies from within bourgeois culture to their extremes – by trying to subvert them from the inside, through *a negation*. This may also account for why the 'cultural revolution' oscillated so rapidly between extremes: total 'opposition', and incorporation. The underground always seemed on the verge of being contained or overtaken by its own dialectic. Although it strained after a *total critique* of bourgeois life, it preserved the character of a massive *disaffiliation*. And since it projected its 'alternatives' from some of the most advanced points within that dominant culture, its projections frequently appeared as 'utopias', fragmentary rehearsals for the future.

It was contradictory developments within capitalism itself, then, which provided the material basis for this qualitative 'break' in the culture and mental universe of capital society – a 'break' which expressed itself, partly, as a *caesura* between the old dominant ethic and a new emergent one. Some aspects which the 'old guard' defined as an assault on traditional values were simply signs of a profound adaptation of the dominant culture to the new and contradictory needs of an expanding capital. Marcuse, for example, was certainly correct to define 'permissiveness' as, in origin, nothing but the result of this *necessary modification* of the dominant ideology: a sign of its repressive tolerance, or what he called 'repressive de-sublimation'. [82] Only subsequently did 'permissiveness' provide the platform for a more sustained and subversive critique and practice. This practical critique, in taking seriously what society had only half-intended, broke through some of the categories and upturned them. The positive content of *liberation* crystallised within the negative limits of the permissible, 'liberated', 'do-your-own-thing' philosophy. The artisan capitalism of the alternative society, which sustained its more fashionable manifestations, did the fashion industry some service by bearing the costs of stylistic innovation – working, as it were, both sides of the street. A glance at some of the new magazines which were the product of this era – like *Playboy* or *Playgirl* – will suggest how easily free sex could be harnessed to the services of the *status quo*. There are many indications that capitalism itself *required* some restructuring of the tight bonds of family life – though the backlash in defence of the family, when the Women's Movement pushed their critique to its limits, suggests that, like all the other liberatory trends, this one was also designed to stop short within well-defined limits. Looking back, we can see now that the 'crisis of authority', associated in the early days of affluence with its advanced party 'youth', was the first symptomatic reaction by the old guard of a dominant culture to a rupture in *its own traditional forms*. Those who identified capitalism with its earlier ethic resisted the onset of the new ethic in the name of the defence of traditional wisdoms and ways of life. They were thus obliged to regard the advocates of the 'cultural revolution' as constituting a conspiracy foisted on society from outside (mainly, as usual, from the United States). They could not see that the bonds of a more austere bourgeois moral regime were being partly dissolved *from inside*, as a by-product of capitalism's own contradictory 'maturity'. The counter-culture produced no material political force, though it infiltrated and inflected, permanently, every other radical movement with which it contracted an alliance. But what it *did* produce was a spectre of 'the enemy' in the heads of its opponents. If its early phases scandalised the bourgeois imagination, the second – including its recruitment into the politics of the street – appeared to challenge its ideological unity and hegemony, and was gradually reconstructed into a moral conspiracy against the state: no longer simply getting and spending, clothes and records, fun and games – but drugs, crime, the withdrawal from work, rampant sex, promiscuity, perversion, pornography, anarchy, libertinism and violence. It became a source of moral–political pollution, spreading an infection in its every form: the conspiracy to rebel. In a profound sense, the dominant culture – face to face with this spectacle – felt itself out of control.

The tremors rippling through British society in 1969, which contributed to the construction of an authoritarian backlash, were not all engendered from within the body politic itself. Indeed, the constant attention to international developments suggests that it was the convergence of forces inside and outside society tending to disrupt its equilibrium which hastened on the reaction. The evolution of the Northern Ireland crisis is of critical importance here, though it concerns us primarily in terms of its impact on the 'control culture' at home. The crisis itself was the product of the long and disastrous history of repression which has characterised Britain's historical relations with Ireland for four centuries or more. It stemmed from the complex economic interests which bind sections of the British economy and its governing classes to the backward structures of economic and social life North and South of the border. More immediately, it stemmed from the extremely backward nature of the political ascendancy in Ulster at whose consolidation of power Britain had connived.

This squalid episode in recent Ulster history – its reactionary heroes, its blackmailing threats of U.D.I., etc. – constituted some of twentieth-century Conservatism's 'finest hours'. The issue which set the torch to Ulster was the systematic repression and economic deprivation of the Catholic minority at the hands of the Protestant ascendancy – a symptomatic form, underpinned by nationalism and religion, of the deeper exploitation of the Ulster working class as a whole. Even the Reverend Ian Paisley is said to have acknowledged the basis of Catholic disaffection in his only private conversation with Bernadette Devlin in 1969, though, he added: 'I would rather be British than just.' [83] No wonder Marx had written to Kugelman, exactly a century before, that:

> I have become convinced . . . that it can never do anything decisive here in England until it separates its policy with regard to Ireland in the most definite way from the policy of the ruling classes. . . . And indeed this must be done, not as a matter of sympathy with Ireland, but as a demand, made in the interests of the British proletariat. If not, the English people will remain in the leading-strings of the ruling classes, because it must join with them in a common front against Ireland. [84]

The left's view of the Northern Ireland crisis was that it was simply one more episode in the long history of British fascism in Ireland. The official view of the crisis was that it was simply the creation of the irrational 'gunmen and bombers' of the I.R.A. Both oversimplify. It was the Civil Rights movement which triggered the crisis; and its leading grouping, People's Democracy, had a critique and supported a strategy in Ireland more advanced, and less confined to the logic of the home-made bomb, than anything which has since emerged. The full involvement of the I.R.A. in the North was a slow and awkward affair. Confronted by the Civil Rights challenge, Labour first backed Captain O'Neill and 'moderate reform' – aimed at improving the everyday lot of Catholics while preserving the structure of capitalist interests under the hegemony of Protestant power. It was this contradictory exercise in reformism which came to grief under pressure from Protestant extremism. When the Civil Rights march was ambushed by the men of Derry at Burntollet Bridge, it was the Royal Ulster Constabulary, technically the law-and-order force, which went on the rampage in the Bogside. This became a regular occurrence – supported, politically, by a transfer of Stormont power to the hands of a tougher reformer, Mr Chichester-Clarke. As the provocative ritual Orange marches of the autumn approached, Labour's dilemma fully crystallised. It had determined that reform should come through the 'constitutional instrument'. But Stormont was no ordinary constitutional body – it was a symbol of the nexus of the power of the Orange ascendancy. On the question of whether troops should go in, and who should order them, Labour was in Stormont's hands, and Stormont was committed to the maintenance of minority power by all necessary means. Once again, Protestant provocation cut through these legal convolutions. In the August rioting, the R.U.C., now openly behind the Protestant marchers, invaded the Bogside, using C.S. gas on one occasion for the first time against U.K. citizens, and, in Belfast, firing on Catholic counter-marchers from armoured vehicles. On the other side of the barricades, 'Free Derry' was born, and the Catholic cause fell, once more, into the keeping of those capable of physical defence – the Provos. On 14 August British troops entered Derry. On 15 August they entered Belfast. Their limited objective was stated as 'getting between' the rioting mobs. It was one of Britain's many Irish euphemisms. In fact, Britain had entered her very own backyard 'Vietnam'. One of the principal factors precipitating this had been the contradictory nature and content of social democracy when it leads in a colony from a declining political and economic base, and seeks to serve as a 'responsible government' of the state within the logic of capital. Across the water from Ulster, the British television viewer, hardly recovered from the scenarios of student confrontations, now accustomed himself to the nightly spectacle of 'our boys' face to face with a full-scale domestic urban insurrection. It was a spectacle calculated to harden British hearts.

WORKING-CLASS RESISTANCE: 'WELL GRUBBED, OLD MOLE!'

> In the signs that bewilder the middle class, the aristocracy and the poor prophets of repression, we recognize our brave friend, Robin Goodfellow, the old mole that can work in the earth so fast, that worthy pioneer – the Revolution. (Marx) [85]

Everything 'comes together' in 1970; it is a watershed, a breaking-point. Here all the contradictions begin to intersect. It felt, at the time, as if Britain alone had escaped the cataclysm which shook the other major Western capitalist societies in 1968. But, in its customary diffused, dispersed, piecemeal way, Britain too passed in and through the furnace of a deep crisis. The foundations moved. Then the forces of stability, the restoration, gathered momentum. The target against which it mobilised seemed, at first, principally composed of the student left and the counter-culture. To this, in 1969, was added the degeneration of the Northern Ireland conflict into open urban warfare. These disparate strands then converged, in the collective consciousness, into the shape of Nemesis: a threat to the cohesion, stability, equilibrium of civil society itself. In response, the balance in the control culture began to swing, slowly at first, then sharply, towards a more openly repressive position. Then what had been simmering and festering not far below the surface, erupted into its very centre, and transformed and redefined the whole balance of the relations of force in society. What commands the transition from this tightening of control at the end of the 1960s into the full repressive 'closure' of 1970, presiding over the birth-pangs of a British version of the 'law-and-order' society, and redefining the whole shape of social conflict and civil dissensus in its wake, is the re-entry to the historical stage of the class struggle in a visible, open and escalating form. A society careering off the rails through 'permissiveness', 'participation' and 'protest' into 'the alternative society' and 'anarchy' is one thing. It is quite another moment when the working class once again takes the offensive in a mood of active militancy. To say 'takes the offensive' might suggest that, for a time, it was absent from the relations of force, resistance and consent in the society. Nothing could be further from the truth. But the *form* which the class struggle assumed in the period of Labourism was different from the form it begins to assume – to assume again – as we enter the 1970s. As the attempt by a social-democratic government to manage the state through an organised version of consensus is finally exhausted and bankrupted between 1964 and 1970, so, gradually, the class struggle comes more and more into the open, assumes a more manifest presence. This development is electrifying. One of its consequences is to translate a struggle which is emerging at the level of civil society and its superstructural institutions (principally the form of the crisis during the period up to and immediately after our '1968') directly on to the terrain of capital and labour, and thus – in the era of organised late capitalism – on to the terrain of the state. Like hanging, such a moment wonderfully concentrates the mind of the ruling class and its parties, whether of the right or the left. In fact, its impact on these two wings is diametrically opposite. The emergence of an open class struggle, in a state temporarily under the command of a government of social-democratic character, undermines and destroys such a government's *raison d'être*. The only rationale for entrusting the management of the corporate capitalist state to social democracy is either (i) that in a tight squeeze it can better win the collaboration of working-class organisations to the state, if necessary, at the expense of their own class; or (ii) that if there is going to be an economic crisis, it is better that such a crisis should be indelibly identified with yet another historic failure of Labourism. When such a government manifestly *fails* to win this class collaboration – as the Wilson government of 1966–70 failed, or when it fails to stem the tide of economic crisis, its days are numbered. The impact of an escalating class struggle on the other side – the real executors of the capitalist class in power – is quite different. In a period of political crisis, this wing can be strong, resisting in depth, recruiting the populace to its side in the active defence of stability and order. In economic crisis, it can be decisive, even brutal in its measures, rallying 'the nation' in a last-ditch effort to 'save the sinking ship'. Either way its hand is immeasurably strengthened, its will hardened – as social democracy's hand and nerve is weakened and destroyed – by the prospect of a coming class struggle. The re-emergence of working-class militancy, combined with what the right regards as a slow erosion of civil society itself, and (in the case of Northern Ireland) the prospect of armed insurrection in nearby provinces, tended to drive the ruling 'bloc' into a much harder, more coercive stance. The return of the Heath government to power, coupled with the resolution which it appeared to offer to nameless fears, threats and anxieties rippling through civil society itself, produced a sort of climax – an ejaculation of control. In such a moment, in and around 1970, with the Heath government mandated to take on and strangle in its bed the resurgence of organised working-class militancy, the long 'crisis of authority' which marks the 1960s finally became absorbed into the 'crisis of the state' itself. Here, the last vestige of a hegemony of consent ends. The appeals to 'the nation', to 'the British people', to 'the national interest', do not of course end. Indeed, they multiply. But the more they are affirmed, the less they refer to anything like an existing consensus of views which holds all ends of the society together under one, dominant, ruling set of purposes, the more they appear as ritual gestures, invocations, whose meaning and purpose is not to refer, but to invoke, create and bring into being a consensus which has almost in fact entirely evaporated. The birth of Mr Heath's government in the disguise of 'the trade union of the nation' is a moment of profound crisis in the exercise of hegemony. The dominant group has nearly exhausted its function to unite and reconcile conflicting interests within the framework of its ideological canopy; its *repertoire* of responses are close to exhaustion; the mechanisms of consent have been decisively undermined. There is precious little left except a vigorous imposition of class interests, a struggle to the death, the turn to repression and control. It is what Gramsci calls the moment of constraint: of police measures, of popular reaction and recourse to the law, of rumours of conspiracies against the state, of panic, of *coups d'état*, of Caesarism from on high. 1970 is such a moment. The state, which ceases to hold together by spontaneous or (as under Mr Wilson) by sponsored consent, must be consolidated by the exercise of a certain kind of force – Mr Heath as 'Bonaparte'.

In 1970 we can pinpoint this 'drift' of the crisis of hegemony up to the level of the state itself. But it is crucial to note the whole trajectory, the whole arc of the movement. Organised capitalism in its 'late' corporate form requires a recomposition of the whole state apparatus and of relations between the different branches of the state, and between the state itself and civil society. This is the beginnings of the state which 'enmeshes, controls, regulates, superintends and tutors civil society from its most comprehensive manifestations of life down to its most insignificant stirrings, from its most general modes of being down to the private existence of individuals'. [86] But since this augmented state is not only itself becoming directly a part of the productive system, but the principal means by which one ruling-class alliance or another can intervene from above in the class struggle, the recomposition of the capitalist state is also, and inevitably, the recomposition 'from above' of the working class. The fact, however, that the ruling 'bloc' intervenes in the class struggle via the intermediation of the state means that the state 'veils the class struggle'. This whole process is not to be equated with the shifting political fortunes of particular parties or their rotation in parliamentary power. We must look behind or through this oscillation on the terrain of parliamentary politics to discern what Marx called 'the peculiar physiognomy of the period'. The recomposition of the capitalist state and of the class struggle in this period is played now through Labourism, now through Conservatism. This is not to make a simple equation between these two 'parties' of capital, any more than Marx simply equated Orleanists with Legitimists or with social democrats. But, in his remarkable *Eighteenth Brumaire* essay, he shows how, through the succession of parties, a particular form of state power is methodically perfected. In their different ways in this period both the major parliamentary parties contribute, at different points, to the reconstruction of the 'late' capitalist state. This development is certainly neither smooth nor without contradiction. This is especially so for the party of social democracy, which cannot become one of the chief architects of the state of capital without generating profound antagonisms. In fact, in the British case the adaptation of Conservatism to this task was almost, if not equally, as traumatic.

Paradoxically, then, both governments preside over the birth of certain key strategies of corporate management. One key strategy is the containment of wages and, occasionally, of prices within the limits of productivity – the 'incomes-policy' strategy, which in its many variants absorbed so much of the parliamentary energies of both sides, and helped to exhaust their *repertoires* of control. When, at the end of the decade, this exercise in guided consent comes to grief, it is, first, a Labour administration, then a Conservative one, which introduces the instrument of legal regulation, and 'perfects it': Mr Wilson fitfully, withdrawing at the eleventh hour; Mr Heath, glorying and revelling in the final showdown. This process is going on behind the back of the 'theatrical show' of parliamentary politics – and, indeed, as Marx also argued, at its expense. Such a far-reaching reconstruction of state power and its exercise has deep complementary movements in civil society as well (we have already noted some) and in the juridical apparatus. The qualitative shift in the mode of operation of the state – from consent to coercion – which is the main sector of the arc which concerns us here, is thus a complex outcome, not simply of developments in the state but in the whole character of the exercise of hegemonic domination.

What forms the *base* of this arc, however, is the persistent and growing weakness of the economic structure of British capitalism. Despite the post-war revival of world trade, Britain's share in the world exports of manufactured goods is halved, between 1954 and 1970. Her level of investment and her rate of economic growth are persistently low. The stable giants like the United States and France, the new competitors – West Germany, Japan and Italy – outdistance British performance on every level. Between 1960 and 1972, investment as a percentage of gross national product is moving, on average, for Japan between 30–35 per cent, for Britain between 16–18 per cent. Between 1955 and 1968, Japan has an annual percentage growth rate of 9.7, West Germany of 5.0, Britain of 2.8. In the 1960s, there is a major influx of foreign investment, which supports the conversion of some sectors of capital into a more 'multinational' form, but it does not match the outflow of direct and indirect investment abroad. The historical structural decline of British capitalism is unquestionable. Everything else that happens in these years must be judged against this backdrop.[87]

In this period the Western capitalist system as a whole suffers a severe crisis in 'profitability', coupled with growing inflation. Increased capitalist competition, the various mechanisms of rescue devised by the I.M.F. and other international financial agencies, the spread of the multinationals, the formation of the E.E.C., all stem in part from this world-wide search for greater shares in the world market to offset the tapering off of the post-war boom and the classic incipient tendency of the rate of profit to fall. Britain is also late or behind in each of these countervailing measures. She is therefore, in consequence, 'at the forefront of the crisis of profitability'.[88] We cannot enter here into the important argument as to the deeper structural roots of the crisis. Certainly, 'wage militancy' is sustained, and relatively successful for a time, though in real terms it is progressively eroded by inflation. This leads directly to the 'political solutions' we examine below. The rate of profit is, of course, different, in a classical sense, from the mass of profits (the latter may be rising even if the former is falling). It is related, not to 'profitability', but to the changing composition of capital itself,[89] and to the increased economic role of the state sector.[90] But ris-

ing wage militancy may affect the share out of profits, limiting how much industry feels able to put into investment, and hence the capacity of capital to
offset a long-term decline.

Whatever its deeper causes and consequences, there can be no doubt that
the growth of wages in the 1950s and 1960s is seen by capital as weakening the
already vulnerable competitive base of the economy.[91] This becomes the most
visible ideological symbol of Britain as a 'stagnant society': the first manifestation of 'crisis'. It is around this pole that the disciplining of the working class is
organised: first, by 'capitalist planning'; then by 'incomes policy'; finally by
statutory and legal control. It is against this pivot that the whole offensive
against the organised working class is mounted. It is through this 'operator'
that the working class is progressively called upon to bear the costs of the
crisis. This is the fulcrum around which the politics of the period turns.

First, we must sketch the outlines of this offensive, and the stages through
which the *repertoire* of voluntary constraints is gradually exhausted. Professor
Beer has argued that the corporate management of the modern capitalist
economy 'depends on governments and producer groups being able to reach
agreements and then on each group being able and willing to implement its part
of the bargain'.[92] The bargain between capital, labour and the state must be
such as to safeguard the long-term survival and profitability of capital, while
generating such growth as will enable each element to rake off something for its
constituency. But fundamentally, labour's share must fall in line behind and be
disciplined by the overall 'productivity' of capital.[93] The British state was
finally converted to this strategy in the period of severe deflation of 1956–7,
one of the most formidable periods of 'stop' the economy has experienced. The
hurried reflation lasted just long enough to secure the 1959 election for the
Tories. Then the balance-of-payments deficit loomed again, prices and wages
began again their upward climb, and 'stop-go' was reintroduced. Selwyn
Lloyd's conversion to 'indicative capitalist planning' dates from this period. He
subsequently confessed to Professor Dorfman (in an interview in 1969) that, as
well as developing 'TUC support for a permanent incomes policy in the planning council', there was an ' "educational" value for the TUC in being constantly exposed to the "broader implications" of government's actions'. Most importantly, he believed the T.U.C. would find it more difficult to play a constantly intransigent role while participating in council decision-making. The great
'educative' offensive to incorporate the working class via its most corporate
representative institution – the T.U.C. – had opened.[94]

The 'conversion to planning' did not begin auspiciously. It began, instead,
with the crisis and recession of 1961. The pay pause was breached before it
was ended formally (most notably by the Electricity Council award), but when
its finale was announced, the National Economic Development Council
(NEDDY) had emerged, and the T.U.C. had agreed to join it. NEDDY was no
raging success. It became – it has been suggested – not the solution to, but the
victim and symptom of 'pluralistic stagnation'. The second phase – under
Harold Wilson – was more decisively interventionist. It was also, characteristically, two-faced. The Labour government discovered a balance-of-
payments deficit of £800 million, and took the pivotal decision to defend sterl-

ing without devaluation, at all costs. This made the matter of bargains with the unions at once more compelling and more difficult: more stick (i.e. recession), less carrot ('growth'). Labour, however, had one major reserve strength – the factor which has made social democracy the 'natural' party of capital through much of the post-war period. This strength was its long-standing alliance with the unions. 'Planning' was retained as an administrative front (indeed, the first and last five-year-plan was published in this phase, though few could now recall its compelling targets). But more central was the *political* construction of a 'long-term voluntary incomes policy' to which the unions would be a party.

The 'long-term voluntary incomes policy' was the last comprehensive attempt, until the Social Contract of 1974, to exercise and enforce restraint over wages and the working class *by consent*. Everything, in this phase, is harnessed to winning the unions to full collaboration with the state in disciplining the working class. It was a failure. It was a strategy beset from the beginning by contradictions. Labour was fully enmeshed in the theology of parliamentarianism. In identifying the defence of sterling with the defence of the nation, it assimilated itself to the goal of the most retrograde, but most powerful, wing of capital. This meant giving in to the severe terms imposed by international creditors. Incomes policy was thus, for the government, a 'long stop' to enable the country to emerge from the crisis with production ahead of wages, and a permanent social contract with labour in its pocket, thereby solving the crisis and securing its political base in one long sweep. The unions, though politically closely aligned with this perspective, occupy a structurally different position: a more 'corporate' one, in Gramsci's sense. No matter how close they are enmeshed in the toils of the state, unless they can be seen to be, in some degree, defending the corporate economic interests of their members, they have no *raison d'être*. The T.U.C., then, had the immediate resumption of growth (and thus of jobs and wages) at the top of their list; that meant getting investment going back again at once. Temporarily, the two contradictory perspectives appeared to be yoked to the same objective – a vista of permanent expansion built on the back of the Labour-labour alliance. Such a deal was, indeed, formally signed and delivered – the *Joint Statement on Productivity, Prices and Incomes* [95] This, too, was not to be. The sterling crisis loomed again in June 1965. Over the heads of the T.U.C., the government introduced a compulsory early-warning system on wages. In response, a disgruntled George Woodcock offered that the T.U.C. should itself once again attempt 'voluntarily' to 'vet' wages: 'the last chance', he said, to show that the unions could manage themselves, were master in their own house, and thus 'offset the legislation which otherwise threatened'. [96] 'Vetting', however, was in practice an empty exercise. The T.U.C. simply had no power – for reasons we examine below – to deliver it. Wage inflation led instead directly to the gigantic balance-of-payments crisis of 1966, the seamen's strike, and a deflationary package of immense severity. The T.U.C. now stood looking directly into the chasm. It was squeezed on all sides like a lemon. With intensely bad grace, covered by the most obsequious collapse before the altar of 'the national interest', the T.U.C. acknowledged that 'the interests of both trade unionism and of the nation as a whole ... compelled them to acquiesce in the Government's proposal'.[97] They accepted the standstill 'with distaste ... in the belief that at this time the need of the nation must necessarily override sectional demands'.[98]

There was worse in store: a standstill on wages; then – the difference escaped most wage-earners – 'severe restraint'; a second crisis, coupled with devaluation; further deflation and a 'nil norm' on wages. The statutory freeze brought wages to a halt; unemployment grew. The zero norm lasted until 1968. When the freeze was officially lifted, it was to a $3\frac{1}{2}$ per cent norm only, breakable by leave of only a few exceptions (of which low pay and productivity deals were, significantly, the main classes). Throughout this period, the Prime Minister noted that 'our own people ... demonstrated great loyalty'.[99] However, in the arctic economic climate, voluntaryism as a corporate strategy withered on the branch. First, it was undermined by the economic crisis itself. Second, voluntaryism had a price, and the state found itself unable to pay up. Under Woodcock's leadership, the T.U.C. expressed no principled opposition to voluntary absorption into the state. But, it required a corporate return for collaboration. As Hugh Clegg put it: 'the unions could only give the government the industrial peace and economic cooperation it required on condition that the government allowed the unions sufficient economic concessions to keep their members from growing too restive'.[100] The government was in no position to do so. But, third, there is some doubt whether, even had the state been able to afford its 'price', the deal would have come off. For the fact is that, throughout this period, the discipline over the working class which the government required was not in the keeping of the T.U.C. It was not the T.U.C. nor the great union leaderships which defended and advanced working-class interests in this period. The real dynamic had passed to another level – one over which the unions and the T.U.C. exerted relatively little power or influence. What sustained 'wage militancy' was not 'the unions' but the infernal coalition between sheer rank-and-file bloody-mindedness and shop-steward 'irresponsibility'. It was this dialectic – this hidden materialism – which undermined 'voluntaryism'. When the state failed to win over the T.U.C. to its offensive, it adopted a more surgical probe for the cancerous source itself. From the mid-1950s to the end of the 1960s the Department of Employment calculated that 95 per cent of all recorded strikes were 'unofficial'. The 'unofficial strike', as Lane and Roberts observe, was raised during Labour's period of office to the status of a crisis issue, closely linked with 'the view that British industry was especially prone' to problems of labour indiscipline – the 'British disease'. This interpretation 'became firmly embedded in popular consciousness'.[101] The fact of utmost significance in the period was the massive shift of the locus of class conflict in industry from management/union disputes to management/shop-floor disputes, and the tilt of the balance from the union-management negotiating table to rank-and-file militancy, spearheaded by shopfloor organisation, the growth of a 'factory consciousness' and the shop stewards.

The immediate cause of this shift in the social organisation of working-class militancy is not hard to find:

> With the revival of national and international trade after 1945 and the readiness of the State to regulate the economy, the trade unions became split

into virtually two parts. At the national level trade union leaders became an established part of the political process: government economic strategies required the cooperation of the trade unions. Union leaders were therefore coopted individually as 'consultants' and collectively as participants in the auxiliary machinery of government. At the local level workers were finding that their strength lay on the shop floor. Union branches, district and shop stewards committees were playing the market with all the vigour of nineteenth-century businessmen. Thus, where the leaders were trying to help governments introduce an ordered capitalism, the rank and file were following traditional laissez-faire policies of taking the market for all it was worth.[102]

The policy of 'co-option', pursued with such vigour and consistency under Labour thus had profound if unintended consequences. Far from following their leaders into the arms of the state, or – as some variants of the 'affluent-worker thesis' predicted – simply disappearing off the face of the earth into the middle classes, the rank-and-file workers in industry found another point of antagonism with the structure of capitalist management and threw up around it a formidable, flexible and militant defensive organisation. Local conditions could be exploited and local advantages taken best in large-scale factory work, especially in engineering, where, as a result of the complex divisions of labour, a stoppage of ten men in one section could bring the whole assembly line to a grinding halt. This vulnerability of large-scale industry was increased under conditions of full or near-full employment with a shortage of skilled labour. It no doubt also owed something – again unintended – to the very ideology of 'affluence' so persistently and effectively propagated by the media and the political parties.

The official structure of collective bargaining involved regular, institutionalised negotiations at national level between 'the union or unions concerned and the relevant federation or association of employers. The resulting national agreements specify rates of pay, hours of work and other conditions of employment for the industry. In theory, this process of national negotiation determines all important aspects of the employment relationship'. In reality, however, 'it is the national agreements which are of minor significance, setting a bare minimum standard for wages and conditions; the worker relies primarily on shop floor organization to win acceptable terms'.[103] Central to this process of negotiating and *implementing* the actual day-to-day details of national agreements were the shop stewards and shop-floor organisation. The power of this level of organisation depended directly on the willingness of the rank-and-file worker to back the stewards by the sudden and unannounced stoppage – the faster, the less expected, the better. Thus the legitimacy of the stewards derived, not from the union structure, of which in the early stages they were at best a residual and marginal part, in the formal sense, but from the immediacy, the closeness, of the steward to 'experiences and grievances at the point of production'.

As the 'unofficial' wildcat strike came to predominate over the official structure of union–management negotiations as the paradigm form of industrial class conflict, the pattern of class conflict in certain key industrial sectors came to pivot around two broad questions, both of them arising, so to speak, in the gap between the 'formal' and 'informal' systems of control. The first was staked out along the line of 'implementation and conditions' – how, and under what precise conditions were national agreements to be made operational in one or another part of the factory at a specific moment? Behind this 'local negotiating frontier' lay a larger question which the whole shift to shop-floor power brought centrally into play within the framework of the class struggle: the issue of the power of the workers directly to define, hold at bay and if possible disrupt or throw back the exercise of 'managerial power and prerogative' over the labour process itself. In its most dynamic, but immediate and localised form, this was no more nor less than the critical issue of *control over production and the rate of exploitation of labour.*[104] National wage agreements established minimal criteria and levels. They overarched the actual division of labour, in an attempt to orchestrate it. In reality, each job or part of a job, divided as it was, differently in each factory, between sections and component plants and ancilliary shops, had a wage rate negotiable from shop to shop, piece-work to piece-work; and the rate depended, not on what had been written and signed at a national level, but on the 'power to intervene', which could be organised on the floor. Of course certain sectors of industry were more vulnerable to the exploitation of this 'formal/informal' gap than others. White-collar workers in public service industries and manual workers in public utilities, for example, could not develop so strong a 'frontier of control', and hence their wages lagged behind the leading sectors in manufacturing and the engineering industry. The point at which the relative success of the shop-floor strategy was demonstrated – and the fact which came most to symbolise both the erosion of trade-union discipline over its workers, and the drain on capital and profits – was the phenomenon of 'wage drift'.

'Wage drift' is the difference between earnings (excluding overtime) in any particular plant or shop and the wage rates arrived at through official wage negotiations and collective agreements. It represents, therefore, the degree to which localised working-class power and organisation has successfully eroded the institutional bargains over wages and conditions struck at national level. The 'graph' of wage drift in this period is telling. After about 1958, real average weekly earnings are not only consistently higher, for manual workers, than the officially agreed rates, but the gap between the two significantly widens, in the workers' favour, right up to the imposition of the freeze. This figure alone demonstrates, not only the failure of the whole incomes policy strategy, but its principal cause and source: 'The more insistently the Labour government focused on incomes policy as an immediate remedial measure, the more that incomes policy worked against the T.U.C.'s ability to deliver an effective incomes policy in any context.' [105]

Thus, little by little – bemused, at first, by its own myths of embourgeoisement and apathy, then victim of its own illusions of 'one nation' and the unremitting ideology of 'moderation' – step by step, did the ruling-class fractions come face to face with the stubborn bloody-mindedness, the 'hidden materialism', of the British working class. Here there was certainly no over-all strategy, no counter-hegemonic trajectory, little strategic leadership, no philosophy for founding a 'new order' or for exercising proletarian power. Shorn, rather, of leadership, denuded of strategy and long-term political perspective, with no organs of influence to wield in the market-places of opinion, few organic intellectual alliances to shape its material practice theoretically, this class disposed of no weapons except the traditional ones of resistance with which to combat the restructuring of capitalism: its leaderships trundling in and out of smoke-filled conferences with the employers at Number 10; the 'party of labour' itself almost sunk without trace beneath the weight of self-righteous platitudinising and Wilsonian double-talk; Marxism as yet a distant toy of the new radical intelligentsia – a class, in short, thrown back on those subterranean anarcho-syndicalist reserve impulses which, in low times, seem to serve the British working class as its last backstop against those forces that are ready to grind it out of existence. This is the working class which, burrowing away through the 1960s, comes to the surface for air, in 1970, catches a glimpse of Mr Heath and his band of hope, the far-off look of 'prosperity' in their eyes, armed with the full majesty of the law, and resolved, if necessary, to take him on.

It was the rise and fall in the tides of voluntaryism – the fever chart, so to speak, of the 'British disease' – which occupied the front pages of public attention in the 1960s. But, as the supports of a voluntary incomes truce were, one after another, knocked sideways, alternative, more subtle strategies of class discipline came to provide the essence of the social-democratic response to the crisis. We may divide them, roughly, into two kinds. First, there were the strategies of containment in the labour process itself: productivity deals, measured-day work systems, tight controls over rates and wage deals, coupled with a tactical assault, in certain key sectors (the motor industry, for example) on the front-line political troops – the stewards. Second, there were strategies of rationalisation and control at the macroeconomic level: the promotion of mergers, takeovers and 'planned' bankruptcies; the redeployment and retraining of labour; the open invitation to foreign capital – especially American – to come in and install a tougher managerial and financing regime than most British managers yet had the stomach for; the scuttle for foreign investment and markets.

The key productivity deal – the Esso Fawley agreement – was signed in 1960; but the years between 1967 and 1970 witnessed what has been described as a 'productivity deals landslide' – rising, in mid-1968, to as many as 200 per month. The aim of the productivity deal, in the context of Britain's declining productive and trade position, was, fundamentally, to reduce unit costs, either by making labour more intensive (i.e. intensifying the rate of exploitation) or by co-opting labour, via the unions, to collude with the peaceful replacement of men by machines (the decomposition of labour). This was the principal instrument in the recomposition of the working class and of the labour process from above. But productivity deals were also directed at the 'drift' of real-wage levels above the negotiated national norms. Here the productivity deal was intended to bind wages firmly behind, and in a fixed relation to, productivity: no increase in output, no wage rise. This was the political cutting-edge of the strategy. One of the key forms through which this disciplining was exerted was the attempt to replace piece-work by fixed rates and wages (thus cutting down the room for plant-by-plant bargaining and cutting into wage drift) – a move which in turn entailed the widespread use of measured-day work procedures. These involved tight job evaluation, grading, rating, timing – and then the imposition of a strict 'production standard' for each part of the productive process. It was a further development of those techniques of 'scientific management' which had spearheaded the restructuring of capital and the labour process in the early years of the transition to monopoly capital. [106] Its *political* content, however, was certainly not missed at the time. That doyen of industrial relations, and arch Fabian militant, Alan Flanders, put it plainly: 'The distinguishing, common feature of all the major productivity agreements is that they are attempts to strengthen managerial controls over pay and work through joint regulation.'[107]

At the other end of the scale, decisive moves were undertaken to reconstruct the shape of British industry into a more rational and corporatist mould. Apostles of statist solutions, and technocratic whiz-kids, like Mr Wedgwood Benn (no other) at the Ministry of Technology, and Charles Villiers at the Industrial Reorganisation Corporation, presided over a really massive wave of induced mergers, takeovers and fade-outs, designed – in the steely philosophy of the I.R.C. – to 'create industrial giants'. This strategy of state-supported monopolisation involved pushing or inveigling competitive capitalist firms into a major concentration of assets, promoting a rationalisation and slimming-down of the major productive units in each sector into their fully oligopolistic form. The purpose of this was to lower production costs, to effect a shake-out and rationalisation in the deployment of labour, to protect profit rates, and to stiffen and shape up the confidence of the industrial elite for the fierce competitive climate of international competition in the era of the multinationals and 'Europe'. Its consequence was the deskilling of significant sectors of the working class and its partial recomposition. In the first half of 1968 the takeover and merger boom was higher (£1,750 million) than the total of all bids and mergers effected in 1967 – the year of the great merger take-off.

It was not enough. Nothing was enough. The nettle of class demand, after all, simply had to be grasped directly. 'The price of securing an incomes policy in Britain', that most persuasive organ of modern enterprise *The Economist* clearly foretold, as early as June 1963, 'will be the willingness to stand up to strikes.'[108] 'Paradoxically,' that foremost economic commentator, Sam Brittan, optimistically predicted in the same year, 'one of the strongest arguments for a Labour Government is that, beneath layers of velvet, it might be more prepared to face a showdown in dealing with the unions.' This weapon of enforced restraint – the last in the Labourist *repertoire* – was infinitely delayed; and one of the principal delaying mechanisms was the appointment of the Royal Commission on Trade Unions and Employers' Associations – the Donovan Commission. Donovan took three long years to report; but finally, in 1968, the Report came out. It clearly and unequivocally labelled the unofficial strike and the shop stewards as the twin demons of the British crisis. Yet, Donovan stayed his hand. Order, regulation, discipline were his watchwords: the integration of what he called the 'inflated power of work-groups and shop stewards' into what Cliff rightly described as a 'plant consensus'. [109] He proposed to build the shop stewards' role *into* the formal management structure and thus weld shop floor and line power into a single structure. It was a strategy of intensified incorporation. The unofficial strike was excluded from the protection of the law and exposed to the whims of employers in the courts; but, at the eleventh hour, no legal sanctions as such against unofficial 'temporary combinations' of workers were proposed. The final epitaph on Donovan was uttered by that stalwart Labour Minister for Employment and rare coiner of biblical mottoes, Mr Ray Gunter: 'Too little,' he said, 'too voluntary, too late.'

Within seven months of Donovan, the Conservatives had published their manifesto on the reform of industrial relations, *Fair Deal At Work*, and the government had replied with its ill-fated package, the Wilson–Castle fiasco, *In Place of Strife*. With this latter document social democracy, its rhetoric of restraint, productive effort and moral fibre exhausted, hesitantly reached for the 'final deterrent' of compulsion. *In Place of Strife* was a woolly and confusing document with a small but extremely dangerous and damaging concept at its core. Unfortunately for its promoters and defenders, management recognised this implicit core at once, and jumped the gun in an effort to push the Cabinet over the line into an explicitly anti-union disciplinary stance. This exposed the document's inner logic and shattered its social-democratic husk. The Wilson–Castle package was abandoned in favour of a paper voluntaryism in which neither the government, the T.U.C. nor the electorate placed much faith. Although the electoral denouement was postponed for almost another year, the 1964 inter-regnum was really at an end, and with it – temporarily – the Labourist version of a managed consensus.

The confrontration which in fact marked its demise was classic. It involved the aggressive, American style, Ford management, which pioneered the managerial crusade against shop-floor power through the decade, and the most disciplined and militant of front-line troops in this period – the Dagenham and Halewood shop stewards. Briefly, the Ford management proposed, with the support of the Joint Negotiating Committee of Ford unions, a package deal modelled around Barbara Castle's White Paper combining long-term wage increases and a scheme to offset loss of earnings through lay-offs, plus enlarged holiday benefits – provided there was no 'unconstitutional action'. The Halewood plant came out on strike. Although the Joint Committee reaffirmed their stand, the big unions – the A.E.F. and the T.G.W. – declared the strike official. With the unions backing the stewards against the package, and the production line at a halt, all seemed set for victory. Then, true to its *In Place of Strife* inspiration, the Ford management took out an injunction against the unions. When the writs finally came to the High Court, Mr Justice Lane was heard to remark that 'I sigh and I sigh only because the whole matter is not a simple matter of law. It is complicated by what people will inevitably do regardless of what the law says is threat. . . . The thing is coloured by a relationship of management and labour.' [110] *The Times*, however, which had urged matters on to a bloody resolution from the beginning, advised the government that 'This is the crunch. . . . If Government needed to be impressed about the

urgency of making unions honour agreements and keeping their members under control, then the time is now.' [111] But neither the government nor the courts
crunched it. By 20 March a face-saving compromise had been struck, and the
men returned to work.

The Ford strike, however, revealed the stark choices: the state had either,
clearly and unambiguously, to intervene, if necessary with the support and majesty of some part of the legal apparatus specifically redesigned for the purpose,
to enforce the 'national will' against sectional class consciousness and militant
materialism, or the defensive power of the shop floor, especially when supported by an official leadership, was unstoppable. The Ford strike formed a bridge
between the 'unofficial' strikes characteristic of the 1960s, and the new wave of
'official' strikes, which were to become a feature of the post-1970 Heath era.
Above all, it foreshadowed the attempt by the state to recruit the law directly in
the service of the management of class struggle − a strategy which precipitated
one of the most bitter periods of class confrontation in recent memory. It
marked 'the watershed between the 1960's and the 1970's'. [112]

Mr Heath, however, not Mr Wilson was destined to preside over the transition. In the summer following the Ford settlement, the Prime Minister initiated
his 'long retreat'. In June, the extraordinary T.U.C. Congress at Croydon supported the T.U.C.'s *Programme for Action* against the government's *In Place
of Strife*. Mr Wilson reported 'positive progress' in his talks with the T.U.C.,
with only one problem remaining: 'the unconstitutional strike where perhaps a
handful of wreckers can wreck a vital sector of our export trade'. Then, at five
minutes to midnight, a 'solemn and binding' agreement replaced the threat of
compulsion. The ditching of this final attempt at a showdown with industrial
militancy was followed by a flood of wage demands, especially in public-sector
industries which had not so far been in the forefront of the wage struggle, flowing through the breach the more militant sectors had opened up: the
phenomenon which became known as 'the revolt of the lower paid' (teachers,
civil servants, dustmen, hospital ancillary workers) − a response to rapid price
inflation, rising unemployment and a period of zero growth, a rehearsal for the
'strike explosion' to follow in 1970. The sight hardened the heart of Mr Heath,
preparing himself in the wilderness, with his colleagues, for a period of open
confrontation with the working class. His epitaph on *In Place of Strife* carried
in it all the promise of this sterner, tougher struggle to come: 'The power,' he
observed, 'resides elsewhere.'

9

The Law-and-Order Society:
Towards
the 'Exceptional State'

1970: SELSDON MAN – BIRTH OF THE 'LAW-AND-ORDER' SOCIETY

> As soon as the dominant social group has exhausted its function, the
> ideological bloc tends to crumble away; then 'spontaneity' may be replaced
> by 'constraint' in even less disguised and indirect forms, culminating in out-
> right police measures and *coups d'état*. (Gramsci) [1]

> The crisis is permanent. The Government is provisional. (Marx) [2]

On the 4 January 1970, the *Sunday Times* noted: 'Among the incipient ghettos
in Britain today, Handsworth, Birmingham displays the classic symptoms:
poor housing, a strained education system, households struggling to make ends
meet, and few social amenities. It also has the usual hustlers, prostitutes and
ponces. Second generation blacks are beginning to show a resistance to all
authority.' This prophetic sketch was based on Gus John's report to the Runnymede Trust, subsequently to form the basis of his book, *Because They're
Black*, written with Derek Humphry.[3] The article was headed – making the by-
now required link – 'Must Harlem Come to Birmingham?' Within a fortnight,
Mr Powell had taken it upon himself to reply, as it were, to the question. In a
challenge to the Tory Party leadership to bring the race question out 'into the
open ... without prevarication or excuse', Mr Powell warned that 'through its
own past sins of omission', Britain was 'menaced by a problem which at the
present rate will by the end of the century be similar in magnitude to that of the
United States'. Except as part of a vigorous repatriation campaign, Mr Powell
added, measures of special aid to high immigrant areas were 'positively
harmful in their net effect'. He referred to his prophecy, twenty months earlier,
of racial bloodshed to come. He made no new predictions. Instead, he quoted a
Leeds solicitor, an Under-Secretary at the Home Office and the Newsletter of
the Manchester Community Relations Council to show that other responsible
spokesmen shared his view that 'racial violence could flare up anywhere in
Britain'.[4] A week or so earlier the Spring offensive against the South African
Springboks tour opened. The Liberal M.P., David Steel, who had helped to
organise a peaceful demonstration, was suddenly confronted by 'a small,
chanting, banner-waving band of about 40 souls', who 'took up positions op-

posite the turnstiles . . . and proceeded to hurl abuse of a fairly virulent kind at both intending spectators and the four-deep line of stationary policemen'. When he asked one of the group who was in charge, he received the reply, 'Nobody in charge of us'. 'Irrational processes,' Mr Steel observed, 'will produce irrational reactions.' [5]

In this sharpening climate, the Tory Shadow Cabinet met in secret conclave at Selsdon Park. There was no mistaking the mood and spirit in which this preparation for power took place, nor the vigorous, pre-election crusading themes which emerged from their deliberations. The *Sunday Times* correspondent, Ronald Butt, entitled the emerging platform, 'A Soft Sell on Law and Order'.[6] Here, the American comparisons — this time with the Nixon–Agnew campaign — were no longer indirect and implicit. The law-and-order theme 'enables the Party to reassure the silent majority of the public that it shares their concern'. The keynote was widely deployed. It referred to 'interference with the liberty of people going about their ordinary business by demonstrating minorities'. Threatening noises — soon to become a scandalous and widespread real practice — were made about the use of the conspiracy charge, a toughening of the law of trespass and the power of the magistracy. The demonstration theme was connected directly, by Butt, with 'vandalism and the rise of organized crime'. Selsdon Man, however, had another, equally important face. This was the side turned in the direction of industrial and economic policy, where abrasive measures, tied to the strict discipline of the market mechanism, were proposed for the shake-up and shake-out of British industry — coupled, of course, with a promise of tough action to curb the power of the unions and to bring the unofficial strike to a dead halt. Buoyed up on a wave of popular and populist enthusiasms, the Shadow Cabinet turned to the electorate, and took to the towns and cities of Britain in its pre-election barnstorm.

The impact of the law-and-order theme was immediate. True, as the *Guardian* remarked, Mr Heath's 'law and order' was not quite President Nixon's — 'the right of the citizens to walk their own streets, free of the fear of mugging, robbery or rape'. True, the Selsdon version was pointed at a nebulous package of popular fears and stereotypes — what the *Guardian* called 'a gallimaufry of subjects — student unrest, political demonstrations, the Permissive Society, long hair, short hair and perhaps in time medium-length hair as well'.[7] True, 'to introduce conspiracy charges for demonstrators, as some have suggested, would be a shameful abuse of the law. . . . Tolerance is a two-way traffic.' But the law-and-order themes orchestrated together in the dim, moral twilight of Selsdon Park, were not intended for the comfort of the *Guardian*'s undoubtedly liberal, undoubtedly minority, readers. There was no silent majority to be won there. The *Sunday Express*, on the other hand, thought the theme powerful enough to give it the front-page headline on the Sunday following the Selsdon Park conclave: 'DEMO CLAMP-DOWN IF TORIES GET BACK.' [8] The crusade in the country was gaining momentum. Lord Hailsham, whom Selsdon Park had released into a renewed burst of moral energy, linked the interruption of high Court proceedings by 'a group of young hooligans', the beating to death of Michael de Gruchy by 'a group of youths', the rise in the proportion of offences in which firearms were used, and the fact that 'an increasing part of the life of every policeman consists of incidents of abuse, insults and provocation nightly hurled ... by street-corner hooligans' with the law-and-order theme. This colourful scenario was entitled 'The Menace Of The Wild Ones'. These fears, he reassured his audience, were not limited to 'imaginary women in flowered hats and prominent teeth'. Organised crime and violence, he suggested, 'cannot be separated from private dishonesty or public demonstration in defiance of law'. Geoff Hammond, sentenced to life for 'queer-bashing', Peter Hain, who endorsed the digging up of cricket pitches, 'the Welsh Language Society and all those who are willing to put their own opinions ... above the law ... undermine the whole fabric of society by challenging the system of law itself on which all of us in the end depend.'[9] The construction of nightmares had commenced in earnest. Within a week, the future Lord Chancellor made a savage attack on Labour for 'presiding complacently' over the biggest crime wave of the century. He invited the Home Secretary to declare that 'he would not parole deliberate killers or assailants of police, warders, innocent witnesses and bystanders'. 'The permissive and lawless society,' he added for good measure, effecting yet another startling convergence, 'is a by-product of Socialism.' [10] 'These questions of law and order,' Mr Heath told his *Panorama* audience, 'are of immense concern to ... almost every man and woman in this country.' [11] Or soon would be, with a little help from their friends. Lord Hailsham added: 'The theme is the safety of the citizen as he lives in his own home with his wife and children, as he goes about the streets, as he attends his places of amusement ... as he tries to accumulate property for his family and his old age free from fraud, as he works, plays and votes.' [12]

In this atmosphere, which the most measured commentators could only describe as one of mounting, often carefully organised, public hysteria, the students at Warwick University occupied the administration buildings and began to consult the personal and political files which this 'community of scholars' had been keeping on them; and a group of Cambridge students noisily interrupted a private dinner being held to celebrate the success of the Greek colonels at the Garden House Hotel. This renewal of student protest moved Mr Heath to contribute another brick or two to the construction of the populist crusade. He traversed in his speech the whole terrain of authority (unions, universities, government) versus disorder (strikes, sit-ins) in a powerful coupling of the two great thematics of Selsdon Man: 'Great factories, railways, airports are brought to a standstill by strike action. . . . Great seats of learning ... are disrupted by rebellious students.' Both, however, descanted towards a political, indeed, an electoral conclusion: 'We [i.e. the Conservatives] are not going to become a nation of pushovers.' [13] It was a threat he intended to honour.

Earlier in the year Mr Powell had re-emerged as another of the key signifiers of the crisis. In April he called the teachers, on strike for higher pay, 'Highwaymen' who 'threatened the fabric of law and order'. [14] A week before the election, at Northfield in Birmingham, he warned of 'the invisible enemy within' – students 'destroying' universities and 'terrorising' cities, 'bringing down' governments; of the power of the 'modern form' of the mob – the demonstration – in making governments 'tremble'; the success of 'disorder, deliberately fomented for its own sake' in the near-destruction of civil government in Northern Ireland; and the accumulation of 'combustible material' of 'another kind' (i.e. race) in this country, 'not without deliberate intention in some quarters'. The government's capitulation to the anti-apartheid's campaign against the South African cricket tour was pinpointed: 'It may have been a happy chance that this particular triumph of organised disorder and anarchist brain-washing coincided with the commencement of the General Election campaign. For many people it lifted the veil; for the first time, they caught a glimpse of the enemy and his power.' [15] Earlier that week, in Wolverhampton, he had implied that the immigration figures had been so consistently underestimated that 'one begins to wonder if the Foreign Office was the only department of state into which enemies of this country were infiltrated'. There is little need to reiterate here how discordant themes are being plotted together, how the motifs of organised disorder and an 'enemy within', with its ambiguous hint of subversion and treason, are serving to raise the nemesis of anarchy to the level of the state itself. It is important, however, to observe how the *race* question had been thematised at a higher level in Mr Powell's new scenario. The problem, he asserted at Northfield, had been deliberately 'miscalled race'. Race was being used to mystify and confuse the people. The real target was the great liberal conspiracy, inside government and the media, which held ordinary people to ransom, making them fearful to speak the truth for fear of being called 'racialist', and 'literally made to say black is white'. It was race – but now as the pivot of 'this process of brain-washing by repetition of manifest absurdities', race as a secret weapon 'depriving them of their wits and convincing them that what they thought was right is wrong': in short, race as part of the conspiracy of silence and blackmail against the silent majority. The intense populism of this line of attack fell on eager ears, especially in Mr Powell's stamping-ground in the West Midlands.

It was 'the enemy and his power' – The Enemy, and his accomplice, the 'conspiracy of Liberal Causes'; the hard conspiratorial centre and its soft, woolly-headed, deluded periphery – around which Mr Powell's penetrating rhetoric in these two speeches circled. It was useless to enquire precisely the shape of this 'enemy'. The point precisely was his protean quality: everywhere and, seemingly, nowhere. The nation's existence was threatened, the country 'under attack by forces which aim at the actual destruction of our nation and society', as surely as when Imperial Germany was building dreadnoughts; but the nation continued, mistakenly, to 'visualise him in the shape of armoured divisions, or squadrons of aircraft'. They failed to see his common presence, now 'in his student manifestation', now in 'disorder, deliberately fomented for its own sake as an instrument of power' in the province of Ulster, perhaps in the very heart of government itself. [16] In dispersing the 'enemy' to every corner and aspect of national life, and simultaneously concentrating and crystallising his protean appearances in the single spectre of 'the conspiracy within', Mr Powell, in his usual extraordinary way, distilled the essence of that movement by which the generalised panic of a nation and the organised crusade of the populists issue at one crucial moment of time, into the ideological figure of a 'law-and-order crusade'. It is quite critical, however, to bear in mind that, though few other speakers in the first half of 1970 achieved so all-inclusive a range and power of reference as Mr Powell did on these occasions, he was only bringing to a conclusion a process to which many, in and outside the Conservative Shadow leadership, had contributed, articulating what many rank-and-file members of the 'silent majority' were thinking, feeling and calling for in those terrifying months. It would be altogether mistaken to attribute the birth of a 'law-and-order' society to Mr Powell. Its midwives were more numerous and varied. Mr Powell simply saluted its appearance with an astonishing display of rhetorical fireworks, sealed its existence with fire and brimstone.

It was the weekend before the Election; and Mr Wilson, whose unflappability on these occasions knows no bounds, still harboured the illusion that Labour could win. . . .

The June election in 1970 marks the official tip of the pendulum, the passage of positions, the formal appearance on the stage of the 'theatre of politics', of a profound shift in the relations of force between the contending classes, and thus in the balance between consent and coercion in the state, which had been initiated at a deeper level in the previous years. This shift in the character of 'hegemonic domination', or, better, the deepening in the crisis of hegemony, which assumes a qualitatively new shape after 1970, must not be missed, nor its specific features misread or oversimplified.

Labour had preserved the parliamentary illusion that, governing with the consent of the trade-union movement in its pocket, it could carry off discipline 'by voluntary consent' where the Tories could not. The Tories knew better — partly because this option was not open to them. But this important difference in political perspective and in the composition of the social alliances favoured by each party should not conceal the fact that, from about 1967 onwards, the state — whichever political colouration it assumed, and in either a soft-sell or hard-sell disguise — was, *structurally* on a collision path with the labour movement and the working class.

This brings us to what may seem a paradoxical feature of the passage which the June election marks. Almost to the edge of the election itself, the pace of the Tory return to power, was set by the law-and-order campaign. In the days immediately before, however, the traditional issues of British electoral politics — inflation, prices, the economy, wages, etc. — come roaring back into prominence; and the election itself *seems* to be decided, after all, on more sensible, calm, rational and reasonable criteria. It is not the first, and by no means the last time that a 'scare' pre-election mood suddenly gives way to more stable electoral issues and, once the poll is over, the 'panic' seems to have been inconsequential. Was the whole law-and-order build-up, then, merely 'sound and fury, signifying nothing'? It is true, as Hugo Young in the *Sunday Times* noted, that though the Tory manifesto offered 'a general deliverance' from all manner of threat, it also marked 'a clear retreat from the trumpetings out of Selsdon Park'.[17] Such discrepancies between the reality of the danger posed, the generality of the way it is perceived and the remedies proposed are a feature of moral panic, which, precisely feeds on such gaps in credibility. However, it is true that no swift and sweeping 'law-and-order' measures were taken by the returning government. As righteous indignants like Mr Heath assumed the mantle of First Minister, apostles of fundamentalism like Mr Powell retired to the back benches, and moral rearmers like Lord Hailsham donned wig and robe and approached the Woolsack, it was easy to imagine that the whole hairy episode had been nothing more than a Spring *divertissement* to keep the Party supporters in good heart.

This may be deceptive. First, we must remember a 'peculiarity' of the English route: the English tendency to do softly softly, pragmatically and piece-meal what other countries do in one fell, dramatic swoop; just as Britain rather sidled up to her '1968', so she edged, bit by bit, towards a 'law-and-order' mood, now advancing, now retreating, moving in a crab-like way, sideways into Armageddon. Second, the *tempo* of reaction *does not* slacken; it quickens – more significantly, it changes direction and character. In this second period there begins the regular, immediate escalation of *every* conflictful issue up the hierarchy of control to the level of the state machine – each issue is instantly appropriated by the apparatuses of politics, government, the courts, the police or the law. What, before January, was a spiralling-upwards movement – local crusading pushing the authorities towards increased repression – becomes, after the mid-1970 tip-over, an automatic and immediate pincer movement: popular moral pressure from below and the thrust of restraint and control from above *happen together*. The state itself has become mobilised – sensitised to the emergence of the 'enemy' in any of his manifold disguises; the repressive response is at the ready, quick to move in, moving formally, through the law, the police, administrative regulation, public censure, and at a developing speed. This is what we mean by the slow 'shift to control', the move towards a kind of *closure* in the apparatuses of state control and repression. The decisive mechanisms in the management of hegemonic control in the period after June 1970 are regularly and routinely based in the apparatuses of constraint. This qualitative *shift* in the balance and relations of force is a deep change, which all the token signs of moderation and retreat, responsibility and reasonableness in the councils of government should not, for a moment, obscure.

Above all (and besides facilitating the routinisation of repression), the law-and-order campaign of 1970 had the overwhelming single consequence of legitimating the recourse to the law, to constraint and statutory power, as the *main*, indeed the only, effective means left of defending hegemony in conditions of severe crisis. It toned up and groomed the society for the extensive exercise of the repressive side of state power. It made this routinisation of control normal, natural, and thus right and inevitable. It legitimated the duty of the state itself, in the crucial areas of conflict, to 'go campaigning'. The first target was Mr Powell's forces of 'organised disorder and anarchist brainwashing'. In the ensuing months the full force of the repressive side of the state is openly and systematically turned against *this* anarchist disorderly flank. But, less obviously, the licensing of the state to campaign had a 'pay-off' in areas which at first sight seemed distant from the enemy of anarchist disorder: namely, in the attempt, now gathering steam, to discipline, restrain and coerce, to bring, also within the framework of law and order, not only demonstrators, criminals, squatters and dope addicts, but the solid ranks of the working class itself. This recalcitrant class – or at least its disorderly minorities – had also to be harnessed to 'order'. If what concerns us here is not a simple unmasking of a temporary 'conspiracy of the state' but its deeper and more structural movements, then it is of critical importance to understand just precisely what it is which *connects*, behind all the appearances, the opening of an official law-and-order campaign in January 1970, and the publication of the Industrial Relations Bill in the closing weeks of December.

What had really united the Conservative Party in the pre-election period was less the rhetoric of disorder, but rather a more traditionally phrased emphasis on 'the need to stand firm', not to give in, to restore *authority* to government. This theme of national unity and authority provided the all-important positive face to the more negative themes of 'law and order'. Shortly before the election, Mr Heath had approached the electorate with the affirmation that 'The Conservative Party is the party of one nation ... the next Conservative Government will ... safeguard the unity of the nation through honest government and sound policies.' The aim was to reaffirm the Nation as unified around a common – and moderate – set of goals, which the Heath government best embodied and expressed. All those who stood outside this 'trade union of the nation' were stigmatised as 'extremists'. The minority activities of squatters and demonstrators most vividly embodied this tendency. But the growing 'extremism' of working-class militancy – strikingly borne in upon the new government by a succession of new wage demands from dockers, miners, local authority manual workers, electricity-supply workers and dustmen – was undoubtedly the larger and more deep-seated trend. It directly threatened the new Heath economic strategy. It posed a direct challenge to the authority of government; and – with the spectre of May 1968 not yet banished from the collective Cabinet mind – it awakened fears of the possibility of the deadly 'student-worker' alliance. It was against this flank that, in the event, the government turned its 'law-and-order' campaign. Within six weeks of taking office, the new Minister for Employment, Mr Carr, told the C.B.I. that the government would support employers who faced strike action over wage demands. The Chancellor, Mr Barber, told the T.U.C. in no uncertain terms that 'there has got to be a steady and progressive cooling down. From now on employers have got to stand firm.' [18] Then Mr Carr sketched out the elements of the Industrial Relations Bill, with soothing thoughts that, after all the trade unions were responsible institutions, would not willingly act against the law of the land, that legal sanctions were envisaged as being used only in rare cases, and that personal liability would only arise where individuals acted outside their union's control and authority.

This application to the class struggle of the thin edge of the legal wedge was overwhelmingly supported by the media – for example (to take the two papers we watched most closely) by both the *Sunday Express* and the *Sunday Times*: the former in its hysterical and instinctive way, the latter in its more sober and rational voice. Both accepted the government's paradigm 'explanation' for industrial unrest: while the *Sunday Express* hysterically saw red militants at the bottom of every strike – in the docks, at Pilkingtons, at the pitheads – and the arrival of the 'suitcase militant', the *Sunday Times*, following the publication of the Industrial Relations Bill, quietly, but decisively, put its editorial weight behind the legislation, and in a manner wholly in line with the conspiratorial version fast becoming received political doctrine: 'The identification of militants as both prime movers of inflation and the prime targets of the Bill has now been clearly spelled out.' [19]

It is difficult, in the calculus of coercion, to measure precisely the combined effect of the 'law-and-order' lead from on high, the sharpening of the legal engine against the working class from within the heart of the Cabinet itself, the steady percolation of a conspiratorial reading of Britain's 'troubles' through the media, and the slow but sure escalation of control against potentially disorderly targets on the ground. There is no evidence of a concerted campaign; but the over-all trajectory is unmistakable.

In July, Mr Justice Melford Stevenson handed down jail terms of nine to eighteen months on six, and borstal sentences on two, of the Cambridge students accused in the Garden House demonstration in Cambridge against the Greek colonels. This was the first post-election occasion in which the full force of the law was seen in operation against political demonstrations, one of the focal points of the 'law-and-order' campaign. The indications it gave were not propitious. Of the 400 participating, sixty were identified (with the help of the proctors), but only a representative, exemplary fifteen were charged. The charges against them were made, progressively, more serious in the period before trial. And though the jury only convicted those against whom some specific unlawful act could be proven, the convicted first offenders were, smartly and summarily, put away.[20] Stephen Sedley, one of the defence lawyers, wrote, after the failure of the appeal:

> The police and the DPP have been encouraged by this trend to strike increasingly hard through the court at those they believe to represent a threat to law and order – demonstrators, Black Power activists, squatters, students. This trend towards politically motivated prosecutions has shown a distinct upswing. 1970 has seen the high point so far, but there is probably worse to come.[21]

Sedley's reference to 'Black Power activists' and the law was no casual aside. Black-power militancy was no doubt advanced in Britain by the steady punctuation of news from the United States. But the rising temperature of race did not require any transfusions of energy from across the water, and it was no process of simple imitation which brought the serious erosion of black–white relations thundering back into the headlines in the second half of 1970. This deterioration was nothing new, as we have seen; what *was* new was the fact that the general race-relations crisis now assumed, almost without exception, the particular form of a confrontation between the black community and the police. John Lambert's judicious survey of this declining situation was published in 1970.[22] It was followed by Derek Humphry's careful but well-documented and damning account, *Police Power and Black People*,[23] which clearly demonstrated the sudden, sharp rise to confrontation which came to a head in the summer of 1970, and extended, on an ever-rising curve into 1971 and 1972. The Liverpool Community Relations Council, established in June 1970, was almost immediately overwhelmed by black complaints of harassment by the police. An hour-long programme on this topic by Radio Merseyside, which referred to the fact that 'in certain police stations, particularly in the city centre, brutality and drug planting and the harassing of minority groups takes place regularly' passed without considered defence by the local police.[24] There were clashes between blacks and the police, in August, in Leeds, in Maida Vale, and at the Caledonian Road station, among others. Notting Hill became the scene of a running battle. The police made raid after raid on the Mangrove Restaurant, which − one constable told the court − 'as far as I am concerned' was the headquarters of 'the Black Power Movement'. (Asked in court if he knew what black power was, he replied: 'I know roughly what black power is − it is a movement planned to be very militant in this country.' That seemed to be enough.)

In October, the British Black Panthers called a conference to complain of what they believed to be a conscious campaign to ' "pick off " Black militants' and to 'intimidate, harass and imprison black people prepared to go out on the streets and demonstrate'. The charge was repudiated by Scotland Yard; but, as Humphry remarks, 'the commendable high-mindedness of the Yard's Press Bureau does not accord with the reality of the situation'.[25] There was no let up of the pressure.

Equally ominous moves were afoot in the areas of legislation and the courts. The Tory concern with civil disturbance had led the Shadow Cabinet to invite Sir Peter Rawlinson, the Shadow Attorney-General, to frame new 'trespass' legislation 'to combat the excesses of demonstrators'.[26] Few lawyers envied him his task; but some at least − had they been able to foresee the outcome of his failure − might have wished him better luck. For the failure to improve on the law of trespass −- clearly, in this case, intended as a legal deterrent against such exploits as the activities of Peter Hain and his anti-South African demonstrators, and the rapid spread of the squatting campaign to Southwark and other parts of south-east London[27] − did not in the least deter the government's resolve. Instead, it strengthened − and *widened* it. The subsequent reactivation of the ancient law of *conspiracy*, the principal form in which legal coercion came finally to be impressed upon the protest movements and industrial militancy in the following two or three years, was the direct consequence of the relative failure of this first stage in the moulding of an alternative legal 'engine of government'. During 1970, it was the giving of a new lease of life to the ancient common law charges of 'unlawful and riotous assembly' which provided the 'law-and-order' campaign with its first political scapegoats − the Cambridge students goaled at the Garden House trial.

Yet, if the 'Garden House' was, from this point of view, the most ominous trial of the year, 'law and order' also had another, less political, meaning in the courtroom, as the following report demonstrates:

'A DETERRENT sentence is not meant to fit the offender, it is meant to fit the offence,' said Mr. Justice Ashworth in the Appeal Court on Monday.

'When meting out a deterrent sentence it is idle to go into the background of each individual', echoed the Lord Chief Justice, Lord Parker. With these words their Lordships confirmed uniform sentences of three years on eighteen Birmingham youths who had been involved in gang fights. There was no regard for the fact that three of them had no previous conviction, that none of them had been found with an offensive weapon and that the police had admitted they had failed to round-up the ringleaders. Most important, perhaps, one of the youths had been receiving psychiatric treatment for a month before the fight. [28]

If everything in 1970 moves up to the threshold of 'law', some commentators were already pointing forward to the threshold which was increasingly to dominate the 1970s: the threshold of violence. Asking 'who is safe in this world of violence?', Angus Maude listed examples from right around the world to demonstrate his thesis that we now inhabited a 'new world of violence': the throwing of two C.S. canisters in the House of Commons; the 'cutting loose' with a tommy gun by Puerto Ricans in the U.S. Congress; the Garden House riot; Bernadette Devlin in Ulster; the banning of the South African cricket tour; and 'the series of airline outrages and kidnappings of Western Ambassadors in South America'. [29] Violence, he added, was a self-perpetuating mindless disease, used 'only too often' by 'weak minorities' to 'blackmail the majorities'. In 1970, in the name of the majority − still unfortunately too silent − the state organised itself to strike back.

1971−2: THE MOBILISATION OF THE LAW

The Heath government initiated a 'new course' in the management of the capitalist crisis − one sharply marked out from the Wilsonian strategy of 'voluntary restraint', and far more attuned to the primitive sentiments germinating in the Tory Party than to the solid centre of the financial and industrial bourgeoisie. It was an adventurist path, aimed at a 'final solution' to the British crisis. Essentially it had three prongs. The first involved setting the face of British capitalism firmly and irrevocably on the road to European integration, and consequently taking a certain distance from the 'special relationship' with the United States which had provided the corner-stone of Wilson's foreign economic policy. [30] The second prong was the economic strategy for British capitalism at home. Here Mr Heath planned a robust and abrasive line of attack. Labour had tried, through the Industrial Reorganisation Corporation, to carve more effective and competitive economic giants by way of a policy of inspired mergers and monopolies. From the Heath viewpoint, this had only served to protect the weak and uncompetitive sectors. Market forces, he believed, must be set free to do their dirty work; if necessary, 'lame ducks' must sink into bankruptcy and liquidation so that 'the great majority . . . who do not need a hand, who are quite capable of looking after their interests and only demand to be allowed to do so', could forge ahead and expand productively (as Mr Davies, the instrument of this side of the Heath policy, so lucidly stated it in the Upper Clyde Shipbuilders debate). [31] It followed that the whole intricate mechanism for 'harmonising' capital, labour and the state, the centrepiece of economic strategy throughout the 1960s, should be abandoned, and if possible dismantled. Much to the astonishment and chagrin of those managers of the political interests of capital – new and old – who had spent so much of their time in and out of Downing Street during the 1960s, Mr Heath did not meet the T.U.C. and C.B.I. in open bargaining until the middle of 1972, when the regression to a revamped *laissez-faire* philosophy had begun to go badly adrift. To the disbelief of *The Times*, the C.B.I., the T.U.C., the National Economic Development Council, prominent figures like Fred Catherwood, Sir Frank Figgueres, many Whitehall economic civil servants, the *Financial Times*, the Bank of England, and even members of Mr Heath's own Cabinet like Reginald Maudling, the central institutional links, pioneered by the state for the management of the economic life of late capitalism, were allowed, temporarily, themselves to go 'into liquidation'. Instead, in a heady, eleventh-hour scamper for growth – at whatever inflationary cost – Mr Heath began to lift the restrictions, promising to dismantle the whole planning apparatus. But the strategy of voluntary restraint had been the principal means by which (once the short interlude of post-war prosperity was over) the pressure on wages and profits and the political demands of the working class had been disciplined. What now would hold labour in line? This brings us to the third prong. Here, the economic pressure of labour must be contained by allowing unemployment, inflation, rising prices and an expanded money supply to rip through. But most crucial of all labour was to be disciplined by *the law* – a tight framework of legal constraints in the industrial-relations field, backed by the courts and fines; an attack on picketting; if necessary, a few exemplary arrests. In order to prepare the ground for this lurch into the coercive regulation of labour, there would have to be a tough, brutal display of 'firm government': in the last resort one or two strategic show-downs. Two sectors of organised labour stood in the front line: the power workers and the Post Office workers. One or other would have to be made an example of.

It was a high-risk strategy – the sort which evoked from the more cautious voices in the ruling class like *The Times*, the paradoxical judgement that Mr Heath was destined to be both 'the best and the worst Conservative Prime Minister we have ever had'. [32] Later events – including both Mr Heath's subsequent conversion and U-turn, and the return, under the Wilson and Callaghan governments post-1974 to 'social contracting' – suggest that it was also fundamentally out of line with the kind of state and government strategies which a weak British capitalism requires. Both its economic and political consequences were soon revealed to be disastrous for capital. To consolidate his rather insubstantial social base, Heath was obliged to give back huge tax reliefs. He failed to lower prices 'at a stroke' – indeed, in these months inflation began to accelerate at fever pace. Price rises weakened Britain's competitive position further, and bankruptcies produced a startling rise in unemployment, before the longed-for productive surge ever appeared. The only sector to gain from the new release of market forces was the speculative wing of finance capital – producing vast, overnight, speculative capital gains and an incomparable

property-market bonanza: a pay-off which blackened 'capitalism's unacceptable face' without in any way touching the core of its economic crisis. The
Heath gamble did not work.

On the political front, however, 1971 opened more auspiciously for Mr
Heath. The power workers work to rule at the end of 1970 had been laid low,
not least of all by the media, which had been 'more concerned to assail the
viewers with emotion over dialysis machines, incubators and old ladies dying of
hypothermia than to discover the facts of the situation or to demonstrate ...
that the union went to considerable trouble to see that hospitals were affected
as little as possible'.[33] The postmen submitted a claim for a 15 per cent increase in wages but they were isolated, could not bring the communication services to a halt, and, after holding out for forty-four days, gave in. In the same
moment Ford workers lost their struggle over 'parity' and had to accede to a
settlement constructed with the help of Mr Jack Jones, Mr Scanlon and Henry
Ford II. By the spring, the ground had been cleared on the back of these
defeats, for the centrepiece of the Heath strategy: the Industrial Relations Bill.

The direct attack on the working class and on organised labour which the
Industrial Relations Act represented had a profound effect on the sharpening
class struggle; for whereas the 'voluntary restraint' policy of the Wilson
government had divided and confused the labour movement, legal restraints,
promulgated by a Tory government, brought even official union leaderships
and the T.U.C. out in opposition, and thus, objectively, tilted the fulcrum of
official trade-union politics to the left. It now became routine media practice to
bring *the whole trade union movement* (including moderate leaderships) into
the orbit of the 'extremist' and 'wreckers' stigma, including a reluctant T.U.C.,
obliged by the logic of its situation to propose demonstrations against, and
'days of non-co-operation' with, the proposed legislation. The February anti-
Industrial Relations Act demonstration was an immense, record-breaking affair. That model of moderation, Sir Fred Hayday, described the March
demonstrators as 'anarchists and professional rowdies ... promoting the
downfall of law and order'. The government – Norman Buchan, Labour M.P.,
was later to complain – 'has made the class struggle respectable'.[34] Mr Heath
pressed on.

The *Industrial Relations Act* required the official registration of unions, with
fines for non-completion; it undermined the principle of the closed shop; it
defined a wide and ambiguous area of 'unfair industrial practices' – by which it
meant 'strikes' – and hedged about with conditions, delays and potential legal
actions the traditional right of workers to withdraw their labour. Above all it
established the Industrial Relations Court, with Sir John Donaldson in command, as the key 'engine' for the disciplined reform of labour.

The mobilisation of legal instruments against labour, political dissent and
alternative life-styles, all seemed to be aimed at the same general purpose: to
bring about by *fiat* what could no longer be won by consent – the disciplined
society. In 1971 the whole society is thus progressively preoccupied with –
rivetted by – the question of the law. This is only in a limited number of cases
the law in what one might call its routine operation. It involved also the framing
of new laws; the dredging up of ancient statutes and activating them in new

settings; the application of laws which, in more permissive times, had been liberally interpreted or allowed to lapse; and the widening of certain crucial legal terms of reference. It involved a toughening in the actual practical administration of the law – longer, exemplary sentences; the use of bail and costs to discourage those charged in the development of their defence; an extension of the arm of the law through administrative procedures, and a bias in favour of police and prosecution in the interpretation of the judges' rules. [35] It involved a widening and toughening of the whole 'anticipatory' use of the police – the activating of the Special Squads, increased surveillance and information-gathering by the Special Branch, dawn raids, heavy questioning, the use of 'verbals' which left doubts when produced in court, restrictions on the freedom of assembly, strong policing of demonstrations, the free use of warrants, the use of suspected charges to 'sweep' whole groups and sections of the population, the collection of literature and private documents on flimsy excuses. [36] This more-than-normal, more-than-routine use of the repressive legal instruments of the state precipitated a change in its whole mode of operation, leading overall to something approaching the progressive corruption of the legal apparatus in the interests of political necessity, and the steady erosion of civil liberties, judicial equality and the rule of law before the more compelling force of *raison d'état*. No doubt, as in the Watergate period in the United States (which, despite its softer form, this period in Britain closely resembles), this steady corruption of the formal 'checks and balances' of the capitalist state was undertaken from the 'highest' of motives – the belief that conspiracy must be met by conspiracy. Indeed, this was the organising viewpoint and the legal framework within which this degeneration took place: the idea of conspiracy.

Rudi Dutschke, the German student leader convalescing in Cambridge from an attack on his life, was, in fact, arraigned and tried before a tribunal, not a court; the tribunal often sat in secret session, from which Dutschke and his counsel were both excluded; hearing evidence from un-named and unidentified people who had clearly been spying on him. The visits to him from students and friends were adjudged to have 'far exceeded normal social activities' – whatever those are. Not only was Dutschke expelled, but, on the basis of this precedent (which even the Attorney-General said had to be gone through 'whether one found it attractive or not'), the immigration appeals procedure was scrapped in cases of political militants and those suspected of urban terrorism – the beginning of that long slide which was to end in 1974 with the occasional suspension of *habeas corpus* and the *Prevention of Terrorism Act*. [37]

During the liberal interlude of the mid-1960s, the law concerning pornography (the new *Obscene Publications Act*) had been allowed to lie fallow, and the boundaries and limits of this murky area left very much open to practical local enforcement: what Cox describes as 'a guerilla war between local police and private do-gooders on the one side, and radical bookshops and the liberal literary establishment on the other'. [38] But as the struggle between the moral guardians and the counter-culture escalated into full-scale warfare, the 'revolt against permissiveness' (as the Archbishop of Canterbury named it) assumed a more organised shape, and took the more tangible form of an attack on a general state of 'moral pollution'. In August, the publisher of the *Little*

Red Schoolbook was convicted by Lambeth magistrates. The Obscene Publications Squad raided the underground press regularly during this period, leaning on them and their printers, seizing letters, subscription files and anything else which looked incriminating. In the middle of the year the sentences against the *International Times* for the charge of conspiring to corrupt the public morals were confirmed by the Court of Appeal. In July, the editors of *Oz* were brought into court on the same charge in relation to their schoolchildren's issue, *Oz 28*. 'There has to be,' the *Daily Telegraph* informed its readers, quoting a senior policeman, 'constant police interest in all these publications because of the volume of public complaint and the implications of these magazines. We suspect that extreme left-wing activities are behind the campaign.' [39] Mr Maude had previously delivered himself of the considered view that 'extreme partisans of sexual freedom were dedicated to the complete destruction of all standards, authority and institutions'. [40] It stretches the imagination somewhat to conceive of Richard Neville and his co-editors as unravelling the whole skein of bourgeois society: and, in the *Oz cause célèbre*, the jury in fact threw out the conspiracy charge, though while the editors were remanded for medical evidence before being sentenced on other charges, 'their hair was forcibly cut by Wandsworth warders'. [41]

Thus the law, in its different branches, came to be actively recruited to complete the informal political work of censorship and control. It was accompanied by a ground-swell of populist and grass-roots reaction. In 1971, behind the legal engine of a repressive state machine working at full throttle, the moral guardians appear, once more, and the two begin to mesh – the beginnings of an organised moral backlash, a law-and-order crusade. This convergence is symbolised at many different points. Lord Hailsham, who had helped to pioneer such a crusade from outside the legal apparatus, was now installed in its highest legal office, as Lord Chancellor. At the symbolic pinnacle of the juridical complex stood a figure who throughout the 1960s had stubbornly insisted, with a transparent and unswerving sense of his own moral rectitude, that these complex matters could be best grasped by their reduction to a few simple moral home truths. It was symbolised at other points: for example, in the Festival of Light march early in 1971, jointly organised by the Chief Constable of Lancashire and the Bishop of Blackburn, who appeared at the head of 10,000 men (no women) in what the *Sunday Times* fittingly called the 'Law and Holy Order March'. [42] Many church and civic groups of a traditionalist inclination rallied in the streets in this crusade of righteousness. When Malcolm Muggeridge addressed a similar gathering the following year in London, he described its purpose as making 'the relatively few people who are responsible for this moral breakdown of our society' know 'they are pitted against, not just a few reactionaries, but all the people who have this light'. [43] Muggeridge, arch cynic of the 1950s, made a brilliant, if belated career out of castigating the evil moral influence of television *on* television. Better late than never!

It was not only those with a practised eye for the political resonance of moral issues, like Lord Hailsham and Mr Maude, who addressed themselves to the connection between moral order and 'law and order'. The National Viewers and Listeners Association, Mrs Whitehouse's organisation, had been gradually widening its campaigning range to take in the larger questions of pornography and sex education. In the Association's house journal, *Viewers and Listeners*, Mrs Whitehouse speculated that 'obscenity in the paperbacks and magazines and on the motion picture screen' was 'a basic and contributing factor to violence';[44] the Autumn issue of *Viewers and Listeners* argued that 'The "Permissive Society", with its much vaunted "freedom", is now seen for what it is − a bitter and destructive thing. The arts are degraded, law is held in contempt and sport fouled by outbreaks of vandalism and violence. The national purse takes the strain of a health service overburdened with increasing abortion, drug addiction, mental disturbance, alcoholism and an epidemic of venereal disease.'[45] The increasingly overtly political nature of this moral backlash is evidenced by the targets about which Mrs Whitehouse publicly protested: they now included all those groups which 'might want to destroy society',[46] Jerry Rubin and the Hippies,[47] Bernadette Devlin and Tariq Ali.[48]

We have commented earlier on the particular role which sections of the entrepreneurial middle class and the 'traditionalist' petty bourgeoisie played in the 1960s in the articulation of grass-roots moral outrage. In the 1970s, moral protest ceases to be a minority and fringe affair, and wins really massive publicity in all quarters of the press and television. Anyone who reads Mrs Whitehouse's autobiography, *Who Does She Think She Is?*[49] must be struck, not only by the good lady's indefatigable energy and commitment, but by the enormous number of public occasions on which she was called upon to advocate her views in the 1970−1 period, the publicity she attracted as well as the prominent figures she won to her cause. Her autobiography is dedicated to The Association's first Chairman, the Midlands M.P., James Dance, whose views were on the far right even of the Heath Conservative Party. The first convention of the Association in 1966 had been addressed by William Deedes, Conscrvative M.P., later to be in charge of information in the Heath government and presently editor of the *Daily Telegraph*. Mr Muggeridge had been, throughout, a constant and close adviser ('Destroy the Denmark myth, Mary', he advised her when, in March 1970, Granada television invited her to go to the Danish Sex Fair).[50] When, in April 1971, she invited Lord Longford to accompany her to the private showing of Dr Martin Cole's *Growing Up* sex-education film, she was in the throes of helping Longford prepare for his House of Lords intervention on pornography.[51] The Longford Committee, with its roll-call of 'the good', and its weighty, if slightly eccentric establishment flavour, was brought into being immediately following in May. Lord Longford himself has drawn attention to this moment, in 1971, when the issues around which his Committee centred precipitated into a high-level 'cause for concern'.[52] It was on the occasion of Tynan's *Oh, Calcutta!* that Ronald Butt, of the *Sunday Times*, reminded his readers of 'the majority who wish to lead decent lives . . . and who are at this moment being forced at every turn to cower before assumptions they reject'.[53] It was also in this period that the Obscene Publications Squad came into its own, beginning with the raid, in 1970, on the Open Space Theatre Club and the seizure of Warhol's *Flesh*. The prosecutions of the *Little Red Schoolbook*, *IT* and *Oz* followed. Tony Smythe quite appropriately described this intensification of legal and police pressure as 'ultimately . . . political'. It was, in short, a 'summer of repression'. [54]

The 1971 period thus allows us to see, in miniature, the dialectical movement by which the 'law-and-order' panic becomes fully institutionalised as an 'exceptional' form of the state. For convenience sake, we can condense this movement into three closely connected phases: first, the overwhelming tendency of the state to move in the direction of the law (the sheer comprehensiveness of the supporting legislative activity in this period, all of it culminating in a tightening of legal sanctions, is staggering); second, the mobilisation, and the extended, routine employment of the law-enforcement agencies in the exercise of 'informal' control; the third and culminating point is the tendency of all issues to converge, ideologically, at the 'violence' threshold. We cite here only some instances of each, as a way of capturing the character of the whole trajectory.

All three aspects, for example, can be seen at work in Northern Ireland. The assumption of an exclusively military definition of the Ulster crisis led to the *Emergency Powers Act* (August 1971) which reintroduced indefinite imprisonment without trial (internment). This placed the army in a quasi-judicial role, and precipitated the widespread swoops on suspects and the opening of the camps. It is precisely in such circumstances that the thin line separating the legal from the arbitrary exercise of 'informal' repression is blurred; and, within a month, the Compton Commission had to be set up to investigate allegations of torture, including 'hooding', continuous questioning, sleep deprivation, 'white noise' and other 'disorientation techniques' perfected in colonial wars farther afield. Although Mr Heath assured Brian Faulkner that 'the charges are substantially without foundation', [55] the Compton Report – calling torture by a more euphemistic name – substantially supported the charge, as, much later (in 1976, with the minimum of help from Her Majesty's Government) did the International Committee of Jurists. As Lewis Chester of the *Sunday Times* (which played a commendably courageous role here, under heavy official pressure) remarked after Compton: 'it now appears that the allegations . . . were substantially with foundation. In some respects they may have been understated.' [56]

The tendency to 'criminalise' every threat to a disciplined social order, and to 'legalise' (i.e. raise to the legal threshold) every means of containment, is witnessed in legislative fields as widely separate as the new *Misuse of Drugs Act* or the new *Criminal Damage Act* – both new departures and remarkably comprehensive in scope. The first related punishment for illegal possession to the alleged harmfulness of the drug, and raised the sentence for 'illegal possession with intent to supply' to as high as fourteen years for trafficking in cannabis. 'Mother's little helper', however – the highly addictive barbiturates which regulate the depressive condition of women – was missing from the list of controlled drugs. The *Drugs Act* cloaked in the sanctity of the law the much-contested theory of 'escalation in drug use' – today's pot-smoker, tomorrow's heroin addict: a thesis which the government's own advisers rejected in their official survey – two weeks or so too late to prevent the Royal Assent. The *Criminal Damage Act* 'modernises and simplifies the law of England and Wales as to offences of damage to property and rationalizes the penalties'. [57] It subordinated the means of damage used and the nature of the property damaged to the simple idea of one basic offence: damage to another's property without lawful excuse – maximum penalty ten years. 'Aggravated damage' carried the recommendation of 'life'. The squat, the picket and the demonstration all potentially fell within its shadow.

The new *Immigration Act*, passed in 1971, represents a slightly different combination of the same elements. The Act must be set in the context of the steady advance of the anti-immigration lobby within the right of the Conservative Party, and the rapidly rising tempo of the undeclared warfare in the ghetto areas between blacks and the police. As the raids on black clubs and social centres and the 'search on suspicion' of any black person on the streets, alone, late at night, became a routine aspect of life in the 'colony' areas, it became the rule of the streets, that in all such encounters the police leaned heavily; gradually, it also became the rule that blacks shoved back. The new Act endowed these routinised forms of informal pressure with the cover of the law. Lowering the boom against 'Commonwealth immigrants', as a whole, the Act in fact excepted whites from the 'Old Commonwealth', thereby making lawful what had so far been merely a part of the system of practical dispensation on the streets. Male labour was permitted entry in strictly controlled numbers, provided they were attached to a contract, stayed put for a period and renewed their permits. The law bore particularly heavily against women, children, dependants and families, many of whom were broken up amidst angry scenes at the ports of entry. Some tried to get in under the net. The battle against illegal entry and the sweep of immigrant communities for suspected illegals was joined. The original bill had proposed that immigrant workers should register with the police. Parliamentary opposition deleted the offending clause. But, as Bunyan has shown,[58] this was a formal and pyrrhic victory. For without reference to Parliament, the National Immigration Intelligence Unit was established (alongside the National Drugs Intelligence Unit, both specialised sectors in a much-expanded information co-ordinating, surveillance and record-keeping section set up by the Home Office and Scotland Yard). When asked, the Home Office Minister of State called this expansion of the surveillance system part of the 'operational activities of the police . . . not normally subject to Parliamentary control'.[59]

The most contradictory development of all – and the factor which served most to lend plausible support to the construction of nightmare dramatisations within the repressive state apparatuses – was the convergence around the theme of violence. Brigadier Kitson's *Low Intensity Operations,* which helped to convert the army to a fully implemented 'counter-insurgency' role, was published in 1971.[60] In the context of the Northern Ireland situation, this study had practical consequences far removed from the level of a philosophic review of military strategies at which it was ostensibly pitched. Kitson's book – which permitted a rare and privileged glimpse into that reticent object, the 'mind' of the Army in a period of escalating domestic political conflict – distinguished between civil disturbance, insurgency, guerrilla warfare, subversion, terrorism, civil disobedience, communist revolutionary warfare and insurrection. The army, Brigadier Kitson argued, with considerable clarity and force, really ought to face up to the fact that in conditions of nuclear stalemate, its principal objects would increasingly be 'subversion ... all measures short of the use of armed force taken by one section of the people of a country to overthrow those governing the country at the time, or to force them to do things which they do not want to do', and 'insurgency ... the use of armed force by a section of the people against a government for the purposes mentioned above'.[61] The knitting of these two together was an ominous development, especially when 'subversion' (defined so widely as to net virtually any form of political action other than standing or voting for Parliament) was understood as a lowly rung on the same escalator leading inexorably to armed insurgency and terrorism. But this logic was rapidly gaining ground – not only in the strategic manuals, and not only in the context of Ulster. The influential Institute for the Study of Conflict was created in 1970.[62] Under its umbrella, experts in world-wide counter-subversion, like its Director, Brian Crozier, counter-insurgency doyens like Major-General Clutterbuck and Brigadier W. F. K. Thompson, ex-Foreign Office diplomats, intelligence officers and high-ranking army personnel like Sir Robert Thompson (former Security Chief for Malaya), senior industrialists and academics, were all associated together in 'scholarly' analyses of 'subversion and revolutionary violence from Santiago to Saigon'.[63] They were also influential and effective in developing 'a network of contacts in Whitehall, the police force, intelligence services and the armed forces'[64] through which they propagated their gospel of world-wide subversion.

Ulster was one context which lent credibility to this vision. Although the break-up of Stormont and the decline into direct rule did not occur until 1972, 1971 was the year in which the Ulster crisis assumed its terminal form – an urban guerrilla war between the British Army and the Provos. In the wake of the Compton Report, the *Sunday Times* Insight Team's book suggested that the most sensitive issue raised by the British involvement in Ulster was indeed the conduct of the army.[65] Richard Clutterbuck, by no means the most reactionary of the new counter-insurgency Establishment, described the book as 'anti-army', 'broadly sympathetic to the IRA'. The iron curtain was beginning to cut down through British thought as well, whenever and wherever the question of political violence was raised. The second context was what Clutterbuck called 'Urban Guerrillas Across The World', and Ian Greig, another specialist, called more simply, 'The Politics of Bloodshed'. As the tempo of the colonial revolution and post-colonial class politics quickened in the developing world, it assumed, more and more, the form of the armed struggle or 'people's war'. Cuba, Algeria, followed by the Vietnam War, the birth of liberation movements in the Congo, then in Portuguese and Southern Africa, all belonged to this category; and they produced, in the writings of Ho Chi Minh, General Giap, Amilcar Cabral, Che Guevara and others, a powerful literature on the waging of a popular political warfare. The wave of armed liberation movements in the next – above all, Latin American – phase (the Tupamaros in Uruguay, Marighela's movements in Brazil, the armed struggle in Venezuela, etc.) were not that of *foco* in the countryside, but of vanguard uprisings in the cities. If the former were intrinsically indigenous, the latter were more translateable to the conditions of the urban developed world. The adoption of guerrilla tactics in or near the metropolitan centres and the use of terrorist attacks on its vulnerable cities hastened the process of 'bringing political violence back home'. Ulster and the Quebec Liberation Front were examples of the first; the kidnapping of businessmen and diplomats, and the hijackings and terrorist attacks by 'Black September' and the Palestine Liberation Front (P.L.O.) were tangible examples of the second.Four P.L.O. hijacks in succession in 1970, ending in the capture of one of their outstanding militants, Leila Khaled, were followed by the Dawson Field hijack, forcing her release. British diplomats were kidnapped in Canada and Uruguay. This urban guerrilla imagery undoubtedly fed *both* the making of extensive preparations against the potential emergence of such movements at home by the army, the police and the intelligence forces, *and* the exacerbation of popular fears and spectres. A classic spiral was entered here – the 'militarisation' of the control response providing exactly the proof, for the urban terrorist, of the authoritarian face behind the liberal mask: the growth of sympathy for such movements and symbolic identifications with them tending further 'to sanction violence in support of the status quo; the use of public violence to maintain public order; the use of private violence to maintain popular conceptions of social order when governments cannot or will not'. [66]

There followed its actual, living apotheosis at home, on native ground. The elements leading to the emergence of the 'Angry Brigade' in Britain at this precise point are too complex to unravel here. They must include: the recognition, on the part of the libertarian left, of a real connection between the 'alienating life conditions' of life in the West and the real structures of corporate capitalist exploitation; the belief that the anti-imperial struggle, now going so well, in the hinterlands, could be strategically and tactically linked with domestic conflict; the symbolic identification with the romantic image of the 'urban guerrilla', made more intense by the routines of privatised domestic apathy against which it was contrasted. There were some theatres of struggle the Vietnam War and the role of the African liberation movements in strengthening Black Power in the United States were two examples – where such connections could indeed be forged: 'bringing the war back home'. There were others where the real and the metaphorical are difficult to disentangle; where a single-minded determination to drive the logic of struggle through to its most extreme conclusion – a 'vanguardism' produced by isolation from any kind of mass struggle – and frustration at the snail's pace of reform, culminated in the formation of the urban terrorist gang: the Weathermen in the United States, the Baader–Meinhof group in West Germany, the Japanese Red Army group and the Angry Brigade were common manifestations of this temptation to vanguardism.

Carr, in his account of the Angry Brigade, argues that it was the group's involvement in ' "normal" criminality' which proved its undoing. [67] And certainly it was a trail of dud cheques and stolen bank-cards which led the police to Jake Prescott, and thus to Ian Purdie, who appeared in court in November charged with the bombing of Mr Carr's and Mr John Davies's houses. More significantly, the trail led through the networks of the alternative society – the communes, collectives, pads and 'scenes' where the libertarian struggle against the Industrial Relations Bill, and movements like Women's Lib and Claimants'

Union intersected. According to Carr, Inspector Habershon confessed: 'I had to get amongst these people because responsibility for the bombing clearly lay in that area.' The police, however, were 'shocked by the conditions they saw.... They could not understand how people could live that way by choice ... it added to and confirmed the prejudices already existing among the police against the so-called alternative society.' The Communiques which prefaced or followed each 'Angry Brigade' explosion attempted to link the bombings with a key class issue: Ireland, the *Industrial Relations Act*, the closure of Rolls-Royce, the Post Office workers' 'sell-out' and the Ford strike. But the 'abstract' nature of the critique which informed the strategy was unmistakeable. Shortly after explosions at Biba's Boutique and the house of the Chairman of Ford, the Bomb Squad was formed and Inspector Habershon took to reading Guy Debord's Hegelian and situationist extravaganza, *The Society of the Spectacle*. When the axe fell, Purdie and Stuart Christie were acquitted: Prescott, found guilty of addressing Angry Brigade envelopes, was given fifteen years by Mr Justice Melford Stevenson. In the following May, another four were sentenced by majority verdict to ten years.

On any reckoning the 'Angry Brigade' episode was a tragic affair. It arose from a deep conviction of the manifest human injustices of the system; and since, in the libertarian cast of thought, the oppression of the state is always direct and unmediated, it could only be met by direct and unmediated means. The recourse to the bomb was therefore *one* possible resolution of the libertarian script inscribed in the cataclysm of '1968'. But the drift towards total resistance in a less than totally revolutionary conjuncture was ultimately a token of isolation and weakness, not strength; and the failure of the spark to ignite other militants, or to connect with any wider mass agitation, indicated the flaw in the abstract nature of the tactical line. Nevertheless, the episode had profound unintended consequences. Unwittingly, it cemented in public consciousness the inextricable link, the consequential chain, between the politics of the alternative society and the violent threat to the state. It made the possible appear inevitable. It gave the forces of law and order precisely the pretext they needed to come down on the libertarian network like a ton of bricks. It strengthened the will of ordinary people, for whom explosions in the night were a vivid self-fulfilling prophecy, to support the law-and-order forces to 'do what they had to do', come what may. The 'Angry Brigade' thus unwittingly provided a critical turning-point in the drift into a 'law-and-order' society. It provided such proof as seemed to be needed that a violent conspiracy against the state *did* exist, and was located in or near the mass disaffiliation of youth. It gave a content to the empty fears of extremism, investing them with the imagery of explosions and arms caches and detonators. It raised reaction to a new pitch.

The second half of 1971 was indeed a 'prelude' – but to a struggle of a quite different order, moving in step with a different logic; and though the principal and dramatic form in which this prelude announced itself – the adoption in the working-class struggle in the Upper Clyde shipyards in Clydebank (and then elsewhere – Plesseys, Fisher–Bendix, Norton Villiers, Fakenham, etc.) of the tactic of the sit-in, first pioneered in the late 1960s by the student left – may have *suggested* all manner of convergences between working-class and middle-class politics, the fact is that, between 1971 and 1972, the direction of the struggle passed decisively to different hands and a different theatre of struggle.

The government announced the closure of the U.C.S. shipyards, a giant which its predecessor in office had rationalised into existence, in June. In July, following several very large Scottish demonstrations against growing unemployment, the shop stewards occupied the yards to prevent closure and protect jobs. The tactic, a defensive rather than an offensive one, was very solidly led and organised, mainly through a communist leadership, and captured the imagination of the growing numbers of workers drawn, through opposition to the *Industrial Relations Act*, into a quickening movement against the Heath government. Then the miners moved into the front line with a major wage claim, and the make-or-break showdown between the Heath 'course' and the organised working class commenced.

1972: THE MOMENT OF THE 'MUGGER'

Mugging is becoming more and more prevalent, certainly in London. As a result, decent citizens are afraid to use the Underground late at night, and indeed are afraid to use the underpasses for fear of mugging. We are told that in America people are even afraid to walk in the streets late at night for fear of mugging. This is an offence for which deterrent sentences should be passed. (Judge Alexander Karmel, Q.C.) [68]

1972 is by any reckoning an extraordinary year: a year of sustained and open class conflict of a kind unparalleled since the end of the war; and elsewhere of shocks and seizures, violence and confrontation. It is the year in which the society falls into deeply polarised sections, and consensus is put into a semi-permanent cold storage. 'It was a year which began and ended in violence,' *The Times* review of the year notes, disconsolately. [69] It opened with Bloody Sunday, in which, in the final moments of a civil rights march in the Bogside, the First Battalion Parachute Regiment lost its head and, in what amounted to a temporary 'army riot', shot wildly and indiscriminately into a Catholic crowd, killing thirteen. It ended with the nightly news of Vietnam, pulverised from the skies by 'the heaviest assault by American bombing that the war – or indeed any modern war – had ever seen'. It was also, *The Times* noted, 'the year of the international terrorist', when terrorism, 'no longer confined to within the borders of colonial occupation . . . struck the soft and open texture of western societies'. It was also the year when 'labour was . . . prepared to resort to strong armed methods to ensure its demands' and unions 'to carry opposition to the Industrial Relations Act to the point of deliberate defiance of the court created by the Act to administer the law'. [70] It was, indeed, the year in which the working class, virtually without political leadership of any strategic kind, at the high point of sheer trade-union resistance, took on, defeated and overturned the whole Heath confrontation strategy, leaving it in ruins, and precipitating that sharp about-turn which led, through the three phases of an incomes policy backed by law, and the dark night of the Emergency, to the political destruction of the Heath government in the second confrontation with the miners in

1974. More strike days were lost in this year than in any since 1919, and this included the first national miners' strike since the General Strike of 1926.

The introduction of the coercive power of the law directly into the management of labour and the economy in the form of the new Act was not tempered by stern Labour parliamentary opposition, nor modified by responsible T.U.C. representations, nor softened by liberal amendments, nor cooled out by the liberal press – the latter, in the early stages of the strategy, positively egged Mr Heath forward. It was taken on, head-first, by organised labour; stopped dead in its tracks and strangled in the last ditch, by sheer bloody-minded working-class opposition. It began in the docks. The container firm, Heaton's Transport, refused access to the Liverpool docks by workers protecting jobs against the inroads of container rationalisation, took up the clear invitation of the new Industrial Relations Court to invoke the power of the law to break the workers and drive rationalisation through. The dockers disobeyed the Court's order to permit access. On 29 March the Court imposed a £5000 fine for contempt on the union, and on 20 April, a further fine of £50,000. The union refused to pay up. The container blackings spread to the London docks. In a series of remarkable legal reversals, the Court of Appeal set aside the Industrial Court's judgement and the fines, only to have their own judgement in turn reversed by the House of Lords in July and the fines restored. Meanwhile, a committal order was made against three dockers leading the London fight. Again, the law wobbled before its clear political duty: the Official Solicitor, a mythical figure of the English legal system, rarely seen before this occasion and almost never since, rescued the men when the Court of Appeal once more set a Court's judgement aside. But the president of the Industrial Court, Sir John Donaldson, was not to be so lightly turned aside, and, on 21 July, amidst scenes of massive protest, five dockers were committed to jail on charges of contempt. The working-class support for the five men was overwhelming, bringing the publication of national newspapers to a halt for six days, and leading, no doubt, to another reversal: the reimposition of the fines on the T.G.W.U. – and the release of the five men. Two days later, amidst scenes of considerable bitterness between the men and their union leaders, the attempt at a compromise solution in the docks – the Jones–Aldington 'modernisation' plan – was rejected and the national dock strike began.

The law had failed to bite. It had depended on the arbitrary might and majesty of the Court, coupled with divisions amongst the working class, for its success, and the first had lost its aura in the course of being recruited directly to the class struggle, and the second was surmounted by an astonishing display of solidarity. When, subsequently, the Court again gambled on the 'silent majority', and forced the railwaymen to obey a fourteen-day statutory cooling-off period and to submit their claim to a ballot, the railwaymen voted by more than five to one in favour of industrial action. Later still, when the Court, taking up the case of the good Mr Goad (a recalcitrant trade-union member who had been refused admission to branch meetings), imposed fines and a threat of sequestration on the A.U.E.W., the latter simply refused to pay up.

This was essentially a *defensive* struggle to hold the coercive power of the law at bay and to protect basic trade-union rights of organisation. The engagement directly with political class power had already, by July, taken place. The miners made a massive wage claim for increases of between £5 and £9, which the government refused. It hoped no doubt that a moderate section of the union leadership would help them to make 'reason prevail' – also, no doubt, to isolate the miners, like they had the postmen, and to keep so many ancillary services going to make the strike action ineffective. Again, the Heath government miscalculated. Although the 'moderate' mining areas were reluctant to undertake industrial action, the more militant sections of the coalfields, strongly supported by miners' wives and reinforced by the solidarity traditional in these communities, moved directly ahead. What is more, on this occasion, the union leadership was, for once, solidly behind the claim, arguing a strong case for the miners having been made to fall behind in living standards as a result of a long period of wage reasonableness; there was a strong and active leadership in the localities and communities – strike action was effectively co-ordinated. Further, the miners took the attack outwards, winning solidarity in other sectors. The key struggle was to prevent the movement of supplies to and from the depots, and thus to enforce the strike at source point; the key tactic was the winning of support amongst other related sectors of workers, and, above all, the mounting of effective picketting. With support from a variety of sources, including students, the miners developed the tactic of the flying picket, which maximised the pressure and made the most effective deployment of available forces at such key points as the ports, power stations and depots. But this brought the strike into the line of fire of that other side of 'the law' – the police – in a struggle with pickets to keep the movement of coal supplies going. This open confrontation came to a head at the Saltley coke depot in Birmingham, where the miners, supported by hundreds of reinforcements from miles away, were able to establish a massive presence and halt the lorries and close the gates. As the police forces began to build up, the Birmingham stewards called the engineering workers out in support: thousands of workers downed tools, bringing the Birmingham factories to a halt in another overwhelming display of class solidarity; a large section marched out to swell the ranks of the pickets. The police backed off, and rapidly, in their wake, so did the government. The miners were speedily declared a 'special case' and the Wilberforce Inquiry was produced, like the Official Solicitor, to help the government put as bold a face on defeat as was possible in the situation. It was an outstanding demonstration, as well as formidable catalyst. It gave a transfusion of class confidence to the forces now arrayed against the government. It turned Mr Heath back in his tracks, and set him on his alternative road to statutory incomes control. It precipitated the swing to the left inside the Labour Party. It no doubt, also, silently steeled the Prime Minister's resolve to bring the miners to heel on some future occasion – a vendetta he never forgot, was drawn back to, like a moth to the flame, in 1974, and by which he was politically destroyed.

One result of the miners' resistance was the inclusion within the industrial-relations law of fresh legislation to outlaw the use of flying pickets – a response to a defeat of legal constraint by the elaboration of further legal constraints which was to terminate, in 1973, in subsequent arrests and conspiracy charges. Another result was to turn Mr Heath, with extreme reluctance and distaste, back into the well-trodden pathways he had so scornfully disdained: the reconstruction of corporate bargaining. The doors of No. 10 Downing Street were grudgingly prised open to admit various representatives of the T.U.C. and the C.B.I. in a new round of 'full and frank discussions'. Mr Heath offered a £2 flat-rate ceiling; the T.U.C. in their spirit of newly discovered militancy declined it. Once again, his instinct for regulation unimpaired, Mr Heath turned to the statutory freeze on wages and prices. Phase 1 of this imposed economic blizzard opened appropriately in November. It was succeeded, in 1973, by Phase 2 (a £1 limit plus 4 per cent), which stimulated a wave of strike resistance, largely led, however, by the low paid and public service sectors (civil servants, hospital workers, gas workers, teachers), not in a strategic position to win. With the line held, Mr Heath moved the notch to Phase 3, and, once more backed by the majesty of the law and the engine of the conspiracy charge, tried to prepare the ground for any further major encounters. Twenty-four building workers in Shrewsbury, where the flying-picket tactic had been employed again to good effect, were sent for trial. Then the miners entered their second massive claim.

Behind the barricades and the 'no-go' signs in Northern Ireland, the Provos came to establish for a time an unchallenged leadership over the Catholic minority; and the daily and nightly encounters between the Catholics and the army, which had begun as street-brawling and stone-throwing and mutual taunting and reprisals, gradually declined into regular armed confrontations. This rapid decline pointed to some inevitably tragic resolution and the Civil Rights Association march in Londonderry on 30 January provided the occasion. When the paras began to shoot rubber bullets into the crowd, marchers were still arriving in preparation for the meeting at Free Derry Corner. Then the troops replaced rubber bullets by live rounds, the stragglers scattered for cover, and when the confusion cleared, there were no less than thirteen Catholics dead on the street. 'Bloody Sunday' not only provided the pretext for a massive escalation into violence but it steeled the heart of the Catholics in the areas and rivetted them to their Provo protectors. The struggle now assumed its full and simplified form of a nationalist – Catholic – Republican struggle against an imperalist occupying force. What had an even greater impact on the public mood *at home* was the planting of a bomb, in reprisal for 'Bloody Sunday', outside the officers mess at the paratroop H.Q. at Aldershot – which killed six people and missed by minutes Brigadier Frank Kitson, architect of the theory of 'low intensity operations'. The war in Ireland had finally 'come home'. The Provo bombing campaign now began in earnest. 'Systematically, street by street, business house by business house, they continued to take the commercial area of the city to pieces. "We are filling in the gaps", they would say. They became very good at it.' [71] Stormont was suspended and Westminster assumed direct responsibility for the province, demolishing the last mediating barrier between the British government and the direct prosecution of a war against the terrorists and bombers. In response, the Protestant paramilitary groups, long in preparation, emerged into the light of day, and threw up their own defensive barricades. The British Army and the new

Secretary of State for Northern Ireland, Mr Whitelaw, had no alternative left but to try to destroy the Provos, and with them the Catholic resistance, by whatever direct means they possessed in order to forestall a Protestant U.D.I. There was a brief cease-fire, ending with a wave of renewed bombings which, on one day in Belfast, accounted for eleven dead and 130 injured. It was a war to the end.

The media were also heavily involved in the forlorn Whitelaw strategy to isolate the 'gunmen' from the bulk of the 'civilian population'. It was a spectacle calculated to chill the heart of British viewers, and to awaken the accompanying fear that the terrorism, slowly perceived as stalking one country after another, was surely, if slowly, already on its way to the heart of the major British cities. The steadily repeated view that the whole terror-laden and explosion-wracked situation was 'senseless', the product of that collective insanity and irrationalism called 'Ireland', did more than perhaps any other factor to signify the Ulster crisis as beyond comprehension, without reason and rationale, a mindless madness. When, at the end of the year, Mr Lynch's government in the south introduced a controversial Anti-Terrorist Bill – the forerunner for a succession of anti-terrorist emergency laws to follow in one Western European country after another – a timely explosion in Dublin (hardly traceable to the door of the I.R.A., since its effect was sure to boomerang against their position), killing two and injuring many more, swept away opposition in the Dáil and ensured its passage into law. It was Dublin's first bomb in the present emergency. It served to confirm the British view that some factor or factors unknown and un-nameable had unleashed a monster amongst the blameless citizens of peaceful and law-abiding countries. This combination – of righteous innocence, frustration, fear at the randomness of the danger and the scale of its prosecution – helped considerably to sharpen the tenterhooks on which the British public, by now, had become thoroughly impaled.

Political kidnappings and hijackings were in no sense the creation of 1972 (one estimate is that there were over 200 aircraft highjacks between 1967 and 1971, only ten of which, however, were political in the direct sense of bringing political pressure to bear on governments). [72] But the year was marked by several particularly dramatic, spine-chilling examples. In March a Turkish guerrilla group kidnapped three NATO technicians, two of whom were British, and, in the course of the ambush, the hostages were killed. In May, however, there was a major escalation in this type of terrorist activity. Three members of the Japanese Red Army Group, acting on behalf of the Palestinian guerrillas, shot down twenty-four passengers in the airport lounge at Israel's Lydda airport. The slaughter was seen as suicidal, indiscriminate and 'almost incomprehensible to Western minds', [73] though there is little doubt it was a revenge attack for the death of three Palestinian hijackers who had taken 100 passengers hostage aboard a Belgian airliner at the same airport three weeks earlier, and who were shot when Israeli troops stormed the plane. Indeed, the position and plight of the Palestinians (which, however one is revulsed by the use of indiscriminate terror as a political weapon, is certainly not 'incomprehensible') provided the main source for the growth of international terrorism, to which all the major international airlines, and airports and the advanced countries in general were especially vulnerable. In this period, it was the 'Black September' Group, emerging alongside the Baader–Meinhof group, the Japanese Red Army fraction and others in what was swiftly seen as an international conspiracy, linking Palestine, Ulster and other centres of urban warfare, which captured the headlines in British papers. This renewed concern with the metropolitan vulnerability to terrorism reached a peak with the invasion by 'Black September' of the Olympic village, the seisure of nine Israeli hostages and the shooting of two others. Here, once again, the ambush went badly wrong, and, in the shoot-out, five of the eight terrorists and all the hostages were killed. The world press and television services, posed for the saturation coverage of international friendship and harmony through sport, picked up instead the reverberations of death and mayhem emerging swiftly and without warning out of a clear blue Bavarian sky. A few weeks later, the three captured terrorists were released when a West German aircraft was successfully hijacked over Zagreb. At this point every one of the two million passengers a month who flow through London airport felt, as he stepped out on to the gangway, that he might be walking straight into the weather-eye of an international holocaust.

Some measure of the distance travelled, on questions of race and immigration between the mid-1960s and the mid-1970s may be derived from the fact that when, in October 1966, Mr Duncan Sandys raised with the Labour Home Secretary, Roy Jenkins, the danger of a new influx of Asian immigrants from Kenya, and was asked to refrain from making his anxieties public, he acquiesced. 'For the moment,' Mr Powell commented in 1967, 'there is a feeling of stabilization, and the subject has disappeared below the surface of public consciousness.'[74] But, he promised: 'there will be subsequent phases, when the problem will resume its place in public concern and in a more intractable form.'[75] Mr Powell returned to the question in October: 'Hundreds of thousands of people in Kenya, who never dreamt they belonged to this country, started to belong to it like you and me.'[76] The question – posed by the *Daily Mirror* in a front-page lead as a choice: 'On Immigration – A free-for-all? Or government control?'[77] – now reappeared, but more often in more dramatic form, the spectre of an 'uncontrolled flood', or what the *Sunday Times* called 'a deluge'.[78] The 1968 Commonwealth Immigrants Bill followed almost immediately, imposing stricter controls on entry and on the right of dependants to join their relatives. The Bill became an Act with indecent haste. The period between the 1968 and the 1971 *Immigration Acts* marks a low-water mark in race relations in Britain; and though the main focus in this period fell on the threat posed by those immigrants already here and the possibility of repatriating them, the danger of a possible fresh influx from abroad of Asians from East Africa who held British passports only added fuel to the fire. One of the main ways of taking the wind out of the Powellite sails was to ensure that stricter control over numbers was exercised; and, in the wake of the new Act, the treatment of new immigrants, especially Asians, by immigrations officers at ports of entry became noticeably more abrasive.[79] But earlier prophecies were realised with a vengeance when, on 4 August 1972, President Amin announced that there was no longer room in Uganda for 40,000 British Asians. Within weeks, Ugandan Asians, carrying British passports but little else of their former possessions, began turning up in large numbers, and a crash programme of accommodation and job-finding had to be put into effect by the government. Considerable confusion surrounded the actual status of the new stateless Asians, many of whom had been caught between the way the Ugandan and British governments interpreted the validity of their citizenship. In this period, as the 'shuttlecocking' of individual immigrants to and from their native place of origin grew into a steady stream, bereft families were separated, or taken to a sort of limbo existence in one of the hastily erected transit camps. By August all the race signals were clearly set at 'panic stations'; what Dilip Hiro has called the 'maritime metaphors' – of floods, deluges, tidal waves, etc. – abounded. The press, by now able to persuade itself that it had done the British people some injustice by deliberately giving race relations a low profile, thus putting itself out of touch with 'ordinary' grass-roots feeling on the issue, lifted its liberal veil and indulged in a bout of healthy realistic plain speaking: Britain was being flooded out.

The really tough 'hassling' of the immigrant communities – the police 'fishing expeditions' for illegal immigrants, the inspection of passports and documents, the routine 'moving on' of groups of black youths, the heavy surveillance of ghetto areas, the raids on black social centres – dates from this period, as does the return of a Conservative government, with a well-organised anti-black lobby and a vociferous anti-immigrant feeling growing amongst its party stalwarts, honouring its election pledges to the right. The 1971 Act was described by Mr Jenkins as 'a highly objectionable Bill ... misconceived in principle and damaging in practice'; but, on his return to office in 1974, Labour did not repeal it, and the panic surrounding the unexpected breach in the control on numbers and entry precipitated by the Amin expulsion escalated.[80] Without pressing the conjuncture too far or too hard, it is worth noting that the beginning of the panic about a new 'deluge' of Ugandan Asians and the panic about 'mugging' occurred in the same month: August 1972.

In 1972, the catchword 'crisis' no longer seems a mere journalistic hyperbole. Clearly, Britain is entering a major social, economic and political crisis. The crisis is differently perceived, differently explained, depending on the point of view applied. But it is no longer merely a witch's mask to scare children with. How the crisis was signified has been linked with our narrative throughout. But the true flavour of 1972, from the viewpoint which principally concerns us here, cannot be adequately communicated without looking briefly at this aspect. The year is absolutely dominated from end to end by two simple abstract terms, linked in a single ideological couplet, and over-arching every single issue, controversy, conflict or problem. The entire year can be summed up, as it were, between these two terms: 'violence' and 'the law'. We have noted before how, in signifying 'trouble', the press or the defining spokesmen in politics, government, public or moral life constantly mapped the themes of social dissent or issues of public concern into wider and wider converging metaphors. By 1970, 'the enemy' has become a single, composite figure, and his presence, hovering numinously over everything, spells out the possibility of large-scale social disorder. Its signifier at the opening of the 1970s is 'anarchy'. But 'anarchy' – the general threat of social chaos – is still something less than (though there is a clear line which connects it with) what follows: the tangible appearance of the forces of anarchy in the shape of violence. Violence is *the* axis around which the public signification of the crisis turns in 1972. It is, as we have argued, the final, the ultimate threshold. For, in violence, anarchy appears at last in its true colours – a conspiracy against the state itself: a conspiracy actually or potentially forwarded by the use of armed force. Violence thus threatens, not this or that aspect of the social order, but the very foundation of social order itself. Violence is thus the crest of the wave – that to which everything which had happened in Britain since the mid-1960s to undermine and erode the 'way of life' naturally and inevitably tended: the end of the road, the parting of the ways. It was also, ideologically, the ultimate convergence. For once a society becomes obsessed by 'violence' – a category which is notoriously difficult to define, but which has the ideological value of appearing quite simple, straightforward and clear-cut (what 'we' are all, ultimately, *against – all* the many varieties of dissent and conflict can be reduced to it), it thus becomes the lowest common denominator, which converts all threats into '*the threat*'. In 1972, the crisis is recurringly signified in terms of its violence; and, it should be noted, this is a violence of a certain kind: anarchic violence. It is mob violence, violence without sense or reason, violence for which no rationale (even those we abhor) can be conceived: lunatic violence, irrational violence, violence for kicks – pointless and incomprehensible.

In February, the *Sunday Express* columnist, Anne Edwards, wrote the following about Bloody Sunday: 'this sort of loudmouthed, lunatic hooliganism is festering all over the country'. Lunatic hooliganism is linked with its 'ugly sister' – 'pointless violence'. 'Perhaps we should have realised sooner that mob violence, which excuses itself by claiming a cause has an ugly sister. And that is the pointless damage inflicted by people with no other purpose in mind than to bash, beat up, break, scar and smash just for the kicks of doing it.' [81] The writer is here 'linking up' through the nexus of violence: the firing of an embassy in a country's capital; the advocacy of violence by a miners' M.P.; the threatening of schoolboys by two youths with a knife; and the tearing up of photographs of a widow's husband in a poor district of London by thugs. The events described are not nice, civilised or humane. Nor are they in any very concrete way political. Englishmen are, anyway, most reluctant to accept that political violence is *ever* justified, though they are the inheritors of a state which has made its wealth and secured its position in the world by many means, including conquest, forced labour and, sometimes, violence. The article does not, however, turn on so sophisticated an argument. The fact is that the things being used here as a peg to hang a thesis on are not 'connected' in any tangible or concrete way at all, except *rhetorically*, ideologically. They may be part of the same nightmare: they are only in the most metaphorical manner part of the same historical phenomenon. It is not the similarity of the events, but the similarity of the underlying sense of panic in the mind of the beholder which provides the real connection. What there is, in fact, in common here is *a felt sense of crisis*. And this, by a series of slides, elisions, descants and metaphorical twists, is projected through 'Bloody Sunday' – an event headlined by the *Sunday Express* reporter as 'When thugs hide behind a cause'. [82] It is not necessary to be a sympathiser with the military policies of the I.R.A. or to fellow-travel with indiscriminate terror as a political weapon to support the view that, whatever else happened, a day or an hour before or after 'Bloody Sunday', the event itself being discussed was a massive blunder *by undisciplined British troops*; and its consequences, politically and militarily, from a British point of view, were an unmitigated disaster – largely because it so transparently confirmed in Catholic eyes what otherwise was rather more difficult to prove conclusively: that a military definition of the Ulster crisis now existed on both sides of the no-go barricades, and when a military logic takes command in a 'colonial' situation, frustrated and action-hungry paratroopers will trigger political issues by acting within an exclusively military – i.e. violent – frame of reference. Such an argument was indeed solidly advanced, on the back of substantial evidence, by a rival paper to the *Express* – the *Sunday Times*. It is even plain to see in the official report on 'Bloody Sunday' by the Chief Justice, Mr Widgery – which, far from being 'soft on the Provos', was widely regarded, as a whitewash job for the Army.

We turn, then, to the paper which has, after all, boldly crusaded on a whole range of liberal and civil rights issues, not excluding the tricky area of race and Mr Powell, and which (unlike its erstwhile 'liberal' rival, the *Observer*) has run some real and financial risks to defend its independent position. Here is a *Sunday Times* editorial of the same period:

> Martha Crawford, Serajuddin Hussein and John Law were murdered thousands of miles apart. In death they acquired a terrible unity. They were all victims, of the utmost innocence, in contests of which they had no part. One was a bystander, one was a hostage, one was a journalist. None was armed, none was defended, none was involved in the political struggles for which their lives were casually taken. One was a housewife, one was a technician, one was an editor. Each pursued as modest and harmless a life as any carpenter's son. Now they are casualties, three among scores, of the barbarism which distinguishes this age. [83]

This subtle passage, too, practices a kind of simplification. The real and terrible, *concrete*, political conflicts, of which these untimely and tragic deaths are one of the many outcomes, are dissolved in the abstractness with which they are raised to the level of sheer violence. The 'terrible unity' is a falsely imposed unity. The only factor these very particular deaths can share here is that they result from the use of violence. To this 'violence' is counterposed another abstraction – the utter innocence of the victims. What the near-anonymity of the passage principally does is to underscore the sheer *meaninglessness* of all conflicts which end this way. Everything here is lifted to the abstract level of 'Everyman' confirmed in the needlessness of death: but it is accomplished at the expense of all historical and political contextualisation. Yet, somewhere behind these deaths, are those other, countless, nameless Palestinian dead, whom the *Sunday Times* cannot name, even for symbolic purposes, because, until a very little while ago, history had altogether forgotten them. It is not altogether far-fetched to see that when institutional or political violence is systematically perpetrated against an exploited people like the Palestinians, it will provoke violence in return. Fanon has written eloquently and with truth on this point. In the deep collusion – not individual, of course, but *collective* – which the British have made with this historical burial of the Palestinian question, there are unfortunately, no 'uninvolved innocents' left. But the *Sunday Times* firmly dispenses with this Fanonist logic. It finds the argument 'baseless in every particular'. These 'are the devices by which all blame is shifted, and valiant martyrdom is claimed, for acts of bottomless cowardice. The imperfections of "the system", that *vademecum* of modern extremists, excuses any attack, however brutal, on any citizen, however uninvolved.' These are impeccable, humanitarian, liberal principles. They do not frighten and terrorise us, as the *Sunday Express* rhetoric does, into seeing and believing what is simply not there. But, in their own rational way, they too perpetrate a sort of 'untruth'. Politics is a harder task-master than is dreamt of in the *Sunday Times* editorial rooms. The 'imperfections of the system' look slightly less like a *vademecum* for extremism from the west bank of the Jordan. Only in the abstract world of classical liberalism can the world be so easily split as this into the public self, which has rights and duties, and the private, unpolitical self, which is wholly 'uninvolved'. The 'politics' of violence comes up out of nowhere and hits us between the eyes, not in spite of the fact that we are 'uninvolved', but *because* the links of exploitation which connect us, collectively, through the imperialist chain to another far-off, forgotten and abandoned section of humanity has been allowed to pass for so long, behind everybody's back. This is a difficult truth. Its outcomes are not at all pretty to behold, or contemplate.

The binary opposite of violence is not peace, love, nor restitution: it is the law. 'This is not just a trial of strength for the Government. It is a test of the whole fabric of our society. The overwhelming majority of British people want peace and justice. Only the law, fairly and legally administered, can in the end guarantee this.' [84] 'The law may need amending. It may produce results which its creators did not intend. Its social effects might be harmful. It might even be a thoroughly bad law. But it is still the law; and although a medieval state may be deemed inoperative for want of modern social consent, a law which has existed for only four months can hardly be similarly dismissed. . . . So even bad laws must be observed.' [85] On and on, through the year, the procession goes. 'But good or bad, it is the law for the moment and the bedrock of a democratic society is that it tolerates laws it does not like until it can change them constitutionally. . . . There has to be a final legal sanction or the rule of force is substituted for the rule of law.' [86] 'There should be no doubt as to the issue that now confronts the country. It had nothing and has nothing to do with the docks or with the redundancy of dockers. It has nothing even to do with the difference between Tory and Socialist policies. It is a simple question as to whether this country is to live by law or by the brute force of anarchy.' [87] And what is the threat to contain which *these* stark, simple appeals to 'the law' are made? Political murder? The shooting of hostages? The kidnapping of innocents? The indiscriminate bombing of civilians? The unobtrusive letter-bomb in the morning's mail? Hordes of bolshevik hooligans in the streets? All four of the editorials and articles quoted are, in fact, mounted in defence of the Heath government's *Industrial Relations Act*, one of the most direct and undisguised pieces of legal class legislation by a ruling political class alliance against the organised strength and unity of the working class enacted in this century.

It has been argued that, by invoking the law in such an extensive and open a manner in the resolution of the crisis, Mr Heath destroyed the necessary fiction of the independence of the judiciary. Barnett has argued that juridical impartiality, enshrined in all developed forms of the capitalist state, provides a framework of legal equality and autonomy which helps to mask the continuing social and economic inequalities stemming from productive relations. [88] But once the state is obliged to intervene more directly, such interventions – especially when they take the exceptional form of positively recruiting the law in the open defence of class interests – 'risk making the "invisible" inequality of the real relationship between workers and capitalists manifestly apparent. The imperative necessity for contemporary capitalism to achieve a new degree of state intervention in the economy ... thus contains a danger for the bourgeoisie: it risks exposing the central ideological mystification of the system, on which the consent of the masses to the reign of capital rests.' [89]

This goes some way to explaining why the introduction of the law into the classically 'neutral' sphere of economic and industrial relations in 1972 served not to pacify but to trigger and detonate a massive class response. In general, though we find the orthodoxy of the American 'new left' in the 1960s – that liberal capitalism is simply a facade for fascist repression – an erroneous simplification, it is true that the more visible and active presence which the legal forces and the courts assumed in political and social life in the 1970s *did* have something of the effect of stripping off certain layers of mystification from the classic benificient model of the state and state power which had previously prevailed. The case could be extended to the sphere of state intervention in general. We have suggested that one of the deep structural shifts under way throughout the whole of our period, which is masked by the more immediate, phenomenal forms of the 'crisis', is indeed the massive reconstruction of the position, role and character of the capitalist state in general. This involved the progressive intervention of the state into spheres – the economic mechanisms of capital itself on one hand, the whole sphere of ideological relations and of social reproduction on the other – hitherto formally regarded as belonging to the independent spheres of 'civil society'. Thus the extension of the law and the courts at the level of political management of conflict and the class struggle is matched, at another level, by the extension of the state into the over-all generalship of the economy and the conditions for capital's expansion; and, at still another level, into the new spheres of welfare and the domestic reproduction of labour-power. It is indeed difficult to tell, as yet, whether the *precise* form which this reconstruction of the capitalist state has assumed in the British case is a feature of developments in the advanced capitalist mode of production as such, which Britain shares with all other developed capitalist countries, or specific to the more 'national' features – such as Britain attempting to carry this reconstruction through on an extremely weak economic base and in face of the most mature industrial working class in the history of capitalism. But the *effects* of this shift can certainly not be denied; and the fact that it has happened, with of course important national differences, both where capitalism is weak (Britain) and where so far it has been strong (the United States) suggests that what we are witnessing is no epiphenomenal movement. It stems from contradictions at the base of the world capitalist system itself in a period of contradictory and uneven development, not simply from the political 'relations of force' in one country or another.

However, we ignore the more conjunctural aspects at our peril. If this recomposition of the state, including the altered role of its juridical arm, is indeed one of the underlying causes of the instabilities we have been analysing, then we must also recognise that, in Britain, it has assumed significantly different *forms*. The 'managed consensus' of Labour's earlier and current phase, with its absolutely central ideological mechanism of 'the national interest', and its complementary ideological strategies of dividing the world into 'moderates' and 'extremists' was *also* a consequence of the extension of the 'interventionist state', though in a different form from that which it assumed under Mr Heath. The difference, then, is not that the extraordinary Heath interlude represented interventionism, in contrast with other periods in our review, but, crucially, that it marked the conclusion of *a critical internal shift in the nature of the balance or equilibrium on which contemporary capitalist state power is founded*. And, though the basic strophe of change may derive from a deeper level of the structure, *this* difference – between a masked and a more open form of repressive regime – arises most acutely at the level of the political class struggle itself. The growth of political dissent, from the mid-1960s onwards, then the resumption of a more militant form of working-class political struggle at the turn of the decade, coupled with the pervasive weakness of the British economic base, have made it impossible, for a time, to manage the crisis, politically, without an escalation in the use and forms of repressive state power. And it is the bringing of this critical shift in the nature of the hegemonic crisis to its culmination which is the 'service' that Mr Heath performed for capitalism – though in the event he got little credit for it. Two further points should be noted. Although we have since returned to a fairer and more regulated, 'contractual', form of interventionism, the opening to the repressive use of the legal part of the state has not disappeared. Consensus remains an enforced not a spontaneous construction; and, in its routine manifestations in the mid-1970s, it assumes an apparently permanent face of repressive force which its previous variants lacked. The second point, not sufficiently acknowledged, is the mobilising power of the recruitment of 'the law' in winning over the silent majority to a definition of the crisis which regularly and routinely underpins a more authoritarian form of the state. The interposition of the law directly into class relations may have destroyed something of its effective neutral 'cover'. But it also had the opposite effect: of making it more legitimate for 'public opinion' to be actively recruited in an open and explicit fashion in favour of 'the strong state'. Anyone who doubts that may tune in to any 'grass-roots' phone-in radio programme at random, and catch the ebb and flow of authoritarian populism in defence of *social discipline*, or they may listen carefully to the cadences of Mr Heath's successor. Mr Heath risked a great deal in his last ditch scramble for the finishing line in 1972. But the ideological effect of this 'extraordinary' period has outlived him and is by no means yet exhausted.

1972 is the point when the 'mugging' panic first makes its full appearance; and thus where the wider historical narrative intersects with our more limited concerns. The date has no other special significance. In terms of the disintegration of the 'Heath course', the rising confidence and militancy of working-class struggle, 1972 is merely a mid-point. From the historical viewpoint, the 'moment of mugging' is only *one* moment in this longer history.

Its position and timing, however, is not adventitious. We are not of course attempting to force this convergence into too tight or neat a fit. We have aimed to expose the accumulation at one point of rupture of a number of different contradictions. If the 'mugging' reaction grows out of the drift of the state, under the crisis of hegemony, into an exceptional posture, it is not, in a simple sense, the direct *product* of that evolution. The reaction to mugging has its own 'inner history', within the juridical and ideological spheres: crime control, the police and courts, public opinion and the media. If it relates to the 'crisis in hegemony', it can only be *via* the shifting balance and internal relations between different state apparatuses in relation to the management of crisis. The internal histories of these apparatuses, in relation to a general history of the capitalist state in this period, remains to be constructed. In its absence, we must not push plausibility further than it will go. A sharp judicial reaction to 'street crime' *could* have occurred at other moments in the post-war period. After all, the 'rising crime rate equation' has been at the top of the agenda of concerns for nearly two decades. Sections of public opinion could be heard calling for a return to capital or corporal punishment, to tougher sentencing and harsher prison regimes throughout most of the period. Race has been the play-thing of Party politics at least since the Smethwick election of 1964. The reorganisation of the police force, which bears so effectively and efficiently against both the black colonies and political dissent, was set in motion as early as 1963 – and for 'organisation' reasons which, at first sight, appear far removed from more manifest threats. A crisis of authority, pivoting around youth, the family and moral conduct, belongs, first, with the 1950s not the 1970s. The seeds of the 'mugging panic' were thus a long time germinating. Yet, undoubtedly, that panic makes a great deal more sense – once set in the context of the 1970s – than at an earlier period. As our earlier discussions showed, it depended on at least five essential conditions: a state of anticipatory mobilisation and 'preparedness' in the control apparatuses; a sensitising of official circles and of the public through the mass media; a 'perceived danger' to social stability – such as when the crime rate is read as indexing a general break-down in social authority and control; the identification of a vulnerable 'target group' (e.g. black youth) involved in dramatic incidents ('muggings') which trigger public alarm; the setting in motion of the mechanisms by which conspiratorial demons and criminal folk-devils are projected on to the public stage. These conditions are all met in full at the moment when the 'mugging panic' precipitates.

That these conditions were not operating exclusively with respect to black crime is certainly part of our case, for it is this which suggests the connection between the reaction in the state to *particular* manifestations of political conflict and social discontent, and the *general* crisis in hegemony. We believe, then, that the nature of the reaction to 'mugging' can only be understood in terms of the way society – more especially, the ruling-class alliances, the state apparatuses and the media – responded to a deepening economic, political and social crisis. Since the phenomenon we are seeking to situate flows most directly from the juridical–political complex, we have traced this crisis preeminently at the level of the state. Thus a crisis, which deserves a fuller and more fundamental analysis in terms of the capitalist mode of production in conditions of a synchronised global recession, is here presented, mainly – and in full knowledge of the limitations – at the level, or in the form of the slow construction of a soft 'law-and-order' society.

AFTERMATH: LIVING WITH THE CRISIS

The period between 1972 and 1976 must be dealt with more summarily. It would be an error to present a roundly concluded story, since the developments precipitated in the 1972–4 period have by no means reached their culmination. We identify, here, four principal aspects: the political crisis; the economic crisis; the 'theatre' of ideological struggle; and the direct interpellation of the race issue into the crisis of British civil and political life. All four themes must be understood as unrolling within an organic conjuncture whose parameters are overdetermined by two factors: the rapid deterioration of Britain's economic position; and the maintenance of a political form of 'that exceptional state' which gradually emerged between 1968 and 1972 and which now appears, for 'the duration' at least, to be permanently installed.

The Heath return to corporate bargaining after 1972 was undertaken in the face of a massive political defeat. It was undertaken with ill grace; and there is every sign that in Mr Heath's mind the final showdown had been simply postponed. Moreover, as the recession, following the world-wide 'crisis boom' of 1972–3, began to bite in earnest, the unemployment figures rose, inflation graduated to rip-roaring Weimar Republic proportions, and the whole balance of world capitalism was thrown sideways by the lurch in Arab oil prices; there was little left in the kitty with which to 'bargain'. Phase 1, therefore, imposed a six-month total freeze on wages; Phase 2 a limit of £1 plus 4 per cent. Phase 3, initiated in the autumn of 1973, with its 'relativities clauses' designed to allow the more militant sectors to 'catch up', was met by the revived strength and unity of the miners' claim: £35 for surface workers, £40 for underground workers, £45 for workers at the coal face. The showdown had arrived. In response, Mr Heath unleashed an ideological onslaught. He pinpointed the unpatriotic action of the miners in timing their claim to coincide with the Arab oil embargo. They were 'holding the nation up to ransom'. The media at once seized on this lead – after all, attacks on those who act against the 'national interest' no longer appeared to contravene the protocol on balanced and impartial news coverage. Between 1972 and the present, as the 'national interest' has become unequivocally identified with whatever policies the state is currently pursuing, the reality of the state has come to provide the *raison d'être* for the media; once any group threatening this delicately poised strategy has been symbolically cast out of the body politic – through the mechanisms of the moderates/extremist paradigm – the media have felt it quite legitimate to intervene, openly and vigorously, on the side of the 'centre'. The phenomenon of the 'Red Scare' is, of course, well documented in British history, and its success has depended before now on a skilful orchestration of politicians and the press. But the virulence of its reappearance in this period is worth noting. In this period the press begins again its deep exploration to unearth the 'politically motivated men' in the miners' union; later (1974) it was to conspire in an organised hounding of the 'red menace' in the person of Mr McGahey, the Scottish miners' leader; later (1976) it was to project Mr Wedgwood-Benn as the 'Lenin' of the Labour Party; throughout the early period of the 'social contract', it was, again and again, openly to intervene to swing elections within the key unions from the 'extremist' to the 'moderate' pole; later it was mesmerised by the spectre of 'Marxism'. All, good, objective, impartial stuff. On occasion, the press opened its feature columns to the sniffers-out of communist subversion: the Institute for the Study of Conflict, the National Association for Freedom, the Aims of Industry Group, the Free Enterprise League, the 'Let's Work Together Campaign'. Later, it required no extreme prod to give front-page treatment to every and any spokesman who could discern the presence of another 'totalitarian Marxist' inside the Labour Party.

Mr Heath then turned to his 'final solution' – one dictated entirely by the political motive of breaking the working class at its most united point. Its damaging economic consequences precipitated Britain's economic decline into 'slumpflation'. The miners had to be defeated, fuel saved; more important, the 'nation' had to be mobilised against the miners by projecting the crisis right into the heart of every British family. The economy was put on a three-day working 'emergency', and the country plunged into semi-darkness. In a wild swipe the 'costs' of the miners' actions were thus generalised for the working class and the country as a whole, in the hope that this would open up internal splits in the ranks: bringing Labour and T.U.C. pressure to bear on the N.U.M., and the pressure of women, having to make do on short-time wages, to bear against their striking men. The splits failed to materialise. When the N.U.M. was finally pressured to a ballot, the vote in favour of a strike was 81 per cent. The 'crisis scare', successfully generated, failed to break that class solidarity which had been tempered in the open two-year season of class warfare with Heath Toryism. To the accompaniment of this fully mobilised 'Red Scare', 'Reds Under the Bed' campaign, Mr Heath called and lost the February election. The February 1974 election 'was more clearly a class confrontation than any previous election since the Second World War'.[90] It was also the most resounding victory, not for Labour (returned in a weak minority position, once Mr Heath could be persuaded to call in the removal men), but for the organised working class. It had brought the government to the ground.

The state of the political class struggle can be briefly summarised, in the two years following, by looking at three strands: first, the level of militancy sustained through the rest of 1974 in the wake of the miners' victory; second, the return to the social democratic management of the deepening capitalist crisis, principally through another variant of the mechanism of the 'social contract' (long mistitled, in a form which inconveniently called to mind its cosmetic aspects – a 'social compact'); third, the articulation of a fully fledged capitalist recession, with extremely high rates of inflation, a toppling currency, cuts in the social wage and in public spending, a savaging of living standards, and a sacrifice of the working class to capital, all managed by a Labour government with its centrist stoical face (Mr Callaghan) turned to the wall of its international creditors, and its belligerent face (Mr Healey) turned against his own ranks. The 'social contract' is the latest form in which British social democracy has attempted to preside over and ride out the contradictory effects of a declining capitalism. Like its predecessors, the 'social contract' is the Labourist version of that corporate bargain, organised within the capitalist state, and struck between the formal leadership of the labour movement (a Labour government in office), the formal representatives of the working class (the T.U.C.) and – a silent and sceptical partner, in this phase – the representatives of capital itself. Once more, in this form, the crisis of capitalism is drawn directly on to the territory of the state. In the concessions, made in the 'contract's' early days, to 'bringing about a fundamental shift in the distribution of wealth', and in its recognition that the whole of the 'social wage' was now the area to be bargained over, the 'social contract' marked the relative strength and cohesiveness of working-class demands, and gave the unions some formal veto over government policies. That strength has, of course, been systematically whittled away in the subsequent conditions of severe cuts in welfare and public expenditure, cuts which the working class have supported with ill grace, to some degree resisted, but – once again bemused and confused by the spectacle of being led into poverty and unemployment by its own side – failed to push to its limits. This unstable social base to the present social contract has had contradictory consequences: formal commitments 'to the left' – just far enough to secure the 'consent' of left trade unionists like Scanlon of the A.E.U.W. and Jones of the T.G.W.U., and to ensure some credibility to the press portrayal of the Labour Party as a party of 'irresponsible leftists'; just centrist enough to persuade the working class to be pushed and bullied, practically, by the Labour pragmatists into tolerating a dramatic rise in the rate of unemployment and a dynamic, staged lowering of working-class living standards. In this way, Labour has 'captured' for its management of the crisis, for capitalism, that measure of working-class and union support required to represent itself as the only 'credible party of government'; while the very presence of the unions so close to the centre of its unsteady equilibrium is quite enough to enable the government to be represented as 'in the pocket of the trade union barons', thereby legitimating the strike of capital investment at home and frightening the currency dealers abroad. (Some of the most virulent examples come from emigrée socialists like Paul Johnson.) [91] A more unstable political 'resolution' can hardly be imagined.

The 'governor' of this stalemate position is, of course, the deep economic trough into which Britain has finally fallen. By 1975, the first synchronised world-wide recession of capitalism was in full swing – one manifesting the un-usual form of productive slump coupled with soaring inflation. How far into recession world capitalism will fall is, still, an open guess. But its consequences for Britain are no longer in doubt. The 'weak reeds' in the capitalist partnership – Britain and Italy especially – have been permanently damaged. The whole Keynesian apparatus for the control of recession is in tatters, with not even a minimum consensus amongst economists as to whether the money supply has anything or nothing to contribute to lowering the rate of inflation. At the same time, the attempt is in progress to transfer the costs on to the backs of the working class. This is no longer the description of an economy suffering en-demic weaknesses. It is an economy being steadily battered down into poverty, managed by a government which is silently praying that it can effect the transfer of the crisis to the working class without arousing mass political resistance, and thus create that mirage of British social democratic govern-ments – 'favourable investment conditions'. If it cuts too fast, the unions will be forced to bolt the 'social contract', and destroy social democracy's fragile social and political base; if it does not cut fast and hard, the international bankers will simply cut their credit short. If it raises taxes, the middle classes – now in a state of irritable, Thatcher-like arousal – will either emigrate in mass or begin, Chilean-style, to rattle their pressure-cooker lids; if it does not tax, the last remnants of the welfare state – and with them any hope of buying working-class compliance – will disappear. Britain in the 1970s is a country for whose crisis there are no viable capitalist solutions left, and where, as yet, there is no political base for an alternative socialist strategy. It is a nation locked in a deadly stalemate: a state of unstoppable capitalist decline.

This has had the deadliest and most profound ideological consequences. Although, under the guardianship of social democracy, Britain backed off a lit-tle from the 'law-and-order' state whose construction was well under way bet-ween 1972–4, the exceptional form which the capitalist state assumed in that period has not been dismantled. The mobilisation of the state apparatuses around the corrective and coercive poles has been coupled with a dramatic deterioration in the ideological climate generally, favouring a much tougher regime of social discipline: the latter being the form in which consent is won to this 'exceptional' state of affairs. Such an ideological thrust is difficult to delineate precisely, but it is not difficult to identify its principal thematics and mechanisms.

Between 1972 and 1974, the 'crisis' came finally to be appropriated – by governments in office, the repressive apparatuses of the state, the media and some articulate sectors of public opinion – as an interlocking set of planned or organised *conspiracies*. British society became little short of fixated by the idea of a conspiracy against 'the British way of life'. The collective psychological displacements which this fixation requires are almost too transparent to require analysis. To put it simply, 'the conspiracy' is the necessary and required form in which dissent, opposition or conflict has to be explained in a society which is, in fact, mesmerised by *consensus*. If society is defined as an entity in which all fundamental or structural class conflicts have been reconciled, and government is defined as the instrument of class reconciliation, and the state assumes the role of the organiser of conciliation and consent, and the class nature of the capitalist mode of production is presented as one which can, with goodwill, be 'harmonised' into a unity, then, clearly, conflict *must* arise because an evil minority of subversive and politically motivated men enter into a conspiracy to destroy by force what they cannot dismantle in any other way. How else can 'the crisis' be explained? Of course, this slow maturing of the spectre of conspiracy – like most dominant ideological paradigms – has material consequences. Its propagation makes legitimate the official repression of everything which threatens or is contrary to the logic of the state. Its premise, then, is the identification of the whole society with the state – the state has become the bureaucratic embodiment, the powerful organising centre and expression of the disorganised consensus of the popular will. So, whatever the state does is *legitimate* (even if it is not 'right'); and *whoever threatens the consensus threatens the state*. This is a fateful collapse. On the back of this equation, the exceptional state prospers.

In the period between 1974 and the present, this conspiratorial world view – once the prerogative of the *East–West Digest*, Aims of Industry, the Economic League and other denizens of the far right only – has become received doctrine. It surges into the correspondence columns of *The Times*, is weightily considered in *The Economist*, mulled over in Senior Common rooms, and debated in the House of Lords. Industrial news is systematically reported in such terms as 'Slim hope for the left in Leyland union poll'. [92] Any industrial conflict is subject to being blackened – as the Chrysler dispute was by Mr Wilson – as the result of 'politico-industrial action'. [93] Peers like Lord Chalfont are given the freedom of the air to propagate against communist 'maggots and termites' dedicated to smash democracy: a thesis supported by the proposition that in Britain all of Lenin's preconditions for revolution have already been fulfilled! [94] Polytechnic Directors, like Dr Miller at North London, facing protests from students he dubs 'malignants', confesses. 'I sit in my office and itch for the ability to say, "Hang the Ringleaders".' [95] The *Daily Telegraph*, now openly an organ of the far right, runs colour-supplement features tracing communism's 'creeping, insidious, cancer-like growth', the 'treachery, deceit and violence of a small minority and ... foreign-directed subterfuge'. The *Birmingham Evening Mail* regards this feature as so authoritative that it reprints it in full. [96] Public opinion is constantly and unremittingly *tutored* in social authoritarian postures by the method of sponsored 'moral panics': the skilfully elevated panic surrounding comprehensive education, falling standards and 'Reds' in the classrooms is one of the most effective and dramatic examples – an instance of how, through an apparently 'non-political' issue, the terrain of social consciousness is prepared for exactly that political *dénouement* required by the 'iron times' into which we are drifting. Meanwhile, the Archbishop of Canterbury, in a statement widely interpreted as 'religious', *not* political (union militants are always 'political', not 'industrial'), casts a spiritual gloss over the national drift into 'insecurity and anxiety' verging on disillusionment and fear. [97]

Not surprisingly, it was – literally – under the banner of the conspiracy charge, an ancient and disreputable statute, retrieved and dusted off for the occasion, that the law was brought into the service of the restoration of 'law and order'. In 1971, some Sierra Leone students who occupied their Embassy were charged and convicted of conspiracy, appealed, and were denied by the Lord Chancellor, Lord Hailsham, in the infamous Karama decision (July 1973). This decision, which laid down a formidable precedent in a contested area of conflict, and represented an actual piece of law-making by the court rather than by Parliament, was unmistakably in keeping with a political rather than a legal chain of reasoning. As John Griffith observed: 'The power of the state, of the police, or organized society can now be harnessed to suppression of minority groups whose protests had formerly been chargeable only in the civil courts.'[98] It perfectly embodied the Lord Chancellor's view that 'the war in Bangladesh, Cyprus, the Middle East, Black September, Black Power, the Angry Brigade, the Kennedy murders, Northern Ireland, bombs in Whitehall and the Old Bailey, the Welsh Language Society, the massacre in the Sudan, the mugging in the tube, gas strikes, hospital strikes, go-slows, sit-in's, the Icelandic cod war' were all 'standing or seeking to stand on different parts of the same slippery slope'.[99] The conspiratorial world view can hardly be more comprehensively stated. 'In that sense,' Professor Griffith remarked, 'Karama was a political decision made by a political judge.' Many others were thrust through the breach thus opened. The editors of *IT* were charged with 'conspiracy to outrage public decency', the editors of *Oz* with 'conspiracy to corrupt public morals'. Mr Bennion and his Freedom Under the Law Ltd entered a private citizen's prosecution against Peter Hain for 'conspiracy to hinder and disrupt' the South African rugby team tour. The judge agreed that Hain had illegally interfered with the public's right in 'a matter of substantial, public concern – something of importance to citizens who are interested in the maintenance of law and order'. The Aldershot bombers and the Angry Brigade both had 'conspiracy' added to their charges. So did the Welsh Language Society protestors who did not, in fact, trespass on B.B.C. property; so did the building workers who had so successfully adopted the 'flying-picket' tactic in the disputes of 1972–3. When their defence lawyer pointed out that a conspiracy was hard to prove among the Shrewsbury pickets who had never previously met, Justice Mais reminded him that 'for conspiracy, they never have to meet and they never have to know each other'.[100] For 'conspiring to intimidate lump workers', Dennis Warren received three years – 'a punishment twelve times heavier than the maximum for direct intimidation provided by the statute'.[101]

As Robertson has shown, the conspiracy charge was perfectly adapted to *generalising* the mode of repressive control: enormously wide, its terms highly ambiguous, designed to net whole groups of people whether directly involved in complicity or not, convenient for the police in imputing guilt where hard evidence is scarce, aimed both at breaking the chains of solidarity and support, and of deterring others, directable against whole ways of life – or struggle. Robertson describes its full-flowering in the 'cartwheel' conspiracy, the 'friendship-cell' conspiracy and the 'roll-up' conspiracy, which even Lord

Diplock commented was 'the device of charging a defendant with agreeing to do what he did instead of charging him with doing so'. Professor Sayre called conspiracy a 'doctrine so vague in its outlines and uncertain in its fundamental nature . . . a veritable quicksand of shifting opinion and ill-considered thought'. Lord Hailsham, defending the Karama judgement, however, admitted, 'I personally prefer a bit of common law which is furry at the edges.' [102] The 'furry' law of conspiracy was to play a key role in the industrial conflicts of 1973 and 1974. In that period it was fashioned into an 'engine of state policy'. Its history became – as C. H. Rolph remarked – 'the history of the class struggle and the regulation of wages'. [103]

One might have expected liberal pragmatists, like the police chief Sir Robert Mark, who knows the checkered history of the relationship between the police and political dissent, [104] to have backed off some distance from this overt recruitment of the law. But he continued to advance his charge – against considerable evidence – that acquittals were too high and that criminals were escaping through 'corrupt lawyers' practices', [105] and his criticisms of trial by jury (with some signs of success in, for example, the Report of the James Committee). [106] He accused the magistrates of 'effectively encouraging burglary and crime' and of failing to discourage 'hooliganism and violence in the punishments handed out', [107] and of 'being too lenient with violent demonstrators'. [108] In an appeal to the press to be more critical of violent protest, he said: 'It is arguable, too, that the police, discouraged by apparent magisterial tolerance of unlawful violence by demonstrators and weary of harrassment by complainants, journalists and political movements alike, have themselves been inclined to show excessive tolerance.' When asked about police problems in the sphere of public order, he defined the main problem as 'inconvenience' – coupled with an unscrupulous and violent minority. [109] A period of rising political dissent is clearly a difficult one for the police to handle – and thus one in which the police can only defend themselves against the charge of colluding with repression by the most scrupulous drawing of lines. Instead, in this period, the police and Home Office clearly came to approve, if not to revel in, the steady blurring of distinctions. Emergency legislation like the anti-terrorist legislation drew the police into that ambiguous territory between suspicion and proof. The Lennon affair revealed the murky terrain between overground policing and the activities of the Special Branch. A number of well-publicised occasions revealed the steady drift towards the arming of the British police force. [110] The striking erosion of civil liberties involved, when remarked upon by bodies like the National Council of Civil Liberties, only won the rebuke, from Tory backwoods M.P.s like Mr Biggs-Davison, that the N.C.C.L. should be renamed 'National Council for Criminal Licence'. When the *Daily Telegraph* asserted that 'the Britain we chiefly treasure and the world admires has grown out of an instinct for freedom, tolerance, justice and legitimacy of rule', it was simply moving about the most powerful ideological counters at its command. The practical defence of practical 'freedoms' and 'tolerances' was obviously not its concern.

We have already referred to the appearance, at the high point of class polarisation, of the conspiracy of the 'Red Scare'. This is not, of course, a recent phenomenon. To take this century alone, Lloyd-George had conjured it into existence in the 1919–21 period; it appeared in the form of the Zinoviev letter during the Labour Minority government; at the time of the General Strike; in the Laski affair; it was ubiquitous for a time in the depths of the Cold War; it received overt confirmation in the revelations of Communist penetration of the electrical trade unions; Mr Wilson had resurrected it in the seamen's strike. In the 1974–6 period, it had a virtual field-day. Mr Heath delivered it, in the very person of Mr Arthur Scargill, to an eager television audience in the warm-up to the 1974 election. Since then, it has surged around such prominent figures as Mr Benn and Mr Scanlon; it has shadowed every key election within any union executive of size; it has become part of the common currency in which media political reporters and commentators trade. Any matter affecting the degree of militancy of a strike, or a union election or vote which *might* tip the balance of forces to the left, and thus endanger the 'social contract', has been recast in terms of 'reds in the executive', 'trotskyists under the bed', or 'moderates/extremists'. The tighter the rope along which the British economy is driven, the finer the balance between compliance with and overthrow of the 'social contract', the greater the power the conspiratorial metaphor has exerted over political discourse. Events as apparently unrelated as progressive education at the William Tyndale primary school, indiscipline in the classroom or agitation at education cuts are instantly reduced to the conspiratorial calculus. Any opposition to anything which does not assume the becalmed form of the well-posed parliamentary question is amenable to being reconstituted as the work of a handful of subversives behind the arras. The Labour Party is entirely discussed in terms of subversion by 'left-wing Marxists' in the constituencies; smear stories, like those floated by Mr Ian Sproat M.P. about fellow-travelling Labour Ministers are extensively examined in the press. The B.B.C. helped to sponsor a whole 'Gulag Archipelago' panic on its own, promoting Solzhenitsyn's uninformed views about the West as the basis for a serious debate about the erosion of British liberties.

This collective paranoia of the conspiratorial enemies of the state is only the most overt side of the ideological polarisation into which the country has fallen. Other themes ride high within its matrix of propositions. One is the charge that, despite all appearances, the country has fallen victim to the stealthy advance of socialist collectivism. This theme – with its attractive counter-posing of the 'little man', the private citizen, against the anonymous, corporate tentacles of the state – has won many converts. While it captures something of the authentic reality of an interventionist state under the conditions of monopoly capitalism, what is obscurely thematised within this populist sleight of hand is the slowly maturing assault on the Welfare State and any tendency towards social equality. Long the target of covert ideological attack from the right, this is now, of course, also the space where social democracy, in conditions of economic recession, is itself obliged to make deep surgical incisions. Under the guise of monetarist orthodoxy, the attempt to dismantle the Welfare State has now received the cloak of economic respectability. (Just exactly what monopoly capital will do without an enormous state edifice to ensure the social and political conditions of its survival remains to be seen.) A related theme is the charge that the government and indeed the whole society is now 'run by the trade unions' – a development of the theme, launched in Mr Heath's era, of the unions 'holding the nation up to ransom', which has now also entered public orthodoxy, and which is peculiarly pointed in a period where the survival of Labour depends exactly on the degree to which the unions are in *its* pocket.

A more powerful ideological thrust is to be found in the co-ordinated swing towards tougher *social discipline*, behind which a general turn to the right in civil and social life is being pioneered. For the first time since the New Conservatives swallowed 'Butskellism', there is an open, frontal attack on the whole idea of equality, a shameless advocacy of elitism, and a complete refurbishing of the competitive ethic. Sir Keith Joseph has not hesitated to give this its full philosophical justification, 'For self-interest is a prime motive in human behaviour ... any social arrangements for our epoch must contain, harmonise and harness individual and corporate egoisms if they are to succeed. ... Surely we can accept ... that the least educated classes in the population should be less open to new ideas, more fixated on past experience...? Anyway, conservatism, like selfishness, is inherent in the human condition.' [111] The economic recession has provided the cover for a return to those 'aggressive' Tory themes – 'patriotism, the family, the breakdown of law, and the permissive society'. [112] His *New Statesman* article, with its defence of the small business entrepreneur ('He exercises imagination. ... He takes risks ... he is sensitive to demand, which often means to people') or his earlier Birmingham speech in defence of the traditional family of modest size, moderate habits, thrift and self-reliance, and its noxious assault on 'mothers, the under twenties in many cases, single parents, from classes 4 and 5', 'least fitted to bring children into the world' who are now producing 'a third of all births', articulate a virulent and unapologetic propaganda for what is euphemistically called 'social market values' which few politicians would have risked uttering in public ten years ago. These themes, in which the dismantling of the Welfare State is strongly advanced, are crosslaced by the usual negatives – 'teenage pregnancies ... drunkenness, sexual offences, and crimes of sadism' – all of which can be laid at the door of the welfare philosophy, supported by 'bully boys of the left', cheered on by some university staffs, 'cuckoos in our democratic nest'. [113] The undisguised effort here is to 'reverse the vast bulk of the accumulating detritus of socialism'. The sustained assault on 'welfare scroungers and layabouts' which has developed in the wake of this line of attack is quite consistent with it – a moral backlash against the vast masses of the unemployed reputed to be living on social security on the Costa Brava. It is evident, also, in the wide-ranging counter-offensive against moral pollution led by Mrs Whitehouse and others ('Let us take inspiration from that remarkable woman', Sir Keith advised), cresting in the anti-abortion campaigns, to which Labour has itself partly capitulated. Another arena in which the authoritarian mood is now much in evidence is, as we already noted, that of public education. The backlash against progressive education is in full swing, with the William Tyndale school chosen as the site of Custer's last stand ('Fascinating! More power to you. I believe we can turn the tide', Mr Rhodes-Boyson wrote to one of the William Tyndale affair's main instigators). [114] Mr Boyson – Mrs Thatcher's second in command at Education

– is, of course, one of the most articulate range-riders on this front, advancing the case for elite education and the voucher system, stimulating the panic surrounding classroom violence, vandalism, truancy and falling academic and literacy standards. The whole Welfare State, he says, is destroying 'personal liberty, individual responsibility and moral growth' and 'sapping the collective moral fibre of our people as a nation'. These scares are attributed to 'little gauleiters' who show 'ignorant, frustrated, aimless young people' how to channel 'their frustration into violent action to further revolutionary aims' (Mrs Walker of the William Tyndale school).[115] These themes are skilfully orchestrated, at a high level, by the education Black Papers, manipulators of 'parent power' like Mr St John Stevas. Tory councils, meanwhile, are making stirring last stands (as at Tameside) to halt comprehensivisation and defend the private and elite education sectors to the limit.

What lends this steady drift into an active authoritarian 'social gospel' its political muscle is the emergence, for the first time since the war, of an organised and articulate fraction of the radical right *within the leadership of the Conservative Party itself.* With the election of Mrs Thatcher and her entourage, this fraction no longer belongs to the Tory fringes and back-benches. It has been installed at its intellectual and political centre. Its principal alibi has been the doctrine of tight money, cuts in public expenditure and a return to the discipline of the free market, which is the main anti-inflation plank advanced by the monetarist doctrinaires who have clustered into the Thatcher camp:

> The more governments have intervened to remove economic decisions out of the market and into the political arena, the more they have set group against group, class against class and sectional interest against public interest. The politicization of so wide an area of the country's economic activities has set up strains which are threatening its social cohesion. In short, what the country is now confronted with is not a crisis of the market economy but a crisis of government interference with the market economy.[116]

This goes hand in hand with the defence of the small businessman, lower-middle-class respectability, self-reliance and self-discipline constantly propagated by Mrs Thatcher, Sir Keith Joseph, Mr Maude and the others at the helm of the Tory leadership. Its ideologues are vociferous elsewhere – in Mr Worsthorne's column in the *Sunday Telegraph,*[117] in Mr Cosgrave's *Spectator* – now virtually a Thatcher house-journal – in *The Economist.* It has its more populist ventriloquists in the Clean-Up Television, Anti-Abortion, Festival of Light campaigns, National Association of Ratepayers Action Groups, the National Association for Freedom, National Federation of the Self-Employed, the National Union of Small Shopkeepers, Voice of the Independent Centre lobbies, who give to the new authoritarianism of the right considerable popular depth of penetration in the aroused middle classes and petty-bourgeois sectors.

It is one of the paradoxes of the extraordinary Heath inter-regnum that, in toying and playing, but only up to a point, with extremist alternatives, Mr Heath – an 'extremist' of the *moderate* sort, and probably ultimately a man of the Conservative middle-ground rather than the far right – nevertheless helped to let extremism out of the bag. He appears to have hoped to ride these dangerous forces through to a defeat of the working class, but then to stop short (in the interests of the more centrist Conservative forces, who were also part of his coalition) of a full elaboration of a moral-political programme of the petty-bourgeois right. The spectacle of a head-on collision with the working class – a collision he seemed doomed to lose – frightened away his centrist support in the Party and his industrialist support in business. But the consequence of his defeat, and the disintegration of the bizzarre class alliance which he yoked together in 1970, was to release the genuinely extreme right into an independent life of its own. He and his supporters are now pilloried as unwitting contributors to the drift into 'creeping collectivism'. The Thatcher–Joseph–Maude leadership, in its breakaway to the right, has pulled those floating themes of extremism and conspiracy into an alternative political programme. It says something for the ability of British capital to recognise its own, long-term, best interests that it settled, after 1974, once more for a management of the crisis by its 'natural governors' – a social-democratic Party. But it says something for the transformed ideological and political climate of the exceptional state that those half-formed spectres which once hovered on the edge of British politics proper have now been fully politicised and installed in the vanguard, as a viable basis for hegemony, by the 'other' party of capital, the Conservatives. As the span of Labour's fragile base is eroded, this is the historical 'bloc' poised to inherit the next phase of the crisis. It is a conjuncture many would prefer to miss.

Those who recall the thematics of the 'English ideology' analysed at some length earlier will not have missed the reappearance of what are essentially these great petty-bourgeois ideological themes on the political stage. There is no doubt that, as recession sharpens the competitive instincts, so the petty-bourgeois civil ethic exerts a stronger appeal to the public at large. In the absence of a well-founded and sustained thrust to democratise education, some working-class parents will certainly be attracted by the promises of 'parent power' and the 'voucher system', if by these means they can ensure that rapidly narrowing education opportunities will be channelled to their own children. The old petty bourgeoisie – the small shopkeeper, clerical and black-coated worker, the small salariat and the small businessman – has certainly been squeezed by the growing power of the corporate enterprises, the state and the multinationals. The middle classes have taken a sharp drop in living standards, and may have to bear more before the crisis ends. Of course, these do not constitute a viable ruling-class fraction on which sustained political power from the right could be based. They might provide the vociferous subalterns in such a class alliance – its political cutting-edge; but it is difficult to see with what fractions of capital they could be combined as a way of 'settling the crisis' under the management of the radical right. But a reorganised capitalist interest, determined to drive through a radical economic solution to the crisis at the expense of the working class, operating – as has happened before in European history in this century – behind a rampant petty-bourgeois ideology, the ideology of 'a petty-bourgeoisie in revolt',[118] *could* provide the basis for a formidable temporary *dénouement*. This *regression* of capitalism to a petty-bourgeois ideology in conditions of political stalemate and economic stagnation is one of the features which makes the equilibrium on which the post-1970 capitalist state is poised an 'exceptional' moment.

INSIDE THE YELLOW SUBMARINE

When we first embarked on this study the use of the word 'crisis' to describe the present 'condition of Britain' had not yet acquired anything like its current status. It is now – almost too conveniently – in fashion. When we started our work on the historical context of 'mugging', we found it extremely difficult to enforce this reading of the general situation in relation to our more delimited concerns. Economic recession, in this sense at least, has wonderfully concentrated the mind. It is now *de rigueur* to refer to 'the British crisis', often without specifying in what respects such a 'crisis' exists. It is necessary for us, then, to define how we understand the 'crisis' whose development we have been delineating. First, it is a crisis of and for British capitalism: the crisis, specifically, of an advanced industrial capitalist nation, seeking to stabilise itself in rapidly changing global and national conditions on an extremely weak, post-imperial economic base. It has become, progressively, also an aspect of the general economic recession of the capitalist system on a world scale. The reason for this global weakness of capitalism is beyond our scope. But we must note, historically, that post-war capitalism in general survived only at the cost of a major reconstruction of capital and labour and the labour process upon which the extraction and realisation of the surplus depends: that profound recomposition entailed in the shift to 'late' capitalism. All the capitalist economies of the world undertook this internal 'reconstruction' differently in the period immediately before and immediately after the Second World War; the comparative history of this period of capitalist reconstruction has yet to be written. Britain attempted such a deep transformation, too – on the basis, we suggest, of an extremely weak and vulnerable industrial and economic base; and this attempt to raise a backward industrial capitalist economy to the condition of an advanced productive one created, for a time, the hot-house economic climate and conditions popularly known and mistakenly experienced as 'affluence'. Its success was extremely limited and short-lived. Britain – in these late-capitalist terms – remains unevenly developed, permanently stuck in 'the transition'. The effects of this stalemate position, this uncompleted transition, have been experienced at *every* level of society in the period since. This main, underlying condition is one to which we continually point, in our analysis, but which we cannot, given the scope of our work and our competence, fill out further or develop, or give its proper weight and dimension. Its centrality to the whole conjuncture must not, however, on that account be neglected.

Second, then, it is a crisis of the 'relations of social forces' engendered by this deep rupture at the economic level – a crisis in the political class struggle and in the political apparatuses. Here, the matter is, again, extremely complicated, and we must settle for a simplification – at the point where the political struggle issues into the 'theatre of politics', it has been experienced as a crisis of 'Party', i.e. of both the ruling-class and the working-class parties. Politically, the key question has been what peculiar alliance of class forces, organised on the terrain of politics and the state in terms of a specific 'equilibrium' of forces and interests, is capable of providing hegemonic political leadership into and through 'the transition'. The question of 'Party' is crucial here, in Gramsci's sense: not at the level of the parliamentary game, but at the more fundamental level of the organised political interests and trajectories of fundamental class forces. We have not been able precisely to delineate the succession of historical class alliances which have made their bid for power in this period, nor on the basis of what kinds of concessions such alliances have been constructed. Once again, this history of Parties and blocs (which is something very different from a history of the Conservative or the Labour Party as such, or of the interplay of parties in Parliament) remains to be written. We cannot undertake it here. We can only note that there has indeed been a succession of such historically constructed class 'blocs' since 1945; we need only think of the particular popular alliance which coalesced in the Labour landslide of 1945; of that which underpinned Macmillan's successful period of 'hegemonic rule' in the 1950s: of the quite distinctive alternative class alliances behind which Mr Wilson attempted to return to power in 1964 – 'workers by hand and brain' (including the revolutionaries in white coats and modern-minded managers of capital); and of the peculiar alliance which supported Mr Heath's return to power in 1970. But, without question, the most important feature of this level of the crisis, for our purposes, is the role of 'labourism' – specifically that of the Labour Party, but also the labourist cast of the organised institutions of the working class. Labourism has emerged as an alternative party of capital, and thus an alternative manager of the capitalist crisis. At the most fundamental political level – and shaping every feature of the political culture before it – the crisis of British capitalism *for* the working class has thus been, also, a crisis *of* the organised working class and the labour movement. This has had the most profound effect, not simply in terms of the massive struggle to incorporate the working classes into the capitalist state, and thus as junior partners in the management of crisis, but also in terms of the consequent divisions within the class, the growth of sectional class consciousness, of economism, syndicalism and reformist opportunism. It has been of profound importance that the major strategies for dealing with the crisis and containing its political effects have been drawn in large measure *from the social-democratic repertoire*, not from that of the traditional party of the ruling class. The dislocations which this has produced in the development of the crisis, as well as the resistances to it and thus to the possible forms of its dissolution, have hardly begun to be calculated.

Third, then, it has been a crisis *of the state*. The entry into 'late capitalism' demands a thorough reconstruction of the capitalist state, an enlargement of its sphere, its apparatuses, its relation to civil society. The state has come to perform new functions at several critical levels of society. It now has a decisive economic role, not indirectly but directly. It secures the conditions for the continued expansion of capital. It therefore assumes a major role in the economic management of capital. Therefore conflicts between the fundamental class forces, which hitherto formed up principally on the terrain of economic life and struggle, only gradually, at points of extreme conflict 'escalating' up to the level of the state, are now immediately precipitated on the terrain of the state itself, where all the critical political bargains are struck. Needless to say this 'corporate' style of crisis management, in which the state plays an active and principal role on behalf of 'capital as a whole', and to which, increasingly, independent capitals are subscribed, represents a *major shift* in the whole economic and political order. Its ideological consequences – for example, the role which the state must now play in the mobilisation of consent behind these particular crisis-management strategies, and thus in the general construction of consent and legitimacy – are also profound.

Fourth, it is a crisis in political legitimacy, in social authority, in hegemony, and in the forms of class struggle and resistance. This crucially touches the questions of consent and of coercion. The construction of consent and the winning of legitimacy are, of course, the normal and natural mechanisms of the liberal and post-liberal capitalist state; and its institutions are peculiarly well adapted to the construction of consent by these means. But consent also has to do with the degree and manner of the 'social authority' which the particular alliance of class forces which is in power can effect or wield over all the subordinate groups. In short, it has to do with the concrete character of that form of social hegemony which it is possible at any moment for the ruling classes to install and sustain. Here we come closer to our immediate concerns so far as 'mugging' is concerned. The degree of success in the exercise of hegemony – leadership based on consent, rather than on an excess of force – has to do, in part, precisely with success in the over-all management of society; and this is more and more difficult as the economic conditions become more perilous. But it also has to do with the development of coherent and organised oppositional forces, of whatever kind, and the degree to which *these* are won over, neutralised, incorporated, defeated or contained: that is to say, it has to do with the containment of the class struggle. Here, the matter of periodisation becomes imperative. It seems to us that, however uncertain and short-lived were the conditions which made it possible, a period of successful 'hegemony' was indeed brought about in the mid-1950s (we have tried, earlier, to say on what conditions and at what cost). But this period of consensus begins to come apart, at least in its natural and 'spontaneous' form, by the end of the 1950s. The state is then obliged to draw heavily on what we have described as the 'social-democratic' variant of consensus-based hegemony. We must not allow ourselves to be confused by this. It matters profoundly that, in however 'reformist' a way, the capitalist crisis in the 1960s can only be managed at the 'expense' of recruiting the party of Labour to the seat of management.

> Undoubtedly the fact of hegemony presupposes that account be taken of interests and the tendencies of groups over which hegemony is to be exercised, and that a certain compromise equilibrium be formed – in other words that the leading group should make sacrifices of an economic-corporate kind. But there is also no doubt that such sacrifices and such a compromise cannot touch the essential.[119]

It is, in any event, difficult to know whether this period can in any proper sense be characterised as one of consensus, of hegemony. It is more akin to what we have characterised as 'managed dissensus' – that undisputed social authority which constitutes 'hegemony' in its proper sense is no longer in place. Consent is won, grudgingly, at the expense only of successive ruptures and break-downs, stops and starts, with the ideological mechanisms working at full throt-tle to conjure up out of the air a 'national interest' – on which consensus might once again come to rest – which cannot any longer be naturally or spon-taneously won. This is no longer a period of ruling-class hegemony: it is the opening of a serious 'crisis in hegemony'. And here, of course, not only do the social contradictions begin to multiply in areas far beyond that of the economic and productive relations, but here, also, the varying forms of resistance, class struggle and dissent begin to reappear. There is certainly no over-all coherence to these forms of resistance – indeed, in their early manifestations, they resolutely refuse to assume an explicitly political form at all. The British crisis is, perhaps, peculiar precisely in terms of the massive *displacement* of political class struggle into forms of social, moral and ideological protest and dissent, as well as in terms of the revival, after 1970, of a peculiarly intense kind of 'economism' – a defensive working-class syn-dicalism. Nevertheless, in its varying and protean forms, official society – the state, the political leadership, the opinion leaders, the media, the guardians of order – *glimpse*, fitfully at first, then (1968 onwards) more and more clearly, the shape of *the enemy*. Crises must have their causes; causes cannot be struc-tural, public or rational, since they arise in the best, the most civilised, most peaceful and tolerant society on earth – then they must be secret, subversive, irrational, a plot. Plots must be smoked out. Stronger measures need to be taken – more than 'normal' opposition requires more than usual control. This is an extremely important moment: the point where, the *repertoires* of 'hegemony through consent' having been exhausted, the drift towards the routine use of the more repressive features of the state comes more and more prominently into play. Here the pendulum within the exercise of hegemony tilts, decisively, from that where consent over-rides coercion, to that condition in which coercion becomes, as it were, the natural and routine form in which consent is secured. This shift in the *internal* balance of hegemony – consent to coercion – is a response, within the state, to increasing polarisation of class forces (real and imagined). It is exactly how a 'crisis in hegemony' expresses it-self.

Control comes to be implemented, progressively, in slow stages. It is dif-ferently imposed on the different 'trouble areas' which the crisis precipitates. Interestingly and significantly, it occurs at two levels – both above and below. Hence it assumes the form of a coercive management of conflict and struggle, which – paradoxically – also, has popular 'consent', has won legitimacy. We must not for a moment abandon the specific form in which the British state slides into an 'exceptional' posture. The simple slogans of 'fascism' are more than useless here – they cover up, conveniently, everything which it is most im-portant to keep in view. A society where the state is abrogated through the seizure of state power, by, say, an armed *coup*, in which the repressive forces openly take command and impose by *fiat* and the rule of the gun, official terror and torture, and a repressive regime installed (Chile and Brazil are examples), is quite different from a society in which each step towards a more authoritarian posture is accompanied by a powerful groundswell of popular legitimacy, and where the civil power and all the forms of the post-liberal state remain solidly intact and in command. Again we have few theoretical and analytic tools, or comparative evidence, with which to characterise more deeply the slow development of such a state of *legitimate coercion*. In their absence, we have settled for a more simple, descriptive term: we have called it 'the birth of a law-and-order society'. It is clear, as we look across the water to the United States or to the erection of 'emergency laws' in one Western European country after another, that, despite its peculiarly British features, this is no idiosyncratic British development. The carrying of the law down directly into the political arena has not, of course, gone uncontested – the intense working-class resistance leading to the defeat of the *Industrial Relations Act* and the political destruction of the Heath government marks, in this context, a development of profound significance; but, in many departments of social life, it has occurred steadily, if apparently haphazardly. The whole tenor of social and political life has been transformed by it. A distinctively new ideological climate has been precipitated.

Again, we have tried to trace this movement – the 'social history of social reaction' – through from its earliest manifestations. Schematically, it begins with the unresolved ambiguities and contradictions of affluence, of the post-war 'settlement'. It is experienced, first, as a diffuse social unease, as an unnaturally accelerated pace of social change, as an unhingeing of stable patterns, moral points of reference. It manifests itself, first, as an unlocated surge of social anxiety. This fastens on different phenomena: on the hedonistic culture of youth, on the disappearance of the traditional insignia of class, on the dangers of unbridled materialism, on change itself. Later, it appears to focus on more tangible targets: specifically, on the anti-social nature of youth movements, on the threat to British life by the black immigrant, and on the 'rising fever chart' of crime. Later still – as the major social upheavals of the counter-culture and the political student movements become more organised as social forces – it surges, in the form of a more focused 'social anxiety', around these points of disturbance. It names what is wrong in general terms: it is the *permissiveness* of social life. Finally, as the crisis deepens, and the forms of conflict and dissent assume a more explicitly political and a more clearly delineated class form, social anxiety also precipitates in its more political form. It is directed against the organised power of the working class; against political extremism; against trade-union blackmail; against the threat of anarchy, riot and terrorism. It becomes the reactionary pole in the ideological class struggle. Here, the anxieties of the lay public and the perceived threats to the state coincide and converge. The state comes to provide just that 'sense of direction' which the lay public feels society has lost. The anxieties of the many are orchestrated with the need for control of the few. The interest of 'all' finds its fitting armature only by submitting itself to the guardianship of those who lead. The state can now, publicly and legitimately, *campaign* against the 'extremes' on behalf and in defence of the majority – the 'moderates'. The 'law-and-order' society has slipped into place.

Let us guard, once again, against a conspiratorial reading of this process. Society is massively more polarised, in every part and feature, in the 1970s than it was in the 1950s. Conflicts, repressed and displaced at an earlier point in time, emerge into the open, and divide the nation. The 'crisis' is not a crisis, alone, in the heads of ruling-class conspirators; it is the form assumed by the class struggle in this period. What are important, however, are the distortions and inflections which are endemic to the ways in which this crisis, and the forces of resistance and opposition ranged against it, are ideologically *perceived* and signposted by those in power, and how those mis-recognitions are communicated to, and come to form the basis for, misconceptions of the crisis in popular consciousness. Ideology is an inflection or misrepresentation of real relations, a displacement of the class struggle, not myths conjured up out of fairy stories. The 'ideology of the crisis', which leads to and supports and finally finds its fulfilment in a 'law-and-order' society, refers *to a real crisis*, not to a phoney one. It is how that real crisis is perceived and controlled which contains the seeds of political and ideological distortion. It is, then, finally, a crisis in and of ideology. The 'consensus' ideologies of the 1950s are clearly inadequate for a period of sharpening conflict and economic decline; in general, these ideologies, constructed around the key post-capitalist themes, give way to more embattled ideologies organised around the issues of national unity and 'national interest'. Not only is there, then, a break in the dominant ideological frameworks, but an enormous variety of oppositional and counter-ideologies develop, presenting challenges of varying force, coherence and effectiveness to the taken-for-granted orthodoxies. Such moments of ideological rupture and transformation are never smooth; the ideological 'work' required, shows through; so do the breaks and dislocations. Above all, there is the question of how the progressive polarisation of society and the 'crisis' of capitalism come to be signified and interpreted, within the framework of these competing ideological constructions. It is of the utmost importance to analyse, precisely, the mechanisms through which the tilt in the crisis of hegemony, from consent to coercion, is publicly signified: how it *wins legitimacy* by appearing to be grounded and connected, not simply in myths, fears and speculations, but in the experienced reality of ordinary people. The actual ideological passage into a 'law-and-order' society entails a process of a quite specific kind. Crucially, in the early years of our period, it is sustained by what we call a *displacement effect*: the connection between the crisis and the way it is appropriated in the social experience of the majority – social anxiety – passes through a series of false 'resolutions', primarily taking the shape of a succession of *moral panics*. It is as if each surge of social anxiety finds a temporary respite in the projection of fears on to and into certain compellingly anxiety-laden themes: in the discovery of demons, the identification of folk-devils, the mounting of moral campaigns, the expiation of prosecution and control – in *the moral-panic cycle*. None of these projected 'workings-through' of social anxiety succeeds for long. The 'trouble' about youth is not appeased by the Teddy Boys, and 'mods' and 'rockers' sent down in court; it surfaces again, now about hooliganism, vandalism, long hair, drugs, promiscuous sex and so on. The fears about race are not expiated by a succession of panics about blacks, or catharsised by Powellite rhetoric or calmed by tougher and tougher measures of control on the entry of immigrants. Up it goes again, now about 'the ghetto', or about black schools, or about the black unemployed, or about black crime. The same could be said for a whole number of 'moral panics' about similar areas of social concern throughout the 1960s – by no means excluding that perennial and continuing public panic, about *crime* itself. The first phenomenal *form* which the 'experience of social crisis' assumes in public consciousness, then, is the *moral panic*.

The second stage is where particular moral panics converge and overlap: where the enemy becomes both many-faceted *and* 'one'; where the sale of drugs, the spread of pornography, the growth of the women's movement and the critique of the family are experienced and signified as the thin edges of that larger wedge: the threat to the state, the breakdown of social life itself, the coming of chaos, the onset of anarchy. Now the demons proliferate – but, more menacingly, they belong to the same subversive family. They are 'brothers under the skin'; they are 'part and parcel of the same thing'. This looks, on the surface, like a more concrete set of fears, because here social anxiety can cite a specific enemy, name names. But, in fact, this naming of names is deceptive. For the enemy is lurking *everywhere*. He (or, increasingly, she) is 'behind everything'. This is the point where the crisis appears in its most abstract form: as a 'general conspiracy'. It is 'the crisis' – but in the disguise of Armageddon.

This is where the cycle of *moral panics* issues directly into a *law-and-order society*. For if the threat to society 'from below' is at the same time the subversion of the state from within, then only a general exercise of authority and discipline, only a very wide-ranging brief to the state to 'set things to right' – if necessary at the temporary expense of certain of those liberties which, in more relaxed times, we all enjoyed – is likely to succeed. In this form, a society famous for its tenacious grasp on certain well-earned rights of personal liberty and freedom, enshrined in the liberal state, screws itself up to the distasteful task of going through a period of 'iron times'. The sound of people nerving themselves to the distasteful but necessary exercise of 'more than usual law' to ensure, in a moment of crisis, 'more than usual order', is to be heard throughout the land. Mrs Thatcher puts it one way; Sir Keith Joseph puts it another; the Archbishop of Canterbury brings the authority of the Church to bear on it in still another way; there is a populist and a social-democratic variant of it as well. In these disparate voices we can hear the closure occurring – the interlocking mechanisms closing, the doors clanging shut. The society is battening itself down for 'the long haul' through a crisis. There is light at the end of the tunnel – but not much; and it is far off. Meanwhile, the state has won the right, and indeed inherited the duty, to move swiftly, to stamp fast and hard, to listen in, discreetly survey, saturate and swamp, charge or hold without charge, act on suspicion, hustle and shoulder, to keep society on the straight and narrow. Liberalism, that last back-stop against arbitrary power, is in retreat. It is suspended. The times are exceptional. The crisis is real. We are inside the 'law-and-order' state. That is the social, the ideological content of social reaction in the 1970s. It is also the *moment of mugging*.

IV

10

The Politics of 'Mugging'

This is a book about 'mugging'; but it is *not* a book about why or how muggers, as individuals, mug. Although using such first-hand accounts as exist, it does not attempt to reconstruct, from the inside, the motives or the experience of 'mugging'. There is, undoubtedly, such a book to be written; but there are many in a better position to do so than us. We have deliberately avoided that kind of reconstructed account because we wanted to show 'mugging' as a social phenomenon in a different light. Our aim has been to examine 'mugging' from the perspective of the society in which it occurs. Even in this final chapter, where we come face to face with what 'mugging' means, our aim is not to provide definitive answers, in terms of the individual biographies of 'muggers' and their victims, but to trace out the terrain on which an answer to the question may be sought, and to identify the elements which such an explanation must include.

This requires us to examine the position of the social group with which, in the intervening period between 1972–3 and the present, 'mugging' has come to be ambiguously identified: black youth. Of course, by no means all those convicted of crimes labelled 'muggings' are black. The official statistics for the more recent period, quoted earlier, reveal significant rises in crimes labelled 'muggings' in areas of some cities where there is no substantial black settlement; and the press continues to report 'muggings' by white youths as well as black. Yet few people would deny that, for all practical purposes, the terms 'mugging' and 'black crime' are now virtually synonymous. In the first 'mugging' panic, as we have shown, though 'mugging' was continually shadowed by the theme of race and crime, this link was rarely made explicit. This is no longer the case. The two are indissolubly linked: each term references the other in both the official and public consciousness. Both are identified with certain areas of dense black settlement, especially in the London area. Mr Powell, whose views on these matters have also become more explicit, has remarked that 'Mugging is a criminal phenomenon associated with the changing composition of the population of some of Britain's larger cities.' He told the Police Federation seminar at Emmanuel College, Cambridge, that 'he was fascinated to notice the police had started not merely to say it, but to criticize those who refused to allow so manifest a fact to be stated. . . . To use a crude but effective word, it is racial.'[1] We shall see in a moment the conditions which have produced this identification.

Even so, it is by no means clear exactly what this equation between 'mugging' and 'black crime' *means*. Perhaps more black youths are indeed involved in the sorts of street crime commonly and casually labelled 'muggings'. There is some evidence that this is the case, especially in the official crime statistics. It may also be that any kind of petty crime which involves black youths is invested with the fearsome 'mugging' label. There is some evidence for that, too, in the way snatchings, pickpocketting and pilfering in the street all seem to attract the 'mugging' label. It may be that 'mugging' is now understood to be, typically, a 'black' crime, even when occasionally white youths actually commit it. There is some evidence for that, as well. Thus even the growth in the scale of 'mugging' in some urban areas is not quite the simple 'fact' that it appears. At least two processes seem to be involved here. First, in some urban areas, black youths are – to a degree which it is impossible, from the statistics, to measure precisely – involved in petty crime, including those which are labelled 'mugging'. But second, 'mugging' has come to be unambiguously assigned as a black crime, located in and arising from the conditions of life in the black urban areas. Let us look at this second development first.

RETURN OF THE REPRESSED

As we have shown, 'mugging', imported into Britain as a label for certain kinds of crime in the 1971–2 period, was already connotatively rich in its racial reference. But, in the early period, this aspect was handled discreetly, euphemistically. The mixed ethnic identity of the three boys sent down in the Handsworth case helped to raise this submerged theme to visibility. But, we have argued, even here it is partially over-ridden or subsumed by a 'public image', which at one and the same time evoked and deflected the racial element. This was the image of the 'ghetto area', discussed in the conclusion to Chapter 4. In this phase, 'mugging' and race play an elaborate game of hide and seek.

In the immediate aftermath of the 1972–3 'mugging' epidemic, the term virtually disappears from the headlines. From the autumn of 1974, however, it begins to make, once more, a fitful and sporadic reappearance. It is once again used in a very imprecise way – a catch-all label for mindless hooliganism rather than anything concretely recognisable as 'muggings' in their more classic form. Thus it is linked, for example, with the problem of attacks on bus and underground crews. Some headlines and stories in the period – all taken from the *Daily Telegraph* – illustrate the range:

> Tube Bus Hooligans Get Tough Move (21 October 1974).
> Police Squad Crack Down on Tube Muggers (21 October 1974).
> 'Get Tough with Thugs' Says Transport Chief (5 November 1974).
> Crack Down On Violence Says Elwyn Jones (16 November 1974).
> Television Watch On Tube Hooligans (15 December 1974).
> Bus Violence Talks Plan By Jenkins (31 January 1975).
> Muggers Find Easy Prey On Tube, Say Police (11 February 1975).

The race theme emerges here very unevenly. Some stories refer to soccer hooliganism – a 'white' rather than a black crime. In at least one case the assaulted bus conductor was black, his assailants white. The specification of certain *venues*, however, reactivates earlier and subsequent associations: Brixton, Clapham.

In the same period when black *crime* appears to have a low profile, the confrontations between the police and black youth in the black urban areas are assuming a more open, politicised, form. One of the most reported of the many similar incidents taking place around this time was the Brockwell Park incident. Here the adult black community actively intervened in a contestation between black youth and the police, transforming the incident into a community-wide issue. Briefly, a firework display at Brockwell Park, half a mile from the centre of Brixton, ended in a scuffle, during which a white youth was stabbed. The police arrived at the scene, felt themselves surrounded and outnumbered by a 'hostile' black crowd; shoving, jostling and a punch-up ensued, in which the police constables seemed to lose their cool, became irate, got involved in scuffles with selected blacks in the crowd – some of whom emerged from the melée badly beaten. By the time police reinforcements arrived, one or two black youths had been picked out and charged; the news of these arrests precipitated a prolonged and intense pitched battle between the police and the black crowd in front of the park. Several youths were charged with serious assault offences; the police went for an Old Bailey trial – and, in March 1974, got heavy sentences. Three things distinguished this incident from the otherwise now-routine rehearsal of 'daily life in the ghetto'. First, the polarisation now appeared as between the police and the whole of a black community – including adults. Second, the substantial, organised and political form of the community resistance which accompanied the sentences and appeal – a response which included support demonstrations and a strike of black schoolchildren.[2] Third, the incident had the effect of pinpointing the source of trouble and disaffection specifically in the black urban localities. It *located and situated* black crime, geographically and ethnically, as peculiar to black youth in the inner-city 'ghettos'. This incident prefigured a massive and dramatic news break, at the beginning of 1975, exclusively orientated around the 'black crime in South London' problem. Thus the three themes, subtly intertwined in the earlier treatment of 'mugging' (cf.: our analysis in Chapter 4) were now fused into a single theme: crime, race and the ghetto. Accordingly, from this point onwards, the explanatory paradigms shift, bringing out more explicitly than before the social, economic and structural preconditions of the black crime problem – and thus contributing the final link in the chain which fused crime and racism with the crisis.

The Brockwell Park incident must not be seen in isolation. As early as December 1973, the White Paper on police–immigrant relations had warned of the necessity, in the coming months, to separate 'the great majority of hard-working, law-abiding citizens' from the 'small minority of young coloured people', discontented with the lack of job opportunities and 'apparently anxious to imitate behaviour amongst the black community in the United States'.[3] The 'hard-working' phrase was no casual reference. The evidence accumulated in this period, not only of the substantial size of black youth unemployment in these areas, but of a growing disaffection from 'work' and even a positive 'refusal to work', especially among second-generation blacks: what *Race To-*

day has articulated and developed as the 'revolt of the wageless'. This was also the period in which those immigrants still at work became fully involved in militant industrial action. The prolonged strike at Imperial Typewriters, sustained with considerable militancy by Asian women workers, lasted fourteen weeks in mid-1974, and its effects rippled into the following year.[4]

In January 1975, the 'mugging' panic recommences. A whole new phase of the cycle begins. Derek Humphry prefaced his piece on black crime in South London with the hope that the facts he retold would not be used to feed prejudice.[5] But this was a forlorn hope. The basic problems behind the crime figures, as Humphry saw them – 'poverty, poor housing, lack of jobs and broken families' – were less dramatic or quotable than the fact that street crime in Lambeth 'had tripled in five years and 1974 was the worst on record' or that 'of 203 muggings' in Lewisham in 1974, '172 were committed by black youths'. Although carefully phrased, the article did invite selective quotation by choosing the highly contentious issue of 'crime' as its main point of entry and in its failure to pinpoint the institutionalised nature of the racism which lay behind 'the basic problems'. In any event, it provoked hostility amongst blacks themselves, partly because of how it was taken up. For when the *London Evening News* opened the first of its four-day 'spreads' on the issue, the language and tone were far less guarded, and the qualifications less carefully drawn. The first, on 12 January, was lurid enough: 'The Violent Truth of Life in London'. It opened with a familiar enough comparison: 'You are more likely to be mugged in Lambeth than in New York.' A list of recent incidents followed, with a truncated version of the *Sunday Times* statistics. In fact the *Evening News* features did not wholly live up to their headlines. Although John Blake's piece, on 12 January, centred on 'frightened local residents', it quoted a number of local officials who were anxious not to 'frighten people'; and both this, and other accompanying pieces, gave far greater emphasis than most features in the previous phase of the cycle to 'environmental' causes: 'no play, no holidays, no presents, youngsters get off to a bad start'; 'the growing sense of isolation felt by blacks'; 'trapped between an education system that seems unable to understand their problems and a white society that seems to thrust humiliating identies upon them'. This changed pattern was not universal. When, in the same period, the *Birmingham Evening Mail* returned to the theme – including two front-page leads between December 1974 and January 1975 – its generalised use of the 'mugging' label was indistinguishable from the 1972–3 pattern: 'bullies, muggers, vandals and exhibitionists have made the subways their own'.

But, elsewhere, there *had* been a notable shift in the pattern of signification. The hitherto ambiguous scenario of black crime had been clarified and focused. Its racial delineation is now unmistakable: victims are middle-aged whites; attackers are black; venues are specified parts of South London. Penal policy questions which dominated the earlier debate are largely absent; a *social-problem* perspective has been almost universally adopted.

This shift in emphasis and explanation must be traced back to its sources. What had triggered off the Humphry article was a special report (never fully released to the public) on street crime in South London, prepared by Scotland Yard and passed to the Home Secretary. Both the panic at the soaring figures for black crime *and* the social-problem, environmentalist explanations of crime appear in this report, and in the subsequent official comments made about it. The figures which Humphry and others quoted from the report revealed: first (an important but hitherto unacknowledged fact about the crime statistics), that the police now recorded the race of victims and assailants in such cases for 'operational reasons'; second, a number of scary comparative statistics. These suggested that street crime was almost as high in other South London boroughs as it was in Lambeth and Lewisham; that '80% of the attackers are black and 85% of the victims are white'; that 'theft from the person' offences had already passed the 1972 peak and a significant majority of these were committed by blacks. *But* the report is also said to have argued that 'it is not a policing problem; soaring street crime is caused by widespread alienation of West Indian youth from white society'.[6] And when Commander Marshall, then head of the Metropolitan Police Community Relations Department, commented on the figures, he went out of his way to cite urban stresses, high unemployment, the generation gap, problems of cultural identity and the influence of 'black extremist voices' as contributory factors. Humphry said his interviews confirmed this line of argument: 'Nowadays they reason that there aren't many jobs available and the blacks won't get them anyway' (a quote from a Peckham youth worker, Norris Richards). What is noticeable about this is that two, distinct and apparently contradictory perspectives are being simultaneously adopted: a police–crime-control perspective, and a social-problem perspective. If the rest of the press fastened first on the electrifying figures, few failed to remark that 'For the first time the police have put the population, housing, school and employment statistics alongside their crime data.'

The use of this double perspective – as compared with the different emphases of the 1972–3 period – requires further examination. Polarisation and hostility between the black community – especially youth – and the police in the ghetto areas had continued to grow. But the tempo and character of the black *response* to casual police harassment was changing. The response had become sharper, quicker, tougher – above all, more organised, collective and *politicised*. This politicisation of ethnic consciousness had also become more *localised* in the black areas. Since the early 1970s, the police have been, effectively, responsible for controlling and containing this widespread disaffection amongst the black population, attempting to confine it to the black areas. However, in the period after 1974, this situation of incipient black revolt was compounded by a new set of factors. For the growing economic recession meant that the black work-force – because of its structural position in the labour force, and especially young black school-leavers, seeking employment for the first time – was coming to constitute an *ethnically distinct class fraction* – the one *most exposed* to the winds of unemployment. This was coupled with signs of a growing industrial militancy amongst black workers. What is more, the recession entailed cuts in public expenditure and in the Welfare State – once again, most calculated to bear directly on exactly those inner urban areas which were also areas of high black concentration. Thus a sector of the population, already mobilised in terms of black consciousness, was now also the sector most exposed to the accelerating pace of the economic recession. What we are witnessing here, in short, is nothing less than the synchronisation of the race and the class aspects of the crisis. Policing *the blacks* threatened to mesh with the problem of policing *the poor* and policing the *unemployed*: all three were concentrated in precisely the same urban areas – a fact which of course provided that element of geographical homogeneity which facilitates the germination of a militant consciousness. The on-going problem of policing the blacks had become, for all practical purposes, synonymous with the wider problem of *policing the crisis*. (This conclusion, unfortunately, was fully borne out by the police attacks on the unemployed, during the *Right to Work March* on 19 March 1976.) Face to face with this fundamental change in the character of the policing exercise, it is little wonder that the police and the Home Office were anxious that the full social and economic dimensions of the race problem should be made plain to – and the potential costs of social unrest borne by – that level in the state most responsible for the over-all situation: the government and the politicians. Hence the steps to shift the problem up the hierarchy of responsibility, and to widen its frame of reference – to include, for example, questions of urban aid and remedial social work, as well as questions of crime and public order. It is to this *synchronisation of the different aspects of the crisis*, that the reference to social indicators alongside the crime indicators points. Contrary to what Commander Marshall and others suggested, it was *because* the blacks and black areas threatened to become a policing problem of a much wider kind that the alienating social conditions of blacks suddenly became a 'police' concern.

That also helps to explain the nature of the official response. As the economic recession deepens, there is evidence of a double strategy, to match the double perspectives we saw emerging. Strategies are designed to 'cool the situation out': expanded urban aid programmes, more direct assistance for 'grass-roots' black welfare schemes, the ill-fated Community Development Projects phase, even the most recent targetting of the 'inner rings' for extraordinary economic support by both Mr Shore, the Minister of the Environment, and Mr Whitelaw, his opposite number in the Shadow Cabinet; as well as steps to maintain a tough, abrasive and intense control through intensified street policing specifically in the urban 'trouble-spots'. This combined strategy – focused poverty funding *plus* vigorous policing of public order – defines the precise nature of the period of intensified 'social concern' which the return of the Labour government initiated. Its character was 'overdetermined' from another direction. Labour was probably more sympathetic to the renewed lobbying by community relations, white liberal and race-relations institutions, which were active in pointing up the deteriorating situation in the ghetto areas. But there is strong evidence, precisely in this period, that, as grass-roots and community-based resistance in the black communities developed, so this was paralleled by a loss of credibility, confidence and legitimacy in the professional race-relations agencies, and a passing of the initiative, finally, to more activist, black organisations and to more politicised black strategies. The growth of a black press, with strong roots in the black communities and of black militant support groups in this period is a crucial – and impressive – part of the picture. But this meant that some counter-measures would also have to be taken, higher up the hierarchy, to strengthen the legitimacy of these crucial 'community-relations' mediating agencies between the state and the black community, lest the initiative pass entirely into more militant hands. The maintenance of the urban aid programme, despite the lowering economic climate, and the reconstruction of the race-relations 'establishment' through the new Equal Opportunities Commission, are products of this same cooling and containing strategy. Throughout this period, then – initiated by events in 1974 – the coupling of 'social-control' and 'social-problem' perspectives appears to be flowing from highly contradictory forces within the urban race problem, as it is intensified and pressured by the crisis. However, as the crisis has lengthened and deepened, even this last exercise in 'disciplined containment' has slipped its official bounds, and society has been obliged to take the full measure of the unplanned coincidence of the race–class problem in the framework of a crisis which is slipping beyond control. As is true of every other moment of the long 'crisis in hegemony' which we have been tracing, *race* has come to provide the objective correlative of crisis – the arena in which complex fears, tensions and anxieties, generated by the impact of the totality of the crisis as a whole on the whole society, can be most conveniently and explicitly projected and, as the euphemistic phrase runs, 'worked through'.

Characteristically, that 'working out' began in a British courtroom. Sentencing five West Indian youths to five years' jail or detention, in May 1975, Judge Gwynn Morris, in remarks not exaggeratedly described as 'a declaration of war against young blacks', observed, with reference to Brixton and Clapham:

> Within memory these areas were peaceful, safe and agreeable to live in. But the immigrant resettlement which has occurred over the past 25 years has radically transformed that environment. Those concerned with the maintenance of law and order are confronted with immense difficulties. This case has highlighted and underlined the perils which confront honest, innocent and hardworking, unaccompanied women who are in the street after nightfall. I notice that not a single West Indian woman was attacked. [7]

In the storm which followed this wide and comprehensive attack on the whole black urban population, the Judge tried to suggest that 'I was making no attack on the great majority of immigrants who have settled in this country and have proved themselves to be law-abiding citizens of whom there can be no criticism.' It is difficult, to say the least, to square this gloss with the content of the speech itself. At any rate, whatever the intentions behind the remarks, they marked the opening of what can only be described as a full-scale 'black panic', sustained without ebb or relief through the rest of that year and, at an increasing pitch, through 1976.

In October 1975, the National Front organised a march through the East End; it was specifically directed against *black muggings* – no qualifications, no inverted commas, no hesitation. It was confronted by a counter-march, organised by blacks. The two were kept separate only by dint of vigilant police marshalling. The race issue had entered the streets. Overt fascist organisations, pivotting on the blacks as before the war they had focused on the Jews, had, of course, been fishing in and around the race issue from the early 1950s. The

Mosleyites were active in the Notting Hill race riots of 1958. Anti-immigrant organisations, putting out racist propaganda in plain envelopes, had been tilling the soil of prejudice throughout the 1960s. In 1966, the National Front was officially formed – an amalgamation of five, extreme right groups (the League of Empire Loyalists, the Greater British Movement, the British National Party, the Racial Preservation Society and the English National Party). Under the leadership of John Tyndall and Martin Webster, it has become the most active agency propagating an open racial fascism at grass-roots level. It has been recruiting steadily in working-class and lower-middle-class areas, and in schools. The sale of its publications – *Spearhead* and *British National News* – has been growing. It fielded its first candidate, Mr Fountaine, in the Acton by-election in 1968, and lost its deposit. Since then, however, it has made significant electoral gains. It fought the three succeeding general elections, each time with more candidates, each time advancing its share of the poll. It or its sympathisers won a number of local council seats. Its interventions in the May 1976 local elections (where it fielded 176 candidates in thirty-four wards and collected 49,767 votes) was strikingly successful. In twenty-one wards it topped the Liberal vote. In Leicester, it took 23.2 per cent of the vote; in Haringey, 13.1; in Islington, 9.4. A sympathiser, Mr Read, was elected to the local council in Blackburn. Its support is growing in areas as diverse as London, the West Midlands, Leicestershire, Yorkshire and Lancashire. Dropping the older themes associated with pre-war fascism, the Front has adopted an explicitly racist, anti-immigrant policy, favouring total repatriation and hard-line policies on law and order, combining these with some classical petty-bourgeois themes from the national-socialist *repertoire* – *anti*-bankers, *anti*-big business and the unions, *for* the oppressed 'small man' – which are most calculated to nourish unorganised white working-class resentment during a period of economic recession. It has of course welcomed the publicity, and the contestation involved in street confrontations with black groups and the anti-fascist left organisations. Its small but potent appearance on the political stage (by no means confined to its extra-parliamentary fringes) has been one of the most powerful forces polarising popular sentiments in an openly racist direction. The Front has been in or near each spasm of racism which has sent tremors through the body politic since the beginning of 1976. And 1976 has been a year when no sophisticated arguments are required to show the *inner connections* between the general crisis and the fever chart of racism. It is a situation which tempts one to the most extreme form of economic reductionism, for every movement in the political and economic indicators of the crisis has been instantly accompanied by a lurch in the race index.

It is difficult to communicate, adequately but briefly, the sequence and severity of the race issues which have passed, like seismic tremors, through society in 1976, or the scale, character and intensity of the media coverage, national and local, to which they have been submitted. In March a new survey was undertaken by the Community Relations Branch of the Metropolitan Police and submitted as a memorandum to the Commons Select Committee on Race Relations. Concentrating on Brixton alone, it revealed that victims' observations about the ethnic identity of their assailants tallied with those revealed by the details of police arrests: both indicated that robberies in the area committed by blacks was 'of the order of 80 per cent'.[9] Mr Powell delivered to the Police Federation 'crime seminar' in Cambridge the speech quoted earlier, in which he roundly declared mugging to be the consequence 'of a divided society and associated with social disintegration. . . . Although there are aspects of mugging which are continuous, permanent and old fashioned,' Mr Powell conceded – qualifying only so far as to confirm the general thrust of his remarks – 'this word is describing a particularly new thing. The new thing . . . is connected with the change in the composition of the population of certain of our great cities.'[10] At the same seminar, Mr John Alderson, Chief Constable of Devon and Cornwall, and former Commandant of the Bramshill Police College, proposed that street crime might be combatted with the help of 'patrols by specially trained volunteers who could be drawn from the ranks of the unemployed'. In April and early May came the news that a number of ex-pelled Malawi Asians holding British passports were seeking settlement in Britain. As had been the case with the Ugandan Asians earlier, this news sparked a panic response of considerable depth, systematically articulated by sections of the national press. Since 1973 the immigration regulations concern-ing the entry of Asian dependents had been administered with peculiar stringency at both the Asian and British ends of the immigration chain; the numbers awaiting entry have grown, the complaints about the lengthy in-vestigations preceding permission and the often humiliating procedures at the ports of entry have swelled (e.g. 1722 letters of complaint from M.P.s to Ministers about delays in 1974).[11] But the spectre of a new 'flood' of displaced Asians set in motion a new wave of reaction. This was triggered by a now-classic scapegoat story – the case of the Suleman and Sacranie families, tem-porarily housed by Crawley Social Services in a four-star hotel: a tale which, by fusing the Asian 'floods scare' with the 'panic' about welfare scroungers, provided the perfect alibi for an 'open season' of racist hysteria. The *Sun* broke the story: 'Scandal of £600-a-week Immigrants – Giant Bill for Two Families Who Live In a 4 Star Hotel'. Others followed ('We Want More Money Say £600-a-week Asians': *Daily Mail*, 5 May 1976; 'Migrants Here Just For Welfare Handouts': *Daily Telegraph*, 5 May 1976). 'Another 4,000 Are On The Way', the *Sun* promised. It could be as many as 145,000, the *Daily Express* warned later in the month. 'The Arnolds are selling their terraced cot-tage to get away from Indian Neighbours. The Barringtons tolerate the Singhs in the nextdoor semi,' the *Mail* embroidered, 'but they wish they weren't there.'[12] In this sustained press onslaught, with its interfusion of anti-race and anti-welfare themes, two aspects of the crisis were once again identified.

Into this cauldron Mr Powell lobbed another explosive. In a remarkable *coup*, Mr Powell got hold of and revealed a private Foreign Office report prepared by Mr Donald Hawley, an Assistant Under-Secretary with special responsibility for immigration matters, which argued that the immigration regulations were being broken and undermined in Asia and too loosely applied in Britain, leading to the threat of a 'rising tide of immigrants' from the Asian sub-continent. This report was, in fact, the product of an internal conflict within the government. Mr Alex Lyon, Labour Minister of State at the Home

Office, also with special responsibility for immigration, had long been exercised by the growing queue of Asian dependents and had set out to 'try to get some justice for blacks in this country'.[13] He was sacked from the government for his pains. He argued strongly against the factual basis of the Hawley document, and the Report was in fact sharply and acutely dissected in the *Sunday Times*.[14] But in the Commons debate following the Powell leak, Mr Bottomley, a former Labour Vice-Chairman of the Commons Select Committee, declared 'there is a lot of truth in this report';[15] and most of the press reported this sensational leak under such headings as 'The Truth Will Out' (*Telegraph*), 'Immigrants – How Britain Is Deceived', 'How Britain Is Fooled', 'When the Conning Had To Stop', 'The Vast Queue of People Planning to Surge Into Britain', 'The Great Fiancée Racket' (all five from the *Daily Mail*).[16]

In this period, at last, the whole media coverage of race came in for trenchant and bitter criticism from black journalists and some media analysts.[17] In the Commons debate on the Hawley leak, Roy Jenkins deplored the Powell prognostication that racial violence in British cities would reach Belfast proportions. But the former Labour Whip, Mr Mellish, commented that enough was enough: 'our own people will take action all of us will regret'.[18] On the same day the *Telegraph* reported that, in areas like Brent, Lewisham and Brixton, or Bradford and Liverpool, black unemployment was 'at least twice the national average' and in some parts of London 'immigrant unemployment is as high as 50 per cent'.

In the editorial of 14 May with which the *Birmingham Evening Mail* concluded its week-long feature-wide series on 'Handsworth – The Angry Suburb' the view was expressed that 'angry unemployed black youth ... are the victims of recession, not the causes of it'. The paper invited its readers to blame, instead, those responsible for the drying up of jobs in the West Midlands – 'pig-headed politicians, bad management, Marxist trade unionists, lazy workers and all of us who have been too greedy in our demands'. 'Birmingham,' it assured them, 'has always been a multi-racial city.' In the wake of the Powell *coup*, however, Bill Jarvis, Labour Councillor and Chairman of the West Midlands County Council, issued a call for a suspension of all immigration to the West Midlands area. And, indeed, the race theme had been at breaking point in this area for some weeks preceding the Powell revelations. At the beginning of May, a Mr Robert Relf had placed a 'For Sale to An English Family' sign outside his Leamington home, had been adjudged to contravene the *Race Relations Act* and, having refused the court order to remove the sign, was jailed for contempt. He went on hunger strike. Mr Relf was instantly adopted by the National Front as an emblem of the self-made, self-reliant 'Briton' willing to stand up for race and country – a 'Des Warren of the Right', the Front called him; and the scenes of Relf's various court appearances provided the stage for a series of bitter confrontations between the Front and the anti-fascist and black groups, ending in a pitched battle in front of Winson Green prison. Relf was released, on the judge's discretion, on 21 June, without rescinding on his sign, and to National Front acclamation.[19] British bull-dog individualism had triumphed again. Only later did the *Sunday Times* reveal the depth and self-conscious nature of Mr Relf's racism. 'So, you bloated black pig,' he wrote to an East African invalid receiving social-security benefits he thought too high, 'Well, you odious venereal ridden black scum, if I had my way I would do the state and the other hard-working Englishmen a favour by putting a rope around your fat slimy neck.' [20]

On 4 June, an 18-year-old Punjabi, Gurdip Singh Chaggar, was murdered by a gang of white youths in Southall. This was the culmination of a wave of assaults by white youths on Asian youths, gradually escalating in the early part of the year, and reaching some sort of crescendo in the middle of the 'Malawi-Asians/four-star-hotel immigrants panic'. The Asian community, hitherto stereotyped as the quieter and less militant of the two 'black' communities, erupted in a wave of community protest, as uncompromising in attitude, and, if anything, better organised than similar movements of protest staged by their so-called 'wilder' West Indian brothers. This critical turning-point in the political role of the Asian community — whose consequences have yet to be fully felt in the race struggle in Britain — and the whole sequence of savage attacks leading up to Chaggar's murder, which was its precursor, was subject to little or no serious analysis in the popular press. The 'Asian siege' of the Southall police H.Q., and the 'rampage of vengeance' were, of course, widely front-paged (*Sun, Daily Mirror*). On August Bank Holiday, the traditional three-day Caribbean Carnival in Notting Hill ended in a predictably fierce, open and uncontainable riot between blacks and the police, in which stones and bottles were thrown, the Notting Hill station was besieged, ninety-five policemen injured and over seventy-five people arrested. The long, unending and unendurable conditions of life in the Notting Hill/Ladbroke Grove ghetto, which had been in a state of more or less permanent siege for nearly a decade, culminated in its all-too-predictable confrontation: Notting Hill's *second* race riot in two decades of 'community relations'. In October, Mr Powell proposed that the government should offer each immigrant family a 'head-start' bounty of £1000 in return for repatriation to the homeland. The proposal was presented as a sort of disguised 'aid to developing countries'. As if to instance exactly how, at each turning-point in post-war race relations in Britain, extremist statements have successfully established a new, acceptable baseline for public debate — each one closer to the adoption of an official policy of racial discrimination — the media began to wonder aloud whether there might not just be some enterprising black families willing and anxious to accept such an offer! Then came the announcement: 'Massive rise in muggings shown in Yard reports', mostly attributable to 'second generation immigrant West Indian teenagers without jobs or prospects';[21] followed by Judge Gwyn Morris becoming, yet again, the centre of controversy when he took the unusual step of postponing the sentencing of six West Indian youths (aged 16/17) for robbing middle-aged and elderly white women in South London, in order to consider the 'immense social problem' such 'gangs' created — in the light of the 'hundreds of letters' from 'petrified' women in the area that he claimed to have received.[22] The result of his weekend deliberations — apart from one deferred sentence — were sentences ranging from Borstal to seven years for the 17-year-old 'leader'; and the suggestion that 'perhaps ... some form or other of vigilante corps ... would become necessary'.[23]

As in the earlier period, this new rising cycle of concern about black crime is sustained and punctuated by a sequence of quantitative indicators. Between 1969 and 1973, Scotland Yard reported, 'mugging' in Lambeth had increased by 147 per cent, thefts from the person by 143 per cent. Overwhelmingly, these involved black offenders against white victims. We will not repeat here the general criticism of the crime statistics about 'mugging' given earlier. Figures computed as these were, and released in this form (a form which later attracted the censure of Sir Robert Mark himself for unduly highlighting the ethnic element), provided the 'hard' quantitative basis for spirals of moral concern and corrective control, whatever their factual base, and rapidly became a part of the spiral they purported to explain. In a larger sense, the figures are irrelevant, even if they could be made more reliable than they are. Black youth are clearly involved in some petty and street crime in these areas, and the proportion involved may well be higher than it was a decade earlier. Black community and social workers in these areas believe this to be the case, an impression more reliable than the figures. The question is not, precisely, how many, but *why*? What is the meaning, the significance, the historical context of this fact? This crime index cannot be isolated from other related indices if we really wish to unravel this puzzle. When examined in context, these various indices point to a critical intersection between black crime, black labour and the deteriorating situation in the black areas. Even these must be contextualised, by setting them in their proper framework: the economic, social and political crisis into which the society is receding. These figures relating to the black population rise as the economic and political temperature rises. The shift, then, is not statistical but qualitative. It is a matter for structural, not quantitative investigation.

The most salient feature of this qualitative shift is the *localising* of the problem. 'Mugging' is now unquestioningly identified with a specific class fraction or category of labour (black youth) and with a specific kind of area: the inner-ring zones of multiple deprivation. In this localising movement, the social and economic aspects of 'black crime' become visible, even for the crime-control agencies. The zones which are specified are the classic urban 'trouble spots', presenting problems of welfare support, of crime prevention and control − but also of social discipline and public order. Here, the infamous 'cycle of deprivation' bears in systematically on the poorer sections of the working class and the sinking and casual poor − black and white. These are the catchment areas for the new, as well as the residual, armies of the unemployed. They are where Mrs Thatcher's 'welfare scroungers' and Sir Keith Joseph's 'single mothers' dwell in ever increasing numbers. This is where the squeeze on welfare and public expenditure, on education and social support, most effectively bites. If they are the classic 'crime-prone' areas beloved by the criminologists, they are also − in conditions of deepening economic recession − potential breeding grounds for social discontent. Overwhelmingly, in the large cities, they are also the black areas. And the black population stands at the intersection of all these forces: an alienated sector of the civil population, now also a significant sector of the growing army of the unwaged, and one vulnerable to accelerating social pauperisation. The many harbingers of doom are constantly reminding us that an economic crisis can eat away the supports of democratic class societies, and expose their inner contradictions. These prophecies of a 'Latin American solution' are designed primarily to adorn a convenient political tale; but they are not wholly without substance. Crises can sharpen antagonisms and awaken apparently abandoned defences, as Mr Heath discovered in 1972 and as the Conservatives would soon discover were they to attempt to put the 'social market philosophy' they espouse fully into operation in the middle of a period of soaring unemployment. Crises can dislocate the 'normal' mechanisms of consent and sharpen the class struggle over how and where the costs of crisis management are to be borne. Crises have to be remedied, their worst effects contained or mitigated. They also have to be controlled. To put it crudely, they have to be *policed.* It is a role which the police – sensitive to the erosion of their traditional position as the state's 'keepers of the peace' – perform but do not relish. It may be one reason why they are beginning to talk more openly about its social and economic dimensions. In their different ways, both the government and the Shadow Opposition know it too. The construction of an authoritarian consensus over a wide range of social issue has already provided the platform on which, if necessary, such an initiative could be launched with public support.

Thus, in its location, the crisis now bears down directly and brutally on the 'colony' areas and the black population. Its consequences are contradictory. As lay-offs increase, and the great majority of black school-leavers drift into semi-permanent unemployment, the traditional distinction within the black community between the hard-working majority and the work-shy minority is levelled. At the same moment differences between the black and white poor are exacerbated. This is not a singular trend. In many of the key industrial disputes which 'create' the crisis – in the motor industry, for example – black and white workers have been involved in a common struggle. In fact, a higher proportion of black employed men belong to unions (61 per cent) than their white counterparts (47 per cent). But outside the work situation, the bonds of solidarity are cross-cut by the virulence of a lingering racism. Although the black and white poor find themselves, objectively, in the same position, they inhabit a world ideologically so structured that each can be made to provide the other with its negative reference group, the 'manifest cause' of each other's ill-fortune. As economic circumstances tighten, so the competitive struggle between workers is increased, and a competition structured in terms of race or colour distinctions has a great deal of mileage. It is precisely on this nerve that the National Front is playing at the moment, with considerable effect. So the crisis of the working class is reproduced, once again, through the structural mechanisms of racism, as a crisis *within* and *between* the working classes. It sets one colonised sector against another. The Labour Party, having transformed its local parties long ago into pure, rather inefficient, electoral machines, has no means of political penetration at its command to stem the tide of this effect, even if it were so minded. In these conditions blacks become the 'bearers' of these contradictory outcomes; and black crime becomes the *signifier* of the crisis in the urban colonies.

THE STRUCTURES OF 'SECONDARINESS'

The crisis intensifies the plight of blacks in society, and especially of black youth; but it should not be allowed to conceal the structural forces and mechanisms at work in relation to black labour throughout the whole of the post-war migration period. This is frequently measured in terms of indices of 'discrimination' against blacks on grounds of colour and race. Discrimination is a major fact of life for black people in this society, and its incidence has been widely and frequently documented. But the measuring of discrimination tends to suggest that black men and women are really in no different a position with respect to the key structures of British society than their white counter-parts, with the exception of that – regrettably large – number who encounter discriminatory practices in housing, education, employment or everyday social life. We believe this gives a false picture; for it treats racism and discriminatory practices as individual exceptions to an otherwise satisfactory 'rule'. Instead we want to examine what the regular and routine structures are and what their effects have been over the period, with special reference to black youth.

It is above all the school and the education system which has the principal function of 'skilling' the different sectors of the working class selectively, and assigning blacks to their rough positions in the hierarchy of occupations. It is the education system which reproduces the wage-earner within the class-structured division of labour, distributes the cultural skills roughly appropriate to each sector within the technical division of labour, and attempts to construct that collective cultural identity and disposition appropriate to the positions of subordination and secondariness for which the majority are destined. The school may accomplish this role of 'reproducing the worker', and the conditions of his labour, well or badly: winning compliance or generating resistance. But these differences in performance do not diminish their over-all function in relation to the world of labour and work. Paul Willis has recently argued that even those 'cultures of resistance' which schools appear to generate, despite themselves, among the less academically inclined (whether capable of academic achievement or not – and many of those who do not choose to be, *are* capable), can provide a sort of intermediary cultural space which *enables* the transition into the troubled but subordinate working-class world of low-skilled manual labour to be accomplished.[24] In relation to black youth, the education system has served effectively to depress the general opportunities for employment and education advancement, and has therefore resulted in 'reproducing' the young black worker as labour at the lower end of employment, production and skill. Superficially, it may seem as if there is little difference in this respect between white and black working-class boys and girls. While true as a general tendency, we neglect the specificity of this process at our peril. The education system has a different effect on the two sexes within the working class – reproducing the sexual division of labour as a structural feature of the class-determined social division of labour, and the same must be said for black youth, male and female. In education, the reproduction of educational disadvantage for blacks is accomplished, in part, through a variety of racially specific mechanisms. The 'cultural capital' of this black sector is constantly expropriated, often unwittingly, through its practical devaluation. Sometimes this takes the form of patronising, stereotypical or racist attitudes of some teachers and classrooms; sometimes, the fundamental misrecognitions of history and culture, as much in the over-all 'culture' of the school as, specifically, through syllabuses and textbooks. This is especially the case in those black or nearly black schools in the predominantly black areas which, despite the ethnic identity and culture of their intake, remain 'white' schools, exclusively geared to the reproduction, at a low level of competence, of white cultural and technical skills. Another significant dimension is that of language. Language is the principal bearer of cultural capital, and thus the key medium of cultural reproduction. Measures which could formally be designed to develop additional competences in the spoken and written language of a new, essentially foreign, culture frequently become, instead, the means by which existing linguistic competences are dismantled and expropriated – as 'poor speech'. Instead of standard English being added as a necessary second language to whatever is the version of patois or Creole spoken by the child, the latter are often simply eliminated as sub-standard speech. The resistance to this now going on in many black schools can be measured, in its intensity, by the growth and spread of Caribbean Creole, rather than its disappearance; and this amongst a generation who have never, as their parents did, heard it spoken around them as 'normal talk'. This *resistance through language* marks out the school as, quite literally, a cultural battleground. The massive dislocations and discontinuities of skills and competences at work here are manifest in the disproportionally high numbers of black children assigned, for want of some more effective remedial measure, to the educationally deprived or 'sub-normal' category. [25] Schools which are predominantly black rarely reflect, as a positive choice, the different cultural tributaries feeding into them. Wherever their culture 'of origin', students tend to be inserted through a narrow filter into a single, unilateral, prescribed cultural stream. The spectacle of black children being systematically incorporated into white cultural identities is a representative one. That it is largely an unintended consequence of how they are being 'schooled' in Britain hardly matters.

The links between school, educational achievement and occupational position are well established. These have served, over-all, to assign them overwhelmingly to certain distinctive positions in the work-force. Black workers are a higher proportion of 'unskilled workers' than the total population, and are also over-represented proportionally in the semi-skilled group. They are well represented in what is called 'skilled work' – though the sectoral distribution here is significant, as we suggest below, and there are important concentrations and absences. In all positions above that in the hierarchy of positions, blacks are under-represented. The following general characterisation is broadly accurate: 'Within the working class, they tend to form the lowest stratum, being mainly concentrated in the unskilled and semi-skilled occupations, while indigenous workers are more frequently in skilled jobs'. [26] The distribution of black labour between the different sectors of capital is, however, even more significant. Black labour is heavily concentrated in some sectors of engineering, in foundry work, in textiles, as general labourers, especially in the building trade, in transport, the low-paid end of the service industries, and in the health service. Three types of work are characteristic of their occupational position, especially if Asian labour is included here. The first is small-scale productive labour in sweat-shop conditions, often associated with small or medium capital. This work is characterised by low piece-work rates, low unionisation and fierce competiton between groups of workers. Often whole shops appear to be 'contracted out' to immigrant labour – frequently women who have to receive instructions in their native language. The second type is lengthy hours under the enervating conditions typical of low-skill work in the catering trades and service sectors. Much of this work, though 'service' occupations, is organised on a 'massified' basis (for example, large-scale catering or London Airport cleaning staffs). The third is in the highly mechanised, heavily capitalised, routinised and repetitive assembly-line types of work, often in the 'local' branch of one of the component firms of the large or multinational engineering plants. These are highly capitalised sectors of industry, with an advanced, assembly-line organisation of the labour process, aimed to ensure the maximum exploitation of labour by expensive machinery. Despite these apparently 'advanced' conditions, such work mainly involves the application of relatively low and interchangeable 'skills', and regular shift-work to ensure the steady flow of production. Although this type of 'detailed labourer' is employed in some of the *leading* sectors of modern production – for example, the motor industry – it is exactly the type of labour which has been subject to the merciless processes of 'deskilling' and 'massification'.[27] Contrary to normal expectations, 43 per cent of black workers are employed in plants of over 500 workers, as compared with $29\frac{1}{2}$ per cent of indigenous white workers. 'Almost a third of black workers work shifts, more than *twice* the percentage of white workers.'[28] The substantial presence of black labour in these advanced sectors of modern production reveals the intensity of the rate of exploitation of black labour in general in the economy. Many of the firms involved are international and multinational concerns, with component factories distributed not only over the country but internationally. Here black labour in Britain stands in precisely the same relation to modern international capital as cheap 'white' migrant labour from the southern half of Europe stands to the workers of the 'golden triangle' (the thriving Northern European capitalist countries). In recent years, therefore, black workers, far from being confined to the backwaters of British industry, have constituted a significant sector of its 'vanguard'; and they have been substantially involved in some of the major industrial disputes (in, for example, Fords, Courtaulds, I.C.I., Imperial Typewriters, Standard Telephones, Mansfield Hosiery).

Two processes have been at work here, with the double effect of a major decomposition and recomposition of black labour – a process with highly significant consequences. The first is the more immediate impact of recession and unemployment. As the recession has deepened, unemployment has become a feature of crisis-ridden British industry, with an immediate impact on black labour already resident in Britain. Figures from the Department of Employment suggest that 'immigrant unemployment may be running at twice the national average of 5.5 per cent ... having grown by a correspondingly faster rate, since 1975'.[29] Unemployment among black school-leavers is four times the national average, and in many urban areas over 60 per cent of recent school-leavers are now without work. This shortage of employment opportunities has the effect of forcing blacks further down in the hierarchy of skilled occupations. If and when the recession ends, it is highly likely that the general position of blacks in the labour force will have deteriorated over all in comparison with indigenous workers.

The second process is more long-term, but in the end more significant. In the early 1950s, when British industry was expanding and undermanned, labour was sucked in from the surplus labour of the Caribbean and Asian subcontinent. The correlation in this period (and indeed throughout the whole cycle) between numbers of immigrant workers and employment vacancies is uncannily close. In periods of recession, and especially in the present phase, the numbers of immigrants have fallen; fewer are coming in, and a higher proportion of those already here are shunted into unemployment. In short, the 'supply' of black labour in employment has risen and fallen in direct relation to the needs of British capital. Black labour has literally been sucked in and expelled in direct relation to the swings and dips in capital accumulation.

In this process, economic, political and ideological factors converge. What has principally governed the 'flow' of black labour is the underlying rhythms and requirements of British capital. But what has *regulated* the flow is, of course, legislative (i.e. political) action. And what has prepared the ground for this use of black labour as a fluid and endlessly 'variable' factor in British industry is the growth of racism (ideology). Here the position of black labour needs to be set against the much wider context of the recomposition of sectors of capital itself. Increasingly, capitalist Europe as a whole has come to depend on the migrant labour system from southern Europe – Italy, Portugal, Spain, Turkey, North Africa. These 'guest workers' are extremely cheap economic units, since they are not resident, do not bring their dependents, and live that temporary existence so graphically described in John Berger's *Seventh Man*. [30] They are recruited in the prime of their productive life. But advanced capital bears none of the costs of the reproduction of their labour power. Not only can their 'flow' be more finely tuned and regulated to the manpower needs of industry in the advanced sectors, but their impermanency, dependency and isolation make them a vulnerable and docile labour force, easily organised into assembly-line conditions. The British pattern up to the mid-1960s was different, and represented a 'worse' deal for Britain as compared with other European countries, for *its* migrant labour force were settlers, with citizenship rights, and dependants, and Britain became responsible for the 'reproduction costs' of this labour force (education, health and pension rights, etc.). Immigration legislation from the mid-1960s onwards must therefore be understood as an attack on the citizenship rights and status of black workers, as the precondition for a tighter regulation of the migrant labour supply. Thus the series of legislative acts in the immigration field has lowered and tightened requirements for specific skills: the severe restriction on the entry of dependants; a transformation of the status of migrant labour – through the patrial/non-patrial and Old/New Commonwealth distinctions – from that of settler to that of 'guest worker'. In the same period, as the flow of black labour has been severely restricted, there is a sharp upturn in the vouchers being given to 'proper aliens' – i.e. 'guest workers' from the poorer European countries. As Sivanandan has succinctly put it: 'those who came from the Commonwealth before the 1971 Act ... are not immigrants, they are settlers, black settlers. There are others who came after the Act; they are simply migrant workers, black migrant workers.'[31] The political restrictions on blacks, the growth of racist ideology and of explicitly anti-immigrant organisations, the toughening of social discipline in the areas of black residence, the general 'unsettling' of the black population cannot therefore be attributed solely to 'discriminatory attitudes' on the part of particular individuals or employers. It is a structural feature of the way in which black labour has been subsumed into metropolitan capital in the post-war period. As has happened before, the conditions of economic recession are being used to drive through a major *recomposition* of black labour by capital itself, through the political and ideological forces aligned with its long-term 'needs'. There is therefore no point in trying to understand the position of black workers and their labour in terms of the immediate contingencies of 'discrimination'. What we are dealing with here is a structural feature of modern capital, and the pivotal role which black labour now plays in the metropoles of capital in a major phase of its recomposition. Castles has recently argued that what we have sketched here represents a *structural* tendency of monopoly capital (though one would have to set it in the context of earlier migrations, and of the movement in and out of employment of female labour to be able to assess precisely how new the phenomenon is).[32] He adds that migrant labour now provides the sector of labour subject to the *highest* rate of exploitation – a feature made more relevant in a period of monopoly, with the pronounced tendency in this phase of the rate of profit to fall. Migrant labour in general is therefore closely integrated with the cyclical movements of expansion and recession of a type of capitalist production which is heavily capitalised (i.e. with a high rate of the organic composition of capital). It is also, he suggests, playing a critical role as a disinflationary factor in periods of capitalist recession – one of the pivotal mechanisms of crisis management in an economy characterised by 'slumpflation'.

The residential concentration of the black immigrant population is one of the most significant features of their structural position. West Indian workers are overwhelmingly concentrated, of course, in the inner-city areas where, alone, relatively cheap housing, tenable in a multioccupancy fashion, was available in the early days as rented accommodation. Subsequent migration has tended to reinforce this pattern. So have such other factors as the search for friendship, kinship and solidarity links, the gap between the low wage levels of blacks and the soaring cost of housing in other areas, the housing policies of the inner-city Councils and the discriminatory practices of some house agents and mortgage companies. The decline and neglect of property by absentee owners, making a short, speculative profit on a deteriorated housing stock, and the strong-arm tactics of extortionate landlords – sometimes, themselves, immigrants, and, whether black or white, exploiting the vulnerable position of the black family – have been constant features of the housing condition of the majority black population. During the housing price inflation of the 1970s, landlords, hemmed in by new legislation with respect to rented accommodation, often found it easier to demolish and develop these properties, or sell for redevelopment, thereby promoting further the decline in the availability of rented property in exactly the housing market most relevant to the black family. It has become even more difficult than hitherto to secure decent accommodation for single black men and women, or for new families to make a start in the housing market. [33] As the housing situation of black adults has worsened, so the situation of single young black men or women, seeking to leave home, has deteriorated at an even faster pace. Young black adults on their own find decent accommodation at modest prices virtually impossible to obtain; in any event, as a higher and higher proportion of them are unemployed, they cannot pay the rents asked for, even where they are 'reasonable'. The growing phenomenon of 'drifting on to the streets', sleeping rough and of 'homelessness' and squatting has thus been underpinned by the structural position of blacks in the housing markets of the contemporary British industrial city.

In each of the structural areas dealt with so far, we can see that the general way in which class position and the division of labour is reproduced for the working class as a whole assumes a specific and differentiated form in relation to the stratum of black labour. There are specific mechanisms which serve to reproduce what almost appears to be a 'racial division of labour' within, and as a structural feature of, the general division of labour. Not only are these mechanisms race-specific; they have a differentiated impact on the different sexes and generations *within* the black labour force. Thus they serve to underpin and support the political fragmentation of the class into racially segmented classes or class fractions, and to set them in competition with one another. It is therefore important to see race itself as a structural feature of the position and reproduction of this black labour force – as well as an experiential category of the consciousness of the class. Race, for the black labour force, is a critical structure of the social order of contemporary capitalism.

History plays a significant part in this story. The period of commercial colonial exploitation, followed by the period of military and economic imperialism, served an important function in securing Britain's past and present economic position. It also imprinted the inscription of racial supremacy across the surface of English social life, within and outside the sphere of production and the expropriation of the surplus. The debate as to whether the British working class as a whole, or, if not, then at least an 'aristocracy of labour', benefited economically out of 'high imperialism' continues. It is certainly the case that colonialism, as well as establishing internal relations of opposition and competition within the British working class (for example, between workers in the cotton industry as against other sectors), also set in motion relations of opposition between the British metropolitan working class as a whole and the colonial work-forces. Further, the imperial period provided the dominant classes with one of the most effective and penetrating ideological weapons with which, in the divisive period of class conflict leading up to the First World War, they sought to extend their hegemony over an increasingly strong, united and confident proletariat, especially through the ideologies of popular imperialism and race superiority. During the decline of the Empire and the rise of post-war national independence movements, these 'colonial relations' were internalised through the importation of immigrant labour. The differentiated structure of class interests between the British and the colonial working classes was then, in a complex manner, reproduced within the domestic economy by the use of imported immigrant labour, under conditions of full employment, often to fill jobs which the indigenous work force would no longer do. Capitalism has continued to reproduce labour in this internally divided form to this day. One significant aspect of this process in the post-war period has been the advantages won in struggle by the more advanced sectors of the white domestic labour force at the expense of the black. Race is one of the main mechanisms by which, inside and outside the work-place itself, this reproduction of an internally divided labour force has been accomplished. The 'benefits' which have also accrued to the dominant classes in Britain, in the light of this history, must therefore be reckoned to include not only the direct and indirect exploitation of the colonial economies overseas, and the vital supplement which this colonial work-force made to the indigenous labour force in the period of economic expansion, but also the internal divisions and conflicts which have kept that labour force segregated along racial lines in a period of economic recession and decline – at a time when the unity of the class as a whole, alone, could have pushed the country into an economic 'solution' other than that of unemployment, short-time, cuts in the wage packet and the social wage.

We have briefly discussed the way different structures combine so as to 'reproduce', in a specific historical form, that black proletariat of which black youth in the cities is a highly visible and vulnerable fraction. We want to stress that we have been concerned with something rather different from the cataloguing of discriminatory practices based on racist stereotypes and attitudes which, throughout, tend to mark the social relations between different ethnic groups – however wretched, demeaning and dehumanising such attitudes are. Our stress also differs from the critique of 'institutionalised racism' which is often made – though the facts certainly support the argument that racism is *not* restricted to the level of social relations and attitudes, but is built into the fabric of such institutional domains as the housing and employment markets (that is to say, racism is a systematic feature of the way these markets function, and is not simply to be ascribed to the 'racist outlook' of the personnel who administer them). However, we have been pointing to the way the different structures *work together* so as to reproduce the class relations of the whole society in a specific form on an extended scale; and we have been noting the way race, as a structural feature of each sector in this complex process of social reproduction, serves to 'reproduce' that working class in a racially stratified and internally antagonistic form. We therefore want to distinguish our approach from the many types of environmental reformism which (as we noted earlier in our review of the mass media) treat structures which are in fact inextricably connected as separate and discrete sets of institutions, and which understands these structures, not in terms of the task which they perform in reproducing the objective social conditions of a class, but in terms of their incidental (and thus eminently reformable) 'discriminatory personal attitudes'. We are concerned with the structures which, working within the dominant 'logic' of capital, produce and reproduce the social conditions of the black working class, shape the social universe and the productive world of that class, and assign its members and agents to positions of structured subordination within it. We have tried to show that the structures which perform this critical task of 'reproducing the conditions of production' for the British working class as a whole also work in such a way as to produce that class in a racially divided and fragmented form. Race, we have argued, is a key constituent of this reproduction of class relations, not simply because groups belonging to one ethnic category treat other groups in a racially discriminatory way, but because race is one of the factors which provides the material and social base on which 'racism' as an ideology flourishes. Race has become a crucial element in the given economic and social structures which each new generation of the working class encounters as an aspect of the 'given' material conditions of its life. Black youth, in each generation, does not begin as a set of isolated individuals who happen to be educated, to live and labour in certain ways, encountering racial discrimination on the path to adulthood. Black youth begins in each generation from a given class position, produced in an objective form, by processes which are determinate, not of their making; and that class position is, in the same moment, a racial or ethnic position.

But race performs a double function. It is also the principal modality in which the black members of that class 'live,' experience, make sense of and thus *come to a consciousness* of their structured subordination. It is through the modality of race that blacks comprehend, handle and then begin to resist the exploitation which is an objective feature of their class situation. Race is therefore not only an element of the 'structures'; it is a key element in the class struggle – and thus in the *cultures* – of black labour. It is through the counter-ideology of race, colour and ethnicity that the black working class becomes conscious of the contradictions of its objective situation and organises to 'fight it through'. This is especially so now for black youth. It is race which provides the mediated link between the structured position of secondariness and subordination which is the 'fate', the 'destiny' inscribed in the position of this sector of the class, and the experience, the consciousness of their being second class people. It is in the modality of race that those whom the structures systematically exploit, exclude and subordinate discover themselves as an exploited, excluded and subordinated class. Thus it is primarily in and through the modality of race that resistance, opposition and rebellion *first* expresses itself. At the simplest, most obvious and superficial level, one can catch this centrality of race for the structures of consciousness in the immediate accounts and expressions of young black men and women themselves: how race structures, from the inside, the whole range of their social experience. Here, for example, is Paul, aged 18, talking about work:

> You always get this thing like when I went for a job up the road and the man he says: 'You don't mind if we call you a black bastard or a wog or a nigger or anything because it's entirely a joke.' I told him to keep his job. Him say, 'I'm not colour prejudiced' and everything like this. But it's foolishness when a man asks a question like that straight away.

Or Leslie, talking about Paul's experience:

> Paul here went for a job and the white man says, you've got an afro haircut and you've got to change your hairstyle. If it had been me I'd have kicked him down. I'd have kicked him rassclatt down. I'd have kicked him in his

c—. F—ing bastard. I don't want to work for no white man. Black people have been working for them for a long time. I don't want to work for them. I never used to hate white people. I still don't hate all of them. But it's them who teach me how to hate.[34]

CULTURE, CONSCIOUSNESS AND RESISTANCE

We turn now to examine more fully this second qualitative dimension: changes in consciousness, ideology and culture, in the modes of black resistance and rebellion. Here, it is important to note once again the different position which black West Indian youth occupy as compared both with their own parents and with their Asian counterparts. Asians, male and female, inhabit a similar *structural* universe to that outlined for West Indian workers earlier. In some ways – through the mechanisms of physical separation in 'Asian' factories, etc. – Asians have been subject, if anything, to a more systematic exploitation on racial lines. Perhaps, as a consequence, their mode of struggle assumed an organised collective industrial form at an earlier stage. However, Asian 'migrant' culture is the product of a different colonialism and dependent economy than that of the Caribbean. Through early transplantation, slavery and plantation society, the latter suffered a more severe process of cultural fragmentation. Asian culture is, therefore, more cohesive and supportive for its youth. In addition to Asians employed in productive labour, there is a significant independent sector – merchants, shopkeepers, small traders – and this sector holds out to its youth a wider range of possible types of employment, including that of the independent self-employed, than is available to West Indian youth. There are, however, clear signs that these distinctions are beginning to break down in the second generation. The position of black Afro-Caribbean youth today also differs in a significant way from that of first-generation migrants from the Caribbean. The fate of the Caribbean labour force – the employed, as well as the seasonally or permanently unemployed – has long been linked with the economy of the metropolis. The economic depression of the inter-war period – coupled with the long decline of West Indian sugar, the major economic export crop – hit the Caribbean later than it did Britain. The men and women attracted to a labour-hungry British economy in post-war conditions, were, in many ways, the reverse side, the alternative face, of metropolitan post-war prosperity: the colonial unemployed, the casual labour and the unemployed of the Caribbean city, rural workers from the plantations, subsistence farmers drawn from the rural masses of the hinterland. Un- and under-employment is a general and apparently permanent feature of their material condition of life. Driven into emigration by endemic colonial poverty, in desperate need for the economic and social rewards their own native islands could not provide, they were massively disciplined on entry, by the wage. Darcus Howe quotes a telling excerpt from an issue of *Punch* (21 August 1965) in which the ruthless logic of capital with respect to black labour in the early period was exposed:

Every immigrant represents a store of capital. It costs £4,000 to raise, educate and train a person for productive employment and this sum is transferred as a free export wherever migration takes place. . . . Britain, with full employment and an immense programme of rebuilding to be tackled, needs immigrants urgently. We have a population of 50 million, a working population of 25 million and it is this productive group that feeds and clothes and shelters all our children and pensioners. Each new immigrant at work helps provide for the unproductive half of the population. Ask the Germans how they have managed to win prosperity from the shambles of 1945. Hard work? Yes. But with a labour force strengthened by millions of immigrants. [35]

The wage was low but the discipline was rigorous. The immigrants found jobs, albeit often the worst and lowest paid. They found accommodation somewhere, albeit sub-standard and decaying, in the inner rings. They settled into an inhospitable climate and an inhospitable culture to 'make a life for themselves'. Heavy work in the factories; long hours and hard stints in London Transport; hot, laborious work for women in the kitchens and other service industries; labouring; sweeping up; low-skill factory labour. It is a dramatic and searing episode in the history of the 'remaking' of the Caribbean working class. In this period, its fate is systematically overdetermined by labour and wages, wages and labour. Nevertheless, in the areas of high black concentration – in Paddington, or Brixton, or Moss Side – alongside the rigours of black labour, the life of Caribbean labour in the 'colony' slowly began to flourish. In the respectable working-class West Indian home, this was often at first a private affair: curtains drawn against the cold and the dark; discreet comings and goings against the prying eyes of neighbours; women muffled up going out to the shops after work; children hustled in from school out of the gloom; winter evenings that started at four o'clock. But in some areas a more variegated 'colony' culture began to take shape, expressing not only the modest achievement of the 'respectables', but the more colourful, more native indigenous rhythms of the urban unemployed, the semi-employed, the club keepers and domino men. In these places a little bit of the West Kingston shanty-town or native Port of Spain was recreated:

> The gambling house where para-pinto (the Jamaican dice game) reigned supreme was an institution in which the wage of the worker circulated into and through the pockets of the unemployed. . . . West Indians actually engaged in direct production found an alternative to the well-defined hours of the public house and the bingo halls, institutions which were governed by state laws and meant to be in harmony with the working day. Thus the gambling hours of the shebeen operating outside and contrary to the rhythm of the working day and independent of state laws proved to be a major obstacle to capital's tendency to control the worker not only in the factory but through every hour of his life. By 1955 these institutions were well established in Notting Hill. . . . By 1957 a newspaper headline screamed 'Black Men, Brothel Keeping And Dope' and called for 'tighter supervision on the rash of clubs emerging in the West Indian community'. [36]

Then came the first, overtly racist onslaught on the West Indian community, the 1958 race riots. We have discussed this historic turning-point in the post-

war history of Caribbean labour in Britain in more detail elsewhere. It is important simply to recall here only the fact that, though the brawling, stone-
throwing and insults on the street, the breaking of windows and daubing with
swastikas of the doors of West Indian homes, was spearheaded by white
youths, egged on in a carefully planned intervention by the organised fascist
movement, the riots represented a major break in the 'friendly relations', not
simply between black people and the Teddy Boys, but between the black and
white communities. It thus marked the watershed between black aspirations for
an accommodated settlement – the policy of 'live and let live' – and the tangible, harsher reality. 'Notting Hill' not only presented the spectacle of the black
community under siege – leading to the first organised political response by the
black community, the rallying of local West Indian organisations and groups;
it also introduced the police – and quickly afterwards, fears of police discrimination – as a control force directly into the black neighbourhoods, establishing a presence from which they have never withdrawn.

By the end of the 1950s, though it remained an objective of liberal social
policy, the strategy of *black assimilation* had already been ruled out, for the
great majority of blacks, as a realistic mode of survival. Blacks could not
become 'white' men and women, in looks, style, culture, even if they wanted to
– and few did. They could not, partly because it is simply not possible for a
group or class to shed its cultural identity just by thought; partly because objectively, they stood on very different terrain, had been assigned to a significantly different social and economic universe, from those sectors of the white population who would have had to provide the models of assimilation; and partly
because the white society to which they would have had to assimilate did not,
in any case, want it to happen in practice, whatever their leaders and
spokesmen said. Lower down the scale was the strategy of *acceptance*. Acceptance meant the black community taking on and accepting as given the proffered role of second-class citizen; it also entailed the white community being
willing to accept that blacks, who would remain different and distinct, lived
amongst them. What was principally at issue in this compromise solution was
the *differential incorporation* of the black community into the white respectable working class. Its outcome would have been, not fusion with, but 'informal segregation' within, the culture of a subordinate class. Many West Indian
families settled, with more or less degrees of success, for this negotiated solution, in the first generation. These included the vanguard, hard-working West
Indian families of the transition period: struggling in their own ways, but
alongside their white respectable counterparts, within the discipline of the
wage, to make a 'decent life' for themselves and their children, keeping themselves to themselves. It was not much of a life, but it could be endured in the
belief that the experience of rejection and relative failure was not necessarily
the systematic fate of their race, and that 'the children' would have a chance of
succeeding in ways in which their parents were destined to fail. This is the now
wellworn path of unending black patience.

Another possible strategy was to develop and extend the *separateness* and
marginality endemic in the 'acceptance' solution into something fuller. But for
a 'West Indian Culture' to take root and survive in Britain, it required a solid

framework and a material base: the construction of a West Indian enclave community – the birth of *colony society*. At one level the formation of the ghetto 'colony' was a defensive and corporate response. It involved the black community turning in upon itself. This emphasis on defensive space becomes more pronounced in the face of public racism, which rapidly developed in the society outside the boundaries of 'the colony' through the 1960s. 'Colony life' was, in one of its manifestations, simply a defensive reaction – a closing of ranks – against official racism, punctuated by the 1964 Smethwick election, the anti-immigration legislation of the mid-1960s, Powellism and the birth of the repatriation lobby. In another sense, the foundation of *colony society* meant the growth of internal cultural cohesiveness and solidarity within the ranks of the black population inside the corporate boundaries of the ghetto: the winning away of cultural space in which an alternative black social life could flourish. The internal colonies thus provided the material base for this cultural revival: first, of a 'West Indian consciousness', no longer simply kept alive in the head or in memory, but visible on the street; second (in the wake of the black American rebellions), of a powerful and regenerated 'black consciousness'. Here began the 'colonisation' of certain streets, neighbourhoods, cafés and pubs, the growth of the revivalist churches, mid-day Sunday hymn-singing and mass baptisms in the local swimming baths, the spilling-out of Caribbean fruit and vegetables from the Indian shops, the shebeen and the Saturday night blues party, the construction of the sound systems, the black record shops selling blues, ska and soul – the birth of the 'native quarter' at the heart of the English city.

The reconstruction of the black 'colony' opened up a new range of survival strategies within the black community. The majority survived by going out from the colony every day to work; but others survived by taking up permanent residence inside the ghetto. The wages of respectable black labour now tended more and more to circulate back through the black 'colony' itself, and thus to provide the economic basis for a distinctive black social world. The 'colony' also provided the material and social basis for a new kind of consciousness – an internally generated black cultural identity. Black people were struggling hard to make ends meet, permanent migrants in a land not their own – but they were no longer apologetic for being what they were: West Indian people, with a homeland and a patrimony, and black with it. As one West Indian girl said: 'If they call me a black bastard I say "I'm black and I'm proud of it, but a bastard I am not." ' [37]

'Colony life' also opened up the possibility of modes of survival *alternative* to the respectable route of hard labour and low wages: above all, that range of informal dealing, semi-legal practices, rackets and small-time crime classically known in all ghetto life as *hustling*. The hustle is as common, necessary and familiar a survival strategy for 'colony' dwellers as it is alien and strange to those who know nothing of it. It is often, erroneously, thought to be synonymous with professional crime. Liberal opinion has frequently drawn attention to the fact that black people were proportionally under-represented in the annual crime figures. But in the later 1950s and early 1960s, the 'colony' comes to be identified with *a particular range* of petty crimes, of which the most common were brothel-keeping, living off immoral earnings and drug-pushing. Darcus Howe quotes a Home Office memorandum of March 1957 which required the police to provide evidence as to 'large-scale crime', the 'degree of mixing with white people', the 'facts of illegitimacy', 'brothel management' and the 'conditions in which they live' in the black 'colonies'. [38] He also recalls that when the Home Secretary made his statement on the 1958 race riots he prefaced it with a reference to 'difficulties' arising 'partly through vice', and suggested that the government might take powers to deport 'undesirables'. This distinction between respectable blacks and the 'undesirable element' has become a commonplace in the syntax of race (it echoes such earlier attempts, discussed above, to drive a wedge between different sectors of a class, such as between the 'deserving poor' and the 'dangerous classes' early in the nineteenth century, and between the 'respectable working class' and the 'residuum' at the end of the century). However, like the simple identification of 'hustling' with crime, this distinction between 'good blacks' and 'undesirable blacks' distorts the nature of the option which hustling offers to those condemned to live in the 'colony'.

Hustling is quite different from professional or organised crime. It certainly takes place on the far or blind side of the law. Hustlers live by their wits. So they are obliged to move around from one terrain to another, to desert old hustles and set up new ones in order to stay in the game. From time to time, 'the game' may involve rackets, pimping, or petty theft. But hustlers are also the people who sustain the connections and keep the infrastructure of 'colony' life intact. They are people who always know somebody, who can get things done, have access to scarce goods, who can 'deal' and service the less-respectable 'needs' of the respectable end of 'colony' society. They hang out around the clubs, organise the blues parties, set the domino game up, know what day the illegal white rum distilleries produce. They work the system; they also make it work. They are indispensable to the 'colony'; for unlike those who live in the 'colony' but work elsewhere, they have chosen to live in, and survive off, the 'colony' itself. By giving up steady and routine work, they settle instead for the upswings and dips of a more unsettled economic existence. When the going is good, hustlers are men about the street *with style*, visibly displaying their temporary good fortune: 'cool cats'. But very few succeed for long in the game. Malcolm X, one of the most famous of all ghetto hustlers, recalls returning, after his 'conversion' from the life of the streets to Elijah Muhammad, to his old haunts and:

> hearing the usual fates of so many others. Bullets, knives, prison, dope, diseases, insanity, alcoholism ... so many of the survivors whom I knew as tough hyenas and wolves of the streets in the old days now were so pitiful. They had known all the angles but beneath that surface they were poor, ignorant, untrained black men; life had eased up on them and hyped them. I ran across close to twenty-five of these old-timers I had known pretty well, who in the space of nine years had been reduced to the ghetto's minor, scavenger hustles to scratch up room rent and food money. Some now worked downtown, messengers, janitors, things like that. [39]

Malcolm was writing about Harlem, the best-established, most prosperous and organised of U.S. ghettos.

In the English 'colonies' of the 1950s and 1960s, there were no lush pickings for those committed to working the street. A certain style there was; and we should not underestimate what highly charged cultural capital the style of 'being cool' and 'doing well' provides for men surrounded by the all-too-evident signs of people struggling to survive in a more respectable way, and just making ends meet. Drifting, unemployment and homelessness, with little or nothing romantic about it, was more characteristic of English hustling than Malcolm's zoot suits and conservative banker's shoes. In the English 'colony', there are fewer full-time and seriously successful hustlers. 'Hustling' should be seen more as a 'survival strategy'. By far the largest number involved are those who simply cannot get steady work; they are into hustling because they are the unemployed sectors of the class – the advance party of black labour's 'reserve army'. For this group, small-scale or incidental crime, or involvement in the rackets, is the difference between survival and starvation. The numbers in the 'colony' living off hustling has therefore increased steadily with the rising curve of black unemployment. Another class of person drawn into hustling are those who simply cannot or will not subject themselves to steady, routine kinds of labouring for 'the Man'. They prefer to risk their fortunes working the street than take in the white man's 'shit-work', or sit it out in his dole queues. Their number, too, has increased. A third group are those who keep the 'colony' life moving, oil the wheels, speed the turnover of the whole gamut of fringe cultural activities which makes the 'colony', despite its material impoverishment, a substitute community, something like home. Scattered amongst these three kinds of people are the petty criminals, con-men, pimps and racketeers. In a larger sense, everyone living in 'the colony' is into the 'rackets'. Respectable black families depend on the rackets as much as the hustler; if the latter need 'the game' to survive economically, the former need it to survive culturally. Naturally, there are unsavoury parts of the hustling networks which respectable, church-going West Indian families would rather not know about. The commitment of first-generation migrants to steady if unrewarding labour, and of the second generation to the life of the street and hustling rather than labouring, are the *principal* forms in which the 'generation gap' is articulated in the black community. However, as the pressures on the 'colony' community – from police surveillance and control, from unemployment and from official or institutional racism – have steadily increased, so the division within the 'colony' between young and old, or between those who have chosen the respectable route and those who have chosen to hustle and survive, has been eroded, and there is an increasing tendency to close ranks, internally, in the face of a common and hostile threat. The 'colony', initially a defensive reaction to the threatening universe of blanket white hostility, has become a defensive base for new strategies of survival amongst the black community as a whole.

Black youth has had to survive and make a life by choosing among the range of strategies pioneered by the first immigrant wave. But they encounter their subordination at a different stage in the historical evolution of their class. The economic and cultural responses which they have developed collectively thus differ significantly from those originally open to their parents. The first wave constructed the 'colony'; the second generation was born into the 'colony'. They are its first true progeny. They have no other home. Their parents are the bearers of that double consciousness common to all migrant classes in the period of transition; the second generation is the bearer of the exclusive consciousness of the black 'colony'. Their earliest experience is of a black enclave in an embattled position at the heart of a white society. They have grown up with racial segregation as a fact of life. As Dilip Hiro pointed out, young blacks see no visual signs of social integration between races in the adult world they inhabit; they do not notice racially mixed groups of adults walking in the streets or leaving the pub; no white friends visit their families; the only whites with which they have contact are people doing a job (postmen, teachers, meter readers) or welfare officers and social workers. [40] The black population in the schools has grown; but they have tended to segregate out along ethnic lines by mutual consent. Black youth has also had an experience of which their parents were deprived: cultural expropriation through the school system. Better equipped in terms of educational skills to take their place beside the white peers of their own class in the ranks of skilled and semi-skilled labour, they feel the closure of the occupational and opportunity structure to them – on grounds not of competence but of race – all the more acutely. English racism, both as a material structure and as an ideological presence, cannot be explained away to them as a temporary aberration, the result of a fit of white absent-mindedness. It is how the system works. In their experience, English society *is* 'racist' – it *works through race*. They cannot avail themselves of the first-generation immigrants' principal source of optimism: that everything improves with time. In fact, things have palpably become much worse. To casual discrimination and the loss of job opportunities must now be added the political mobilisation of white hostility, new legal disabilities governing the movement of their relatives – above all, the constant pressure of police harassment on the streets. Nothing makes one aware of living in a 'colony' so much as the permanent presence of an 'occupying force'. They have no greener memories of home to turn back to: 'home' is Willesden Junction, Handsworth, Paddington, Moss Side, St Annes. These people are permanent internal exiles. As 'Paul' told Peter Gillman:

> I call Barbados home. This isn't home. I call Africa home. That's home. Because I don't belong here. Even though I was born here I don't belong here and I don't call myself an Englishman. I don't call myself nothing to do with the English race in fact. They look upon me as a stranger so I look upon myself as a stranger in their country. [41]

This negative picture needs no further elaboration here. It is also true, on the more positive side, that this 'colony' generation is less outfaced than their parents were by the reality of life in the metropolis: less willing to endure and survive in patience; less deferential to white society; and more aggressively confident about who they are. In this sense the 'colony' has provided a basis for the construction of positive alternative cultural identities. Many first-generation blacks had to pass painfully through this transitional point. It is eloquently expressed in the autobiography of the West Indian Carpenter, Wallace Collins:

> I decided to quit the disenchantment, the uncompassionate yet impolite monstrosity of the white man's society. . . . This metamorphosis took place within me without my knowing it, until I began to intermingle with my own people. . . . I felt wanted and desired by my own people. . . . I belonged.[42]

The second generation simply *is* a black generation, knows it is black and is not going to be anything else but black. Its consciousness has received what the Ras Tafarians would call its 'groundation' in that fundamental and necessary knowledge. It is most unlikely, then, that this generation would ever set its feet, willingly, on the path to assimilation. As a collective solution, the option of assimilation has not only been officially closed by white society, but blacks have actively closed the door on it themselves, from the inside, and turned the key. What we have called an 'acceptance' strategy no longer has much to recommend it either. Black youth has come to see the infinite endurance of their parents as too quietist a solution – it too often involved giving in, knuckling under, to 'the Man'. One of the principal arenas in which black youth resist and reject what, unwillingly, their parents have had to accommodate, is in the sphere of work itself. A 17-year-old engineering apprentice told Dilip Hiro the story of how 'The foreman told me to brush the floor. . . . There was a white labourer (whose job it was) doing nothing, so I refused. I got the sack. I told my dad and he said, "You should have swept". I told my dad, "You're white-washed, those English people have corrupted your mind".'[43] The 18-year-old 'Paul' told Peter Gillman: 'I get kicked out of me house. Me old man didn't like the way I was going on. I was hustling, raising money here and there, not working for it, and he didn't like that so I just said I was leaving. I went out on the Saturday night and he locked the door and wouldn't let me in again.'[44] Another youth put it differently:

> My ambition is to get my father off London Transport. . . . I don't feel ashamed because he works there, that's nothing because he is a working man and he has brought up a big family and he has to be respected for that. It is just that he is on that bus collecting tickets all day and it's so uncool. I would just like to go up to him once and say, 'dad, just give them your cards and rest, take your cards and just rest'. He says he's proud working hard and everything, but really who would like going out on a bus in this cold in this country. Nobody. And no matter what he said, I know because I check him and I know he don't dig it. But he knows it's too late for him to say, 'well, boy, I'm not working, I will hustle or I will do this or I am going to play music – be an artist or gambler.' It's too late. He has responsibility, but for a young guy you have to look on him and say, 'well, look at my old man, he come to this country looking for a fortune and he's on a bus every day climbing up and down the stairs crying out, "any more fares"!' You got to say the way this system works I will only be one step above that and then my son would have to be one step above what I was . . . and so on. There has to be one in the family who leaps, so that the whole family goes up.[45]

So long as the labour market could absorb black school-leavers, it tended systematically to assign them to what they call the 'shit-work' end of the occupational spectrum. But, as unemployment deepens, those heading for the bottom end of the labouring pile become the unemployed reserve army of their class. The system which needed them as workers does not need them even for that any longer, so their objective position has deteriorated. But the dynamic factor is the change in the way this objective process is collectively understood and resisted. Thus, the social content and political meaning of 'worklessness' is being thoroughly transformed from inside. Those who cannot work are discovering that they do not want to work under those conditions. The unemployed are developing a new form of 'negative consciousness' around the condition of being unemployable. Of course, this may be a temporary situation, and thus a transitory form of consciousness; we will discuss below whether, if this is so, it is possible to organise from such a position anything but a temporary negation of the system. Meanwhile, this black sector of the class 'in itself' has begun to undergo that process of becoming a political force 'for itself':

> Economic conditions ... first transformed the mass of the people of the country into workers. The combination of capital has created for this mass a common situation, common interests. This mass is already a class as against capital but not yet for itself. In the struggle ... this mass becomes united and constitutes itself as a class for itself. The interests it defends become class interests. But the struggle of class against class is a political struggle. [46]

The shift is a momentous one. It does not, of course, follow the classic line sketched out by Marx. It is the common experience of 'worklessness' rather than the discipline of combination in social production which seems to be providing the catalyst – though for those sectors still at work the tempo of militancy has also considerably advanced. This qualitative shift has not happened spontaneously. It has a history. It began with the discovery of black identity, more specifically the rediscovery, inside the experience of emigration, of the African roots of 'colony' life. The 'African' revival in the 'colony' population was fed and supported by the post-war African nationalist revolutions. But it derived its positive content – as well as its clear materialisation within the life and confines of the 'colony' – from the black liberation movements in the United States from the early 1960s onwards and the black rebellions which spread through the ghettos, behind the mobilising slogans of 'black is beautiful' and 'black power':

> Once I used to think I'm the same as everybody else. But then I started realising. The first time was in 1965 when they had the riots in Watts. I started looking at all the things in the world and realised I got to act like a black man and got to be proud of it and everything. [47]

This is also the most intense period of active politicisation of the black community by political activists, and includes the visits to Britain of Stokely Carmichael and Malcolm X. It was the style of black resistance developed by groups like the Black Panthers, and the positive images of ethnicity generated by leaders like Seale, Cleaver, Newton, George Jackson and Angela Davis, rather than 'black power' as a political doctrine, which first seized the imagina-

tion of black youth in the 'colony'. One of the most significant points of identification between British and American developments was precisely the way
the latter movement built on the 'politics of ghetto survival', giving a new
political significance to 'the hustler'. This wholly negative stereotype role of the
black working class was positively redefined in the black cultural renaissance
of the 1960s. Not only had many of the prominent leaders and spokesmen of
the black American rebellion started their careers in the life of street-corner
crime, but the whole thrust of this movement was designed to build a political
movement among black people from the bottom up – and that meant from a
base inside the 'colony', from the defensive space of the ghetto. The only
'troops' the Black Panthers could aspire to command were lumpen-blacks from
the ghetto working class. The 'comrades in arms' were the brothers and sisters
of the streets.

Between the late 1960s and the 1970s, the seeds of cultural resistance have
not only sprouted in Britain's 'Harlems' up and down the country, they have
blossomed – but now in a distinctively Afro-Caribbean form. There was no
need to borrow, literally, styles or images from the North American ghetto,
since the street life had its own distinctive roots in Afro-Caribbean soil. The
revival among 'colony' blacks of the apocalyptic religio-politics of Ras
Tafarianism, the sounds of Anglo-Caribbean 'colony' music – rock-steady
Blue-beat, ska and reggae – and the 'hard' style of the Jamaican 'Rude Boy',
combined to provide a new vocabulary and syntax of rebellion much more
closely attuned to the material existence as well as to the emergent consciousness of those condemned to the drifting life of the streets. In and through
the revivalist imagery of the 'dreadlocks', the music of the dispossessed
(dispossessed, it should be added, in Kingston as much as it was in Brixton or
Handsworth) and the insistent, driving beat of the reggae sound systems came
the hope of deliverance from 'Babylon'. The 'culture' of the back-to-Africa
sect, the Ras Tafari, is crucial here; both in Brixton and in Kingston, in recent
years, it is the dress, beliefs, philosophy and language of this once marginal and
despised group which has provided the basis for the generalisation and
radicalisation of black consciousness amongst sectors of black youths in the
cities: the source of an intense black cultural nationalism. It is this 'religion of
the oppressed', as embodied in the rhythm and imagery of reggae, which has
swept the minds as well as swayed the bodies of young black men and
women.[48] Britain, the country where black people are oppressed, are 'suffering', the land which they are *in* but not *of*, the country of estrangement, dis-
possession and brutality, perfectly recapitulates the 'Babylon' of the Ras
Tafarian credo. Inside their own 'house' the brothers may greet each other with
'peace and love'. But for 'Babylon', the music promises the 'rod of correction',
and for the brothers, it promises 'power' – '*let the power fall*'. In the wake of
this cultural upheaval, coursing through Lambeth and West Kingston alike,
which inverts and transforms every sign of white domination into its negative
and opposite, which rereads the culture of oppression from 'the roots' up as the
culture of suffering and struggle, every activity touched is given a new content,
endowed with a new meaning. It is the ideological point of origin of a new
social movement amongst blacks, the seeds of an unorganised political

rebellion. The extent of police supervision of the 'colonies', the arbitrariness and brutality of the 'hassling' of young blacks, the mounting public anxieties and the moral panic about 'young immigrants' and crime, and the size of the welfare and community projects designed to relieve tension and 'cool' the problems in the ghetto, serve only to reinforce the impression, both inside and outside the 'colony', that, in some as yet undefined way, a 'political' battleground is being staked out.

Many respectable black adults still regard a full-time life of 'worklessness' and petty crime as a desperate and illegal solution to the survival problems which confront the community. They hope and pray it is temporary. At the same time they are increasingly enraged at the level of exploitation which is driving the young people of the 'colony' progressively towards this option, and at the arbitrary oppression which is now the routine control response to those who cannot survive in any other way. There is an older element of the 'colony' population for whom the drift into and out of crime has already become a stable aspect of their unstable and precarious economic existence. The situation with respect to black youth seems to differ from both these dispositions. It is impossible to tell, for example, at the present time, how many black school-leavers cannot get jobs, how many would not take those kinds of jobs, and how many are refusing to work as a positive and political strategy. The uncertainty of the 'hustling' life may be preferable to the predictable monotony of unskilled factory work. Presently, in any event, the choice is simply not open for the majority of those who have come on to the labour market for the first time. The attempt, in these circumstances, to draw such fine distinctions may be a fruitless exercise. It takes no account of the way choices are conditioned. It treats the concrete material issues of survival as if submittable to a clear calculus of rational choice by free agents. It reduces social behaviour to the level of decisions in the head, made in terms of universal moral criteria, which happen, fortuitously, to coincide with the way the legal boundaries are currently drawn. The ambiguous relation of black youth to crime cannot be understood in this way. The available accounts clearly show that few young blacks confront a clear choice between the options of hard labour and crime, and settle permanently for one strategy or another. One of the precipitating factors is precisely a difference in attitude to the problems of survival between the two generations. Young blacks, unable or unwilling to work, and attracted by the more free-wheeling life of the street, find themselves unable to live without conflict in their parental home. But once outside it there are neither places to live nor any steady source of income on which to survive unemployment. Hustling or occasional pilfering constitute an immediate and thoroughly predictable temporary solution to this condition, as does homelessness, 'dossing out' and drifting. Every black colony area has its rooms, cafés or hostels, sometimes provided, more often simply taken over – colonised – where alert and intelligent black youths, in their overcoats and knitted caps, are simply sitting out the crisis. Often, a local black café-owner has taken pity on them and cleared a room or a space in which they can at least be warm. In other areas, black community workers, on practically no resources, attempt to organise the permanent 'free time' of these youths into some kind of useful or profitable activity.

But the drifting in and out, the precariousness, is endless. This fraction of the black labouring class is engaged in the traditional activity of the wageless and the workless: doing nothing, filling out time, trying to survive. Against that background it is not too much to say that the question 'why do they turn to crime?' is a practical obscenity.

Certain patterns begin to emerge here. The first step into the twilight zone of crime comes through sporadic pilfering: pinching off open stalls or from super-markets. The second is the lure of a bigger take – pickpocketting, snatching from a shopping basket, lifting a wallet. The chances are better, and the take bigger, in the open street, in the ambiguous urban spaces and wastegrounds, or in the labyrinth of the tube station. A certain amount of drifting 'uptown' begins, and the activity – working in pairs, or arranging a chain of connections along which a snatched purse can be passed on – requires more social organisation, a more stable network. Life comes to depend more and more on these successes. A fraction of the class is *being criminalised*. All the evidence suggests that the numbers now forced to survive in these ways on the margin of the legal life are increasing, directly in line with the numbers unemployed, and that the age limit of those involved is dropping. Some of these boys are now ripe for recruitment into the life of professionalised crime, where crime – not the unpredictable, sporadic snatch but the planned breaking and entry of unoc-cupied houses, often in broad daylight – promises to become a regular occupa-tion, a *substitute job*. The numbers involved in petty pilfering and snatching are confined to a limited age range. Beyond that, the tendency is either to give it up, especially if you are lucky enough to land a job, or to graduate into a more set-tled criminal life-style. All the evidence clearly points to the fact that, while still involved in the 'twilight zone' of crime, most of the youths are still regularly seeking employment. 'Mugging', the more violent, planned and ruthless form of survival crime, represents only a tiny fraction of this larger pattern, is indulged in by only the more hardened section of the drifting population, and tends to be given up by those obliged either to move on into conventional crime, or to move out.

The way in which these massively overdetermined options are recovered and transformed in consciousness by those caught up in their logics is a different matter. For these are no ordinary white boys and girls, with a well-developed, ascribed consciousness of subordination already available to them. They are an excluded black group in a dominant white world. And their growing black con-sciousness has given them, however rudimentarily, a sort of awareness of the systematic nature of the forces driving them into certain pathways, and of the structuring principle of racism at work of which they are the victims. Few young blacks consciously *choose* crime as a form of political revenge against white society. But consciousness and motives do not work in that way. It is more likely that, finding themselves drifting or driven into one of the few remaining strategies for survival open to them, they develop a collective defini-tion of their situation; and, in doing so, they draw on the available reservoir of charged feelings and emotions about racism and its system. Reasons and rationales, vocabularies of action, meaning or motive, frequently, in concrete experience, follow rather than precede practical actions. This does not mean that they are simply convenient excuses, cover stories. It means that certain patterns of action can be retrospectively glossed and reinterpreted in the light of meanings which progressively emerge. What seems, at first, the product of circumstances – fate – comes to be understood as the product of particular social and historical arrangements. Modes of existence, inertly inhabited as unchangeable, 'given' in the structures which inscribe men as the bearers of their conditions, can, in this way, be transformed into a more positive agency or practice. Thus it comes about that the attitudes towards and the understanding of crime amongst black youth remain profoundly ambiguous, suffused with the ethos of racism which bounds their life on all sides, yet with no clear precipitation as a conscious or organised political strategy. Some of those involved in crime appear to have no special feelings about it. That is how they live; the job of the police is to prevent or apprehend them. They know that, if picked up, they may well be singled out for special, harsh and abusive treatment. The preoccupation of the professional criminal is to stay out of the hands of the police, as a condition of his existence. A spell in jail is one of the hazards of the trade. For many others, however, the sense of being pressured into the twilight zone of crime only makes sense as part of a wider configuration. Those whites with whom they come into contact – whether victims or the police – are seen as representatives, 'personifications', of a society which is systematically exploiting and excluding them. Thus crime is ambiguously invested with more politicised feelings and ideas. It relates to the traditional status of the ghetto 'wide-boy' and 'hard man', in the same moment as it expresses – often in a muffled, generalised or apocalyptic manner – a new means of struggle and resistance against white oppression. Both structures of feeling coexist within the same pattern of activity, and may be seen in the way it combines the brazen recklessness of the daylight robbery in crowded places with the deliberate choice of white victims and the planned exploit out of the ghetto to the richer pickings of London's West End:

> 'We don't touch our own people. I never thought of doing it to a black man', one youngster confessed. 'A black man wouldn't do it to me. But I know a white man would do it to me. A black man knows that we are all suffering the same. We all try and hustle in our own way', a second observed. [49]

A certain glamour may temporarily attach itself to the life of petty crime; but the accounts of those who have to survive in this way for long, or those now languishing in detention centres or in prison, clearly show that there is nothing remotely romantic about it. It is a precarious, haphazard, desperate existence, always on the edge of a violence which brutalises all those who engage in it, for whatever motives. It brings in its wake the constant attentions and harassment of the police, who lump in this category any young black person who happens to be on the streets after dark. The common, root cause of it can be traced back to simple, sheer material need. Brother Herman of the London Harambee was certainly correct when he observed:

> There is no professional criminal intent there. What happens is that at some point they are hungry and need money; a boy is on the street and has no

food to eat and nowhere to live. I go along to the courts every day and the kinds of boys I see and the nature of the offence – I don't see any criminal ability there at all. But I don't think the courts recognize their predicament. [50]

Although it is not possible to reconstruct the particular biographical path which each young black person has taken to the 'mugging' solution, it is quite easy to construct a typical biography of this kind. Here is the black adolescent at the point of leaving school: 'When you go to school, you realize the difference, you're made to realize it. They (the white kids) pick on you. First you try to bribe them – sweets, ices, the lot. But then one day you can't stand it any more. You get vicious, real vicious and you lick them.' [51] (The violence of the 'mugging' which such a boy may one day come to commit, and which the press headlines, the judge's homily and the Home Office statistician will abstract from its context, is already inscribed in this biography, however far from his mind the possibility of a criminal career still is.) His prospects are none too good, and they are getting worse. If he is lucky, a series of 'dead-end' jobs interspersed with long periods of unemployment – increasingly, not even that. His parents know he is having a rough time; but they also know from bitter experience what awaits him if he cannot find steady employment. He starts to drift with friends, and the rows at home become sharper and more frequent. He is already too big for home, too poor for an independent life; but sooner or later, if nothing changes, he will leave home. He is now permanently on the streets. He may move in with a friend; he may find a bed at one of the black hostels or he may be sleeping rough. He cannot be seen too often on the streets. If the police find him after dark, they will stop and question him, perhaps search him. He has no permanent address. He has not yet committed an offence; but a group of black youths, loitering with no intent whatsoever, good or bad, after dark, are a sitting target. The police do not like their look, their walk, their knitted tea-cosy caps, their manner and insolence. The youths do not much like the look of that official white face beneath the helmet. Each expects the other to jump. On most occasions, someone does. (This boy is not yet 'an offender', not yet a 'disturber of the peace'; but both these identities, which the desk sergeant will swear to and the sentencing judge will rehearse against him, are already inscribed in his fate.) There is a fight with the 'coppers', and the bous break away. They are now on the run; but there is nowhere to run to except further up the street. The 'nigger-taunting' still hangs on the night air: 'all of a sudden you see this guy and you say, well. . .'. [52]

But *can* crime provide the basis of a resistance which is capable of transforming or even modifying the circumstances which force more and more young people to enlist in its ranks? *Is* hustling and petty crime the potential basis for a viable class strategy? Or is the 'criminal consciousness' destined to remain a quasi-political form of consciousness only, which, apart from providing the immediate and spontaneous basis for opposition, also permits *an accommodation* to the very structures which are producing and reproducing crime as a viable 'solution'? Is not crime precisely that form which, while it swallows up the extruded part of the surplus labouring class, renders that section inactive, politically, by binding it to its fate – by *criminalising and brutalising it*? This is not a question which can be answered in terms of consciousness alone. It is not one which can be solved through an exclusive preoccupation with crime as such.

BLACK CRIME, BLACK PROLETARIAT

We must depart, at this point, from the immediate logic driving certain sections of black youth into 'the mugging solution'. To assess the viability of 'crime' as a political strategy, we must re-examine the criminalised part of the black labour force in relation to the black working class as a whole, and the relations which govern and determine its position – above all, in terms of its fundamental position in the present stage of the capitalist mode of production, the social division of labour and its role in the appropriation and realisation of surplus labour. We must include these structural relations in our assessment of the relation of crime to political struggle in the present conjuncture.

In recent years social historians have given increasing attention to forms of social rebellion and political insurgency adopted by classes other than that of the classical proletariat of the developed industrial capitalist societies of Western Europe. This is the result, in part, of the long political containment of the working class in such societies, coupled with the fact of major historical transformations elsewhere which have been spearheaded by classes other than the proletariat – the role of the peasantry in the Chinese Revolution being only the most significant example. In addition, then, to the study of peasant revolutions, and questions of strategy arising from those societies (for example, Latin America) which contain both substantial peasant and developing industrial working-class sectors, there have also been studies of other forms of social rebellion – pre-industrial riot and rebellion, the city mobs, rural unrest, social banditry, etc. Despite this, the orthodox view seems to prevail that, where developed industrial societies are concerned, the 'rebellions' of the poor and the lumpen classes, or the forms of quasi-political resistance inscribed in the activities of the criminal elements and 'dangerous classes', cannot be of much long-term interest to those concerned with fundamental social movements. Professor Hobsbawm, who has himself made a major contribution to the studies referred to above (with his books on primitive rebels, insurrections amongst the landless proletariat and social banditry[53]) has stated the limits in admirably clear terms. Criminal underworlds, he argues, 'are anti-social insofar as they deliberately set their values against the prevailing ones'. But:

> the underworld (as distinct from, say, peasant bandits) rarely take part in wider social and revolutionary movements, at least in Western Europe. . . . There are obvious overlaps, especially in certain environments (slum quarters of big cities, concentrations of semi-proletarian poor, ghettoes of 'outsider' minorities, etc.) and non-social criminals may be a substitute for social protest or be idealised as such a substitute, but on the whole this type of criminality has only marginal interest for the historian of social and labour movements.[54]

This is because, in advanced industrial capitalist societies, the fundamental revolutionary class is the proletariat, which has not only been formed in and by capital, but whose struggle against capital is organised – made collective and 'methodical' – because it is the struggle of a class schooled by the discipline of the wage and by the conditions and relations of social labour. There is a phased or staged history of class conflict present here which makes the struggles of organised labour the historical agency with the most advanced form of struggle at the present stage of the development of capitalism:

> as a conscious social movement and especially as a labour movement develops, the role of 'criminal' forms of social protest diminishes; except, of course, insofar as they involve 'political crime'. . . . For the historian of labour movements, the study of 'social criminality' is important during the prehistoric and formative periods of the movements of the labouring poor, in pre-industrial countries, and possibly during periods of great social effervescence, but otherwise he will be only very marginally concerned with it. [55]

Elsewhere, Hobsbawm has argued:

> The underworld (as its name implies) is an anti-society, which exists by reversing the values of the 'straight' world – it is, in its own phrase, 'bent' – but it is otherwise parasitic on it. A revolutionary world is also a 'straight' world. . . . The underworld enters the history of revolutions only insofar as the *classes dangereuses* are mixed up with the *classes laborieuses,* mainly in certain quarters of the city, and because rebels and insurgents are often treated by the authorities as criminals and outlaws; but in principle the distinction is clear. [56]

This argument poses questions of far-reaching importance.

Hobsbawm and others are pointing to the conditions which might seem to make the movements of the 'criminal poor' what Gramsci called 'conjunctural' rather than 'organic'. This entails three propositions. The criminal classes cannot play a fundamental role in such social movements, first, because their position is marginal to the productive life and relations of social formations of this kind; second, because, historically, they have become marginal to the proletariat which has replaced them at the centre of the theatre of political struggle; third, because the form of consciousness traditionally developed by this stratum is not adequate to that required by a class which aims to supplant one mode of production by another. Thus, though the life and values of the 'dangerous classes' represent an inversion of the bourgeois world, they remain ultimately enclosed by it – confined by it and thus in the end parasitic upon it. The effect of this orthodox interpretation on the development of a 'Marxist theory of crime' has been noted. Alvin Gouldner, for example, once commented:

> Viewing criminals and deviants as *lumpenproletariat* that would play no decisive role in the class struggle and, indeed, as susceptible to use by reactionary forces, Marxists were not usually motivated to develop a systematic theory of crime and deviance. In short, being neither proletarian nor bourgeois, and standing off to the periphery of the central political struggle, criminals and deviants were at best the butlers and maids, the spear carriers,

the colourful actors perhaps, but nameless and, worst of all, lacking in a historical 'mission'. They could be, indeed, *had* to be, ignored by those devoted to the study of more 'important' issues – power, political struggle and class conflict.[57]

Some Marxist writers would indeed argue that the very concepts required to 'think' the problems of crime and deviance are foreign to Marx's conceptual field – to the problematic of historical materialism as a theory. Hirst argues, on this basis, that there *cannot* by definition be 'a Marxist theory of crime'.[58] In his mature work, Hirst argues – the work, essentially, of *Capital* – Marx adopts a viewpoint on crime which breaks with a moral critique and bases himself instead on the scientific propositions of a fully materialist viewpoint. Within this framework, crime (theft) is merely redistributive; like prostitution, gambling or racketeering, it is a form of 'unproductive' rather than 'productive' labour and though it may be 'illegal' with respect to the norms which govern normal capitalist relations, it is most often 'capitalistic' in form (e.g. organised criminal enterprises) – i.e. adapted to the system on which it is parasitic. This analysis of the 'marginal' position of crime may be extended by looking at the role and nature Marx ascribed to the 'criminal classes'. The centrality of the proletariat to any transformation of the capitalist mode of production lies in its role in production, as the source of surplus value. This position is ascribed to the proletariat by the mode of production. It is this *position* – rather than that process of coming to consciousness as a collective historical agent, of which Marx spoke in *The Poverty of Philosophy*[59] and elsewhere in the earlier works – which defines productive labour as the only class capable of carrying through the struggle to transform the capitalist mode into socialism. Now the proletariat and the bourgeoisie are, in this schema, the fundamental political forces. Other classes exist as a result of the combination within any social formation of more than one mode of production; but they cannot be the decisive forces in the political class struggle. Marx does suggest that, at certain moments of struggle, the proletariat will seek alliances with other subordinate classes; and these allies may include the petty bourgeoisie, the lumpenproletariat of the cities, the small peasants or agricultural labourers. But, Hirst concludes, Marx believed the lumpenproletariat to be unreliable class allies. Since, through theft, extortion, begging, prostitution and gambling, the lumpenproletariat tends to live parasitically off the working class, 'their interests are diametrically opposed to those of the workers'. Further, because of their precarious economic position, they are bribable by 'the reactionary elements of the ruling classes and the state'. Thus, the argument runs, individual acts of crime are the volitionless acts of the victims of capitalism, 'not in effect forms of political rebellion against the existing order but a more or less reactionary accommodation to them'.[60] Even the more obviously 'political' crimes, like the machine-breaking of the Luddites, represent immediate, spontaneous but ultimately inadequate forms of struggle since they are directed 'not against the bourgeois conditions of production but against the conditions of production themselves'. As the basis for a revolutionary struggle, such acts are useless; the only task is to 'transform such forms and ideologies of struggle'.[61]

How historically specific was Marx's analysis of the composition and nature of the *lumpenproletariat*? He and Engels seem clearly to have had the 'dangerous classes' of mid-Victorian England and of Paris in mind as they wrote. One of the key passages is the analysis of their role in the crisis of 1851 which Marx offered in the *Eighteenth Brumaire*. The *lumpenproletariat* appears in that graphic passage as the criminal detritus of *all* classes – the *déclasses* at the bottom of the human pile:

> Alongside decayed *roués* with dubious means of subsistence and of dubious origins, alongside ruined and adventurous off-shoots of the bourgeoisie, were vagabonds, discharged soldiers, discharged jailbirds, escaped galley slaves, swindlers, mountebanks, *lazzaroni*, pickpockets, tricksters, gamblers, *maquereaus*, brothel-keepers, porters, *literati*, organ-grinders, ragpickers, knife grinders, tinkers, beggars, – in short, the whole indefinite, disintegrated mass thrown hither and thither, which the French term *la boheme*.[62]

The list will be familiar from the pages of Engels's *Condition of the Working Class in England*,[63] or from Mayhew's account of life in East London.[64] It is open to question whether a class stratum with this precise social composition could so easily be identified under the conditions of monopoly capitalism. This is not simply a way of saying that Marx's historical and political predictions are out of date. The old petty bourgeoisie, about which Marx and Engels were occasionally more optimistic as allies of the proletariat, still survives, though greatly reduced in number. When they do appear on the political stage, they tend to play the reactionary role which Marx believed predictable from their position – for example, in the various types of Poujadism in France, and in the rise of fascism in Germany in the 1930s. But alongside this, stemming from the fundamental reorganisation of capitalist production consequent on the shift to monopoly forms, new strata have arisen – what is sometimes designated as the 'new petty bourgeoisie'. Its economic identification, and its political and ideological character, present real and complex problems for contemporary Marxist theory. Such internal shifts in the strata and composition of the classes is perfectly in line with Marx's mature reflections. He was about to plunge into its complexity where the manuscript of *Capital* breaks off. The question, then, of who and what corresponds to the *lumpenproletariat* in contemporary capitalist social formations is not an idle speculation. And the further question of whether all those involved in crime as a way of life belong, analytically, to the category of the 'lumpen' is a matter requiring serious theoretical and definitional work, not a problem of simple empirical observation.

The relationship between classes constituted in the economic relations of capitalist production and the forms in which they appear as political forces in the theatre of political class struggle is no simple matter either, especially when considered from the standpoint of Marx's more mature theory. But the later work – the analysis of the economic forms and relations of capital accumulation conducted in *Capital* – differs from some of Marx's earlier writings, especially in the position of the working class with respect to the 'laws of motion' of capitalist production. Whereas, earlier, Marx had tended to see the proletariat as the 'oppressed' class in a political struggle with the oppressors, *Capital* thoroughly reconstitutes his argument on the terrain of capitalist production itself and the circuit of its self-expansion. It is the exploitation of the labourer within production, the identification of labour-power as the 'commodity' on which the whole process rests, which finds in surplus labour the source of surplus value which is realised as 'capital'; this provides the basis of Marx's 'immense theoretical revolution' in *Capital*. Capital had at its disposal many ways of exploiting labour-power and extracting the surplus − first, by lengthening the working day, then by intensifying the exploitation of labour-power through augmenting the productive power of advanced machinery, in the form of constant capital, to which the labourer is increasingly directly subsumed. But, in whatever form, capital could not exist for a day without production; and production was not possible without the exploitation of productive labour in the class-structured relations of capitalist production. Marx then lodged the fundamental mechanism of capitalist societies in the contradictions which arose in this fundamental relation − that between the 'forces' and 'relations' of production. Many other forms were necessary, outside the sphere of production proper, to ensure the 'circuit of capital' − the relations of market, exchange and circulation; the spheres of the family, where, through wages, labour-power was renewed; the state which superintended the society in which this mode of production was installed; and so on. Ultimately, the whole circuit of capitalist production depended on these other related spheres − what have come to be called the 'spheres of reproduction' − and on the various classes and class strata exploited by them. But production relations dominated the whole complex circuit 'in the last instance'; and other forms of exploitation, other social relations, had to be thought, ultimately, in terms of the essential contradictions of the productive level. Marx makes the point in several places in *Capital*:

> The specific economic form, in which unpaid surplus labour is pumped out of direct producers, determines the relationship of rulers and ruled, as it grows directly out of production itself and, in turn, reacts upon it as a determining element. . . . It is always the direct relationship of the owners of the conditions of production to the direct producers − a relation always naturally corresponding to a definite stage in the development of the methods of labour and thereby its social productivity − which reveals the innermost secret, the hidden basis of the entire social structure, and with it the political form of the relation of sovereignty and dependence, in short, the corresponding specific form of the state. This does not prevent the same economic base − the same from the standpoint of its main conditions − due to innumerable different empirical circumstances, natural environment, racial relations, external historical influences, etc., from showing infinite gradations and variations in appearance. [65]

From this perspective, it follows that, even if we depart from the strict implications of the earlier discussion of crime and the *lumpenproletariat* outlined above, a political struggle arising from a sector of a class living through crime cannot be, analytically, so central to the contradictions stemming from its relations of production; at the simplest level of analysis, it is simply not strategically placed with respect to capital's 'laws of motion'. This, however, omits the question of what the role of the criminalised part of a class is, structurally, *to the waged*, to the productive sectors, of that class. And this returns us to the question of what the relation is between the 'waged' and the 'wageless' sectors of the black labour force in relation to capital in its present form. Marx had something critical to say about this in *Capital*, in terms of the relation of what he called the 'reserve army of labour' – the different strata of the unemployed – to the fundamental rhythms of capital accumulation, and we will turn to this in a moment.

First, however, we must enter a brief caveat against treating Marx's theory of capital as, essentially, what has been called a form of *productivist* theory – as if nothing mattered, for capital, but that sector of the labouring masses involved *directly* in 'productive labour'. Marx did, following but differing in his definition from the classical political economists, use the distinction between 'productive' and 'unproductive' labour. Productive labour was that sector directly involved in the production of surplus value, exchanging directly against capital. Many other sectors of the work-force, though equally exploited by capital, did *not* directly produce surplus value, and exchanged, not against capital, but against revenue: 'Labour in the process of pure circulation does not produce use-values and therefore cannot add value or surplus-value. Alongside this group of unproductive labourers are all workers supported directly out of revenue, whether retainers or state employees.' [66]

The theory of productive and unproductive labour is one of the most complex and contested areas of Marxist theory, and its ramifications do not directly concern us here. In the capitalism which Marx knew, 'unproductive labour' was relatively underdeveloped, and often confined either to idlers, parasites on the labour of others, or to marginal producers. The same cannot be said of modern forms of capitalism, where the service and 'unproductive' sectors of the work-force have been enormously expanded, performing what are clearly *key* functions for capital, and where the largest proportion of workers exchange against revenue (state employees, for example) and the proportion involved in the direct production of surplus value appears to be growing smaller. In these circumstances, the line – apparently relatively simple for Marx – between 'productive' and 'unproductive' labour has become increasingly difficult to draw with any clear result. The distinction may, nevertheless, be important for identifying the position and identity of the many new layers and strata in the modern working class. However, it seems clear that the argument has also been bedevilled by a clear misunderstanding of the distinction, even as Marx made it. 'Unproductive' labour has sometimes been interpreted exclusively in Marx's pejorative and more frivolous sense – as economically and politically insignificant. This was clearly not his meaning, as a reading of volume II of *Capital*, where Marx deals at length with circulation and reproduction, soon reveals. The whole argument in *Capital* demonstrates how vital and necessary to the realisation of capital, and to its expansion and reproduction, are those relations which are not directly tied to the surplus-value producing sphere of capital. Capital could not, literally, complete its passage or circuit without 'passing through' these related spheres. Further, he stated directly that it is not only the sector of the class which directly produces surplus value which is *exploited* by capital; many other class sectors are exploited by capital, even if the form of that exploitation is not the direct extraction of surplus value. Thus, even if we need to retain the terms 'productive' and 'unproductive' for purposes of analysis, relating to the identification of the different strata of the working class, there is no warrant in Marx for treating the classes and strata exploited outside production proper as unnecessary or 'superfluous' classes, beyond capital's contradictory dialectic:

> the aim of Marx in developing the concepts of productive and unproductive labour was not to divide the workers. Exactly the opposite. . . . With the aid of these concepts it proved possible for Marx to analyse how value is expanded in the direct process of production and how it is circulated in the reproduction process. [67]

The point is seminal for, and can be nicely illustrated from, the recent debate within Marxism and the feminist movement about the position of female domestic labour with respect to capital. In an early contribution to this debate, Seccombe argued that 'housework' must be judged, from a Marxist perspective, 'unproductive', and seemed to imply that, for that reason, no decisive political struggle, capable of striking back against capital, could be organised from that base. [68] (Similarly, it could, by analogy, be argued that no fundamental political struggle which could affect capital could be mounted from a base constituted by black wageless, black hustlers involved in the essentially redistributive activities of 'crime', and black men and women largely confined to the service and 'unproductive' sectors.) Many aspects of Seccombe's argument were challenged in the course of a lengthy and important theoretical debate. [69] In a subsequent contribution, Seccombe has clarified his position. [70] Housework may be strictly speaking 'unproductive', but 'the working class housewife contributes to the production of a commodity – labour power . . . and through this process participates in social production'. [71] Indeed, the reproduction of labour-power, through the family and the sexual division of labour, is, in Marx's strict terms, one of the fundamental conditions of existence of the capitalist mode of production, to which capital devotes a part of what it has extracted from the labourer – variable capital – and 'advances' to him and his family, in the form of wages, so that this 'reproduction' can be effected. Domestic labour may be 'unproductive', but it produces value, Seccombe agrees. It is exploited by capital – indeed, doubly exploited, through the sexual division of labour; and is fundamental to the laws of motion of capital. It is through the sexual division of labour that capital is able to seize 'not only the economic but every other sphere of society . . . value regulates labour conducted beyond the direct auspices of capital'. [72]

Although not directly linked with our main argument, this digression on domestic labour has some significant pay-offs for our consideration. The housewife appears to 'do nothing' productively; she *labours* but does not appear to *work*. Her sphere – the home – is thus perceived as lying at, apparently, the opposite end of the spectrum to capital's productive heart: spare, marginal, useless. Yet, by her contribution to the reproduction of labour-power, and by her role as the agent of the family's consumption, the housewife sustains a necessary and pivotal relation to capitalist production. What is important is that this is hived off, segmented, segregated and compartmentalised from the production process proper. And what simultaneously connects and obscures this relation is the intermediation of the *sexual* division of labour as a structure within the *social* division of labour. *In this specific form,* capital extends, without appearing to do so, 'its auspices'. And, when women are drawn into work outside the home, they substantially appear in work which is not only at the unskilled, ununionised and 'unproductive' end of the occupational spectrum, but in kinds of work which are often similar in nature to, and are experienced like, 'housework' or 'women's work' – only done outside the home (service trades, textiles, catering, etc.). Braverman argues that in the U.S. economy women have become 'the prime supplementary reservoir of labour', a movement essentially 'to the poorly paid, menial and "supplementary" occupations'.[73] Seccombe points out that one of the crucial ways in which capital extends its sway over domestic labour is in regulating what proportion of it will be drawn into or thrown back out of 'productive work'. 'It [capital] structures the relation of the working population to the industrial reserve army of which housewives are a latent and often active component.'[74] Without attempting to draw the parallels too tightly, we may then point to the following: (1) the struggles of both women and blacks present acute problems of strategy in aligning *sectoral* struggle with a more general class struggle; (2) this may have something to do with the fact that both occupy a structurally segmentary position, or are related to capitalist exploitation through a 'double structure' – the *sexual* division within class relations in the first case, the *racial* division within class relations in the second; (3) the key to unravelling the relation of both is not the question of whether each directly receives a *wage* or not, since a proportion of each is, at any time, in employment – i.e. 'waged' – while the rest are 'wageless'; (4) the key lies in the reference to capital's control over the movement into and out of the *reserve army of labour.*

In the debate with Seccombe, the strongest case in favour of regarding housework as 'productive' was advanced by Selma James and Mariarosa Dalla Costa, in *The Power of Women and the Subversion of the Community.*[75] 'Wages for housework' was, for them, a strategy of feminist mobilisation, with subversive potential, directly against capital. In Selma James's *Sex, Race and Class* this analysis is extended to black struggles.[76] The introduction to the earlier pamphlet put the nub of the argument clearly, highlighting the strategic value of the refusal to work:

> The family under capitalism is a centre ... essentially of *social production.* When previously so-called Marxists said that the capitalist family did not produce for capitalism, was not a part of social production, it followed that they repudiated women's potential *social power.* Or rather, presuming that women in the home could not have social power, they could not see that women in the home produced. If your production is vital for capitalism, refusing to produce, refusing to *work,* is a fundamental lever of social power.[77]

In *Sex, Race and Class* Selma James also extended the argument into a novel interpretation of how the struggles undertaken by such groups as women and blacks relate to class struggle as a whole. It is based essentially on a reworking of the notions of *caste* and *class*. 'Manufacture,' Marx argued in *Capital*, 'develops a hierarchy of labour powers, to which there corresponds a scale of wages.'[78] The international division of labour, argues Selma James, leads to an accentuation in the 'hierarchy of labour powers', which splits the working class along racial, sexual, national and generational lines, and confines each sector of the class to its position within this 'caste', at the expense of its position in the class as a whole. 'The individual labourers,' Marx added, 'are appropriated and annexed for life by a limited function ... the various operations of the hierarchy are parcelled out among the labourers according to both their natural and their acquired capabilities.'[79] (Marx, of course, was writing here of an early phase of capitalist development. 'Modern industry', he argued, involved a *different* division of labour. Selma James does not defend her extension of the 'hierarchy of labour-powers' concept to this later phase of capitalist development.) This segmentation of the classes – hierarchy of labour-powers – represents a weakness in the face of capital. But at present, it is argued, no alternative 'general' class strategy is possible. (The argument at this point closely follows that of C. L. R. James, perhaps the most seminal and influential Caribbean Marxist to date, in his insistence that no vanguard party of the Leninist mould can claim to 'speak for' a class so internally divided.) The accent of struggle thus (in line with James's own stresses) falls on the autonomous self-activity of each sector of the class. *Each sector* must make its 'autonomous power' felt first; and, by using 'the specificity of its experience ... redefine class and the class struggle itself. ... In our view, identity – caste – is the very substance of class.'[80] Only through autonomous struggle in each sector will the 'power of the class' as a whole come to be felt. This line of argument, theoretically developed in *Race Today*,[81] has become the most powerful political tendency within active black groups in Britain. It is predicated on the autonomy and self-activity of black groups in struggle; and it identifies the most significant theme of this struggle as the growing 'refusal to work' of the black unemployed. The high levels of youthful black unemployment are here reinterpreted as part of a conscious political 'refusal to work'. This refusal to work is crucial, since it strikes at capital. It means that this sector of the class refuses to enter competition with those already in productive work. Hence, it *refuses* the traditional role of the 'reserve army of labour' – i.e. as an instrument which can be used to break or undermine the bargaining power of those still in work. Thus it 'subverted Capital's plan for maximum surplus-value from the immigrant work force'.[82] Police activity, which is principally directed against this 'workless' stratum of the class, is defined as an attempt to bring the wageless back into wage-labour. The 'wageless' are not to be equated with the traditional disorganised and undisciplined 'lumpenproletariat'. This false identification arises only because the black working class is understood exclusively in relation to British capital. But, in fact, black labour can only be adequately understood, historically, if it is also seen as a class which has already developed in the Caribbean – *vis-à-vis* 'colonial' forms of capital – as a cohesive social force. In the colonial setting 'wagelessness' was one of its key strategies. It is not surprising that this wageless sector has reconstructed in the metropolitan 'colony' a supporting institutional network and culture. Finally, the entrance of young, second-generation blacks 'into the class of unemployeds represents not only an increase in numbers but also a qualitative change in the composition of the class'. This new generation now brings to the struggle through 'wagelessness' a new confidence and boldness. [83]

The position originally outlined in Selma James's *Sex, Race and Class* has been extended and developed in the Power of Women Collective's pamphlet, *All Work and No Pay.* [84] Here, the original argument about the 'hierarchy of labour powers' is repeated, with an interesting and relevant addition. The wagelessness of housework is now shown to be disguising its real character as capitalist commodity production; and the payment of the 'family wage' to the male worker structures the dependency of the female labour force on the male. This is called the 'patriarchy of the wage' – one product of which is sexism. On this analogy, the structurally differentiated position of black labour as a whole to the white working class, may be similarly understood as a form of structured dependence, one product of which is racism – the 'racism of the wage relation', to coin a phrase. (But see the penetrating critique by Barbara Taylor which questions whether an analysis of female and domestic labour can be so directly based on an assumed homogeneity or perfect homology between production and ideology, structure and superstructures. [85] This is also one of the main critiques of the *Race Today* position advanced by Cambridge and Gutsmore in *The Black Liberator.*)

It should be added, that though there is not as yet a fully theorised account of the present stage of metropolitan capitalist development in the *Race Today* position, some parts of their analysis of the position of blacks is quite close to that elaborated by a major current in contemporary Italian Marxist theory (what is sometimes called 'the Italian school'). [86] Very crudely, this tendency identifies the present phase of capitalist development as it was characterised by Marx in volume III of *Capital* as 'social capital'. This involves the subsumption of 'many capitals' into one capital, based on a vastly expanded reproduction process; the progressive abolition of capital as *private* property and the socialisation of the accumulation process; and the transformation of the whole of society into a sort of 'social factory' for capital. In this phase, the state is progressively synonymous with social capital – its 'thinking head' – and assumes the functions of integration, harmonisation, rationalisation and repression hitherto partly the responsibility of capital itself. This massive concentration of capital – on an international scale – is matched by the growing concentration (again, on an international scale) and massification of the proletariat. The higher the organic composition of capital, the greater the 'proletarianisation' of the worker. The recomposition of capital along 'social-capital' lines has been accomplished, principally, by three factors: the reorganisation of the labour process, through the application of 'Fordist' techniques to production; the Keynesian revolution in economic management; and the 'integration' of the organised institutions of the working class through social democracy and reformism. The recomposition of capital has therefore, in turn, 'recomposed' the working class. The tendency, progressively, to deskill the working class, and to subsume it into massified processes of production is tending to create the 'mass worker'. Although operating in advanced modes of production, the 'mass worker' is not the old skilled worker of an earlier capitalism, but literally a worker who can be moved from one part of a fragmented and automated labour process to another, and from one country to another (the use of migrant labour in the more advanced capitalist countries of Europe is a key instance of this). This 'productive' recomposition of the class also involves a political recomposition – the old reflexes and organisations of class struggle belonging to an earlier phase being dismantled, and class struggle tending to generate new forms of militant resistance directly against the exploitation of the new labour process, often directly at the 'point of production'. Hence, many of the forms of direct workers' resistance – of 'organised spontaneity' – hitherto thought of as syndicalist in character, represent an advanced mode of struggle face to face with the new conditions of capitalist accumulation and production. This 'mass worker' is a concrete embodiment of Marx's 'abstract labourer'. Without going into this argument further, it can be seen at once how this analysis can be extended to illuminate the specific position of black labour (and other migrant 'labours') in the 'advanced' sectors of modern British industry; but also how forms of 'direct resistance' – like the refusal to work – can assume a quite different meaning and strategic position, as forms of class struggle, not of a marginal but of pivotal sections of the working class.

It is useful at this point to turn to the altogether different analysis of the position of black labour and the black wageless advanced by *The Black Liberator* collective. Cambridge and Gutsmore are critical of the *Race Today* position, and the main arguments advanced against them are as follows. The refusal to work amongst black labour, and black youth especially, is a real phenomenon, but it represents an ideological not a political struggle. It does not 'subvert capital' directly, since even if the whole working class, black and white, were employed, the rate of exploitation of labour by capital would not necessarily be intensified. Black workers are therefore conceived in more classical terms as a 'reserve army of labour' (of a special, racially differentiated type). They are used, productively or unproductively, in relation to the needs and rhythms of capital. As such they constitute a black *sub-proletarian stratum* of the general working class. When productively employed, they are 'super-exploited', in that a relatively higher level of surplus value is extracted from them. They are exploited and oppressed at two different levels: as black workers (super-exploitation) and as a racial minority (racism). The idea that the function of the police in relation to this sector is *directly* to regulate the conditions of class struggle and to tie the working class to wage-labour is undercut on the grounds (mentioned above) that it constitutes a false reduction of the level of the state (political) to the level of the economic. The position adopted here is directly and explicitly in line with Seccombe's argument on domestic labour, [87] and it shares *something* with the Hirst argument at least in seeing the 'refusal to work' of this wageless sector as, at best, a quasi-political rebellion, not as a fully formed class perspective. [88] There are critical differences of theoretical analysis between the two positions here, and both – necessarily – lead to very different political assessments of the correct strategy for the development of black political struggle. Whereas the *Race Today* position stresses the self-activating dynamic of a developing black struggle, with the black wageless clearly providing this struggle with one of its key supports, Cambridge and Gutsmore, in *The Black Liberator*, while supporting the developing industrial and community struggles of blacks against exploitation and oppression, are obliged to define these as, inevitably at this point in time, 'economist' or corporatist in form.[89] Both positions, however, agree in defining the various sectors of black labour as 'super-exploited'; and both analyse blacks as constituting a racially distinct stratum of the class, different in character from the traditional notion of the 'lumpenproletariat' as advanced, for example, by Hirst.[90]

Marx, it will be recalled, called the lumpen 'the social scum, the passively rotting mass thrown off by the lowest layers of the old society'.[91] Engels characterised them thus:

> The lumpen proletariat, this scum of the depraved elements of all classes, which establishes its headquarters in the big cities, is the worst of all possible allies. This rabble is absolutely venal and absolutely brazen ... every leader of the workers who uses these scoundrels as guards or relies on them for support proves himself by this action a traitor to the movement.[92]

This is a very different picture to that presented by Darcus Howe:

> And now I want to speak specifically of the unemployed. In the Caribbean it is not simply that you are unemployed and you drift in hunger and total demoralisation from day to day. That is absolutely untrue. I know how I first got the idea that people thought about that was from the White Left. When they talk about the unemployed, they talk about a miserable, downtrodden, beaten population that does not constitute itself as a section of the working class and in one way or another carry on struggles of their own, and so the unemployed I talk about in the Caribbean, that has not got a wage, an official wage of any kind, no wealth, is a vibrant powerful section of the society. It has always been that. Culturally, steel band, Calypso, reggae come from that section of the population. What little there is of *National* culture in the Caribbean, came out of the vibrancy of that section of the population.[93]

This section of the class typically survives by 'hustling' — which Howe describes as 'eking out' a survival in a wageless world, *not*, usually, by resorting to crime. The same sense of vibrancy emerges in the positive stress on avoiding the humiliation of work, and also, in the way the class can be *disciplined* by such activities:

> In my view the *minority* would be carrying on activities called criminal, in the sense of robbery and burglary and things like that. What normally happens in those days would be somehow your whole social personality develops skills by which you get portions of the wage. Either by using your physical strength as a gang leader, or your cunning — so that section of the working class is disciplined by that general term and form called 'hustling'.

Ganja in Jamaica, anything like that – I do not think ganja is a crime in that sense. All different ways, you eke out, which does not involve, in my view, a kind of humiliation.[94]

Survival by these means produces a *political* awareness. Talking of the intervention of the Prime Minister of Trinidad and the Commissioner of Police to end one of the fiercest of local gang wars, and the need to do this by 'winning over' the gangs, rather than by confrontation, Howe has this to say:

They could not choose confrontation because by and large that section of the working class was the military arm of the Nationalist movement, of the African section of the Nationalist Movement. So that when the Indian had a tendency to attack the African political leaders with guns at meetings and things, we constituted the military arm of the African section. So that we always had to be courted. So the Prime Minister comes and negotiates with the gang leader and the police to terminate the war. At which point the class now begins to see itself as a section with formidable power, so we begin to raise the question of unemployment.[95]

The steady drift of youngsters with 'O' levels into the ranks of the wageless helped to transform the class; and this is, again, exemplified by the refusal of the Army (largely made up of the unemployed) to quell the mass demonstrations during the 1970 political crisis in Trinidad:

So that this section of the working class, although not disciplined, organised and unified by the very mechanism of capitalist production itself, were necessarily concentrated and socialised through hustling, in some kind of quasi-disciplinary way, to make an intervention in the society and break up the army, and leave the opening for the working class to come on the stage.[96]

This interpellated history of the Trinidadian wageless has direct relevance, Howe maintains, for an understanding of the British situation, though he is aware of the dangers of suggesting such simple political parallels. Furthermore, he does not deny that this section of the class displays negative tendencies (that, for example, the criminal element supplies most of the police informers). But he insists that these tendencies exist in the class as a whole, and are not specific to the wageless. This conception of the black wageless is very different from that offered by the editors of *The Black Liberator*. For them, the *whole* of the black proletariat is best conceived of as a *sub-proletariat*: a stratum of the working class that is the object of two specific mechanisms – *super-exploitation* and *racial oppression*:

The *interlacing* of these specific mechanisms operate such that they pervade the reproduction process of *surplus value extraction* where the *rate of exploitation* – i.e. super-exploitation – is high with the sub-proletariat; such that where unemployed, the Black Masses form a disproportionate section of the *reserve army of labour*; such that their class struggle combine forms, against *racial oppression* and *cultural-imperialism*, other than those specifically practised by the indigenous white working class.[97]

Although, as Cambridge goes on to say, 'the mechanisms whereby surplus-value extraction is specified as peculiar to Black workers in the metropolitan economy is still to be worked out', the introduction of the notion of the *reserve army of labour* and of the black masses, where unemployed, forming a disproportionate section of this, marks a crucial departure from the 'wageless' argument of *Race Today*. Cambridge defines the reserve army this way:

> Along with the accumulation of capital, the life blood of the *capitalist mode of production* created by the surplus labour of the working class and vital for *expanded reproduction of the conditions of production* goes the reproduction not only of their means of exploitation (employment) but also of their own dispensability (unemployment). The reproduction of the *capitalist mode of production* depends on its constantly finding new markets and unproductive sectors of production must go. In this connexion, capitalism has a two-fold need – on the one hand, for a mass of labour-power always ready for exploitation which allows for the possibility of throwing great masses of productive workers on the decisive point of production without upset to the scale of production, and on the other, to dispose of these workers when their exploitation is no longer profitable. Capitalist production depends, therefore, upon the constant transformation of a part of the labour force into an *'unemployed'* and *'under-employed'* disposable 'industrial reserve army of labour'. In the Imperialist dominated world economy, where unemployed, the *Black Masses* form a substantial section of this industrial reserve army of labour, increasingly unlikely to be used in production as the productivity of labour increases in the context of centralised capital.[98]

Some of the analytic difficulties now begin to emerge fully from the juxtaposition of these positions – all of them, it must be noted, posited within a Marxist framework. Marx and Engels clearly regard the *lumpenproletariat* and the 'dangerous classes' as 'scum' – the depraved element of all classes. Parasitic in their modes of economic existence, they are also outside the framework of productive labour which alone could hone and temper them into a cohesive class capable of revolutionary struggle at a point of insertion in the productive system which could limit and roll back the sway of capital. Darcus Howe regards this element, not as the dregs and deposit of all classes, but as an identifiable sector of the working class – that sector which, *both* in the West Indies and in Britain, have been consigned to a position of *wagelessness*, and which has developed, from such a base, an autonomous level of struggle capable, in economic and political terms, of inflicting, through the wageless strategy, severe damage on capital and 'subverting' its purposes. This is clearly not a description any longer of a *lumpenproletariat* in the classic Marxist sense. Cambridge and Gutsmore regard the whole of the black labour force as a *super-exploited stratum* of the proletariat. Its more or less permanent position, structurally, below the white working class makes it a *sub-proletariat*. Its exploitation is then 'overdetermined' by racial exploitation and oppression. The wageless part of this sub-proletariat does not have either the 'lumpen' character ascribed by Marx and Engels, nor the strategic political role predicted by *Race*

Today. Classically, they are *that sector of the black sub-proletariat which at the present time capital cannot employ*. Thus they perform the classic function of a 'reserve army of labour' – they can be used to undermine the position of the waged sectors, but their own wagelessness, far from constituting a striking base on capital, is a token of their containment.

One of the main sources of the difference between these descriptions arises from the different historical periods and phases in the development of capitalism to which they refer. Marx and Engels were observing the transitional period from domestic to factory labour and the historic epoch of 'classical' capitalist development. The decanting of rural populations into the centres of factory production, the development of the discipline of factory labour and the break-up of older systems of production created in their wake, at one end, the first industrial proletariat, at the other end, the casual poor and the destitute classes. In Hobsbawm and Rudé's studies,[99] the Wilkes, 'King and Country' and city 'mobs' and 'crowds', which appear at the end of the eighteenth century, are the last occasion when the latter are seen – in combination with skilled artisans in declining trades and the petty-criminals – in a leading role on the political stage. After that, to be sure, this human detritus of the capitalist system – its massive casualty list – accumulates in the hovels and wens, often (as Hobsbawm argued) overlapping through their occupancy of certain slum areas of the cities with the 'labouring classes', but already declining in historical importance. Both *Race Today* and *The Black Liberator* base their analyses on accounts of the *subsequent* phase of capitalism – that period of growing monopoly which, under the title of 'imperialism', Lenin characterised as capitalism's 'highest' – and hopefully, its last – stage. The main outlines of Lenin's thesis are too well known to rehearse at length – the growing concentration of production; the replacement of competition by monopoly; the shift of power within the ruling fractions of capital from industrial to finance capital; the deepening of the crises of overproduction and underconsumption; leading to the sharpening competition for overseas markets and overseas outlets for profitable capital investment; and thus the period of 'imperialist rivalries' and of world wars.[100] What is important for us is the impact which Lenin assumed this new phase in the development of capitalism would have on the *internal* structure and composition of the proletariat. He argued that the much higher profits obtainable through overseas investment and the exploitation of the hinterlands by a global capitalism would enable the ruling classes to bribe or buy off an 'upper' stratum of the proletariat at home – incorporate it in the imperialist net and blunt its revolutionary edge. This would create *sharper* distinctions *within* the proletariat, between its 'upper' and 'lower' sectors. The term he coined for that stratum successfully bought off in this way was the 'aristocracy of labour'. Lenin also believed it would widen the gap between the British proletariat *as a whole* (upper and lower) and the 'super-exploited' colonial proletariat at the other end of the imperialist chain. The concept of an 'aristocracy of labour', as a way of accounting for the sectionalism and internal divisions of the proletariat, was not new. Hobsbawm notes that the phrase 'seems to have been used from the middle of the nineteenth century at least to describe certain distinctive strata of the working class, better paid, better treated and generally regarded as more "respectable" and politically moderate than the rest of the proletariat'.[101] Lenin, in fact, had quoted with approval Engels's letter to Marx (7 October 1858), in which the former noted that 'the English proletariat is actually becoming more and more bourgeois, so that the most bourgeois of all nations is apparently aiming ultimately at the possession of a bourgeois aristocracy and a bourgeois proletariat *alongside* the bourgeoisie. For a nation which exploits the whole world, this is of course to a certain extent justifiable.'[102] Already contained within Engels's ironic exasperation is (i) the appearance of new internal stratifications within the metropolitan working class; and (ii) the germ of the idea that the proletariat of an imperialist power benefits economically (and so the ruling classes profit politically) from the super-exploitation of the colonial proletariat. Looked at from the underside, within the global framework of the capitalist system, the colonial proletariat which is excessively exploited so as to produce the super-profits with which to placate the proletariat at home is, structurally, *already* a *sub-proletariat* to the latter. It is hardly surprising, then, that when, at a later stage, sections of this colonial proletariat are attracted to work in the metropolis, they are inserted into the productive relations in a sectionally appropriate role – as an *internalised* sub-proletariat. The subordinate economic role which this black sub-class has always played, historically, to the white metropolitan working class is reproduced in the metropoles: in part, through ideological distinctions based on racism, the effects of which are to reproduce that subordination, ideologically, within the metropolitan economy, and to legitimate it as a 'permanent' – or caste – division within the working class as a whole. But the picture is not complete until we look at those underside conditions in which, before emigration, the colonial proletariat was constituted. And here, of course, we find, as a constant and apparently *necessary condition* of its super-exploitation, the condition of 'wagelessness':

One of the major features of the contemporary Third World is the explosive growth of urban populations composed of immigrants from the countryside and the smaller towns who are not established proletarians either in terms of occupation – since they live in a chronic state of unemployment or under-employment – or of political culture, since they have not absorbed the life-style and mentality of established urban workers. Countries like India and China are indeed overwhelmingly peasant societies. But in Argentina, Chile, Venezuela and Uruguay, 40% and more of the population live in towns or cities with more than 200,000 inhabitants. . . . Every year thousands of new recruits flock to the favelas, barridas, bidonvilles, shanty-towns or whatever you like, in encampments made out of cardboard, flattened petrol tins and old packing cases. Whatever term we may use to describe this social category it is high time to abandon the highly insulting, inaccurate and analytically befogging Marxist term *lumpenproletariat* which is so commonly used. 'Underclass' or 'subproletariat' would seem much more apt characterizations of these victims of 'urbanization without industrialization'.[103]

Such an 'underclass', as Worsley describes in his important essay, may, in strict terms, be 'unproductive', in that its members are not in regular productive employment. But in Third World societies, where shanty-towns are a permanent and structural feature of life, they cannot be considered 'marginal' in any other sense. They are large in number, and growing; their economic activities, however transient and precarious, are of crucial importance to the whole society; and their strength must be compared to what, in many cases, is a very small, and sometimes non-existent urban proletariat in the classical sense. The Portuguese-African leader, Amilcar Cabral, who spoke of *two* categories within the 'rootless' – 'young folk come lately from the countryside', and 'beggars, layabouts, prostitutes, etc.' – said, of the latter category, it 'is easily identified and might easily be called our lumpenproletariat, if we had anything in Guinea we could properly call a proletariat'. [104] And, so far as political role is concerned, it was, of course, just this group of urban dispossessed, in and out of work, chronically un- or under-employed, scraping a living by all means – straight, illegal, and in between – permanently on the border of survival, whom Fanon believed constituted 'one of the most spontaneous and the most radically revolutionary forces of a colonised people'. [105] They, with the peasantry, *were* the 'wretched of the earth'.

We have here two, apparently divergent ways of attempting to understand the nature and position of the black working class and of the types of political struggles and forms of political consciousness available to it. These divergent paths may be summed up in the following way. If we focus on *wagelessness*, as a pertinent and growing condition for a greater and greater proportion of black labour, but limit our treatment of it to its British metropolitan context, then the wageless appear as a sinking class fraction, expelled into poverty as superfluous to capital; then the temptation to assimilate it, analytically, to the classic 'lumpenproletariat' of Marx and Engels's earlier descriptions is a strong one. *Race Today* breaks with this ascription, by redefining black labour in terms of two 'histories'. First, it is a sector of *Caribbean* labour, and, as such, central to the history of struggle and the peculiar conditions of the Caribbean working class from which it originates. Second, it tends to be inserted into metropolitan capitalist relations as the deskilled, super-exploited 'mass worker'. In redrawing the historical boundaries of black labour in this way, so to speak, the *Race Today* collective is able to redefine 'wagelessness' – in two different contexts – as a positive rather than as a passive form of struggle: as belonging to a majority rather than a 'marginal' working-class experience, a position thoroughly *filled out* and amplified, culturally and ideologically, and therefore capable of providing the base of a viable class strategy. From this combination of Third, and 'First', World perspectives, the black wageless are very different indeed from the 'passive and rotting scum' of the traditional lumpen. *The Black Liberator* is as concerned with Caribbean and 'Third World' politics as is *Race Today*. But it analyses the position of black labour in Britain principally in relation to the present class relations of British capital, into which the migrant labour force has been directly subsumed; that is to say, not historically, in terms of the mechanisms of 'colonial' capital in the past, but structurally, in terms of the mechanisms of British capital and in the present conjuncture. What matters is how black labour has been subsumed under the sway of capital in the metropolis – i.e. as a sub-proletariat – and how its relations to capital are governed – i.e. in terms, not of the cultural struggle expressed in the strategy of 'wagelessness', but through the more classic mechanisms of the reserve army of labour.

Another way of examining the same terrain would be to distinguish more carefully between the determinacy over black labour of the level of the *economic*, and the *political and ideological* practices of struggle. We cannot push this argument too far at this point; but it is sufficient merely to sketch out the possibilities it entails.

What determines the size of the wageless sector of the black working class at any point may be less the political strategy of a minority 'not to take shit-work any longer', and more the fundamental economic rhythms which Marx analysed as structuring the size and character of the different strata of the 'reserve army of labour'. However, it is still possible for those so ascribed (economic class relations) to develop this into a more positive strategy of class struggle (political and ideological). The forms of *political* class struggle would then relate to previous modes of survival and resistance by that class, deriving, essentially, from its pre-metropolitan past. This latter position is not as constrained by a 'history of origins' as it may at first appear. For there may be political factors *in the present* recreating for black labour the possibilities of waging a political struggle of this kind from such a base. In the section which follows, we trace some of the factors which may have helped to determine the forms of political struggle face to face with metropolitan capital in the present conjuncture. On the other hand, this type of explanation remains open to the objection that it tends to be 'historicist': it explains *present* forms of struggle in terms of traditions derived from the past. It is of critical importance at this point to remind ourselves of the economic mechanisms which do, indeed, appear to have the effect of fundamental determinate forces governing the size and position of the black wageless today. This returns us to Marx's analysis of the 'reserve army' of labour. For Marx, the industrial reserve army of labour (the 'relative surplus population') becomes a permanent feature of capital accumulation only after the transition from manufacture to modern industry, when capital takes 'real control'. Modern industry requires 'the constant formation, the greater or less absorption and the re-formation, of the industrial reserve army or surplus population'. As capital advances into new areas of production, 'there must be the possibility of throwing great masses of men suddenly on the decisive points without injury to the scale of production in other spheres'.[106] Capitalism, thus, not only required a disposable reserve army, but attempted to govern its size and character – that is, the rate at which, in accordance with capital accumulation, sections were drawn into production or expelled into unemployment. Thus, for Marx, the question of the reserve army was centrally linked to the capitalist accumulation cycle. As the proportion of 'dead' to 'living' labour (machines to labourers) increased, so a section of the waged force was 'set free' to be available elsewhere as and when capital required. The presence of the reserve army thus also helped to determine the conditions and wages of those in employment. When the reserve army was large, employed workers were obliged to accept lower wages since they could easily be replaced by their substitutes. The presence of a 'permanent' reserve army therefore was considered to have a competitive effect on the employed, tending to lower the value of labour-power to capital. If the reserve army is small, workers are in a better position to demand higher wages. But the resulting fall in profits and capital accumulation leads to workers being thrown out of work and a consequent growth of the reserve army, and a fall or slower rise in wage levels.[107] In the different phases of this cycle, capital continually composes and recomposes the working class through its own dynamic movement: it generates a certain level of unemployment as a necessary feature of that movement, unless this tendency is counteracted in some other way. The 'recomposition of the labour force' argument here is a critical one. For sections of the waged, thrown temporarily into the reserve army, may not necessarily be re-employed either in the same sectors of production, or at the same levels of skill. Both 'deskilling' and substitution – replacing one sector of labour by a cheaper one – are therefore central aspects of the process of the formation and dissolution of the reserve army. This 'then raises the question of the sources of labour which become part of the working class' when labour is being attracted into production from the reserve army, 'while the tendency to repulsion raises the question of the destiny of the labourers, whether employed or unemployed (for example, the tendency towards the marginalization of certain groups of workers)'.[108]

Marx, in fact, distinguished several different layers or strata *within* the 'reserve army': the *floating* strata were those repelled and drawn back into production in the heart of the productive sector; the *latent* strata were principally those in agricultural production displaced in the course of the capitalist advance into the rural economy; the *stagnant* were those 'permanently' irregularly employed. All three were distinct from the 'lumpenproletariat' – the 'dangerous classes', and from *pauperism* – 'the demoralised and ragged and those unable to work ... the victims of industry'. Pauperism, he added, is the 'hospital of the active labour-army and the dead weight of the industrial reserve army'.[109] As we shall see, there is no intrinsic reason why these mechanisms should not operate at the marginal poles of capitalism as a global system – i.e. in the colonial hinterlands – as well as in the metropolis. Thus we must modify, now, the argument outlined a little earlier. The size and significance of the unemployed, the wageless, the semi-employed and the 'marginalised' sectors of the colonial proletariat may differ from that in the metropolitan society; but *vis-à-vis* colonial capital, too, its formation may well be governed by the kinds of rhythms outlined by Marx in this crucial argument in *Capital*.

The industrial reserve army of the unemployed is as fundamental to the laws of capitalist accumulation as the size of the productive 'labour-army'. But in the developed countries of Western Europe in the post-war period, it has proved increasingly difficult to sustain it in its classical form, at least until recently. As a result of a complex set of factors which cannot be rehearsed here – including the growing strength of the labour movement itself – capitalism, in order to survive, had to aim for continuous productive expansion and 'full employment' for the native work-force. This ran counter to the need for a 'reserve army'. A substitute 'reserve army' was therefore needed: one neither costly nor politically unacceptable – as unemployment resulting from capitalism's cyclical movement then was. Modern capitalism has made use of two principal 'reserve' sources: women and migrant labour. 'The solution to these problems adopted by West European capitalism has been the employment of immigrant workers from under-developed areas of Southern Europe or from the Third World.' [110] These had always played a part; but in post-war conditions they became a *permanent* feature of the economic structure of these societies (as, according to Braverman, Latin American and Oriental labour has become for the American post-war economy). Migrant workers now form *the permanent basis of the modern industrial reserve army*. In the period of productive expansion, labour was sucked into production from the Caribbean and Asian sub-continent. Gradually, as economic recession began to bite, a more restrictive practice was instituted – in effect, forcing a part of the 'reserve army' to remain where it already was, in the Caribbean and Asian homelands. Now, in the depths of the economic crisis, we are in the alternate pole of the 'reserve-army' cycle: the phase of control and expulsion. In the intervening period, both women and some southern European labour had already begun to 'substitute' for the black reserve army. In the 1970s, the political assault on 'full employment' has demolished the political barriers; and the reconstitution of the layers of the 'reserve army' is proceeding full tilt. The black youths roaming the streets of British cities in search for work are its latest, and rawest, recruits.

THE 'WRETCHED OF THE EARTH'

We have followed the argument through, from the new stratifications in the working class of the metropolis set in train by imperialism, to the very different disposition of the strata of the work-force in Third World colonial societies, through imperialism and neo-imperialism. The connection between the latter and the black working class in Britain must now be pursued further. First, in order to take up the theme that the black working class as a whole belongs to *two*, different, though intersecting, histories: the history of Caribbean labour and the history of the British working class. One line of argument, which could follow from attempting to hold these two histories in mind, is that when black labour, pulled in by an expanding phase of British capital, is thrown temporarily or permanently into unemployment as a result of a recession, it develops a way of survival, outlook and modes of class struggle which appear similar to that of the white 'reserve army' or the *lumpenproletariat*, but which are far better understood in terms of its *other*, previous, colonial history. Thus this proposition of the 'double positioning' of the class throws a different light on how we assess the potential politics and trajectory of its more self-conscious strata. Second, the Third World connection puts the relationship between unemployment, marginality *and crime* in a new perspective. In Britain, the distinction between those described by Marx, Engels and others as 'lumpen' and those sectors of productive labour thrown temporarily into the reserve army of the unemployed may remain a sharp one. But, for example, Keith Hart, in one of the few (though growing) studies of a colonial sub-proletariat (in Nima, Accra), goes so far as to reject the categories of 'unemployed' and 'underemployed' altogether, preferring to think instead of 'formal' and 'informal' income opportunities. Even the employed have to supplement their meagre incomes, Hart observed, and hence 'money-lending, moonlighting, dependence

on kin and living on credit, the working of land within the city, and crime
become central features of everyday economic life'. [111] Third, theories of the
potential political role and consciousness of these 'rootless' poor in colonial
economies, such as those propounded by Fanon, have had a major retrospective impact *on* the emergent consciousness of black people *in the metropoles*. In
Britain, for example, the impact of Fanonist perspectives has been exercised,
partly through the African revolutions, and partly through the mediation of the
black movement in the United States. Thus, on several levels, the problem of
the colonial 'underclass' or *lumpenproletariat* is directly germane to any discussion of the position and potential political consciousness of that black 'underclass' which now increasingly appears, in Britain, in a marginal or
criminalised form. The size, social complexion and economic position of the
rootless poor of the colonial cities will vary considerably, of course, from one
area of the Third World to another. Chris Allan, in a useful summarising essay,
describes the typical, large sector of the urban poor in colonial cities as unemployed, of low status, with little contact with other dominant social groups, living a marginal economic existence, usually in a distinct area of the city or
town, and generally regarded as 'social outcasts' by the rest of the
community. [112] Within these 'outcasts', he distinguishes between those who are
born into the status – children of 'outcast' families born and reared in 'outcast'
slum areas – and those who have been through the process of 'becoming outcast'. He also distinguishes between those who have lost jobs and become permanently or semi-permanently unemployed, and those who have never really
been employed since drifting into the cities. Many in both categories will be internal migrants from the countryside (one of Marx's 'reserve-army' categories).
Both kinds of adult outcast groups will scrape a living by a host of occasional
jobs, petty-trading – and crime. Speaking of the African experience, he writes:

> If as is increasingly the case, he fails to find some permanent occupation, the
> migrant will then move along a series of contacts, initially relatives and then
> acquaintances, with and off whom he will live, until he ceases to be suppor-
> ted by the last member of the series, and has to live entirely from parasitic
> occupations: sporadic petty-trading, car-cleaning and watching, begging,
> pimping, or prostitution, petty theft, minor bullying for political leaders,
> shoe-cleaning, bottle-cleaning, portering and occasional unskilled labouring.

Give or take some items in this list of occupations, it could be immediately
referred to, for example, the 'outcast' areas of West Kingston in Jamaica. The
group may include those occasional or street traders involved in the economic
activity which Sol Tax called 'penny capitalism'. [113] Allan stresses both the
heterogeneity of this group as a whole and the different modes in which outcasts exist:

> The unemployed become shunned, and move into areas of cheap housing;
> they steal to live, and may become full-time criminals, moving to yet more
> isolated areas of town. Blacks find both jobs and housing hard to get, and
> are in any case treated by most persons as both socially and psychologically
> outcast. Any of such outcasts can become, in Fanon's words, 'the hopeless
> dregs of humanity, who turn in circles between suicide and madness'. [114]

More recently, Latin American economists have been studying the growth of a permanently 'marginalised labour force'. As one sector of the economy becomes progressively adapted to the international capitalist market, so a substantial sector of the labour force at the other end is driven towards the 'marginal pole' of the economy. Obregon, for example, considers the position of what he explicitly calls this growing 'reserve surplus population'. [115] Such a population, he notes, exists in several forms, again corresponding to Marx's distinctions. There are the 'floating' sectors, drawn into and expelled from employment by turns, depending on the cycles of economic expansion and contraction. There are the 'latent' sectors – rural workers, thrown out of employment or unable to get it in the countryside, who drift into the cities. There is an 'intermittent' sector – in permanent but irregular employment, outworkers for example. Then there is the 'lumpenproletariat' or the ragged proletariat, often comprised of vagrants, prostitutes and criminals; and the pauperised – those totally unemployed and lacking any source of income, destined for a state of permanent poverty. Obregon goes on to argue that, in the particular circumstances he is examining (that of a Latin American economy with an advanced, leading capitalist sector), this 'surplus population' is no longer, strictly speaking, a 'reserve army'; since it is unlikely to be re-employed, even in prosperous economic circumstances; hence it ceases in many ways to be a 'lever' on capital.

One of the confusions arises from the fact that, since the internal distinctions between the different layers of the 'underclass' are not clearly defined, and differ considerably from one society of this type to another, they tend to have been saddled with the catch-all label of 'lumpenproletariat' and then to have ascribed to them the derogatory descriptions reserved by Marx and Engels for one sector only – the 'lumpen', which is taken from a quite specific set of historical circumstances, the destitute classes of the industrial cities of Western Europe in the mid-nineteenth century. The revisions have thus been seen as running counter to a classical or orthodox version of the theory. In fact, these revisions are not so much economic as political. They stem in part from the fact that, since 1917, revolutions have assumed anything but a 'pure' or classical shape. There has been a decisive shift in the location of revolutionary struggle from Europe to the Third World – i.e. to societies with strikingly different economic and class structures from those of Western Europe. In these situations, the industrial proletariat is relatively weak and small, and sometimes non-existent. This shift has therefore brought to the fore the vexing question of the form of alliance between the oppressed classes and the 'national bourgeoisie', especially in a period dominated by nationalism rather than a social revolution (the distinctions, of course, are never so clear-cut). In practice, these questions have been answered differently, in different settings. But whether one takes Asia, Latin America or Africa, each form of the solution contains certain clearly 'unmarxist' or revisionist strands. China provides the example of a nationalist struggle which became during its course a social revolution, spearheaded by the peasants, the Party and the Red Army, culminating in a military victory. It also, through its theoretical elaboration in 'Maoism', embodied a stress on the over-riding importance of the collective, 'subjective' will, as compared with objective conditions, and on the key role of the peasantry *qua* peasantry (necessarily under the leadership of a proletarian party). It included Mao's own enthusiastic recruitment of what he called *déclassés elements* (soldiers, bandits, robbers, etc.) into the revolutionary struggle. Schramm, for example, remarks:

> The episode of Wang and Yuan [a reference to two bandit chiefs Mao had united with in 1928 in preference to the central committee instructions to 'workerise' the cadres of the Party and the Army] has in fact broad implications. It reflects the accent on the human will, rather than on objective factors, which still characterises Mao's version of Marxism. A little later, commenting on the presence of an extremely high percentage of *elements déclassés* in his army, Mao affirmed that the only remedy was to intensify political training 'so as to effect a qualitative change in these elements'. [116]

In the Cuban case, the revolutionary leadership under Castro effected, by a masterly combination of political and military strategies, a further 'Latinised' deviation from the pure European model of revolutions. Here, the concern was with a military solution, based on the use of roving guerrilla *focos*, leading to a social revolution, after the nationalist one, from 'on top' – a strategy which, as elaborated by writers like Debray, played a directly influential role in Latin America, at least up to the death of Guevara in the Bolivian jungle. Debray reminds us how Guevara set out the preconditions of this *foco* strategy in his preface to *Guerilla Warfare*: [117]

> The Cuban revolution has made three fundamental contributions to revolutionary strategy in Latin America: 1: The popular forces can win *a war* against the army; 2: It is not necessary always to wait until all the conditions for revolution are fulfilled – the insurrectionary centre can create them; 3: In underdeveloped America the terrain of armed struggle must basically be the countryside. [118]

There is no need to follow through the successes and defeats of this strategy in Latin America, and the reappraisal which has followed its containment, to see how distinctive this scenario is from any classical one, above all in terms of the composition of the classes which will be principally involved in political and military struggle.

It is Fanon, however, writing of the Algerian and other African struggles, whose 'revisions' are most apposite to our concerns. Fanon laid particular stress on a *violent* (as opposed to a purely military) solution to the question of colonial oppression, since the practice of violence binds the colonised 'together as a whole', as well as, individually, freeing 'the native from his inferiority complex and from his despair and inaction; it makes him fearless and restores his self-respect'. [119] Worsley has made the important point that Fanon is not an apostle of unorganised expressive violence but of violence 'as a social practice'. [120] More germane for us. Fanon regarded the key social classes in the colonial struggle as the peasantry – 'the only spontaneous revolutionary force of the country' – and the *lumpenproletariat*, 'one of the most spontaneous and the most radically revolutionary forces of the colonised people':

It is within this mass of humanity, this people of the shantytowns, at the core of the lumpenproletariat that the rebellion will find its urban spearhead. For the *lumpenproletariat*, that horde of starving men, uprooted from their tribe and from their clan, constitutes one of the most spontaneous and the most revolutionary forces of a colonised people. . . . The lumpenproletariat, once it is constituted, brings all forces to endanger the 'security' of the town, and is the sign of the irrevocable decay, the gangrene ever present at the heart of colonial domination. So the pimps, the hooligans, the unemployed and the petty criminals, urged on from behind, throw themselves into the struggle for liberation like stout working men. [121]

It is important to remember that Fanon also regarded as crucial the role of the revolutionary nationalists – the 'illegalists' – who, disaffected with the reformist nationalist parties, retreat to the countryside, identify with the peasantry and learn from them, and come to provide the vanguard stratum in the revolutionary coalition – a 'potent political force'. [122] He also acknowledged that the spontaneous peasant uprising, by itself, could not win a revolutionary war. And he recognised that the 'oppressor . . . will be extremely skilful in using that ignorance and incomprehension of the *lumpenproletariat*'. [123] They had, he said, to be 'urged on from behind'. Nevertheless, he believed that the *lumpenproletariat* – which is clearly a very broad and rather ill-defined category in Fanon's analysis – is capable of a revolutionary, as well as a reactionary, political role. His writings were clearly attempting to generalise outwards from the Algerian experience, where 'tens of thousands of the volatile lower depths of the city slum population were transformed from being an anarchic, hopeless, depoliticised mass into a reservoir for the revolution'. [124]

Fanon's thesis has been substantially criticised in the years which have followed his death. Worsley, for example, seems to be correct in his judgement that Cabral's more sober assessment of the role of the lumpenproletariat, and *déclassés* in general, has been historically more accurate than Fanon's. It is Cabral's rather than Fanon's version which seems most sensitive to the specific social and cultural factors helping to determine the political role of the different class strata in the specific conditions of Guinea: 'Lima is not Bissau, and Bissau is not Calcutta.' However, Worsley also argues that what these instances reveal is that a particular form of consciousness, mode of struggle and position in the revolutionary spectrum cannot be *permanently ascribed* to any one sector: 'Similar things were said in history about women, Blacks, the proletariat, colonial peoples, and so on.' Although the forms of consciousness of the *lumpenproletariat* will *tend* to be, at best, corporate, or 'communal', Worsley reminds us that slum life is in fact a highly organised and structured form of existence, not the 'total social disorganisation' which has often been fostered on those living within the 'cultures of poverty'. And they *can* be won to a different mode of struggle provided conditions, organisation and leadership intervene in their material modes of existence to break the existing chains of inaction, and develop amongst them the basis for an authentic political struggle. Others, often working from a different basis, have been more sceptical of the potential for collective action amongst the marginal classes. [125]

Worsley, however, also observes that Fanon's arguments have found their greatest resonance in places very different from his native Algeria – especially 'in the revival of direct action in Paris and Berlin, but above all in the Black ghettoes of the United States where his books have sold in thousands'. The 'taking up' of a Fanonist perspective amongst white revolutionary youth does not directly concern us here. Terrorism and violence as revolutionary weapons, and the key role of the *lumpenproletariat*, form central strands within certain historical traditions of anarchism, which came to the fore in the 1960s and 1970s as the Communist Parties of the West were outpaced by the revolutionary and extra-parliamentary groups of the extreme left. It also stemmed from the ideological identification, especially by the student movements, with Third World revolutionary struggles. But the adoption and adaptation of Fanonism within the *black* movement in the United States is more directly germane: first, because of its impact on the developing consciousness of black people everywhere, including those in Britain; second, because it suggested that a political analysis, initiated in terms of colonial society and struggle, *was* adaptable or transferable to the conditions of black minorities in developed urban capitalist conditions. During the high tide of the black movement in the United States, there were always a number of rhetorics and ideologies competing for hegemony amongst blacks; but, despite this competition, the decisive shift was from the reformist, integrationist perspective of the civil rights phase to the revolutionary and separatist phase identified with Black Power, the Afro-American cultural nationalists, the Muslims and (though they were not 'separatist' in the same manner) the Black Panthers. If we try to reconstruct the key ideological elements common to many of these different tendencies within the black movement, we can discover how the transposition was attempted from African to American circumstances: how Cleaver's *lumpenproletariat* was grafted on to Fanon's.

The identification with Africa meant, for the black American movement, a rediscovery of a common, black, African historical and cultural identity. In the same moment, it engendered a rediscovery of underdevelopment, oppression and super-exploitation. Amongst the black population in the United States, all these were to be discovered most evidently in the black ghettoes of American cities, which therefore ceased to be regarded, statically, as 'resource-starved enclaves' of social disorganisation, and came to be reconstructed as *internal colonies*. Integration into the white economic and social system through the extension of equal opportunity became less experientially relevant as compared with a struggle for the liberation of the black 'colony' from the imperial 'metropolis'. As Worsley notes, these internal colonies were in fact conceived as parts of the Third World *within* the 'First World' – the term 'Third World' thus coming to signify a set of characteristic economic, social and cultural exploitative relations, rather than a set of geographical spaces. Other struggles – for example, the Vietnam War – may have been more significant in the development of a strategy aimed to 'bring the war of liberation back home'. But Fanon was critical for his analysis of the 'colonial mentality' amongst blacks, its appositeness for an understanding of the culture of the ghetto, and his thesis of the possibility of the transformation of this mentality as the struggle developed from the limited aim of 'rights' to the more extended revolutionary aim of 'liberation'.

In economic terms, the American black population is a distinct, super-exploited class within the wider (white) working class. At any time, it is substantially recruited to the lowest rungs of the occupational ladder, and a substantial majority are permanently marginal, under- or unemployed. Black politics has, therefore, never been able to function exclusively with the advanced industrial vanguard, or to develop exclusively around the point of production. It has been obliged to adopt a more 'populist' approach to its constituency, and to work from a *community* base. Here, the base in the ghetto and the importance of the politicisation of the unemployed became key political factors. The Panthers, for example, basing themselves on a broad non-sectarian programme, went out to recruit the unemployed to the struggle, not in the first instance because of a romantic identification with the 'hustling' life of the colony, but because this was the representative condition and experience of their potential constituency. They approached it in full awareness of the difficulties involved in bringing a degree of political discipline and organisation to this typically unorganised class stratum. Racial oppression was *the* specific mediation through which this class experienced its material and cultural conditions of life, and hence race formed the central mode through which the self-consciousness of the class stratum could be constructed. The importance of race as a structuring feature of life for this whole sector can hardly be denied. Indeed, the important gains made for some blacks during the Poverty Programme period and the failure of such reforms to undermine structural poverty for black workers, must have positively contributed to the recognition of the centrality of race as a key component of their oppression.

But for the Panthers to address themselves to the politicisation of the ghetto inevitably involved their also finding a strategy, a positive cultural identity and political role, for the ghetto's main economic activity: hustling. The hustler was the product of the combination of racism and unemployment. But he also provided one of the few positive role models for young blacks on the block: one of the few not cowed by oppression, not tied to the daily grind of low-wage poverty. By no means everyone in the ghetto was a hustler. But the image of the hustler was positively *sanctioned* – and this is of key importance (what marked out Hobsbawm's 'social bandits' from traditional criminals was their 'sanctioned' place in the community). [126] In the transformation of black politics which Huey Newton, Bobby Seale and the rest of the Panther leadership attempted, what was posed was a form of black revolutionary politics alternative to the worlds of low-wage work, hustling, the middle-class politics of 'civil rights' and the separatism of cultural nationalism. This meant recruiting those blacks still attached to one or other of these survival strategies. But the solution which the Panthers adopted was predicated, neither on the world of the black father, nor of the black worker, but on the world of his lately awakened *brother*. And if a political alternative to the sanctioned potency of the 'brother' who was also invariably a hustler, was to gain command, it *had* to be a 'lumpen politics'. This perspective was not limited to the tactics of the Panther Party, though they took it further than most, and it had major successes. The well-known cases – the conversion from hustling and crime of Malcolm X, Eldridge Cleaver and George Jackson – were only the best known of countless other examples. A lumpen politics meant, in the first place, developing a resistance within the defensive space of the ghetto, against the most immediate features of oppression. And this led straight to the open warfare between black activists and the police. The traditional role exercised within the ghetto of policing 'the colony' was politicised in the process. This, together with examples drawn from other revolutionary struggles, contributed to the complementary strategy of 'armed self-defence'. Amongst the Panthers, specifically, this was no simple, adventurist adoption of spontaneous violence. It was that measure of self-defence which the severe repression by the police on the black community required. It was also *exemplary work*: to demonstrate to the community that, if it exercised its power and stood on its rights, and prepared to defend itself 'by all means necessary', the most immediate forms of oppression could be held at bay. In this way, a powerless community, schooled to the mentality of colonial subordination, could be transformed into an organised, self-conscious, active social force. The second strategy was the attempt to base activities on community self-help. Again, this had two aspects: to establish the rudiments of an alternative social infrastructure within the community; but also, to give the community a sense of its own capacity to organise, control and develop its authentic forms of self-activity. The important point to remark, here, is the way the strategies of groups like the Panther leadership were designed, at one and the same time, to *take root in* the conditions of life of the majority of people in the ghetto colony, and to *transform* those conditions through a conscious political practice. It is important to bear both aspects in mind, since in recent years the perspective has come to be equated with a simpler, spontaneous, affirmation of anything and everything which the ghetto people choose to do in the face of their oppression. The Panthers never believed nor argued that all survival strategies of the black masses could become political without an active process of political transformation. [127]

The 'armed struggle' side of the black movement has tended to command greater attention in recent years, as compared with its more complex politics, in part because, since the Panthers and other black movements have been decimated and destroyed in the confrontations with the police, urban terrorism and guerrilla warfare have been more widely adopted as modes of struggle in the developed Western world. But, in assessing the impact of the Panthers on black people in other parts of the developed world, this conflation of two rather distinct tendencies hinders rather than aids our understanding. Seale, Newton and Cleaver were, of course, perfectly well aware that they were departing from any of the classical recipes for revolutionary struggle. This is clear from Cleaver's writings, where the ascription of the label 'lumpenproletariat' is positively welcomed; or in Seale, who once remarked that 'Marx and Lenin would probably turn over in their graves if they could see lumpenproletarian Afro-Americans putting together the ideology of the Black Panther Party'. [128] They were also aware of the complicated strands and cultural influences which they were attempting to weave together in this programme for a black politics in the heartland of industrial capitalism. Seale records that:

When my wife Artie had a baby boy, I said, 'The nigger's name is Malik Nkrumah Stagolee Seale.' Because Stagolee was a bad nigger off the block and didn't take shit from nobody. All you had to do was organize him, like Malcolm X, make him politically conscious.... 'The nigger out of prison *knows*', Huey used to say. 'The nigger out of prison has seen the man naked and cold, and the nigger out of prison, if he's got himself together, will come out just like Malcolm X came out of prison. You never have to worry about him. He'll go with you.' That's what Huey related to, and I said, 'Malik for Malcolm [Malcolm's Muslim name was El Hajj Malik Shabazz] Nkrumah, Stagolee Seale.' [129]

HARLEM TO HANDSWORTH: BRINGING IT ALL BACK HOME

In this chapter we have attempted to explore the social content of 'mugging', and so pose some questions about its 'politics' in relation to the black struggle. Our aim has not been to provide definitive answers, but to examine what seem to us the component elements of an explanation, and thus the basis of a political judgement. Here, we wish only to resume, in summary form, the path which the argument has taken.

The criminal acts labelled 'muggings' and the patterns of black crime to which 'muggings' have been assimilated constitute the starting-point, only, of this examination. We insist on the requirement to *go behind* the criminal acts to the conditions which are producing black crime as one of their effects. We examined, briefly, the structures which directly affect the social group most concerned with this pattern of crime: black youth. Black youth, we argue, can only be properly understood as a class fraction – a fraction, defined by age and generation, but also by its *position* in the history of post-war black migration, of the constitution of a metropolitan black working class. We then looked at the structures which produce and reproduce this class as a class of black wage-labourers, which assign them, through specific mechanisms, to specific positions within the social and economic relations of contemporary metropolitan capitalist society. We defined these, not as a set of discrete institutions which exhibit 'racially discriminatory' features, but as a set of interlocking structures which *work through race*. The position of black youth, defined in terms of the reproduction of class relations through the education system, the housing market, the occupational structure and division of labour, cannot be properly analysed at all outside the framework of racism. Racism is not simply the discriminatory attitudes of the personnel with whom blacks come into contact. It is the specific mechanism which 'reproduces' the black labour force, from one generation to another, in places and positions which are race-specific. The outcome of this complex process is that blacks are ascribed to a position within the class relations of contemporary capitalism which is, at one and the same time, roughly coterminous with the position of the white working class (of which black labour is a fraction), and yet segmentally differentiated from it. In these terms, ethnic relations are continually overdetermined by class relations, but the two cannot be collapsed into a single structure. The position which results from this combination of race and class we have called a position of *secondariness.* In the present conjuncture of crisis, defined in the two previous chapters, the position of the working class in general is under pressure. Unless society can be radically transformed, that position will continue to deteriorate along each of the crucial dimensions. Economically, the class is now subject to growing unemployment, at the same time as it is called upon to bear the costs of the crisis and the forms in which it is to be resolved. Politically, positions won in an earlier period by a process of uneven reform are being drastically eroded and reversed. Ideologically, the most advanced positions of the working class and its representative organisations are subject, in the crisis of hegemony, to a systematic ideological onslaught aimed at transforming the ideological terrain into an 'authoritarian consensus' favourable to the imposition of strong remedies and reactionary policies. The position of black labour, subordinated by the processes of capital, is deteriorating and will deteriorate more rapidly, according to its own specific logic. Crime is one perfectly predictable and quite comprehensible consequence of this process – as certain a consequence of how the structures work, however 'unintended', as the fact that night follows day. So far, there are no problems at the explanatory or theoretical level. There *are*, of course, the most massive and critical problems of strategy and struggle: the 'so-called rising black crime rate', which presents a problem of containment and control for the system, presents a problem for black people too. It is the problem of how to prevent a sizeable section of the class from being more or less permanently *criminalised.*

Here, however, the problems begin, for just as the structures which reproduce the black worker, male and female, as a sub-proletariat, work through race, so the forms of resistance and struggle which have begun to reveal themselves in response, also – naturally and correctly – tend to crystallise *in relation to race.* It is through the operation of racism that blacks are beginning to comprehend how the system works. It is through a specific kind of 'black consciousness' that they are beginning to appropriate, or 'come to consciousness' of their class position, organise against it and 'fight it out'. If race is the conductor of black labour to the system, it is also the reversible cir- cuit along which forms of class struggle and modes of resistance are beginning to move. And black crime, including 'mugging', has a complex and *ambiguous* relation to these forms of class resistance and 'resistance-consciousness'. By examining the history of the formation of the black 'colony' – itself a defensive strategy in reaction to earlier phases of 'secondariness' – we have tried to show the complex process by which crime, semi-crime, fringe-dealing and hustling became appropriate modes of survival for the black community, and thus how the terrain and the networks were formed, and certain cultural traditions es- tablished, by means of which what appears to those outside the 'colony' as the criminal life of the minority became, if not fused, then inextricably linked to the survival of the black population as a whole. It is perfectly clear that *crime*, as such, contains no solution to the problem as it confronts the black worker. There are many kinds of crime which, though arising from social and economic exploitation, represent, in the last result, nothing but a symbiotic adaptation to deprivation. Crime, as such, is not a political act, especially where the vast number of the victims are people whose class position is hardly distinguishable from that of the criminals. It is not even necessarily a 'quasi-political' act. But in certain circumstances, it *can* provide, or come to be defined as expressing some sides of an oppositional class consciousness. Without hailing crime as a resolution to the problem of the secondariness of the black working class, it requires only a moment's reflection to see how acts of stealing, pickpocketting, snatching and robbing with violence, by a desperate section of black unemployed youth, practised against white victims, can give a muffled and displaced expression to the experience of permanent exclusion. It is essential, here, not to reduce the political content of what is expressed to the 'criminal' forms in which it sometimes appears.

The questions of crime and of black youth, then, consistently drive us back to a consideration of the whole black class – the black sub-proletariat – of which those who are, temporarily or permanently, involved in crime constitute a criminalised fraction. How to understand the position of this black working class? How to relate the question of crime to its forms of struggle?

Here we encountered one powerful interpretation. The connection it is said, lies, not in the fact of 'crime', but in the position of *wagelessness*. What crime is concealing, at the same time as it 'expresses' it, is the growing wagelessness of the black proletariat. But there are two ways of understanding that condition of 'wagelessness' and the forms of political organisation and ideological consciousness which arises or could arise from its base. One interpretation sees in 'wagelessness' principally the presence, already, of a quasi-political consciousness: the consciousness of the new mass worker – often a migrant worker – expressed in the growing 'refusal to work'. Those who 'refuse to work' must continue to survive, and crime is no doubt one of the few available modes of survival left to the 'wageless'. But this is incidental to the positive rejection of 'secondariness' represented in the refusal of one of the principal defining structures of the system – its productive relations, which have systematically assigned the black worker to the ranks of the deskilled labourer. There is good evidence of a growing resentment by blacks to the limited opportunities for work which the capitalist system holds out to the black worker. It is also clear that this has coincided with a growing willingness to resist, struggle and oppose the forms of racist oppression which then inevitably follow. This interpretation, therefore, has the strength of helping us to 'make sense' of the material base of the uneven transformations of consciousness now in progress in the black communities. It helps, that is to say, to make sense of developments at the ideological and political levels. But, as the recession deepens, so it becomes clear that those blacks, in larger numbers, who are 'refusing work' are making a virtue of necessity; there is hardly any work left for young black school-leavers to refuse. As large as is the section who have just found it possible to survive through the hustling life of the street, the numbers of blacks who would take work if they were offered it *is larger*. Thus the 'wagelessness' argument appears weaker when it comes to understanding the economic level at which the reproduction of the class now proceeds. There is an appropriation of a limited form of economic struggle as if it were a full economic, political and ideological confrontation with capital. Something of vital importance to this argument is no doubt added by insisting that black labour is the product of *two* intersecting histories, not one. Alongside the direct subsumption of black migrant labour in the metropolis, one must set the history of the extended subsumption of the black colonial proletariat to capital on a world scale through imperialism. This accounts for certain essential specific features of the black working class in Britain; but it does not explain adequately what the mechanisms are, in the *present* situation, in the present conjuncture, which govern its social reproduction, especially at the level of economic relations.

At this level the alternative explanation seems to have greater explanatory power. This treats the racially segmentary insertion of black labour into the productive relations of metropolitan capitalism, and thus its position as a subproletariat to the white working class, as the central, all-important feature with respect to how capital now exploits black labour-power. This structural position accounts both for the structured relation to capital, and for the internally contradictory relation to other sectors of the proletariat. Thus it is able to account for the growing condition of 'wagelessness' in terms of the classic mechanisms of capital accumulation and its cycles: the constitution of the 'industrial reserve army of labour'. Struggles by black workers, whether waged in the industrial sector or outside, by the section of the class which remains waged or by the 'wageless', have a critical political and ideological significance in terms of the growing cohesion, militancy and capacity for struggle of the class. But they are, from this position, less significant at the economic level: still clearly 'corporate' in character – pursued within, rather than against, the whole 'logic of capital'. Here, then, arose the questions about the role of black labour in the reserve army of labour: the dependence of capital on its formation; the specific role which 'migrant labour' – whether black, southern European, North African or Latin American – now plays in advanced capitalism everywhere; and questions concerning the position of those who, at this point in the cycle, are being rapidly expelled from productive work – marginalised. By looking at this question from several points of view, we were able to show that capital *needs* to exploit not only those who remain in productive work but those who are expelled from production, pauperised out of work, or assigned to a position of more-or-less permanent 'marginality', or who, when recruited back into capital's fitful productive cycle, are taken up through the operation of its secondary labour markets.

Now there are several ways of understanding the position of a whole class fraction which appears systematically vulnerable – as migrant workers are now everywhere, in the period of capitalist recession – to these mechanisms; and one of them is in terms of the traditional *lumpenproletariat*. What makes this assignation tenable is the fact of its growing dependence on crime and the dangerous life of the street as its principal mode of survival. But it can clearly be shown that this is not, in any classical or useful sense, a *lumpenproletariat* at all. It does not have the position, the consciousness nor the role in relation to capital of the *lumpen*. It may be rather more like the 'lumpenproletariat' of the colonial hinterlands underdeveloped by capitalism. But this, too, is not a traditional lumpenproletariat in any meaningful sense, and to call it so is to gloss over some of the most fundamental mechanisms of capital in the colonial and post-colonial world. The growth, size and position of 'marginalised labour' in those areas is not the fate of a small, sinking, Lazarus-like fraction, but a common, necessary and rapidly expanding condition. In the colonial city, this layer corresponds exactly to Marx's *latent* stratum of the reserve army – those thrown out of agricultural labour by the uneven fluctuations of capital. The fact that both this sector *and* the traditional 'lumpenproletariat' tend to live, partly, off crime is neither here nor there, as a way of identifying what this stratum *is* in relation to capital.

The problem about this more 'classical' kind of analysis is that it is the obverse of the first argument. It has considerable explanatory power at the level of economic and productive, or 'unproductive', relations. But it does not sufficiently explain things at the political, cultural and ideological level. The 'unwaged' sector of black labour in Britain may be a floating or stagnant stratum of the 'reserve army'. But it does not exhibit the forms of political consciousness traditional to this stratum. It was at this point that we were obliged, once more, to redirect the path of the argument. By examining what we have called the 'wretched of the earth' and its contemporary history of political struggle, we attempted to bring back into the picture, now clarified and to some degree 'corrected' at the economic level, a contingent history which might help to explain some recent developments among blacks in Britain. This does not represent an 'answer' to the problems posed, even if it contributes something significant to their resolution, for it is, at best, an ambiguous history. Its greatest and most profound successes have been achieved far from the metropolitan heartland of capitalism. The closer it has approached the centre of the most advanced forms of capitalist development, the less political purchase it exhibits. The transformations of Africa, China and Cuba are one thing: but, heroic as has been the struggle of the black masses in the United States, its transformatory power, so far, has been severely limited. If this goes some way to explaining what is now in train amongst militant black youths in the metropolis, it certainly does not hold out any possibility of immediate success. And part of its weakness here, even in comparison with the U.S. instance, may be accurately measured by its general failure, so far, to transform the 'criminal' consciousness into a political one.

Without exaggerating the position, we are left, then, apparently with a difficult problem of analysis – one with pertinent effects at the level of developing a theoretically informed political practice and strategy. This is the problem of the discontinuities, the discrepancies, the divergences, the non-correspondences, between the different levels of the social formation in relation to the black working class – between the economic, political and ideological levels. This question is being widely debated at this time, but it is not our intention to go into these theoretical issues further here. Rather, we want, if anything, to point to the practical, strategic and political consequences of this debate. To put it directly, the problems which now confront us are those of developing forms of political struggle amongst blacks *adequate* to the structures of whose contradictions they are the bearers. This political knot cannot be untied here. Indeed, this is not the book and we cannot presume to offer quick solutions to these problems of strategy and struggle. We have deliberately refrained from entering directly into this question, because it is a matter which we believe must be resolved in struggle, rather than on paper. We hope, nevertheless, that our argument has served to highlight certain aspects and to clarify the terrain on which answers can be sought.

There is, however, one dimension along which we can begin to rethink the issues posed in this section. Our readers will recall our insistence at an early point in the chapter on the strategic and structural position of *race*. The structures through which black labour is reproduced, we argued, are not just coloured by race; they work by means of race. We can think of the relations of production of capitalism articulating the classes in distinct ways at each of the levels or instances of the social formation – economic, political, ideological. These levels are the 'effects' of the structures of a capitalist mode of production. The 'relative autonomy' of the levels – the lack of a necessary correspondence between them – was discussed earlier. Each 'level' of the social formation requires its independent 'means of representation' – the means by which the class-structured mode of capitalist production 'appears' at the level of the economic class struggle, the political struggle, the ideological struggle. Race is intrinsic to the manner in which the black labouring classes are *complexly constituted* at each of those levels. Race enters into the way black labour, male and female, is distributed as economic agents on the level of economic practice – and the class struggles which result from it; into the way the fractions of the black labouring class are constituted as a set of political forces in the 'theatre of politics' – and the political struggle which results; and in the manner in which that class is articulated as the collective and individual 'subjects' of emergent ideologies and forms of consciousness – and the struggle over ideology, culture and consciousness which results. This gives the matter of race and *racism* a theoretical as well as a practical centrality to all the relations and practices which affect black labour. The constitution of this class fraction as a class, and the *class relations* which inscribe it, function *as race relations*. The two are inseparable. Race is the modality in which class is lived. It is also the medium in which class relations are experienced. This does not immediately heal any breaches or bridge any chasms. But it has consequences for the *whole class*, whose relation to their conditions of existence is now systematically transformed by race. It determines some of the modes of struggle. It also provides one of the criteria by which we measure the *adequacy* of struggle to the structures it aims to transform.

This has consequences, first for how we think, and organise to contest, the internal divisions within the working class which currently articulate themselves 'along racial lines'. These are no mere impositions from above. If they serve capital, they are not one of its better con-tricks. If they are elaborated and transformed into practical ideologies, into the 'common sense' of the white working class, it is not because the latter are dupes of individual racists, or prey to racist organisations. Those who seek to articulate working-class consciousness into the syntax of a racist ideology are, of course, key agents in the struggle at the ideological level: they have pertinent effects. But they succeed to the measure that they do because they are practising on real relations, working with real effects of the structure, not because they are clever at conjuring demons. Racism is, therefore, not only a problem for blacks who are obliged to 'suffer' it. Nor is it a problem only for those sections of the white working class or those class organisations which are infected by its stain. Nor indeed can it be overcome, as a virus which can be treated by a heavy dose of liberal innoculation. Capital reproduces the class as a whole, structured by race. It dominates the divided class, in part, through those internal divisions which have 'racism' as one of their effects. It contains and disables the representative class organisations by confining them, in part, to strategies and struggles which are race-specific, which do not surmount its limits, its barriers. Through race, it continues to defeat the attempts to construct, at the political level, organisations which do in fact adequately represent the class *as a whole* – that is, which represent it *against capitalism, against racism.*

The sectional struggles which continue to appear are the *necessary* defensive strategies of a class which is divided against itself, face to face with capital. They are, therefore, also the site of capital's continuing sway over it. The white working class and its economic and political organisations (it has, currently, *no* ideological organisations which adequately represent it) fundamentally mistakes itself and its position when it extends itself, out of fellow-feeling or fraternal solidarity, to struggle against racism on behalf of 'our black brothers'; just as black organisations misrecognise the nature of their own struggle when they debate whether or not to form tactical alliances with their white comrades. This is certainly *not* to be interpreted as a tactical call for a united struggle, a common front – 'black and white, unite and fight!' It is said fully confronting the impossibility of developing the struggle in this form *at this time.* It is said in the full awareness that, at every critical moment in the post-war history of the class in advanced capitalism, the struggle has *necessarily divided* into its separate, strategic parts. But the analysis has a certain logic, which must drive through to its conclusion. We must *add* that every time the struggle appears, once again, in its divided form, capital penetrates through and occupies the gap. The theoretical argument compels us to say that each section of the class requires to confront capital *as a class*, not out of solidarity with others, but *for itself.* Otherwise, as Marx observed in the *Eighteenth Brumaire*:

> in so far as millions of families live under economic conditions of existence that separate their mode of life, their interests and their culture from those of other classes and put them in hostile opposition to the latter, they form a class. In so far as there is merely a local interconnection among these . . . and the identity of their interests begets no community, no national bond, and no political organization amongst them, they do not form a class. They are consequently incapable of enforcing their class interests in their own name.

This brings us back to crime: for now we can see how black crime functions as one of the vehicles of this division. It provides the separation of the class into black and white with a material basis, since, in much black crime (as in much white working-class crime), one part of the class materially 'rips off' another. It provides this separation with its ideological figure, for it transforms the deprivation of the class, out of which crime arises, into the all too intelligible syntax of race, and fixes a false enemy: the black mugger. Thus it sustains the political separation. For the moment black organisations and the black community defend black youth against the harassment to which they are subject, they appear on the political stage as the 'defenders of street criminals'. Yet not to defend that sector of the class which is being systematically driven into crime is to abandon it to the ranks of those who have been permanently criminalised.

We have been trying, throughout this study, to follow the logic which unfolds from an apparently simple beginning in the 'mugging' scare. We have attempted to reconstruct this logic as fully as we can. It should be clear that this does not entail approving of 'mugging' in some simple moral way, or positively recommending it as a strategy, or romantically identifying with it as a 'deviant solution'. As the *Race Today* editorial expressed it: 'The resort to mugging at this time represents that the youth failed to grasp that getting money by force or stealth from members of the white working class is itself subversive of their struggles against the slavery of capitalist work. It is not white workers who have the money.' In addition, the violence which is sometimes involved has the effect of disabling and degrading those who perpetrate it in the same moment as it 'pays back' those enemies against whom it is principally directed. Seen in this way, 'mugging' by blacks may appear as the same set of behavioural acts as 'mugging' committed by other young people; but in its social content and position in relation to the problematic of its class as a whole, it is *not* the same. The *Race Today* editorial also added: 'We stand openly with the refusers to work. We have explained how this action is a source of power for the whole class. We are uncompromisingly against mugging. We see the mugging activity as a manifestation of powerlessness, a consequence of being without a wage.'[130] The two propositions contained there will appear to be contradictory only to those who believe that 'mugging' is a simple, open-and-shut 'moral issue', and who think they can comprehend its social meaning by transparently reading it off from its most immediate surface appearances.

Whether, in itself, this condition is a 'source of power for the whole class' we have had cause to doubt, when formulated in that way. When we confront, not crime, but the economic, political and ideological conditions producing crime, as the basis of a possible political strategy, the issues become necessarily more complex. They bring together the most difficult matters of strategy, analysis and practice. We hope that those who do not accept our way of making that analysis will nevertheless have found our examination of it useful. It is conducted in that spirit, directed to that end. There are, we saw, important historical examples where precisely such a class stratum *has* become the basis of a significant political struggle. But the conditions are somewhat different from those prevailing here – if only because the ways in which the class as a whole has been subsumed into the sway of capital is different here. Worsley is right to remind us that it was the French Paras, not Ali-la-Pointe, the *lumpen* hero of Pontecorvo's film, who won 'the Battle of Algiers' – and that, though the national struggle was successful, it was not the *lumpen* who inherited the Algerian earth. The Black Panthers represented one of the most serious attempts to organise blacks politically in the heart of the capitalist world; but they have been decimated and destroyed. The fact is that there is, as yet, no active politics, no form of organised struggle, and no strategy which is able adequately and decisively to *intervene* in the quasi-rebellion of the black wageless such as would be capable of bringing about that *break* in the current false appropriations of oppression through crime − that critical transformation of the criminalised consciousness into something more sustained and thorough-going in a political sense. This is certainly *not* an argument for failing to do political work in this area. But it constitutes a powerful reminder that we should not mistake a proto-political consciousness for organised political class struggle and practice. It sets up a necessary warning about any strategy which is based simply on favouring current modes of resistance, in the hope that, in and of themselves, by natural evolution rather than by break and transformation, they could become, spontaneously, another thing.

Notes and References

CHAPTER 1

1. K. Chesney, *The Victorian Underworld* (Harmondsworth: Penguin, 1972).
2. Ibid. pp. 162–5; see also J. J. Tobias, *Crime and Industrial Society in the Nineteenth Century* (London: Batsford, 1967) pp. 139–40.
3. See F. H. McClintock and E. Gibson, *Robbery in London* (London: Macmillan, 1961) p. 1; and J. W. C. Turner, *Kenny's Outline of Criminal Law*, 17th edn (Cambridge University Press, 1958) pp. 291–2.
4. See *The Times*, 1 November 1972.
5. *Sunday Telegraph*, 5 November 1972.
6. See *Daily Express*, 20 March 1973.
7. See the report of the crime at the time; *Guardian*, 17, 19, 23 April 1969.
8. *Sunday Times* and *Sunday Telegraph*, both 5 November 1972.
9. S. Ross, 'A Mug's Game', *New Society*, 5 October 1972; C. McGlashan, 'The Making of a Mugger', *New Statesman*, 13 October 1972.
10. *The Times*, 20 October 1972.
11. *London Evening News*, 7 October 1972.
12. *Sunday Mirror*, 15 October 1972.
13. *Guardian*, 3 November 1972.
14. *Daily Mail*, 26 October 1972.
15. See *The Times*, 1 November 1972.
16. *The Times*, 2 November 1972.
17. For example, *Daily Mail*, 7 December 1972.
18. See *Daily Mirror*, 25 January 1973.
19. See *Guardian*, 8 March 1973.
20. *The Times*, 12 March 1973.
21. *London Evening Standard*, 30 March 1973.
22. *Daily Telegraph*, 17 April 1973; *London Evening Standard*, 16 April 1973.
23. *Daily Mail*, 4 May 1973; *Sunday Mirror*, 6 May 1973.
24. *London Evening Standard*, 11 May 1973.
25. *Daily Mail*.
26. *Daily Mirror*, 23 May 1973.
27. *Observer*, 29 July 1973.
28. *Daily Mirror*.
29. *Report of the Departmental Committee on Criminal Statistics* (Perks Committee) Cmnd 3448 (London: H.M.S.O., 1967).

30. For example McClintock and Gibson, *Robbery in London*; and F. H. McClintock (ed.), *Crimes of Violence* (London: Macmillan, 1963).
31. For a more extended treatment of the problems of criminal statistics and the rising crime rate, see P. Wiles, 'Criminal Statistics and Sociological Explanations of Crime', in *Crime and Delinquency in Britain*, ed. W. G. Carson and P. Wiles (London: Martin Robertson, 1971); N. Walker, *Crime, Courts and Figures* (Harmondsworth: Penguin, 1971); and L. McDonald, *The Sociology of Law and Order* (London: Faber, 1976).
32. W. I. Thomas, *The Unadjusted Girl* (Boston: Little, Brown, 1928).
33. F. H. McClintock and N. H. Avison, *Crime in England and Wales* (London: Heinemann, 1968) pp. 18–19.
34. *Annual Reports* of the Metropolitan Police Commissioner and the Chief Inspector of Constabulary.
35. *Guardian*, 30 June 1972.
36. *Guardian*, 13 February 1970.
37. Data from F. H. McClintock, quoted in N. Fowler, 'The Rewards of Robbery', *The Times*, 7 April 1970.
38. Data from *Annual Reports* of Metropolitan Police Commissioner and the Chief Inspector of Constabulary.
39. *Guardian*, 8 March 1973.
40. McClintock and Avison, *Crime in England and Wales*.
41. McDonald, *The Sociology of Law and Order*.
42. See, for example, Sir Robert Mark, 'The Disease of Crime – Punishment or Treatment', paper delivered to the Royal Society of Medicine; reported in the *Guardian*, 21 June 1972; and Sir Robert Mark, *The Dimbleby Lecture*, broadcast on B.B.C., 5 November 1973.
43. S. McCabe and R. Purves, *The Jury at Work* (Oxford: Blackwell, 1972); reviewed in the *Guardian*, 17 July 1972.
44. S. J. Elgrod and J. D. M. Lew, 'Acquittals – a Statistical Exercise', *New Law Journal*, vol. 123, no. 5626, 6 December 1973; reviewed in the *Sunday Times*, 9 December 1973.
45. R. F. Sparks, *Local Prisons: the Crisis in the English Penal System* (London: Heinemann, 1971).
46. *People in Prisons*, Cmnd 4214 (London: H.M.S.O., 1969).
47. *The Regime for Long-Term Prisoners in Conditions of Maximum Security: Report of the Advisory Council on the Penal System* (Radzinowicz Report) (London: H.M.S.O., 1968); S. Cohen and L. Taylor, *Psychological Survival: the Experience of Long-Term Imprisonment* (Harmondsworth: Penguin, 1972) pp. 15–17.
48. L. Radzinowicz, 'Preface' to McClintock and Gibson, *Robbery in London*, p. xvi.
49. McClintock and Avison, *Crime in England and Wales*.
50. R. Baxter and C. Buttall, 'Severe Sentences: No Deterrent to Crime?', *New Society*, 2 January 1975.
51. Metropolitan Police District Statistical Unit, *Robbery and Kindred Offences, 1968–72* (London: Metropolitan Police, 1973).
52. S. Cohen, *Folk Devils and Moral Panics: the Creation of the Mods and Rockers* (London: MacGibbon & Kee, 1972) p. 28.

53. Ibid.
54. R. Lejeune and N. Alex, 'On Being Mugged: The Event and its After-math', Paper presented at the 23rd Annual Meeting of the Society for the Study of Social Problems, August 1973; see also D. W. Maurer, *Whizz Mob* (New Haven, Conn.: College & University Press, 1964) p. 171; and G. Myrdal, *An American Dilemma* (New York: Harper, 1944).
55. See E. Partridge, *A Dictionary of Historical Slang* (Harmondsworth: Penguin, 1972).
56. See National Commission on the Causes and Prevention of Violence, *Final Report* (New York: Award Books, 1969).
57. Lejeune and Alex, 'On Being Mugged'.
58. See Henry Brandon, 'America in a State of Rebellion', *Sunday Times*, 27 October 1968; Andrew Kopkind's review of 'Wallace-Mania', *Sunday Times*, magazine, 3 November 1968; and 'The Year the World Swung Right', *Sunday Times*, magazine, 29 December 1968.
59. See *Sunday Express*, 3 March 1968, 17 August 1969, 28 September 1969.
60. For example, 'Mobbing and Mugging', *Daily Sketch*, 25 June 1970; see also 'Violent Crimes', *Daily Telegraph*, 25 August 1971 (both editorials).

CHAPTER 2

1. See K. T. Erikson, *Wayward Puritans: a Study in the Sociology of Deviance* (New York: Wiley, 1966) pp. 8–19.
2. On the importance of the symbolic role of the judiciary, see T. Arnold, *The Symbols of Government* (New York: Harcourt, Brace, 1962); S. Lukes, 'Political Ritual', *Sociology*, vol. 9, no. 2, May 1975; on the grounding of ideology in ritual practice, see L. Althusser, 'Ideology and the State' in *Lenin and Philosophy, and Other Essays* (London: New Left Books, 1971).
3. *Evening Standard*, 8 November 1972.
4. *Daily Telegraph*, 10 October 1969.
5. *Guardian*, 30 October 1969.
6. *Guardian*, 14 January 1972.
7. *Guardian*, 20 May 1972.
8. See *Report of the Parole Board for 1972* (London: H.M.S.O., 1973); 'Conflict over Numbers in Juvenile Courts', *Guardian*, 8 February 1972; M. Berlins and G. Wansell, *Caught in the Act: Children, Society and the Law* (Harmondsworth: Penguin, 1974) pp. 77–98; and *Guardian*, 30 December 1972, on the *Criminal Justice Act*.
9. For a more general assessment of the Act, see Berlins and Wansell, *Caught in the Act*; and D. Ford, *Children, Courts and Caring* (London: Constable, 1975).
10. Berlins and Wansell, *Caught in the Act*, p. 36.
11. Ibid. p. 83.
12. Ibid. pp. 63–84.
13. L. Blom-Cooper, 'The Dangerous Precedents of Panic', *The Times*, 20 October 1972.
14. *Report of the Parole Board for 1972*, p. 8.

15. A. Morris and H. Giller, 'Reaction to an Act', *New Society*, 19 February 1976.
16. See J. Paine, 'Labour and the Lawyers', *New Statesman*, 11 July 1975.
17. See J. Young, *The Drugtakers: the Social Meaning of Drug Use* (London: MacGibbon & Kee, 1971); J. Young, 'Mass Media, Deviance, and Drugs', in *Deviance and Social Control*, ed. P. Rock and M. McIntosh (London: Tavistock, 1974); and S. M. Hall, 'Deviancy, Politics and the Media', in *Deviance and Social Control*, ed. Rock and McIntosh.
18. See L. Wilkins, *Social Deviance: Social Policy, Action and Research* (London: Tavistock, 1964); and Young, *The Drugtakers*.
19. *Evening Standard*, 25 September 1972.
20. *Evening Standard*, 8 November 1972.
21. *Time Out*, 27 October–2 November 1972, 17–23 November 1972, 11–17 May 1973.
22. *Sunday Times*, 5 August 1973.
23. *Time Out*, 11–17 May 1973; *Sunday Times*, 5 August 1973.
24. *Robbery and Kindred Offences, 1968–72*.
25. Young, *The Drugtakers*, p. 189; but see also M. Stellman, 'Sitting Here in Limbo', *Time Out*, 23–29 August 1974.
26. See T. Bunyan, *The History and Practice of the Political Police in Britain* (London: Friedmann, 1976).
27. C. McGlashan, 'The Making of a Mugger', *New Statesman*, 13 October 1972.
28. See the resulting *Deedes Report, House of Commons Select Committee on Race Relations and Immigration: Police/Immigrant Relations*, vol. 1: 'Report'; vols 2–3: 'Minutes of Evidence' (London: H.M.S.O., 1972); and the analysis of the structuring presuppositions of the Committee in relation to black evidence in J. Clarke *et al.*, 'The Selection of Evidence and the Avoidance of Racialism: a Critique of the Parliamentary Select Committee on Race Relations and Immigration', *New Community*, vol. III, no. 3, Summer 1974.
29. *The Times*, 12 March 1973.
30. *Time Out*, 17–23 November 1972.
31. Young, *The Drugtakers*, p. 171.
32. H. Becker, *Outsiders: Studies in the Sociology of Deviance* (New York: Free Press, 1963).
33. Cohen, *Folk Devils and Moral Panics*, p. 168.
34. J. Lambert, *Crime, Police and Race Relations* (London: Institute of Race Relations/Oxford University Press, 1970) p. 190.
35. *The Times*, 26 August 1972; *Sunday Times* and *Sunday Telegraph*, 1 October 1972; see also *London Evening News*, 7 October 1972; *Sunday Mirror*, 15 and 22 October 1972.
36. *Daily Mail*, 26 October 1972.
37. *The Times*, 1 November 1972; *Guardian*, 3 November 1972; *Sunday Telegraph*, 5 November 1972; *The Times*, 25 January 1973.
38. *Sunday Mirror*, 6 May 1973.
39. Reported in *Daily Mail*, 15 May 1973.

40. *Daily Mirror*, 7 June 1973.
41. *Daily Mirror*, 1 October 1973.
42. *Sunday Times*, 5 August 1973.
43. D. Humphry, *Police Power and Black People* (London: Panther, 1972).
44. Lambert, *Crime, Police and Race Relations*.
45. Ibid. p. 183.
46. See the re-analysis of this evidence by Clarke *et al.*, 'The Selection of Evidence and the Avoidance of Racialism'.
47. *Guardian*, 28 January 1972.
48. *Guardian*, 11 February 1972.
49. *Guardian*, 9 March 1972.
50. *Guardian*, 28 April 1972 and 11 May 1972.
51. See evidence of Mark Bonham-Carter, Chairman of the Community Relations Council, to the Select Committee, *Guardian*, 12 May 1972.
52. *Deedes Report*, vol. 1, p. 69.
53. National Council for Civil Liberties, *Annual Report 1971* (London: N.C.C.L., 1972).
54. *Guardian*, 5 May 1972.
55. *Guardian*, 18 July 1972.
56. For a fuller account of the Lewisham police 'affair', see *Time Out*, 21–27 July 1972.
57. Quoted in Humphry, *Police Power and Black People*, pp. 109–10.
58. S. Pullé, *Police Immigrant Relations in Ealing: Report of an Investigation conducted on behalf of the Ealing CRC* (London: Runnymede Trust, 1973).
59. See J. Rex and R. Moore, *Race, Community and Conflict: a study of Sparkbrook* (London: Institute of Race Relations/Oxford University Press, 1967).
60. See Lambert, *Crime, Police and Race Relations*, pp. 123–4.
61. See Stellman, 'Sitting Here in Limbo'.
62. This being a process recommended by the Royal Commission on the Police, *Final Report*, Cmnd 1728 (London: H.M.S.O., 1962) ch. VII.
63. See the conclusion to M. E. Cain, *Society and the Policeman's Role* (London: Routledge & Kegan Paul, 1973); for a summary of other important police changes between 1964–74, especially the development of a wider political role, in the areas of computerised surveillance, pre-emptive policing and co-operation with the military, see Bunyan, *History and Practice of the Political Police in Britain*, pp. 74–101.
64. See the *Reports* of the Metropolitan Police Commissioner for the relevant years for details.
65. *Time Out*, 23–9 March 1973.
66. Ibid.
67. See Bunyan, *History and Practice of the Political Police in Britain*.
68. J. Young, 'The Role of the Police as Amplifiers of Deviancy' in *Images of Deviance*, ed. S. Cohen (Harmondsworth: Penguin, 1971).
69. See A. C. H. Smith *et al.*, *Paper Voices: the Popular Press and Social Change, 1935–1965* (London: Chatto & Windus, 1975); and J. Clarke, S.

M. Hall, T. Jefferson and B. Roberts, 'Subcultures, Cultures and Class: a Theoretical Overview' in *Resistance through Rituals*, ed. S. M. Hall and T. Jefferson (London: Hutchinson, 1976).

70. See, *inter alia*, Mark, *The Dimbleby Lecture*.
71. See E. C. S. Wade and G. G. Phillips, *Constitutional Law* (London: Longmans, 1960), quoted in P. Laurie, *Scotland Yard* (Harmondsworth: Penguin, 1972) p. 113.
72. Laurie, *Scotland Yard*, p. 116.
73. Data from McClintock and Avison, *Crime in England and Wales*, pp. 127, 140.
74. *Guardian* (extra) 16 January 1973.
75. See T. Tullett, 'The Thin Blue Line', *Daily Mirror*, 17 February 1970; and M. De-La-Noy, 'Stress and the Law: The High Cost of being a Policeman', *Guardian*, 29 July 1974.
76. For race relations in the period, see C. Mullard, *Black Britain* (London: Allen & Unwin, 1973); and D. Hiro, *Black British, White British* (Harmondsworth: Penguin, 1973).
77. Lambert, *Crime, Police and Race Relations*, p. 181.
78. Ibid. p. 183.
79. Young, 'The Role of the Police as Amplifiers of Deviancy', p. 39.
80. Lambert, *Crime, Police and Race Relations*, p. 183.
81. *Report* (London: H.M.S.O., 1971).
82. *The Times*, 9 June 1971.
83. *The Times*, 24 August 1971.
84. *The Times*, 25 August 1971.
85. See *Guardian* and *The Times*, 25 August 1971; *Sunday Times* and *Observer*, 29 August 1971.
86. *Evening Standard*, 25 September 1972.
87. *Daily Telegraph*, 25 August 1971.

CHAPTER 3

1. C. MacDougall, *Interpretative Reporting* (New York: Macmillan, 1968) p. 12.
2. For a fuller account of the impact of these 'bureaucratic' factors in news production, see P. Rock, 'News as Eternal Recurrence', in *The Manufacture of News: Social Problems, Deviance and the Mass Media*, ed. S. Cohen and J. Young (London: Constable, 1973).
3. See J. Galtung and M. Ruge, 'Structuring and Selecting News' in *The Manufacture of News*, ed. Cohen and Young.
4. See ibid; K. Nordenstreng, 'Policy for News Transmission', in *Sociology of Mass Communications*, ed. D. McQuail (Harmondsworth: Penguin, 1972); W. Breed, 'Social Control in the Newsroom? A Functional Analysis', *Social Forces*, vol. 33, May 1955; and S. M. Hall, 'Introduction' in *Paper Voices*, ed. Smith *et al.*

5. L. Wirth, 'Consensus and Mass Communications', *American Sociological Review*, vol. 13, 1948.

6. *The Times*, 28 February 1973; quoted in G. Murdock, 'Political Deviance: the Press Presentation of a Militant Mass Demonstration', in *The Manufacture of News*, ed. Cohen and Young, p. 157.

7. Rock, 'News as Eternal Recurrence'.

8. G. Murdock, 'Mass Communication and the Construction of Meaning', in *Rethinking Social Psychology*, ed. N. Armistead (Harmondsworth: Penguin, 1974) pp. 208–9; but see also S. M. Hall, 'A World at One with Itself', *New Society*, 18 June 1970; and J. Young, 'Mass Media, Deviance and Drugs', in *Deviance and Social Control*, ed. Rock and McIntosh.

9. Rock, 'News as Eternal Recurrence', p. 77.

10. Murdock, 'Mass Communication', p. 210.

11. For a historical account of the evolution of those rules, see J. W. Carey, 'The Communications Revolution and the Professional Communicator', *Sociological Review Monograph*, vol. 13, 1969.

12. H. Becker, 'Whose Side are We on?', in *The Relevance of Sociology*, ed. J. D. Douglas (New York: Appleton-Century-Crofts, 1972).

13. K. Lang and G. Lang, 'The Inferential Structure of Political Communications', *Public Opinion Quarterly*, vol. 19, Summer 1955.

14. J. D. Halloran, P. Elliott and G. Murdock, *Demonstrations and Communication: a Case Study* (Harmondsworth: Penguin, 1970).

15. See S. M. Hall, 'The "Structured Communication" of Events', paper for the Obstacles to Communication Symposium, UNESCO/Division of Philosophy (available from Centre for Contemporary Cultural Studies, University of Birmingham); Clarke *et al.*, 'The Selection of Evidence and the Avoidance of Racialism'.

16. F. Parkin, *Class Inequality and Political Order* (London: MacGibbon & Kee, 1971) p. 83.

17. On the *Mirror*'s transformations, see Smith *et al.*, *Paper Voices*.

18. L. Goldmann, *The Human Sciences and Philosophy* (London: Cape, 1969).

19. See I. L. Horowitz and M. Liebowitz, 'Social Deviance and Political Marginality', *Social Problems*, vol. 15(3), 1968; and S. M. Hall, 'Deviancy, Politics and the Media', in *Deviance and Social Control*, ed. Rock and McIntosh.

20. See Hall, 'Deviancy, Politics and the Media'.

21. J. Westergaard, 'Some Aspects of the Study of Modern Political Society', in *Approaches to Sociology*, ed. J. Rex (London: Routledge & Kegan Paul, 1974); see also S. Lukes, *Power: a Radical View* (London: Macmillan, 1974); and J. Urry, 'Introduction', in *Power in Britain*, ed. J. Urry and J. Wakeford (London: Heinemann, 1973).

22. Urry, 'Introduction', p. 10.

23. For a more detailed analysis of this relationship, see S. M. Hall, I. Connell and L. Curti, 'The Unity of Current Affairs Television', *Working Papers in Cultural Studies No. 9*, C.C.C.S., University of Birmingham, 1976.

24. Erikson, *Wayward Puritans*, p. 12.

25. *Daily Mail*, 13 August 1966; quoted in S. Chibnall, 'The News Media and the Police', paper presented to National Deviancy Conference, University of York, September 1973.
26. See A. Shuttleworth *et al.*, *Television Violence, Crime-Drama and the Analysis of Content*, C.C.C.S., University of Birmingham, 1975.
27. See Chibnall, 'The News Media and the Police'.
28. See M. Douglas, *Purity and Danger* (Harmondsworth: Penguin, 1966).
29. See P. Rock and F. Heidensohn, 'New Reflections on Violence', in *Anarchy and Culture*, ed. D. Martin (London: Routledge & Kegan Paul, 1969); and S. Cohen, 'Protest, Unrest and Delinquency: Convergences in Labels or Behaviour?', *International Journal of Criminology and Penology*, vol. 1, 1973.
30. Galtung and Ruge, 'Structuring and Selecting News', p. 65.
31. Hall, 'Deviancy, Politics and the Media'.
32. See Cohen, *Folk Devils and Moral Panics*, p. 39.
33. See *Daily Mirror*, 7 September 1972; and Daily Express, 1 December 1972.
34. See *Sun*, 6 January 1973; *Daily Mail*, 9 February 1973; and *Daily Mirror*, 28 June 1973.
35. See also *Daily Mail*, 29 March 1973; *Sun*, 14 April 1973; and *Daily Mail*, 6 April 1973.
36. See *Daily Mirror*, 12 August 1973.
37. *Report*, p. 44.
38. See B. Roshier, 'The Selection of Crime News by the Press', in *The Manufacture of News*, ed. Cohen and Young.
39. Ibid, pp. 34–5.
40. *Daily Telegraph*, 21 March 1973.
41. Althusser, 'Ideology and the State'.

CHAPTER 4

1. See, for examples, *Evening Standard* and *Daily Mirror*, 6 October 1972; and *Sunday Mirror*, 22 October 1972.
2. See, for example, *Sunday Times* and *Sunday Telegraph*, 5 November 1972.
3. H. Marcuse, *One Dimensional Man* (London: Sphere, 1968) pp. 79, 84.
4. R. Barthes, *Mythologies* (London: Paladin, 1973) p. 153.

CHAPTER 5

1. But see K. Pearson, 'Letters to the Editor', *New Society*, 30 January 1975; and E. P. Thompson, 'Sir, Writing by Candlelight', in *The Manufacture of News*, ed. Cohen and Young.
2. R. Williams, 'Radical and/or Respectable', in *The Press We Deserve*, ed. R. Boston (London: Routledge & Kegan Paul, 1970).

3. Ibid.
4. But see *Daily Mail*, 27 March 1973; and *Daily Telegraph*, 30 March 1973.
5. See Baxter and Nuttall, 'Severe Sentences'.
6. This is the only letter to shift the terrain of the debate completely – it connects Charles Simeon's statements about the 'rule of law' to the level of politics: 'Ireland must have gone to their heads'.
7. See *Evening Mail*, 21, 22, 23, 26, 27 March 1973; and *Birmingham Post*, 22, 23, 24, 28 March 1973.
8. But see *Evening Mail*, 23, 24, 28 March 1973; and *Birmingham Post*, 27 March 1973.
9. See C. Pawling, 'A Bibliography of the Frankfurt School', *Working Papers in Cultural Studies No. 6*, C.C.C.S., University of Birmingham, Autumn 1974; E. Fromm, *The Fear of Freedom* (London: Routledge & Kegan Paul, 1960); T. Adorno *et al.*, *The Authoritarian Personality* (New York: Harper, 1950); and W. Reich, *The Mass Psychology of Fascism* (Harmondsworth: Penguin, 1975).

CHAPTER 6

1. See D. Marsden and E. Duff, *Workless* (Harmondsworth: Penguin, 1975).
2. See E. P. Thompson, 'Time and Work Discipline', *Past and Present*, December 1967.
3. See Young, *The Drugtakers*.
4. See Westergaard, 'Some Aspects of the Study of Modern Political Society'; H. Moorhouse and C. Chamberlain, 'Lowerclass Attitudes to Property: Aspects of the Counter Ideology', *Sociology*, vol. 8(3), 1974.
5. R. Jessop, *Traditionalism, Conservatism and British Political Culture* (London: Allen & Unwin, 1974); but see also J. Westergaard, 'The Rediscovery of the Cash Nexus', in *Socialist Register 1970*, ed. R. Miliband and J. Saville (London: Merlin Press, 1970); H. Moorhouse, 'Political Incorporation', *Sociology*, vol. 7, no. 3, September 1973; and Moorhouse and Chamberlain, 'Lowerclass Attitudes to Property'.
6. Reich, *The Mass Psychology of Fascism*.
7. G. Playfair, *The Punitive Obsession* (London: Gollancz, 1971).
8. See G. Pearson, *The Deviant Imagination* (London: Macmillan, 1975); and L. Chevalier, *Labouring Classes and Dangerous Classes* (London: Routledge & Kegan Paul, 1973).
9. G. Orwell, 'Lion and the Unicorn', in *Collected Essays, Journalism and Letters* (Harmondsworth: Penguin, 1970) vol. 2; see the development of the argument in relation to the war in S. M. Hall, 'The Social Eye of Picture Post', *Working Papers in Cultural Studies No. 2*, C.C.C.S., University of Birmingham, Spring 1972.
10. See, for example, B. Jackson, *Working Class Community* (Harmondsworth: Penguin, 1968) chapter entitled 'Riot'.

11. J. Young, 'Working Class Criminology', in *Critical Criminology*, ed. I. Taylor, P. Walton and J. Young (London: Routledge & Kegan Paul, 1975).

12. See P. Anderson, 'Origins of the Present Crisis', *New Left Review*, vol. 23, 1964; reprinted in *Towards Socialism*. ed. P. Anderson and R. Blackburn (London: Fontana, 1965); T. Nairn, 'the British Political Elite', *New Left Review*, vol. 23, 1964; T. Nairn, 'The English Working Class', *New Left Review*, vol. 24, 1964; reprinted in *Ideology in Social Science: Readings in Critical Social Theory*, ed. R. Blackburn (London: Fontana, 1972); E. P. Thompson, *The Making of the English Working Class*, rev. edn (Harmondsworth: Penguin, 1968); R. B. Johnson, 'Barrington Moore, Perry Anderson and English Social Development', *Working Papers in Cultural Studies No. 9*, C.C.C.S., University of Birmingham, 1976; E. P. Thompson, 'The Peculiarities of the English', in *Socialist Register 1965*, ed. Miliband and Saville.

13. K. Marx, *The Poverty of Philosophy* (Moscow: Foreign Languages Publishing House, 1956) p. 115.

14. A. Dummett, *Portrait of English Racism* (Harmondsworth: Penguin, 1973).

15. N. Poulantzas, *Political Power and Social Classes* (London: New Left Books, 1973) p. 223.

16. See T. Nichols and P. Armstrong, *Workers Divided* (London: Fontana, 1976).

17. R. Hoggart, *The Uses of Literacy* (Harmondsworth: Penguin, 1958) pp. 72–3.

18. Ibid. p. 102.

19. Ibid. p. 103.

20. A. Gramsci, *Selections from the Prison Notebooks* (London: Lawrence & Wishart, 1971) pp. 421, 419.

21. Ibid.

22. G. Nowell-Smith, 'Common Sense', *7 Days*, 3 November 1971.

23. See Anderson, 'Origins of the Present Crisis'; and Parkin, *Class Inequality and Political Order*.

24. Parkin, *Class Inequality and Political Order*.

25. See Moorhouse, 'Political Incorporation'.

26. N. Harris, *Beliefs in Society* (London: Watts, 1968) p. 54.

27. Dummett, *Portrait of English Racism*.

28. K. Marx and F. Engels, *The German Ideology* (London: Lawrence and Wishart, 1965).

29. Harris, *Beliefs in Society*.

30. F. Engels, 'Ludwig Feuerbach and the End of Classical German Philosophy', in *Marx–Engels Selected Works*, vol. 2 (London: Lawrence & Wishart, 1951).

31. See Harris, *Beliefs in Society*, and C. Geertz, 'Ideology as a Cultural System', in *Ideology and Discontent*, ed. D. Apter (New York: Free Press, 1964).

32. See the eloquent portrait by A. Maude in The *English Middle Classes*, a

seminal text, written in this period, and representing an important, early moral *Cri de coeur.*

33. G. Steadman-Jones, 'The Remaking of the English Working Class', *Journal of Social History*, vol. 7, Summer 1974.
34. See Cohen, *Folk Devils and Moral Panics;* and Clarke *et al.,* 'Subcultures, Cultures and Class'.
35. Clarke *et al.,* 'Subcultures, Cultures and Class'.
36. See R. Glass, *Newcomers: The West Indians in London* (London: Allen & Unwin, 1960).
37. Cohen, *Folk Devils and Moral Panics,* p. 192.
38. See Clarke *et al.,* 'Subcultures, Cultures and Class'; J. Clarke, 'Style' in *Resistance Through Rituals,* eds Hall and Jefferson; and P. Cohen, 'Subcultural Conflict and Working Class Community', *Working Papers in Cultural Studies No. 2,* C.C.C.S., University of Birmingham, Spring 1972.
39. J. Seabrook, *City Close-up* (Harmondsworth: Penguin, 1973) p. 62.
40. Ibid. p. 57.
41. See C. Critcher *et al.,* 'Race and the Provincial Press', Report to UNESCO, 1975; also available as *C.C.C.S. Stencilled Paper No. 39.*
42. Seabrook, *City Closeup,* pp. 79–81.
43. Ibid. pp. 198–9.
44. Gramsci, *Selections from the Prison Notebooks.*
45. C. Levi-Strauss, *The Savage Mind* (London: Weidenfeld & Nicolson, 1966).
46. K. Marx, 'The Eighteenth Brumaire', in *Marx–Engels Selected Works,* vol. 1.
47. *The Times,* 28 June 1973.
48. P. L. Berger and T. Luckmann, *The Social Construction of Reality* (Harmondsworth: Penguin, 1971).
49. Ibid.
50. On behavioural ideologies, see V. N. Volosinov, *Marxism and the Philosophy of Language* (New York: Seminar Press, 1973).
51. Berger and Luckmann, *The Social Construction of Reality.*
52. Volosinov, *Marxism and the Philosophy of Language.*
53. Poulantzas, *Political Power and Social Classes*; and Althusser, 'Ideology and the State'.
54. K. Marx, *Grundrisse: Foundations for a Critique of Political Economy,* trans. M. Nicolaus (London: Penguin, 1973).
55. H. Maine, *Ancient Law* (London: Dent, 1917); selected in *The Sociology of Law,* ed. V. Aubert (Harmondsworth: Penguin, 1969).
56. Quoted in I. Taylor, P. Walton and J. Young, *The New Criminology: for a Social Theory of Deviance* (London: Routledge & Kegan Paul, 1973) p. 1.
57. Ibid.
58. Quoted in L. Radzinowicz, *Ideology and Crime: a Study of Crime in its Social and Historical Context* (London: Heinemann, 1966).
59. Chevalier, *Labouring Classes and Dangerous Classes.*
60. Pearson, *The Deviant Imagination.*

61. But see Taylor, Walton and Young, *The New Criminology*; and S. Cohen, 'Criminology and the Sociology of Deviance in Britain', in *Deviance and Social Control*, eds Rock and McIntosh.
62. Cohen, 'Criminology and the Sociology of Deviance'.
63. But see, *inter alia*, G. Steadman-Jones, *Outcast London* (Oxford University Press, 1973); Pearson, *The Deviant Imagination*; R. Bailey and M. Brake (eds), *Radical Social Work* (London: Arnold, 1976) for some of the elements of social work's development.
64. See J. Clarke, 'The Three R's: Repression, Rescue and Rehabilitation: ideologies of control for working class youth', *C.C.C.S. Stencilled Paper*, University of Birmingham, 1976.
65. See E. J. Hobsbawm, *Labouring Men* (London: Weidenfeld & Nicolson, 1964); I. Taylor, P. Walton and J. Young, 'Critical Criminology in Britain: Review and Prospects', in *Critical Criminology*, ed. Taylor, Walton and Young.
66. On this ambiguous relation, see Taylor, Walton and Young, 'Critical Criminology in Britain'.
67. R. Nisbet, *The Sociological Tradition* (New York: Basic Books, 1966).
68. Gramsci, *Selections from the Prison Notebooks*, p. 210.

CHAPTER 7

1. *Deedes Report*.
2. D. Humphry, *Police Power and Black People* (London: Panther, 1972).
3. See D. Humphry, *Sunday Times*, 31 October 1976.
4. Steadman-Jones, *Outcast London*.
5. See Hobsbawm, *Labouring Men*; F. Mather, *Public Order in the Age of the Chartists* (Manchester University Press, 1959); G. Rudé, *Wilkes and Liberty* (Oxford University Press, 1962); G. Rudé, *The Crowd in History* (New York: Wiley, 1964); G. Rudé and E. J. Hobsbawm, *Captain Swing* (London: Weidenfeld & Nicolson, 1969); F. O. Darvall, *Popular Disturbance and Public Order in Regency England* (Oxford University Press, 1934); E. P. Thompson, 'The Moral Economy of the English Crowd in the Eighteenth Century', *Past and Present*, no. 50, February 1971; F. Tilly, 'Collective Violence in European Perspective', in *Violence in America*, ed. H. Graham and T. Gurr, Task Force Report to the National Commission on the Causes and Prevention of Violence (1969); and J. Stevenson and R. Quinault (eds), *Popular Protest and Public Order* (London: Allen & Unwin, 1974).
6. For example, E. J. Hobsbawm, *Bandits* (Harmondsworth: Penguin, 1972); Thompson, *The Making of the English Working Class*; E. P. Thompson, *Whigs and Hunters* (London: Allen Lane, the Penguin Press, 1975); D. Hay, P. Linebaugh and E. P. Thompson, *Albion's Fatal Tree: Crime and Society in Eighteenth Century England* (London: Allen Lane, the Penguin Press, 1975).

7. See R. Samuel, 'Conference Report', *Bulletin*, no. 25, Autumn 1972, Society for the Study of Labour History; and L. Taylor and P. Walton, 'Industrial Sabotage: Motives and Meanings', in *Images of Deviance*, ed. Cohen.

8. For example, Steadman-Jones, *Outcast London*; Chevalier, *Labouring Classes and Dangerous Classes*; and G. Lefebvre, *The Great Fear of 1789* (New York: Vintage, 1973).

9. E. J. Hobsbawm, 'Conference Report', *Bulletin*, no. 25, Autumn 1972.

10. Hay, Linebaugh and Thompson, *Albion's Fatal Tree*, p. 14.

11. See Clarke *et al.*, 'Subcultures, Cultures and Class'.

12. See H. Mayhew *et al.*, *London Labour and the London Poor* (London: Griffin, Bohn & Co., 1862) vol. IV.

13. Thompson, *Whigs and Hunters*, p. 194; see also E. P. Thompson, 'Patrician Society, Plebeian Culture', *Journal of Social History*, vol. 9, no. 4, 1974.

14. See Chevalier, *Labouring Classes and Dangerous Classes*; and Steadman-Jones, *Outcast London*.

15. Steadman-Jones, *Outcast London*.

16. See Clarke *et al.*, 'Subcultures, Cultures and Class'.

17. See M. McIntosh, 'Changes in the Organization of Thieving', in *Images of Deviance*, ed. Cohen; and M. McIntosh, *The Organisation of Crime* (London: Macmillan, 1975).

18. Thompson, *Whigs and Hunters*.

19. See Cohen, 'Protest, Unrest and Delinquency'; Horowitz and Liebowitz, 'Social Deviance and Political Marginality'; Hall, 'Deviancy, Politics and the Media'; Rock and Heidensohn, 'New Reflections on Violence'; and T. Bunyan, 'The Reproduction of Poverty', unpublished MS, 1975.

20. Cohen, 'Protest, Unrest and Delinquency'.

21. Malcolm X and A. Haley, *The Autobiography of Malcolm X* (Harmondsworth: Penguin, 1968).

22. See G. Jackson, *Soledad Brother* (Harmondsworth: Penguin, 1971); and E. Cleaver, *Soul on Ice* (London: Panther, 1970).

23. P. Linebaugh, 'Conference Report', *Bulletin*, vol. 25, Autumn 1972, Society for the Study of Labour History.

24. See L. Radzinowicz, *A History of English Criminal Law and its Administration from 1750* (London: Stevens & Sons, 1948) vol. I.

25. See ibid; Thompson, *Whigs and Hunters*; and Hay, Linebaugh and Thompson, *Albion's Fatal Tree*.

26. Thompson, 'Preface' in *Albion's Fatal Tree*.

27. D. Hay, 'Property, Authority and the Criminal Law', in *Albion's Fatal Tree*, p. 55.

28. Thompson, *Whigs and Hunters*, p. 191.

29. Hay, 'Property, Authority and the Criminal Law', p. 25.

30. Ibid. p. 58.

31. Ibid. p. 62.

32. Thompson, in *Albion's Fatal Tree*.

33. W. Blackstone, *Commentaries on the Laws of England* (London: T.

Cadell, 1793–5), vol. II; quoted in Hay, 'Property, Authority and the Criminal Law'.

34. Linebaugh, 'Conference Report', *Bulletin,* no. 25, Autumn 1972.
35. Thompson, 'Conference Report', *Bulletin,* p. 10.
36. See K. Marx, 'Introduction' (1857) to *Grundrisse*; L. Althusser, 'Contradiction and Overdetermination', in *For Marx* (Harmondsworth: Penguin, 1969); Poulantzas, *Political Power and Social Classes*; and S. M. Hall, 'Marx's Notes on Method: A "Reading" of the "1857 Introduction" ', *Working Papers in Cultural Studies No. 6,* C.C.C.S., University of Birmingham, Autumn 1974.
37. See Hay, 'Property, Authority and the Criminal Law'.
38. J. Griffith, 'The Politics of the Judiciary', *New Statesman,* 4 February 1977.
39. Quoted in ibid.
40. E. M. Lemert, *Social Pathology* (New York: McGraw-Hill, 1951).
41. Becker, 'Whose Side are We on?'
42. K. Marx, 'Preface to Critique of Political Economy', in *Marx–Engels Selected Works,* vol. 1.
43. Marx, *Grundrisse.*
44. K. Marx, *Critique of Hegel's Philosophy of Right* (Cambridge University Press, 1971).
45. Marx, *Grundrisse.*
46. Engels, 'Ludwig Feuerbach and the End of Classical German Philosophy', p. 359.
47. Ibid.
48. K. Marx and F. Engels, *The German Ideology* (London: Lawrence & Wishart, 1965).
49. Ibid. p. 66.
50. V. I. Lenin, *The State and Revolution* (London: Lawrence & Wishart, 1933) p. 13.
51. Poulantzas, *Political Power and Social Classes,* p. 150.
52. See N. Geras, 'Marx and the Critique of Political Economy' in *Ideology in Social Science,* ed. Blackburn; J. Mepham, 'The Theory of Ideology in Capital', *Working Papers in Cultural Studies No. 6,* C.C.C.S., University of Birmingham, Autumn 1974; M. Nicolaus, 'Foreword', in *Grundrisse*; Hall, 'Marx's Notes on Method'; and J. Rancière, 'The Concept of Critique', *Economy and Society,* vol. 5, no. 3, 1976.
53. Gramsci, *Selections from the Prison Notebooks,* p. 158.
54. F. Engels, 'Socialism: Utopian and Scientific', in *Selected Works.*
55. K. Marx, *Capital* (London: Lawrence & Wishart, 1974) vol. 1, ch. 23, p. 572.
56. Ibid. part VII.
57. Ibid. ch. 23, pp. 568–9; part VII, p. 565.
58. Ibid. ch. 6, p. 176.
59. Marx, 'The Eighteenth Brumaire', in *Selected Works.*
60. Ibid.
61. See Engels, 'Socialism: Utopian and Scientific', in *Selected Works.*

62. Althusser, 'Ideology and the State', p. 127.
63. K. Marx, *The Poverty of Philosophy* (Moscow: Foreign Languages Publishing House, 1956).
64. Marx in a letter to Ruge.
65. Gramsci, *Selections from the Prison Notebooks*, p. 247.
66. Ibid. p. 246.
67. See Althusser, 'Ideology and the State'.
68. Gramsci, *Selections from the Prison Notebooks*, pp. 181–2.
69. Ibid.
70. Anderson 'Origins of the Present Crisis'.
71. See E. P. Thompson, 'The Peculiarities of the English', in *The Socialist Register 1965*, ed. R. Miliband and J. Saville (London: Merlin Press, 1965); and Johnson, 'Barrington Moore, Perry Anderson and English Social Development'.
72. K. Marx and F. Engels, *On Britain* (Moscow: Foreign Languages Publishing House, 1962).
73. F. Engels, 'Socialism: Utopian and Scientific'.
74. E. Mandel, *Late Capitalism* (London: New Left Books, 1975) p. 479.
75. F. Engels, *Anti-Dühring* (London: Lawrence & Wishart, 1954) p. 386.
76. See Poulantzas, *Political Power and Social Classes*, p. 53.
77. Ibid. p. 53.
78. Ibid. p. 211.
79. A. Hunt, 'Law, State and Class Struggle', *Marxism Today*, June 1976.
80. Thompson, *Whigs and Hunters*, p. 258 ff.
81. Althusser, 'Ideology and the State'.
82. Hunt, 'Law, State and Class Struggle'.
83. K. Polanyi, *The Great Transformation* (Boston: Beacon Press, 1957).
84. E. J. Hobsbawm, *The Age of Capital* (London: Weidenfeld & Nicolson, 1973).
85. See D. Melossi, 'The Penal Question in *Capital, Crime and Social Justice*, Spring/Summer 1976.
86. Gramsci, *Selections from the Prison Notebooks*, p. 210.

CHAPTER 8

1. Althusser, 'Contradiction and Overdetermination'.
2. See K. Marx, 'Population, Crime and Pauperism', *New York Daily Tribune*, 16 September 1859.
3. For example, L. Wilkins, *Social Deviance: Social Policy, Action and Research* (London: Tavistock, 1964); and Young, *The Drugtakers*.
4. Horowitz and Liebowitz, 'Social Deviance and Political Marginalty'.
5. Hall, 'Deviancy, Politics and the Media', p. 263.
6. See V. Greenwood and J. Young, *Abortion on Demand* (London: Pluto Press, 1976).
7. R. Moss, *The Collapse of Democracy* (London: Temple-Smith, 1976).
8. Ibid.
9. Gramsci, 'Modern Prince' in *Selections from the Prison Notebooks*.

10. B. Barker (ed.), *Ramsay MacDonald's Political Writings* (London: Allen Lane, the Penguin Press, 1972).
11. Quoted in A. Gamble, *The Conservative Nation* (London: Routledge & Kegan Paul, 1974).
12. R. Titmuss, *Essays on the Welfare State* (London: Allen & Unwin, 1958).
13. See R. Miliband, *Parliamentary Socialism* (London: Allen & Unwin, 1961); T. Nairn, 'Anatomy of the Labour Party', in *Towards Socialism*, ed. Anderson and Blackburn; J. Saville, 'Labourism and the Labour Government', in *Socialist Register 1967*, ed. R. Miliband and J. Saville (London: Merlin Press, 1967); and D. Coates, *The Labour Party and the Struggle for Socialism* (Cambridge University Press, 1975).
14. See Gamble, *The Conservative Nation*; and N. Harris, *Competition and the Corporate Society* (London: Methuen, 1972).
15. See G. Kay, *Development and Underdevelopment* (London: Macmillan, 1975); and E. J. Hobsbawm, 'The Crisis of Capitalism in Historical Perspective', *Marxism Today*, October 1975.
16. Quoted in Kay, *Development and Underdevelopment*.
17. Quoted in M. Pinto-Duschinsky, 'Bread and Circuses: the Conservatives in Office, 1951–64', in *The Age of Affluence: 1951–1964*, ed. V. Bogdanor and R. Skidelsky (London: Macmillan, 1970).
18. P. Addison, *The Road to 1945* (London: Cape, 1975).
19. Barthes, *Mythologies*.
20. Kay, *Development and Underdevelopment*.
21. *The Economist*, 16 May 1959; quoted in S. M. Hall, 'The Condition of England', *People and Politics* (Notting Hill Community Workshop Journal) 1960.
22. See the longer discussion in Clarke *et al.*, 'Subcultures, Cultures and Class'.
23. See P. Rock and S. Cohen, 'The Teddy Boy', in *The Age of Affluence*, ed. Bogdanor and Skidelsky.
24. For an analysis of the Teddy-Boy style, see T. Jefferson, 'Cultural Responses of the Teds', in *Resistance through Rituals*, ed. Hall and Jefferson.
25. *The Times*, 5 September 1958.
26. Marx, 'The Eighteenth Brumaire', in *Selected Works*.
27. L. Panitch, *Social Democracy and Industrial Militancy* (Cambridge University Press, 1976).
28. Ibid.
29. Cohen, *Folk Devils and Moral Panics*.
30. Gramsci, *Selections from the Prison Notebooks*.
31. P. Hansford-Johnson, *On Iniquity* (London: Macmillan, 1967).
32. *Sunday Express*, 16 January 1966.
33. *Sunday Express*, 8 May 1966.
34. Analysed in Young, *The Drugtakers*.
35. P. Foot, *Immigration and Race in British Politics* (Harmondsworth: Penguin, 1965).

36. P. Foot, *The Rise of Enoch Powell: an Examination of Enoch Powell's Attitude to Immigration and Race* (Harmondsworth: Penguin, 1969).
37. See Hall, 'Deviancy, Politics and the Media'; and Young, 'Mass Media, Deviance and Drugs', both in *Deviance and Social Control*, ed. Rock and McIntosh.
38. *Sunday Express*, 1 January 1967.
39. K. Marx and F. Engels, *The Communist Manifesto* in *Selected Works*.
40. G. Cohn-Bendit and D. Cohn-Bendit, *Obsolete Communism: the Left-wing Alternative* (London: Deutsch, 1968).
41. N. Mailer, 'The White Negro' in *Advertisements for Myself* (London: Deutsch, 1961).
42. *Sunday Express*, 7 April 1968.
43. See Hall, 'Deviancy, Politics and the Media', in *Deviance and Social Control*, ed. Rock and McIntosh.
44. Halloran, Elliott and Murdock, *Demonstrations and Communication: a Case Study*.
45. 'End this Menace', *Sunday Express*, 27 October 1968.
46. *The Times* and the *Daily Mirror*, 28 October 1968.
47. 'Can we afford to let our Race Problem Explode?', *Sunday Express*, 9 July 1967.
48. Quotes from Foot, *The Rise of Enoch Powell*.
49. E. Powell, M.P., text of speech delivered in Birmingham, 20 April 1968, *Race*, vol. X, no. 1, July 1968.
50. See T. Nairn, 'Enoch Powell: the New Right', *New Left Review*, vol. 61, May-June 1970.
51. *Sunday Times*, 14 July 1968.
52. Open letter to the Underground from the London Street Commune; quoted in P. Stansill and D. Z. Mairowitz (eds), *BAMN: Outlaw Manifestoes and Ephemera, 1965–70* (Harmondsworth: Penguin, 1971) p. 224. (The style, viewpoint and rhetoric show unmistakably the hand of 'Dr John' of the 144 Piccadilly Squat.)
53. *Sunday Times*, 28 September 1969.
54. Hiro, *Black British, White British*.
55. Foot, *The Rise of Enoch Powell*.
56. 'Living around the Crime Clock', *Sunday Times*, 9 March 1969.
57. *Sunday Express*, 23 February 1969.
58. *Sunday Times*, 6 April 1969.
59. *Sunday Times*, 23 February 1969.
60. *Sunday Times*, 26 October 1969.
61. *Sunday Times*, 7 December 1969.
62. *Sunday Times*, 20 April 1969.
63. 'Anarchy at Large', *Sunday Times*, 2 November 1969.
64. *Sunday Times*, 27 July 1969.
65. M. Whitehouse, *Who Does She Think She Is?* (London: New English Library, 1971) p. 107.
66. See the analysis of this period in Young, *The Drugtakers*.
67. *Sunday Times*, 20 July 1969.

68. D. Phillips, 'The Press and Pop Festivals: Stereotypes of Youthful Leisure', in *The Manufacture of News*, ed. Cohen and Young, pp. 323–33.
69. Whitehouse, *Who Does She Think She Is?*, p. 107.
70. A. Arblaster, *Academic Freedom* (Harmondsworth: Penguin, 1974) p. 29.
71. B. Benewick and T. Smith, *Direct Action and Democratic Politics* (London: Allen & Unwin, 1972) p. 206.
72. See E. P. Thompson, *Warwick University Ltd.* (Harmondsworth: Penguin, 1970).
73. See P. Hain, *Don't Play with Apartheid* (London: Allen & Unwin, 1971).
74. B. Seale, *Seize the Time: the Story of the Black Panther Party* (London: Hutchinson, 1970).
75. Stansill and Mairowitz, *BAMN*.
76. J. Mitchell, *Woman's Estate* (Harmondsworth: Penguin, 1971).
77. Gramsci, *Selections from the Prison Notebooks*; and Althusser, 'Ideology and the State'.
78. Mitchell, *Woman's Estate*.
79. T. Nairn, 'Why it Happened', in *The Beginning of the End*, ed. A. Quattrocchi and T. Nairn (London: Panther, 1968).
80. Mitchell, *Woman's Estate*, p. 32.
81. Ibid. p. 32.
82. Marcuse, *One Dimensional Man*; and *Eros and Civilization* (London: Sphere, 1969).
83. *Sunday Times* Insight Team, *Ulster* (Harmondsworth: Penguin, 1972).
84. In Marx and Engels, *On Britain*.
85. K. Marx, Speech at the Anniversary of the *People's Paper* in *Surveys from Exile* (Harmondsworth: Penguin, 1973) p. 300.
86. Marx, 'The Eighteenth Brumaire' in *Selected Works*, vol. I, p. 258.
87. For example, A. Glyn and B. Sutcliffe, *British Capitalism, Workers and the Profits Squeeze* (Harmondsworth: Penguin, 1972); D. Yaffe, 'The Crisis of Profitability: a Critique of the Glyn–Sutcliffe Thesis', *New Left Review*, vol. 80, July–August 1973; Mandel, *Late Capitalism*; and P. Bullock and D. Yaffe, 'Inflation, the Crisis and the Post War Boom', *Revolutionary Communist*, no. 3/4, 1975.
88. Yaffe, 'The Crisis of Profitability', p. 53.
89. Ibid.
90. I. Gough, 'State Expenditure in Advanced Capitalism', *New Left Review*, vol. 92, 1975; and Bullock and Yaffe, 'Inflation, the Crisis and the Post War Boom'.
91. Glyn and Sutcliffe, *British Capitalism, Workers and the Profit Squeeze*.
92. S. H. Beer, *Modern British Politics: a Study of Parties and Pressure Groups* (London: Faber, 1965).
93. G. A. Dorfman, *Wage Politics in Britain, 1945–1967: Government vs TUC* (Iowa State University Press, 1973).
94. Ibid. pp. 101–2.
95. Signed December 1964.
96. Quoted in R. Hyman, *Strikes* (London: Fontana, 1972) p. 22.

97. Ibid. p. 121.
98. Dorfman, *Wage Politics in Britain*, p. 140.
99. H. Wilson, *The Labour Government, 1964–70* (Harmondsworth: Penguin, 1974) p. 591.
100. H. A. Clegg and R. Adams, *The Employers' Challenge: a Study of the National Shipbuilding and Engineering Disputes of 1957* (Oxford University Press, 1957) p. 20.
101. T. Lane and K. Roberts, *Strike at Pilkington's* (London: Fontana, 1971).
102. T. Lane, *The Union Makes Us Strong* (London: Arrow, 1974) p. 155.
103. Hyman, *Strikes*, p. 144.
104. See the excellent study by H. Beynon, *Working for Ford* (Harmondsworth: Penguin, 1973).
105. Dorfman, *Wage Politics in Britain*, pp. 133–4.
106. See H. Braverman, *Labor and Monopoly Capital* (New York: Monthly Review Press, 1975).
107. Quoted in T. Cliff, *The Employers' Offensive* (London: Pluto Press, 1970) p. 140.
108. *The Economist*, 5 June 1965.
109. Cliff, *The Employers' Offensive*, p. 126.
110. Quoted in P. Jenkins, *Battle of Downing Street* (London: Charles Knight, 1970) p. 58.
111. Quoted in Beynon, *Working for Ford*.
112. Ibid. p. 243.

CHAPTER 9

1. Gramsci, 'Notes on Italian History' in *Selections from the Prison Notebooks*, p. 61.
2. Marx, 'The Crisis in England and the British Constitution' in Marx and Engels, *On Britain*, p. 424.
3. D. Humphry and G. John, *Because They're Black* (Harmondsworth: Penguin, 1971).
4. Manchester C.R.C. letter in the *Sunday Times*, 18 January 1970.
5. *Guardian*, 7 February 1970.
6. *Sunday Times*, 8 February 1970.
7. *Guardian*, 7 February 1970.
8. *Sunday Express*, 1 February 1970.
9. *Sunday Express*, 8 February 1970.
10. *Sunday Express*, 22 February 1970.
11. Quoted in *Sunday Times*, 8 February 1970.
12. Lord Hailsham, quoted in *Guardian*, 12 February 1970.
13. *Sunday Express*, 8 March 1970.
14. *Sunday Times*, 5 April 1970.
15. *Sunday Times*, 14 June 1970.
16. Ibid.
17. *Sunday Times*, 7 June 1970.
18. *Sunday Times*, 11 August 1970.

19. *Sunday Times*, 6 December 1970.
20. See *Sunday Times*, 12 July 1970.
21. *The Listener*, 8 October 1970.
22. Lambert, *Crime, Police and Race Relations*.
23. D. Humphry, *Police Power and Black People* (London: Panther, 1972).
24. Ibid.
25. Quotes from ibid.
26. *Sunday Times*, 1 February 1970.
27. See R. Bailey, *The Squatters* (Harmondsworth: Penguin, 1973).
28. *Sunday Times*, 18 October 1970.
29. *Sunday Express*, 26 July 1970.
30. See R. Blackburn, 'The Heath Government: a New Course for Capitalism', *New Left Review*, vol. 70, November–December 1971.
31. Quoted in A. Buchan, *The Right to Work* (London: Calder & Boyars, 1972) p. 49.
32. *The Times*, 22 July 1972.
33. Stuart Hood in *The Listener*, 25 February 1971.
34. Quoted in Buchan, *The Right to Work*, p. 71.
35. See B. Cox, *Civil Liberties in Britain* (Harmondsworth: Penguin, 1975).
36. See Bunyan, *The History and Practice of the Political Police in Britain*.
37. See, for quotes, Stuart Hood in *The Listener*, 14 January 1971.
38. Cox, *Civil Liberties in Britain*.
39. Quoted in T. Palmer, *Trials of Oz* (London: Blond & Briggs, 1971).
40. *Sunday Express*, 2 May 1971.
41. Cox, *Civil Liberties in Britain*.
42. *Sunday Times*, 3 January 1971.
43. M. Muggeridge, 'Foreword', in F. Dobbie, *Land Aflame* (London: Hodder & Stoughton, 1972).
44. *Viewers and Listeners*, Summer 1970.
45. See R. Wallis, 'Moral Indignation and the Media: an Analysis of N.V.A.L.A.', unpublished ms, University of Stirling (1975).
46. *The Times*, 21 December 1970.
47. *Viewers and Listeners*, Spring 1971.
48. *The Times*, 27 April 1972.
49. M. Whitehouse, *Who Does She Think She Is?* (London: New English Library, 1971).
50. Ibid. p. 110.
51. Ibid. p. 110.
52. Lord Longford, *The Longford Report: Pornography* (London: Coronet, 1972) p. 26.
53. Quoted in ibid. p. 22.
54. Cox, *Civil Liberties in Britain*, p. 117.
55. *The Times*, 18 October 1971.
56. *Sunday Times*, 21 November 1971.
57. *Current Law Statutes Annotated 1971* (London: Sweet & Maxwell, 1971).
58. Bunyan, *The History and Practice of the Political Police in Britain*.

59. See ibid.
60. F. Kitson, *Low Intensity Operations* (London: Faber, 1971).
61. Ibid.
62. See *Time Out*, no. 284, 29 August–4 September 1975; *Guardian*, 16 July 1976.
63. *Time Out*, no. 284, 29 August–4 September 1975.
64. *Guardian*, 16 July 1976.
65. *Sunday Times* Insight Team, *Ulster* (Harmondsworth: Penguin, 1972).
66. T. Rose (ed.), *Violence in America* (New York: Random House, 1969).
67. G. Carr, *The Angry Brigade* (London: Gollancz, 1975).
68. Quoted in *London Evening Standard*, 25 September 1972.
69. *The Times*, 30 December 1972.
70. Quotes from ibid.
71. E. McCann, *War and an Irish Town* (Harmondsworth: Penguin, 1974).
72. R. Clutterbuck, *Protest and the Urban Guerrilla* (London: Cassell, 1973) p. 234.
73. Ibid.
74. *Daily Telegraph*, 16 February 1967.
75. Hiro, *Black British, White British*, p. 222.
76. Ibid.
77. *Daily Mirror*, 15 February 1968.
78. *Sunday Times*, 18 February 1968.
79. See R. Moore, *Racism and Black Resistance in Britain* (London: Pluto Press, 1975).
80. See, *inter alia*, ibid. or *Race Today, passim*, for an account of the immediate effects of this on the black communities.
81. *Sunday Express*, 6 February 1972.
82. Ibid.
83. *Sunday Times*, 2 April 1972.
84. A. Maude, 'Now Anarchy has shown its Face', *Sunday Express*, 30 July 1972.
85. *Sunday Times* editorial, 8 June 1972.
86. *Sunday Times* editorial, 23 July 1972.
87. *Sunday Express* editorial, 30 July 1972.
88. A. Barnett, 'Class Struggle and the Heath Government', *New Left Review*, vol. 77, January–February 1973.
89. Ibid.
90. I. Birchall, 'Class Struggle in Britain: Workers against the Tory Government, 1970–1974', in *Radical America*, vol. 8, no. 5, 1974.
91. P. Johnson, 'The Know-Nothing Left', *New Statesman*, 26 September 1975; and 'Towards the Parasite State', *New Statesman*, 3 September 1976.
92. *Guardian*, 12 January 1976.
93. *Guardian*, 21 May 1975.
94. *Sun*, 27 February 1975.
95. *Guardian*, 9 June 1975.
96. *Birmingham Evening Mail*, 12 June 1975.

97. *Guardian*, 17 October 1975.
98. J. Griffith, 'Hailsham – Judge or Politician?', *New Statesman*, 1 February 1974.
99. Quoted in ibid.
100. J. Arnison, *Shrewsbury Three* (London: Lawrence & Wishart, 1975).
101. G. Robertson, *Whose Conspiracy?* (London: N.C.C.L. Publications, 1974).
102. Ibid.
103. *New Statesman*, 3 August 1973.
104. See J. C. Alderson and P. J. Stead (eds), *The Police we Deserve* (London: Wolfe, 1973).
105. *Observer*, 16 March 1975.
106. See *Guardian*, 26 November 1975.
107. *Guardian*, 7 November 1975.
108. *Guardian*, 18 March 1975.
109. *Observer*, 23 March 1975.
110. Robertson, *Whose Conspiracy?*; and Bunyan, *The History and Practice of the Political Police in Britain*.
111. *New Statesman*, 13 June 1975.
112. So described in the *Spectator*, 26 April 1975.
113. *Sunday Times*, 20 October 1974.
114. *Guardian*, 5 February 1976.
115. See ibid.
116. Centre for Policy Studies, *Why Britain Needs a Social Market Economy* (London: C.P.S. pamphlet).
117. See 'Why High Marx means Low Marks', *Sunday Telegraph*, 12 October 1976.
118. Poulantzas, 'Marxist Political Theory in Great Britain', *New Left Review*, 43, 1967.
119. Gramsci, *Selections from the Prison Notebooks*, p. 161.

CHAPTER 10

1. *Daily Telegraph*, 12 April 1976.
2. See the full and detailed account in *Race Today*, June 1974.
3. See I. MacDonald, *Race Today*, December 1973.
4. See M. Dhondy, *Race Today*, July 1974; see also *Race Today*, March 1975.
5. 'Danger Signals from the Streets of Lambeth', *Sunday Times*, 5 January 1975.
6. Quotes from the *Sunday Times*, 5 January 1975.
7. Quoted in the *Daily Mail*, 16 May 1975.
8. *The Times*, 2 July 1976.
9. *Sunday Times*, 28 March 1976; see also M. Phillips, 'Brixton and Crime', *New Society*, 8 July 1976.
10. *The Times* and *Guardian*, 12 April 1976.
11. See *Race Today*, June 1976.

12. *Daily Mail*, 24 May 1976.
13. *Daily Telegraph*, 26 May 1976.
14. 'The Facts and Myths', *Sunday Times*, 30 May 1976.
15. *Daily Telegraph*, 26 May 1976.
16. *Daily Mail*, 25 May 1976.
17. See C. Husband (ed.), *White Media and Black Britain* (London: Arrow, 1975); and Critcher *et al.*, *Race and the Provincial Press*.
18. *Daily Mirror*, 25 May 1976.
19. See *Birmingham Evening Mail*, 21 June 1976.
20. *Sunday Times*, 4 July 1976.
21. *Sunday Telegraph*, 17 October 1976.
22. See *Daily Telegraph*, 23 October 1976.
23. See *Daily Mail*, 26 October 1976.
24. P. Willis, *Learning to Labour* (London: Saxon House, 1977).
25. See B. Coard, *How the West Indian Child is made Educationally Sub-Normal in the British School System* (London: New Beacon Books, 1971).
26. S. Castles and G. Kosack, *Immigrant Workers and Class Structure in Western Europe* (London: Oxford University Press/Institute of Race Relations, 1973) p. 116.
27. See Braverman, *Labor and Monopoly Capital*; and A. Gambino, 'Workers Struggles and the Development of Ford in Britain', *Red Notes Pamphlet*, vol. i, 1976.
28. C.I.S. and Institute of Race Relations, *Racism: Who Profits?*, 1976 (our italics).
29. Ibid.
30. J. Berger, *The Seventh Man* (Harmondsworth: Penguin, 1975).
31. A. Sivanandan, *Race, Class and the State* (London: Institute of Race Relations, 1976).
32. Castles and Kosack, *Immigrant Workers and Class Structure in Western Europe*.
33. See Notting Hill People's Association Housing Group, *Losing Out*, 1972, Notting Hill People's Association Housing Group, 60 St Evan's Road, London W.10; and J. Greve, D. Page and S. Greve, *Homelessness in London* (Edinburgh: Scottish Academic Press, 1971).
34. Quotes from P. Gillman's account of black youth at the Harambee hostel in Holloway: 'I blame England', *Sunday Times*, colour supplement, 30 September 1973.
35. D. Howe, 'Fighting Back: West Indian Youth and the Police in Notting Hill', *Race Today*, vol. 5, no. 11, December 1973.
36. Ibid.
37. Quoted in Gillman, 'I blame England'.
38. Howe, 'Fighting Back'.
39. Malcolm X and Haley, *The Autobiography of Malcolm X*, pp. 315–16.
40. Hiro, *Black British, White British*, p. 81.
41. Quoted in Gillman, 'I blame England'.
42. Quoted in Hiro, *Black British, White British*, p. 80.

43. Ibid.
44. Quoted in Gillman, 'I blame England'.
45. 'The Black Youth Speak', *Race Today*, April 1975.
46. Marx, *The Poverty of Philosophy* (Moscow: Foreign Languages Publishing House, 1956).
47. Quoted in Gillman, 'I blame England'.
48. See D. Hebdidge, 'Reggae, Rastas and Rudies: Style and the Subversion of Form', *C.C.C.S. Stencilled Paper No. 24*, C.C.C.S., University of Birmingham, 1974; reprinted, in shorter form, in *Resistance through Rituals*, ed. Hall and Jefferson; and R. Nettleford, *Mirror, Mirror* (London: Collins–Sangster, 1970).
49. Quoted in Gillman, 'I blame England'.
50. Ibid.
51. Hiro, *Black British, White British*, p. 79.
52. Quoted in Gillman, 'I blame England'; see also V. Hines, *Black Youth and the Survival Game in Britain* (London: Zulu Publications, 1973).
53. E. J. Hobsbawm, *Primitive Rebels* (Manchester University Press, 1959), *Labouring Men, Bandits*.
54. Hobsbawm, 'Conference Report', *Bulletin*, no. 25, Autumn 1972.
55. Ibid.
56. Hobsbawm, *Bandits*, p. 98.
57. A. Gouldner, 'Foreword', in Taylor, Walton and Young, *The New Criminology*, p. xii.
58. P. Q. Hirst, 'Marx and Engels on Law, Crime and Morality', in *Critical Criminology*, ed. Taylor, Walton and Young.
59. Marx, *The Poverty of Philosophy*.
60. Hirst, 'Marx and Engels on Law, Crime and Morality', p. 218.
61. Ibid. p. 219.
62. Marx, 'The Eighteenth Brumaire', p. 267.
63. F. Engels, *The Condition of the Working Class in England* (London: Panther, 1969).
64. Mayhew *et al.*, *London Labour and the London Poor*, vol. IV.
65. K. Marx, *Capital* (London: Lawrence & Wishart, 1974) vol. III, pp. 791–2; for a relevant discussion, see J. Gardiner, S. Himmelweit and M. Mackintosh, 'Women's Domestic Labour', *Bulletin of the Conference of Socialist Economists*, vol. IV, no. 2 (II), June 1975.
66. I. Gough, 'Productive and Unproductive Labour in Marx', *New Left Review*, vol. 76, 1972.
67. P. Howell, 'Once more on Productive and Unproductive Labour', *Revolutionary Communist*, nos 3–4, November 1975.
68. W. Seccombe, 'The Housewife and her Labour under Capitalism', *New Left Review*, vol. 83, 1973.
69. For example, M. Benston, 'The Political Economy of Women's Liberation', *Monthly Review*, September 1969; P. Morton, 'Women's Work is Never Done', *Leviathan*, May 1970; S. Rowbotham, *Woman's Consciousness, Man's World* (Harmondsworth: Penguin, 1970); J. Harrison, 'Political Economy of Housework', *Bulletin of the Conference of*

Socialist Economists, Spring 1974; C. Freeman, 'Introduction to "Domestic Labour and Wage Labour",' *Women and Socialism: Conference Paper 3,* Birmingham Woman's Liberation Group – available from 26 Lonsdale Rd, Harborne, Birmingham B17 9RA; J. Gardiner, 'Women's Domestic Labour', *New Left Review,* vol. 89, 1975 (from a paper originally printed in *Women and Socialism: Conference Paper 3,* 1974); M. Coulson, B. Magas and H. Wainwright 'The Housewife and her Labour under Capitalism – A Critique', *New Left Review,* vol. 89, 1975 (from a paper originally printed in *Women and Socialism: Conference Paper 3,* 1974); and Gardiner, Himmelweit and Mackintosh, 'Women's Domestic Labour'.
70. W. Seccombe, 'Domestic Labour: Reply to Critics', *New Left Review,* vol. 94, November–December 1975.
71. Coulson, Magas and Wainwright, 'The Housewife and her Labour under Capitalism'.
72. Seccombe, 'Domestic Labour'.
73. Braverman, *Labor and Monopoly Capital.*
74. Seccombe, 'Domestic Labour'.
75. S. James and M. Dalla Costa, *The Power of Women and the Subversion of the Community* (Bristol: Falling Wall Press, 1972).
76. S. James, *Sex, Race and Class* (Bristol: Falling Wall Press, 1975).
77. James and Dalla Costa, *The Power of Women,* p. 6.
78. K. Marx, *Capital* (London: Lawrence & Wishart, 1974) vol. I.
79. Ibid.
80. James, *Sex, Race and Class,* p. 13.
81. For example, in Howe, 'Fighting Back'; I. MacDonald, 'The Creation of the British Police', *Race Today,* December 1973; and F. Dhondy, 'The Black Explosion in Schools', *Race Today,* February 1974.
82. Howe, 'Fighting Back'.
83. Ibid.
84. Power of Women Collective, *All Work and No Pay* (Bristol: Falling Wall Press, 1975).
85. B. Taylor, 'Our Labour and Our Power', *Red Rag,* no. 10, 1976.
86. See M. Tronti, 'Social Capital', *Telos,* Autumn 1973; M. Tronti, 'Workers and Capital' in *Labour Process and Class Strategies,* Conference of Socialist Economists pamphlet, 1976; S. Bologna, 'Class Composition and the Theory of the Party' in *Labour Process and Class Strategies*; Gambino, 'Workers Struggles and the Development of Ford in Britain'; G. Boldi, 'Theses on the Mass Worker and Social Capital', in *Radical America,* May–June 1972.
87. See A. X. Cambridge, 'Black Workers and the State: a Debate Inside the Black Workers' Movement', *The Black Liberator,* vol. 2, no. 2, October–May 1973–4, p. 185 n.
88. Hirst, 'Marx and Engels on Law, Crime and Morality'.
89. See A. X. Cambridge and C. Gutsmore, 'Industrial Action of the Black Masses and the Class Struggle in Britain', *The Black Liberator,* vol. 2, no. 3, June–January 1974–5.

90. Hirst, 'Marx and Engels on Law, Crime and Morality'.
91. Marx, 'The Eighteenth Brumaire', p. 44.
92. F. Engels, 'Preface to "The Peasant War in Germany"', in *Marx–Engels Selected Works*, vol. 2, p. 646.
93. Howe in a personal interview.
94. Ibid.
95. Ibid.
96. Ibid.
97. A. X. Cambridge, 'Glossary', *The Black Liberator*, vol. 2, no. 3. June–January 1974–5, p. 280.
98. Ibid. p. 279.
99. See G. Rudé, *Paris and London in the Eighteenth Century* (London: Fontana, 1952); G.Rudé, *The Crowd in The French Revolution* (Oxford University Press, 1959); Rudé, *Wilkes and Liberty;* Rudé, *The Crowd in History;* and Rudé and Hobsbawm, *Captain Swing.*
100. V. I. Lenin, 'Imperialism, The Highest Stage of Capitalism', *Selected Works in One Volume* (London: Lawrence & Wishart, 1969); see also R. Owen and B. Sutcliffe (eds), *Studies in the Theory of Imperialism* (London: Longmans, 1972).
101. Hobsbawm, *Labouring Men*, p. 272; see also J. Foster, *Class Struggle and Industrial Revolution* (London: Weidenfeld & Nicolson, 1975).
102. Quoted in Lenin, 'Imperialism', p. 247.
103. P. Worsley, 'Fanon and the "lumpenproletariat"', in *Socialist Register 1972*, ed. Miliband and Saville.
104. Quoted in ibid.
105. F. Fanon, *The Wretched of the Earth* (New York: Grove Press, 1963).
106. Marx, *Capital*, vol. I, p. 633.
107. See Castles and Kosack, *Immigrant Workers and Class Structure in Western Europe*, p. 4.
108. V. Beechey, 'Female Wage Labour and the Capitalist Mode', unpublished mss, University of Warwick, 1976.
109. Marx, *Capital,* vol. I, pp. 640–5.
110. Castles and Kosack, *Immigrant Workers and Class Structure in Western Europe.*
111. Quoted in Worsley, 'Fanon and the "lumpenproletariat"', n. 23.
112. C. Allan, 'Lumpenproletarians and Revolution', *Political Theory and Ideology in African Society*, seminar proceedings, Centre for African Studies, University of Edinburgh, 1970.
113. S.Tax, *Penny Capitalism: A Guatemala Indian Economy* (Washington, D.C.: Smithsonian Institute, 1953).
114. Allan, 'Lumpenproletarians and Revolution'.
115. A. Q. Obregon, 'The Marginal Pole of the Economy and the Marginalised Labour Force', *Economy and Society*, vol. 3, no. 4, 1974.
116. S. Schram, *Political Leaders of the Twentieth Century: Mao Tse-tung* (Harmondsworth: Penguin, 1966) p. 127.
117. C. Guevara, *Guerrilla Warfare* (Harmondsworth: Penguin, 1969).
118. Quoted in R. Debray, 'Castroism: the Long March in Latin America', in

Strategy for Revolution (Harmondsworth: Penguin, 1973) p. 39; see also R. Debray, *Revolution in the Revolution?* (Harmondsworth: Penguin, 1968).

119. Fanon, *The Wretched of the Earth*, p. 73.
120. Worsley, 'Fanon and the "lumpenproletariat"'.
121. Fanon, *The Wretched of the Earth*, pp. 103–4.
122. I. L. Gendzier, *Franz Fanon: A Critical Study* (London: Wildwood House, 1973) p. 207.
123. Fanon, *The Wretched of the Earth*, p. 109.
124. Worsley, 'Fanon and the "lumpenproletariat"', p. 40.
125. See, for example, R. Cohen and D. Michael, 'Revolutionary Potential of the African Lumpenproletariat: a Sceptical View', *Bulletin of the Institute of Development Studies,* vol. 5, nos 2–3, October 1973.
126. See Hobsbawm, *Bandits.*
127. See Seale, *Seize the Time*; and H. P. Newton, *Revolutionary Suicide* (New York: Ballantine Books, 1974).
128. Seale, 'Foreword', in *Seize the Time.*
129. Ibid. p. 4.
130. 'The Police and the Black Wageless', *Race Today*, February 1972.